alfredo boulton and his contemporaries

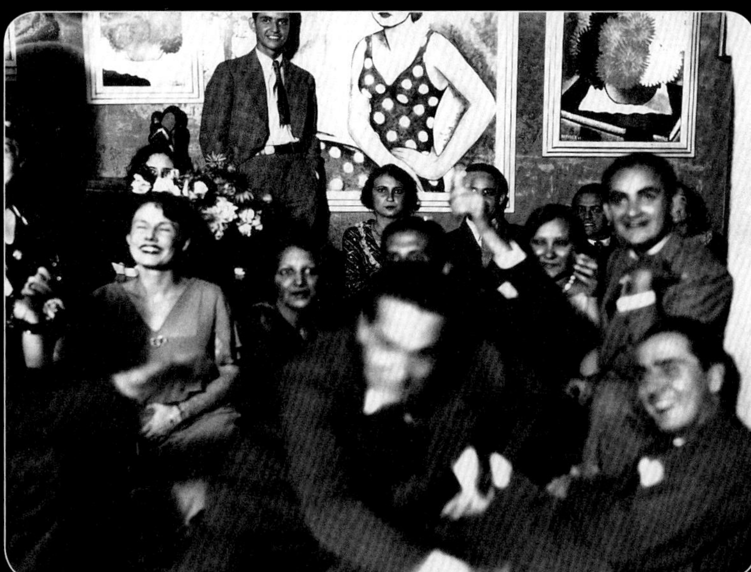

alfredo boulton and his contemporaries

critical dialogues in venezuelan art 1912–1974

edited by **ariel jiménez**

the museum of modern art, new york

This publication was generously sponsored by The International Council of The Museum of Modern Art. Additional support was provided by Mercantil Servicios Financieros (Venezuela), Ignacio and Luis Alfonso Oberto, the Reed Foundation, Juan Ignacio Parra, the Alberto Vollmer Foundation, Inc., Jean Hartley Boulton, Estrellita B. Brodsky, Harry Mannil, Gonzalo Parodi, Patricia Phelps de Cisneros, Byron Meyer, and William L. Bernhard.

Produced by the Department of Publications, The Museum of Modern Art, New York

The contents of this book were selected and compiled by Ariel Jiménez, who was assisted by Jessica Hankey. Paulo Herkenhoff, Jay A. Levenson, Juan Ignacio Parra, Luis Pérez-Oramas, and Edward J. Sullivan served on the book's advisory committee.

Edited by Diana C. Stoll
Design by Gina Rossi
Production by Christina Grillo
Printed and bound by Editoriale Bertolazzi-Stei s.r.l., Verona

This book is typeset in Avenir Next by Linotype. The paper is 150 gsm Euro Bulk.

Published by The Museum of Modern Art, 11 W. 53 Street, New York, New York 10019

Distributed in the United States and Canada by D.A.P./Distributed Art Publishers, Inc., New York
Distributed outside the United States and Canada by Thames & Hudson Ltd, London

Library of Congress Control Number: 2008924417
ISBN: 978-0-87070-710-0

Cover: Universidad Central de Venezuela's Plaza Cubierta (covered plaza; detail). Photograph by Paolo Gasparini. 1985–89. Collection of the photographer

Back cover: Fishing net (detail). Photograph by Alfredo Boulton. c. 1952. See p. 23 for full image and caption information

Inside flaps (front): Universidad Central de Venezuela's Plaza Cubierta (covered plaza; detail); (back): the Plaza Cubierta's access ramp to the balcony of the Aula Magna (great hall; detail). Both photographs by Paolo Gasparini. 1985–89. Archivos Fundación Villanueva, Caracas

Frontispiece: Alfredo Boulton (seated, far right, foreground) and friends at the atelier of Francisco Narváez (seated behind Boulton). c. 1932. Photographer unknown. Alberto Vollmer Foundation, Inc., Caracas

Chapter frontispieces:

Chapter 1, p. 13: Alfredo Boulton. *Vista de El Ávila desde Los Guayabitos de mañana* (El Ávila mountain seen from Los Guayabitos in the morning; detail). c. 1943. See p. 142 for full image and caption information

Chapter 2, p. 75: Alfredo Boulton. *Desnudo con Cambures* (Nude with bananas; sculpture by Francisco Narváez; detail). 1933. See p. 138 for full image and caption information

Chapter 3, p. 155: Carlos Cruz-Diez. *Ambientación cromática* (Chromatic environment; detail). 1974. See p. 307 for full image and caption information

Chapter 4, p. 323: Aerial view of Caracas's El Silencio district, with an outline indicating the zone to be occupied by the El Silencio urban-redevelopment project. 1942. Archivos Fundación Villanueva, Caracas

References, p. 367: View of Alejandro Otero's *Torre solar* (*Solar Tower*, 1986). Photograph by Alfredo Boulton (detail). 1987. See p. 309 for full image and caption information

Printed in Italy

contents

chapter three **the challenge of the times**

chapter four **critical nexus**

references

acknowledgments

The series of documentary anthologies to which this volume belongs began in 2002 with the publication of *Primary Documents: A Sourcebook for Eastern and Central European Art since the 1950s*. At that time, Paulo Herkenhoff, who was then MoMA's Adjunct Curator of Latin American Art, proposed that we address Latin America in the next volumes of the series and conceived an initial group of publications focusing on writings from Argentina, Venezuela, and Brazil. The first of these was *Listen Here Now! Argentine Art of the 1960s: Writings of the Avant-Garde* (2004), which was subsequently published in Spanish as *Escritos de vanguardia: Arte argentino de los años '60* (2007), with the collaboration of Fundación Proa and Fundación Espigas of Buenos Aires.

Following the success of *Listen Here Now!*, we are delighted to present the next offering in this program, *Alfredo Boulton and His Contemporaries: Critical Dialogues in Venezuelan Art, 1912–1974*. Alfredo Boulton was a key personality in the creation of the discourse on modernity in Venezuela, a significant historian and critic of the visual arts, an important photographer in his own right of the Venezuelan landscape and people, and a long-time member of the International Council of The Museum of Modern Art, serving as its Chairman from 1970 to 1974. His figure provides an ideal focus for the study of this fascinating era in the history of Venezuelan art.

We are deeply indebted to Ariel Jiménez, Chief Curator at the Colección Patricia Phelps de Cisneros, for his complete commitment to this book and his impeccable work as its editor. He devised its organization and structure, wrote the introduction to each group of texts, selected the images to include, and, in collaboration with our advisory committee, identified the writers of the newly commissioned essays and selected the historical texts for the volume. Jessica Hankey, Editorial Associate in MoMA's International Program, worked closely with him, and we are very grateful for her zealous coordination of the project and her insightful research. I served on the Museum's advisory committee for this project, along with Paulo Herkenhoff, Edward J. Sullivan, Luis Pérez-Oramas, and Juan Ignacio Parra; we are all grateful to these scholars for their generous advice and help. We would also like to thank the writers of the new essays – Hugo Achugar, Roldán Esteva-Grillet, Elías Pino Iturrieta, Marco Negrón, Luis Pérez-Oramas, Sandra Pinardi, Maciá Pintó, and Rafael Castillo Zapata – whose work so sensitively places the historical texts in their original context and explains their significance to a contemporary audience. We also owe thanks to Carlos Palacios, who contributed the chronology to this volume.

The International Council of The Museum of Modern Art is the principal sponsor of our entire series of documentary anthologies. We are deeply grateful to Jo Carole Lauder, the Council's President; Agnes Gund, its Chairman; and Carol Coffin, its Executive Director. We have also received generous contributions toward the production of the book from Mercantil Servicios

Financieros (Venezuela), Ignacio and Luis Alfonso Oberto, the Reed Foundation, Juan Ignacio Parra, the Alberto Vollmer Foundation, Inc., Jean Hartley Boulton, Estrellita B. Brodsky, Harry Mannil, Gonzalo Parodi, Patricia Phelps de Cisneros, Byron Meyer, and William L. Bernhard.

Many members of MoMA's staff helped with this publication. In the Department of Publications, we owe thanks to Christopher Hudson, Publisher, Kara Kirk, Associate Publisher, David Frankel, Editorial Director, and Marc Sapir, Production Director. We would especially like to thank the Production Manager, Christina Grillo, for her invaluable help in the realization of this volume. Outside the Museum, Diana Stoll, the editor of the English-language edition of the book, brought aplomb and expertise to the project, and Elise Nussbaum cast a sharp editorial eye on the historical texts. We are grateful to the book's designer, Gina Rossi, who has been responsible for all the volumes in this series, for an original design that is both handsome and thoughtful. In the International Program, thanks go to Sylvia Renner for taking on so many of the organizational details with enthusiasm and rigor, and to Gwen Farrelly for her adept assistance with rights and reproductions. We are grateful to Majlena Braun, Inés Katzenstein, and Miriam Basilio for their work and feedback in the early stages of the project, in addition to Kristopher Kersey, Kip Michel, Max Kaplan, and Julia Meuse. We also owe thanks to Peter Reed, Senior Deputy Director for Curatorial Affairs; Jennifer Russell, Senior Deputy Director for Exhibitions, Collections, and Programs; Elizabeth Burke, Foundation Relations Director; Alexis Ferguson, Development Associate; Geaninne Gutiérrez-Guimarães, Curatorial Assistant, Drawings; Michelle Elligott, Milan Hughston, Jenny Tobias, and Taína Caragol of the Library and Archives; and MoMA interns Erica Huang, Isabel Bohrer, Lilit Sadoyan, Jamieson Bunn, and Heather Cleary. We are especially grateful to Glenn D. Lowry, the Museum's Director, for his support of the entire publication project from its conception.

We would like to thank the dedicated translators who provided new translations for this volume: Kristina Cordero, Jen Hofer, Catalina Ocampo, Richard Moszka, and Laura Pérez. We offer special thanks to Carlos Riobó for his sensitive translations of the work of Alfredo Boulton, to Mónica de la Torre, Spanish-language coordinator and translator, for her spirited guidance, and to Lara Tucker for her assistance with issues of research and translation.

We are very grateful to the many individuals—critics, artists, historians, and writers (and, in some cases, their heirs), as well as private collectors—without whose generous support and assistance this publication would have been unimaginable. We would like to thank in particular Sofía Vollmer de Maduro, who helped us in innumerable ways throughout the publication project, including assisting us with the all-important task of locating the necessary sponsorship. We are also indebted to Victoria Apostolatos, Antón Apostolatos, Ada Castro, Carlos Cruz-Diez, María Antonia González Arnal, John Paul McDonald, José Navas, Ignacio Oberto, Valentina Oberto, María Omaña, Carlos Palacios, Juan Ignacio Parra, Luis Pérez-Oramas, Delia Picón Salas, María Esther Pino, Maciá Pintó, Tahía Rivero, Rafael Romero D., Rafael Santana, Hélène Soto, Anne Soto, Isabelle Soto, Edward J. Sullivan, Paulina Villanueva, and Zuleiva Vivas.

In addition, a number of public institutions and collections, and private collections provided vital assistance to the project. The Alberto Vollmer Foundation, Inc., of Caracas was an especially important supporter of this project, providing us with, among other things, full access to Alfredo Boulton's texts and photographs. The Fundación Villanueva of Caracas helped us enormously in locating texts by Carlos Raúl Villanueva and photographs by Paolo Gasparini and Ricardo de Sola. We also wish to thank: Colección Archivos Nacionales de Venezuela. Instituto Autónomo Biblioteca Nacional, Caracas; Asociación Civil Proyecto Armando Reverón, Caracas; Centro de Estudios Latinoamericanos Rómulo Gallegos, Altamira; Colección Banco Central de Venezuela, Caracas; Colección Mercantil, Caracas; Colección Fundación Museos Nacionales Galería de Arte Nacional, Caracas; Colección Fundación Museos Nacionales Museo de Arte Contemporáneo de Caracas; Colección Fundación para la Cultura Urbana, Caracas; Colección Ignacio y Valentina Oberto, Caracas; Colección Patricia Phelps de Cisneros, Caracas; Fundación Alejandro Colina, Caracas; Fundación Casa Arturo Úslar Pietri, Caracas; Fundación Francisco Narváez, Caracas; Fundación Gego, Caracas; and Fundación Jesús Soto, Caracas.

Jay A. Levenson
Director, International Program
The Museum of Modern Art

foreword

The aim of *Alfredo Boulton and His Contemporaries: Critical Dialogues in Venezuelan Art, 1912–1974* is to provide readers interested in Latin American cultural processes with a series of essential tools with which to delve into the universe of works and ideas that drove Venezuelan art practice in the twentieth century. For this purpose, we have adopted as a guide the person and work of Alfredo Boulton, art historian, critic, and photographer, who held a commanding perspective on the art made in his country. Indeed, no one before Boulton had attempted a comprehensive analysis of the region's art from colonial times to the present; thus his work has become a mandatory reference for Venezuelan art historiography and criticism.

Using Boulton's work to guide our selection of texts determined the volume's chronological parameters, as well as its strict focus on what we may call the "modern Venezuelan project," beginning with the advent of Impressionistic painting in the early twentieth century and ending in the mid-1970s, when the country's will to modernization reached its peak. Boulton's preferences, opinions, and understanding of Venezuelan art provided a point of view for us; in order to delineate it, we were obliged to document the main works and artists that Boulton discusses in his criticism, as well as a number that—for methodological or ideological reasons—he purposefully chose *not* to discuss.

Boulton did not limit himself, however, strictly to the purview of Venezuelan art practice. From very early on, he maintained a far-reaching dialogue with artists and intellectuals in Latin America, Europe, and the United States—especially with The Museum of Modern Art in New York City, where his photographs were included in the 1946 exhibition *New Photographers*, curated by Nancy and Beaumont Newhall. But it was not only as a photographer that Boulton was engaged with MoMA: he was an interlocutor deeply involved in the Museum's international activities, to the extent that he was appointed Chairman of the Board of MoMA's International Council in 1970. In this role, Boulton shared with the Museum the benefits of his understanding of the art of his time from a perspective that encompassed work made in the most diverse national and regional settings and that went beyond a narrow reading of modernism.

For the reader familiar with the evolution of what we have come to call modern Western art, the dates 1912 to 1974 that serve as this publication's framework may seem curious. Indeed, the choice of this particular chronological period says much, not only about the discrepancy that characterizes Venezuelan processes vis-à-vis their European models, but about their specificities—about that difference that makes the Venezuelan reality unquestionably distinct.

This volume is divided into two essential sections and periods: "Figuring Venezuela, 1912–1949" and "The Challenge of the Times, 1949–1974." In both sections, the reader will find historical documents selected to illuminate the issues that distinguished the period in question; most of these texts have never before been published in English. The historical sections that constitute the heart of the book are preceded by a series of introductory studies by contemporary scholars. The purpose of these essays is to give readers the frame of reference needed to understand the political, demographic, and cultural context in which ideas were fomenting. The book concludes with a "critical nexus": four essays by contemporary critics discussing issues addressed by Boulton that characterize Venezuelan modernity. At the end of this publication, a chronology and selected bibliography offer useful complements for readers who wish to continue their research and broaden their knowledge of the period.

Due to the inevitable limitations of the book's physical size, we have abridged some of the selected historical documents, in particular the more extensive ones (such editorial abridgments are acknowledged by ellipses in brackets within the texts; a note at the end of these pieces indicates both the fact of abridgment and the full publication information should readers wish to consult the complete texts). Lastly, if the dates of certain texts do not coincide with the period of the section in which they are included, it is because the issues discussed by the writer correspond in essence to the concerns of the era in question. This is the case, for instance, with Arturo Úslar Pietri's essays on *mestizaje* (racial mixing), a topic that clearly corresponds to concerns typical of the first half of the twentieth century—especially after 1920—although Úslar Pietri dealt with it in the 1970s.

Specialists may lament the absence of a specific image, or the fact that an important artist or group is mentioned only cursorily here. Our hope is that interested audiences will find in this book a broad and representative introduction to the individual artists and movements cutting across the twentieth century in Venezuela—their achievements and failures, their expectations, and their remarkable collective initiatives—and may proceed from this grounding to further investigations.

—Ariel Jiménez

chapter one introductory studies

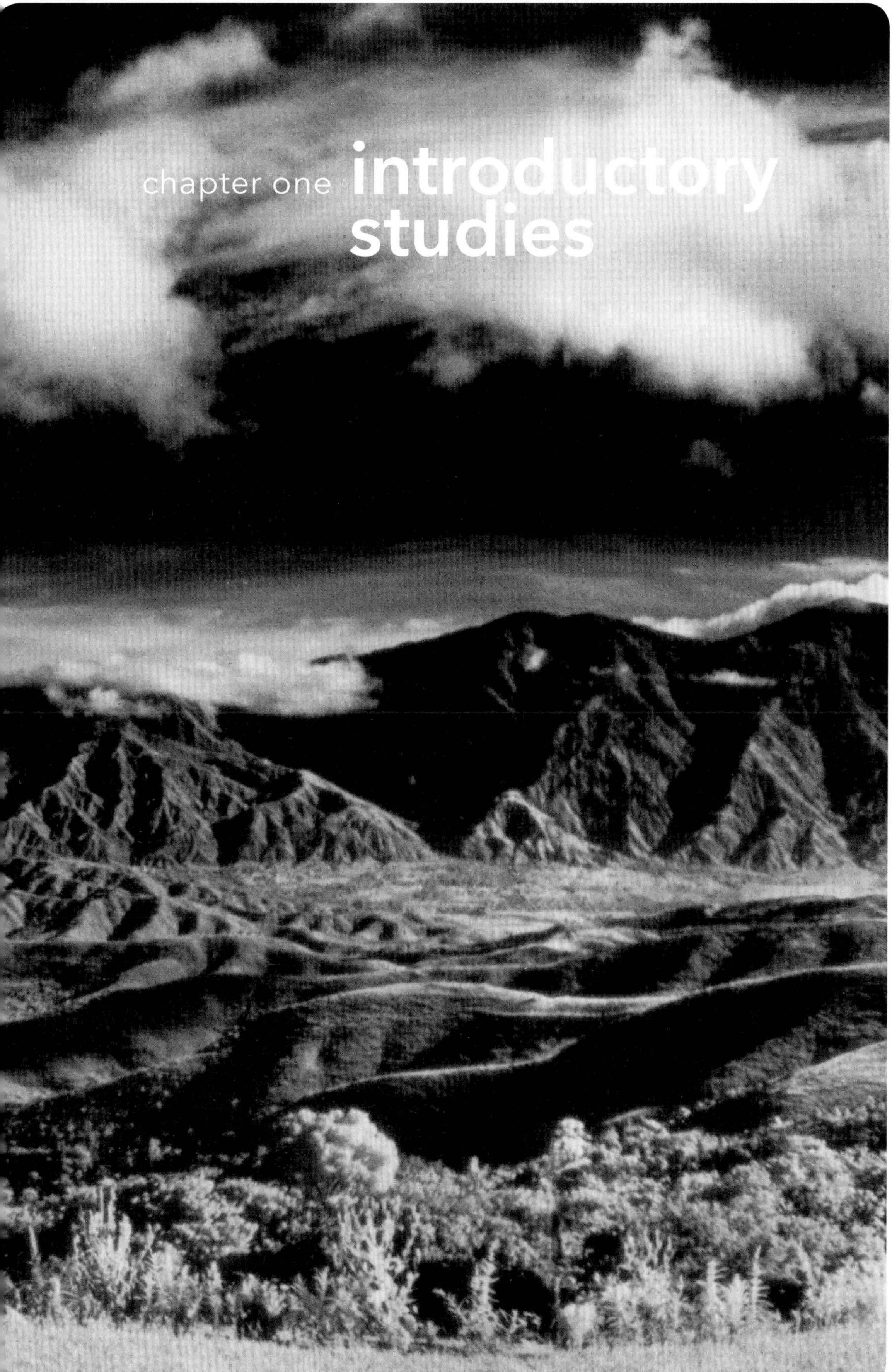

latin american modernities **hugo achugar**

latin american scenarios

According to Hegel, the American continent was incapable of developing its own theoretical approach.[1] Other thinkers of the so-called First World have seen Latin America, specifically, as a premodern realm of handicrafts and magic realism. In much of the discourse on Latin America, the region is synonymous with great rivers, abundant tropical rainforests, and an alarming accumulation of dictators, malnourished children, and drug dealers. These scenarios have "orientalized" Latin America, making it the home of the savage, of the cannibal, of Shakespeare's Caliban.

The history of such scenarios and representations of Latin America begins before 1492.[2] During the twentieth century these representations changed in accordance with global events such as the Bolshevik Revolution, the two world wars, and the Cold War, and with regional events such as the Mexican Revolution of 1910, the Cuban Revolution of 1959, the dictatorships of the 1970s, and the more recent emergence of left-wing or "populist" governments in various countries of the region, particularly Venezuela since the time of Hugo Chávez's rise to power in 1999.[3]

Throughout history, many of the images of Latin America—those constructed both locally and abroad—have had a common tendency: a will toward homogeneity. The reasons for this have often been political and economic. However, if anything characterizes Latin America it is its radical *heterogeneity*—its geographic, ethnic, and social diversity, of course, but also its cultural heterogeneity, marked by the dichotomy of oral and written culture,[4] the trichotomy of indigenous, African, and European cultures, as well as the experience of living simultaneous temporalities or "mixed times";[5] in other words, it is possible to find a variety of cultural, social, and economic temporalities coexisting within Latin America, and even within a single country. Paradoxically, these multiple scenarios provide one of the region's fundamental—and unifying—traits: its supranational diversity and multiplicity.

This does not mean that it is impossible to identify a single element that cuts through these countries' heterogeneous historical and cultural realities, allowing us to establish a few common factors. There is certainly at least one such element—heterogeneous in itself—that would eventually underlie all Latin American modernities: the experience of speed, both in the sense of movement from one place to another and also in relation to the propensity for change and the acceptance of novelty and difference. Different speeds in Latin America have made it possible for highways and skyscrapers to multiply in Caracas at an ever-increasing pace since the mid-twentieth century, while in other regions of Venezuela, which remain untouched by successive waves of modernization, indigenous groups still live on the fringes of the country's modernity in spite of their relatively small size in comparison to those in the Andean region, in Guatemala, or in Mexico.

In Venezuela differences and tensions are played out between the city and the countryside, the Western and the indigenous, the literate and the illiterate, the cosmopolitan and the provincial, but also within each of these categories. Thus, the cosmopolitan may be illiterate and rural, the urban may be provincial and literate. This heterogeneity of scenarios is not a recent phenomenon, although it intensified throughout the twentieth century and now, at the start of the twenty-first, goes hand in hand with the current technological, media, and audiovisual revolution.

As a consequence, it is increasingly difficult to understand various Latin American phenomena in exclusively national or regional terms. To speak of the radical heterogeneity of the vast majority of these countries is also a way of describing their social and cultural fragmentation. Perhaps this is why, among the discourses that sought to provide a general image of Latin America—including those developed by Latin Americans—the most meaningful ones were constructed from afar. This was the case with the Venezuelan Andrés Bello[6] during his exile in London around 1820, with the Cuban José Martí[7] who was writing from New York in 1891, with other Latin Americans such as Carlos Quijano,[8] Arturo Úslar Pietri,[9] Alejo Carpentier,[10] Julio Cortázar,[11] and with many others as well, ranging from the early twentieth century to the present, as general visions of Latin America are still being developed in the context of a globalized world and from a globalized perspective.

Situating Venezuela within the diversity and heterogeneity of Latin America poses two risks: the first, of committing the "sin" of exceptionalism, and the second, of failing to recognize the particularities of a country that is itself multiple and heterogeneous. Any attempt to make homogenizing assertions about a nation that harbors the Andean foothills, long stretches of Caribbean coast, wide plains, and the northern section of the Amazon basin—plus a significant Afro-Venezuelan community, an indigenous minority, and a sizeable population of *mestizos* (people of mixed races)—is destined to fail. However, the many Venezuelan cultures do possess certain traits that distinguish them from the rest of Latin America; these result from the interrelation of natural, demographic, and social circumstances and from the fact that the country has developed a particularly sophisticated artistic practice in close contact with Western centers of power, an important cultural industry of its own, and a popular culture that is diverse, secular, and both urban and rural.

modernity is multifarious

There is more than one modernity in Venezuela and Latin America. This is due not only to Latin America's diversity and heterogeneity but also to the different stages that characterized the development of the region's modernities.

That development itself was, furthermore, uneven and asynchronous: while Venezuela was living through Juan Vicente Gómez's dictatorship during three decades of the twentieth century (1908–35), Mexico was in the throes of a revolution that began in 1910 and would last long into the century, as other countries, such as Argentina and Brazil, were engaged in an accelerated process of modernization. In addition, the various stages of modernization were experienced differently by different people: while some enthusiastic Latin Americans welcomed modernity as a synonym for progress, for others it was experienced as a brush with the Apocalypse.

These ambivalences and conflicting visions have pervaded the imagery of Latin American artists and intellectuals since the mid-nineteenth century. For example, in 1845 the Argentinean Domingo F. Sarmiento[12] coined the problematic phrase "civilization or barbarism" as an illustration of the contradictions between the "barbarous" characteristics of local culture and Eurocentric modernizing impulses. This problematic vision has been reiterated, questioned, and finessed up to the present century, thus confirming the fact that the representations and imagery of different modernities have not been able to escape their own diversity or the conflicts intrinsic to the region.[13]

By the end of the nineteenth century, Latin America was in the midst of an uneven integration into the Western project of modernity. The process of decolonization had ended in almost all countries – with the exception of Cuba and Puerto Rico, which were involved in the Spanish-American War of 1898 – and a series of administrative reforms had been achieved at the state level, notably the creation of public education and the abolition of slavery.[14] The transition from a precapitalist system of exploitation to economic rationalism was already a fact for the majority of the region's countries. Once again, such processes were neither homogeneous nor simultaneous; whereas modernizing impulses were evident in southern Brazil, Mexico, Argentina, and other countries of the Southern Cone, some countries persisted in the colonial rhythm.[15] Although Venezuela was beginning to emerge from the civil wars that had put an end to the multiple presidencies of Antonio Guzmán Blanco[16] – who spearheaded a number of reforms to modernize the state and the educational system – this was not necessarily linked to the transformations of the time.

This diversity and heterogeneity of circumstance meant that in some regions and countries the influx of icons representative of modernity's productive and technological revolution coexisted with lifestyles, behaviors, and modes of production that were characteristic of the colonial era and sometimes incompatible with Western versions of modernity. Thus by the first decades of the twentieth century, vast regions of Latin America continued to live within cultural, social, and economic parameters set by indigenous traditions barely altered by their contact with European colonizing practices. At the same time Buenos Aires, São Paulo, Mexico City, Montevideo, and a few other cities were undergoing a period of particularly dynamic growth with regard to media, transportation, the new products of the cultural industry (especially film, radio, and music), dialogue with European cultural production, and the establishment of new literary and artistic centers. Venezuela, for example, witnessed the appearance of its first movies in 1897, the first full-length film in 1916, the first automobile in 1904, and the first radio broadcasts in 1926.

These were not yet mass phenomena; many modern icons were linked to the powerful or most educated socioeconomic classes. Dialogue between the educated class, or the "lettered city,"[17] and cultural production in cosmopolitan centers – particularly France – was, however, a common practice in all Latin America, and especially Venezuela, as the correspondence between Arturo Úslar Pietri and Alfredo Boulton or between the latter and Julián Padrón[18] from the 1920s to the 1930s demonstrates. For example, in a letter of October 11, 1939, sent to Boulton in Paris, Padrón asks for James Joyce's *Ulysses* in French and suggests that Boulton acquire "*Finnegans Wake*, Joyce's latest work, along with the recordings in which he himself reads several passages," a recommendation that illustrates the modern cosmopolitanism characteristic of the period's educated class.[19]

The "lettered city's" cosmopolitan dialogue was accompanied by migratory processes that altered the demographic landscape and contributed to an increase in the population of various Latin American cities. The population of Buenos Aires went from 890,000 inhabitants to almost 1,500,000 between 1903 and 1913, and Mexico City's grew from little more than 340,000 to more than a million between 1910 and 1930. New York City grew from almost three million to nearly seven million between 1900 and 1930. Caracas's expansion was not as pronounced: the city had close to 90,000 inhabitants in 1900 and some 150,000 in the 1920s.

The quick growth of Buenos Aires and New York has been explained in terms of strong migratory currents from Europe. But those two cities were not the only ones affected by the influx of European immigrants; a similar wave occurred in Santiago de Chile, Montevideo, and other cities of the region. This was compounded by immigration from non-European countries, contributing to the region's present cultural and ethnic diversity—from Japan to São Paulo; from China to some countries on the Caribbean and Pacific coasts, such as Peru; from India (in particular) to some Caribbean countries. There was a substantial Jewish migration to various countries, especially those in the Southern Cone. In Venezuela's case, the greatest impact came from the colonial slave trade. From the early nineteenth century on, however, immigration was subject to a number of vicissitudes both at home and abroad that, in spite of its importance, weakened the impact of European immigration—from Germany, Italy, and Spain especially—on the country in comparison with other regions of the Americas.

All the changes that characterized the rise of modernity in the early twentieth century—including immigration to Latin America, the impact of World War I, the Mexican Revolution of 1910, and the Bolshevik Revolution of 1917—helped to reinforce an imagery of renewal; this was further strengthened by the daily experience, already acquired and assimilated, of the transformations in the media and transportation systems.

Although trains, electricity, and automobiles were still privileges enjoyed by few, they had long been part of everyday life in the Americas. By the early twentieth century, mass transit systems—one of the most obvious symbols of modernity—had already been in existence for half a century. In his *Arcades Project*, Walter Benjamin wrote that in Paris, "on January 30, 1828, the first omnibus began operation on the line running along the boulevard from the Bastille to the Madeleine."[20] In New York the first horse-drawn streetcar appeared in 1832, and in Latin America three lines opened simultaneously in 1858 in Mexico City, Havana, and Santiago de Chile. Latin America's first railroad opened in Cuba in November 1837, eleven years before trains ran in the capital of the Spanish empire that ruled over the island. In Venezuela, the main railroad lines were inaugurated before the turn of the century, though their construction had begun much earlier: the lines from Puerto Cabello to Valencia (1888) and from Caracas to Valencia (1894) were linked to the one between La Guaira and Caracas (1883), the two most important ports and cities of the central region. The horse-drawn streetcar, on the other hand, arrived here in 1882 and the electric streetcar in 1908.

The purpose here is not to list modern means of transportation but to highlight the emergence of a different perspective, a new gaze. Our main interest is not the railway per se, but the experience of modernity and, above all, a gaze lived and experienced through the new means of movement from one place to the next. This new gaze, introduced by the icons of modernity—photography is paradigmatic of such a gaze—was a key element of the technological innovations that transformed the experience of the "new" in Latin America.

avant-gardes and modernity between the wars

The panorama set up by the first modernity was already well established by the time the "historical avant-gardes" burst onto the scene in Latin America: the São Paulo Semana de Arte Moderna (Modern art week)[21] in 1922 is held as a key date,[22] and 1925 is considered a fundamental year as both the start of the Mexican muralist movement and the year in which the Venezuelan Úslar Pietri, based in Paris, coined (or adapted) the term "magic realism" as a form of Latin American "cultural capital" (to borrow a term from sociologist Pierre Bourdieu).

The technological, social, and cultural transformations at the beginning of what has been called the "short century"[23] gave rise to great cultural productivity, an intense dialogue between the two shores of the Atlantic Ocean, and an energetic revitalization of ideas that had an impact on the image of Latin America, especially among the region's intellectual and artistic elites. This enthusiasm, transformation, and dialogue produced a kind of generalized upheaval that sparked political, artistic, and literary as well as ethnic and cultural movements: Andean indigenism, the Mexican Revolution, Caribbean negritude—which occurred at the same time as the New York Harlem Renaissance—and the *americanismo*[24] championed by various authors and countries.

Enthusiasm and unlimited faith in the potentials of the New World in the face of European decadence were not, however, the only aspects of Latin American modernity during this period. Like those in Western Europe, Latin American modernities also had their dark side, their apocalyptic elements.

The promise of Futurism was epitomized in Filippo Tommaso Marinetti's 1909 proclamation that "a speeding car . . . is more beautiful than the Victory of Samothrace," but little of that zeal is to be found in Charlie Chaplin's representation of modern malaise in the film *Modern Times* (1936). Likewise, Rómulo Gallegos[25]—the future president of Venezuela and an enthusiastic proponent of the power of education and civilization in Latin America—observed the following in his September 1931 talk at the Nicholas Roerich Museum of New York: "The Empire State Building is large. Grand. They say it will hold five thousand offices. Five thousand abodes of toil with their corresponding instruments of torture for five thousand typists. Five thousand bankruptcies. The crisis continues indeed."[26]

There is no doubt that the experience of modernity was ambivalent and even contradictory, or that the modernity depicted in *Modern Times* (or in Fritz Lang's 1927 film *Metropolis*), and which Gallegos satirized, was merely one of modernity's many manifestations. In fact, if one compares the critical spirit with which Gallegos engages the modernist icon of the Empire State Building in his 1931 speech with his stance in the 1929 novel *Doña Bárbara*, in which he fleshes out his belief in civilization and modernization, it is obvious that the ambivalences of modernity were due not only to economic or financial factors but to conflicting feelings generated in many Latin Americans by the enthusiasm and frustrations of the modernizing process.

From the mid-nineteenth century to the present, contradictory experiences and ambivalent reactions to the successive stages of modernization were common in both the West and peripheral Latin America. In January 1928 Venezuela was still controlled by Gómez and barely a decade had passed since the discovery of its tremendous oil reserves, which put an end to the cocoa production that had dominated Venezuelan agriculture since the nineteenth century.[27]

That year, a group of students wrote the words that would serve as a kind of generational manifesto: "We are a group of young men with faith, with hope, and with no mercy."[28] These young men would later become known as the "Generation of 1928,"[29] a group that included future Venezuelan presidents Rómulo Betancourt[30] and Raúl Leoni,[31] as well as other figures such as Jóvito Villalba, Miguel Otero Silva,[32] and Isaac Pardo, all of whom played important roles in Venezuela's cultural and political life (and to whom Úslar Pietri, among others, had close connections). Their "faith" and "hope"—and even their lack of mercy—are emblematic of the enthusiasm of the educated class at the forefront of one of Latin America's many modernities. Proponents of this modernity believed not only in cultural renewal but also in the transformation of life in all its aspects, most particularly in the democratization of public life. It was this belief that inspired the student movement and the 1918 reforms to the university system in Córdoba, Argentina; it was this same belief that motivated the Nicaraguan Augusto César Sandino's[33] actions in the 1920s and mobilized artists, writers, politicians, and social activists in various parts of Latin America. In the United States, meantime, the "roaring twenties" saw the return home of veterans of World War I, the growth of jazz, the emergence of the modern woman (the flapper), and the beginning of the Great Depression.

In Venezuela and the rest of Latin America, along with enthusiasm, willfulness, and experimentation came frustrations, the rise of dictatorships, economic disasters, the failure of projects, isolation, and tense relations between Latin America and its great northern neighbor, which invaded or engaged in conflicts with Cuba, Mexico, Nicaragua, Panama, Puerto Rico, Venezuela, and others between 1898 and 1934. These years were marked by the fall of dictatorships, including Gómez's in Venezuela (1936), the Argentine military coup, the rise of Getulio Vargas's populism in 1930 in Brazil,[34] the Chaco War between Paraguay and Bolivia (1934), Gerardo Machado's period of despotism in Cuba,[35] the beginning of the Somoza dynasty in Nicaragua,[36] but also Mexican president Lázaro Cárdenas's nationalization of the petroleum reserves (1937),[37] Sandino's insurrection in Nicaragua, and Farabundo Martí's insurrection in El Salvador.[38]

During these years, the presence of North American multinational companies assumed ominous overtones, as happened with the United Fruit Company's involvement in the "Banana Massacre" (fictionalized in Gabriel García Márquez's 1967 novel *One Hundred Years of Solitude*). Companies also finished consolidating their power, making the Rockefeller family the owner of 95 percent of Venezuela's petroleum production through the Standard Oil Company in 1940.

These events helped establish the stereotype of the "banana republic" that has been grafted onto the region's countries from the mid-twentieth century to the present, as well as other stereotypes that would follow: the tropical exoticism of Carmen Miranda, or the world of the Buenos Aires and Montevideo mafia, as seen in the 1946 Rita Hayworth vehicle *Gilda*.

This was also a time of fevered *americanismo*, strong nationalist sentiments, and close contact with cosmopolitan centers. The maxim of the Brazilian avant-garde—"Tupí or not Tupí, that is the question"[39]—references the desire to hybridize cultures, that deliberate cultural cannibalism that would elsewhere be termed *mestizaje* (Úslar Pietri), or the universal "melting pot," as in the Mexican José Vasconcelos's *La raza cosmica* (*The Cosmic Race*),[40] or Uruguayan artist Joaquín Torres-García's version of *americanismo*, in which Constructivism was engaged with Inca symbols.

In Venezuela, this period coincides not only with the cultural and educational renewal ushered in by the "Generation of 1928" but also with the construction of a society in which petroleum would play a key role. The phrase "sembrar el petróleo" (to sow the oil), coined by Úslar Pietri in 1936, was put into practice by Gómez's successor, General Eleazar López Contreras,[41] toward the late 1930s. In 1936, some of the country's most valuable intellectuals, among them Rómulo Betancourt and Mariano Picón Salas[42] (a central figure in the realm of education), returned to Venezuela; both of these men founded a political movement whose goal was to democratize and modernize the country.

This was a rich and diverse time in Latin America, during which the cultural dialogue with Europe and the United States resulted in collaborations not only among Latin American and European painters but also among writers from many countries; the hotbed of artists included Vicente Huidobro, Alejo Carpentier, César Vallejo, Miguel Ángel Asturias, Nicolás Guillén, José Lezama Lima, Robert and Sonia Delaunay, Pablo Picasso, Jean Arp, Langston Hughes, Wallace Stevens, and Edward Weston. It was during this time that the filmmaker Sergei Eisenstein discovered Mexico, and French writer Blaise Cendrars was captivated by Brazil. Venezuela not only participated in this multifaceted dialogue, but in fact produced numerous artists and writers (Úslar Pietri and Boulton, as mentioned, but also Francisco Narváez,[43] Jesús Rafael Soto,[44] Guillermo Meneses, Sofía Imber, and the architect Carlos Raúl Villanueva[45]), each of whom became a paradigmatic example of the Latin American intellectual's role as a "culture broker" for his or her country of origin.

The somewhat arbitrary list above seeks to show yet another face of the multiple heterogeneities and temporalities experienced during the emergence of modernity between the wars in Latin America: the modernity of transatlantic and transcontinental dialogue, an exchange shaped by the time period and by the cosmopolitan and globalizing aspects implicit in both past and present irruptions of modernity.

midcentury or contemporary universalism

Modernizing impulses in Latin America underwent a very particular transformation at the end of the 1930s and the beginning of the 1940s. This transformation can be understood as the weakening of artistic and cultural projects, the emergence of existentialist thought, or the consequence of economic and political changes that began with the economic crisis of 1929 and with the regional and global consolidation of political movements that resulted in the Spanish Civil War, World War II, and the Holocaust.

Although these events happened outside Latin America, their effects were felt within the region. They played, after all, a predominant role in the restructuring of world power that took place after 1945 once Mussolini's and Hitler's fates were decided and Roosevelt, Churchill, and Stalin had divided up the planet at Yalta. During this new stage of globalization and modernization, Latin America not only served as a refuge for various groups—Spanish exiles, Jewish communities, and other European émigrés—but also as a supplier of food and oil, and as repository for European capital. In some cases (particularly in Brazil) Latin America would participate by sending soldiers off to fight in Europe, and in others (such as the Río de la Plata) it felt, to a lesser extent, the effects of a naval battle. Venezuelan oil would play a crucial role both in World War II and in the new global order.

By the end of the 1940s, other effects of the major transformations brought about by global reorganization came into focus: the beginning of the Cold War, the Bretton Woods Agreement (1944), the beginning of the atomic era with the bombing of Hiroshima (1945), the creation of the U.S. National Security Council (1947), the creation of the Organization of American States (OAS) (1948), and the Truman government's implementation of the Marshall Plan. The effects of the Truman Doctrine and the National Security Act would be felt throughout Latin America, particularly with the establishment of authoritarian regimes in countries as diverse as Guatemala, Paraguay (1954), the Dominican Republic, and Colombia, as well as in Brazil, Uruguay, Chile, and Argentina during the 1960s and '70s.

In Venezuela's case, after López Contreras's government, a revolutionary junta led by Betancourt deposed President Isaías Medina Angarita[46] in 1945 and took provisional power in order to guarantee presidential elections and establish direct, universal secret suffrage. Three years later, in 1948, Rómulo Gallegos assumed the presidency with the intention of initiating educational reforms and renegotiating petroleum contracts, but was ousted by the end of the year. The new world order, as well as internal turmoil in Venezuela, facilitated the establishment of dictatorial governments that would control the country until January of 1958, with Marcos Pérez Jiménez[47] as their central figure.

There was another aspect to this scenario, intimately linked to certain aspects of midcentury modernization. The European conflicts and the new world order provided, in effect, economic "benefits" to some of the countries in the region due to an increase in exports and the localization of some global assets. During these years, the architecture of cities such as Caracas, São Paulo, Buenos Aires, and Mexico City underwent profound transformations. Latin America's modernizing impulse and the urban transformation of the late 1940s and early 1950s are key to understanding midcentury modernity in Latin America (although it must be remembered that the vast majority of Latin America was excluded from these transformations).

It has been argued that the most evident signs can be seen in Havana, which remained frozen at this stage of modernization; but perhaps

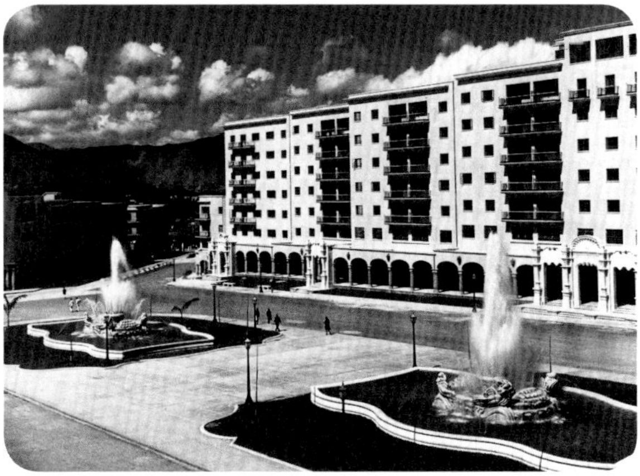

El Silencio building complex in Caracas. Photograph by Alfredo Boulton. c. 1945. Alberto Vollmer Foundation, Inc., Caracas

Caracas and São Paulo are even clearer examples of the post-World War II drive to modernize. The redevelopment of the El Silencio district (1941–45) and the construction of the Universidad Central de Venezuela (1944–58)—two Caracas projects by the architect Carlos Raúl Villanueva—had an enormous impact on the city's inhabitants, which numbered barely more than a million in 1950; and the buildings and highways in São Paulo—which in the same year had a population of 2,200,000—are eloquent examples of modernity's face at that time. The urban and architectural growth of Caracas and São Paulo in the 1950s is indicative of the vitality that characterized this phase of modernity. Oscar Niemeyer's Brasilia project (1956–60) is a particularly revealing example of the spirit of the time.[48] It epitomizes the idea of modernity as a civilizing mandate, as the inscription of culture on nature, as omnipotent reason's control over natural chaos; the city's construction in the middle of the Mato Grosso jungle was a geometric operation kindred, concordant, and convergent with a modernity that was seeking its own path.

This is perhaps the key to this stage of Latin American modernity: the desire to make the universalism of reason coincide with a new regard for the particular and local. During this period, universalism and localism inspired multiple projects, similar to those attempted in the years between the wars but of a different tenor. The difference lay in Latin America's midcentury efforts to attain self-sufficiency, which converged with import-substitution policies. The impulse to construct new societies, modern cities, and universal spaces was complemented by an effort to create national industries, at least in some countries (as others remained mere producers of raw materials for the industries of developed countries).

This oscillating perspective, this gaze trapped between contemporary universalism and nationalist localism also crystallized in projects as dissimilar as Jorge Luis Borges's anti-realism, Miguel Ángel Asturias's and Rosario Castellanos's magic realism, Juan Carlos Onetti's blurring of boundaries between the real and the imaginary, and Alejo Carpentier's "real maravilloso" (marvelous real). Although most of these authors began writing before World War II, the midcentury decades brought new interest to their particular visions.

In fact, this entire period is a battleground between those who held on to the strictly local and those who aspired to enter into dialogue with the global, between the populist nationalism of president Juan Perón and his wife Evita in Argentina and the universalism of intellectual currents that attempted to distance themselves from the local.

This polarization, however, does not account for everything that was happening at the time. Numerous writers, artists, art critics, photographers, and intellectuals were speaking out on both sides of the issue. The term and the notion of the "glocal"—a conflation of "global" and "local"—had not yet been coined, yet the "glocal" spirit and, in particular, "glocal" production already existed in Latin America.[49]

Boulton's *La Margarita* (1952), an ethno-historic photo-essay about the Isla de Margarita, off Venezuela's northern coast, is closer to artistic creation than to photographic record, and embodies the "glocal" spirit. The book is, on one hand, a detailed and carefully documented historical account, and on the other a photographic record with ethnographic ambitions, both of which are brought together through a "modernist" aesthetic.[50] Nature, everyday objects, and human beings are treated not only in terms of their referential value—that is, as documents—but also as aestheticized images or objects valuable in and of themselves. Two good examples of this are the image of the fishing net (which can almost be envisioned as one of sculptor Gego's weblike Reticuláreas),[51] and the aerial photograph of the Isla de Margarita in which the "real object" is defamiliarized and given the status of an "artistic object."[52]

This spirit—which we may anachronistically call "glocal" because of its attempt to give new worth to the local and national while simultaneously inscribing itself within the universalist aesthetics of contemporary Western modernism—is present in the work and thinking of other Latin American authors, artists, and intellectuals of the time. To a great extent, this aesthetic-ideological project can be found in the writings of Octavio Paz, in the essays of the art critic Romero Brest, and in the architectural work of Oscar Niemeyer. The "glocal" allowed enthusiasm for the French films of the Nouvelle Vague and a preference for the films of the Swede Ingmar Bergman over Hollywood's productions to coexist with Pérez Jiménez's nationalist cultural project and his celebration of the patriotic Semana de la Patria (Homeland week) and Danzas Venezuela (Venezuela dances) as two faces of a divergent, cosmopolitan, Americanist project.

There were, however, other positions, other faces to this divergent project. Villanueva's correspondence with Alexander Calder dates to these years; it is the same period in which Roger Caillois translated the work of Borges and made

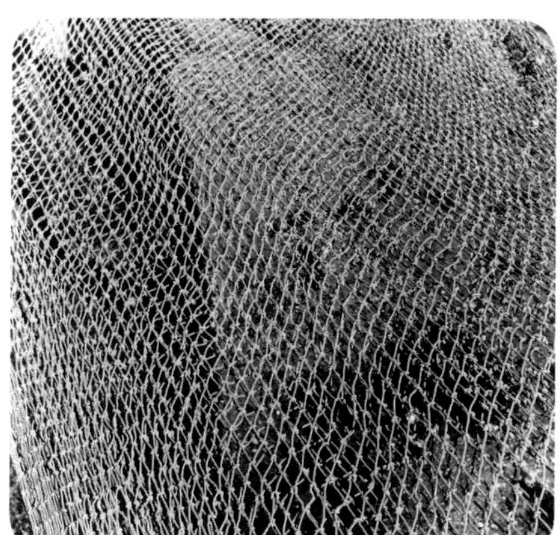

Fishing net. Photograph by Alfredo Boulton. c. 1952. Alberto Vollmer Foundation, Inc., Caracas

it accessible to Europeans; Lezama Lima established contact with Wallace Stevens; Witold Gombrowicz roamed around Buenos Aires; and Malcolm Lowry was entranced by Mexico – these and other projects during this time period confirm Latin America's cultural heterogeneity. Such endeavors opted for the inward-looking *americanismo* of Pablo Neruda's *Canto General* (1950), Heitor Villa-Lobos's *Bachianas Brazileiras* (Brazilian Bach-pieces), and the Argentine Alberto Ginastera's "objective nationalism." In Venezuela's case, they included in the realm of music Inocente Carreño's *Suite Margariteña* (1954) and Antonio Estévez's *Cantata Criolla* (1954).[53]

Around 1950 there were two sites of "progressive Venezuelan art," according to Miguel Cabañas Bravo:[54] Caracas and Paris, where two groups emerged in short succession – the Taller Libre de Arte[55] (Free arts workshop, 1948) and Los Disidentes (The dissidents, 1950).[56] Many of the latter's members returned to Caracas during the 1950s, espousing an abstract-geometric vision that challenged the prevailing artistic conservatism in Venezuela; they fell into step with contemporary Western artistic production and with the work of Latin Americans such as Wifredo Lam. This group – which included Alejandro Otero,[57] Mateo Manaure,[58] and Oswaldo Vigas,[59] among others, and which maintained close contact with Carlos Cruz-Diez[60] and Jesús Rafael Soto – epitomized that moment of midcentury modernity in which contemporary universalism entered into a dialogue that exceeded the merely local, reaching its ultimate expression in Villanueva's Universidad Central de Venezuela (just one example among many). This work by Villanueva involved the participation of such international artists as Jean Arp, Victor Vasarely, Alexander Calder, and Fernand Léger.

Venezuelan and Latin American midcentury modernity continued its dialogue with Western European culture, but for the first time it experienced the euphoria of seeing one of its projects validated and assimilated, at least by the West; the euphoria of having attained a modernity that carried its own signature – a modernity "made in Latin America" that could engage as an equal, if not with the rest of the planet, at least with the old empires and the recently forged superpowerful "American dream." The distinctly Venezuelan stamp on this modernity lay in the audacity of its proposal and its progressive character within the Latin American context.

from the 1960s to the turn of the twenty-first century: hopes and disappointments

Boulton concluded the 1952 edition of his photography project *La Margarita* with these words: "Rejecting all other industries, the island will continue living on what has always been nearest to its heart. It will live off the sea, fishing, and pearls." In the edition that was reissued thirty years later, the preliminary note reads:

> I would like travelers today to recognize the change that the island has suffered. I hope these images encourage them to prevent this harsh turn of events from becoming even more desolate and sterile. I hope they do their utmost to preserve and protect whatever still remains of the landscape and its people, for if it loses its current charm, the island will have lost its reason for being.[61]

The quote reveals a love of popular customs, traditions, and the surviving natural landscape, and expresses a desire to preserve local values or "authenticity" in the face of modernizing forces. Boulton's sentiment betrays the characteristic ambivalence of a modernity that he himself admired and celebrated in his commentary on Cruz-Diez and Soto, while at the same time proclaiming his adherence to the disingenuous naïveté of Armando Reverón,[62] and marveling at the colonial cultural production or reveling in Venezuelan popular culture and the country's natural landscape.

The Isla de Margarita was not the only place affected by these changes. As Boulton himself put it in 1981: "The tremendous difference between the Venezuela of 1950 and the one of 1981 is obvious." Summarizing the changes that Venezuela and Latin America underwent during these years is not an easy task. Those intervening thirty years included the Bolivian Revolution (1952), the Cuban Revolution (1959), the return of democracy to Venezuela, the creation of OPEC, the emergence of guerrillas in the 1960s, the heyday and fall of Che Guevara, the beginning of the "space age" and the landing on the moon, dictatorships in the Southern Cone, the Vietnam War, the fuel crisis and economic turmoil of the mid-1970s, the breakdown of the Bretton Woods system, the appearance and apotheosis of television, the democracy of so-called "petro-bolívars," the development of Pop art, the rise of Latin America's "boom" generation of writers, the new *aggiornamento*, or "openness," of the Catholic church, and the spread of the liberation theology, in addition to innumerable other cultural, technological, and artistic transformations.

In Venezuela, the nationalization of the iron and oil industries, as well as the tremendous increase in the international price of oil in the 1970s, fueled significant cultural developments such as the international theater festivals begun in 1973, the Rómulo Gallegos International Novel Prize (which helped establish the reputations of the writers Gabriel García Márquez, Mario Vargas Llosa, and Carlos Fuentes), and other initiatives that turned the country, and particularly Caracas, into a cultural point of reference for all of Latin America.

Latin America had entered another phase of its successive modernities, this time characterized by the rise of television and the advent of the "telenovela"—in whose production Venezuela, Mexico, and Brazil played a preponderant role—as a specifically Latin American cultural product distinct from the North American soap opera. However, cultural modernity and the emergence of new forms of popular culture were also accompanied by profound sociopolitical transformations, increased immigration from rural areas to the city, and the exponential growth of megalopolises such as Mexico City and São Paulo. By the end of the 1950s, in particular with the triumph of the Cuban Revolution and the worldwide success of Latin American literature,[63] the region became fashionable and captured the world's attention—with the Cuban Missile Crisis of 1962, among other things—but also passed from the stereotype of a continent filled with "banana republics" to that of the home place of the "bearded revolutionary."

Cultural and revolutionary modernity was not, of course, an exclusively Latin American phenomenon. It was also embodied by the turmoil and protests of May 1968 in France, the civil-rights movement in the United States, the Vietnam War and the antiwar movement in the United States, the Chinese Cultural

Revolution, postcolonial independence movements in Africa, Prague Spring, the second wave of feminism, and the start of the gay-rights movement. The synchronization of times that Latin America had aspired to in the early twentieth century seemed to be falling in step with the planetary clock during this period.

According to cultural critic Charles Jencks, modernity ended on July 15, 1972 at 3:32 P.M. with the demolition of the functionalist Pruitt-Igoe housing project in St. Louis, Missouri.[64] The nostalgia expressed by Boulton and numerous others between the end of modernity and postmodernity's beginnings points to the inevitable state of every change in eras: simultaneous discontent and glimmers of future potential.

One can understand postmodernity as the conclusion of modernity. One can argue that the project of modernity remains unfinished, that it is still valid. One can also argue that modernity and postmodernity—or better, modernities and postmodernities—*still* coexist. In spite all this—and in spite of discussions about whether postmodernity begins with the "short century," after World War II, with the crisis of 1973, or even, as some suggest, in 1492[65]—it seems obvious that something called "postmodernity" had taken root in Venezuelan awareness at the beginning of the 1980s, when Boulton expressed his nostalgia for the past of the Isla de Margarita and the revolutionaries of the 1960s began to lose heart.

These were years of transition, from the experimentalist impulse of Latin American art—whose centers were the Instituto Di Tella in Buenos Aires, the São Paulo biennials, Mexico City, and Caracas—to the millennium's threshold when the last stage of modernization in the region was (for the time being, at least) finally assimilated. It was during this period that the group known as El Techo de la Ballena (The roof of the whale),[66] representatives of the 1960s Venezuelan avant-garde, developed much of its work, which combined informalist rupture, the influence of Surrealism, and the liberating political blitheness of the time.

The final stage of development, which extends to the present, is something more than just modernity's new face. It is most likely a *civilizational* change, not only in the realm of the arts, but also in the social, the political, and particularly the technological realms. This civilizational change, which is occurring in Venezuela as well as in the rest of Latin America, is marked not only by the sociopolitical transformations sparked by the "Caracazo" protests and brutal military response on February 27, 1989,[67] but also by the conclusion of an era, by the demise of a certain way of understanding the cultural and political life that shaped Venezuelan history in the twentieth century. There have been similar changes throughout Latin America, but the events that transpired since the late 1980s and early 1990s in Venezuela entailed a rupture greater than those in other countries.

The Venezuelan process is, however, inscribed within more generalized phenomena. One need only enumerate words that have entered the vocabularies of the vast majority of Latin Americans and the rest of the world's inhabitants: *fax, Internet, DVD, CD, credit card, money wires, email, cell phone, laptop, iPod, Blackberry, AIDS, space stations, artificial satellites, European Union, MERCOSUR, Chavismo*. One need only enumerate words that have lost their currency: *Soviet Union, telex, telegram, Berlin Wall, apartheid, Cold War*, and so on. One need only enumerate words that have always been meaningful and are still in use: *war, genocide, poverty, discrimination, torture, populism, dictatorship, illness, border, church, drugs, terrorists* (they existed even before World War I), *theater, film, dance, radio, car, avant-garde, artistic experimentation, censorship*. One need only enumerate all these words to understand that modernity and contemporaneity—terms that are not synonymous—embody the tremendous changes we are living through at the present stage of globalization. This is all one needs in order to understand that Latin American modernities—and pertinently Venezuelan modernities—have undergone a tortuous process of rapprochement and dialogue with other contemporary modernities around the world, and have taken on a never-ending search for their own path.

Translated by Catalina Ocampo

notes to the text

1. "Of America and its grade of civilization, especially in Mexico and Peru, we have information, but it imports nothing more than that this culture was an entirely national one, which must expire as soon as Spirit approached it. America has always shown itself physically and psychically powerless, and still shows itself so." G.W.F. Hegel, *The Philosophy of History* (Kitchener, Ontario: Batoche Books, 2001), p. 98.
2. See Miguel Rojas Mix, *América imaginaria* (Madrid: Lumen, 1992).
3. Eric Hobsbawm established 1914 (World War I) and 1991 (the end of the USSR) as the beginning and end dates of what he terms the "short" twentieth century; the Venezuelan phenomenon of Hugo Chávez's rise to power thus falls outside the period delineated. Hobsbawm, *The Age of Extremes: The Short Twentieth Century, 1914–1991* (London: Michael Joseph, 1994).
4. See Antonio Cornejo Polar, *Escribir en el aire: Ensayo sobre la heterogeneidad socio cultural en las literaturas andinas* (Lima: Horizonte, 1994).
5. Fernando Calderón, "América Latina: Identidad y tiempos mixtos, o cómo tratar de pensar la modernidad sin dejar de ser indios," *David y Goliath* (Santiago de Chile), 1987: 4–9.
6. Andrés Bello was a Venezuelan lawmaker, politician, and poet committed to Latin American independence early on in his career. In 1842, he founded the Universidad de Chile. He was the author of the *Código civil* (1857) or the Chilean civil code, the *Silvas americanas* (American verses; 1823–26), a collection of poems dedicated to Latin America, and the *Gramática de la lengua castellana destinado al uso de los americanos*, the first Spanish grammar book written specifically for Latin Americans (1847).
7. José Martí was a Cuban poet, writer, and hero of Cuban independence. He was the author of the influential essay "Nuestra América" (Our America) (1891).
8. Carlos Quijano was a Uruguayan journalist and intellectual, and a founder of the Latin American student association in Paris at the start of the twentieth century. He founded the influential journal *Marcha* (1939–74), in which Jean-Paul Sartre, Che Guevara, Julio Cortázar, and many intellectuals worldwide published writings.
9. Arturo Úslar Pietri was a Venezuelan writer, lawyer, and politician who later had a fruitful career as an essayist. He is the author of *Las lanzas coloradas* (*The Red Lances*; 1931), one of the major works written during the first stage of modernity in Venezuela. In 1936 he published his influential article "Sembrar el petróleo" (To sow the oil), a slogan used to this day by Venezuelan politicians. Úslar Pietri coined the term "realismo mágico" (magic realism) in the 1930s.
10. Alejo Carpentier was a Cuban writer whose work had a considerable impact in Latin America. He is the author of *El reino de este mundo* (*The Kingdom of this World*; 1949), in whose prologue he developed his theory of the "real maravilloso" (marvelous real) to describe the power of eliciting wonder through an unexpected alteration or revelation of reality. Unlike "realismo mágico" or "magic realism," most commonly used to describe a writer's deliberate transformation of reality, Carpentier considered the "real maravilloso" to be an intrinsic characteristic of Latin American reality.
11. Argentine writer Julio Cortázar was one of the main representatives of the Latin American "boom" generation of writers. He is author of the novel *Rayuela* (*Hopscotch*; 1963) and many short stories.
12. Domingo Faustino Sarmiento served as Argentina's president from 1868 to 1874. He was the author of *Civilización*

y barbarie (*Civilization and Barbarism*; 1845), an influential book about the caudillo Facundo Quiroga.

13. Of course, the ambivalence toward modernizing impulses or different stages of modernity is not an exclusively Latin American phenomenon. One can trace enthusiasm as well as uneasiness, disruptions, and fears to the beginning of the nineteenth century in both France and England, to name only two centers in which modernity had a particularly powerful impact. The era's experience of the *frisson nouveau* that interrupted tradition's narrative and imposed an uncertain future was best described by Charles Baudelaire: "L'air est plein du frisson des choses qui s'enfuient": "the air is a-shudder with things on the wing." (See "Le crepuscule du matin" in Baudelaire, *Les fleurs du mal*, introduction by Jean Paul Sartre [Paris: Gallimard, 1965], pp. 120–21.) Although many saw the nineteenth century as the embodiment of modern progress and blind faith in the future, the discovery of the crowdedness and anonymity of the new cities, human exploitation, and the scandal of slavery also gave rise to an unpleasant malaise that prompted insurrections like those that broke out in various European cities, the beginning of a series of utopias that set universal salvation as their goal, and the beginning of the abolitionist movement.
14. The abolition of African slavery in Latin America began in 1804 in Haiti and continued throughout the nineteenth century until 1888 when it was achieved in Brazil. In Venezuela slavery was abolished in 1854 and free, public elementary education was established in 1870.
15. José Martí wrote: "La colonia continuó viviendo en la república" (The colony continues to live within the republic). "Nuestra América," in *Nuestra América de José Martí*, prologue by Juan Marinello; chronology by Cintio Vitier; ed. and notes by Hugo Achugar (Caracas: Biblioteca Ayacucho, 1977), p. 30.
16. Caudillo Antonio Guzmán Blanco controlled Venezuela between 1870 and 1888 and played an important role in the symbolic construction of the nation. He promoted the construction of significant urban and architectural works in the capital, as well as the first important wave of iconography centered on the struggle for independence and its heroes.
17. See Ángel Rama, *La ciudad letrada* (Hanover N.H.: Ediciones del Norte, 1984); in English as *The Lettered City*, trans. John Chasteen (Durham: Duke University Press, 1996).
18. Julián Padrón was a Venezuelan writer and lawyer, as well as a founder (with Úslar Pietri and Boulton) of the literary journal *El ingenioso hidalgo*.
19. Julián Padrón to Alfredo Boulton, letter in the Boulton Archive at the Alberto Vollmer Foundation, Inc., Caracas.
20. Walter Benjamin, *The Arcades Project*, ed. Roy Tiedemann, trans. Howard Eiland and Kevin McLaughlin (Cambridge, Mass.: Harvard University Press, 1999), convolute no. M3a, 8.
21. The São Paulo Semana de Arte Moderna was a public repudiation of academic art and an endorsement of modern art. Held in February 1922, it gathered a significant number of artists and intellectuals for a week of exhibitions, concerts, and conferences. The date is considered a crucial moment in the development of modern art in Brazil.
22. Jorge Schwartz, *Las vanguardias latinoamericanas: Textos programáticos y críticos* (Madrid: Cátedra, 1991).
23. Hobsbawm, *The Age of Extremes*.
24. The term "*americanismo*" (or "Americanism")—here and throughout the essay—embraces the entire continent and not just the United States; it refers to an enthusiasm for and a championing of the New World over and against Europe. *Trans.*
25. Rómulo Gallegos was a writer and statesman. He served as president of Venezuela from February to November 1948.
26. Rómulo Gallegos, "Las tierras de Dios" ("God's Lands"), in *Rómulo Gallegos: Una posición ante la vida* (Caracas: Centauro77, 1977) pp. 112–44. This speech is included in the present volume, pp. 103–7.
27. In 1914, the so-called *reventón* (or "blowout") of the Zumaque 1 oil well in the Mene Grande field on the eastern coast of Lake Maracaibo unearthed the oil reserves that would grant Venezuela access to the world's energy markets.
28. Arturo Úslar Pietri, "Somos" ("We Are"), *Válvula* 1, no. 1 (January 1928), included in this volume, pp. 98–99.
29. The phrase "Generation of 1928" refers to a group of university students who staged an important public protest against Gómez during the carnival of 1928.
30. Rómulo Betancourt served as president of Venezuela from 1959 to 1964.
31. Raúl Leoni was a founding member of Acción Democrática, and president of Venezuela from 1964 to 1969.
32. Miguel Otero Silva was a writer and

politician. In 1943 he founded *El Nacional*, one of the two most influential newspapers in Venezuela. He was a member of the Communist party and wrote a number of novels, including *Fiebre* (Fever; 1931) and *Casas muertas* (Dead houses; 1955).

33. Augusto César Sandino was the central Nicaraguan nationalist leader, well known for his struggle against U.S. occupation in the 1920s.
34. Getulio Vargas was president of Brazil on four occasions (1930–34, 1934–37, 1937–45, and 1951–54). He was known as "the father of the poor."
35. Gerardo Machado was a general in the Cuban Army during the Spanish-American War and president of Cuba from 1925 to 1933.
36. Anastasio Somoza García, head of Nicaragua's Guardia Nacional in its fight against Augusto César Sandino, assumed power over Nicaragua in 1936. After his assassination, power was transferred to his son Luis Somoza Debayle, who ruled from 1956 to 1963. Luis Somoza's brother Anastasio Somoza Debayle was president from 1967 to 1972, and was reelected for the term 1974–79.
37. Lázaro Cárdenas del Río was a Mexican general of the revolutionary forces; he served as president of Mexico from 1934 to 1940.
38. Agustín Farabundo Martí was a Communist revolutionary who founded the Salvadorian Communist party in 1930 and was one of the instigators of the rural uprising in El Salvador.
39. See Oswald de Andrade, "Manifiesto antropofágico," *Revista de antropofagia* 1 (São Paulo, May 1928): 1. The Tupí are an indigenous people of Brazil.
40. José Vasconcelos was an important Mexican writer and politician. His *La raza cósmica* (1925) was an influential book about what he believed was the destiny of the Americas: to be the land of *mestizaje*, the place where "the synthetic race that shall gather all the treasures of History . . . will be created." Vasconcelos, *The Cosmic Race*, trans. Didier T. Jaén (Baltimore: Johns Hopkins University Press, 1997), p. 18.
41. Eleazar López Contreras was the minister of war during the last years of Juan Vicente Gómez's dictatorship and assumed the presidency of Venezuela from 1936 to 1941.
42. Writer and historian Mariano Picón Salas was the author of *Formación y proceso de la literatura venezolana* (Form and process of Venezuelan literature; 1940) and *Comprensión de Venezuela* (Understanding Venezuela; 1949).
43. Francisco Narváez was a painter and sculptor and one of the protagonists of the nativist movement in Venezuela. He participated in the most important attempts by Carlos Raúl Villanueva to integrate the arts into architecture: the development of El Silencio in Caracas (1941–45) and the Universidad Central de Venezuela (1944–67).
44. Jesús Rafael Soto was one of the founders and principal representatives of European and Venezuelan kinetic art. A significant number of his works have been integrated into urban architecture in cities around the world.
45. Architect Carlos Raúl Villanueva designed and developed some of the largest architectural complexes in Venezuela; the best-known among them is the Universidad Central de Venezuela (1944–67), which spearheaded the project of integrating art and architecture.
46. Isaías Medina Angarita was a politician, a member of the military, and chief of staff during the dictatorship of Juan Vicente Gómez. After Gómez's death, he was appointed minister of war and the navy by López Contreras. He was elected president of Venezuela by the country's national congress in 1941 but was overthrown by a coup d'état in 1945.
47. Marcos Pérez Jiménez was a politician and a member of the Venezuelan military. He participated in the 1948 coup d'état against Rómulo Gallegos and established himself as dictator from 1952 to 1958.
48. Designed in 1956 by Oscar Niemeyer and city planner Lúcio Costa, the city of Brasilia was officially inaugurated as Brazil's capital on April 21, 1960.
49. The term "glocalization" was introduced by Manfred Lange to indicate "local and global change," on the occasion of the touring exhibition *Global Change: Challenges to Science and Politics*, which opened at the German Chancellery in Bonn, May 1990. Since then, the term "glocal" has been used by numerous authors (among others recently Zygmunt Bauman). (See writer.zoho.com/rss/public.ximl?id=suite.)
50. Here "modernist" is used in its Anglophone sense—that is, as the aesthetics established and consolidated by the early twentieth-century avant-gardes.
51. Gego (Gertrude Goldschmidt) was a Venezuelan sculptor born in Germany, known for her abstract geometric works, including the Reticuláreas series.
52. In Boulton's own text; he affirms: "I am working on a book about the artistic value of our aboriginal ceramics in light

of contemporary aesthetic concepts. I am taking the archaeological object as an artistic work, and applying my own concept of beauty to it." In "El arte en nuestra cerámica aborigen" (Caracas: Alfredo Boulton; printed by S.p.A. Antonio Cordani, Milan; designed by Carlos Cruz-Diez, 1978), p. 11.

53. This period also produced a number of works that fit multiple categories, or works that have been given divergent interpretations. One example of this is the Mexican Juan Rulfo's narrative *Pedro Páramo* (1954), which has been taken as the purest expression of the Mexican spirit but also as a prime example of a work inscribed in the Western biblical tradition.
54. Miguel Cabañas Bravo, "Caracas, un intento frustrado de continuidad en las bienales hispanoamericanas de arte (I)," in *Espacio, tiempo, forma* (series 7, *Historia del arte*, no. 8; Madrid: Universidad Nacional de Educacíon a Distancia, 1995), pp. 325–64.
55. The Taller Libre de Arte was inaugurated on July 10, 1948 as a response to the demands of dissatisfied young artists who insisted that education, still mired in the work of Paul Cézanne and the Cubists, needed to be modernized. As with the Círculo de Bellas Artes in 1912, the Taller attracted the most progressive artists and generated influential exhibitions, such as the one featuring the Argentine organization Arte Concreto-Invención, also founded in 1948. During its first few years the Taller was directed by the painter Alirio Oramas.
56. Los Disidentes group was created in Paris by young Venezuelan artists and intellectuals, primarily Alejandro Otero, Mateo Manaure, J. R. Guillent Pérez, Perán Erminy, Aimée Battistini, Pascual Navarro, Dora Hersen, Narciso Debourg, Luis Guevara Moreno, and Carlos González Bogen. Los Disidentes produced a journal by the same name through which they voiced their ideas and demands.
57. Artist Alejandro Otero's work triggered various currents of abstract art in Venezuela. He was a founding member of Los Disidentes.
58. Mateo Manaure is a Venezuelan visual artist and a founding member of Los Disidentes. He participated in the Universidad Central de Venezuela project.
59. Artist Oswaldo Vigas participated in the Universidad Central de Venezuela project. Although his work tended toward geometric abstraction in the early 1950s, he always maintained a nationalistic approach, using themes drawn from local history and mythology.
60. Carlos Cruz-Diez was a staunch advocate of painting as a tool of political dissent before becoming one of Venezuela's most important kinetic artists in the 1960s.
61. Alfredo Boulton, *La Margarita* (Caracas: Macanao Ediciones, 1981), unpaginated prefatory text.
62. Armando Reverón was one of the most important Venezuelan artists of the twentieth century. He was a member of the Círculo de Bellas Artes.
63. The 1960s was the decade in which Jorge Luis Borges achieved global recognition, Gabriel García Márquez's *One Hundred Years of Solitude* appeared, and Carlos Fuentes, Julio Cortázar, Mario Vargas Llosa, and numerous other writers of the Latin "boom" generation published their major works.
64. Charles Jencks, *The Language of Postmodern Architecture* (London: Academy Editions, 1977), p. 9.
65. Serge Gruzinski, *El pensamiento mestizo* (Barcelona: Paidós, 2000), p. 18.
66. El Techo de la Ballena (1961–68)—"The roof of the whale"—was an artists' organization in Venezuela that was heavily influenced by Surrealism. It was, in a sense, the cultural manifestation of political battles that led to the armed uprising of pro-Cuban guerrillas in the 1960s. Carlos Contramaestre, Daniel González, Adriano González León, Caupolicán Ovalles, and Juan Calzadilla were among its members.
67. The 1989 "Caracazo" uprising was marked by looting and riots in protest against the economic measures instituted by the newly elected president Carlos Andrés Pérez. The harsh military response to the events caused thousands of deaths and had a profound impact on Venezuela.

an appraisal of contemporary venezuela **elías pino iturrieta**

As the first decade of the twentieth century came to a close, the people of Venezuela had begun to indulge in the idea that their country might be embarking on an auspicious new path. The so-called Restauración Liberal (Liberal restoration) regime of Cipriano Castro (1899–1908) offered some measure of distance from the tumult of the nineteenth century, but his administration ended in a tyranny that replaced hope with pessimism. It was during Castro's time in power that the country finally overcame the political disintegration it had suffered, and progressed toward the development of a centrist administration that had never before existed. But the defeat of past powers was not used as an opportunity to evolve truly republican forms of government; instead, a leadership style evolved that was rooted in the "cult of personality." Lost amid its banalities and unconcerned about improving the economy, the new leadership brought only hardship to the lives of the people it governed. The president-turned-dictator fomented corruption and instigated protracted disputes with the European powers and with the dynamic and enterprising United States, which provoked a state of affairs that was untenable for all parties involved. When Castro was ousted in a bloodless coup d'état, the great thinkers of the day predicted the start of a promising new period for Venezuela.

change and permanence

The Venezuelan people had high hopes for Juan Vicente Gómez when in 1908 he rose to the rank of president, where he would remain through 1935. A quiet man known for his austere habits, he provided a stark contrast to the recently deposed head of state. At the time, no one anticipated the extent of his appetite for power, to which he would cling until he died, an old man, having committed countless offenses against his people and country—from making legislative changes at whim to pillaging the public treasury, appropriating private property, and issuing orders for horrific torture.

Initially, though, the new leader's inscrutable nature and disinterest in striking dramatic poses were qualities that led some people to believe that the dawn of a new era was on the horizon, and prompted young writers like Rómulo Gallegos to declare that the country had reached the end of a barbaric age. There was much evidence that seemed to support this belief. A new age seemed to be in the air—still, there were many people who feared that it might be only an illusion.

The possibility of real change for the nation would ultimately depend on the country's ability to take advantage of the copious flow of oil that bubbled forth from its subsoil. Before the government began to make use of its hydrocarbon resources, some very concrete steps were taken to ensure their future: first, the regime put an end to its conflicts with foreign governments; it implemented a new system of roadways that helped transform the country's dismally poor internal communications, and it established the national army, an institution that reinforced the strength of a dictatorship with lifelong aspirations. The visit of U.S. Secretary of State Philander Knox, who met with Gómez in a closed-door meeting in 1912, was a sacramental blessing for the new head of state. Hydrocarbon operations

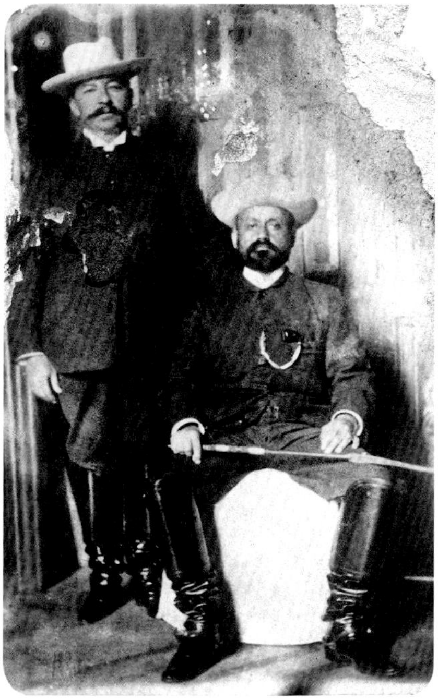

Juan Vicente Gómez (left) and Cipriano Castro. 1901. Collection Fundación para la Cultura Urbana, Caracas

in Venezuela began in 1914, when the first commercial well was tapped in Mene Grande, the first oil pipeline was built, and work started in the district of Colón in the state of Zulia. The wealthy Bolívar district would soon follow, entering the market in 1915. Companies with British capital were the first to take control of exploration rights in the country, but American consortia began receiving advantageous concessions of their own as of 1918.

And so began the empire of strong interests, such as that of Maracaibo Oil Exploration (a forerunner of Standard Oil of New Jersey). These were the companies that would transform the life of the nation as they introduced the Venezuelan people to an odd kind of opulence, a great change that required no effort whatsoever on their part. Soon foreign companies operating in the country began to see returns on more than twenty million tons of hydrocarbons, and while their profits were generous, the regulations governing them were not—a detail that was taken care of between their managers and the Venezuelan government. Through these efforts, the earnings that remained in the country sparked a metamorphosis that was beyond anyone's wildest dreams.

Venezuela's governmental sector began to exhibit unprecedented levels of efficiency in many areas. The administration overhauled the treasury and instituted a bureaucracy that was capable of handling every last bit of state business, on every corner of the map. The foreign debt was paid off and new commercial, legal, and criminal codes were drafted and enacted.

These were the realities of 1922, when the country had been sailing along its river of black gold for scarcely eight years. Finally, in the waning years of the dictatorship, twelve million hectares were designated for subsoil exploration, a blessing that gave way to a number of critical consequences for the traditional way of life in Venezuela and for the coexistence of its citizens. The regime grew stronger thanks to the exorbitant taxes that went straight into its coffers.

The daily lives of Venezuelan people were radically transformed. Decisions that had previously been made within the context of rural life were now thrust into the realm of the urban neighborhoods that were just beginning to take shape. The country now boasted a half-dozen dynamic urban centers that controlled the flow of this unexpected bounty. Now that Venezuela had joined the club of capital-rich countries, its citizens could hardly recognize themselves in the mirror of the rural, deplorably impoverished country that had been languishing until so very recently.

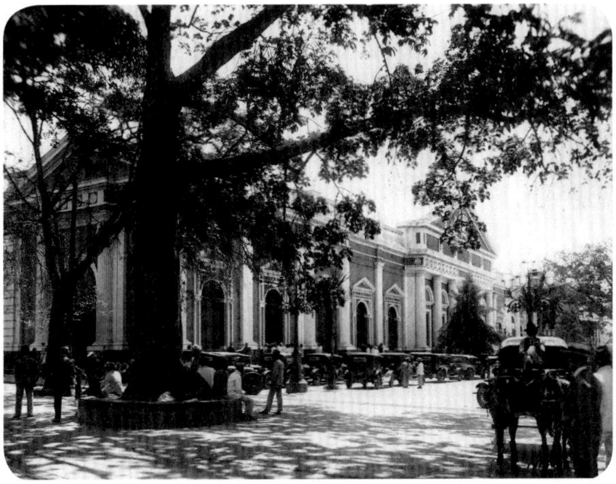

Corner of the church of San Francisco, Caracas. Photograph by Luis Felipe Toro Mujica (Torito). c. 1920. Collection Instituto Autónomo Biblioteca Nacional. Archivos Nacionales de Venezuela, Caracas

That old country continued to exist in emblematic figures like Gómez and many members of his clan—strongmen wallowing on their ranches, impassive in the face of the government's often cruel modus operandi, acolytes who were always loyal to their master but never to any kind of legality. Everyone had to make the same decision: either resist the avalanche of change or become a part of it.

A new kind of life and coexistence began to take shape in Venezuela, the likes of which would have been unthinkable in the early years of the nation-state with its crippled economy, its feeble executive branch, and the disruptions of so many civil wars. This sudden windfall of material resources precipitated a change that, as time went by, set up patterns of behavior that some people believe to be defining characteristics of the nation's contemporary history—as well as stumbling blocks on the path of establishing a true, mature republican state. What evolved might be described as a parasitic sensibility that lingered on indefinitely thanks to the money spread around by political operators and the lack of individual commitment to the pursuit of a common good.

The country that had come of age during a period of tyranny began to enjoy all the benefits of modern comforts, acquiring the most coveted goods the market had to offer and sending its young people off traveling to the capitals of the Western world. At the same time Venezuelans grew accustomed to remaining silent as crimes were committed in certain places that would become synonyms for atrocity, such as the Caracas jail La Rotunda, or the colonial castle in Puerto Cabello. The horrors of these places circulated by word of mouth, though the news never prompted any meaningful protest. The Venezuela of the day was also a country that looked on, unfazed, as its agriculture industry fell into decline, poverty gripped a broad swath of the population, and education and public health were all but abandoned by the government. As more and more luxury goods flowed into the country, 60 percent of Venezuelan oil workers suffered from venereal diseases, 65 percent of the population remained illiterate, and malaria swept through the countryside.

The novelist Manuel Díaz Rodríguez lamented the paralysis that had afflicted and dominated Venezuelan society since the period of independence.

In his 1920 book *Idolos rotos* (Broken idols), he described a nonexistent nation burdened by the weight of its omissions, a place where nothing had moved forward since 1830. The influential essayist Rufino Blanco Fombona had already insisted in his 1905 work *El hombre de hierro* (The man of iron) that the country lacked a "national soul." José Rafael Pocaterra, enemy and prisoner of the regime, described his experiences in 1927 under the title *Memorias de un venezolano de la decadencia* (Memoirs of a Venezuelan in the age of decadence), a text that underscored the inescapable quality of that unfettered decline. Only Gallegos managed to avoid reaching the most damning conclusions. In his deeply analytical novel *Doña Bárbara* (1929), he described a battle that barbarity would ultimately lose when civilization arrived at the goal that had been declared at the very birth of the nation.

Venezuela had indeed changed, but these changes inspired terribly pessimistic interpretations, because the country had been hijacked, so to speak; it stifled the majority of its inhabitants while allowing a select few to partake in the delights of capitalist consumer culture.

One of the results of this clash was the student movement that was launched in 1928 with the goal of making improvements within the university faculty and administration, and obtaining financial aid for their more disadvantaged classmates. The majority of these young activists—who later became known as the "Generation of 1928"—were sent to jail. The undergraduates at Venezuela's Universidad Central who meekly proposed a change through the vehicle of the ephemeral journal *Válvula*, and who sought resources for their poorer classmates, became the victims of ruthless punishment: some were sent to concentration camps while others endured torture (both standard practices at the time) before being released into the comparative relief of ostracism. At the time, these were not significant names among the protests of the day, which were still fairly elemental and tame; some of the radicals, however, went on to become important figures who would establish political parties of a more modern orientation. At the center of all this, two future presidents of the republic, Rómulo Betancourt and Raúl Leoni, were also finding their way in the political sphere.

The year 1936, just after Gómez's death, marked the beginning of a renaissance in literature, nonfiction writing, science, and the visual arts; it was a time of change that found its voice in various members of this movement. At the time, though, it seemed like only the vaguest hint of something that could not possibly materialize in a country with wealth so capriciously distributed among its people, and with so many age-old shortcomings and conflicts.

timid first steps

Following the death of Gómez, power fell into the hands of General Eleazar López Contreras, the former dictator's war and naval minister. His regime, which lasted from 1936 to 1941, was clearly a continuation of the previous one; indeed, to a large degree it was a fulfillment of the late tyrant's express wishes. Nevertheless, the country that had been bitten by the oil bug was also enthused by the return of exiles; this provided some relief within Venezuelan society.

The new head of state, a soldier who had risen up through the ranks during the dictatorship until making it into the military's supreme command, was not like his predecessor. López Contreras presented a bold new plan, the so-called Programa de febrero (February program), with the aim of finding solutions to the country's main problems, such as health, education, and agriculture. It was an agenda unlike any that had come before. López Contreras instituted constitutional reforms that shortened the administrative period and blocked the immediate reelection of the first magistracy, but also prohibited Communist and anarchist propaganda, declaring adherents to be traitors to the nation. He abolished torture in the nation's prisons, and announced that he would give his countrymen the freedom to form political parties (although he created a labyrinth of legal subterfuge—detailed forms, interrogations with the attorney general, petitions for good conduct, certificates that appeared in documents on an ad hoc basis—to discourage the establishment of organizations that might be inclined toward "radical" political options). The straitjacket was subtler and more comfortable now, but it remained a straitjacket.

Close to twenty parties, representing a limited political spectrum, began to enjoy an intermittent presence in the country. The Venezuelan students' federation encouraged the scenario with their battalions, holding demonstrations that occasionally overshadowed those of the political parties. The reemergence of extremist conduct at the core of one of these student groups led to an important splintering: the seed from which the Christian Democratic movement came to life.

This was the moment when young Rómulo Betancourt began his long and steady rise to prominence. A student of the "Generation of 1928" and an indefatigable champion of the radical opposition in exile, he fought for organizations that would keep republican institutions from succumbing to the cronyism represented by the first magistracy—a cronyism that could easily be replayed in the future if ideas did not prevail over individual prestige. In exile, Betancourt and a group of his friends had drafted a plan of action for a structural metamorphosis that, they believed, might finally pave the way toward democracy. Starting in 1931, the Plan de Barranquilla[1]—outlining actions to be taken against the Gómez regime—was circulated among a select group of people; it was one of the first testimonies of political modernity in twentieth-century Venezuela. After 1936, members of political movements that were not sympathetic to the administration were often expelled or imprisoned. The autocratic regime that had only recently ended was no doubt the inspiration behind the new administration's desire to quash its opposition, but the changes wrought by the hydrocarbon industry over the previous decades, in addition to the experience acquired abroad by Gómez's exiles, were by now unstoppable forces. The oil business had expanded all the way to the eastern coast of Lake Maracaibo, the Monagas savannahs, the plains and the foothills of the Andes. After Gómez's death, a number of politicians—both old-school and just-out-of-school—finally dared to return to Venezuela. Were these the engines that would propel the inevitable change?

In order to fulfill an array of increasingly specific demands, the governmental structure underwent a transformation of sorts. New executive departments were created through an initiative that signified, beyond the mere construction of new offices, a renewed desire to focus on areas that had traditionally been neglected. To this end, certain central governmental departments were expanded to make room for newly minted, contemporary-minded entities such as the Banco Industrial de Venezuela, the national institute of hygiene, the department of labor, and the national children's council. The activities of these new agencies implemented a large number of new regulations and achievements (such as the national finance-office law, the labor law, the code for minors, and the agricultural census), as well as programs that offered financial assistance and subsidies to farmers and cattle ranchers, international trade agreements governing commercial reciprocity, and a new scheme for the employment of currency.

At the same time, the government was taking a closer look at the oil industry, the immediate result of which was the suspension of new concessions and a full review of the existing system. The administration also stopped ignoring education and culture, and began to implement significant changes in those spheres—including the foundation of the Instituto Pedagógico Nacional (National pedagogical institute), the creation of geology and veterinary schools at the university level, improvements in the education and training of primary-school teachers, the erection of new buildings to house the museums of fine arts and natural sciences, and the publication of the journal *Revista Nacional de Cultura*.

In 1937 the economist Alberto Adriani, a champion of this bureaucratic overhaul, wrote the book *Labor venezolanista* (Venezuelan labor), in which he speaks of planting new trees in an age-old land—that is, initiating activities linked to Venezuelan traditions. The notion encapsulates the spirit of an administration in which the most illustrious spokespeople, such as the writer Arturo Úslar Pietri and the historian Caracciolo Parra Pérez, wanted to gradually close the chapter on the Gómez era.

When all was said and done, however, the intensity of this long and tumultuous voyage would depend not on moderates but on discoveries made by the more outré thinkers, and the conflicts sparked by the pioneers of a new cultural movement that, perhaps to their surprise, found all doors flung wide open to them. After *Doña Bárbara*, Gallegos continued producing his masterful works, while a new generation of fabulists changed the way people thought about writing. Distinguished authors such as Guillermo Meneses, José Rafael Pocaterra, Miguel Otero Silva, Ramón Díaz Sánchez, Antonio Arráiz, and Jacinto Fombona Pachano broke with the old formal ways of thinking. The movement of essayists that began to emerge at this time generated a great deal of serious reflection about the direction in which society was headed, in what was a quest to challenge notions and answer questions. Positivism languished, while other systems of thought, more liberated concepts of the environment, sought to envision and shape a multifaceted destiny for the nation. The most important among the essayists of this period were Mario Briceño Iragorry, Mariano Picón Salas, Augusto Mijares, Joaquín Gabaldón Márquez, Miguel Acosta Saignes, and Rodolfo Quintero. The brains at the center of the governmental machine (including Adriani, Úslar Pietri, and Parra Pérez, along with their colleagues Amenodoro Rangel Lamus and Tulio Chiossone) continued to operate, all of them placed at the highest strata of the bureaucracy.

The situation was ripe for a new form of expression also in the plastic arts, the values of which were perhaps best represented by the most significant artists of what came to be called the Escuela de Caracas, such as Pedro Ángel González, Marcos Castillo, Elisa Elvira Zuloaga, and Antonio Alcántara, who began to achieve recognition among refined arbiters of culture as well as (for the first time) the public at large.[2] Their versatile, newly emancipated talent provided both a contrast to the stiff purity of those who had come before them and yet another testimony to the transition that Venezuelan society was experiencing at the time.

This transition continued with even more intensity during the regime of Isaías Medina Angarita (1941–45), whom López Contreras handpicked to succeed him as head of state, though in doing so he created a crisis within the avalanche of more mass-oriented politics. With López Contreras at the helm, the administration tended to be perceived as the instrument of a select cast of characters—a coterie of intellectuals, high-ranking bureaucrats, qualified professionals, and confidants that surrounded the head of state, all with a common cause. This group believed that the Venezuelan people were not yet ready to control their own destiny, a point of view that sparked a heated reaction of varied consequences for Venezuelan society. The advisors surrounding the president did not fall silent, but they were eventually overcome by the leftist forces that had been incubating. By granting freedom to political parties, they allowed matters of the state to be aired with greater liberty and facilitated a more careful analysis of economic entanglements, but their sensibility was marked by a paternalistic attitude that confined all decision making to their inner circle. The most significant decision they made emerged with the passage of the country's new "hydrocarbon law" in 1943, which gave the state an increased level of participation in the country's oil earnings by substantially raising the taxes levied against foreign companies that were granted concessions to operate in the country. The law also gave the state greater control over oil-industry operations, as well as product commercialization, by unifying contracts and imposing requirements that governed the processes of refining crude oil on national territory.

A handful of regulations that garnered praise, however, was not enough for the Venezuelan people to shake the feeling that the promoters of those regulations smacked of elitism and small-mindedness. This became still more apparent when the government eliminated the legal obstacles that had blocked the establishment of emerging organizations. At the center of this new scene was Acción Democrática (AD), the party founded by Betancourt and legalized in 1941 through a constitutional reform.[3]

Acción Democrática instantly set out on a propaganda and organizational campaign that established its presence throughout the country. The party's platform, presented and launched with ease, underscored the importance of responding to the needs of the poor through the fairer distribution of oil revenue and by encouraging the Venezuelan populace to play a more active role in public affairs. The focal point of all the party's speeches, however, was the demand for direct and universal suffrage, through secret ballots, for the election of public officers, a stance that garnered increasing popular support over time. The newspaper *El País,* Acción Democrática's mouthpiece, reached multitudes of readers. After their party was legalized the Communists ultimately supported the government and found endorsement from two papers of a more contemporary orientation, *El Nacional* and *Las últimas noticias*. It was on the pages of these two dailies that the destiny of Venezuelan newspaper tradition would be decided.

The conservative faction that had broken off from the federation of students became the Comité de Organización Política Electoral (Political electoral organization committee, or COPEI), the forerunner of Christian Democracy.[4] The two flags under which the nation's destiny would be monopolized for much of the rest of the century had now been raised. In 1936, Venezuela had a population of 3,364,347 inhabitants, whose senses had been numbed by the Gómez regime. By 1941, at the dawn of a surprising new horizon, the census registered that the country was home to 3,850,772 people tempted by voices they had scarcely dreamed of hearing.

splendors and miseries of the revolution

The strings that had been pulled in so many directions finally broke when the regime bristled at the changes that AD had proposed regarding universal suffrage. The disagreement over what appeared to be a widespread demand from the people became the perfect excuse for a coup d'état. Leaders of the AD party were invited to participate by a group of midlevel officers that had come together, in secret, to create the Unión Patriótica Militar. During their clandestine meetings, members became convinced that they had to upend the military order and bring technology and professionalism to the army.

The movement triumphed in October 1945. Betancourt's rise to power ushered in a three-year stretch that offered hope for the country's future. Though it was brief, that rocky period left deep and lasting marks on Venezuelan society, and also served as a harbinger of the conflicts to come. At the time, the instigator of the change appeared to be Betancourt, president of the civilian-military governmental junta, though it was in fact the founder of the Unión Patriótica Militar, Marcos Pérez Jiménez, who exerted increasing influence from behind closed doors.

Popular participation was the hallmark of these three years. Finally the demon of politics had gotten under the skin of laborers and artisans, the workers and the common people, all of whom took to the avenues and alleyways in an endless parade of demonstrations. At no other point in its history had the country witnessed such a groundswell of people, from all corners of society, exhibiting their willingness to become part of Venezuela's political future.

The political analysts who took the time to consider the events of 1945 were forced to take a hard look at those multitudes that were so willing to change their own destiny. The campaign for the election of a constituent assembly and the radio coverage of the debates regarding the matter were a mirror of the drive and the scope of an unprecedented social upheaval that would reach its pinnacle with the election of Rómulo Gallegos as president of the republic in December 1947.

Never before had Venezuela experienced such a vast collective mobilization as this. Politics had finally ceased to be a small-town phenomenon. Joseph Stalin's speeches and the editorials in *Pravda* were openly discussed, and socially oriented encyclicals were no longer pious reading but topics for heated debate. Foreign political figures and intellectuals—including Haya de la Torre, León Felipe, Juan Marinello, Germán Arciniegas, and Nelson A. Rockefeller—came to celebrate the rise of Gallegos. Both friends and foes of the revolution joined with the parties of the day as protagonists of this motley, momentous struggle.

The country was without question on the precipice of a very promising future, but there were certain factors threatening to tip the situation into the abyss. The governmental party suppressed all demonstrations of other parties, and its strong-arming caused a great deal of friction. People generally assumed that the power monopoly was under the control of Betancourt, whom the opposition denounced as circumventing the purposes of democracy and transparency that had been heralded at the start of the new administration. The demonstrations and rallies held by opposition parties were subject to acts of sabotage that generally went unpunished, while the red carpet was rolled out for governmental events. The mounting list of excesses reached such a peak that the government began to incur the wrath not only of its opponents, but also of the military officers who were part of its own power structure. Many officers were already disgruntled, as the majority of the jobs in the new administration had been commandeered by sectarian politicians. When rumors began to circulate about an incipient Bolshevik-style revolution, the resentful officials began to distance themselves from the "insolent" party that had granted them so few positions within its inner circle. Not even Gallegos, the discreet and intellectual politician so highly regarded for the quality of his literature, escaped reproach.

A few measures that the junta had approved in advance only caused suspicions to fester. One was the creation of a jury for civil and administrative responsibility against the illicit enrichment of previous governmental authorities, which arrived at debatable sentences (sentences that could not, however, be appealed) against figures such as ex-president López Contreras and the writer Úslar Pietri. Another measure was a decree regarding evaluations of secondary-school education that discriminated against private-school students, as the Church disclosed in communiqués that prompted a number of public demonstrations.

Considering these circumstances, the sea change that occurred after October 18, 1945, was crucially important; it was during this time that Venezuela obtained the tools it needed to make its way in the twentieth century with confidence. The development firm Corporación Venezolana de Fomento was created; the government raised taxes on oil companies after aborting its policy of awarding concessions to private interests; a daring transportation system was drafted; the autonomous railway system, the Merchant Marines of Greater Colombia, and an agency for the docks and shipyards were all established. Great emphasis was placed on the development of the country's human resources, as evidenced by the foundation of new patrimonies and institutes for national literacy, public nutrition, and immigration—all of which produced very tangible results. When Gallegos rose to power, this legacy became clear in a number of ways: an investment of 430 million bolívars in public works; the construction of residential low-income apartment housing; the allotment of fifty million bolívars for the construction of the Universidad Central campus, and the first steps toward the building of the Caracas-La Guaira highway. Of greatest note, however, were the advances made in the state of education: in two years 37,000 adults had learned to read and write, and a record number of 5,500 people entered the halls of higher education. Who could possibly doubt, after the burial of the Gómez era and the start of two long years marked by such overwhelming numbers, amid the heat of the bonfires that raged in the country, that Venezuelan society was finally blazing the trail of its own contemporary history?

a military officer in power

Rómulo Gallegos was overthrown in a coup d'état on November 24, 1948. A military junta, presided over by Carlos Delgado Chalbaud and comprised of the lieutenant colonels Marcos Pérez Jiménez and Luis Llovera Páez, attempted to change the course of the country. At first it was assumed that the rule of law would be interrupted for a brief period as a kind of prerequisite for a new institutional experience, but Delgado Chalbaud's death by assassination in 1950 eliminated the one person who was perceived as a possible mediator between left and right in the march toward contemporaneity. The path to an open democracy was clearly impossible now, as was made evident by the prohibition of the Acción Democrática and Communist parties, and the dissolution of the national congress, as well as the electoral council and the municipal councils.

With the legitimate institutions abolished, the regime refused to recognize an overwhelming defeat in the elections for a new constituent assembly, selected an acquiescent parliament, and proclaimed Pérez Jiménez the "constitutional" president. The atmosphere was rife with dark prophecies that began to come true in April of 1951, when more than three hundred political prisoners were sent to the Guasina concentration camp.[5] The ruthless attack launched to quell a peasant uprising in Turén and the murder of the celebrated resistance leader Leonardo Ruíz Pineda signaled the direction of the regime. During 1953 and 1954 the repression remained intense, but as time went by, what had begun as a general policy evolved into a crusade against specific intractable opposition leaders. Given the circumstances, bankers, business leaders, and bishops felt no shame as they offered their support to the president and his plans for material development.

From the start of the dictatorship, the residents of Caracas were surprised by the amount of work they saw being carried out on the avenues of the capital city: the construction of buildings in depressed areas, the plans laid out for new urban development zones. Prestressed concrete was the new darling of the building industry. In the areas of mining and oil, solid advances were achieved as well, such as the inauguration of the refineries at Amuay and Puerto La Cruz, the discovery of the oil-rich fields at Oriputano and Doción, and the initial phase of iron-ore extraction. The new Caracas-La Guaira highway plan[6] won a Pan-American prize for Pérez Jiménez and untold millions under the table for his cronies; but it also gave the Venezuelan people what they needed to take possession of their national territory. The citizenry embraced the pompous style of the monuments, street intersections, and traffic circles that were built during this period. The dynamic spirit of urbanism sparked a transformative change in lifestyle, which was made even more interesting by the influx of European immigrants arriving on Venezuelan shores. The expansion of the radio industry and the advent of television, air travel, and modern telephone communication became factors of cohesion as well as development.

There was, however, less encouraging data to contend with as well: 30 percent of the populace was illiterate. Only .08 percent of all Venezuelans had more than a secondary-school education. A troubling 46.7 percent of the cities were blanketed with shantytowns, and as many planned urban projects had been summarily halted. Other, less quantifiable measures and attitudes were adopted by the government – censorship of the press, terror inspired by the national-security agents, hubris of the armed forces, a dizzying rise in corruption, and constraints instituted in the educational system to prevent people from dreaming up subversive ideas – revealing that the panorama in Venezuela was perhaps less promising than it appeared on the surface.

Still, the burgeoning cultural life of the country was not to be stopped. This period, in fact, produced many essential works of thought and artistic creation that would become cornerstones of the evolution of the Venezuelan spirit. Writers produced books and poems that soon became fundamental texts for understanding the country, including *Guzmán, elipse de una ambición de poder* (Guzmán, ellipse in one man's quest for power; 1950) by Ramón Díaz Sánchez; *Mensaje sin destino* (Message without destiny; 1950) by the exiled Mario Briceño Iragorry; *Buenas y malas palabras* (Good and bad words; 1960) by Ángel Rosenblat; *Los días de Cipriano Castro* (The days of Cipriano Castro; 1953) by Mariano Picón Salas; and *Esta tierra de gracia* (This land of grace; 1955) by Isaac Pardo. The literary awakening was evident in other essential works such as *El falso cuaderno de Narciso Espejo* (The false notebook of Narciso Espejo; 1952) by Guillermo Meneses; *La tuna de oro* (The golden *tuna* plant; 1951) by Julio Garmendia; *Casas muertas* (Dead houses; 1955) by Miguel Otero Silva; *Elena y los elementos* (Elena and the elements; 1951) by Juan Sánchez Peláez; and *Florentino y el diablo* (Florentino and the Devil; 1940–57) by Alberto Arvelo Torrealba.

In the area of plastic arts, the principal name is of course Armando Reverón, along with his contemporaries Alejandro Otero, Héctor Poleo,[7] Luis Guevara Moreno,[8] Pascual Navarro[9] and the young Jacobo Borges.[10] The founding of the Maracaibo symphony orchestra and the premieres of Antonio Estévez's *Cantata criolla* (1954) and Inocente Carreño's *Suite margariteña* (1954) serve as proof of the great strides made in the field of academic music, and inspired many to tout the virtues of "nationalist music."

Venezuelan society never fully surrendered to the Pérez Jiménez dictatorship. From the most varied disciplines and trades, from artistic production to other outlets of fame and fortune, people managed, with a certain amount of determination, to go about their business. They confronted the regime with demonstrations of autonomy that gained momentum as the government contemplated the conundrum of a new constitutional period: Pérez Jiménez had been appointed by Venezuela's constituent assembly until April 19, 1958, a deadline that forced him to manipulate the legality of his situation to keep the army and the citizens from rising up in protest of his excesses. An insurrection in the army barracks that quickly turned into a massive popular mobilization put an end to this lull, and on January 23 of 1958, a critical year, the doors were opened anew to democratic coexistence. Until this date, twentieth-century Venezuela had enjoyed a period of only three short years of democracy. Now, once again, the country would try to make it work.

an outline for a new approach

It was the administration of Rómulo Betancourt, from 1959 to 1964, that heralded Venezuela's return to democracy. The nation's vision for the future, however, soon broke off into two distinct paths, creating a rift between the political forces at play. The debate now revolved around the difference between real freedoms and "formal" freedoms, between the promises made in the political discourse and the real need to fulfill them in order to truly redress historical wrongs. This crossroads began to take shape through three of the issues that were most pressing for Venezuelan society at the time: agrarian-reform, urban reform, and nationalization. The struggle to resolve these things, however, became linked to armed violence in all its myriad manifestations. The influence of the Cuban Revolution and the belligerence of the Communist party played their parts in cultivating another kind of radicalization of thought, the influence of which was felt among intellectual circles as well as in the rank and file of the government.

It was in this atmosphere of premature conflict that the rule of law was established, along with a republican culture that had been on hold since the beginning of the twentieth century. These early confrontations were characteristic of the process from this point forward, and they left wounds that would never fully heal.

Within the framework laid out by the 1961 constitution and controlled by the 1945 parties AD and COPEI, new foundations were established for the modernization and industrialization of Venezuelan society, which entailed the exclusion of Communism and its adherents. Further moves were made through a broad program focused on rebuilding the nation, the initiatives of which included the creation of national institutes for cooperative education and for culture and fine arts, and the enactment of the agrarian-reform law. With regard to the employment of natural resources, significant goals were achieved in the diversification of energy sources and the establishment of the groundwork for heavy industry, as evidenced by the inauguration of the Caroní Hydroelectric Complex and the creation of OPEC.

However, all these steps happened amid widespread unrest that Betancourt managed to control only through his stubborn insistence on an ideal model of democracy. Not only did the president have to respond to foreign threats from Caribbean powers like Rafael Trujillo in the Dominican Republic[11] and the Somozas in Nicaragua, and the armed factions of army officers sympathetic to the recently deposed dictator, he also had to pay close attention to the subversive designs of the left that found inspiration in the Cuba of Fidel Castro. The Frente de Liberación Nacional (National liberation front) and the armed forces of Liberación Nacional led a rebellious period that grew more intense as the constitutional period reached its peak in 1964.

It was during the term of the new president, Raúl Leoni (1964–69), a seasoned leader of the governmental party, that the democratic experiment began to reveal its cracks. Apart from the forces controlled by AD and COPEI, many elements began to cluster around the figure of Úslar Pietri. Beyond his personal dynamism and other qualities, Úslar Pietri represented the Venezuela of past regimes—while the leftists raged against the elections with a spirited chorus of intellectuals supporting them. But Úslar Pietri and other figures who had come to power just after the Gómez era were not the only ones who felt they had been excluded from the country's democratic destiny—the guerrillas and the domestic intelligentsia felt the same way, and they expressed their objections in public without reservations.

Nonetheless, the policies that Betancourt's administration had implemented over the course of the previous five years were continued in the new regime. By 1968 the country was producing 3,600,000 barrels of oil per day. The expansion of the Orinoco iron and steel works and the success of the Venezolana de Navegación shipping company produced plentiful profits from their business ventures. The country's network of highways was expanded by more than three thousand miles. Considerable sums of money were invested in housing and the social security system was revamped with very favorable results.

Leoni's supreme skill, however, was in his handling of the problems he faced during an era of armed struggle and opposition from the intellectual community. His awareness of these problems led him to instigate a complex confrontation with the armed elements and a deft reconciliation with the country's artists and thinkers. And while he supported the use of force to an unacceptable degree, he did enact a law for the commutation of sentences through pardon or expulsion, an action that was aimed at releasing some 250 left-wing militants from prison. The poets, writers, and painters who had distanced themselves from the regime and from public institutions were now called in to participate in promoting culture from official or semi-official posts. The Instituto Nacional de Cultura y Bellas Artes (National institute of culture and fine arts) would now serve not just for those urgent ends but also to promote, with renewed energy, a practice that would become a constant in future administrations: governmental sponsorship of the very broadest range of activities of artistic creation or cultural promotion.

When the COPEI party candidate Rafael Caldera[12] rose to the presidency (1969–74), the friction seemed to abate somewhat. He was an opposition candidate, and his election confirmed for the first time that the dream of republican alternation in power was in fact possible in Venezuela. Negotiations with the guerrillas led to an open policy of peacemaking—which brought subversive elements back toward the path of democracy. But former dictator Pérez Jiménez's supporters also emerged boldly from their clandestine existences, and it came as no surprise when they garnered a healthy number of votes for their nationalist Cruzada Cívica Nacionalista (Nationalist civic crusade).

Ultimately, during Caldera's first term as president continuity trumped change in decisive areas such as iron- and steelworks, energy, petrochemicals, and aluminum. Caldera upheld the legacy that had begun in the 1940s, when he embodied the greatest legal challenge to Acción Democrática. Both he and his party had changed, but more importantly, the country had changed. By this point, the national population had passed the ten million mark, and was 75 percent city-based. The modernization that had taken place in areas like communications and the circulation of ideas, as well as the influence of all that was happening outside the country, became increasingly important. But the reverse was true as well: Venezuelan cultural and economic events now had an impact beyond the country's borders. For example, when Venezuela's status dropped to fifth place among the world's oil-producing nations, the United States took notice, warning that the descent was due to the country's limited competitive capacities and its failure to take sufficient advantage of its mineral resources.

People who had lived in the belief that Venezuela was the first in oil production were forced to realize the ephemeral nature of the very privileged circumstances that they had enjoyed since the beginning of the twentieth century. The path would become more and more fraught with peril every time this reflection went unheeded. Today, as the democratic coexistence that prevailed back then has begun to wend its way down some very twisted paths, it is clear what went unnoticed by the individuals who should have been busy reflecting upon the plummeting numbers of the hydrocarbon business. Neither the country's leaders nor its intellectuals, in all their searching, realized that what Venezuela most desperately needed was not the resolution of urgent economic matters, but rather a metamorphosis in the way of thinking about how leaders and society alike might operate to bolster the common good. It was a perfect opportunity to remedy the missteps of a democracy that had already begun to show patent signs of deterioration – and about which the majority groups of the population began to grow extremely concerned and disgruntled. The details of a political landscape that was growing hazier escaped the shortsighted mindset of the day, and this was what allowed the historical chapter that began in 1958 to take a turn that might give way to a complete breakdown – in other words, the conundrum we are facing today.

Translated by Kristina Cordero

notes to the text

1. The Plan de Barranquilla was a document drafted in Barranquilla, Colombia, in 1931 by a group of Venezuelan exiles. The document offered an analysis of the situation in Venezuela at that time, and itemized actions to be taken against the Gómez dictatorship. In a way, it was the manifesto of the leftist collective Agrupación de Izquierda (ARDI), which counted among its members two future presidents of Venezuela: Rómulo Betancourt and Raúl Leoni.
2. The artists of the Escuela de Caracas were focused on capturing the unique spirit of Venezuela, particularly through landscape. González, one of the Escuela's central figures, was well known for his depictions of the iconic El Ávila mountain. Castillo painted landscapes as well as still lifes and nudes; he is considered one of Venezuela's masters of color. Zuloaga was a painter and printmaker; in 1948 she became the cultural director of Venezuela's ministry of education, and in that post issued study grants to a group of young people who would go on to establish the group Los Disidentes in Paris. Alcántara was a landscape painter.
3. This was the "democratic, multiclass, popular, revolutionary" party founded in Caracas in 1941 by Betancourt, Leoni, and Gonzalo Barrios, among others. After participating in the coup d'état against Medina Angarita in 1945, the party went on to become a primary influence upon the politics of Venezuela in the second half of the twentieth century.
4. COPEI was a political party with a Social Christian orientation, founded by Rafael Caldera in 1946. Along with Acción Democrática, COPEI was one of the political parties that had the greatest impact on Venezuela in the second half of the twentieth century.
5. The Guasina concentration camp was established by the revolutionary junta

of the government following the coup d'état that overthrew Gallegos. More than three hundred political dissidents, the majority of them members of the Acción Democrática party, were incarcerated at this camp, which was located on an island in the estuary of the Orinoco River.

6. The Caracas-La Guaira highway, which connects Caracas to its seaport, was inaugurated by Pérez Jiménez in 1953 and became an emblem of the modernization process initiated by the dictatorship.
7. Héctor Poleo was one of the pioneers of socially engaged art in Venezuela. He was influenced by the Mexican mural painters of the early 1940s. After World War II, Poleo's work began to move toward Surrealism, and his later output was marked by a more abstract and decorative style.
8. Luís Guevara Moreno was a founding member of Los Disidentes. A champion of geometric abstraction during the 1950s, he later returned to figurative painting.
9. Pascual Navarro was a founder of Los Disidentes. Like many other Venezuelan abstract artists, he returned to figurative painting in 1955.
10. Among visual artists, Jacobo Borges is the most representative of the "new figuration" in Venezuela of the 1960s, during which time he created paintings that revealed his strong opposition to the political situation of the day.
11. Rafael Trujillo was the dictator who governed the Dominican Republic between 1930 and 1961. In 1960 he engineered an unsuccessful assassination attempt against Betancourt.
12. Rafael Caldera, the founder of COPEI, was president of the republic from 1969 to 1974 and again from 1994 to 1999.

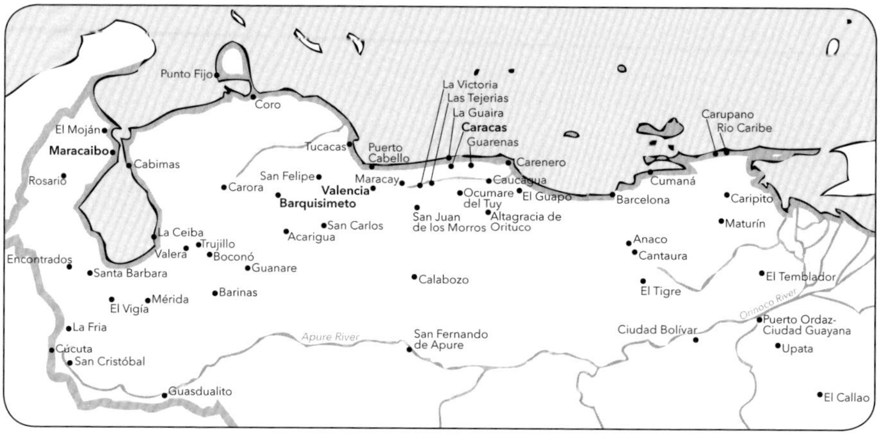

Coastline and Principal Cities of Venezuela

transformations in venezuelan territorial development and construction from the 1920s to the 1950s

marco negrón

In the period of the 1920s to the 1950s, Venezuela underwent a number of crucial transformations in the interdependent realms of politics, economics, and demographics. These changes were largely, though not exclusively, the result of the country's new oil wealth, the impact of which was both hugely beneficial and stunningly complex. It was a time of exponential growth and migratory shifts: factors that were both pivotal in Venezuela's coming modernization and its new role on the international stage.

the oil economy, modernization, and urbanization

During the early twentieth century, the Venezuelan nation was still a physically scattered entity comprised of four poorly interconnected regions, each made up of subregions that also suffered from weak communications systems. To the west, Maracaibo was the port from which export goods were dispatched to international markets; it was also the focal point for the fragmented region of Los Andes and its then-flourishing coffee economy. The country's eastern region had little internal physical integration. Its principal city of Carúpano – home to a significant and very entrepreneurial population of Corsican immigrants – was the principal port of the region of Paria, shipping coffee and cocoa from its harbor, though its narrow strip of coastline proved difficult to integrate into the region as a whole. At the center of the country, Caracas asserted its status as the nation's capital. Despite its weak links with other regions, Caracas prevailed over Venezuela's other cities in terms of population, politics, and culture. Since the late nineteenth century, the Caracas region had had the benefit of a road and rail system connecting its cities and two ports, La Guaira and Puerto Cabello; by the early twentieth it was the only region in Venezuela that was fully integrated in terms of transport and communication. In the south of the country and the plains, a sparsely populated area where the principal economic activity was large-scale ranching, the chief transport system was comprised of the Orinoco

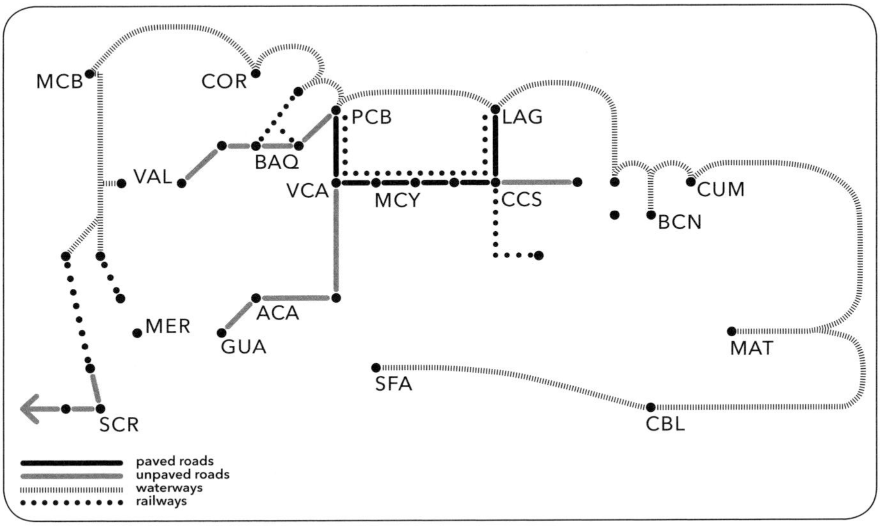

Fig. 1: Venezuela's National Transportation Infrastructure, 1920. Source: *Urbanización en Venezuela*, 3 vols. (Caracas: CORDIPLAN-United Nations, 1971).

and Apure rivers, and the main urban center and nexus to the rest of the world was Ciudad Bolívar (see fig. 1).

The process of urbanization in contemporary Venezuela, as well as the physical integration of the nation's territories, is associated with the rise in oil-export activity that transformed the Venezuelan economy beginning in the 1920s. In 1926, for the first time, oil exports were worth more to the country than its traditional agricultural exports, and from that point on the predominance of oil exports would continue to grow. By 1929, oil outpaced agricultural exports by four to one.[1]

At the beginning of the 1920s, no city in Venezuela had more than 100,000 inhabitants, and only seven boasted more than 10,000, representing 8.5 percent of the country's population.[2] Caracas alone represented 3.7 percent of Venezuela's population with just over 92,000 inhabitants, as the urban population (that is, in localities of more than 2,500 inhabitants – the census's definition of an "urban center") scarcely grazed 16.4 percent of the country's total.

During these years significant changes began to take place within Venezuela's demographic indicators. The country's great economic catalyst was the return value of its oil exports: that is, the rent the State took in and subsequently redirected into the country's domestic economy. In this period of growth, internal production activities were relatively insignificant economically, and were dependent on the performance of oil exports.[3] To this we may attribute the fact that by 1941, when oil exploration and development activities were at their peak, the population of the seven significant oil-industry cities of the day – Cabimas, Punto Fijo-Cardón, Ciudad Ojeda Lagunillas, El Tigre, El Tigrito, Bachaquero, and Mene Grande – represented 1.3 percent of the overall population of Venezuela, having multiplied their 1920 population numbers by 3.5 percent[4] (while Caracas now boasted 8.4 percent of the population). At this time the population tended to cluster not around those urban centers most directly connected to the extraction of hydrocarbons, but rather in those where the distribution of the return value of the exports was determined.

A second important factor in Venezuela's demographic history was the widespread presence of malaria in the national territory, which lasted until at least the 1940s. It has been noted that in the early 1930s, two-thirds of the 570,000 square miles of Venezuelan territory were affected by malaria. The first attempts to put an end to the epidemic were made at some point in the mid-1920s, but more sustained efforts began in 1936. There was a qualitative leap forward starting in December 1945 with the introduction of the mosquito-killing pesticide DDT, which ultimately eradicated the disease.[5] This achievement, too, was linked to the country's oil exports, which generated the funds necessary to finance such a vast undertaking.

Geographic factors also played a part in the uneven territorial occupation of Venezuela. The country was naturally divided into three large geo-economic regions: the coastal-mountain region comprised of the Andes, the Maracaibo Lake basin, the northern mountain range, and the Caribbean coast; the *llanos*, or plains, comprising the mesas and savannahs of the country's central zone; and Guayana, covering the territories to the south of the Orinoco River, and comprising the Amazon jungle. The first region (which includes the islands) represents 20 percent of the national territory, and is the home of the country's most fertile agricultural land. For this and other reasons, the main cities of Venezuela have been centered in this region since the colonial era. In the second region, which makes up 35 percent of the country's territory, the predominant economic activity has long been large-scale cattle ranching, with its high demand for land, low demand for labor, and relative incompatibility with the presence of urban conglomeration. The third region, which makes up the remaining 45 percent of the nation's territory, is a rich but complex area, generally focused on ore extraction and generation of hydraulic energy, activities that started to become particularly valuable in the middle of the twentieth century. In this region, the few human settlements have tended to concentrate along the Orinoco River, no doubt because of the advantages it offers for transportation.

In 1873, when the first national census was conducted in Venezuela, the first of these regions was home to 65 percent of the population, the second to 32 percent, and the third to 3 percent. By 1936 – early in Venezuela's modern demographic transition – the third region remained more or less the same, but the first region had jumped to constitute 80 percent of the population, and the second had slipped to 18 percent. This change was related to two phenomena that had a tremendous impact upon the territorial distribution of the population and the location of production activities: the bloody wars of the nineteenth century, which took place largely in the region of the *llanos*, and which did not end until the early twentieth century;[6] and the malaria epidemic, which affected the plains regions most severely.[7]

Another factor was the belated integration of the Venezuelan territories: while in 1920 the country's central area boasted a network of paved roads and railways that guaranteed its internal integration, interregional connections were virtually nonexistent. Regions were either completely isolated from one another or were connected by a few precarious waterways and dirt roads. Trains

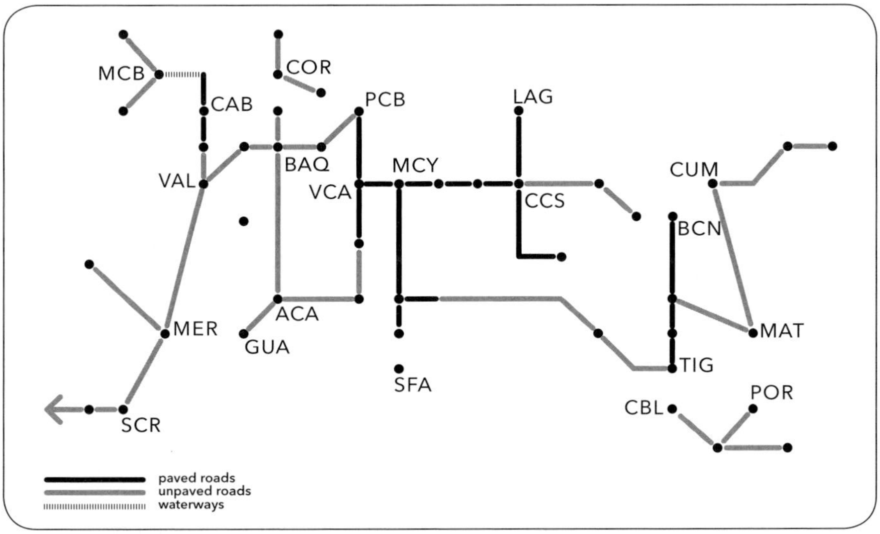

Fig. 2: National Roadways Infrastructure, 1947. Source: *Urbanización en Venezuela* (1971)

existed in some of these areas, but (with the partial exception of the Caracas-Valencia axis) there was no comprehensive rail system, even on the regional level, which meant that they had virtually no overall territorial impact.

The transportation-integration process was spurred by the growth of Venezuela's oil economy. By 1947 there was a relatively comprehensive national transport network (see fig. 2), although the majority of the roadways were still unpaved and the old railways and coastal navigation routes had been abandoned.

By 1947 the new paved roads had expanded beyond the Caracas-Valencia region into the oil-producing regions, along the eastern coast of Lake Maracaibo and between the oil fields to the south of Anzoátegui and Puerto La Cruz.

1920–45: modernization in the making

In the maturation of the so-called petro-state,[8] the years 1920–45 constitute a key period: a nexus between what might be termed the "agro-colonial" phase and the modern era. During this period Venezuela began to witness economic, political, and sociocultural transformations that would form the contemporary nation.

What set off this great change was of course the surge of oil-export activities that began in the 1920s and marked Venezuela's definitive entry into the world-trade system, from which it had long been marginalized (indeed, it was partially excluded from this system for a significantly longer period than were other Latin American countries). During this era, oil was virtually the sole engine of the Venezuelan economy; it was a time of what might be described as "simple growth," when economic accumulation was not greatly significant. It was only toward the end of World War II that conditions became ripe for the advent of a second economic engine: the building industry. Ambitious construction projects brought jobs and incited growth in ancillary industries, accelerating the expansion of Venezuela's internal market, as well as in the areas of accrual and urbanization.

Before the oil boom, Venezuela's development had been precariously based on agricultural exports that had a low intensity of capital and were closely connected to economic fluctuations. The modest surplus that these exports brought tended to go straight into the pockets of the emerging bourgeoisie of the central region, affording leverage to the financial, real estate, commercial, and transportation sectors. The country's work force was vulnerable, dispersed, and greatly lacking in education and cultural sophistication; all this allowed the bourgeoisie to consolidate its power – occasionally in alliance with landowning sectors – in the domestic political sphere. The bourgeoisie favored investment in the fertile region that constituted the bedrock of its hegemony, a process that naturally compounded its own power.

Nevertheless, in these pre-boom years, the Venezuelan economy saw few benefits from the surpluses, as an internal investment structure was not yet in place. The modernization project that Antonio Guzmán Blanco had initiated at the end of the nineteenth century was atrophied. The profits were further diminished by the ruling class's reluctance to reinvest them – although these were the activities that constituted the basis of its power. All these factors played a part in Venezuela's slow development, its negligible urbanization, and the widespread consolidation of a subsistence economy.

the expansion of the oil business after 1920

The table below offers an illustration of how oil exports altered the dynamics of the Venezuelan economy.

years	coffee and cocoa		oil	
	value (in millions of bolívars)	% of total exports	value (in millions of bolívars)	% of total exports
1920	101	50.0	26	12.9
1926	118	24.2	325	66.6
1929	158	17.0	721	77.4
1940	26	3.8	616	90.2
1947	89	3.0	2,746	93.4

Table 1: Venezuelan exports, 1920 – 47 (indicating economic values and percentages of total exports)
Source: Asdrúbal Baptista, *Bases cuantitativas de la economía venezolana 1830 – 2002* (Caracas: Fundación Empresas Polar, 2006), pp. 218 – 22.

Thus, in a short span of years, oil overwhelmingly replaced agriculture in the nation's exports. Interestingly, however, 1929 data reveal – contrary to what is widely believed – that the decline of the agriculture economy was not attributable solely to the emergence of the oil market. The worldwide economic crisis of the 1930s dealt the deathblow to Venezuela's traditional export business,[9] leading to a national agricultural crisis, the repercussions of which were felt at least until the 1960s. For obvious reasons, the Depression had a far less dramatic effect on oil production.

Venezuela's oil production was determined by and dependent upon foreign countries; the demand for oil came exclusively from outside the country's borders, from industrialized nations that were major participants in the world's economic processes. Foreign companies had the technology and capital to take control of the markets and the commercial channels—indeed, of the entire scope of oil-production activities.[10] As a result, Venezuela's oil industry had its main economic impact abroad; operations within the country became a kind of enclave: the only direct effect of oil production upon its domestic market was through the payment of salaries and wages.[11] What would revolutionize the domestic economy was not oil production itself, but rather the return value of its exports.

Since Venezuela's national constitution has historically adjudicated ownership of the country's subsoil to the State, all of that return value entered the country through the government. Whoever was at the helm of the country at a given point played a critical role in the distribution of returns—and thus in establishing the general state of the country's economy. Just 16 percent of Venezuela's oil income generated between 1920 and 1936 went directly to private citizens, through wages and salaries paid out by oil companies; the remaining 84 percent went toward taxes and royalties charged by the government.[12] This situation only strengthened the politically powerful bourgeoisie's domination over a range of social processes, in addition to helping it withstand the collapse of the export agriculture business—its original source of power—in 1930.

Venezuela's ruling classes were hence further empowered economically. The Proyecto Nacional,[13] which had been incubating since 1864, quickly became identified as the only conceivable framework for the organization and operation of society.[14] This, however, did not initially imply a substantive expansion of the country's internal-production apparatus, either through the source of this new wealth[15] or any use that was made of it.

Corruption was rampant. According to historian Germán Carrera Damas, it would not be an exaggeration to consider embezzlement as the "decisive factor in the maturation process of the Venezuelan bourgeois class."[16] Rómulo Betancourt proposed that proximity to power was in itself an essential link to wealth.[17] There was little financial risk for the ruling class, and this new source of wealth had unprecedented stability, in comparison to the unstable and weak economic activity that had previously predominated in Venezuela.

It has been argued that none of the Latin American societies that suffered infrastructural crises at the end of the eighteenth century was able independently to generate the dynamic economic factors that might have allowed them to overcome their difficulties. On the other hand, it has also been suggested that by the 1930s and '40s there already existed viable options for internal reinvestment of the oil rent—in theory, at least. In practice, because of the manner in which it originated, the distribution and use of such revenue among socioeconomic agents were determined on the basis of political rather than economic reasoning. The criteria for the distribution of wealth were largely determined by the ruling class and its desire to ensure the status quo.

This state of affairs did not come about easily or rapidly: as Venezuelan society grew increasingly complex, the debate regarding the management of oil income also became more complicated and contradictory. At stake was the dialogue of power between the different strata that comprised Venezuelan society. The ramifications of this dialogue would be felt far into the future.[18]

"sowing the oil" and the role of the state

Under the Gómez administration the Venezuelan ruling class recognized that, given the complexity of the oil business and the lack of education among the vast majority of the country's citizens, there would be no feasible way to integrate Venezuelan society into this economic system through the means of production. They did, however, see the possibility of integration through rent. But while some people favored the participation of private landowners, others felt the oil business should belong primarily to the State, as owner of the country's subsoil. The first option would have meant placing the country's wealth in the hands of a social class operating with a pre-capitalist mentality, whereas the second option at least offered the possibility that the wealth might be channeled into productive means and toward the modernization of the country.

After Gómez's death in 1935, the influential voice of Alberto Adriani[19] maintained that oil represented an ephemeral source of wealth that was best left aside, so that the agricultural sector – especially the coffee industry – might be strengthened and modernized. Adriani had little understanding of the characteristics of the oil business, but the notion of a rent-based economy was anathema to him. His premature death in 1936 helped clear the field so that ultimately a different approach would be adopted.

In ethical terms, the position of Arturo Úslar Pietri, a writer, lawyer, and politician who exercised considerable influence upon the Venezuelan governments between 1936 and 1945, was perhaps not so different from that of Adriani, but in practical terms he took into account the great relevance that oil income would soon have for the country. Úslar Pietri understood this market to be about not only rent but "natural capital," a concept that legitimized the revenue from its very roots. In this sense, the oil rent did not exist as the result of a relationship between a landowner and a capitalist businessman, but was equitably positioned between two entities possessing capital that came together to form an association: the Venezuelan nation, owner of the "natural capital" of oil, and the foreign oil companies, owners of the technology that facilitated the extraction and production of that oil.

All that remained to be determined was the fate of that income – that is, how to keep it from being directed toward purely consumptive ends, which would drive the nation toward an increasingly parasitic existence. This was a risk that would rise as the previous internal production business – export agriculture – had collapsed with the Depression. The proposed solution was to put the oil income in its entirety toward *investment* instead of operating expenses, a notion that was synthesized in the slogan "sembrar el petróleo" (to sow the oil): in other words, turn the oil rent into the "seed" that would eventually grow to become a national, production-based capitalist system. To allocate this income for consumption would not only be an ethically unacceptable position (according to Úslar Pietri's way of thinking), it would also lead to the swift disintegration of this clearly vast source of "natural capital."

Within this program, the State would be responsible for defending national interests against those of foreign companies, as well as administering and distributing the income. Direct investment, on the other hand, would be the responsibility of the private sector, following the idea that voluntary individual initiative is the firmest foundation for the efficient management of such things, and for the construction of a true democracy. In operational terms, however, there was a problem: not only was this income effectively "rent," it was a level of rent so extraordinary that it would always tend to exceed the capital absorption capacity of the society that enjoyed it. This represented an enormous obstacle to the objective of "sowing the oil."

In 1945, the national-populist ticket, with the help of military powers, overthrew the "old executors" of the Gómez legacy, placing Rómulo Betancourt and the Acción Democrática party in power. For the new ruling party, the legitimacy of the rent's origin was accorded with the same basic criteria—but with one important difference: the new leaders declared that the direct participation of "the people"—and not just private capital—was crucial in determining the manner in which the country's income was to be spent. Betancourt made it very clear that the popular, democratic claims and demands were at one with the national interests regarding revenue. He also well understood the forces he would have to face in this stance: the foreign oil companies and the ruling elites that were his domestic allies.

This was how the Venezuelan government legitimized the use of oil revenue for consumption. One of its primary objectives was to improve the living conditions of "the people" through salary raises in the public sector (a measure that trailed behind the private sector), and to increase the job market and citizens' services, especially in the areas of education, health, and housing. But the State would be given a newly important role in the area of production as well, due to the private initiatives' inclination to take the path of least resistance.

The populist strategy may be summarized in the following terms: rent from oil, initially, was intended to help develop "human capital" and create a domestic market—in other words, to establish the foundations that would allow the oil to be "sown." Once this objective was fulfilled, and oil rent had been channeled toward consumption, the country would be ready to enter a second phase, in which the emphasis would be on accumulation, on investing the oil rent in the development of productive activities, specifically industry. If the phase of consumptive absorption of the rent were prolonged beyond what was absolutely necessary, however, there was a risk that the money might begin to be squandered.

The members of the Acción Democrática party would not have the chance to prove their ability to handle this new system. In November 1948, the same military officers who three years earlier had brought the party to power overthrew the recently elected president, Rómulo Gallegos, and instituted a radically different kind of political program, ostensibly focused on the "transformation of the physical environment" (although in this respect the new administration continued in more or less the same vein as the previous). In the 1950s, as

Venezuela's oil production soared higher than ever, these policies were translated in a short span of years into the construction of a physical infrastructure that was arguably without parallel in all of Latin America.

migratory processes and the logic of urbanization

In 1920 Venezuela was an overwhelmingly rural country: nearly 80 percent of its 2.3 million inhabitants lived in the countryside and all its cities had fewer than 100,000 residents. According to certain estimates, the active rural population in 1926 came close to one million people;[20] by 1937, the country's agricultural census reported that this figure had dipped to just under 650,000.[21] Nevertheless, these statistics reveal that as time went on, in addition to the accelerated growth of its population, Venezuela also experienced an intensification of internal migration that, as is traditional in such contexts, originated in the rural environment and was directed toward the country's urban centers. By 1941, the overall population of Venezuela was approximately four million, and the two cities that had more than 100,000 inhabitants, Caracas and Maracaibo, together represented 10.8 percent of the country's population. At the other end of the spectrum, the rural population grew in absolute numbers but suffered a drastic reduction in relative terms, tumbling to 60 percent of the overall population.

Contrary to what one might conclude at first glance, the final destinations of those migrants were not the cities that had recently sprouted up around Venezuela's oil fields, the source of the nation's newfound wealth. Instead, they gravitated toward the country's more traditional cities, despite the fact that significant development in any kind of large-scale production had not yet occurred. The 1936 census listed only two oil-industry cities, Cabimas and Lagunillas, both on the eastern shores of Lake Maracaibo, the combined population of which was no more than 23,425 inhabitants, scarcely 0.7 percent of the country's overall population. The subsequent census, however, taken in 1941, identified seven oil-industry cities, the majority of which were clustered around Lake Maracaibo, with two others quite far away in eastern Venezuela. The total population of these cities had just barely increased to 48,813 inhabitants, representing 1.3 percent of the overall population. Studies carried out later reveal that between 1936 and 1941, the final balance of the migration toward the oil-producing districts totaled 31,500 people, a number that was almost doubled by the migratory flow into Caracas, which absorbed some 58,000 people during this same period.[22]

The reason for the weak demographic pull of these new oil-industry cities is that their principal activities were carried out with a high level of productivity. Again, oil-industry employment reached its peak during this period with 27,000 employees in 1929, the year in which the value of oil exports was almost five times greater than coffee and cocoa exports (see table 1), which required, as we have pointed out, a much greater volume of labor.

Given all these factors, oil-production activities cannot be described as having been directly responsible for the population growth that took place in urban centers during this period, nor can this growth be explained by any processes of modernization in the agricultural sector, because in fact such modernization never occurred. On the contrary, the collapse of the export agriculture business in 1930 was what prompted this wave of internal migration.

This demise, coupled with the demographic increase in the countryside due to the decreasing mortality rate and the continued concentration of agricultural property,[23] quickly created a surplus rural population whose only option was migration. In addition, the migratory flow into Venezuela's traditional cities cannot be attributed to any transformations in the urban-industrial apparatus (such transformations had not yet taken place); it was, rather, due to the political nature of the decisions relating to the distribution of oil income. These decisions determined the concentration of that distribution according to the presence of the dominant social strata in these cities—and led to increased employment possibilities in the areas of commerce and services.

developing and constructing the national territory

The 1939 "Plan Monumental," the urban-renewal plan for Caracas, designed by the directorate for urbanism of the government of the federal district, in consultation with a group of distinguished European urban planners,[24] was the definitive inauguration of Venezuela's new tradition of urban planning. Because of bureaucratic obligations, the project's leaders were forced to limit the agenda to the area that is now known as the Libertador municipality within the metropolitan district of Caracas; it was, nonetheless, a plan of massive dimensions.

According to the 1939 publication *Revista Municipal del Distrito Federal* (Municipal journal of the federal district):

> In its goal of achieving a total resurgence on the national level, Venezuela has the advantage, thanks to its favorable economic conditions, of access to all the modern equipment and the most effective, rational methods that the time-tested experience of other countries suggests for the improvement of the administrative mechanism. As such, the country is in an unparalleled position to **modify and rebuild those great cities** that the government, industry, and commerce need. The country will, additionally, be able to **stimulate growth in certain regions**, while at the same time avoiding the intermediate agglomerations that were necessary in other times due to the lack of roadways.[25]

This mission would be revived toward the end of World War II by the national commission for urbanism, which carried out the country's first regional-planning efforts and executed projects on a national level until it was disbanded in 1957. Its responsibilities were then transferred to the directorate of urbanism under the country's public-works ministry.

In the same vein, in 1947, the recently created national highway-administration commission formulated a preliminary highway plan, which was implemented swiftly and would remain in use for the rest of the century. In 1936, Venezuela had some 3,000 miles of roads, of which only 300 were paved. By 1948 those numbers had risen to 4,700 and 1,000 respectively; and by 1957, the global road network in Venezuela had increased by more than 200 percent, while the number of paved roadways grew by 300 percent.[26] In contrast with the 1947 roadways, which were primarily concentrated in the area around Caracas and the oil-producing regions (see fig. 2), they now covered practically the entire surface area of the territories to the north of the Orinoco and Apure rivers (see fig. 3).

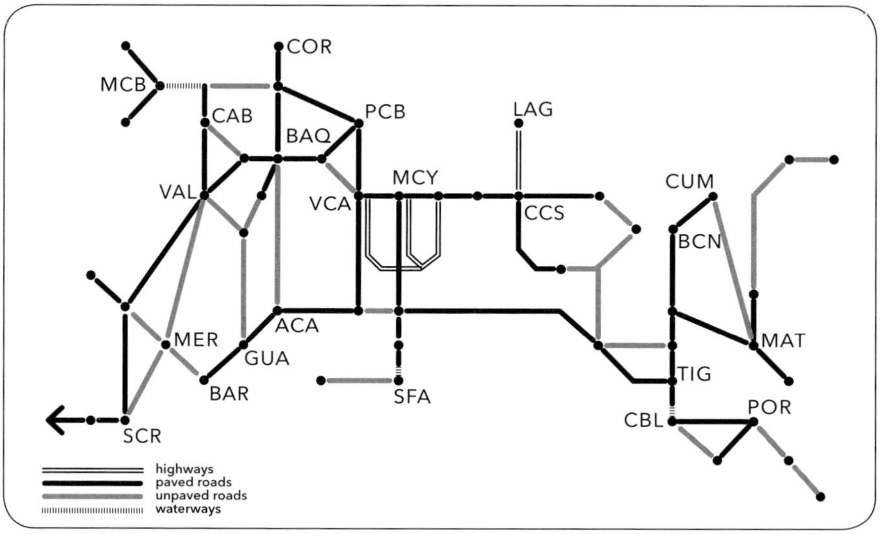

Fig. 3: National Roadways Infrastructure, 1957. Source: *Urbanización en Venezuela* (1971)

In 1971 Venezuela's institute of state railroads formulated a national rail plan, but it was barely executed, and thus had little or no impact on Venezuelan life.

the great architectural projects

In the aftermath of Gómez's death, Venezuela experienced a boom of formidable architectural projects, including a network of primary and secondary schools built across the country. Caracas in particular benefited from a number of extraordinary urban-renewal plans, many of which incorporated the work of modern artists, in a newly inspired vision of a "synthesis of arts" and architecture. Between 1943 and 1945, Carlos Raúl Villanueva's El Silencio complex was erected at the very center of Caracas, comprised of seven blocks of 747 apartments and 207 commercial units – all in a city with a population that had yet to reach 500,000. Villanueva brought in the artist Francisco Narváez, who created the fountain-sculpture around which the entire project is conceived. In 1949, just one street east of El Silencio, construction began on the Centro Simón Bolívar, an ambitious complex of offices and commercial space designed by Cipriano Domínguez.[27] With 400,000 square meters of space, the center featured murals by Oswaldo Guayasamín[28] and César Rengifo,[29] among other works, and was crowned by two towers that ascended thirty floors skyward – an unprecedented and almost inconceivable height for the Caracas of those days.

In 1955, on an ample stretch of land scarcely separated from El Silencio by the Calvario hill,[30] work began on what would eventually be known as the 23 de Enero community,[31] a facility for 55,000 residents. The project was developed by the architecture workshop of the Banco Obrero under the stewardship of Villanueva, who on this occasion invited the participation of the artist Mateo Manaure, creator of the polychromes on the façades of the complex's fifteen-story apartment blocks.

In 1944, during the presidency of Isaías Medina Angarita, work began on Caracas's Ciudad Universitaria (the campus of Venezuela's Universidad Central), again under the direction of Villanueva.[32] The Aula Magna (great hall) and Plaza Cubierta (covered plaza), the two most exceptional elements of this architectural complex, were completed between 1952 and 1953. In these two spaces Villanueva most clearly enacted his vision of a "synthesis" of all the arts, incorporating works by the most celebrated young Venezuelan artists of the day, as well as by a distinguished selection of the international avant-garde, from Jean Arp to Fernand Léger, as well as Victor Vasarely, Henri Laurens, Baltasar Lobo, Antoine Pevsner, and Alexander Calder, whose remarkable 1953 *Acoustic Clouds* hang in the great hall.

Despite their impressive scale and formal attributes, Venezuela's modernist architectural achievements are unlikely to be deemed "grand urban projects" as we conceive of them today. There is no doubt, however, that they strengthened the Venezuelan capital, helping to place Caracas on the map of great Latin American cities, and transforming it into an attractive destination for international migration as well as for the intellectual elites in the rest of the country.

Indeed, Venezuela's position and identity in the global context had changed radically in a relatively short span of years: from the inchoate, impoverished land it had been in the 1920s, it was now a country to be reckoned with, entering the future on an equal footing with other nations.

Translated by Kristina Cordero

notes to the text

1. Asdrúbal Baptista, *Bases cuantitativas de la economía venezolana, 1830–2002* (Caracas: Fundación Empresas Polar, 2006), p. 219; Miguel Izard, *Series estadísticas para la historia de Venezuela* (Mérida: Universidad de Los Andes, 1970), pp. 186, 200.
2. Julio Páez Celis, *Ensayo sobre demografía económica de Venezuela*, 2nd edition (Caracas: Edoven, 1975). The seven cities were: Caracas, Maracaibo, Valencia, Barquisimeto, La Guaira-Maiquetía, San Cristóbal, Cumaná.
3. Luís Carlos Palacios, "El desarrollo y la planificación urbana en Venezuela," *Urbana*, no. 12 (Caracas), 1993: 11–26.
4. Marco Negrón, "Los orígenes de la urbanización contemporánea en Venezuela: El crecimiento sin acumulación entre 1920 y 1945," *Urbana*, no. 4 (Caracas), 1982: 71–92.
5. Germán Yépez Colmenares, "La lucha para controlar y erradicar la malaria en Venezuela entre los años 1936 y 1948," *Anuario* vol. 2, no. 6 (Caracas: Instituto de Estudios Hispanoamericanos, Universidad Central de Venezuela, 1994).
6. The dictatorial regime of Juan Vicente Gómez (1908–35) put an end to the civil wars of the nineteenth century.
7. In 1916, "an intense and catastrophic malaria epidemic that . . . decimated the Venezuelan plains" was recorded. Official statistics indicate that between 1905 and 1935 more than 220,000 people died as a result of malaria in Venezuela, that is, 12.5 percent of the total deaths in the country during that period. See Jeannette Rodríguez and Víctor Pinzón, "La aplicación del DDT en la lucha antimalárica en Venezuela (1945–1948)," *Anuario* 2 , no. 5 (Caracas: Instituto de Estudios Hispanoamericanos, Universidad Central de Venezuela, 1993).
8. The term "petro-state," coined by Terry Lynn Karl in 1995, refers to those peripheral economies that rely heavily on income from oil exports, and for which the state plays a central role in channeling income toward the domestic sphere. From this perspective, Karl states that "culturally, Venezuela belongs to Latin America; structurally, its economy and patterns of stability and instability are more similar to those of such other relatively populous oil exporters as Algeria,

Iran and Nigeria." Cited in Fernando Coronil, *The Magical State: Nature, Money, and Modernity in Venezuela* (Chicago: University of Chicago Press, 1997), p. 5.

9. Irene Rodríguez Gallad, "Perfil de la economía venezolana durante el régimen gomecista," in Elías Pino Iturrieta (coordinator), *Juan Vicente Gómez y su época* (Caracas: Monte Ávila, 1985), p. 83.
10. During this time, it was the policy of these foreign companies not to operate oil-refining plants on Venezuelan soil, with the exception of a very few that were intended to satisfy a small part of the country's own demand for fuel. The Venezuelan government neither hindered nor objected to this policy.
11. Even this portion of the economy was weak, as the labor required in these oil-production activities is relatively low: for the entire period that ended in 1945, labor demand never exceeded 27,000 workers, the number that was recorded in 1929. Until the nationalization of the industry in 1976, it never exceeded 3.5 percent of Venezuela's overall employment. See Baptista, *Bases cuantitativas de la economía venezolana*, pp. 916–17; Chris Tanner, *Venezuelan Migration* (Diessenhofen, Switzerland: Rüegger, 1980), p. 92.
12. Armando Córdova, *Inversiones extranjeras y subdesarrollo*, 2nd ed. (Caracas: Universidad Central de Venezuela, 1979), p. 150.
13. Venezuela's Proyecto Nacional, or "national project," first defined in the country's 1864 constitution, was a comprehensive plan for the construction of a liberal, democratic state, including the consolidation of government, the bolstering of the bourgeoisie, and the modernization of the economy. The project was reformulated in the constitutions of 1947 and 1961 to comprise a socially oriented rule of law; increased individual, social, and economic rights; and the implementation of new policies with regard to the nation's oil wealth.
14. Germán Carrera Damas, *Una nación llamada Venezuela*, 4th ed. (Caracas: Monte Ávila, 1991), p. 137.
15. According to Max Flores, oil income, in terms of the domestic economy, "does not express a social product per se—that is, a product for which a direct effort is made by people, the economic subjects that are involved in the production process and who, as such, are part of a global accumulation process through which the majority of the surplus is generated, recirculated within and reinjected into the economy." See Flores, "El capitalismo en la Venezuela actual," *Economía y Ciencias Sociales* 18, no. 1 (Caracas), 1979. Bernard Mommer considers it a form of rent "in Ricardian and Marxist terms." See Mommer, *La nueva situación energética enfocada desde la teoría ricardiana y marxista de la renta de la tierra* (Mérida: Universidad de los Andes, Economics Department, publication 76-02, 1976). A similar formulation, but inclusive of the entire range of basic export products, is in B. Widyono, "Empresas transnacionales y productos básicos de exportación," *Revista* CEPAL, no. 5 (Santiago de Chile: CEPAL, 1978).
16. Carrera Damas, *Una nación llamada Venezuela*, p. 112.
17. Rómulo Betancourt, *Venezuela, política y petróleo*, 3rd ed. (Caracas: Editorial Senderos, 1969), chaps. 6, 7, and 8. Betancourt's observations are based on data provided by Edwin Lieuwen.
18. An in-depth analysis of this debate can be found in Asdrúbal Baptista and Bernard Mommer, *El petróleo en el pensamiento económico venezolano* (Ediciones IESA, 1987). The paragraphs that follow synthesize many of the ideas of these authors; I hope to have faithfully represented them in my own attempt to understand the debate surrounding the territorial question.
19. Alberto Adriani was an economist, writer, and politician. He was Venezuela's agricultural and wildlife minister, then treasury minister during the administration of Eleazar López Contreras.
20. See Federico Brito Figueroa, *Venezuela siglo XX* (Havana: Casa de las Américas), 1967.
21. See Marco Aurelio Vila, *Geoeconomía de Venezuela*, 2 vols. (Caracas: Corporación Venezolana de Fomento), n.d.
22. See *Urbanización en Venezuela*, 3 vols. (Caracas: CORDIPLAN-United Nations, 1971).
23. According to the national agricultural and farming census, in 1937, 89 percent of the agricultural lands of Venezuela were in the hands of 4.7 percent of the landowners. See Vila, *Geoeconomía de Venezuela*.
24. French urban planners Henri Prost, Jacques Lambert, and Maurice E. H. Rotival worked with an engineer named Wegenstein. For practical purposes, Rotival assumed the leadership of the team and returned to Venezuela on several occasions as advisor to both the Comisión Nacional de Urbanismo and the Centro Simón Bolívar.

25. *Revista Municipal del Distrito Federal, Posición y función geográfica de Caracas: Su porvenir* (Caracas: Gobierno del Distrito Federal, 1939), p. 19 (boldface in ms.). Facsimile edition of 1985.
26. Rafael S. Valery, *Los caminos de Venezuela* (Caracas: Cuadernos de Lagoven, 1978), p. 47.
27. Cipriano Domínguez was one of the founders of the architecture school of the Universidad Central de Venezuela.
28. Ecuadorian painter Oswaldo Guayasamín's work was influenced by Mexican muralism; his work decried the humiliation and misery of indigenous Latin Americans and all those living in poverty.
29. César Rengifo was a Venezuelan painter and playwright. Influenced by the Mexican muralists, he sought through his work to denounce the suffering of the poor.
30. Calvario hill was a park in the center of Caracas, with Gothic-inspired architecture that was designed by French landscape architects during the administrations of Guzmán Blanco (1870–88).
31. A residential complex designed by Villanueva in the 1950s, under the dictatorship of Marcos Pérez Jiménez. The name by which it is now known, 23 de Enero, commemorates the date (January 23, 1958) of the popular rebellion and coup d'état staged to overthrow the dictator.
32. The Ciudad Universitaria project was carried out without interruption until 1967. It was designated a World Cultural Patrimony of Humanity site by UNESCO in the year 2000.

alfredo boulton and the historiography of venezuelan art

roldán esteva-grillet

I analyze time through the artist or artists who best manage to express it.
—alfredo boulton, 1973

death to the colony, long live independence

In the late 1950s, anyone interested in Venezuelan art history who went to a library looking for information would have found very little material. The oldest book was published in 1883, the centennial of Simón Bolívar's birth. The date is no coincidence; Venezuela's then-president, Antonio Guzmán Blanco, had commissioned two works: an enormous painting, *La firma del acta de la Independencia* (The signing of the declaration of Independence), by the academic painter Martín Tovar y Tovar for that year's Exposición Nacional, and a book titled *Ensayos sobre el arte en Venezuela* (Essays on art in Venezuela) by historian Ramón de la Plaza.[1] If anything besides State secularization distinguished Guzmán Blanco's nearly two-decade hegemonic rule (1870–88), it was his support of the arts and sciences.

De la Plaza's *Ensayos sobre el arte en Venezuela* became required reading in Venezuelan schools. The author held patently negative opinions about art of the colonial period, but took a more sympathetic view of two Republican painters—Pedro Castillo in Valencia and Juan Lovera[2] in Caracas—from the era of General José Antonio Páez.[3] Readers of the book were introduced to the academic painters who, after completing their advanced studies in Rome, formed the teaching staff of Caracas's Instituto de Bellas Artes (from 1877 under the direction of de la Plaza). In both his book and his review of the Exposición Nacional, de la Plaza propounded the idea of overcoming colonial "backwardness" with a new art of patriotic themes, in the academic French tradition.[4]

Tovar y Tovar was de la Plaza's great favorite. Relegated to painting society portraits after his studies in Madrid and Paris, Tovar y Tovar was given the opportunity to make a name for himself as a historical painter with Guzmán Blanco's 1883 commission. *La firma del acta de la Independencia* was massive, measuring some twenty-three by fifteen feet (7 by 4.8 meters), and was awarded a gold medal at the Exposición Nacional. The following year, it was the subject of a detailed study by Arístides Rojas, a well-known chronicler and collector of art (and later great-uncle of Alfredo Boulton). Rojas also published writings on petroglyphs and indigenous effigies, and urged the establishment of an official system of art patronage. After his death in 1894, some twenty years would pass before another major contribution to the field of art history would be made in Venezuela.

Both de la Plaza and Rojas were fully in step with the period's positivist trends, and the two of them championed an academic art that glorified the nation's military past. Spurning Spanish colonialism, they were instrumental in turning Venezuela's focus toward the products of its own indigenous culture.

the landscape is the nation

During Juan Vicente Gómez's lengthy dictatorship (1908–35), Tito Salas—the official painter of the Gómez regime—took up the cause of academic art, and created a celebrated series of large-scale paintings of the life of Simón Bolívar. At the same time, the younger generation of artists began to turn away from commissions, painting scenes of their own milieu, such as the iconic mountain El Ávila, in the hopes that a market would emerge to purchase their work.

As early as 1906, critic and journalist Jesús Semprum[5] spoke of younger students' predilection for landscapes at Caracas's Academia de Bellas Artes. His speech at the 1912 inauguration of the Círculo de Bellas Artes[6] was broadminded and welcoming: "Along with supporters of the strictest classicism," he stated, "along with those most stubborn defenders of Romanticism and its derivatives, the fervent followers of the new schools—no matter how outrageous or absurd they may seem to us, including those ascribing to esoteric Symbolism or the frenetic lovers of Futurism—should also join us."[7] (Nonetheless, in his 1919 survey of Venezuelan art history, Semprum seemed more keen to recount the immediate academic past than to discuss the artistic innovations whose emergence he was witnessing.)

There was a need for more critics to foster an audience and market for art. In the newly formed Círculo de Bellas Artes were two important writers: Leoncio Martínez,[8] a champion of Venezuela's new art from 1912 to 1918, and Enrique Planchart, who took up the cause from Martínez in 1918. Often credited with engendering the first wave of modern criticism in Venezuela, Planchart was keenly attuned to formalist concerns, and generally refrained from the sort of literary and patriotic tangents that were typical of de la Plaza and Rojas. He would continue his advocacy of the modernist agenda until his death in 1953.

The painters, poets, and novelists of this generation—several of them founders of the Círculo de Bellas Artes—began to take over both new and established institutions after Gómez's death in 1935: the painter Antonio Edmundo Monsanto became the director of the Escuela de Artes Plásticas y Aplicadas, an important position that he held for the next decade; landscapist Manuel Cabré was at the Museo de Bellas Artes; writer Rómulo Gallegos became the country's minister of education; and Planchart was named head of the Biblioteca Nacional.

Adopting Martínez's point of view, Planchart extolled a naturalistic portrayal of the landscape and its regional traits, a style that drew on that of the European post-Impressionists. But as this generation was joined by younger converts, and as the art market developed during the 1940s, Planchart stopped working as a critic and became an art historian, focusing above all on the nineteenth century. He claimed, however, to know practically nothing about art of the colonial era, and presumed that most works of the period were in fact Spanish imports. Although he generally refrained from criticizing works of the colonial period, in 1938 he did speculate that much colonial art was created by "la mano esclava" (that is, by slaves)—a theory he later rescinded. Planchart unearthed period documents about the nineteenth century and did formal analyses of works from the recent past—especially by Lovera, Tovar, Arturo Michelena, and Cristóbal Rojas—providing well-researched biographical information on each artist.

the colony, without prejudice

By the 1930s, writers who had managed to shake off their positivist prejudices were ready to contend with the colonial period. They may be categorized together as humanists, although some were conservative (such as Caraciolo Parra Pérez and Mario Briceño Iragorry) and others liberal (among them Augusto Mijares, Arturo Úslar Pietri, Mariano Picón Salas, Ramón Díaz Sánchez, and Guillermo Meneses). These writers' engagements with the topic of Venezuelan art were uneven, with the exception of Picón Salas and Meneses, both of whom wrote surveys about Venezuelan art for exhibitions (in 1954 and 1961 respectively). These two also were the first to bring attention to Armando Reverón – the most original artist of the Círculo de Bellas Artes generation – writing about his work in the late 1930s. Rather than dwelling upon Reverón's eccentricities and sometimes outlandish persona, they focused on his luminous painting. The writer Alejo Carpentier likewise felt that the theatrics of the "hermit from Macuto" – as painter and critic Pascual Navarro dubbed Reverón in 1947 – should be disregarded in order to concentrate attention upon his work (Boulton would later concur emphatically with this approach).

While Planchart established himself as the new historian of a specifically Venezuelan tradition in art (a tradition that in his view came into being only in 1920),[9] Carlos Manuel Möller wrote essays that dwelled on the colonial tradition's importance in the fields of architecture and the decorative arts. Although neither of them had an academic background, they contributed much to both the research and the appreciation of Venezuelan artistic and architectural heritage. Even so, they published only one book each, compilations of their articles: Planchart's *La pintura en Venezuela* (Painting in Venezuela), issued in 1956 after his death, and Möller's *Páginas coloniales* (Colonial writings), published in 1962. These were pioneering (though modest) studies with documented sources, bibliographical references, illustrations, and competent – in Möller's case, sometimes even evocative – writing. To these two books may be added José Nucete Sardi's *Notas sobre la pintura y la escultura en Venezuela* (Notes on painting and sculpture in Venezuela), which was awarded the prestigious Premio de la Raza from the Real Academia de la Lengua Española when it was first published in 1940, and had the distinction of being twice reprinted.

two crucial decades

At the end of his *Notas*, Nucete Sardi speaks of an emerging genre: an "Americanist" art that values folk customs and indigenous or mulatto identity. He mentions the artist Francisco Narváez and boldly brings up the work of the sculptor Alejandro Colina, who was at the time practically unknown.[10] Though his book does not feature the same level of formal analysis as Planchart's, it does bear abundant references to lesser-known provincial artists. Local production was also a topic of interest for the writer Eduardo Rohl, who published a series of essays about nineteenth-century travelers, all of whom were scientists, and some (such as Ferdinand Bellerman and Anton Goering) artists at the service of science.

The year 1942 would be especially significant for Venezuelan art history and historiography. That year, the Museo de Bellas Artes presented an imposing show titled *Paisaje Venezolano* (Venezuelan landscape), which was reviewed by Planchart and the Catalan writer Albert Junyent. The Salón Oficial de Arte awarded a privately sponsored prize for the first time—called the "John Boulton," after Alfredo Boulton's father—to the Mexican-educated figurative painter Héctor Poleo. In the same year, the Asociación Venezolana de Amigos del Arte Colonial (Venezuelan association of friends of colonial art) was formed following a show of colonial art in 1939 at the Museo de Bellas Artes. Finally, an exhibition about Simón Bolívar was presented at the same museum to celebrate the centennial of the repatriation of his remains from Santa Marta, Colombia. It was a time of coinciding themes—themes that set off a new, strictly documentary historiography, an objective approach that Boulton believed was necessary in order to form a true understanding of Venezuelan heritage.

Between 1945 and 1948, there was much political turmoil at all levels: General Isaías Medina Angarita's rule came to an end in 1945, to be followed by the first of Rómulo Betancourt's two presidential terms (1945-48); and Rómulo Gallegos's subsequent social-democratic government was ousted after less than a year in power in 1948. Unrest at the Escuela de Artes Plásticas y Aplicadas led to the foundation of the Taller Libre de Arte (Free arts workshop). The Taller was a forum for discussion—more intuitive than rational or pragmatic—about the new trends that broke with post-Impressionism and social realism, as a number of artists began to gravitate toward avant-garde abstraction.

The reform of Venezuelan art education in 1945 was split between two factions: the anthropologist Gilberto Antolínez championed a socially and politically committed art, whereas the painter Pascual Navarro Velásquez advocated an independent, libertarian art legitimized by its formal inquiries and entirely "devoid of dogma."[11] Intellectual artists such as Miguel Arroyo (who was educated in the United States) and César Rengifo (schooled in Mexico) discussed abstract art and realism at the Centro Venezolano Soviético de la Amistad (Center for Venezuelan-Soviet friendship) in 1948.

The 1950s was the defining decade for Venezuelan modernism, aided by a sharp rise in oil prices that was fed partly by the Korean War. During this period, Caracas's Ciudad Universitaria (the main university campus) was designed by Carlos Raúl Villanueva, who conceived it as a great "synthesis of the arts"; the space incorporated the work of both Venezuelan and foreign artists associated with the avant-garde. There was a much-publicized controversy about abstract art involving artist Alejandro Otero—one of the founders of the renegade group Los Disidentes—and leftist writer Miguel Otero Silva in 1957. While Otero defended his own modernity-related rationalist avant-garde (which embraced such artists as Piet Mondrian, Kazimir Malevich, and Antoine Pevsner), Otero Silva accepted *only* the work of Pablo Picasso, and furthermore felt that modern artists' participation in the putative "synthesis of the arts"—as at the Ciudad Universitaria—was tantamount to a subordination of painting to architecture, a relegation common in the Middle Ages.

Reverón's death in 1954 and his retrospective exhibition at the Museo de Bellas Artes in 1955, with an accompanying text by Boulton, marked the end of one era and the dawn of a new one.

from word to image

The time was ripe for a new proponent of Venezuelan art history to enter the scene.

Though Boulton was admitted as a member for life to the Academia Nacional de la Historia (National academy of history) in April 1959,[12] he was in fact more a connoisseur than a scholar. His induction to the academy of history—which he attributed to its members' generosity—was based on a single book: *Los retratos de Bolívar* (Portraits of Bolívar, 1956). Up to that point, Boulton had been known primarily as a photographer and less as an art critic; with this volume he demonstrated to what extent an image could serve as a record of history.

Boulton's education was typical of members of the upper middle class of the day: he had private tutors in Caracas and five years of secondary education at a Swiss boarding school, followed by a year studying business in England. What made this basic education unusual was his family—one of recent European extraction (from England and Italy) that nonetheless had deep Venezuelan roots and a heartfelt commitment to the arts. Among his ancestors, a great-grandfather was a painter, his great-uncle Arístides Rojas an art collector and chronicler, and his father a businessman and collector who was friends with many artists. His mother had been educated in France for twelve years. In the years during which Boulton lived in Europe, he went regularly to galleries and museums, accompanied by his parents when they visited him. As a young man, he also demonstrated his own artistic predilections, which he explored with a small camera given to him by an uncle.

When Boulton returned to Venezuela in 1928 at the age of twenty, he was surprised to encounter a burgeoning avant-garde—though, like all the independent cultural initiatives that arose under Gómez's dictatorial regime, it was having little public impact. But a new generation—which would become known as the "Generation of 1928"—was rising to challenge this dictatorship. At the beginning of the year a group of young intellectuals published the first and only issue of the journal *Válvula*, with a Cubist-inspired illustration on its cover and texts on Surrealism and Futurism in its pages. Among the writers featured in *Válvula* were Arturo Úslar Pietri, Miguel Otero Silva, Antonio Arráiz, José Antonio Ramos Sucre, Pedro Sotillo, Carlos Eduardo Frías, Fernando Paz Castillo, and José Nucete Sardi. During the ensuing Semana del Estudiante (Students' week), inflammatory anti-government speeches were made by university students—among them Raúl Leoni and Jóvito Villalba—bringing an end to a relatively quiet period in the country. The university was in for a painful trial: two hundred students, some of whom had collaborated on *Válvula*, were arrested and sent to prisons or forced labor. Boulton immediately aligned himself with this "Generation of 1928."

Other factors indicated that change was in the air in 1928. The young Carlos Raúl Villanueva received his architecture degree from the École des Beaux Arts in Paris and made his first visit to Venezuela to begin his career working for the government in Maracay, an important city in the center of the country, near Caracas. The following year, the distinctly regionalist novel *Doña Bárbara*, by Rómulo Gallegos, then a psychology teacher and the director of the Caracas Lycée, was published in Spain; this event buoyed many Venezuelans' hopes for the future.

Since the Círculo de Bellas Artes had formed in 1912, a rift between two positions had become apparent: one inward-looking, seeking a form of nationalistic expression (Martínez was the chief proponent of this stance) and the other open to the coexistence of currents from all parts of the globe (advocated by Semprum). Still, it was clear, even within the country's general climate of repression, that there was another Venezuela striving to express itself culturally.

In 1931, a private institution for the promotion of culture was established in the capital: the Ateneo de Caracas. Here, the educated bourgeoisie paid tribute to music, theater, intellectual pursuits, and the fine arts. It was on the occasion of a Venezuelan art show at the Ateneo in 1933 that the twenty-five-year-old Boulton took his first steps as an art critic, with a review in the pages of *El Universal*.[13] (Because his family was well known, he used the pseudonym "Bruno Plá," based on the initials of his two last names, Boulton and Pietri.) Disregarding the Cuban writer José Martí's famous mandate that "one should not concern oneself with bad art," Boulton brazenly panned the works of the widely admired painters Manuel Cabré and Marcos Castillo, along with other pieces that he felt should simply not have been exhibited; he also stated flatly that Reverón and Narváez were the only interesting contemporary painters. His words invited a sharp response: a Basque journalist, Francisco de Villanueva de López y Uralde, defended Cabré and Castillo as accomplished artists, and asserted that Alejandro Colina's work at the Aborigen de Tacarigua park was an example to follow in terms of "authentic" Venezuelan art.[14]

Boulton contributed writings (under the pen name Bernardo Pons) to *Élite* magazine in 1934, and in the following year (again as Bruno Plá) to *El ingenioso hidalgo*, where his text appeared alongside those of his friends Julián Padrón, Pedro Sotillo, and Úslar Pietri. This rather Europeanist and liberal journal was attacked by *La gaceta de América*, whose staff of writers included the leftist nationalists Inocente Palacios and Miguel Acosta Saignes.[15]

In tandem with his work as a critic, Boulton began organizing shows at the Ateneo de Caracas, to help Reverón and Narváez gain the attention of Venezuela's limited buying public. He organized a Reverón exhibition in 1934, which was a failure in terms of sales. According to a review by Padrón, Narváez's show in the same year garnered some nine hundred bolívars (despite Marcos Castillo's castigation of Narváez's painting as "naïve").

from image to word

Boulton married Yolanda Delgado in 1937 (the couple received a set of bedroom furniture designed by their friend Narváez as a wedding gift), and they settled in Maracaibo. He spent his vacations traveling around western Venezuela with the Rolleiflex he had received from his cousin Úslar Pietri during a trip to Venice. Boulton's first photography exhibition took place at the Ateneo de Caracas in 1938, and it brought him wide recognition. Two years later, he traveled to New York and returned home with his first published book of photographs, *Imágenes del Occidente venezolano* (Images from the Venezuelan West), with texts by Padrón and Úslar Pietri. It was the first publication of its kind in Venezuela.

The country was undergoing huge and rapid transformations with the profits of the oil industry. Boulton photographed the new cityscape that arose with Villanueva's redevelopment of Caracas's El Silencio district between 1943 and 1945. In 1944, Boulton turned to the Isla de Margarita, where he had bought an old country house; his photographs of the island were shown at the Museo de Bellas Artes in 1944 to great acclaim. Around this time, Boulton befriended the painter Rafael Monasterios and took him along on one of his trips to the Andes so that Monasterios could paint landscapes while Boulton photographed them.

During Medina Angarita's presidency (1941–45), Boulton's cousin Úslar Pietri worked for various government ministries. In October 1944 a group of seventy-four intellectuals, including Boulton, penned a letter in defense of the "climate of total freedom in which all intellectual and artistic manifestations are gaining such a powerful momentum, which expresses the fruitful and creative will of this democratic government."[16] Medina Angarita's liberal-democratic government came to an end in a civil-military coup on October 18, 1945, and was replaced with the Junta Revolucionaria de Gobierno, led by Rómulo Betancourt. In 1948 Boulton showed a series of portraits of his intellectual friends at the Salón Planchart—all of them opposed to the incoming Gallegos regime—under the title *30 hombres para el 48* (30 men for 1948). At the end of that year, the much-reviled Gallegos government was ousted by yet another coup d'état.

Venezuelan politics affected every aspect of the country's cultural development. The government-sponsored folkloric traditions and ceremonies—always with nationalistic references to the regime—during the Semana de la Patria (Homeland week) celebrations. In 1950—the year General Carlos Delgado Chalbaud was assassinated—Boulton published his book *Los llanos de Páez* (Páez's plains), judged by Úslar Pietri to be a model geography and history manual. For this project, Boulton revisited the sites mentioned by José Antonio Páez in his 1867–69 autobiography, documenting in photographs the landscape of broad horizons and floodplains, as well as the *llaneros* at work and at leisure. In 1952—the year of Pérez Jiménez's electoral fraud—a new book appeared that marked the beginning of Boulton's documentary research into history: *La Margarita*. Here, his photographs of the Isla de Margarita were accompanied by his text describing his dogged research for obscure news items among old documents in the island's archives.

Boulton had made the transition from image to word. Just as he had investigated people and landscapes in his photographs, he investigated their roots in his writings.

After his work on Páez, it was natural that Boulton should choose Bolívar as the subject of his next project. His research, the undertaking of a man educated by and thoroughly engaged with images, began with the hero's famous portraits. Boulton first looked at the Venezuelan paintings, all of which were copies of works by artists from other countries; he then tracked down the original renderings, which more accurately represented the features of Bolívar as they changed over the course of his life. "El Libertador" had never been painted in life by a Venezuelan, but had posed for painters from Ecuador, Peru, and Colombia, where he had spent more time and where the arts had reached a more advanced stage of development.

In 1954, Manuel Pérez Vila came to work as Boulton's assistant; the presence of this Spanish scholar would be fundamentally important to Boulton's education as a historian. Pérez Vila had studied at the universities of Bordeaux and Toulouse and had been employed for five years at the Archivo de El Libertador (Bolívar archives). He would work for Alfredo Boulton and for the John Boulton Foundation over the course of twenty-seven years.

While Boulton was deeply involved with his documentary research, as a collector of art he also understood the importance of examining period painting on a formal level. During travels with his camera—which he now used to document works of art—he began to draw connections between the Venezuelan copies of Bolívar's portraits and the originals from which they derived, through an analysis of the paintings' imagery, which included comparing them to physical descriptions from the period. The results of his intensive research were collected in *Los retratos de Bolívar*, published in Venezuela in 1956—the first of Boulton's books to be produced in his homeland.

A year later, Boulton entrusted Marcel Floris with the design of an exhibition summing up his Bolívar research. The show opened in the Diego Ibarra square in Caracas and had a total attendance of more than thirty thousand people. Boulton then organized a similar show with the original portraits at the Museo Nacional in Bogotá. Critic Marta Traba's review of the show noted "a sense of pedagogy and of historical research."[17]

criticism, curation, and research

As a critic, Boulton was very involved with the art of his period, helping and advising young artists, acquiring works for his collection, acting as a juror at the annual Salones Oficiales exhibitions, reviewing and organizing shows. As a historian, he undertook a thorough study of nineteenth-century Venezuelan art in search of faithful likenesses of Bolívar—an interest that led him to the paintings of Juan Lovera, many of which were scattered among several private collections. Boulton curated an exhibition of Lovera's work at the Museo de Bellas Artes in Caracas in 1961; it was the first time that a Venezuelan artist of such a distant era had been featured in a major show. The exhibition came as a revelation to many about the substance and value of the nation's history.

For approximately eight years, Boulton focused his research on ecclesiastic archives, and uncovered a vast amount of information that helped to give form to the specter of Venezuela's colonial painting. How could the anonymous makers of so many paintings be identified? The Museo de Arte Colonial had been established at the Casa de Llaguno in 1942 to exhibit the collections of the Asociación Venezolana de Amigos del Arte Colonial. As a member of this association—with personal ties to some of the country's few serious collectors and antiquarians—Boulton had the opportunity to examine many colonial paintings closely; he measured them against information gleaned from estates as well as certificates of baptism, marriage, and death, as well as other documents. He examined the imagery on all levels—formal, stylistic, academic—and combined this examination with documentary research.

In the course of this study, Boulton happened upon a painting that was dated and signed by one Juan Pedro López, who had until then been identified simply as "El Caraqueño" (or alternately as "El pintor de los ángeles mofletudos": "The painter of chubby-cheeked angels"). In 1963, Boulton presented the first exhibition of López's work at the Museo de Bellas Artes—the preeminent site for important art events since its founding in 1938.

The first volume of Boulton's monumental three-part historical study of Venezuelan painting was published in 1964. *Historia de la pintura en Venezuela*: *Época colonial* (History of painting in Venezuela: Colonial period) was enthusiastically received; it also revealed to the Venezuelan public how much of their history had been overlooked. The country was just developing an anxious sense that its own artistic production was perhaps not of a level comparable to that of the Spanish viceroyalties, while other means of research—such as economic studies—showed that the *mantuanos* (people of Spanish heritage, sometimes with aristocratic titles, generally in possession of vast households) had made their fortunes in the cocoa trade in the eighteenth century. With thorough documentation, Boulton demonstrated that while many works of art had indeed been imported to Venezuela, others had been made within the country. Although the ravages of time, war, and above all ignorance and negligence had destroyed much of the work to which wills and inventories testified, those pieces that had been conserved must, Boulton insisted, be valued as evidence of Venezuela's important collective past.

The second volume of Boulton's study, *Historia de la pintura en Venezuela: Época nacional*, was published in 1968; it dealt with Venezuela's post-independence period. This book concluded his historical research, which spanned from the early nineteenth century (with Lovera) to the early twentieth (with the formation of the Círculo de Bellas Artes). It drew upon a wide variety of sources, from period newspapers and magazines to legal documents, public and private archives, and artists' personal correspondence. Boulton debunked many myths of the colonial period—including the attribution of certain folk works to "la mano esclava"—and shed new light on figures of the post-independence period, such as the academic artist Cristóbal Rojas, whose paintings—like Arturo Michelena's while they shared a studio—often depicted social miseries and destitution, and revealed a rebellious, tortured personality.

While Boulton's first volume had met with great acclaim, the second, which dealt with more recent art, was not so well received. Other critics, and the general reading public, were not satisfied with Boulton's use of the Círculo de Bellas Artes generation as the endpoint of his study. Many wished for him to go on to address truly contemporary art—but Boulton was reluctant to comply with a third volume, feeling that his own "scientific" research went only as far as the 1940s with the Círculo de Bellas Artes. Boulton's rebuttals to various critical reviews[18] were relatively unconvincing, in arguments on such topics as the complexity of art practice after Picasso, the oil industry's transformation of the Venezuelan lifestyle, and the diversification of art practice after World War I. It would seem that Boulton lacked the temporal distance from which to venture an objective, well-grounded assessment.

In the four years between the publication of the first and second volumes of his *Historia de la pintura en Venezuela*, Boulton produced three monographs that presaged his future focus: that is, in-depth studies of individual artists. He became engrossed first in the work of Camille Pissarro, who was born in the West Indies and spent time in Venezuela as a young man before moving to France. In Boulton's investigations into the nineteenth century, he had placed much focus on "traveling" artists, and Pissarro was itinerant for much of his early life. Boulton took a particular interest in the artist's drawings and watercolors that were informed by his time in Caracas. Boulton's second monograph was on Armando Reverón, whom Boulton knew and with whom he was in touch up until the artist's death in 1954. Boulton organized an exhibition featuring four hundred of Reverón's works at the Museo de Bellas Artes in 1955, and a smaller selection that traveled to various cities in the United States. The last of Boulton's three monographs was on Alejandro Otero, whose work in 1966 was at the forefront of kinetic art.

the creation of hegemony

It is not surprising that Boulton's first monograph on Otero was published in 1966 by the country's Oficina Central de Information (Central office of information). The democratic period, beginning in 1958, was characterized by high oil revenues and technological advances (highways, iron- and steelworks, high-rise buildings), alternating political powers, and great respect for private capital; with these advances, the new democratic period managed to stanch old wounds. After Venezuela's Social Democratic party—which reintroduced militarism to the country—had overthrown the last dictatorship and faced leftist insurgents (inspired by the Cuban Revolution), those social sectors the party had once spurned for being liberal and bourgeois were now welcomed as supporters of the new regime. This political situation suited Boulton's own aspirations, and as for Otero, he was fully identified with the democratic regime.

The Venezuelan government had much to gain in spreading the word abroad about artists such as Otero and Jesús Rafael Soto, who garnered new prestige for the nation's culture. The Venezuela Pavilion at the 1967 World's Fair in Montreal was a minimalist construction designed by Carlos Raúl Villanueva. Its interior featured Soto's ephemeral environment *Volume suspendu* (Suspended volume, 1967). The presence of these two Venezuelan artists at world-class events became increasingly common. Soto's inclusion in President Rafael Caldera's retinue during the president's first trans-American trip in 1971 was indicative of the new status artists had achieved in Venezuela. Undoubtedly, the international success of kinetic art kindled a sense of national pride, and the government was sensible enough to support projects that allowed these artists to make monumental works in Venezuela itself.

But kinetic art was of course not the only genre in Venezuela in the 1960s. New *art informel* and neo-figurative tendencies played parts in expressing the malaise and contradictions of a democratic system that had to defend itself against guerrilla movements triggered by the Cuban Revolution.

It was in this context that the debate arose over Boulton's third volume of historical research, *Historia de la pintura en Venezuela: Época contemporánea* (History of painting in Venezuela: Contemporary period), published in 1972. With the second volume in his trilogy, some readers had felt that Boulton underplayed the importance of such figures as Franco-Venezuelan

Emilio Boggio (whom he called an "outdated Impressionist") and Marcos Castillo (although Boulton adopted a somewhat more favorable view of Castillo in this third volume). For the most part, Boulton limited his study to those great figures that were, in his view, the outstandingly original artists of their generation. What he categorized as "contemporary" began with the Taller Libre de Arte in 1948 and the central members of Los Disidentes around 1950. He was criticized also for excluding foreign artists and disregarding social realism as well as the Informalist and neo-figurative trends. (It is likely that these movements' political and social underpinnings made Boulton feel uneasy about stating a negative opinion.) He claimed not to know of any outstanding foreign artists, though he acknowledged the importance of critics José Gómez Sicre from Cuba and Gaston Diehl from France, and the influence of Mexican artist José Luis Cuevas.

Boulton's central point was that art may be understood as a narrative, in which certain individuals are eminently worth mentioning for their unique contributions, or for best expressing the spirit of their time. Much of Boulton's thinking was influenced by Thomas Carlyle's historical approach and the importance he attached to heroes, and by Hegel's idealistic conception of the zeitgeist. In his earlier volumes Boulton had adroitly juggled the roles of "connoisseur" and rigorous researcher—tackling major and minor artists, locals and foreigners, and referencing a gamut of writers, from Renaissance authority Bernard Berenson to modern theoretician Pierre Francastel. In this third volume, turning to his own time and place, Boulton based his ideas largely on his own *auctoritas*.

The publication of this third volume coincided with Boulton's being awarded the Premio Nacional de Literatura (in the essay category) for the years 1969–71. It was a new phase in the country's democratic history, bringing a successful peace process, the end of guerrilla insurgencies, booming oil revenues, and new cultural policies that met with the intelligentsia's widespread support. This prosperity led to the foundation of a large number of museums, at a time when U.S.-influenced art movements were emerging (among them Pop art, Conceptual art, performance art, body art, and video art).

Boulton played a crucial role in the development and establishment of the Museo de Arte Contemporáneo in Caracas. In the museum's impressive exhibition spaces, he had the opportunity to organize countless shows of his favorite artists, accompanied by substantial catalogues. The institution's professed "contemporary" mission was sometimes set aside to allow for Boulton-curated shows that might be more logically expected at the Galería de Arte Nacional: a collection of indigenous ceramics; works by a seventeenth-century religious painter known as "El Pintor del Tocuyo"; and the art of the self-taught painter Bárbaro Rivas.

In 1978 an article by Marta Traba appeared in the journal *Revista Medellín*, making spirited claims concerning Boulton's responsibility in the creation of what she saw as an "artistic hegemony" in Venezuela—that is, kinetic art. She labeled Boulton a "futurologist."[19] For Traba, the work of such figures as Gego (Gertrude Goldschmidt), Harry Abend, and Gerd Leufert—artists of European origin, now residents of Caracas—was of far greater value than that of the kineticists, who, she felt, had crafted a rarefied experiment and transformed it into a luxury object for a sophisticated elite. The environments they constructed fed the illusion of a technological society, she stated, without the "greatness of the structural pioneers." Kineticism monopolized recognition, commissions, and even scholarships, as if nothing else existed in the Venezuelan art world.

final recognition and appraisal

In 1987, shortly before Boulton's eightieth birthday, the Museo de Arte Contemporáneo organized an event in acknowledgment of his lifetime achievement. The president of the republic himself decorated Boulton with the highest of Venezuelan honors, the Orden del Libertador. The catalogue that accompanied this homage provides a wealth of information about Boulton's career. It features transcripts of a number of interviews he granted the press – including one titled "No le debo nada a nadie" (I do not owe anything to anyone) – that reveal a singular, multifaceted persona: a businessman (in the fields of transportation and insurance); a patron of the arts and sciences; a promoter of museums; a collector; a scholar of the colonial period and nineteenth century; an expert in the imagery of Bolívar, Páez, Sebastián Francisco de Miranda Rodríguez, Antonio José de Sucre,[20] and Manuela Sáenz;[21] and finally, a photographer of Venezuelan landscapes and people, of artists and intellectuals who were his friends, of native populations, and of indigenous works.

Even the most adamant critics of the 1970s had to admit that Boulton was an important and unique figure, and that in spite of certain mistakes and occasional class-conscious posturing, he indubitably deserved credit for what he had accomplished and was still accomplishing in his various fields of interest.

Boulton had the integrity and humility to recognize in the late 1980s that Carlos F. Duarte – who had delved into many of Boulton's chosen subjects – had notably improved upon his own earlier findings on Lovera. Boulton acknowledged the possibility that a portrait he had identified as depicting Sucre was not actually of the "hero of Ayacucho" (in view of claims and evidence presented by a great-great-grandnephew of Sucre's). Boulton did not live to realize that he had been the victim of a swindle: two portraits he had bought – a pastel of Bolívar supposedly made in Haiti, and another of Miranda, allegedly made in the United States – turned out to be forgeries, as did a miniature of Bolívar attributed to José María Espinosa, a work that Boulton had recommended to the Galería de Arte Nacional for acquisition. Ironically, he himself had spoken out against the unscrupulous trade in forgeries, especially of Reverón's works.

Boulton wished to be thought of as a researcher. He denied being a critic on more than one occasion – although he was in fact the president and founder of the Venezuelan chapter of the International Art Critics' Association, and had taken on all the tasks normally associated with the profession: reviewing and curating shows, working as a juror, penning catalogue texts and articles for magazines and newspapers, and writing artists' monographs. He also balked at the title "historian," although some of his books certainly meet all the requirements of historical treatises. When he did adopt the role of historian, he regarded his task as that of relating an artist's adventures; he was a narrator, ultimately allowing the artist to explain his concerns in his own words. (This might be considered an act of modesty on Boulton's part, or a way of justifying the author's stance as mere chronicler.)

Boulton focused exclusively on painting, perhaps because he found in it a kinship to the photographic image as he understood it, with similar rules of composition, light, and framing. He dealt with sculpture only in exceptional cases—such as that of Narváez, who was originally a painter but more successful as a sculptor, in both his *criollista*[22] and abstract *nuevas formas* (new forms) phases. When speaking of the kinetic artists—Alejandro Otero, Jesús Rafael Soto, and Carlos Cruz-Diez—Boulton's critical language tended to give way to personal, descriptive account.

His work as a photographer was exceptional in its own right, but he wrote and spoke little about his photographs or the medium in general. Two exceptions are an article from 1952, in which he asks himself if photography can be considered art (his answer is yes), and a course he taught on the theory and aesthetics of photography at the Universidad Católica Andrés Bello—but here he was careful to tailor his discussion of the trajectory of this medium's development in Venezuela, a trajectory in which he had played such a significant role.

In 1978—the year of Traba's controversial article—the faculty of arts was founded at the Universidad Central de Venezuela. To this day, anyone conducting research in visual art will encounter the work of Boulton, now considered a "classic," especially when it comes to certain topics and artists. His œuvre has been complemented by the research and writings of new generations who have strived to fill the gaps and carry Boulton's investigations forward. We will remain indebted to his work for many years to come.

The author wishes to thank Simón Noriega and Lourdes Blanco for their critical revision of the manuscript.

Translated by Richard Moszca

notes to the text

1. Historian Ramón de la Plaza was a general in the Guerra Federal and the first director of the Instituto Nacional de Bellas Artes (1877). He died in 1886, at the age of fifty.
2. Juan Lovera was one of the initiators of Venezuela's nationalist art, and is responsible for two classics of Venezuelan Republican art: *El 19 de abril de 1810* (April 19, 1810) and *El 5 de julio de 1811* (July 5, 1811).
3. José Antonio Páez was the chief commander of the Venezuelan independence army. He was considered the archetypal *llanero* leader, and played a central role in the country's history between 1821 and 1863. He was the first constitutional president of Venezuela after the unified territory of Great Colombia, established by Simón Bolívar, was split into separate countries in 1830.
4. De la Plaza also took a deep interest in music, and was a pioneer in writing about the importance of the Escuela de Chacao, the music school founded by Father Pedro Ramón Palacios y Sojo in Caracas in 1781, where a considerable number of composers and other musicians were educated in the late eighteenth century.
5. Jesús Semprum was a doctor, writer, journalist, and literary critic who collaborated regularly on the journal *El cojo ilustrado* from 1905 to 1915.
6. The Círculo de Bellas Artes was a group of young artists (painters, writers, musicians, and journalists) who, following the model of Madrid's Círculo de Bellas Artes (1880), sought to renew the way art was taught in Venezuela. It was formed during strikes against the Academia de Bellas Artes (1909) and its then-director Antonio Herrera Toro.
7. Jesús Semprum, "El Círculo de Bellas Artes," speech delivered at the inauguration of the Círculo de Bellas Artes, September 1912, at the Teatro Calcaño in Caracas. In *Visiones de Caracas y otros temas* (Caracas: Corporación Venezolana de Fomento, 1969), p. 108. See Semprum's full speech in this volume, pp. 96–98.
8. Leoncio Martínez was a journalist, caricaturist, art critic, and a founder of *Fantoches* magazine (1923). His 1912 manifesto "Ideas y propósitos: Palabras en la instalación del Círculo de Bellas Artes" ("Ideas and Aims: Some Words on the Establishment of the Círculo de Bellas Artes") is included in this volume, pp. 94–96.
9. In a 1920 article discussing the previous year's exhibitions, Planchart mentions several shows of works by foreign artists—such as Emilio Boggio, Nicolas Ferdinandov, and Samys Mützner—emphasizing the dearth of true Venezuelan painting. Planchart refused to acknowledge the academic tradition as endemically Venezuelan because of its French influence in both style and subject matter.
10. Alejandro Colina lived in various indigenous communities in western Venezuela for eight years. Two sculptures of indigenous figures and various archaeological motifs of his form part of the Indio del Tacarigua Plaza (Maracay, 1933); other well-known sculptures by Colina include *María Lionza* (1951) and *El cacique Tiuna* (Tiuna the cacique, 1951).
11. Pascual Navarro Velásquez, "Arte sí . . . pero sin dogmas," *El Nacional* (Caracas), December 2, 1945; reprinted in Roldán Esteva-Grillet, *Fuentes documentales y críticas de las artes plásticas en Venezuela: Siglos XIX y XX* (Caracas: Consejo de Desarrollo Científico y Humanístico, Universidad Central de Venezuela, 2000), vol. 1, pp. 1022–26.
12. Boulton was thus honored after presenting an essay on the imagery of Sebastián Francisco de Miranda Rodríguez (1750–1816), a Venezuelan military man and a forerunner of Venezuelan independence, who fought in the French Revolution and in Spanish campaigns during the American Revolutionary War.
13. Alfredo Boulton (as "Bruno Plá"), "La pintura venezolana como valor internacional" ("Venezuelan Painting as International Value"), in *El Universal* (Caracas), August 20, 1933. The essay is included in this volume, pp. 107–10.
14. Francisco Villanueva de López y Uralde, "Hay arte venezolano?" *El Heraldo* (Caracas), September 5, 1933. On the other hand, the painter Marcos Castillo was offended by Boulton's criticism, and protested his dismissal of landscape in favor of the still life.
15. Over the years, curiously, a number of thinkers who were initially accused of being "pro-foreign" were eventually acknowledged as champions of a Venezuelan agenda, and the inverse happened as well: Inocente Palacios went on to become a promoter of international contemporary music festivals, an expert on Arnold Schönberg, and a collector of abstract art.
16. "Carta pública de los escritores y artistas al Presidente de la República," *El*

Nacional (Caracas), October 7, 1944; reprinted in Esteva-Grillet, *Fuentes documentales y críticas*, p. 986.

17. Marta Traba, "El verdadero rostro de Bolívar," *El Tiempo* (Bogotá), June 12, 1957; reprinted in *Marta Traba* (Edición del Museo de Arte Moderno de Bogotá, Editorial Planeta, 1984), p. 154.
18. The most important critiques of Boulton's book were penned by José Ratto-Ciarlo, Rafael Pineda, Marco Figueroa, José Antonio Rial, Luis Alfredo López Méndez, and José Nucete Sardi.
19. Marta Traba, "Venezuela: cómo se forma una hegemonía artística," *Revista Medellín*, April 1978; reprinted in *Marta Traba*, p. 217.
20. Antonio José de Sucre y Alcalá was a Venezuelan military man, a hero of Latin American independence. Known as "the great marshal of Ayacucho," he was president of Peru and of Bolivia.
21. Manuela Sáenz was a revolutionary of Ecuadorian origin. The wife of English doctor James Thorne, she lived in Lima, the capital of the Viceroyalty of Peru, and developed an interest in politics. In 1822 she became Simón Bolívar's lover and followed him on his campaigns until his death.
22. Narváez's *criollista* period took place in the 1930s and '40s, when he focused on racial and social topics (mulattos, fishermen), which he depicted with stylized, geometric realism, inflected by Art Deco.

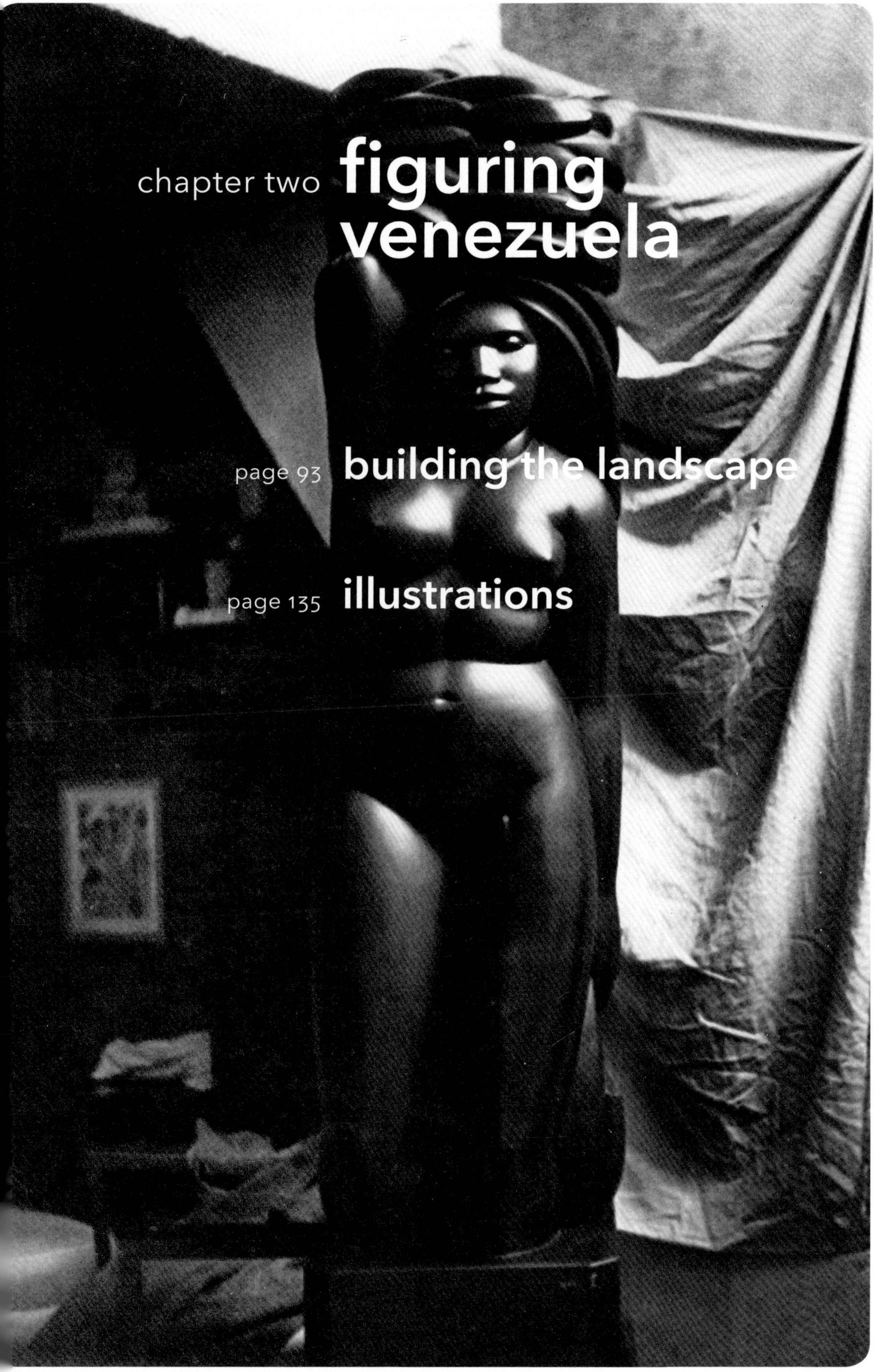

chapter two figuring venezuela

figuring venezuela **ariel jiménez**

One cliché among the critiques of geometric abstraction in Latin America – and in Venezuela in particular – is the accusation that it is an imported art form, an artificial construction imposed by the dominant classes, who turned their backs on the country and its history.[1] In this critique's terms, an art form that exists in such contrast to the social reality of Latin American countries could never be the *authentic* expression of their people. At issue, therefore, is a contrast that collapses in the face of anyone who seeks an unbiased analysis of what we might call the initial stage of Venezuelan modernity.

During the first half of the twentieth century the country's modernist movement set itself the fundamental task of *figuring* Venezuela – that is to say, of endowing the nation with an iconography within which its inhabitants might recognize themselves, and from which they might draw support when it came time to consider the future. This task fueled all projects that could be classified as "modern," whether on the right or the left politically, both in Europe and in the Americas. That contrast, however, between art and social reality was not the result of an artificial imposition on the part of elite sectors of society, but was rather one of many elements constituting a multifaceted reality that was impossible to reduce to any single factor.

The modernist agenda in Venezuela was unswervingly oriented toward the future; indeed, all hopes were invested in it. One of the factors that characterized the movement was the disparity between the purity of form through which modernism was materialized and the cruel reality of social inequities in Venezuela that were impossible to resolve and increasing to explosive proportions. These inequities finally dismantled the impeccable spaces of the modern.

There is perhaps no better way to exemplify the dichotomy between the modernist agenda and society's ills in Venezuela than through the work of two central proponents of the modernist project: the photographer and critic Alfredo Boulton and the author Arturo Úslar Pietri. As first cousins, they both belonged to what the writer Marta Traba[2] called the "dominant class": that is, white, cosmopolitan, and generally Eurocentric. Like many artists of their generation, they were driven by a sense of the dire necessity of defining Venezuela, a country whose identity – mutable though it may be – was as yet unexpressed, and allowing it to have its own features, drawing a face that Venezuelans might turn toward the rest of the world as equals. Their work formed part of what may be thought of as the primary impulse of the country's early modernity: to locate the essential qualities of what it is to be Venezuelan, and to accord those qualities their "universal" value – that is, a value that might be perceived outside national boundaries, and that would be understood as a positive contribution to humanity, and not just as a belated echo of what had been produced in Europe. Such essential characteristics would, as Úslar Pietri put it, cause a story written by a Venezuelan to *smell* like Venezuela, even if it were translated into Russian.[3]

Deriving from a clearly elite milieu, these two artists might naturally have contributed to an art world that critics like Traba condemned as lacking in historical significance, a world far removed from the sad reality of the country's dismal poverty. But their work took another route from that prescribed. The aristocratic Úslar Pietri's 1928 "Miralejos" (Far-gaze)—a short story that "smells like Venezuela"—describes a rural population, poor and diseased, condemned irrevocably to the hard labor of the land, with no future other than death. The characters in Úslar Pietri's stories and novels of that era (as in the works of his contemporary Rómulo Gallegos) are marked by tragic destinies; their bodies are battered by the primitive harshness of their environment, their dreams frustrated by their surroundings. Indeed, the tragedy of these characters is as systematic and somber as the landscape—constructed with the same systematic insistence—is serene and luminescent in Boulton's photographs, in the paintings of Manuel Cabré, Pedro Ángel González, and Elisa Elvira Zuloaga, or in the uninhabited interior scenes by Federico Brandt.

There is no question that this duality derives from the tensions and hopes that constituted the backbone of the Venezuelan will to modernize, which attempted to put down roots in the subsoil of the nation's history. These tensions were different, even opposing, but complementary in the sense that the purity of the landscapes produced during the early stages of modernity (purity that would later be traded in for the search for formal perfection with the geometric and kinetic abstraction of the 1950s and '60s) were efforts to redress Venezuela's misery—social conditions that literature denounced with such harsh clarity, and with a directness rarely attained in the visual arts.

Thus art and literature presented themselves as forces born under opposing signs. Literature did not, of course, have exclusive domain over the recognition of society's difficulties; the clean and ostensibly tranquil imaginary presented in the visual arts was proposed as a kind of antidote to society's deplorable conditions, intended to confront them through the sheer potency of visual ideas. Similarly, in the 1950s and '60s, when Venezuelan abstract and kinetic artists—continuing the "purist" line of thinking—attempted to intervene in the realm of architecture (as they did at the Universidad Central in Caracas), it was above all with the hope (or perhaps it was a dream) that they were working against the country's ills, against its lack of structure, and against the alienation that threatened the inhabitants of cities that had become so very inharmonious.

The discrepancy between the visual arts' and the literary arts' engagement with society's troubles was a factor not only in Venezuelan modernity but in all of Western modern art, beginning at the time of the Impressionists and moving, via Cubism, toward a new art of invention. Was the contrast less pronounced between the work of French Impressionist landscape painters and the writings of, say, Émile Zola? During the horrors of the Franco-Prussian War of 1870, many of the best artists continued painting peaceful landscapes and naïve peasant scenes. And Cubism was a cerebral, intellectual, and speculative art form that evolved just at the moment when the century was discovering the destructive powers of all the inventions that had until that time illuminated it.

The problem, however, was now posed in completely different terms, and the varied functions of landscape depictions in modern painting had as much to do with the subjects addressed—and of course those that were *not* addressed—as it did with the way those subjects were handled, the manner in which that visual *work* was realized. The works also made manifest other intellectual issues, beyond the symbolic and political exigencies of the "national project" in which their authors believed themselves to be participating. Modernism signaled the launch of self-reflexivity in painting, of a contemplation of the individual and his or her chosen mediums—as seen in landscape painting, and particularly in the phenomenon of light as a primary motif and as a central element of consideration among painting's aspects.

a scenario of origin

Any nation, no matter how small, must create for itself a "scenario of origin": a series of tales describing the nature of the ties that bind it to the space and time in which it exists. These tales outline the occurrences and characters that made it possible for this nation to come into existence at a specific time in a specific place.

Nineteenth-century Venezuelan painting, particularly during the Antonio Guzmán Blanco government (1870–88), played an important part in fulfilling this task: impressing in the public's mind the most outstanding events of the wars for independence, and the images of its heroes' faces. During this period, recourse was taken in the figure of Simón Bolívar, known as "El Libertador" (the Liberator), a figure that provided a first basis of legitimacy for Venezuela.[4]

Little attention was paid, however, to the landscape in which all these events had transpired. In contrast to other countries in the Americas—Mexico and the United States, for example, where artists were investigating their indigenous environments and applying themselves to creating symbolic ties between the landscape and the nation—Venezuela seemed incapable of working with the image of its own landscape, of creating a unifying imaginary based on the symbolic inscription of the nation onto the natural environment. As the twentieth century opened, this task was yet to be accomplished; such explorations into the local landscape would be undertaken only by later generations—particularly after the cessation of Venezuela's civil wars, under the long regime of Juan Vicente Gómez.

With the fall of Cipriano Castro in 1908 and Gómez's subsequent assumption of power, Venezuela experienced a moment of new hope. The magazine *Alborada* was founded in 1909 by a number of young writers (notable among them Rómulo Gallegos), and its pages are infused with the excitement energizing them during this period—which would last until 1913–14, when Gómez's maneuvering to maintain power signaled the onset of a different reality. In short time, a group of young artists, animated by a spirit of freedom that would allow innovative practices of plein-air landscape work, came together to form the Círculo de Bellas Artes.[5] A 1912 article in the journal *El Universal* by critic Leoncio Martínez declares the death of "the barbarian years," and celebrates the arrival of "the days of incense and salves."[6]

The initial stage of the modernist project in Venezuela[7] was thus marked by an eruption of interest in the landscape as a central theme of the new trend in painting, and also by the predilection of the military government for images of Bolívar and nationalist heroics, as depicted in the paintings of Tito Salas. Salas's work from the 1910s to the early 1940s embodied patriotic iconography, particularly his painting cycles about the life and work of Bolívar, located at the house where El Libertador was born and at the Panteón Nacional, the monument to Venezuela's heroes where he is buried. Upon his return from a stint in Europe in 1911, Salas was met with acclaim at home, and his work was perceived as a living echo of the past—particularly as the authoritarian nature of Venezuela's dictatorship was reinforced.

The country's younger artists were almost unanimously turning their focus toward the potential role of landscape in an art that would belong unquestionably to Venezuela; those in the Círculo de Bellas Artes felt duty bound to enrich the national iconographic panorama. The primary and most salient function of their work as painters was to create a record of Venezuela's national territory—although for a time their purview was limited almost exclusively to the Caracas Valley. Interestingly, the landscape mission had been initiated previously by photographers (Henrique Avril is a notable example), who published their images in the pages of the magazine *El cojo ilustrado* between 1892 and 1915. The journal's publishers had expressed their intention to familiarize their audience with the monuments of Venezuela's principal cities, and with the country's most characteristic landscapes.[8]

The need to understand Venezuela fully, to make the nation known in its entirety, became an increasingly urgent mission among artists and intellectuals. And the general difficulties in traversing Venezuela in order to come to such an understanding drew attention to the shocking deficiencies in the country's communication and transit systems. Yet the artists of the Círculo de Bellas Artes wished to go further; they sought not merely to depict the exterior image of that landscape—as did the photographic "vistas" published in magazines such as *El cojo ilustrado*—but to express its very soul, to isolate and define the particularities of a national psychology. As Martínez urged in his 1912 article:

> Let us make art that is our own, genuine art, Venezuelan art, availing ourselves of the simple, beloved elements around us, without taking recourse in exotic practices that do not fit our subject matter and our aims: art is nothing more than seeing and transmuting, [. . .] appreciating the souls' moments in our gestures and the soul of the landscape in the environment.[9]

Martínez's call to artists outlines one of the axes upon which the Venezuelan context would be balanced over the course of the twentieth century. Within that context were numerous distinct attempts to produce an "authentic" art (with all the contradictions such an essentialism might imply). These attempts tended to oppose other currents within Western traditions—traditions that often purposefully disregarded the particularities that would link them to their region of origin. The words of the journalist Jesús Semprum[10] attest to the fact that some figures were open to all possible ideas, with an enthusiasm whose naïveté showed, early on, characteristics of the cosmopolitanism and "futurism" that would deeply aggravate nationalistic thinkers. This enthusiasm, however, is unquestionably a part of the history of one of the "open" Latin American countries–as opposed to the "closed" (*ostra*, meaning "oyster") countries, to use Marta Traba's terminology.[11]

Certain factors thus distinguish Venezuela from other Latin American countries that were undergoing similar processes: it lacked early landscape traditions, which caused a number of symbolic exigencies to come to the fore simultaneously. Venezuela's early, impressionistic landscape period coincided with the moment when the country's modernist project was producing the edenic images that seem to be inscribed in all national traditions. Simon Schama refers to "the timeless universalism of the way symbols operate in our cultural consciousness";[12] it is for this reason, in part, that the self-reflexivity of modernist painting coexisted in Venezuela with artistic impulses and exigencies that might be seen as "anachronistic," even "exotic," in comparison with developments in Europe, the United States, and Mexico. But, in the realm of landscape especially, Venezuela's artistic expressions were impossible to reduce to any universal or canonical reading. Yet these differences, the odd mixture of modernity and anachronism, naïveté and pertinence, are fundamental to the particular and distinct charm of Venezuela's early twentieth-century landscape-oriented work.

The often innocent images of haciendas that surrounded Caracas in the early twentieth century contain, hidden within them, a vital essence that might be described as anachronistic, but is nonetheless indispensable. In a leafy grove, a red *apamate* tree may from time to time break the harmony of the greens; the rivers are tranquil and limpid, and above all there appears in those images, with purposeful insistence, El Ávila, the mountain that forms the northern border of Caracas, separating it from the sea and its port. So systematic is the depiction of these calm spaces in Venezuelan painting and photography of the era, so central is the presence of the mountain, so clear as well the marginal appearance of the city and its inhabitants, that it is impossible to ignore the symbolic value these images hold in the modern Venezuelan context—regardless of how stereotyped and kitsch they may have seemed to us since the 1950s.

These spaces were the staging grounds where Venezuelans of the period dreamed of building a modern country; their Arcadia, the primal dwelling place of the nation. This was the case, at least, in the urban imaginary; however, in this country of such marked contrasts between the capital and the provinces, between the city and the country, it was inevitable that other staging grounds—and personages—would challenge the centrality of this one.

Germany had its dark forests where the hero Arminius—with his hordes of savages—vanquished the Roman troops; the United States had the West, the untrodden landscapes of Yosemite and its ancient sequoias; Argentina was home to infinite pampas and the barbarism of the gaucho. In Simón Bolívar, Venezuela had its historic hero; and that clean landscape provided the inspiration for an art that Pablo Neruda would later describe, clearly and meaningfully, as "the joy of a grand, pure game, of an essential cleansing."[13]

Although the country's many problems, its deficiencies in infrastructure and public health, and the ignorance of its "masses" all far outweighed the enthusiasm of its governors, there existed the hope of constructing here a modern society in a new world. This hope gave rise to a tireless drive to locate, in the landscape and in the country's history, the support it needed in order to project itself into the future, in order to take shape in the Venezuelan mind.

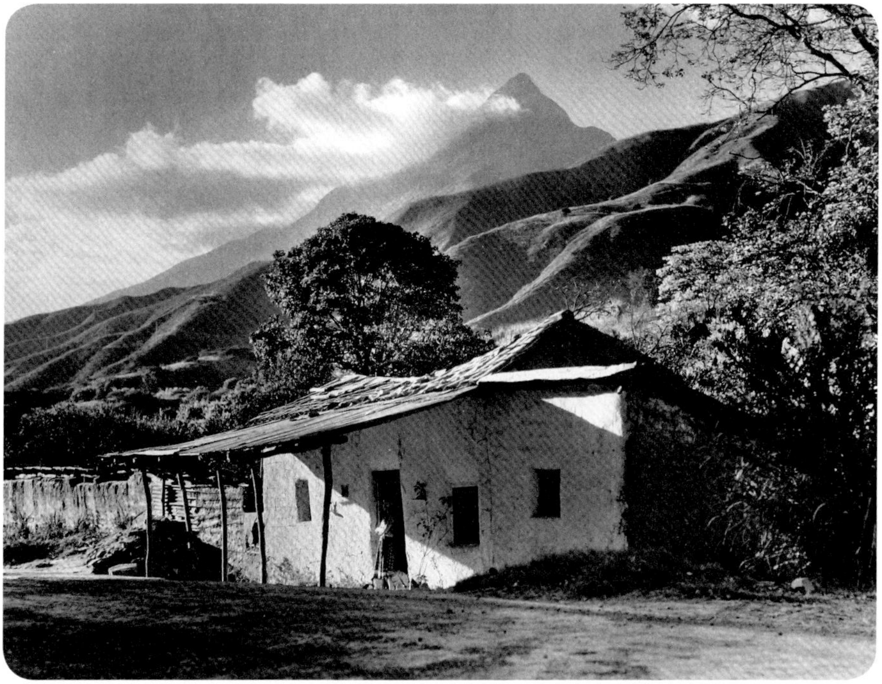

View of El Ávila mountain with illuminated house. Photograph by Carlos Herrera. 1953. Collection Fundación Museos Nacionales. Galería de Arte Nacional, Caracas

the symbolic axis of el ávila

The insistence and systematic regularity with which El Ávila mountain appears in these Venezuelan landscapes gradually turns the mountain into a real-life character, a central figure in the genre. One reason for this is that El Ávila is not a mere geographic formation, but a true natural monument, to which national pride is firmly anchored in those communities in which – according to the German naturalist and explorer Alexander von Humboldt[14] – works of art did not constitute a sufficiently memorable ensemble of images. For this reason, the wise German affirmed, one could not cast doubt on the exaggerated dimensions that Venezuelans attributed to the mountain "without harming nationalist sentiment" (especially since the measurements Humboldt took indicated that the mountain's height was in fact lower than that of the Plaza Mayor in Quito).[15]

For the inhabitants of the valley, the mountain held great significance: it was part of their national identity, part of the sentiment that linked them to their native landscape. It was thus natural that artists should take El Ávila as a central subject, and that they might associate all sorts of merits with the mountain – immeasurably huge proportions, and the notion that it was a geologically "young" body: young like the new country they sought to construct (although such theories were proposed without the benefit of any scientific support). This was one of the characteristics that the painter Manuel Cabré noted in explaining his own fascination with the mountain:

> El Ávila – I've said it many times – has the charm and sweetness of young bodies, and its triangular structure is a repetition of the same volumes that would be achieved if one let a handful of sand fall softly to the ground. When compared with old European mountain ranges, with the Alps and the Pyrenees, El Ávila seems to have been formed quite recently.[16]

The renascent country thus found an eloquent echo in the geology of the place.[17] This correspondence between landscape and nation in the process of construction was not, of course, exclusive to Venezuela – on the contrary, it was taking place in most of Latin America – but here the link had a particular salience. First of all, there was in Venezuela that dearth of early landscape traditions, already mentioned, that might have allowed for a more gradual, continual development of the symbolism of the genre. Furthermore, the country's landscape imagery was firmly centered on scenes in and around Caracas – only later introduced into the collective imaginary were such elements as the Orinoco River, the Gran Sabana, and the Amazon jungle of the Escudo Guayanés (or Pico Bolívar) in the Andes. The focus on the area around the capital city was undoubtedly due to the country's urgent need for symbolic foci, which coincided with the destruction of the landscape around Caracas beneath the treads of the tractors constructing the modern city.

It was no coincidence that Boulton began his "national photography project" – an attempt to capture the totality of his country's landscapes in photographs – in the late 1930s, after the death of the dictator Juan Vicente Gómez in 1935.[18] The country was possessed by a spirited enthusiasm for modernization, which found in urban planning and architectural projects – and in the inevitable occupation of the landscape – some of its most authentic and powerful manifestations.

The new Venezuela was taking shape, both physically and symbolically. The landscape was glorified, as were its inhabitants, who were given the role of prototypes, national icons. (Not by chance, this recalls the Soviet photographers' exaltation of the image of the worker and the power of the machine, working together to construct the new motherland, the world to come.) Figuring Venezuela implied traversing the country, experiencing its wonders – and this was finally becoming a possibility: the development of a national system of roadways permitted people to travel through the land to an extent that would have been nearly impossible fifteen or twenty years previously.

In 1933, Boulton had read works by the French novelist Jean Giono, in whose loving descriptions of the Provençal landscape and the deep communion his characters experienced with the land Boulton found the impetus he needed to capture the image of his own surroundings. The few photographs he had made up to that time had generally been either Surrealist-inspired experiments or straightforward Caracas landscapes. Now he focused wholeheartedly on his local environment, creating photographs that would provide the basis of his ambitious national project. He thus set out to capture the image of the Venezuelan landscape from the Andes and the central plains to the Isla de Margarita, in a process that both recalls and dovetails with Rómulo Gallegos's efforts to describe the life of the nation in all its characteristic beauty and conflicts.[19]

The concept of documenting a "national landscape" was to a great extent prompted by the massive transformations that the country, and particularly Caracas, underwent in the 1930s. Conscious of the rapid changes the city was experiencing, government authorities, led by General Eleazar López Contreras from 1936 to 1941 – heeding the three-part maxim "to clean up, to educate, and to populate" – contracted the services of the well-known French urbanist Maurice E. H. Rotival, who was to design a plan that would bring order to the city's development. Indeed, since the implementation of Rotival's design (completed in 1939) Caracas has benefited from an urban plan that extends to the entire valley, from the old colonial downtown to the nearly uninhabited valleys to the east and the south.

The perception and depiction of El Ávila as a natural monument reached a heated point in the 1940s. There was pressure exerted on the collective Venezuelan imaginary by large-scale urban planning projects and construction – the landscape was changing, possibly disappearing. And this pressure extended to the private sphere. Old haciendas that were located near or on the mountain were making way for the coming urbanization. Before beginning their work projects, however, the owners of some haciendas made use of the services of Manuel Cabré (as did, for example, the Vollmer-Boulton family); the painter was hired to depict those landscapes that would soon be gone. One account has Cabré running in front of the tractors, hurrying to capture the scene that was about to disappear so that he might complete his depiction of that calm, green valley where the new city would soon rise. There was much significance attributed to these painted images of places that had been the settings of the lives of *caraqueños* throughout the entire colonial period. Photographic records were not enough; they lacked the touch of meaning and soul that paintings might offer.

Parallel to the urbanizing projects of the private sector, Venezuela's Medina Angarita government undertook, between 1941 and 1945, one of the most ambitious city projects of the early modern era: the renovation of the El Silencio district of Caracas. This was the initial phase of a process that would transform the city, following the general guidelines of Rotival's urban plan. El Silencio, one of the poorest and most unhealthy neighborhoods in the old urban center, was to be transformed into a model of what much of the city would become in the immediate future. The rural, wretchedly poor past would be converted into a vigorous and healthy future.

Significantly, Boulton's most expressive images of El Ávila – those in which the mountain is clearly depicted as the last refuge of the Caracas landscape – also date from this period. It is telling that in those images, even as the city was overflowing its old colonial limits on all sides and beginning to cover the valley, Boulton chose a vantage point that completely erases the city's encroaching presence[20] in order to focus on the totally naked figure of the mountain.

So while architects and urban planners were busily constructing a dream city, painters and photographers were applying themselves to their work with equal fervor, inventing an idealized imaginary that might serve as the symbolic foundation for the new construction. The importance of El Ávila, then, became ever clearer: it was an icon – both real and symbolic – around which a certain modern visual vocabulary was organized. The mountain provided an emblem of the relationships that united the city with the nation, the landscape with its history, its present, and its future.[21]

Thus an initial trajectory of meaning was drawn within the country's visual traditions over the first half of the twentieth century – at least from the perspective of those artists who were most firmly committed to the ideals of collective progress and well-being. But the larger reality was more complex, and the internal contradictions unavoidable.

The context of Venezuelan landscape art was dense enough to engender a truly unique artist. Such a figure would bring together the features of modern Venezuelan painting with the radical contradictions inherent to the modernizing impulse, all the while turning his critical gaze toward the irreconcilable tensions of national life. That artist was Armando Reverón.

Perhaps by chance – but the fact is nonetheless important – Reverón settled on the margins, on the nether side of El Ávila, which had become such a symbolic axis for the country, there to produce an œuvre that his contemporaries would recognize as the most genuine and universal manifestation of Venezuelan art. And indeed, his painting may have been the purest and most complex example of the country's early phase of modernity, but his isolated life in this rural region clearly contradicted the ideas of material progress that were guiding the country. Reverón is thus the most modern artist of his time, in maintaining – as St. Augustine put it in his day – a complete disinterest in the illusions of his century.[22] This is the modernity, fully conscious of its own contradictions, that most clearly characterized a country that believed it could leave behind, buried in the past, the poverty of a population whose existence was still light years away from the progressive ideals of the country's elites. It was for these reasons that Reverón was admired as much by those who saw no salvation outside his inscription into "universal history" as by nationalists who were eager for an identity – which seemed to vanish at the very moment it was grasped.

Certainly the landscapes and characters from Reverón's so-called White period (1925–35), with the crystalline purity of their light, are powerful manifestations of painting that reflects back upon itself. Reverón worked with color, form, and material to achieve an aesthetic order that parallels the natural order; his facture – the trace of his craft – stands up against the work's status as a salient example of modern painting. It was this balance that led Boulton to study Reverón's work as a new and original Latin American contribution to the European art-historical tradition. For Boulton, Reverón's White period in particular represented a culmination of creative power and intimate communion with his surroundings that made his work simultaneously deeply Venezuelan and genuinely universal.[23]

In the 1930s, Reverón's White period reached a peak with paintings such as *El árbol* (*The Tree*; 1931) and *Paisaje blanco* (*White Landscape*; 1934). Soon thereafter, the artist's life and work seemed to become enclosed in a world of shadows; he felt besieged by the ghosts of his nation's history. Not only did his palette shifted from whites toward tones Boulton identifies as "sepia," but his own *rancho* was now filled with cryptic machines and objects (fake telephones, cardboard guitars, paper and plastic crowns, and other objects that created—as they do for children—a double artifice in the world of adults); and the figures in his paintings were often imbued with explicitly sexualized or racialized attributes—or were outright caricatures. In his final self-portraits, of the late 1940s and early 1950s, Reverón seems to embody the contradictions of the entire country: his shirt is unbuttoned, his beard overgrown; he is shown surrounded by carnivalesque characters; his head is crowned with a ridiculous *pumpá* hat. It is as if with this willfully incongruous image of himself—both imposing and pathetic—he was expressing his enormous indignation with Venezuela's inequities, just as the country was reaching the greatest intensity of its modern agenda.

the country and its inhabitants

The developments of Reverón's late period—the increased carnality of his figures, the focus on Venezuela's port and its activities, the appearance of machines, dolls, and games in his works—were surely related, at least in part, to the social changes that, little by little but ineluctably, were transforming his rural environs into a suburban and marginalized zone, the habitat of that "people" who had no place in the modern city.[24] In this sense, his work echoed one of the central problems of Venezuelan reality—of Latin American reality in general—the elusive self-image: a "figure" in which *all* the country's people might recognize themselves. It was a question that was ceaselessly repeated in Latin America, from the very instant that each country began to see itself as an independent reality.

The task of "figuring Venezuela" did not merely imply the depiction (or invention) of a landscape and its links to history, to the country's past and future. It also entailed defining a face for its inhabitants, a human prototype in which all that was Venezuelan could be recognized. This task was particularly difficult in a country marked by such cultural and ethnic diversity, in which any one of several figures might qualify for the role. There were of course the great heroes of the struggle for independence, most often personified in Simón Bolívar. There was the *llanero* (plainsman, or gaucho); there was the *criollo mestizo* (person of mixed lineage)—a product of the European encounter with the American continent; and there was the eternally excluded *indio*, the aborigine who had resisted the Spanish conquest. And finally, a less clearly defined figure who combined of all these elements: the *pueblo*—the "people"—those inhabitants of the urban peripheries, of the *ranchos*, who formed the heart of the nation. The image of each of these Venezuelan prototypes, and their respective surroundings, had begun to emerge at the time of the country's independence.

In the 1920s and '30s, and to a lesser extent into the 1940s, two of these figures dominated the collective imaginary: Bolívar (iconized by many artists, but most famously by Tito Salas)[25] and the "*belleza criolla*" (*criollo* beauty, so dubbed by Boulton). In the latter figure, authors such as Úslar Pietri believed they had located an element that not only defined Latin America, but also indicated its future role in the history of humanity.[26] The *belleza criolla* was an ideal product of *mestizaje*, or racial mixing, among blacks, whites, and *indios*, and thus provided an apt metaphor for American diversity and universal synthesis.

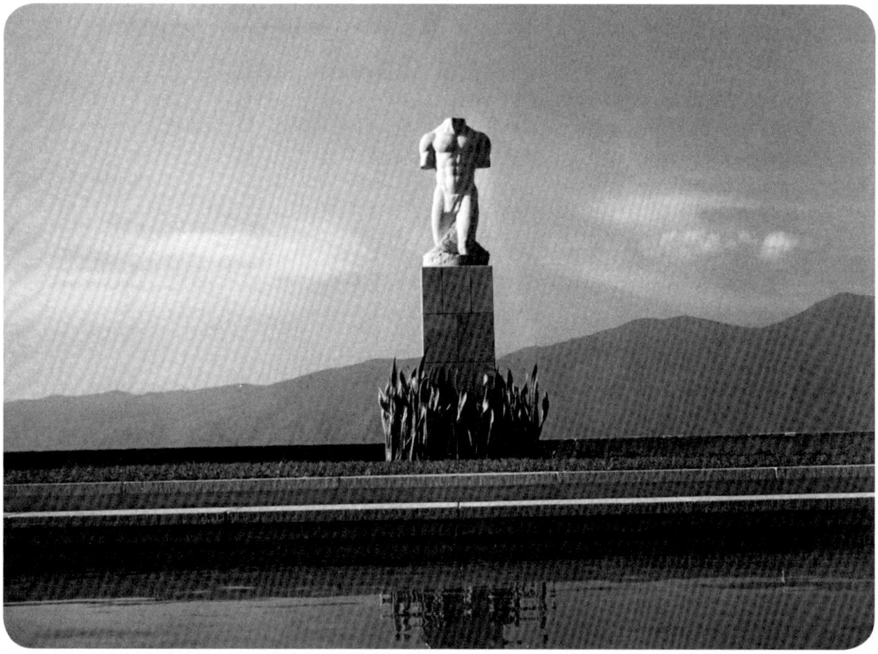

Barutaima by Francisco Narváez. Photograph by Alfredo Boulton. 1947. Alberto Vollmer Foundation, Inc., Caracas

The sculptor and painter Francisco Narváez was one of the principal artists working to conflate Venezuela's various racial types into an ideal of *belleza criolla*. This was the idea that Úslar Pietri emphasized about the young man who came to Paris in 1928 and who continued, even there, to paint black *margariteñas* and the fishermen and bathers he had known from his childhood on the Isla de Margarita. But even when Narváez's figures can be identified racially as black, *indio*, or white, they tend toward an oddly universalized, undifferentiated form: their faces are usually depicted as basic circles or ovals, with individual features often erased or highly stylized, expressing a synthesized visual ideal. Narváez's subject matter, too, was universalized: bathers, fishermen, men or women who are rarely identifiable. When Narváez did desire to express specific concepts or customs typical of his country (as he did in the mural paintings made for Gómez's children in 1934), he identified those that might be capable of achieving a certain popular consensus among his viewers—entertaining subjects such as *bolas criollas*, cockfights, *joropo*, or *toros coleados*.[27] Such activities were practiced in nearly all parts of the nation, and particularly on the plains, where the *llaneros* were held up as the true prototype of *belleza criolla*, sometimes more black or *indio* than white, other times *catire* (fair-haired), like the formidable commander José Antonio Páez.[28] It is significant, furthermore, that even when Narváez sought to represent an *indio* chief, as he did in his 1947 *Barutaima* (created for Boulton's home), the figure is presented without a face or arms, like an ancient Greco-Roman sculpture, but with an idealized robust torso, an homage to the glory of the men who opposed the Spanish during the conquest.

Narváez's paintings and sculpture draw a literal illustration of the Venezuelan native as universal icon; his work thus provides a clear connecting point between modernity's earliest manifestations in the country and its later "mature" iterations: the geometric and kinetic abstractions of the following decades. His art parallels at least two urban projects that were vital to the advent of Venezuela's early modernity: the development of Caracas's El Silencio district and the first phase of the construction of the Universidad Central de Venezuela. Both of these projects linked modern architecture to native traditions, leading the way to an open engagement with modern sculptural forms later (particularly during the second phase of the university's construction), and even to clearly abstract forms beginning early in the 1950s. Narváez, similarly, shifted from "nativist" to abstract sculpture during the 1950s – a transition that was in fact fairly natural, in that universalization was a denominator common to both modes.

Not all socially conscious artists and intellectuals followed this path, of course. Although sensitive to the new political and social demands that had originated with the Mexican Revolution and the Communist party, which began its public activities during the 1940s,[29] many leftist thinkers identified "the oppressed classes" (including the indigenous *indios*) as the "Other," clearly to be excluded from the modernizing tactics of the governing sectors. For these "Others" – who likewise aspired to modernization, to the construction of a politically, economically, and culturally independent society – the models that had been followed up to this point led inevitably to the exploitation of the weakest; in their view this situation would be rectified by the establishment of a Communist society. This hope was further buttressed by the successes achieved during this period by the Soviet Union and its highly efficient information campaigns.

Thus a clear difference was delineated between two opposing currents at the heart of early Venezuelan modernity, among both literary and visual artists: those who sought to extract universal value from native elements, and those who, concurring with the former group in the value they placed on the national, nevertheless focused their attention on radically different social and political ideals. The "nativism" of such artists as Narváez, Boulton, and Úslar Pietri had as its ultimate goal the attainment of universality – and in this they would later agree with the ideals of abstract artists. More politically committed leftist groups, on the other hand, rejected the Eurocentrism of the first modernists, and consistently advocated for a purely Latin American identity, a destiny fully independent from Europe and the rest of the world – even if they never successfully defined what that might be, beyond sheer rebellion itself.

Some of the earliest manifestations of these opposing currents can be sensed in the paintings of artists such as César Rengifo,[30] Gabriel Bracho,[31] Héctor Poleo,[32] and later Carlos Cruz-Diez (in his early period);[33] these artists discovered in Chilean political and cultural movements and in Mexican mural painting models for a struggle that grew more radical as the Venezuelan Communist party offered them the tools to orient their social demands. In addition, these influences on the Venezuelan iconography of the 1940s solidified the presence of another prototypical figure – the urban workingman – and more generally the inhabitants of marginalized and impoverished communities, abandoned lots,

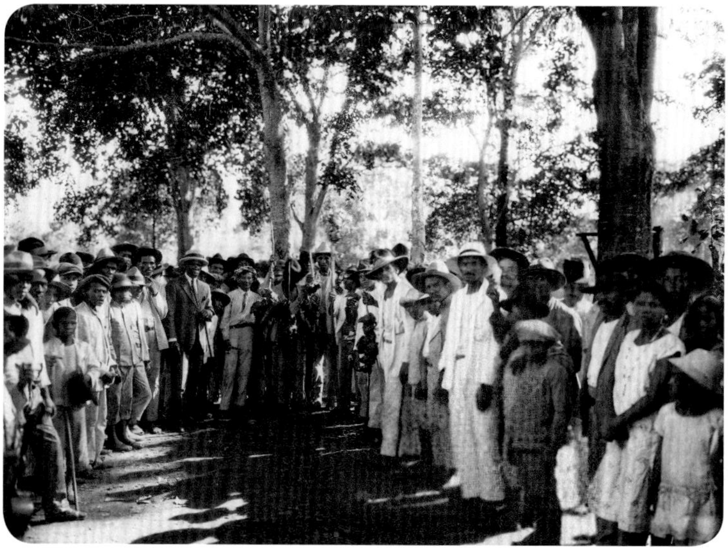

Venezuelans at a traditional outdoor meal. Photograph by Luis Felipe Toro Mujica (Torito). c. 1930. Collection Instituto Autónomo Biblioteca Nacional. Archivos Nacionales de Venezuela, Caracas

ravines, and hills around Caracas, that small city with its aspirations to become an orderly, clean metropolis. Beginning at this point, these downtrodden figures are a constant in Venezuelan art, sometimes exalted, other times caricaturized to the point of stigma.

Perhaps only a photographer could succeed in showing the real, rough face of this population, a population that despite itself—because of its ignorance, because of its abandonment by the world and its mistrust of the elites—represented the most entrenched obstacle to dreams of modernity. The impressive photographs by Luis Felipe Toro Mujica (Torito),[34] severe in their documentary candor, were neither idealized nor politicized: they simply depicted the image of the *pueblo* that only sporadically appeared here and there among the calm landscapes of the so-called Escuela de Caracas.[35]

The *indio*, the last of the figures in the Venezuelan collective imaginary, was perhaps the humblest of them all, and the iconography of this prototype appeared only later, beginning in the 1940s. This was because Venezuela's native inhabitants did not leave memorable monuments (such as the remarkable ancient edifices of Peru or Mexico), and their descendents were relegated to the most remote areas of the country; furthermore, *indios* were generally looked down upon by the nonindigenous populations. Indeed, they were excluded even among the excluded, scarcely recognized in the programmatic documents produced by the Communists, who did not see in the Venezuelan *indios* a base sufficient to merit their political propaganda (as they had, by contrast, in Peru's indigenous people). Nonetheless, the Venezuelan natives' radical otherness was powerfully represented in the work of a handful of artists in the 1940s and early '50s, among them Alejandro Colina[36] and César Rengifo. In the works of these artists, the *indio* ceased to be just another figure, one idealized ingredient in the makeup of the *mestizo*, the distant and ethereal origin of the nation. Instead, here was an energized, living presence, always in an attitude of struggle or resistance. For many, in fact, the *indio* represented the origin of another nation that had not yet found its true place, and was anathema to everything symbolizing progress in the cities.

Thus the first version of modernity that existed in Venezuela comprised certain central currents and others that radically countered them. The establishment of a "national" literature and painting movement, and great urban design projects in El Silencio and the Universidad Central, as well as the inauguration of the Centro Simón Bolívar in Caracas, all marked a moment of culmination, and also a point of fracture. Dramatic tensions—both political and cultural—rapidly transformed Caracas, which had for centuries been a simple town, into an increasingly complex urban center. These tensions would continue to have profound consequences on all facets of life in the country.

A series of occurrences between 1945 and 1949 would indicate that the rules of the game were changing: a new population had appeared on the scene that wanted to elect its own governors, and would no longer accept leaving such decisions of state in the hands of the country's members of congress. The vision of a rural country dominated by the enormity of the landscape—as Rómulo Gallegos describes it in his short stories and novels—no longer adequately addressed the growing complications of urban life. The coup d'état against Isaías Medina Angarita in 1945 and the subsequent election of Gallegos in 1948 indicated a change on the political plane that was as radical as the changes to the visual arts—as symbolized by the establishment of the Taller Libre de Arte (Free arts workshop)[37] and the exhibition of the first abstract works by Alejandro Otero in 1949.[38] All of these occurrences signaled the arrival of new generations, and with them, a litany of new and very different cultural needs.

Translated by Jen Hofer

notes to the text

1. It is simplistic, at the very least, to claim that the Venezuelan project of modernism did nothing more than construct a fiction that was completely disconnected from the country and its history, as if the "dominant classes" in Venezuela were not also a product of that same history, as if they had not seen the existing inequalities, and had made no effort whatsoever to resolve them. There were attempts at resolutions, without question, and numerous urban-design projects are proof of those. It is true, however, that all these attempts were dramatically insufficient, and that the ideals of progress that made their most significant achievements possible were unable to pinpoint mechanisms that would be capable of transmitting their energy to the rest of society. Among the failures were systems we might call "geared mechanisms" (systems of education, health, and efficient social services), caught between different worlds inherited from the colonial period—worlds that coexisted and continue to coexist in the midst of a hushed mutual distrust.
2. Marta Traba was one of the most prolific and exacting critics on the Latin American art scene during the second half of the twentieth century, and one of the first art-world personalities to achieve continental renown. Her books and articles delineated the essential arguments about Latin American art, particularly from the 1950s to the 1980s. Three of her articles are included in chapter 3 of this volume, pp. 274–84; 289–94.
3. On this point, see Úslar Pietri's letter to Boulton dated June 1928, regarding the former's short story "Miralejos" (Far-gaze), in this volume, p. 101.
4. During the various governments led by Guzmán Blanco, the figure of Bolívar on horseback was erected in Caracas's Plaza Mayor, in 1874; the Panteón Nacional (tomb of the nation's heroes) was inaugurated in 1875, to which the following year the remains of El Libertador were brought. In 1879, the "bolívar" was created; this has been the Venezuelan national currency ever since.
5. The Círculo de Bellas Artes (1912–17) was a group of young painters, writers, musicians, and journalists who, following the example of a similar group in Madrid (founded in 1880), sought to renew arts education in their country. The Círculo was formed by opponents to Venezuela's conservative Academia de Bellas Artes, headed by Antonio Herrera Toro.
6. Leoncio Martínez, "Ideas y propósitos: Palabras en la instalación del Círculo de Bellas Artes" ("Ideas and Aims: Some Words on the Establishment of the Círculo de Bellas Artes"), *El Universal* (Caracas), September 4, 1912. This text is included in the present volume, pp. 94–96.
7. In his outlines of Venezuela's cultural processes, Boulton insisted upon the immense transformation the country underwent during the twentieth century. In the introduction to the third volume of his *Historia de la pintura en Venezuela* (History of painting in Venezuela; 1972), he wrote, "A few statistics might serve as indicators of the magnitude of this transformation. At the beginning of the century, Venezuela had two and a half million inhabitants. By the time of this writing, the population has reached ten million." The distribution of that population had changed drastically as well: at the beginning of the century, 80 percent of the population was living in rural areas; by the 1970s nearly 80 percent had moved to urban centers.
8. See the introduction to the first issue of *El cojo ilustrado*, 1892.
9. Martínez, "Ideas y propósitos" ("Ideas and Aims").
10. Jesús Semprum was a doctor, writer, journalist, and literary critic. He was a regular contributor to *El cojo ilustrado* between 1905 and 1915, and the author of one of the texts read during the opening ceremony of the Círculo de Bellas Artes in 1912, included in this volume, pp. 96–98.
11. Marta Traba divided the countries of the region into two large categories: Venezuela, Brazil, and Argentina were "open" to outside influences and exchanges, and countries such as Peru, Colombia, and Ecuador were *ostra*—meaning literally "oyster," indicating "closed." See Traba's articles in this volume, pp. 274–84; 289–94.
12. Simon Schama, *Landscape and Memory* (New York: Alfred A. Knopf, 1995), p. 211.
13. Pablo Neruda, *Revista nacional de cultura*, nos. 217–18 (November 1974).
14. Alexander von Humboldt visited Venezuela and other parts of North and South America at the beginning of the nineteenth century. He was the author of *Ensayo político sobre el reino de la Nueva España* (Political essay on the kingdom of New Spain; 1811) and *Viaje a las regiones equinocciales del nuevo continente* (Voyage to the equinoctial regions of the new continent [first published in France under the title *Relation du voyage aux régions équinoxiales du nouveau conti-*

nent]; 1814), two texts that had enormous influence on the countries of the region. The latter text, on New Spain, played an important role in U.S. policy toward Mexico not long before the Mexican-American War, after which the United States took possession of a large portion of Mexican territory.

15. Humboldt, *Viaje a las regiones equinocciales del nuevo continente* (1814) (Caracas: Ediciones Monte Ávila, 1991), pp. 335–36.
16. Manuel Cabré, interviewed by Gloria Carnevali in *Manuel Cabré* (Caracas: Museo de Arte Contemporáneo, May 1980), n.p.
17. That echo between landscape and nation was not necessarily a consistent one. At times, it was not the newness but the ancientness of the geological setting that was highlighted. Alejandro Otero was one artist who attempted to establish a relationship between the modernity of his work and the oldness of the Guyanese region from which he came: his distinctly modernist work arose from one of the oldest territories on the planet. Hence Venezuelan modernity might be considered to be united to the earth with millenarian ties.
18. Boulton's photographic project on Venezuela was realized between 1938 and 1952, and provided the material for numerous publications, including *Imágenes del occidente venezolano* (Images from the Venezuelan West; 1940), *Los llanos de Páez* (Páez's plains; 1950), and *La Margarita* (1952).
19. By 1938–39, when Boulton decided to bring his full focus to the Venezuelan landscape, Gallegos had already published *El último Solar* (The last of the Solars; 1920), a novel that takes place in the Caracas Valley; *Doña Bárbara* (1929) and *Cantaclaro* (Chanticleer; 1934), both set in the plains; and *Canaima* (1935), set in the Amazon jungle. It was clear that Gallegos's intention was to create a narrative that took place in the theater of the entire national territory.
20. When, in the 1970s, Cabré himself was unable find even one space in the valley that had not yet been urbanized, he turned to photography in order to be able to make his paintings; in these, he erased the buildings and added trees and fictitious fields, except when depicting the golf courses at the "country club," where he could gain a clear perspective of the mountain.
21. In 1958 El Ávila was declared a national park in an effort to preserve it from urban encroachment. Apart from that, the projects undertaken on the mountain (such as the Humboldt Hotel), like those that were planned but never realized (a monumental statue of Bolívar proposed by the sculptor Alejandro Colina), say a great deal about the relationships that link the country and its history to the landscape, and to the particular natural monument El Ávila represents.
22. St. Augustine, *Confessions* (Paris: Garnier-Flammarion, 1964), p. 123.
23. This drive to locate universal values in the authentically Venezuelan crossed artistic boundaries. Reverón's induction into this universal history had clear parallels with Úslar Pietri's pursuit of a Venezuelan essence in his stories. The same principle led Gallegos to write his 1919 novel *Pataruco*, providing a lucid metaphor: it is the story of the son of a rural popular musician; the son is married to a white woman from the city, and he re-encounters "the voice of his blood" after years of musical education in Europe. The young man learns to create a new music that is truly his own, music that contains "the landscape's fiery desolation, on the one hand, and the furious nostalgia of the Africans who came in slave ships and the melancholy sadness of the Indian that make up the Venezuelan race, on the other." And yet this music is no longer primitive and coarse, like his father's rustic tunes.
24. Boulton maintained that the changes in Reverón's style toward the end of his career were essentially due to the impact of his mother's death in 1943, but it seems clear that this event only intensified a shift in Reverón's work that had begun some time earlier.
25. Between 1913 and 1931 Salas created great mural paintings about the life and work of Bolívar, located at the birthplace of El Libertador in Caracas. The house had been acquired by the government in 1912 via popular subscription through the so-called "Sociedad patriótica" (patriotic society) and was restored by Gómez's government between 1916 and 1921. Once Salas had finished this mural commission, he began work on his iconographic painting cycle for Venezuela's Panteón Nacional, which he finished in 1942.
26. Úslar Pietri was following in the conceptual footsteps of Mexican writer and politician José Vasconcelos, author of *La raza cósmica* (*The Cosmic Race*; 1925), an influential text on what he considered to be the destiny of the Americas, a land where, according to Vasconcelos, "the synthetic race that shall gather all the treasures of

History . . . will be created." Vasconcelos, *The Cosmic Race*, trans. Didier T. Jaén (Baltimore: Johns Hopkins University Press, 1997), p. 18.

27. *Bolas criollas* is a popular game akin to bocce; *joropo* is a style of music and dance originally from the plains, practiced all over Venezuela and Colombia. *Toros coleados* is a popular sport played on the plains, in which a rider runs after a bull on a horse, with the goal of capturing it by the tail in order to bring it to the ground.
28. José Antonio Páez, general-in-chief of Venezuelan independence, was considered a *llanero* leader par excellence. He played a central role in Venezuelan history between 1821 and 1863. He was the first constitutional president of Venezuela, after Simón Bolívar's much-desired Great Colombia was dismantled in 1830.
29. In 1927, the Partido Revolucionario Venezolano was founded in Mexico as an outgrowth of the Communist party. The party was legalized in 1945 by the government of Isaías Medina Angarita.
30. César Rengifo, painter and playwright, studied in Chile (1936) and then in Mexico (1937–38), where he was influenced by the muralists, particularly Diego Rivera. With Gabriel Bracho, Rengifo would be the most important representative of a style of painting thought of as a weapon of political denunciation. The principal figures in his work were the inhabitants of the suburban neighborhoods and *ranchos* around Caracas.
31. Gabriel Bracho was a painter and muralist whose work is highly representative of socially conscious art. Between 1939 and 1942 he studied at the Escuela de Artes Aplicadas in Chile, where he discovered and was influenced by the work of the Mexican muralists, particularly that of David Alfaro Siqueiros.
32. Héctor Poleo was strongly influenced by the Mexican muralists, particularly during his early career (1938–41). Although Poleo was never a politically militant artist, and his painting—like that of Narváez—would later move closer to the basic principles of abstraction, the Andean figures and landscapes he painted during the early 1940s also marked the beginning of a thematic interest traditionally associated with nationalist currents.
33. Carlos Cruz-Diez was a fervent defender of painting as a tool of political denunciation, before he became, in the 1960s, one of the most important Venezuelan kinetic artists.
34. Luis Felipe Toro Mujica, called "Torito," was the official photographer of Juan Vicente Gómez; during Gómez's regime, he made many of the most famous photographs of the period. He also worked with Carlos Raúl Villanueva during a time of great development in photography in Caracas.
35. Generic term coined by the critic Enrique Planchart in reference to those artists—both before and after the advent of the Círculo de Bellas Artes—who took as their central thematic focus the landscape of the Caracas Valley and its environs.
36. The sculptor Alejandro Colina lived for eight years with various indigenous communities in western Venezuela. Among his best-known works are *Tacarigua* (1933); *María Lionza*, and *El cacique Tiuna* (both 1951).
37. The Taller Libre de Arte was launched on July 10, 1948, as a response to the dissatisfaction of young artists who insisted on the modernization of arts education that they felt was stagnating. As occurred with the Círculo de Bellas Artes in 1912, it was here that the most progressive artists came together, among them Jesús Rafael Soto and Mateo Manaure, and they created extremely influential exhibitions, such as the show of the Argentinean group Arte Concreto-Invención in 1948. The Taller was initially directed by the painter Alirio Oramas.
38. In the late 1940s, Otero was one of the best-known young artists in Venezuela. The 1949 exhibition of his Cafeteras (Coffeepots) at the Museo de Bellas Artes had a significant impact on his generation. This was the first time a Venezuelan artist had undertaken abstract work, without a doubt opening a new era for visual arts in the nation.

building the landscape

ideas and aims: some words on the establishment of the círculo de bellas artes **leoncio martínez**

Sirs:

The Círculo de Bellas Artes platform encompasses, in brief, ideas that it would benefit us to elucidate for the purposes of propaganda and the greater clarification of the aims that unite us. As I have taken on the responsibility of distributing these ideas, there will be no need for me to confess my ineptness for the task, in the humble rhetoric dictated by such customary rituals. [. . .]

While they are yet in the classroom, science students have associations and societies that bring them together; the very organization of their classes affords them spaces at the universities to enjoy a consistent and close interaction, and, as a result, the easy exchange of ideas and the demonstration of what they glean from their daily studies. Workers form mutual societies in order to nibble at the crumbs strewn along their rivers of sweat, to be secure in death even when they do not strike for benefits in life. Wholesalers, too, form unions and groups in their frustration, and all of urban existence takes heart and reaches out toward this steady gathering of men. Our souls are linked by a web of affection; social status is defined; society constructs the city and the wave of love expands, sheltering entire peoples, and as if beneath a bronze cupola, the crystal tears of an immense luminescent spider; our hearts remain trapped in the great heart of our fatherland, and when it is wounded, we reverberate, all of us, with a unanimous echo.

Artists [. . .] in Venezuela are still finding themselves without a common space, dispersed and itinerant. For some, the rigid regimentation of official institutions is not sufficient. For others the consecrated groupings symbolize retreats into senile repose as the ultimate conclusion of their ambitions: the same may be said of that repose that is told of at insane asylums, only in the opposite sense: "All those who are mad are not there, nor are all those who are there mad."

And if those first bodies always restrict, try as the legislators might to broaden the codes, how much more confining still are the others, for young people who have not yet experienced the dejected wings of exhaustion. Seeking free flight, we formed the Círculo de Bellas Artes on an extremely liberal foundation, molding our ideal in the forge of the requirements of our national character, welcoming the inspiration of many and the sage advice of a few with more experience. Thus our association has no rules nor statutes, no board of directors, no parliamentary procedures as to how to accept projects: everything is resolved via a jovial camaraderie in which there are no titles conferring prerogatives. Thus our idea springs forth naked, it expands and breathes, breaking bonds. [. . .]

Those were our beginnings, humble and lacking in intent, reduced to climbing step by step toward success, as our continual efforts and unflagging will laid the groundwork for other souls to realize that we exist, that in active silence we were training the forces of an adolescent ideal in order to prime it—like a prizefighter. But the embryonic seed was already present in the thirsty furrow and thus, at the initiation of our project, its blossoming was sudden and well-tailored. [. . .] As if a natural law of attraction were propelling them, disparate artistic elements came together suddenly in a vertigo of excitement to form this nucleus, which today is barely chaos in evolution, but which might mark, perhaps before too long, a luminous disturbance for those who are unaware of how to contemplate the blue—how to gaze often at the sky—which, according to the classical Latin expression, is the only way to avoid having so much mud before our eyes.

Understanding and approachable spirits have lent their support so that from the very beginning the Círculo de Bellas Artes might present itself at a level its founders could view as nothing less than a utopian promise. These are the gentlemen who appear on our list of Advisory Members, for whose kindness we take this opportunity to publicly express our oath of gratitude. [. . .]

Our first Salón Independiente, which will take place in four months, will carry this message: if we know how to respond not just to that oath of appreciation and veneration, but also to many others, commitments we made from the very instant we declared the establishment of the Círculo de Bellas Artes and joined our lives with the life of the art of the fatherland—to these things bring our energies, our love—then may we mark the conclusion of the barbarian years,[1] when voracious altars ran purple with the blood of useless sacrifices, and may the days of incense and salves come. [. . .]

Let us work, dear comrades, for art and for the fatherland. Let us make art that is our own genuine art, Venezuelan art, availing ourselves of the simple, beloved elements around us, without taking recourse in exotic practices that do not fit our subjects and our aims: art is nothing more than seeing and transmuting, feeling more deeply than people generally feel, appreciating the soul's moments in our gestures and the soul of the landscape in the environment. It is to express and to make manifest, always distancing ourselves from other influences that are not those of our own feeling, to signify first the individual's personality and later the character of the race.

Pueblos are worthy as unmistakable entities when their artists have successfully matched the patterns of characteristic features externally, and have, in interior depths, hit upon the blurry, uneven terrain of national psychology; this is why some, who in my view are a bit timid, affirm that a national community cannot have representative artists except when they have adapted their work to certain defined traits in a process of extremely slow evolution. On the contrary, I think that it is artists who clear the path toward the masses, discovering in the precious mine of our collective soul rich veins of beauty. [. . .]

Our land, abundantly endowed with the luxuries of a tropical sun, sets before our eyes its uncultivated models, landscapes of flourishing verdure, surprising decorations for retinas unaccustomed, in the hazy Nordic mists, to such extravagances of light. In the language and the thinking and the living of our *pueblo*, there are possibilities, easily apprehended by artists, for those who labor industriously and delve somewhat deeper into the national soul, moving along with barely a glance at those false inductions that have resulted in what we call *criollismo*,[2] just a varnish of Venezuelan language upon an everlasting universal vulgarity. The mere phonetic value of words, or the exterior appearance of the figures, does not suffice to make a national art if the work is not animated with the philosophical meaning inherent to each *pueblo*: a sap that runs hidden yet revitalizing; if our art does not transcend the customs of the race, constituting a rigorous apostrophe to our errors, an annotation of our moment, in order to leave for the future truthful data that will both foster and conserve traditions.

Where have our representative Venezuelan artists been up until now? Where are our genuine interpreters, free of the taint of alien schools?[3] Without ceasing to understand the legitimate merit of those who adapt their practice to cosmopolitan traditions, to the models provided by legends, history, and religions – realms that may be conquered by generality – let us work for greater merits, for the formation of our art in exaltation of the heroes of our own astonishing epic, to secure the fleeting soul of our landscapes, to perpetuate with our work the forward motion of the century in which we live, and to create a chronicle of our race. [. . .]

Let us work, I repeat, for art and for the fatherland, in a great brotherhood, with neither restrictions nor quarrels, beneath the precious shade of this roof. Let us think that we have achieved but the very initial stages of our work, and that now is the time to fight – and we have begun – against small acts of malice, against the meanness some people exhibit, and against the fury some would impose on us. Now, you all know this, comrades: we have suffered ignoble attacks and silent acts of sabotage, which I will not enumerate because the greatness of our ideal places us far above those wretched miseries that cannot reach us, and if they perhaps distract us on our march toward the future it is just for a minute – sufficient time for us to place the sole of our shoe upon the head of the snake and continue calmly on our way.

Let us evoke no bitterness on this first day, which is like a new dawn for us. May the generous gestures of the hands outstretched in our favor erase any fatal threat, and may we ready ourselves to work from morning onward toward the fulfillment of the aims of the Círculo de Bellas Artes, raising no flag other than our national colors, symbol and figure of our fatherland, in whose bands redound the gold wings of glory, the purest blue of dreams, and the purple of sacrifice. [. . .]

– "Ideas y propósitos: Palabras en la instalación del 'Círculo de Bellas Artes,'" *El Universal* (Caracas), September 4, 1912.
Translated by Jen Hofer
This text has been abridged for the present volume.

the círculo de bellas artes **jesús semprum**

In just a few words, [William Makepeace] Thackeray expressed an idea that I would like to see engraved in your spirits, as a slogan for action and a branded ideal. The great English writer said that for man, life is like a mirror that reproduces his gestures and attitudes: he whose existence is populated by dark thoughts and ugly actions will find darkness and evil in the world; he who illuminates his existence with the clear smiles of good will encounter clarity and smiles reproduced in the world.

At first, this might seem to be just a simple moral formula, but in reality it is an aesthetic canon: it is not just that conscience reproduces actions, bringing us happiness as a reward for our beautiful acts and imposing the punishment of trouble for evil ones, but rather that the exterior world, too, gives back to us in loveliness and pleasure the efforts we undertake toward beauty. What else is the joy of work well executed if not the payment with which that work expresses appreciation for our efforts in executing it? As we contemplate a work and find that it is good, we see a part of our spirit crystallized in material elements, and we can enjoy a pleasure beloved by the gods: the pleasure of feeling ourselves capable of creating beauty simply by the efforts of our spirit, the pleasure of the father contemplating his son, gallant and robust and triumphant.

When you gather to establish this humble art movement, you should ask nothing more of your companions than their simple intention not to make any gesture that might be clumsy or brutal or ugly. Everyone's thought must be unanimously fixed on producing beauty.[1] At the beginning, it might perhaps seem that such an intention does not provide many palpable benefits, but you may be sure that on the tree you believe to be dry and sterile, eventually flower buds will initially burst forth and later the fruits of our reward will take shape and ripen. [. . .] But at no time should we think that the mere fact of being fervent cultivators of an art means that we are absolved from any other obligation of our existence. The true artist has an even greater responsibility to love and comprehend beauty intensely and joyfully, to exercise his influence over others, and additionally to provide an example of ethical conduct and decorum. There exists a pernicious concept recklessly broadcast by some of the same people who should be fighting it: that artists, simply by virtue of being artists, should avoid all conventional restraints and live in total abandon, trampling every law and all human respect. [. . .] Perhaps living is only to write elegant prose, to paint magnificent canvases, to sculpt harmonious assemblages? No: life imposes other obligations, and their uncompromising fulfillment is as important as art itself, because they ensure and complete the truth of art and its beneficial influence over men. Those who counsel and practice the divorce of art from life are not generally good artists or good men. Life and art should run parallel and harmoniously, like streams of analogous music. The more perfect the harmony and consonance between art and life, the more the vitality of art and the beauty of life are assured.

Gathered in fraternal agape, we must first think of dispensing with dogmas, regardless of their provenance. In art, as in everything, disparity, divergence, and contradictions among opinions is a condition without which all possibility of advancement would be destroyed. Human knowledge, which is today enormously vast, has been acquired thanks to a series of successive contradictions. Each theory, each philosophical, aesthetic, literary, and political formula has deposited what it unquestionably and incontrovertibly comprises in the common storehouse of knowledge. Yet the very errors of past doctrines and schools have been useful—perhaps because they have provoked their own refutations—as error is not a crime except when it is preached by one who knows from the start that he is preaching error. [. . .]

And there is not, cannot be, one art. We might desire that, along with supporters of the strictest classicism, along with those most stubborn defenders of Romanticism and its derivatives, the fervent followers of the new schools—no matter how outrageous or absurd they may seem to us, including those ascribing to esoteric Symbolism or the frenetic lovers of Futurism—should also join us.[2] The more varied our circle, the greater the force we shall have. You must direct your aims so as not to be a docile herd of uniformed lackeys, like a mob of slaves, but rather a group of free men who gather to confer: each chooses his own path, each enjoys his own whims and will to the fullest capacity. Tolerance is the grandest virtue of the spirit. Tolerance, like a magic wand, turns animosities to smiles, ensures peace, breaks the narrow mold of evil passions. But in order to tolerate, it is necessary to understand. Try, then, to understand. To understand an error is to have conquered it already. And you will be victorious over error, and you will reach the heights of true triumph the day it can be said that this Círculo is veritably a spacious temple of Tolerance.

–"El Círculo de Bellas Artes," speech delivered at the inauguration of the Círculo de Bellas Artes, Teatro Calcaño, Caracas, September 1912. In *Visones de Caracas y otros temas* (Caracas: Corporación Venezolana de Fomento, 1969), pp. 103–9.
Translated by Jen Hofer
This text has been abridged for the present volume.

we are **arturo úslar pietri**

We are a handful of young men with faith, with hope, and with no mercy. We consider ourselves called upon to fulfill a tremendous duty, one we have posited and imposed upon ourselves: to renew and to create. The aim of our work will become clear in time. We will labor whether we are understood or not! We know quite well that giving birth is accompanied by pain and toward that end we offer our new flesh. We do not categorize ourselves in schools or with literary labels, nor will we allow anyone to do so; we are of our time, and the rhythm of the world's heart will be our guiding principle.

On the other hand, we are here to recuperate the true concept of the new art, which has already been abused by Pharisees and disfigured in caricatures without talent, or else too easily discredited by the facile posturing of all the deserters and all the incompetents.

The new art does not allow for definitions because its freedom rejects them, because it is never stationary enough for its profile to be traced. The only concept capable of approaching all the aims of the newest literary, pictorial, or musical modes—we repeat, the only one—is that of suggestion.

Its ultimate goal is to suggest, to say everything using the fewest possible elements (thus its need for metaphor and double or multiple images) or via synthesis, so that the artwork, the aesthetic complex, might be produced (with all the immense added possibilities) more through the spirit of the person directing the experience than through the limited raw material of the instrument itself.

Our hope is that an image might surpass or at the very least compress all that a dense treatise might communicate to an intellect. That four brushstrokes on a canvas might capture more transcendence than all the drawing manuals of the pompous, defunct schools. That, in music, a single note might wholly contain a state of the soul.

In sum, that the material might receive its due as collaborator in our artistic work, or that the work of art be completed in the mind with the fullness that the physical instrument denies it.

Our global aim has already been said: TO SUGGEST. . . .

We know that rank antiquated tradition will surely close itself off to us, and in fact has already wielded some of its most typically cloying words: *nihil novum sub sole*. As honorable fighters we would like to concede the enemy's advantage: let us accept a priori that there is nothing new, in the academic sense of the term, but on the other hand – and who will dare deny it? – there are many virgin elements that have not yet been illuminated by the light of the sun. The possibility of discovery still stands!

We abhor halfway measures, all discretion; we believe solely in the efficacy of silence or outcry. *Válvula* is the little lid on the machine out of which the gas of the explosions of future art will escape. To begin: we believe, which is already a force; we hope, which is already a virtue; we are willing to torture the seeds, to exhaust time, because the harvest belongs to us and we have the right to demand it whenever we want.

We are a handful of young men with faith, with hope, and with no mercy.

– "Somos," *Válvula* 1, no. 1 (Caracas), January 1928.
Translated by Jen Hofer

auto-da-fé **leopoldo landaeta**

Comrades:
Despite my determination that you should turn your backs on the past, you have expressed your desire that I contribute something to the début issue of *Válvula*. As it is not possible for me to reverse time to arrive again at your age, I will limit myself to explaining my idea of the reaction I hope the new spirit and the new sensibility will occasion, though the likes of [Leopoldo] Lugones[1] may grumble from El Guaire to El Plata.[2]

The past offers you nothing more than rhetoric, oratories, and frivolities of an artificial literature, alienated from the reality of Venezuela; throw all that into the fire, with no fear of committing an injustice, for if anything of any value exists there, it will resist this trial by fire, and you yourselves will take charge of gathering up the truly shining gold from among the cinders. For my part, following the example of Botticelli and his paintings, I will fling my load of false literature into the flames.

It is not a fussy, ladylike scrutiny, but rather an auto-da-fé that I propose to you. Until now our literature has provided only thrushes, magpies, and birds of ill omen: those birds with their eternal monotonous song, their eternal shrill clamor, with their equally eternal cawing of desolation, the results of a physical and spiritual impotence from which you should protect yourself as if from premature death.

You represent the future. You belong to a democracy that despite its youth has produced Bolívar, [Antonio José de] Sucre, [José Antonio] Páez himself, and Fermín Toro, who despite his terrible rhetoric overcame his own literary school with the masterful dignity of a personality to which Napoleon's concept regarding Goethe could readily pertain: "Voilà un homme" [Here is a man]. And this is all one might need to be in life, in order to address the collective problems you are called to solve. For the moment, you are faced with a literary problem, close at hand, which you begin to clarify with such excellent common sense: you have definitively wrung the neck of the peacock of eloquence, with your verse that renounces meter and rhyme as if in utter repudiation of verbiage and oratory.

You bring intellectualism to defeat: you know that the man who engenders a son and the man who plants a tree constitute literary substance, and that when one is set against the other, it is worth more to engender the son and to sow the tree than to write a book, when that book does not imply an exaltation of life.

For your own good and for the good of the country, this distances you from the academy, that factory of pedantry.

Young men of the twentieth century, you see the world in your own way and you express it accordingly; the idea of wanting to fix you with bolts and screws to the contemplation and admiration of a bygone day that now says nothing to you is deplorable: you feel with the soul of a youthful era, the unconscious manifestation of an ancient poetic and philosophical dream, emanation of that virile Hellas, instinctive and harmonious, that lived life in the fullness of beauty and art.

We, the intellectualists of the generation preceding yours, we gorge ourselves on whiskey and on rhetoric, because the "masters" relished that nectar, that ambrosia. You, off to a better start, you go to baseball games, you devour space and hear the world's vibration, and with your spiritual antennae attuned, you profess a cosmopolitanism in which the domestic, the *criollo*, become jumbled with the harmony of the universe.

To lend credence to your labors: it is the case – though odd – that at the same time that the professionals of rhetoric abhor the new sensibility, people less inclined toward the literary understand the beauty of this new song, made of familiar words, images, and emotions: it is the sincerity of the poet coming into contact with the sincerity of the masses.

The avant-garde has molded itself out of spirit, and thus partakes of that superiority attributed to the spirit over force itself by a great man, Bonaparte, who used and abused his force to the maximum degree. Your actions must be directed toward human ends; otherwise it would be utterly superfluous to found a journal simply to publish pretty verses and literary criticism with intellectualist aims. If that were your goal, you might as well toss your rag onto the fire with everything else. May it be said, in order both to remember and to move beyond a romantic phrase from the Venezuelan annals – the world belongs to the poets.[3] In this case, the poet has no affinity with the minstrel, with the bohemian, with verse virtuosos who declaim their ballads for a handout of bread, a handout of wine, or a handout of applause.

Meanwhile, the avant-garde might take refuge in Walt Whitman's approach: "Solitary, singing in the West, I strike up for a New World."

– "Auto-da-fé," *Válvula* 1, no. 1 (Caracas), January 1928.
Translated by Jen Hofer

letters from arturo úslar pietri to alfredo boulton

Caracas, June 7, 1928

[. . .] I have written a story I like *un rato largo*—"quite a bit," as the Spanish say.

It is called "Miralejos" [Far-gaze]. It will be published in *El Universal*.

With this story, I have succeeded at something I've been trying to do for quite some time: to give a Venezuelan impression without Venezuelanisms and without coarseness. I suspect that even translated into Russian, "Miralejos" would smell of Venezuela.

I have now found a path, and I'm pleased. I think it's one of the best stories that has been written around here.

I must also write a Venezuelan novel in the same form. It will be my most solid work and will probably be titled *Relato de la Tierra* [Story of the land].[1] I'll give it a dedication something like this:

"To the men of my generation, I dedicate these humdrum lives."

[. . .] Rafael Rivero has drawn me a cover image for *Barrabas*,[2] and I can't find a way to describe it. It is the most sober, the strongest, and the most beautiful image you can imagine.

In September you'll have it in your hands!

[. . .] I'm currently reading [G. K.] Chesterton and [John] Ruskin. A polygraph and an art critic—two cathedrals!

I read [Nikolai] Evreinov's *The Comedy of Happiness*. Simply: disconcerting.

And now I will end. I have to study. Those vexing, starchy law books await me.

I have turned solitary and surly like an oyster.

It would not be strange if I shaved my eyebrows after my exams, so as not to have to go out.

I love this solitude populated by my own self. This tower of my pride: *turris superbiae*, the decadent Latins would say, comforts and defends me.

Meanwhile: you in Paris, I in Caracas, weaving this slow tapestry of our communication over the sea.

—et nunc et semper—

Arturo

Translated by Jen Hofer
This text has been abridged for the present volume.

Paris, June 4, 1931

I didn't believe that a conspiracy of silence would be created around *Las lanzas* [*coloradas*] [*The Red Lances*]. I still don't believe it. Even when they've had three weeks to comment and have only mentioned the work out of courtesy, in allusions filled with banal adjectives. I'm still waiting; I'm waiting for Pedro Sotillo, for [Fernando] Paz Castillo, for Fco [sic]. When a book, especially one with the accurate and moving tone in which mine has been executed, has laid bare the entire soul of a people, the men who believe themselves to be the antennae of that soul cannot keep silent. If indeed Venezuela is alive, I must receive some response to what I have said to Venezuela.

Las lanzas coloradas is a painful cry of love. Total and impassioned love for that land that is made of my body, for that world that populates my spirit, for those concerns that rip my heart to shreds. I know of nothing like it that has ever been done in Venezuela: not in its evocative transcendence nor in its sincerity of sentiment, nor in the pain without rhetoric of its description of souls.

It is a work of infinite comprehension. Because I love I have understood. Because I adore anxiously and I suffer, I have been able to see and to speak of the entirety of divine simplicity. Because I am wracked with anguish I have been able to make that entire world mine. Mine for always. *Las lanzas coloradas* is my property title.

That action of harnessing the Venezuelan soul must not go without a response. I await the voices of those who have heard me. They will come! They will come, because they are already latent in the message itself, because they already vibrate within the very emotion of the voice that speaks to them; they will come, even when they remain silent, because their hearts will betray the lie their faces and attitudes seek to dissemble. They will come, and victory will be mine, because even when they—those whom I have addressed directly—keep silent for all eternity, keep silent like the dead, like the tombs that guard the dead, like the tombs of flesh that guard dead spirits, the word is spoken and its resonance must touch the virgin souls, the ardent spirits, all those who must come someday to give themselves entirely to me, to absolve me, to manifest me; even when I myself, alone, am enough to manifest myself and absolve myself, and I feel better.

It was apt that a man of my generation would turn his eyes toward Venezuela and speak just words. I have done this; it is now not for human hands to detain it, nor to extinguish it, nor even to diminish it. When a message corresponds profoundly to a reality it extends beyond the human radius, in spite of men, to enter into the radius of the forces that determine historical processes.

All this regards the reception *Las lanzas coloradas* might merit from a certain group. That justification I owe to my book, and I state it before you.

As for me, nothing matters other than what happens to the book. *Las lanzas* is a prelude, a fleeting form, an exordium, a prior recapitulation of my personal action. Once it was written, my own person was extracted from it. Due to a profound demand within my very being, my psycho-physiological composition, I have imposed a single rule in life upon myself: *to serve!* May my life become fertile and useful for thousands of other, less empowered lives; my life begins to be imbued with a deep fervor: the necessity of service. Petty literary glories, wealth, personal happiness, all that seems to me devoid of true value, true greatness, when compared to the extraordinary satisfaction (and by "extraordinary" I mean that harmony between dream and achieved, harnessed reality) of one who might, as a fine day elapses, feel himself to be the very roots of the race, the udder of the spirit, the powerful sling of a people, the creator of a thousand destinies, the helm of a retinue of free fighters, the legitimate proprietor of the world's morning.

I have joyfully accepted a transcendental destiny; in the gravity of my earliest hour I have said the word that prepares the way and compels it. Born of the fervor of painful flesh, it must let loose a harvest of fervor. Alone, or better yet already surrounded by ghosts, by the shadow of those who are to come, before beginning on this path I have silently served up my blood, wine for the shadows, my flesh, bread for ghosts, and I have said, solemnly, the offertory prayer: Take this and eat. . . .

Now I do not want to, I cannot, I must not turn back. Within my heart, silently, I celebrate the glory of my first day walking this path—

I embrace you fraternally,
Arturo

—Letters in the archives of the Alberto Vollmer Foundation, Inc., Caracas.
Translated by Jen Hofer

god's lands **rómulo gallegos**

A rather strange title, this—as much, perhaps, in my mouth as in the ears listening to me—but it is not without purpose, because it is a good thing, from time to time, to let loose onto the hardened fields of positivism[1] the mystical content of certain words, bushel-bins heaped with an antiquated seed that is no longer sown, and because it is natural for this to be done by someone, like myself, who tends more toward sowing the perfumed flowers of chimeras than the substantive bulbs of reality.

At first glance, it might seem that to call certain lands "God's" reveals a desire to aggrandize them as the best lands: ones that give more than 100 percent, that neither breed sorrows nor nourish vices, lands refreshed by gentle air, covered by tender shade and allowing for an easy life. If, however, we recall that even in the Bible the harsh lands of Judea were those that Jehovah preferred, we might begin to comprehend that perhaps we cannot expect too much good to result from the divine possession under which I place these lands to which I will refer, in order to distinguish them from ones we might say are "man's."

For there are some lands where God still works and others where it is now men who work; lands where the lightning-flashes of creation still storm and lands where by now they have calmed.[2] And the case is that the days of creation were long and the work began at dawn and lasted through the night, and the lands that appeared in the morning had already had time to mature, while those that were created in the afternoon were still unripe. For this reason there are old lands and young lands, lands where man has already had time to build his works, and others that are just now emerging from God's hands. These, still hot from the warmth of the creator's hands; those others, growing cold already. And this is also the explanation for why there is a torrid zone and others that are more temperate and cool.

Has it not happened to some of you, walking distracted through the Cuban jungle, the Brazilian forest, the Andean cave, or the Venezuelan prairie, that you quiver suddenly with the idea that you will imminently happen upon an already-adult man, recently born, naked, covered only in his own pelt, not born of parents but rather sprung up from the earth, standing immobile, with his feet still buried in the sludge, devouring the strangeness of the world with an astonished gaze, his mouth half-open with his first stammered sound?

This has happened to me at any rate, on a number of occasions. And that is because in these lands of ours, with their impressive silence and tragic solitude, it is easy to feel that the sixth day of Genesis has not yet ended, that the creator's breath still blows through them. And that is why I call them "God's lands."

But there is no need to remain confined to the dense woodlands in order to come across this creature—unnerving, more or less hairy, more or less babbling, new and at the same time ancient, like any anachronistic thing. For it is familiar already with the ways of cities; it has sprung out of the maternal brambles and reigns upon them, with some clothes on his body by now—very colorful ones, naturally, as befits his childish taste, garments not quite perfectly human, some colored rags with braided decorations and golden epaulets, with various brightly shining medallions and crosses on his chest.

I know of one who does not take his off, though nobody knows where he might have acquired them, one of these anachronistic savage eruptions beneath whose barbarian rule my people have moaned for the past twenty-three years.[3] And this merely serves to explain why I signaled that there is not much good to expect, not with regard to a pleasant life, and, at least for the moment, not from the lands to which I have been referring.

Did I say "barbarian"? That is how the species is designated in merciless scientific language; I, however, prefer to continue working with the symbolism of the title I have given to these paragraphs and to explain its origin and condition in the following bizarre way:

As the whirlwind of creation has not yet ceased its flurrying over those lands—though what now spins within it is cosmic rubble, the leftovers from more favored creations—and as, on the other hand, the end of the sixth day draws near, and it is time to hurry so the remains of that tempestuous matter will not continue circling the world, God grabs it in huge handfuls, gives it two or three human touches, and flings it down to fall as it will. But the sad thing is that they almost always fall on their feet, because the devil walks those roads and stands them up.

And now that I mention the Devil and make reference to the ill-fated past that causes us to be upright and to sing the praises of the works flowing from the creator's lap, I wonder if it would not have been more apt to classify these as "satanic lands," though I've been calling them "God's."

I take the expression from Gabriela Mistral,[4] from whom I heard it just a few days ago, as we were talking about certain aspects of our America and she asked me if my Venezuelan lands really are as they are described in *Doña Bárbara*. Lands prone to barbarian outbreaks, lands that turn the depths of the soul upside-down and fling open the cages of blackbirds with grim instincts; but robust lands, irascible, equally good for hard work and for heroic exploits. Lands of the profound virgin silence of the human voice, of deep solitude, of the majestic landscape that disappears if it is not contemplated, as does the water of its great rivers if they are not navigated, lands of infinite prairies where the heartiest shout turns into a verse of song, of dense forests where the raspy sound of a wild bird can frighten you and your heart clenches into a fist at the funereal bell tolls of the *yaacabó*,[5] lands of steep cliffs and solitary plateaus one should move through silently so as not to arouse their rage. Lands of macho men, as they say in those parts.

That is how these lands are, and their satanic influence molds barbarism into the souls of all who surrender to them. For myself, I can say with certainty that being on the Arauca,[6] before the immense savannah, I felt that if I were to fling my leg across a wild horse's back and succeed in lassoing a bull, I'd stay on the prairie forever.

What is so strange about the fact that those lands should produce men like the one with all those medallions upon his chest to whom I have just alluded? He descended from the Andean peaks, together with another just like him,[7] at the head of a crowd of rough, fierce barbarians, and I believe things happened in the following way:

One day a storm broke out over the plateau: wind, lightning, and thunder inside a black cloud. The Creator's whirlwind. Suddenly the cloud cracked open, the whirlwind passed, and two brand new men were left standing on the plateau. One, sallow and simian, was all restless nervous system, ragged and broken;[8] the other, fashioned from a block of cork-oak carved by ax-blows, was coarse, brutish, vastly patient.[9] That one, lewdness and cruelty; this one, greed and cruelty. The first, with a blue military jacket, warrior's clothing and a kerchief around his saluting right hand; the second, with a grotesque checkered suit made of rough flannel cut by a country tailor, and a fighting cock under his arm. They were riding two shaggy mules, all four of the same substance. [. . .]

And it was as if an avalanche spilled from the plain, a spontaneous eruption from the satanic land.

Is the Cuban jungle like that? It would be a good idea to investigate whether anyone has ever found himself with that hairy Don Gerardo, emerging from the intricately tangled underbrush.

But do not grow alarmed, gentle reader, because you hear me attributing this nearly divine origin to our men of prey. First, this idea is not singularly my own: it is by now an established custom among us, at least in Venezuela, to use the word *providential* in reference to that species of men who sprang up from the chaos of armed revolt, whose existence and predominance in villages that consider themselves civilized cannot be explained in even a remotely dignified manner—instead, the phenomenon must be ascribed to the work and misfortune of miracles that obey the inscrutable designs of the God of nations;

in this way, we silence the reproaches of our civic conscience in the face of the prevalence and perpetuation of such scourges. And on the other hand, that nearly divine genealogy that I have attributed to my country (debatable, as is any genealogy) is worth at least as much as that of our Basque ascendancy—now the Basques are all the rage given our democracies' keen enthusiasm for nobility—which a certain writer of articles of the Venezuelan sycophancy recently attributed to [Juan Vicente] Gómez, so as to make him a match for Bolívar, and comparable to [Joseph] Joffre.

To which the Basques would say: Who would demand that our forebears leave their houses? And now they blame this on us!

NONETHELESS, I HAVE FAITH

So much faith that I do not hesitate to intone my panegyric to the tropics, defying the disdain of the solstices, that same disdain the sun has as it pauses there and turns its back on them, twice a year.

But it is not the disdain of the geographic zone that "around its beloved sun circumscribes its vague course," where "the pineapple's ambrosia grows ripe" and "the almond nestled sparkling gourds fills coral urns abundantly," to which my dear Andrés Bello[10]—yours and mine, our Chilean brother—has already pronounced this paean, using these and other beautiful metaphors. It is, rather, that of the spiritual zone of a tropical psychology, which, beyond the solstices, has been most disgraced.

For just as there is a land marked by heat from the ardor of the creator's hands that continue to work upon it, there is a soul recently emerged from the forge: pure ostentatious fire.

Two remarkable features characterize it: a combustible imagination and a ferocious propensity toward individualism. Both so disgraced, in the face of the exaggerated praise afforded the virtues of colder races, set in opposition to them: reflexive intelligence and good sense.

It is not difficult to praise imagination. To put it better: such praise is by now taken for granted as accepted, even in these parts. It is already known that imagination is the great creative force and perhaps the truly distinctive defining characteristic separating men from animals, since it would be relatively easy to demonstrate that reason is but a special—and incidentally quite pedantic—form of the human capacity for imagination. On the high planes of the spirit, imagination precedes scientific discoveries, and deserves sole credit for those marvelous long-lived creatures, myth and art, the latter to beautify our transitory lives and the former to promise us eternity; and on the lower planes of ingenuity—although it is somewhat dangerous to classify those planes as "lower" in these parts—imagination has populated the world of that multitude of great and small mechanical monsters, from the airplane to the tobacco pouch, to which we modern men owe the tremendous complications of our comfort.

Now, if imagination is all this, we men of the tropics do not have to worry much if we are branded as "imaginative." It is more than clear that those who give us this moniker do not intend to attribute to us the capacity for creation that such talents entail; instead they ascribe to us all that is less useful and estimable in them: verbal pyrotechnics, the fatuous fire of projects never executed, will squandered along a thousand different paths, reluctance to engage in persevering action, lack of practical spirit—and given all of the above, the fact that we have not yet succeeded in producing any positive and stable good.

Positive and stable good! Look who's talking! The Empire State Building is large. Grand. They say it will hold five thousand offices. Five thousand abodes of toil with their corresponding instruments of torture for five thousand typists. Five thousand bankruptcies. The crisis continues indeed.

And yet.

"What rubbish you say!"—some might respond. That is not the way to argue, nor does the famous skyscraper have anything to do with this. The point was to demonstrate that our virtues are better. . . .

No, the point was simply to defend our ways. To say that we are men among men and we have a right to the world's respect, and if I made allusion to the famous skyscraper, it was, first of all, because the magnificence it symbolizes buttresses the pride of those who look down on us, and then because there never cease to be those among us who think we will not be great and happy as long as we do not have our own skyscraper. I do not share this opinion and I was attempting to demonstrate, with all my talk about the imaginative, that we have done something uniquely our own that is not bad at all and that we would already have done more and better if it were not for. . . .

But let us leave all this about praising the imagination, because, really, it is a chore. I will now endeavor to locate better reasons to defend our individualism. [. . .]

—"Las tierras de Dios," lecture delivered at the Nicholas Roerich Museum in New York City on September 1, 1931 (sponsored by the Latin American Federation of Students); in *Rómulo Gallegos: Una posición ante la vida* (Caracas: Centauro77, 1977), pp. 112–44.
Translated by Jen Hofer
This text has been abridged for the present volume.

venezuelan painting as international value
alfredo boulton (as bruno plá)

The artistic near-uselessness implied by the Venezuelan art exhibition at the Ateneo de Caracas demonstrates a lack of pictorial personality. Artistic concern with color and form, and the artistic whole do not seem to be of interest to most of our painters. This group of paintings indicates an artistic apathy that is characteristic of most of today's Venezuelan painters. Painters should be aware of the artistic significance that painting has in every era—indeed, the result of that concern is what defines an era, and if our painter is not committed to being concerned about art, it would be better if he abandoned it completely. Faintheartedness is not compatible with painting, and the work that is on exhibit at the Ateneo is sopping in it. A painter should understand that what matters above all else is character—that anybody, with a small effort, can paint, but to be a truly interesting painter, it is not enough to have been praised by friends or by people with little artistic understanding. No. It is necessary to have been born a painter, to feel strong enough to reach beyond what one may have seen; to discover, to assert oneself, to create, to be constantly preoccupied, constantly searching for colors, forms, or impressions, to continue advancing, to evolve, and to avoid the greatest danger to art—which is to stand still. And this is precisely what has taken place here. The great majority of the painters in this exhibition find themselves at this dead end, some because they believe that they are already confirmed as artists, and others because they have joined a school in which individuality does not exist. Consequently, the artist's initiative, ideas, or personal concepts find themselves blocked by academic form.

And now let us move on to look superficially at the submissions of the "cream of Venezuelan art."

Antonio Alcántara has submitted *Cabo blanco* [White cape], with a blue light rarely seen here in Venezuela. His pointillism is sincere until it reaches the vertical foreground, when he forgets about it and drags his brush across some trivial cactuses.

A[lejandro] Alfonzo Larrain's two watercolors are remarkably surprising. It was disconcerting. Some were pictures for an advertisement calendar.

C[ruz] Alvarez Sales displays a dirty palette in the portrait of Pedro Zerpa. His technique is undefined.

J[osé] M[anuel] Betancourt's two gouaches would be very successful as illustrations for a children's storybook.

Miguel Bousquet uses pretty colors and has a happy composition. The impression given is that of a feminine painting.

Julia Brandt reveals a certain degree of preoccupation with stylization of figures in the portrait she has submitted. We recommend that J.B. work on her subjects with greater depth.

Manuel Cabré loves the baroque in nature. His Venezuelan landscape seems to have been painted at different times of day. We cannot find a consistent use of light. The olive groves have a greater freedom of execution, but the painter is always stymied by rococo detail.

María Luisa de Capriles has two sketches that are inferior to her previous submissions.

Marcos Castillo has reached a standstill as a portrait painter and Cézanneian Impressionist. We cannot discern any innovation in his portrait of Julio Morales Lara, with respect to his previous portraits. His still life's greens and blues create a pleasant effect. Castillo seems to have completely given up landscape, in which he had once achieved a certain character.

Luis Eduardo Chaves—still life no. 24—contains shades of Japanese lacquer, an unexpected discovery in this medium.

Pedro Centeno Vallenilla resides at a dead end. His *Sinfonía heróica* [Heroic symphony] did not manage to give us the impression of an ensemble of triumphant lives. He has found a formula and abuses it. His technique is essentially scholastic, and thus lacks personality.

Alberto Egea López is a better portrait painter than a landscape painter. He presents his North American oil painting with uncertainty—as if he wishes to see how the land lies. Its colors, among which yellow prevails, obscure the painting a bit. His *El cementerio* [The cemetery], which we saw before the exhibition opened, was run by the admissions jury. It was chosen from among three watercolors, and is superior to the images of boats that were shown. That painting had a series of very well-conceived hues.

Francisco Fernández reminds us of the Cabré of days gone by. And the same may be said of Pedro A. González with respect to his landscape, although Fernández and González have different approaches.

Mimí González Rincones surprised us with her vigorous pastels. She achieved a collection of unexpected values and hues, with cheerful colors and a very personal craftsmanship.

Leopoldo La Madriz did not manage to create a unified whole on his large canvas. It is completely lacking in atmosphere. On the other hand, his landscape, which uses greens, sepias, and grays, is well harmonized. His brushstroke is quick and his motif's effect is very successful. Might La Madriz have seen the Boulton collection's [André Dunoyer de] Segonzac?

We regret that Antero López submitted only one work. *El negro Altagracita* [The black Altagracita] is one of the few interesting things in the exhibition. Despite its poor location, it managed to attract attention because of its strength of color and freedom of execution. His very well-applied gouache managed to give the skin a very realistic glow. López should continue working with interest, for he promises to have that pictorial feeling that is so rare in our medium: personality.

La calle [The street], by Rafael Monasterios, shows great technical progress. It is airy and the canvas is worked with ease. The background is well painted in watercolors. Monasterios's colors are pleasant and poetic. His blues, yellows, and greens form a very interesting mixture. His purified Impressionistic technique gets better every day.

Las magnolias [The magnolias], by Francisco Narváez, indicates an indisputable progress in this artist's sense of ornamentation. His technique remains as it was, while he makes use of highly contrasted colors. He has a clear personality. If Narváez were to worry more about composition and technique, his progress would be faster. He must realize that he is just beginning, and that he has a series of problems before him, which can only be resolved by dint of sincerity. As for *Las lavanderas* [The washerwomen], the composition is unfortunate.

Carlos Otero has not managed to infuse his portrait with life. His color is soft and his composition very cold.

Elena de Pecchio shows a small canvas that is fairly interesting. In the short range she gives us, she proves to be a good colorist, if a bit influenced by [Maurice de] Vlaminck.

Gloria Pérez Guevara paints in the style of the French *pompiers* [firemen].[1]

César Prieto continues to evolve favorably. His blues reach a crude white and his use of color is very distinct. The two canvases that he exhibited are a testament to his progress.

The much-discussed Armando Reverón is undoubtedly one of our most interesting painters. The use of color fading almost to white is an area that is very skillfully exploited by this artist. The composition of *La hamaca* [The hammock] is the work of a person with admirable mastery. If Reverón were to exhibit in Europe, we are sure that he would be welcomed with very favorable criticism. Without a doubt, Reverón and Narváez are the only two interesting cases in contemporary painting.

Rafael Rivero is not a painter. He is a good caricaturist who knows his métier. His two drawings have no transcendence whatsoever.

Tito Salas exhibits a sketch. His approach and evolution have been the same for several years now.

Raúl Santana has two somewhat confusing drawings: *La burriquita* [The foal] gave us an impression of reality that we do not find in *El café* [Coffee].

Magdalena Schlooman made a nice portrait, *Elisa Elvira Zuloaga*; it is an adequate likeness.

Manuel Salvatierra (Mas), like Rivero, looks at his characters with a certain influence from Narváez. He achieves skin tones that are pleasant enough.

Julio Salas's submissions are of a contradictory technique. His *Calle* [Street] adheres closely to its landscape. It has a pleasant coloring.

Elisa Elvira Zuloaga apparently visited Valle Abajo on a cloudy day. However, her *El lavandero* [The laundryman] has a very skillfully rendered, dazzling sun.

In the drawings section, Otero's sketch drew our attention. His little figure is engraved well and his drawing is made accurately and with ease.

Nina Crespo, Tomás Golding, Gregorio García, and many others whose current production we would have been very interested to see, have stopped submitting their work.

We have left out a great number of submissions because they seem to us of very little interest and because we fear repeating ourselves even more than we have already done.

What the exhibition of paintings at the Ateneo de Caracas conveys, and I shall say it again, is an almost complete absence of pictorial personality. Impressionism is only now peeking through in Venezuela. All the other trends that have already been accepted in Europe and in North America are in practice unknown to our artists. Our painters are now doing what was done in Europe in 1900 and this can only be due to the scant artistic interest that exists in our midst. Venezuela at present does not possess any painter of this generation who might have authentic international value. We conclude by asking ourselves if, in effect, the group of painters who admire [Henri] Matisse, [Amedeo] Modigliani, [André] Derain, or Segonzac—and we only name these few so as not to create a quarrel—can be truly sincere when praising Joan Miró, Paul Klee, or Max Ernst, because what is exhibited at the Ateneo does not confirm this sincerity, and by no means substantiates it.

—"La pintura venezolana como valor internacional," *El Universal* (Caracas), August 20, 1933.
Translated by Carlos Riobó

brief notes on the fringes of venezuelan painting

alfredo boulton (as bruno plá)

Art demands a great dose of sincerity—total and absolute sincerity—to be valuable, to stand up to the greatest sacrifices and the greatest doubts. We should consider our pictorial scene with a certain generosity, because of social problems, cultural phenomena: our specific circumstances. We consciously assume this kindly attitude solely because of the events that have taken place in our past and are taking place in our artistic present. Let us be tolerant, then, as we take a brief glance around our pictorial panorama, and let us not qualify it as overly crude since facts and circumstances have a fundamental influence on both its progress and its stagnation. It might be difficult to understand our problem at first, but we should admit that deep down, at the core of this stagnation, a certain artistic impulse has always existed; although it might not always have been constant, it has proven at least to be admirably tenacious: it is there when its greatest contributions and enthusiasm are required.

Some years ago, we used to say that our painting—from an international perspective, considering its commercial and commodified aspects—was utterly worthless. These days, we are still under that same sad and undisputed impression. When it comes to painting, especially, we cannot give ourselves the luxury of doubt. Painting is either made with sincerity or there is no painting whatsoever. Anything between the two is—in art as in real life—of little interest; how few interesting people we have! We must therefore not accept in-between position. We must try to achieve the impossible, so we will no longer observe this disinterested attitude toward things of great significance, things of the highest cultural merit, here where our people live and debate.

We consider it a great breach of artistic responsibility to keep silent about the failings that fall within our purview. We must be fully convinced, first, of the need to fight in earnest to bring to light such failings as have existed and undoubtedly still exist, so that tomorrow we will be able to speak proudly about the victorious struggle through which we have come. We must abide by this attitude, as it pertains to artistic Ethics. The age of bribery, deception, and enforced silence is fortunately in the past.[1] Let us focus now on the problem facing our painter. He has seen himself surrounded by a society whose absolute lack of intellectual enjoyment is crystal clear. The painter in our midst has not encountered the open support of the rich and powerful—support that is so necessary to sustain the enthusiasm of those who have barely enough on which to live. With only a few exceptions, the wealthy classes have always shown a preference for works that have the least artistic value. Perhaps it is these works that are most readily accessible to the wealthy. It is a matter of intellectual education, but sadly, intuitive intelligence has also been notably lacking. As we can see, painters find themselves trapped in a cycle of absolute incomprehension—with the problem of survival, and no way of solving it. Few enough follow the path of sincere art, but it is clear that, even among these few, not all have the kind of pure devotion required for true artistic sensibility.

In sum, now that we have turned our focus to the grave problem of Venezuelan painting, let us make some observations about the better-known painters in our country. The job of analyzing an activity that stands out so little, as our painting has always shown itself to do, is always difficult: it is a task that requires a certain degree of patience. Let us leave that laborious task to other patient and tolerant beings.

We shall first speak of those painters whom death has placed before public opinion in the dangerous and difficult circle known as "the classics." For Venezuelans (and to be clear: the word "Venezuelan" refers here to the vast majority of us, not just to the small group of cultured people who have always been intensely preoccupied with displays of art)—for Venezuelans, our painting came to resemble reality with the appearance on the pictorial stage of [Arturo] Michelena, [Cristóbal] Rojas, [Antonio] Herrera Toro, [Martín Tovar y] Tovar, etc. Here it is worth pointing out why "cultural phenomena" were previously mentioned. We note the great veneration with which the prestige of our painters—those who are considered classics—has been respected. Michelena, Rojas, Herrera Toro, etc. have heroic reputations, but this is precisely where we see that a grave error has been made—an error that is understandable given our country's useless pictorial education. We all know that these painters have devoted great canvases and a great many hours to painting battle scenes: Ayacucho, Bomboná, Carabobo, etc. People have been deliriously excited by these war scenes, and this enthusiasm has had repercussions on the quality of the painter as an artist. This veneration, this enthusiasm, is due to the spiritual union that exists—or rather that some think should exist—between an artist and his work, between a painter and the subject at hand. We have come to exaggerate this sentiment to such a degree that we have turned our painters into untouchable grandees of our national painting. The public, unaware of what is going on, finds it very difficult to understand that in the era when these illustrious painters were winning bronze, silver, or cardboard medals with the tips of their sword-brushes, the real creators of contemporary painting were already convinced of the errors and of the erroneous path taken by those others who preferred the tried-and-true school of painting over that of rebellion. It was a matter of choosing between what had already given up its original essence, was already too well worn, and what was a new step toward unknown and revolutionary art. We should remember that [Édouard] Manet, [Camille] Corot, [Eugène] Delacroix, and the other creators of modern painting (and also, certainly, painters of other schools) lived through that time of struggle, of doubt, and of hunger. Their accomplishments, however, did not result from a stroke of genius after excessive fasting; they came from having a broader and clearer vision, and from recognizing the true responsibility that one has to world culture: to keep fighting for one's own ideas. It was a matter of aptitudes, not attitudes. We may make the same observation, in support of this theory, if we examine painters of religious paintings. We have found the most tangible proof in Cristóbal Rojas. We have spoken much, with people who have studied painting, regarding the universal pictorial value of Cristóbal Rojas. We have noted that the vast majority of these people allege, as a forceful argument, that C.R. won a medal in the Paris Salon with his *El Purgatorio* [Purgatory]. Despite its awards and despite its lofty placement in a niche, this painting has not borne the severe criticism of time. I doubt that anyone who knows a little about painting and who is sincere in his judgment would declare *El Purgatorio* by Cristóbal Rojas a painting of merit. We have a sufficiently poor opinion of the French art salons to believe that if the aforementioned painting were to be exhibited now, it would be deemed *hors-concours* [out of the running] for its creator. This theme of Purgatory is one that once tended to cause great commotion, a great style with a burst of acrobatic and anatomical tricks, with exuberant imagination, à la Gustave Doré. The theme lends itself what Michelena accomplished in his *Pentesilea* [*Penthesilea*]–a burst of anatomical acrobatics, unimaginable leaps, giving (as Michelena does) the feeling of an avalanche, of confusion, and of explosion. On the other hand, Cristóbal Rojas is content with a few tense bodies that do not cause much excitement. With his "golden brush," he places a most serene, gliding angel, precursor of motorless flight, in the painting's upper portion.

In mentioning Michelena, we should point out that he is our finest pictorial proponent, from the last century to date. We have come to believe–even in this period of artistic revival, in which art may yield its best harvest to date–even in this time, we consider Michelena to be a good Venezuelan painter. Comparisons are often thought of as odious, and following this notion, we shall not compare Michelena to his European contemporaries. Let us remember very vividly that painters such as [Léon] Bonnat and [Fernand] Cormon have received medals, diplomas, and degrees, but despite all these distinctions, they are mediocre exemplars of French art. Merit is not found in medals. We consider Arturo Michelena to be a good painter, and we understand that to most Venezuelans, who know little about painting, he is indeed an excellent painter.

Tovar y Tovar is a part of this same group. His painting *La firma del acta de la Independencia* [The signing of the declaration of independence] has brought him national admiration as a painter, for rendering on canvas a glorious act of our history.

It would be an overwhelming task to name all our painters and to comment on them individually; let us, however, remember Emilio Mauri, who has the great distinction of having founded our Academia de Bellas Artes. Let us equally remember Federico Brandt,[2] a talented artist with a fine sensibility. We would have to mention many if we wanted to comment fully on the national pictorial scene. We shall leave such a patriotic task to more tolerant figures.

The current situation of our painting is quite interesting. We have two incompatible camps, each of which has been able to prove itself the better theorist and expert with regard to modern painting. But these differences of opinion are not greatly relevant; we mention them only so that later on we might be able to discuss the happy execution that one of these theories has had when put into practice. When we study current public opinion regarding painting, we observe that this opinion is useless because people are absolutely ignorant about who our best painters are. We may make an exception when it comes to Tito Salas, whom the public cannot ignore due to the opportunities he has had to make his painting known. Tito Salas is, if we may refer to him thus, our official painter. He knows how to interpret different stages in Bolívar's life with spirit, in paintings located at the Casa Natal de El Libertador and in the Panteón Nacional. On the subject of Salas, it is worth noting that he is the only portrait painter of merit whom we now have. Those painters among us who devote themselves to portraiture are scarce and we can only explain this scarcity by the fact that the very small group of buyers that exists has always shown a preference for landscape.

We cannot cite any outstanding figure in our pictorial panorama. It seems that the vast majority of them, if not all of them, find themselves tied to a series of problems that prevent them from acting freely. In art, what is important is to obtain moral and material freedom, and we know that it is extremely difficult to achieve the latter. As we have already noted, we are aware of the useless contribution that our people are making to the plastic arts. We can discern a very marked Impressionist influence among all of our good landscape painters: [Rafael] Monasterios, [Armando] Reverón, [Manuel] Cabré, [Marcos] Castillo, [Tomás] Golding, [Alberto] Egea [López], [Cruz] Alvarez Sales, etc.; all of them are fervent landscape painters and the best representatives of our plastic arts. They are all young men whose work is currently evolving, and let us hope that this small artistic resurgence may guide them toward a greater pictorial sincerity. It is worth remembering here [André] Gide's words upon his return from the USSR: "I consider that if ever sincerity is important, it is surely when the beliefs of great masses of people are involved together with one's own."[3] We demand of them that essential sincerity that is necessary at this time, a sincerity that some have already displayed and that we admire fully. They should know how to be thoroughly responsible to their charges and to their beliefs. We must make special mention of the young phalanx that is under the artistic supervision of the Escuela de Bellas Artes. We sincerely believe that Venezuela might one day have a good example of the pictorial culture that it deserves among civilized nations, and that it could come from the Escuela of today. We have seen the latest results obtained by this new generation, and we truly admire the conscientiousness and sincerity of the work shown.[4] These results allow us to believe in the artistic recourse that our people have. We do not believe it necessary to talk about this or that painter of today. We are now beyond that; we believe it and we will reiterate it: now, as before, there is no one capable of saving Venezuelan painting from its present state of anonymity. Those who head governmental departments, responsible for the artistic education of the people, shirk a very great responsibility when they do not watch over a nation's best cultural product, which is art. Let us hope that they act favorably for the benefit of our culture, for the time to achieve a sincere work of art is here. Each one of us should calmly weigh our own responsibility and contribute as much as possible to the true culture of our homeland. If we make an effort to advance our culture, let us do it sincerely since, as Gide says, the beliefs of great masses of people, including ourselves, are at stake.

– *"Breves comentarios al margen de la pintura venezolana," Maracapana* (Caracas), September 1937.
Translated by Carlos Riobó

armando reverón **mariano picón salas**

Physically, Armando Reverón (one of the most important Venezuelans alive today, though he may not seem so) cuts one of those strange figures who illustrate that in Venezuela, through indefinable racial processes, there exists an Arab even further bronzed by the sun of our hot land and by the caciques whose language of many generations runs in their blood. Andalusian Arab and indigenous Venezuelan: these are not—as we will see later—negligible aspects of his mysterious personality.[1] Reverón's entire personage and life's work are expressed under a sign more mysterious than that observed by Sunday tourists who reach that fortress, part Incan and part Venezuelan peasant, which he constructed in Macuto[2]—or rather, which he has not finished constructing—and which is the most arbitrary living structure in our country. There, half-naked, girdled by his reed belt (which, according to Reverón's theory, functions as a closed borderline between his sexual organ and his head)—between the material and spiritual, in the peculiar company of the trained monkeys he teaches to wield paintbrushes and dresses in the most surrealist suits, ruled by the gentle instruction of his cook or attendant, Juanita, who brims with miraculous comprehension and faithfulness—Reverón plays the extravagant, wild artist: with genteel innocence he capitalizes on his reputation as a lunatic. Now that the Carribean Sea has demolished the walls of the ancient baths, now that the democratic taxi-van makes the old romantic beach a plebeian and sweaty franchise of the most plebeian and sweaty Caracas neighborhoods, Reverón has become, more aptly than the doves and sea-grapes of the baths, Macuto's greatest tourist attraction. Some parents lead their children here to show them how artists are naturally crazy; young girls who are avid readers of novels observe how novelesque beings can also live in reality. "Robinsons" who raise settlements on their deserted islands and Yankee tourists who make a quick weeklong circuit from New York to gulp down everything picturesque from the "West Indies" encounter here a delicious subject for their Kodaks.

In the presence of tourists, Reverón is the most dazzling Fregoli,[3] and has made many preparations to affect and frighten them: indigenous loincloths; feather necklaces; gaudily made-up mannequins among rough and copper-colored corkscrew-shaped bodies—Reverón's own mannequins, sitting on rattan chairs or hanging in maguey hammocks like great dead caciques. In the "attic"—and all the floors in Reverón's house have one—lurk characters, dolls, or simply one of the monkeys receiving painting lessons. Reverón, who grinds and emulsifies dirt to prepare his box of paints; who makes his own brushes with maguey fibers; who drinks and offers guests black coffee in aboriginal calabash gourds; who has his extremely special case of conch shells—he is one of the few Venezuelans who has no need of Western civilization. He has discovered the formula of an odd natural economy and flaunts his Robinsonian personality before the world. It is true that he puts on a show for the tourists; but it is also true that no one knows how to love and avail themselves of the humble things—things cast out by the sea and the earth—as he does. And on stormy nights he is like a weather-beaten mariner, atop the highest beam of his hut as if it were the foremast of a fantastic ship, scanning the horizon. There is something simultaneously magical

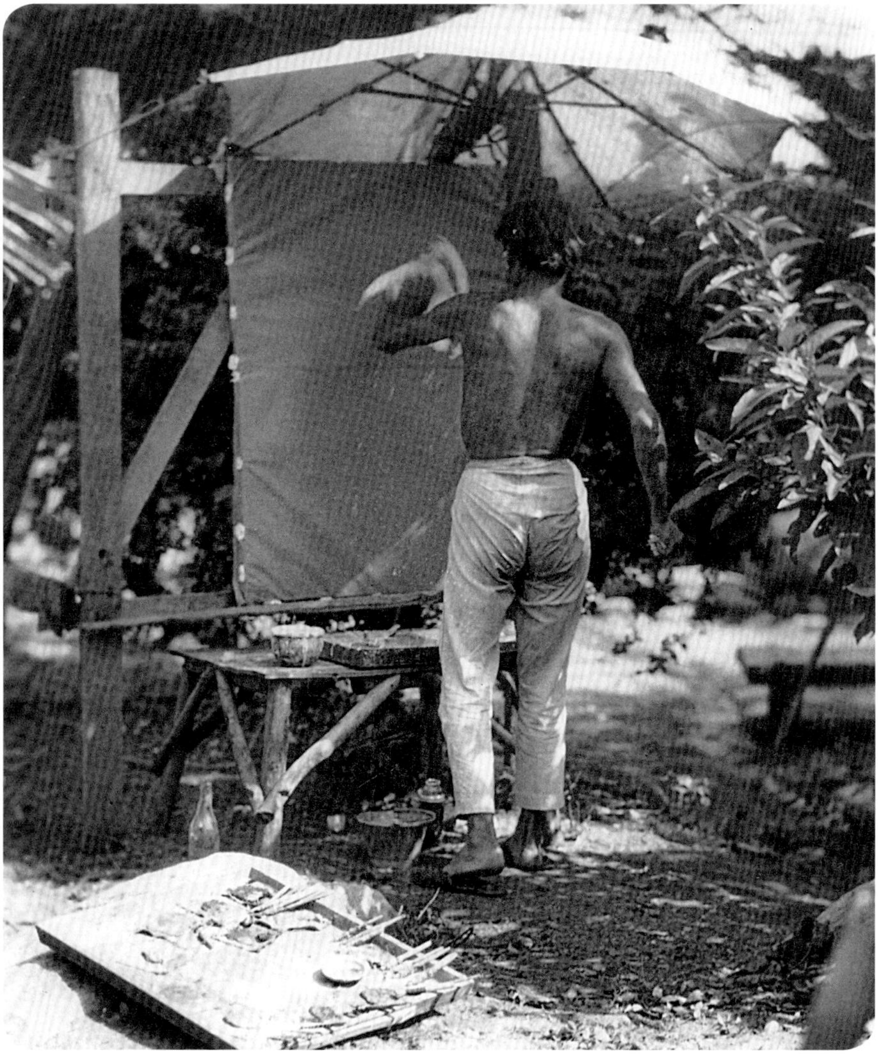

Armando Reverón painting Luisa Phelps. Photograph by Alfredo Boulton. 1934. Alberto Vollmer Foundation, Inc , Caracas

and animal in his gestures, his agility, his ears, and his hunting dog's sense of smell. And a conversation, perfectly illogical. A conversation in which his trip to Spain and Paris—the complicated tale of a small house he mortgaged and resold to the original owner in the city of Valencia[4] so he could go to Europe—is transcribed like a Freudian dream. Listening to him recount his trip to Europe in fleeting, simultaneous images, one thinks of a man who on a rainy night might suddenly happen into the Gare Saint-Lazare, get lured into a car, and see a city reflected in the damp pavement where colors, lights, and forms are separated from one another in a pressed, sparkling bouquet. And one doesn't know—I do not know, even after numerous dialogues with Reverón—if there is something calculated, something conscious disguised as the unconscious in his manner of exhibition and storytelling. (Only one other artist in South America made a similar impression on me—the Peruvian poet José María Eguren.)[5] These are the two most peculiar and inspired messengers of the air that it has been my privilege to meet, but in Eguren there is something of a physical destitution that does not exist in the Venezuelan painter, who is infinitely more agile, more astute.

How has Reverón learned, how has he arrived at such singular grace and refinement, such profound synthesis, that dematerialized and at the same time voluptuous elegance, which ensure his unique place among Venezuelan painters? How was he born in our midst, how did he develop here, this artist who is simultaneously our [Auguste] Renoir and our Henri Matisse and also, in a certain sense, our Goya? I have here an absolutely inexplicable problem, something that was generated and resides in the deepest and most mysterious spaces of personality, because all the circumstances of his life led to the exact opposite path. He did not experience the methodical apprenticeship of a [Manuel] Cabré in Europe; he was not an attentive visitor to museums, nor did he delve into those abstruse mathematics problems with the same concern exhibited by some of our researchers, such as Bernardo Monsanto. However, neither is he a spontaneous painter who, like Rafael Ramón González, paints the joyous things he sees, his walls and his small *criollo* plazas, the gigantic trees, the colorful people passing near him. There is in Reverón an extraordinary decorative geniality, and there is much to lament in the fact that many of his works have been realized on those fragile papers and with those paints, all of his own invention, that are destined to fade. The fact, however, that a Venezuelan man has arrived at a solution to decorative modernity that is extremely similar to Matisse's is something that might fill us with excitement and pride, above all when we consider how Reverón has lived and how he has developed. (A note to readers: Reverón's paintings, like Renoir's, are not photographable. The fineness of his color, the music of his brushstrokes, and even the unrefined material he uses to paint his works resist any photographic lens. It is necessary to see Reverón's works directly, to see them beneath a certain light and from an adequate distance.)

When the strange Valencian kid—who would continue, as a man, to be an enigma to his contemporaries—began his learning process as a painter, Tito Salas reigned in Venezuela. He had come from Europe, loaded with adventures and prizes, sparkling with Andalusian spirit, blessed with an easy and colorfully romantic skill with language he had learned in the Spanish school of [Ignacio] Zuloaga and [Julio] Romero de Torres. This same ease would, in the long term, hurt Tito's work. He was a friend to the literati; indeed, his painting became a bit literary. Established at the very center of Caracas, in a spot no less venerable than the birthplace of El Libertador,[6] the artist's studio was a magnetic center where anecdotes were spiced up; it was the customary gathering place for the most adept conversationalists and the most beautiful girls in the city. Over the course of twenty years of Caracas's history, Tito Salas was like a Rafael to our small tropical Rome; extravagant in his living, he was the Dictator of Art, and of each of us. His Sistine Chapel, where he was unconditionally offered walls and rooms to decorate, was the very House of Our Hero. And in a "prestissimo," in an abundance at odds with the happy self-assurance of his life, Tito's works are populated with tremendous passion. There, without symbology, depicted at times in an excessively hasty manner, are Bolívar's life and exploits. Certain oils that might have done well with more repose grow thin-skinned, treated like fidgety romantic etchings. Tito's talent tends to disintegrate there in the tiny details; he does a good job with a face and an object; he narrates charming fables, such as that in the large painting *El matrimonio de Bolívar* [Bolívar's marriage], but in the work as a whole the forms and groupings tumble headlong, as if to achieve merely a certain striving for effect. Tito does not achieve that great compositional tranquility of which [Arturo] Michelena was a master, and if we compare, for example, the horses and figures in a painting like *Pentesilea* [*Penthesilea*] with those of Tito's painting *La expedición de 1814* [The expedition of 1814], we observe the difference between real horses and riders and others that are lit up, tired-looking, in a phantasmal and nightmarish atmosphere. A certain Spanish picturesque mode, his own narrative facilities, and his tendency to consider art more as impression than form have all undoubtedly prevented Tito Salas's prodigious talent from manifesting its most lasting and full potential. But who knows whether this may be precisely what constitutes the secret of his success. When faced with the art made by earlier Venezuelan painters, the grave uprightness of a [Martín] Tovar y Tovar, Michelena's linear classicism, the tormented pathos of a Cristóbal Rojas, Tito Salas created – even with historical paintings – his animated bohemian fiesta.

Given the somnambulistic trance in which Reverón began his passage through the world, he was absolutely immune to the general influence the young monarch called Tito enjoyed over both painters and literary figures in 1910. If at any point they had met, each would have repelled the other, as profound temperamental contrasts and differences formed insurmountable barriers between them. Using a simple sociological formula, we might say that Tito is the Spanish *criollo*, with a facility for language and pleasant anecdotes, whose evident ease and ready extroverted nature lend themselves to the necessities of the exterior world and in turn yield to the demands of that world. In Reverón's soul, by contrast, something more mysteriously Venezuelan is concentrated, something magical, subjective, and decorative all at once, which might explain for us some of his biographical enigmas. The idea of an artist's "yoga," of a certain vital asceticism – a deep and obsessive concern that years later would lead him to shut himself in that small Robinsonian fort or dwelling built in Macuto, to impose a severe control over his own senses, and even to frighten the fusty bourgeoisie with his peculiar theories – suddenly shows Reverón to be quite sensitive. Without defining it – like Leonardo da Vinci – from a very young age he began to think of painting as a "mental thing." Hence his tendency to surround himself with defenses against sensuality in a nearly maniacal way. And he once explained to me that his most beautiful feminine figures came exclusively from his head – unlike Adam, from whose ribs they derived – because while he was painting, Reverón kept the lower part of his body firmly girdled. About these subjects and about his disquieting spiritualist calling he seems to have conversed quite a bit with that curious and dazzling Russian decorative painter Nicolás Ferdinandov,[7] who appeared in Caracas around 1920 and in whose studio, decorated with old icons and acquatic motifs—a studio that seemed to be the sanctuary of an esoteric religion—Reverón learned to drink tea in the Slavic manner, to pronounce a few Russian words, and to argue and seek the existence of God like one of Fyodor Dostoevsky's characters. From this moment on, something out of his own existence penetrated his art in those certain figures treated with a technique like that of Byzantine mosaic, submerged in a mysterious photic background, reaching for a vague symbology, as in the painting titled *Las hijas del sol* [*Daughters of the Sun*], owned by Carlos Eduardo Frías. Without knowing it—because Reverón has anything but an archaeologist's cultural view—he arrived at nearly magical figures and portraits, much like those of fourth-century Ravenna. Out of the decorative background emerges the face, swathed in a nocturnal light, in a mass of dispersed colors, in absolute spiritual flight.

And here it is worth pausing to consider other aspects of his work and the development of his style.

A young Venezuelan man arrives in Madrid on a winter's day in 1912. At the guesthouse he asks for a professor of painting, and is given the name of Señor [José] Moreno Carbonero, a coarse specimen of the art of folkloric painting, in whose solid figurines the pages of *Quixote* or the history of Spain are rigidly transcribed. In a dense world of honorific ceremonies and academies—a very formal world without a whit of daring—as a friend to the monarchical authorities, that painter represents, not decadence (because there is something tragic in any decadence), but rather the thickest platitude of Art. Sancho and his burro, Don Quixote and his lance, the dukes and their ruffs and all the elements of a colorless set of stage props—all these affirm Moreno Carbonero's fame and support his professorial appointment. At that moment there is great painting in France, but the Pyrenees and the heavily mustachioed customs officials do not let it through. If it exists in Spain, it is not seen or it is not shown in places as serious as the Academia de San Fernando. There is also great Spanish painting, but to admire El Greco leads directly to the Decadent movement; Velázquez's *Las lanzas* [*The Lances*] has nothing to do with guesthouses; Goya—"that Aragonese Goya," as Señor Moreno Carbonero calls him—was too mischievous. There are also the Romantics—Don Mariano Fortuny—but you already know the fate of the Romantics. Señor Moreno Carbonero recommends a healthy realism, like that with which he himself inundates the illustrated magazines: *Blanco y negro*, *La esfera*, *La ilustración española y americana*. With his good conduct and his realism, Señor Moreno Carbonero has reached old age loaded down with crosses and with salaries.

The easily chilled Venezuelan notices that Señor Moreno Carbonero's studio has a magnificent heater. That heater justifies the professor. And thus he has resolved his principal problem with Madrid. The professor recommends that you, the students, study one of the great compositional subjects. For example—you there, the American—when the Spanish arrived in the Americas and the Indians were going to surrender to them in servitude. (For Señor Moreno, universal history is a permanent kiss of the ring. Christopher Columbus should have established a court in Guanahani.) But at that moment, the hushed, indomitable caciques begin to speak within Armando Reverón. I'm just not so good at that, Señor—he tells him one day. And you have your clipped way of speaking with your American-style diminutives. Better just leave me here to one side of the little stove. If you'll allow me, I'll pay you my rent in advance.

While Señor Moreno expounds and maps out his paintings taken from a literal reading of El Quixote, on his paper Reverón sketches subjects from a distant land.

(When he left Caracas all the young people were painting seascapes. Those Macuto landscapes, with the same old sea-grapes and the same breakers, were selling by the dozen. A timid Impressionism insinuated itself into the worn, yellow debris and those undefined cliffs in the background, which seemed about to take off from the painting.)

—You still haven't seen Goya? the Venezuelan writer Salustio González Rincones, then a visitor to Madrid, asked him one afternoon.

And that afternoon, at the Prado, with the two *Majas* and Charles IV's family, Goya made his presence known.

Goya, subjected to the distillation of a mysterious soul, at times forgotten but always at work, would leave a lasting legacy in Reverón's art.

If Reverón had been a writer, he would have written something the day he met Goya. I would hear him say so twenty-seven years later.

> The most palpable difference between my new Master, Goya, and my older professor, Moreno Carbonero, is that the latter's painting ends with the canvas. It finishes exactly in the place where the molding of the frame begins. In contrast, with Goya, something stays with me, floating on my retina. That old señora's little dog from the portrait seems to me to vibrate still. The ribbon used to adjust the Marquesa de la Solana's mantilla, I take it away with me, in my eyes. It's material more beautiful than material itself. I leave with that tumultuous rhythm, that music—I can't say it any other way—contained in the painting *Carga de mamelucos* [*Charge of the Mamelukes*] at the Prado.

The day that Reverón visited Goya, some of the figures we Venezuelans would later adore began to come into existence: two paintings, Goya's great-grandchildren, which would appear twenty-some years later in Enrique Planchart's collection. As they did not have names, I've baptized them with the nicknames "Dama del clavel" [Lady of the carnation] and "Odalisca del manto azul" [Odalisque with blue robe].

Goya's influence would create in Reverón the same process, the same alchemy, that it created in modern art, affecting all the Impressionists, including [Édouard] Manet and Renoir, and even the extremely purified decorative language of Matisse.

More slender, more Oriental, yet unforgettable and insistent, Goya's *Maja* continues, stretching out over the entirety of an immense lyrical and ornamental territory of contemporary art. It is because she exists and still perturbs us that we set her in opposition to [Paul] Cézanne's more abstract bather or Pablo Picasso's version of "maternity."

An artistic era's style—as those in the know claim—is produced by the alternation or simultaneity of two ways of conceiving form. These sometimes close in on one another and intercommunicate within a great cultural current, like that which resulted in the great discipline of the Italian Renaissance, with varied contributions, both Nordic and Southern. But at other times the opposing currents battle, coexist, and confront one another, as when the decorative lyricism of Siena came up against the shapely line and sculptural and architectural tendencies of Florence, as when [Jean-Auguste-Dominique] Ingres's linear art encountered [Eugène] Delacroix's colorist art, or as occurs now when Cubist and Cézannesque constructivism stand against the fantastical worlds and lyric evasions of the Surrealists and Expressionists. And if we were to seek out the nearest genealogy of contemporary art we would encounter two branches, two great family trees, which, to define them by a single name, we might call the "pictorial-constructive" and the "lyric-decorative." At the head of the first current would appear names of antecedents like Ingres and Cézanne; atop the second would be one of the most important forebears, that is, Goya. Do the rebellious Surrealists and Expressionists of today know that Goya appears in their most venerable and robust line of ancestry?

Pedantic contemporary critics, with their pretensions of reaching the deepest secrets in the development of forms and styles, construct a history of art as if it emanated from inside artists; in that territory where signs are forged, they tend to give little importance to subject matter. The fact that Cézanne has painted bathers or card players or large olive trees in Provence is not what matters—they say—it is, rather, the *way* he painted them. Nevertheless, there are subjects that in themselves express and manifest fundamental chapters in the history of culture, subjects that are born, evolve, and become new curves or currents like bends in a great river. Thus it would be possible to write an entire history of art following the progress and avatar provided by subject matter. (Jacob Burckhardt, in his old and admirable *Cicerone,* has for example traced the formal and psychic trajectory of themes such as "Apollo" and "Aphrodite" in the development of Greek culture.)

Let us pause here to consider the subject of the reclining woman, as it is one of the themes repeated most consistently in Reverón's painting; let us consider the "Sleeping Venuses" which by the eighteenth century had already lost the idealization imposed on them by the Italian masters and became Goya's *Majas*. What has the fate of this subject been over the hundred-some years of its existence? One daughter of Goya's *Maja* is Manet's *Olympia*, which is both French and universal. The feminine body is now no longer an outlined silhouette and sculpture, as it was in the work of Ingres and the classics, but a vibrant mass of color. And in Renoir's nudes, the same subject continues as a luminous vibration, an ephemeral reflection, a musicality. Matisse's odalisques are outlined upon their blue tapestries, interpreting, stylizing, and shifting with their largely decorative motif the voluptuousness of our times; they come from the same lineage. And in the same way, the Yugoslav [*sic*: Bulgarian] artist [Jules] Pascin's "*jeunes filles*" share more than one analogy with our very own Armando Reverón. These are the manifestations of a lyric, luminous, and decorative art, in contrast to that other art of abstraction and form intuited as geometry, which is also inscribed into our contemporary reality.

Reverón has thus given Venezuelan art an immensely varied decorative feast. The problem of his "good taste," of his well-balanced refinement, his color harmonies—even when he uses muted tones—is what makes his painting stand out as having a unique and purified value. The process of distilled interior development that his art constitutes is all the more admirable as he did not have his documentary material at hand—miniatures, mosaics, or Oriental tapestries—through the study of which Matisse could come to create an entire twentieth-century ornamental style. Transferring what Reverón suggests to other arts, we might say that he is the greatest musician and the greatest poet of our painters.

Reverón is permanently in flight through the realm of color, possessed by his own internal rhythm; for him the object has not been—above all in his most recent works—anything more than a vague poetic leitmotif. He is the creator of an enchanted territory where enormous women descended from Goya's *Maja* recline, yet their bodies are now experienced as vibratile reflections, where the blue or red stain of a tapestry, the trembling of a flower or a ribbon or a certain mossy green, function as a background to the painting, and only accentuate that impression of mystery, of delicacy, and of celebration. The Venezuelan note (for one who is so far from the folkloric and the historical) suddenly gives her a detail that seems as if extracted from an ethical subconscious, a detail on which he never insists and which he would never describe. In one case it's that small parrot in the hand of the strong, sensual *criolla* woman from one of his gouaches, the one I permitted myself—in order to give it a name (and one should baptize Reverón's paintings)—because of her air of rural ferocity, to call the "wife of the Civil Chief." Or it is that pair of girls hanging in the hammock with an air so unmistakably familiar, or the poor circus clown in whose brightly colored suit the light and grace of all the circuses of our childhood converge in rebellion. Or it is—and we haven't spoken at all about Reverón as landscape painter—that wall enveloped in the dazzling and milky light of a tropical midday; in that seeming silence of heat, that wall on a lone street, on which two twin acacias recline.

An artist of inexhaustible thematic range and refined, intimate elegance (one might call him a "chamber painter," just as there are exhibition painters, academic painters, and court painters), Reverón is to us like no other born in Venezuela.[8]

—"Armando Reverón," *Revista nacional de la cultura*, no. 13 (November 1939): 63–80; reprinted in *Armando Reverón: 10 ensayos* (Caracas: Consejo Municipal del Distrito Federal, 1975), pp. 43–50.
Translated by Jen Hofer

creative *mestizaje* **arturo úslar pietri**

In 1609, one of the strangest books of the time appeared in Lisbon. It was called *Comentarios reales* [*de los Incas*] [*Royal Commentaries of the Inca*] and it was penned by Garcilaso de la Vega. It recounted the fabulous story of an immense and exotic empire from the still little-known American continent. It was written by a meticulous, refined man with a strange physiognomy, a Catholic priest who had been a captain in the Spanish infantry, and who was a direct descendent of the Inca kings. He wrote at the time of Felipe III's Spain, but he was born in faraway Cuzco, the day after the conquest of Pizarro. He lived in a city where the majority of the population were indigenous people who did not speak Spanish, where the greatest monuments were the millennial works of the Inca, where Christian churches were raised on the walls of the Indian temples and forts, in a strange and enormous house where his father, the Spanish captain Garcilaso de la Vega, lived in one wing, surrounded by his clerics and soldiers, while in the other lived his mother, the Inca princess Isabel Chimpu Oello—baptized perfunctorily—who spoke in Quechua with her relatives, the dispossessed dignitaries of the Atahualpa court.

During the three centuries of the Spanish Empire in America, numerous churches and other buildings arose in both new and old viceregal cities, from the cathedral of Santo Domingo, which is a nostalgic reproduction of a beautiful Italianate Renaissance temple, to religious and government buildings that were built in the eighteenth century and exhibit distinct characteristics and styles that make them quite different from their European counterparts.

Anyone who has ever climbed a small hill near Tlaxcala, in Mexico, and has seen rising up amid the tall surrounding pines the marvelous vision of the Ocotlán sanctuary, must have felt the inherent revelation of the original work, invested into this new geographic setting by its colonial builders. "The most delightful church in the world," it has been called, without exaggeration. It is, in fact, a work of extraordinary grace, full of humanity's joy—and it is not a reproduction of any European temple. The façade is like an immense stucco, brick, and tile altarpiece in vivid contrasts of red and white, with statues and ornaments on its various surfaces culminating in two tall, graceful towers, which seem more like the work of a jeweler than that of an architect. What is expressed here is an impulse different from the one that led to the building of the Spanish cathedrals, and it is expressed in a visual language that has no explanation other than the fertile meeting of cultures.

The churches were changed in the New World, but also the people who populated them were different.

The Spanish in Spain witnessed, with curious and not infrequently derisive wonder, the changes in custom, character, manners, and even ways of speaking of the Spanish who lived in America or were born there. An image, and often a caricature, of the "Antón Pirulero," the "*indiano*," and the "*criollo*" arose, with their macaws and their *indio* and black servants, with their archaic and byzantine way of speaking, with their extravagance and ostentation, with their tendency toward idleness and digression. They were different because they lived in cities that were different, in a society that no longer resembled Spanish society, in the midst of a natural landscape that had nothing in common with Europe's. When they spoke of a river, it was of those bodies of sweet water called the Amazon, the Orinoco, the Magdalene, the Plate, and not the modest trickles of the Duero or the Guadalquivir; when they spoke of mountains, it was not of the diminished European sierras, but of the immense ranges, snowy and inaccessible, stretching out like a spine from the north to the south of the New Continent. Their music, their dances, their foods, their folklore—all were different. From the music and dances of the Spanish, *indios* and blacks had extracted other music, other dances. The *areito*, the *chacona*, the *habanera*, the *danzón*, the *joropo*, the *pericón*, the *jarabe*. They had strange remedies and strange foods: cocoa, potato, corn, yucca, tomatoes, tobacco, and *guaiacum* branches that cured the strangest illnesses.

They came to have such a particular concept of the uniqueness of their situation that in some instances they attempted to repudiate the example and imitation of all things European. They thought that theirs should be a New World for many more reasons than simply its recent discovery and colonization. It should be a New World because there the tragic and failed history of Europe would not be repeated. They wanted to create a world and a society that would be different from those of the old continent. They believed that the American *indios* were the survivors of the Golden Age: good, pure, naked, with neither gunpowder nor swords, and without greed for gold or property. This was the image of the noble savage, which would have such a deep influence on the revolutionary thinking of a convulsively changing Europe in the eighteenth century. When Thomas More dreamed of a more moral and just society from his vantage point, as part of Henry VIII's cruel and corrupt court, he called it "Utopia" and located it on an island in America. Vasco de Quiroga, a Spanish priest established in Mexico, resolved to undertake More's Utopia; he created a communal group in Michoacán and wrote to Charles V:

> For not in vain, but rather with great cause and reason, this is called the New World, not because it was newly discovered, but rather because it is, in its people and in nearly every aspect, just as that early age, the Golden Age. . . .

In the vast savage solitudes of the riverfront territories near the Paraguay River, for over two centuries the Jesuits maintained an indigenous society that was completely segregated from any contact with European elements. There, neither property ownership nor commerce were allowed, and even Spanish was prohibited, in order to avoid infection, as if with a sanitary quarantine, from the bad example of the vices and sins of Europe. With amazement the ancient chronicles describe those reform-oriented, moralizing communities, where the *indios* were like eternal pupils of a strict pedagogy that proceeded from the cradle to the grave in order to avoid evil, hate, greed, wretchedness, and injustice. Life there was lived in one great brotherhood directed by the priests; here everyone shared the same benefits and the same duties, and the beating of a drum at night signaled that it was time for married couples to fulfill their conjugal duties.

All this reveals the consciousness of belonging to a different world, in which it was not just possible but necessary to attempt a new and different chapter in the history of man on earth. They knew they would not be able to maintain their indigenous civilizations—which in many ways, nonetheless, belonged to them and remained alive inside them—but they were also convinced that they could not create a New Spain, a mimetic and almost exact overseas extension of Castile. Spanish people, *indios*, and black people had contributed elements that were incorporated into their life and their character: the combination was sometimes contradictory, but always fertile.

They often felt tormented by the anguish of wondering what they were, or of endeavoring to be what they could not be. At the moment of the heroic fight for independence they invoked Atahualpa and Cuauctémoc as their forefathers, to buttress support for their rights, but at the same time they asserted that the Mayan and Aztec myth of the plumed serpent was nothing more than a blurry memory of the miraculous arrival of Saint Thomas the Apostle in America in the times of Claudius or Nero, and they claimed as title Charles V's old certificates and the treatises of the Spanish theologians. Bolívar himself, a supremely significant actor in Latin American history, observed the larger implications of the situation and would come to say: "We are not Europeans . . . we are not *indios*. . . . We are a small, human genus."

This condition of being a compound, a mixture—the product of the meeting of cultures and societies separated by history—in one of the most powerful and varied geographic landscapes, was what created and allowed for an explanation of the originality of this possible New World.

They were *mestizos* [of mixed race], but they did not dare to recognize it. When they began to examine their past, the word *mestizo* designated solely those beings of mixed blood, those hybrid products of different and even opposing races, those who descended from the genetic mixture of whites, *indios*, and blacks. It was a disgraceful and even slanderous word in the context of the predominance of racist beliefs in nineteenth-century Europe, when one still spoke of pure Aryans, of the superiority of whites, and even the superiority of Anglo-Saxons. No one wanted to be classified as *mestizo*. But the truth was that the color of one's skin had little to do with the powerful creative processes of *mestizaje*. In any case, that was not nor has it ever been inherent to those processes, nor is it less fundamental. There was *mestizaje* in European history between peoples of white races who were from different civilizations. Because what is truly important and creative about the process of *mestizaje* exists in the encounter and mixing of different cultures.

Those Gothic, Frankish, or Lombard tribes who invaded the decadent space of the Roman Empire unleashed an immense and dark process of intermingling in which their languages, their institutions, their beliefs, and their customs mixed with those of the Romans in order to give birth to other, different things: the church, the languages and the political structures of the West. From corrupted Latin, from the imitations of Caesarian majesty, from the mixture of the *corpus juris* and barbarian customs they created the civilization that would dominate Europe and the world until the present day. The entirety of that rich development constitutes a prodigious example of cultural *mestizaje*.

Latin America has been the site of this extraordinary process of *mestizaje* throughout its existence, from the time of Columbus until the present day. Its fundamental characteristics, its originality and its destiny are determined by this great fact, even in those cases where there are no traces—or it seems there aren't any—of the mixing of bloodlines, even in those regions where one might claim that a certain racial homogeneity exists, whether we are talking about the city of Montevideo or the town of Pisac in the Peruvian sierra.

That situation, and the tendency toward creative mixing of cultures and influences, is present in the greatest and most original Latin American works and devotions, whether painting from Cuzco or Rubén Darío's poetry.

Rubén Darío's case, like those of all the great figures who were part of the so-called Literary Modernism that he spearheaded, constitutes one of the best examples of cultural *mestizaje* and the destiny of the New World. He could manage to deceive himself and believe that he was a faithful follower of French poetry written by Parnassians and Symbolists. But he was not. He was a marvelous creator of poetry that contained the elements of cultural *mestizaje*, of which his work was both product and expression. Perhaps unconsciously, he used elements of the popular poetry of his land and forgotten forms of Spanish literature from the Golden Age, alongside French models provided by [Paul] Verlaine.

More than a few people have thought that Latin American art is what is known as baroque art. That in its ornamental, complicated, exasperatingly decorative, and labyrinthine tendencies this style came to express Latin American uniqueness better than any other. This is possible, but it is not quite the truth. Rather, the truth might be that the characteristics of the baroque, as they were known via European art, came to coincide astonishingly with certain characteristics of the Latin American sensibility and reality, because the baroque is the artistic style perhaps best suited to allow the process of cultural *mestizaje* its fullest expression and development.

This element of mixing, of impurity, of commingling and union of different eras and heterogeneous tendencies—which is nothing other than the creative characteristic of cultural *mestizaje*—is present in all of the great originary moments in Latin America.

The great works of the Mexican muralists demonstrate this with total clarity. At a moment when painting al fresco was seen in the West as a relic of the remotest artistic past, and when language and visual subjects were disintegrated and reconstituted in the explorations of Cubism, one man who managed to escape that critical yet fertile moment in European painting, Diego Rivera, rediscovered Mexico—its drama, its people, its hunger for expression and affirmation. He set to work covering enormous walls, in a form that was perhaps anachronistic for Europe at the time—as if he were giving new life to Simone Martini's condottieres in fourteenth-century Siena, or Orcagna's passion for death in the Pisa cemetery, or the candid themes of good and bad government that Ambrogio Lorenzetti had painted five hundred years earlier—in order to find a way to narrate to the Mexican people their tragedy and their greatness in the most immediately contemporary images.

Without question, the possibility that Latin America might come to be a New World resides principally in its calling and in its destiny of cultural *mestizaje*. It resides in repeating now, by means of the extraordinary conditions of its formation, the experiment in fertile encounter and synthesis of cultures that all great peoples in history have undertaken. That is how the Greeks and the Romans became what they were. And that is how, in more recent times, the countries of Western Europe became what they are, through a long and magnificent process in which the Germanic, the Roman, the Christian, the Greek, the Byzantine, and the Arab were mixed and combined.

Instead of being ashamed of its *mestizaje*, Latin America should recognize in that unique condition the most powerful foundation of its originality and of the great synthesizing role it is called to fulfill in the immediate future.

This, to summarize, is nothing other than to accept and to recognize the marvelous enterprise that was established and promised from the time of Columbus's arrival: to make a New World—that is, a new epoch and a new way for the civilization of man.

—"El mestizaje creador," in *No somos un subcontinente: La otra América* (Madrid: Alianza, 1974), pp. 21–27.
Translated by Jen Hofer

three eras in caracas **carlos raúl villanueva**

(Introduction)

To the living memory of Diego Nucete Sardi,[1] who fought enthusiastically for the betterment of Caracas, and whose dynamism and good will resulted in the felicitous creation of the El Silencio project.

Among the cities of America, Caracas is singularly important as the birthplace of Simón Bolívar, El Libertador; of Francisco de Miranda, the precursor of independence; and of the great scholar Andrés Bello. The city was founded in the year 1567 by Diego de Losada, on a charming and blessed site with a healthy climate, and given the name Santiago de León de Caracas. It is located 922 meters above sea level, not too far from the ocean, in a smiling valley of the Cordillera de la Costa mountain range; it reaches from the foothills of the Ávila to the Guaire River, and possesses one of the most original topographies in the world.

The city was constructed in the narrowest part of the valley, at the intersection of two roads: one leading to the maritime port of La Guaira,[2] and the other leading to Los Teques gold mines.[3] [Alexander von] Humboldt lamented that the city was not founded more to the west, "where the valley widens, on the Chacao side, onto an expansive plain that seems almost flattened by the permanent presence of the waters"; today the new city extends into this area. At that time, Caracas was a large village surrounded by vast savannahs and cultivated fields, without suburbs, its outlines demarcated by the modes of transit of the era—the horse and the mule—and bordered by the abundant waters of multiple rivers.

The original design of the city—a legacy and lesson drawn from the Spanish, an example of order and organization—was like a chessboard, characterized by straight perpendicular streets, with a main plaza situated in the center of the composition. This was the type of design established by the "Leyes de Indias" [Laws of the Indies],[4] common to all Hispano-American urban spaces. We would do well to recall here the importance of the instructions these laws contained: indeed, these were excellent rules and regulations full of good sense and clarity, which might still serve as a model in our times. Two causes of development influenced the growth of the city during this era; one was political:

the shift of the provincial capital, which was originally in Coro and moved to Caracas during the sixteenth century; the other was economic: the prosperity that reigned during the eighteenth century when agriculture was flourishing, due largely to the famous Compañía Guipuzcoana,[5] established in 1730.

Caraqueños would meet in the Plaza Mayor—later called Plaza de la Catedral and finally Plaza Bolívar—which was the political and administrative nucleus of the city. This was the plaza where justice was imparted, military and religious festivals were celebrated, and the market was situated. Government buildings, such as the Casas del Cabildo [town-council hall], the barracks, and the royal prison, were constructed around the plaza. It was here, too, that the most symbolically significant church of the era was built: the cathedral, with a façade that was nothing other than an enlarged altarpiece, originally with an elegant three-part tower. The cathedral was built around 1665, on the site where a humble adobe church with a palm-thatched roof had been primitively constructed previously. In areas near this vital center, other churches were built as well, near the convents, following designs identical to those used for some Spanish or American churches. Some of these, facing small plazas, like that of San Pablo or Candelaria, were organized into parishes, vital hubs of the neighborhoods of the time; others, like the churches at San Francisco, Altagracia, or San Jacinto, were set back from the facing walls, leaving a space or atrium that would later be absorbed by the expansion of the adjacent streets.

The city's basic component, the living space, was established around these vital centers and with them formed the body of Caracas. At that time, families—the fundamental organ and building-block of the era—lived in simple, humble houses that were spacious enough to fill the greater part of each city block. These houses were built out of materials native to the region, which were culled from the earth—mud or adobe—and were usually one story high. The slightly sloping roofs were covered with traditional Spanish tile, attached with functional materials like mangrove beams and spiral ginger, sometimes with triangular roof supports of exposed wood. Crowning the smooth façades, classic cornices made of heavy masonry molding or tiled eaves fastened to wood planks and brackets created ingenious plays of light and shadow. The façade consisted of a main door at the entranceway and high, latticed windows at regular intervals; these were well-proportioned, with shutters to protect the interior from the intensity of the light. Some of the entries were designed simply in stone brought from El Ávila, while others were built of brick and lime, their tops ingenuously finished with touches reminiscent of rococo or "Churrigueresque"[6] exuberance. A rich polychromy gave singular power to this architecture: the red of the tiles and the yellowish ochre or pink tint of the smooth façade created a contrast with the white of the entrance gate or the green or indigo of the doors and windows.

The design of the houses, inherited from the Greeks and Romans, was brought by architects from the south of Spain and represented a Mediterranean style, with a familiar sequence of patios with bedrooms arrayed around them, all adapted to the customs and traditions of the era. The carriage entrance constituted a transitional space between the bustle of the street and the tranquility necessary for family life. The main patio, constructed between

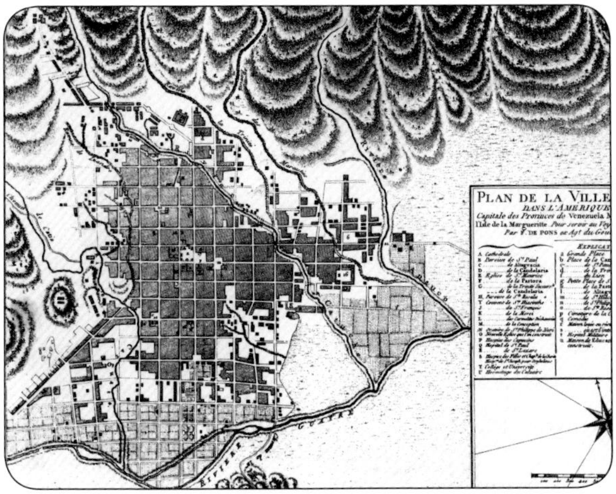

Plan of the city of Caracas by Francisco Depons. 1806. Archivos Fundación Villanueva, Caracas

depressed arches resting upon Tuscan-style or squat pillars, with portico walls painted at the bottom with bright colors in imitation of dazzling Spanish tile work, formed the distribution center around which were arranged the main rooms, designated as the anteroom, dining room, and bedrooms, and adorned with plants and trees growing in the dirt borders that framed the romantic fountain. Other, smaller patios led out from the first, all intelligently distributed in an order that allowed for proper ventilation; at the very end were the servants' quarters. In the back, gardens and orchards of all types were cultivated. Those immense green spaces that came together at the center of each city block almost in opposition to the cobblestone streets, which were wide for the traffic of the time, gave the city a certain gardenlike quality, just as in the very human-scale cities of the Middle Ages.

It was unquestionably during the eighteenth century that the colonial city achieved full equilibrium and perfected its most vital institutions. Caracas, head of a simple general captaincy during the time of the colony, was transformed overnight due to Venezuelan petroleum wealth, and became a vital command post as the capital of one of the richest countries in America.

Unfortunately, beginning at the end of the last century, the finely woven checkerboard pattern of the colonial city was allowed to expand infinitely, without at any moment taking into account the topography of the valley or changes to the systems of transit: the plazas thus lost their function as central forums. The family unit, too, began to lose its vitality. City blocks fragmented; in the areas originally destined to be gardens and orchards, houses were built and in turn divided into smaller units and long narrow lots; patios were reduced in size; and city blocks lost the vast green spaces they once had as their center.

Years passed and Caracas continued to expand rapidly, like an oil stain, into all corners of the valley, without order and without clearly defined principles. It is now not a city, precisely, but rather an entity formed by distinct molecules; it is the dislocation of the urban center: within a short time the colonial city literally exploded.

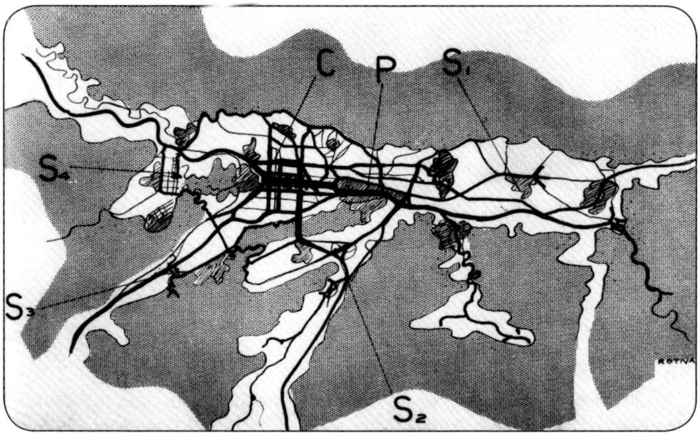

Draft of the master plan for Caracas by Maurice E. H. Rotival. 1939. Archivos Fundación Villanueva, Caracas

In 1937, based on its realization that the city had lost its equilibrium, the government[7] created a commission on urbanism in the capital. This commission was made up of Venezuelan architects, and its mission was to seek logical solutions to all these vital problems. This step was followed by the nomination of a group of French urbanists as advisors; among them was Maurice E. H. Rotival, who presided over the studies for a regulating design. The plan for regulation and development was approved in 1939 and anticipated, among other things, the promotion and conservation of the city's most vital features: as in the colonial era, the concentration of similar elements through the formation of different zones; studies of residential areas based on community housing projects; a new and rational distribution of green spaces and areas for play and relaxation; a new road plan based on a new design.

In 1942 the first step was taken with El Silencio.

The El Silencio neighborhood, one of the oldest in the capital, had begun to pose a danger to public health and public morals. Located at the intersection of two main access roads into the city, it was impeding the flow of traffic due to its labyrinth of narrow alleys affixed to the flanks of El Calvario hill, swarming with a rowdy population confined in unsanitary living spaces. The governing urban design had made this neighborhood the starting point of an entire modern urban system, the central avenue of which was dedicated to El Libertador, Simón Bolívar. But it was necessary to undertake the total reurbanization of the area, despite the considerable technical difficulties presented by a deep ravine located in the very middle of the unsanitary islet, and the usual opposition of some of the landowners, who were often against even the most minor change due to the interests involved.

Nonetheless, demolition began in the area on January 4, 1943, with the groundbreaking blow of the pick made as a ceremonial act by General Isaías Medina Angarita, president of the republic at that time; from then on, initially with the support of the press and later with that of unanimous public opinion, he did not for a moment cease to move forward with building projects. The operation was directed with mastery and enormous economic competence by Diego Nucete Sardi, director of the Banco Obrero, a nationally administrated institution; it was finished by Carlos Luis Ferrero, who succeeded him at that post. The job of project director was given to Carlos Blaschitz, a technician and administrator, and to the Banco Obrero's technical services team, which had already provided proof of its efficient construction skills when it built various workers' cities. This local company, organized in groupings delineated by the successive segments of work to be done, knew just how to position itself so as to be equal to this immense task, which was made easier—it must be emphasized—by the professional conscience and eagerness of innumerable Venezuelan workmen, artisans, foremen, and master builders.

I believe it may be useful at this point for me to outline the principle of the general design with which the national government entrusted me. First and foremost, I set myself the task of conceiving a solution that would make use of the central axis of the city, which would in the future be demarcated as the Avenida Simón Bolívar. The design balanced upon this axis culminates in a plaza where the arrangement of streets was imposed by the urban layout, at the convergence of the principal avenues leading into the city from the west.

The neighborhood was situated at the very heart of the city; the solution thus had to be essentially urban. It was necessary to locate open spaces not by creating flexible designs, as in the outskirts of the cities, but rather within rigidly graphed squares inside of which the axes of the streets would cut the space into distinctly defined sectors. Beginning from this division into independent sectors, I have sought to locate, around one central point—the patio—the first modern configuration of human activities that Gaston Bardet calls "the domestic stepping-stone." This is comprised of the first cooperative consisting of 50 to 150 families, units that should bring together their human activities and common interests: parks for children, stores, restaurants, laundries, etc.

The Calvario park, situated at the very center of the composition, serves as the natural park for a group of seven blocks that almost compose a "housing complex" of which one element, Block 1, has already been defined as a shopping and business center. It is easy to understand that in this case it would be impossible to conceive of a "housing complex" separated from other equivalent complexes by green spaces, since we are in the middle of the city. This is the initiation of a composition that should link El Silencio, via the new Avenida Bolívar, to forthcoming areas of the city and that will eventually constitute the entirety of the urban organism.

With regard to what should rightly be called the "style," I considered it necessary to establish some connection with the colonial city, which is losing its typical antiquated character more and more each day, and to retain certain elements of its basic architecture. When I resolutely adopted the archway—perhaps unnecessary in Nordic countries where one requires greater illumination, but indispensable in a country that needs to protect itself from the violence of the sun and the rain—the primary elements of the design extended logically from these fundamental principles.

By contrast, the upper sections of the archways are constructed with the simplicity of the great smooth surfaces of our colonial era, which, in my opinion, should today be a signal feature of modern architecture; additionally,

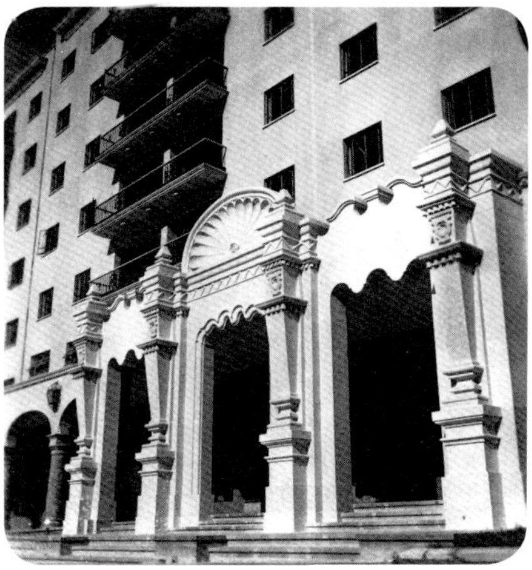

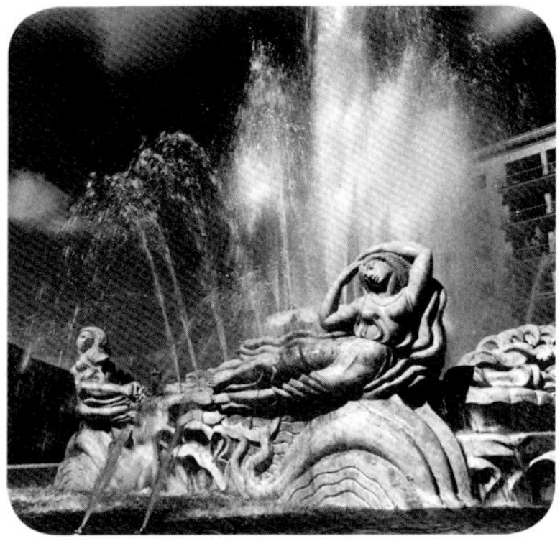

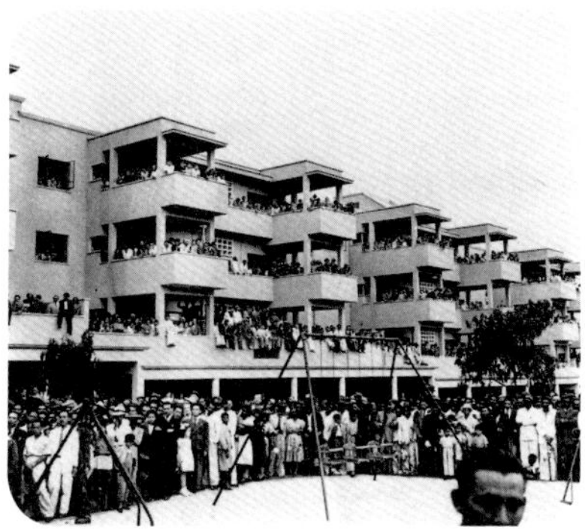

Above: Entryway to El Silencio. Photograph by Ricardo de Sola. 1945. Archivos Fundación Villanueva, Caracas

Above, right: Francisco Narváez's *Las toninas* (The river dolphins) fountain in El Silencio, Caracas. Photograph by Alfredo Boulton. c. 1945. Alberto Vollmer Foundation, Inc., Caracas

Right: The inauguration of Caracas's El Silencio complex. Photograph by Ricardo de Sola. 1944. Archivos Fundación Villanueva, Caracas

due to the similarity of their origins, they recall the formation processes of new colonial cities in North Africa, built under the masterful direction of Henri Prost. The original sculptures in the monumental fountains of the Plaza Urdaneta, by the Venezuelan sculptor Francisco Narváez, bear witness to the vigorous creative conceptual capacities of our America, capacities that have been felt with tremendous force over the course of these recent years.

Finally, the basic element of the design, that is to say, the living element that underlines the social aspect of its conception—the patio—has been considered freely, with a succession of terraces, true platforms where housewives work, from which they can be in communication with their children and their neighbors. These same patios recal some of the colonial patios that overflowed with life, with that Latin life that will be a distinguishing feature of our South American countries for a long time to come. [. . .]

—Introduction to the first edition of *Caracas en tres tiempos* (Caracas: Comisión de asuntos culturales del Cuatricentenario de Caracas, 1966).

Translated by Jen Hofer

This text has been abridged for the present volume.

editor's notes to the texts

martínez/ideas and aims: some words on the establishment of the circulo de bellas artes, pp. 94-96

1. Here Martínez is referring both to the civil wars that scarred Venezuela in the nineteenth century and to Cipriano Castro's regime, which ended in 1908. Like the majority of intellectuals of his time, Martínez saw the early years of Juan Vicente Gómez's dictatorship as a guarantee of progress and stability. The atmosphere would soon change and the dictatorship would reveal itself as a less than felicitous phenomenon.
2. The term *criollismo* is used here to describe the preoccupation in Latin American art with issues of national identity or types. *Trans.*
3. The desire to create an entirely autonomous art, the expression of an independent way of thinking, led many Latin American intellectuals to a naïve form of nationalism. This included the notion that "national" art can be made only by using the local landscape as one's subject; it went unacknowledged that in undertaking this type of work, the artist is unavoidably conscripted into a broad visual tradition that breaches national boundaries.

semprum/the círculo de bellas artes, pp. 96-98

1. This mandate of "producing beauty" illustrates the difference between Semprum's views and the nationalist position that Leoncio Martínez was defending. To produce beauty, and not to make national art, was Semprum's rallying cry. Thus the two lines of action that would mark the development of Venezuelan art throughout the twentieth century were clearly drawn.
2. Semprum's cosmopolitan openness is, in essence, exactly what would be criticized in Venezuelan abstract and kinetic artists from the 1950s to the 1970s.

landaeta/auto-da-fé, pp. 99-100

1. Leopoldo Lugones was an Argentine poet and essayist known for his glorification of nationalist values. He was initially associated with Socialist movements, but ended up supporting more nationalist and authoritarian political trends in his country in the first decades of the twentieth century. Landaeta was oriented, by contrast, toward a clear cosmopolitanism.
2. The Guaire is the river that crosses the Caracas Valley from west to east; the Río de la Plata is the river along the shores of which Buenos Aires developed.
3. Here, Landaeta may be echoing the well-known exchange between José María Vargas, president of Venezuela in 1835-36, and Pedro Carujo, a soldier of the so-called Revolución de las Reformas, waged against the Carujo government. Vargas was held prisoner for a time in his own home by Carujo, who famously said to the president, "Doctor Vargas, the world belongs to the brave," to which Vargas replied, "The world belongs to the just man."

letters from arturo úslar pietri to alfredo boulton, pp. 101-3

1. This work would be published as *Las lanzas coloradas* (*The Red Lances*) in 1931.
2. This was Úslar Pietri's first book of short stories, published in 1928.

gallegos/god's lands, pp. 103-7

1. Gallegos is referring here to the considerable weight that positivist ideas had in Venezuela at the time, particularly among the intellectuals surrounding the dictator Juan Vicente Gómez; Gallegos himself shared these ideas during his early career as a novelist. It was against these intellectuals that he launched a romantic defense of imagination and individualism, which in his understanding characterized the "tropical" psychology: "still, pure ostentatious fire."
2. This sentence and the following lines clearly illuminate the concept of the preeminence of the landscape in Venezuela and in Latin America: a landscape that was still virgin, not yet domesticated. This image of an untainted landscape is also found among the landscape artists of the Círculo de Bellas Artes, and later, even among abstract artists in the 1950s. It still persists today, when the fragility of the purportedly virgin forests and rivers is now obvious, even dramatically so.
3. Here Gallegos is referring to Juan Vicente Gómez.
4. Lucila de María del Perpetuo Socorro Godoy Alcayaga, known by her pen name Gabriela Mistral, was a Chilean poet and diplomat. She was awarded the Nobel Prize for Literature in 1945.
5. The author creates a wordplay here: *yaacabó* is the name of a bird, while the term *ya acabó* means "it's all over now." *Trans.*
6. The Arauca is a region in Apure state, located in the southwest of Venezuela.
7. A reference to Cipriano Castro.
8. Idem.
9. Here Gallegos is referring to Gómez.

10. Andrés Bello was a Venezuelan lawmaker, politician, and poet; he founded the Universidad de Chile in 1842.

boulton / venezuelan painting as international value, pp. 107 - 10

1. *L'art pompier* was a derisive term for the grand, allegorical work favored by the French Academy. The name derives from the similarity between old-fashioned French firemen's helmets and the helmets of the Roman soldiers often featured in such work. *Trans.*

boulton / brief notes on the fringes of venezuelan painting, pp. 111 - 14

1. Boulton is referring here to the end of the Gómez dictatorship, in December of 1935.
2. Federico Brandt was one of the few intimist painters of what is known as the Escuela de Caracas. His work is delicate in its execution; his depictions of interiors are almost systematically uninhabited.
3. The English translation of Gide's quotation is from André Gide, *Return from the U. S. S. R.*, trans. Dorothy Bussy (New York: Alfred A. Knopf, 1937).
4. Boulton is referring here to the efficiency of the work of Antonio Edmundo Monsanto as the head the Escuela de Bellas Artes y Aplicadas de Caracas.

picón salas / armando reverón, pp. 115 - 22

1. Alfredo Boulton was opposed to any sociological reading of the work of Reverón, believing that the value of painting resides in its "plastic" quality, rather than in social circumstances. Still, the particular vision of the country and its history that is seen in the work of Reverón is marked by the sort of distance – at once distrustful and full of admiration – that sometimes characterizes people who live at the margins of society, even though they may be immersed in it.
2. The author is referring to "el Castillete," the precarious residence built gradually by Reverón on the Venezuelan coast, on the nether side of El Ávila, in the district of Macuto.
3. Leopoldo Fregoli (1867 - 1936) was a famous Italian stage actor and quick-change artist.
4. Reverón was born in Valencia, in the north central region of Venezuela, west of Caracas.
5. José María Eguren was a Peruvian poet and photographer, author of *Simbólicas* (Symbolisms, 1911), and *Canción de las figuras* (Ballad of the figures, 1916).
6. That is, Simón Bolívar.
7. Nicolás Ferdinandov was a Russian painter who traveled to Venezuela at the beginning of the twentieth century. The symbolic and nocturnal dimensions of his work had a decisive influence on Reverón during the Venezuelan artist's youth.
8. Reverón and the author of this seminal essay established a close and abiding friendship. The artist presented Picón Salas with a significant example from his White period, the 1927 painting *Paisaje* (Landscape), which remains in the Picón Salas family's collection.

villanueva / three eras in caracas, pp. 127 - 32

1. Diego Nucete Sardi was a Venezuelan businessman and government official. As director of the Banco Obrero during Isaías Medina Angarita's regime he developed the financial plan for the El Silencio redevelopment project.
2. La Guaira is the port that serves Caracas and the country's central region.
3. Los Teques, a city located near Caracas in north-central Venezuela, is the capital of the state of Miranda. An important gold mine was located on the city's outskirts.
4. The "Leyes de Indias" was a collection of laws enacted by the Spanish monarchs to govern its colonies in the Americas. They originated in traditional Castilian law, which was expanded over time through capitulations (agreements established between the monarchs and the conquistadors), papal bulls, and certain forms of civic organization established by indigenous law, particularly those relating to *cacicazgo*, the code governing indigenous land possession, and *Ayllú*, the nucleus of Incan communal and tribal life.
5. The Real Compañía Guipuzcoana de Caracas was created in 1728 by a royal decree issued by King Felipe V and began operations in 1730. Its purpose was to guarantee exclusive trade relations between Spain and the province of Venezuela. The company functioned until 1781, mainly from the ports of the Guipúzcoa province in northern Spain.
6. "Churrigueresque": a general term used to describe certain manifestations of eighteenth-century Spanish Baroque architecture. This expression is derived from the last name of the Churriguera family of architects, whose work is recognized for its lavish and intricately detailed ornamentation.
7. That is, the government of General Eleazar López Contreras.

illustrations

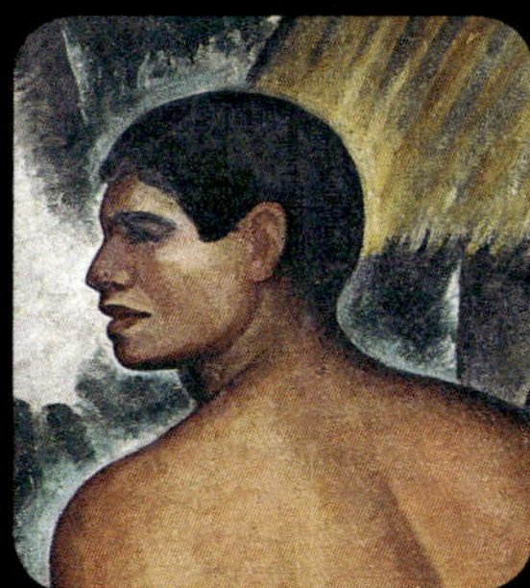
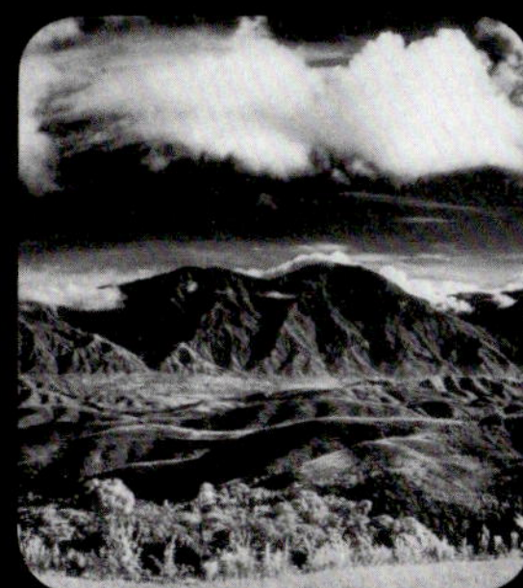
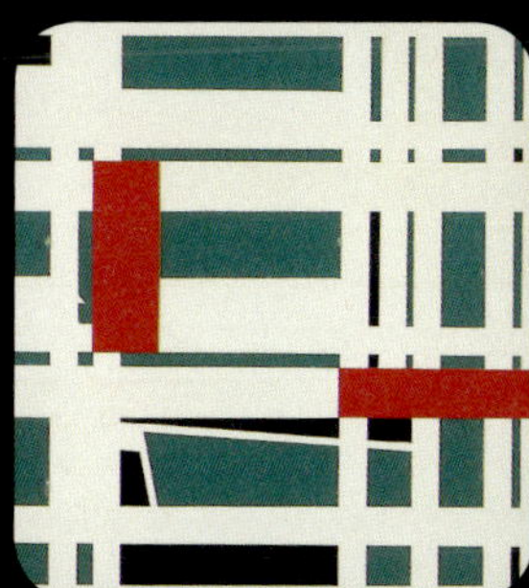
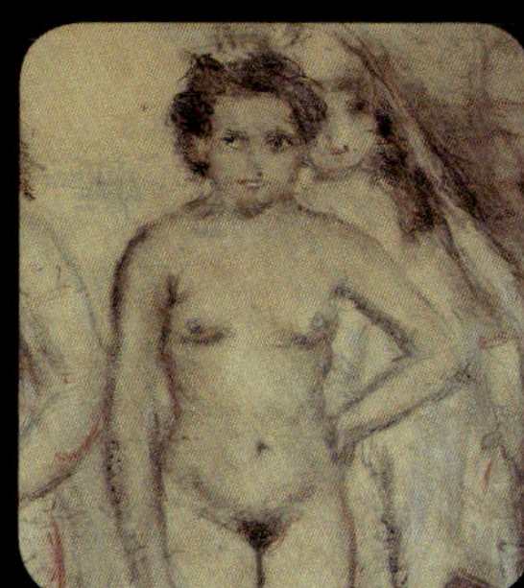
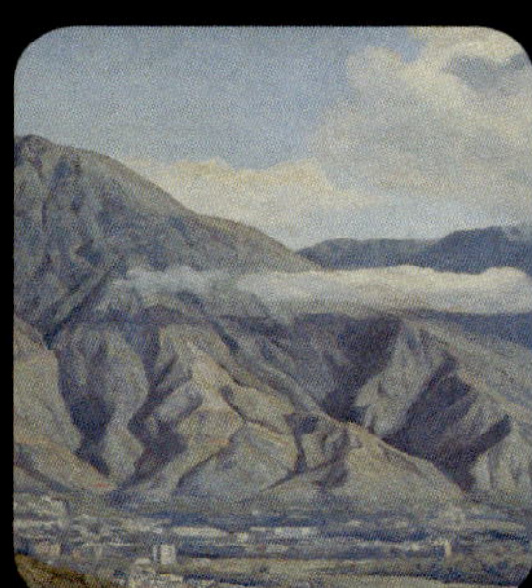
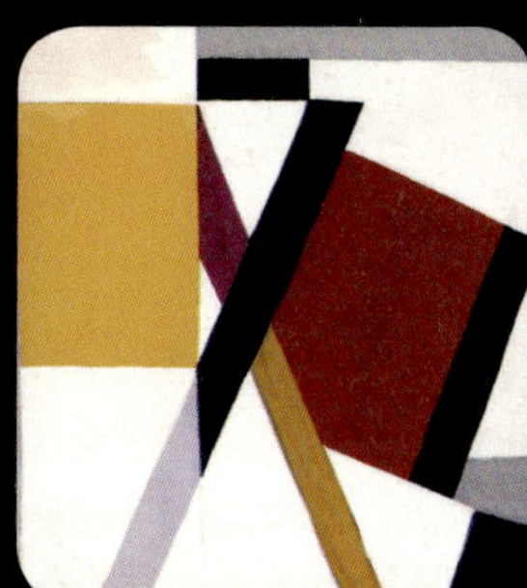

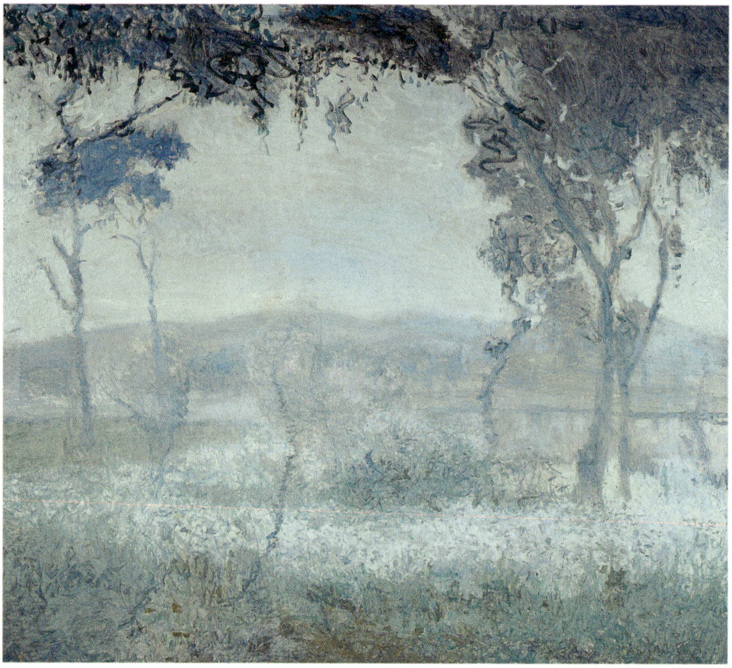

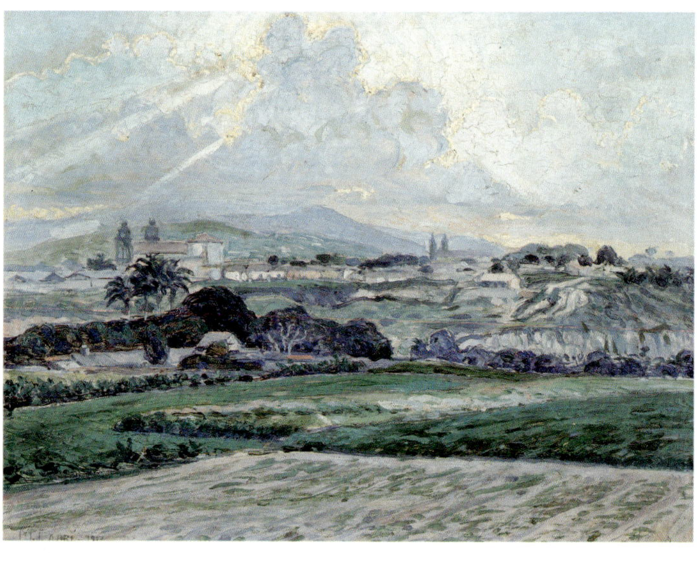

opposite, top: **armando reverón**
Paisaje (*Landscape*). 1922. Oil on canvas. 35 x 38 3/16" (89 x 97 cm). Private collection

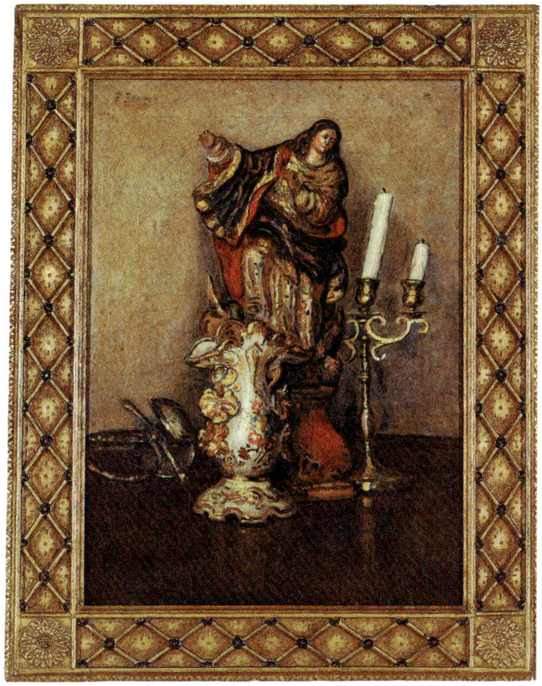

right, top: **federico brandt**
Naturaleza muerta con Virgen (Still life with Virgin). c. 1925. Oil on canvas. 23 5/8 x 15 3/4" (60 x 40 cm). Collection Fundación Museos Nacionales. Galería de Arte Nacional, Caracas

opposite, bottom: **manuel cabré**
Paisaje (*Landscape*). 1917. Oil on wood. 13 x 15 3/4" (33 x 40 cm). Collection Mercantil, Caracas

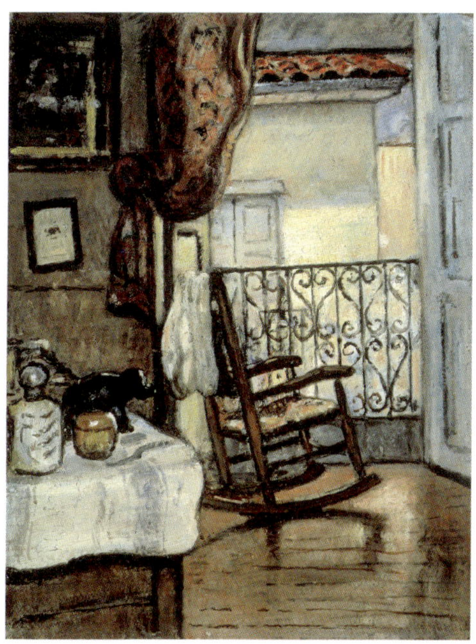

right, bottom: **federico brandt**
Interior con mecedora (Interior with rocking chair). c. 1931. Oil on Masonite. 18 11/16 x 13 7/8" (47.5 x 35.3 cm). Collection Fundación Museos Nacionales. Galería de Arte Nacional, Caracas

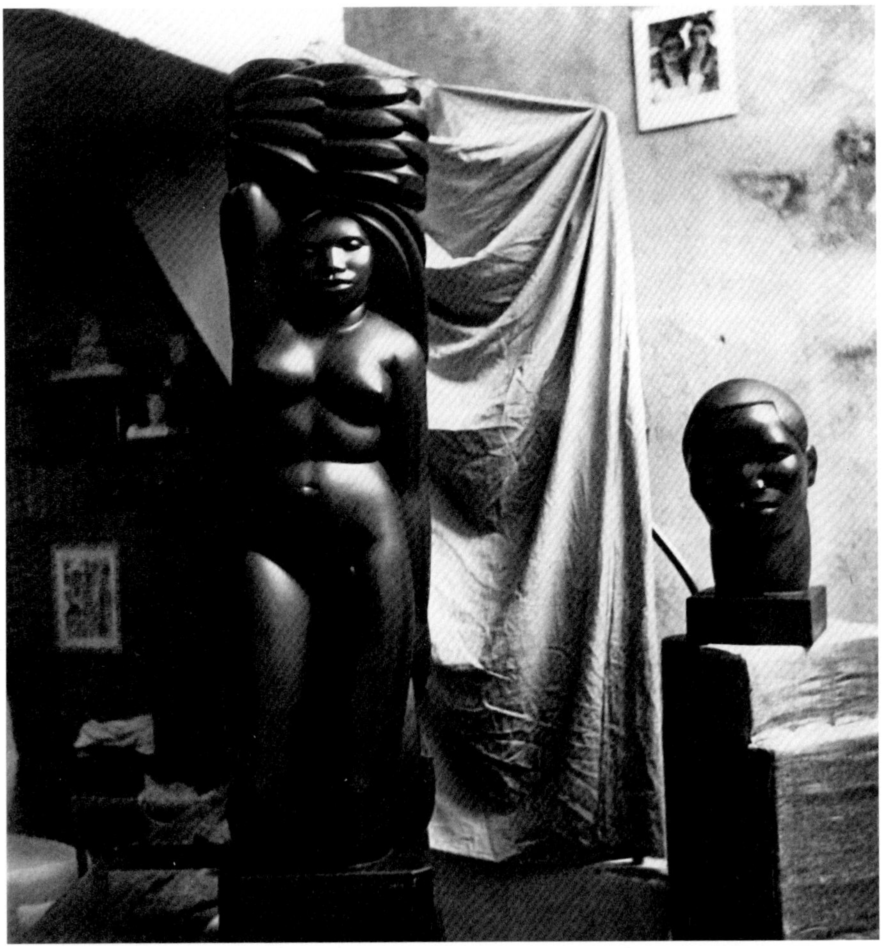

alfredo boulton
Desnudo con cambures
(Nude with bananas; sculpture by Francisco Narváez). 1933. Gelatin-silver print. 8 5/16 x 7 5/8" (21.2 x 19.4 cm). Alberto Vollmer Foundation, Inc., Caracas

francisco narváez
Bolas criollas (*Criollo* ball game). 1934. Oil on canvas. 9' 10 1/8" x 13' 2 1/4" x 1" (300 x 402 x 2.5 cm). Collection Patricia Phelps de Cisneros, Caracas

francisco narváez
Pelea de gallos (*Cockfight*). 1934. Oil on canvas. 9' 8 1/2" x 13' 2 1/4" x 1" (296 x 402 x 2.5 cm). Collection Patricia Phelps de Cisneros, Caracas

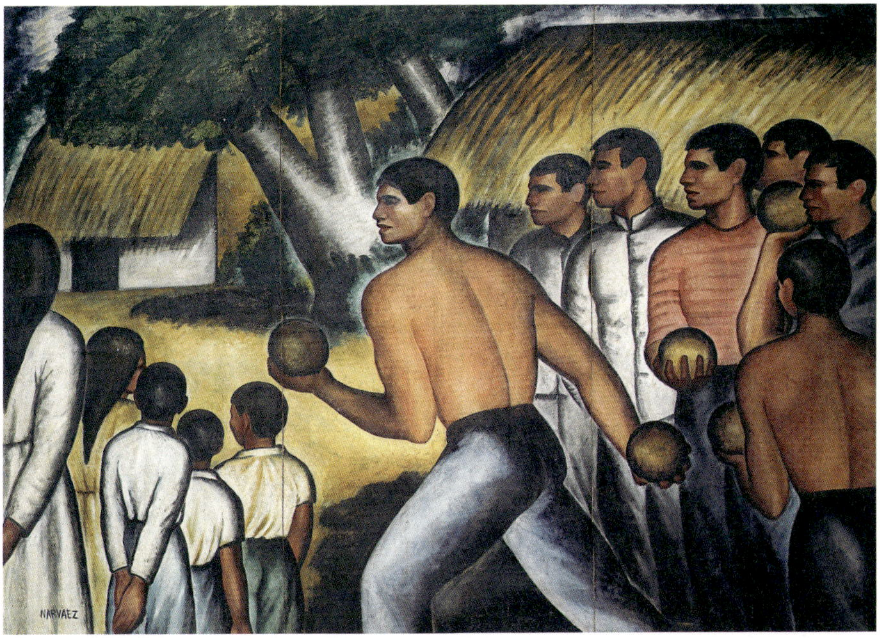
NARVAEZ

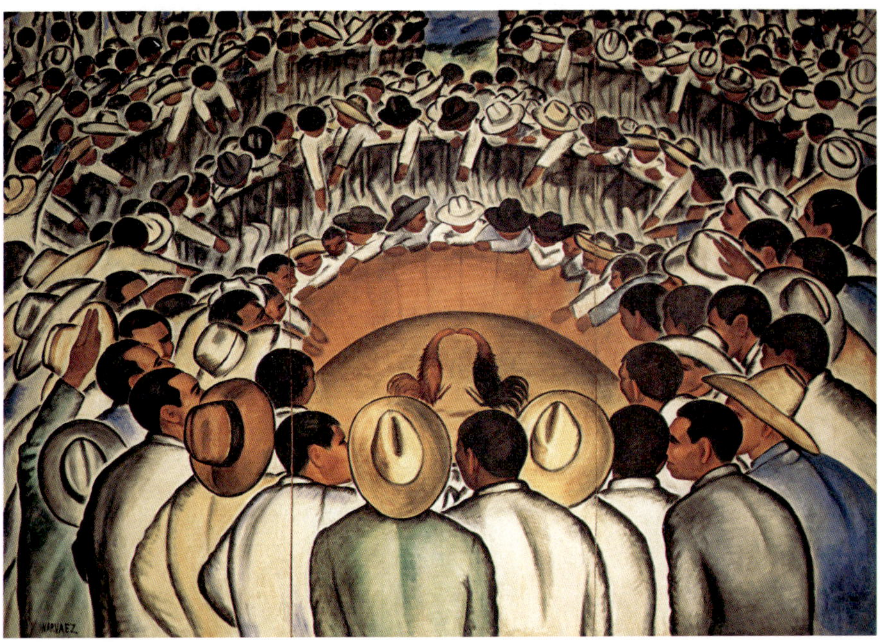
NARVAEZ

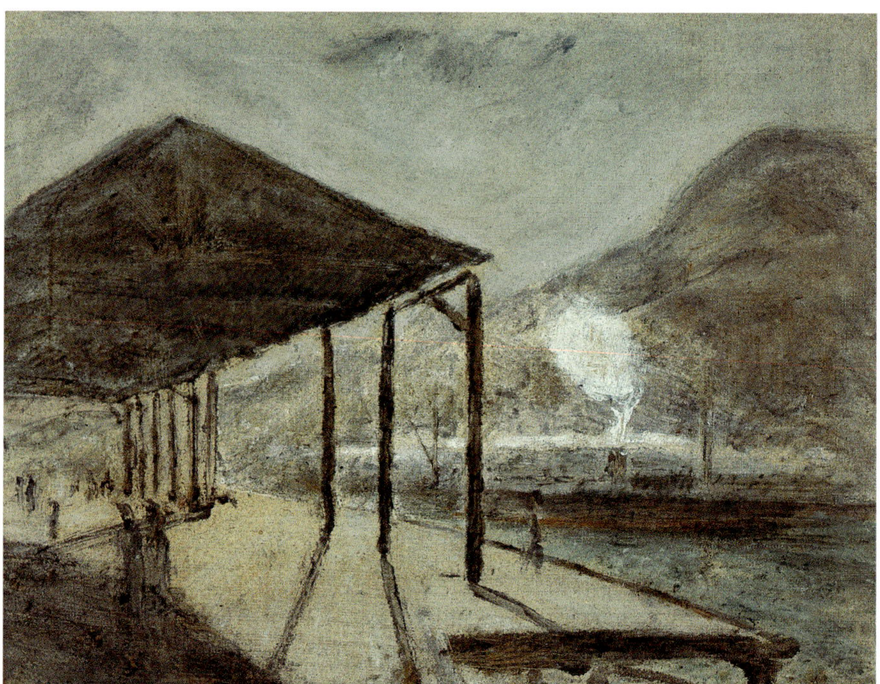

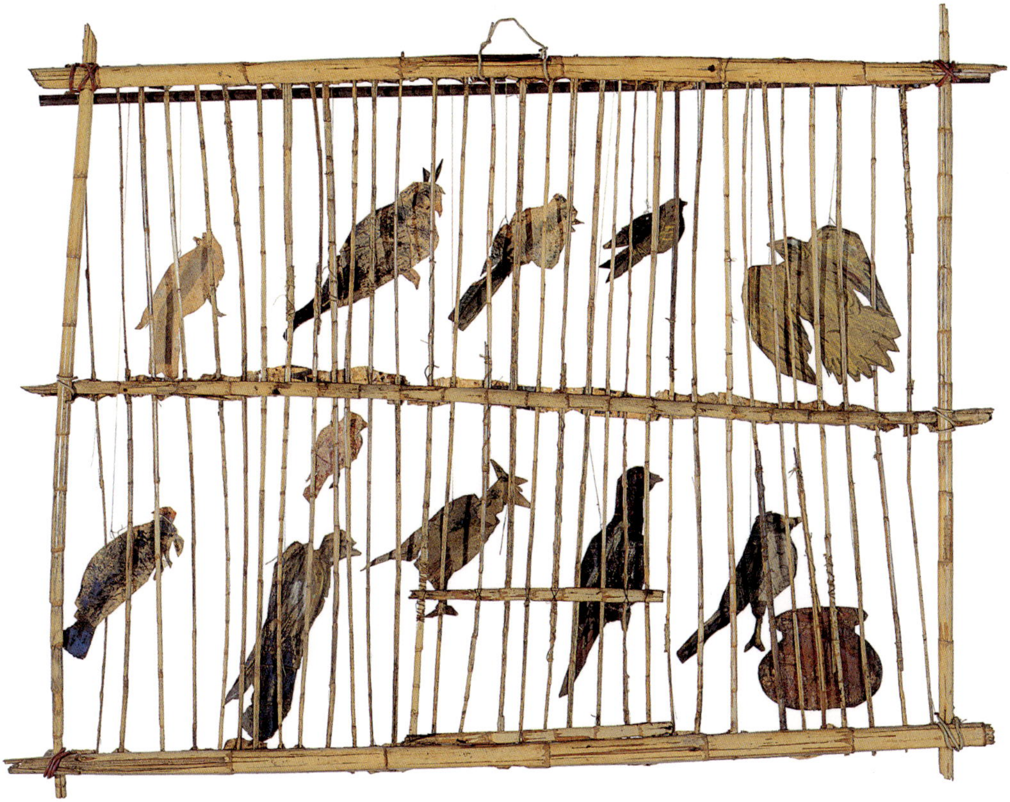

armando reverón
Pajarera (*Birdcage*). 1940s. Wood, wire, paper, and aluminum. 33 7/16 x 41 15/16 x 1 7/16" (85 x 106.5 x 3.6 cm). Collection Fundación Museos Nacionales. Galería de Arte Nacional, Caracas

armando reverón
Paisaje blanco (*White Landscape*). 1934. Oil on canvas. 24 3/8 x 31 1/2" (62 x 80 cm). Private collection

armando reverón
Puerto de La Guaira (*Port of La Guaira*). 1941. Oil and tempera on canvas. 25 5/8 x 31 7/8" (65 x 81 cm). Private collection

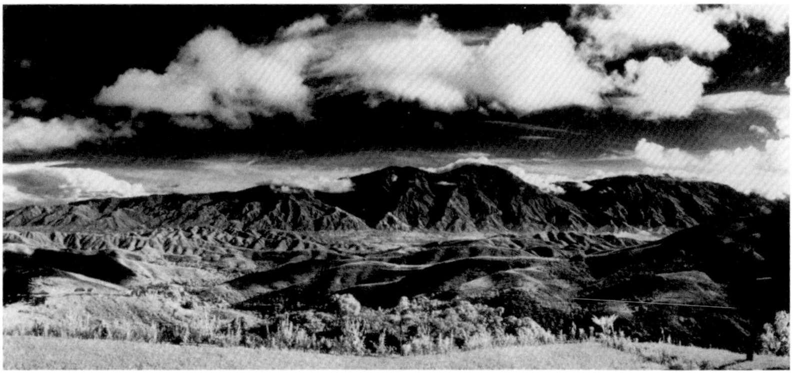

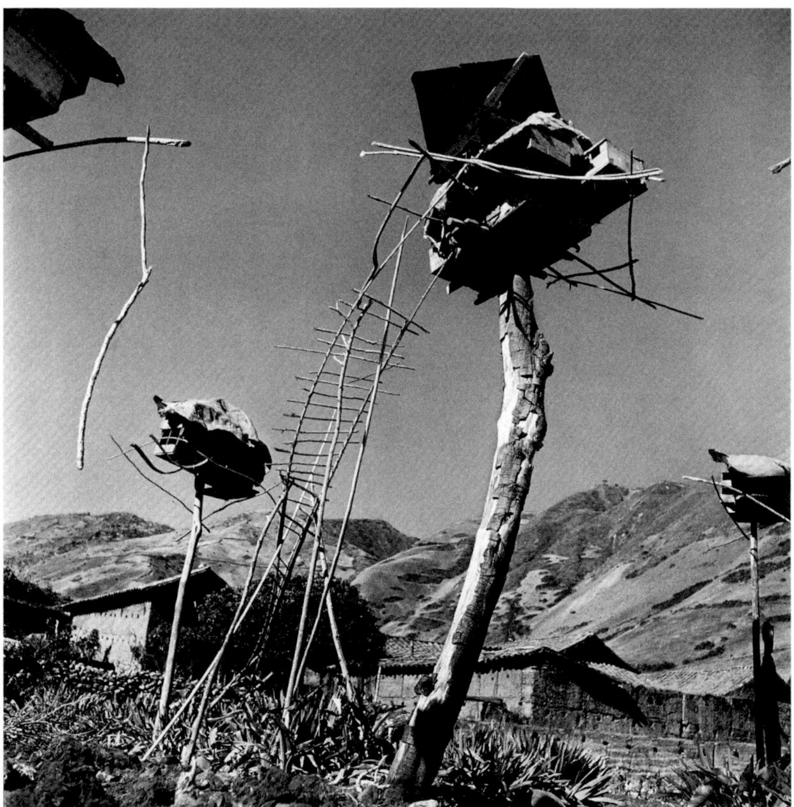

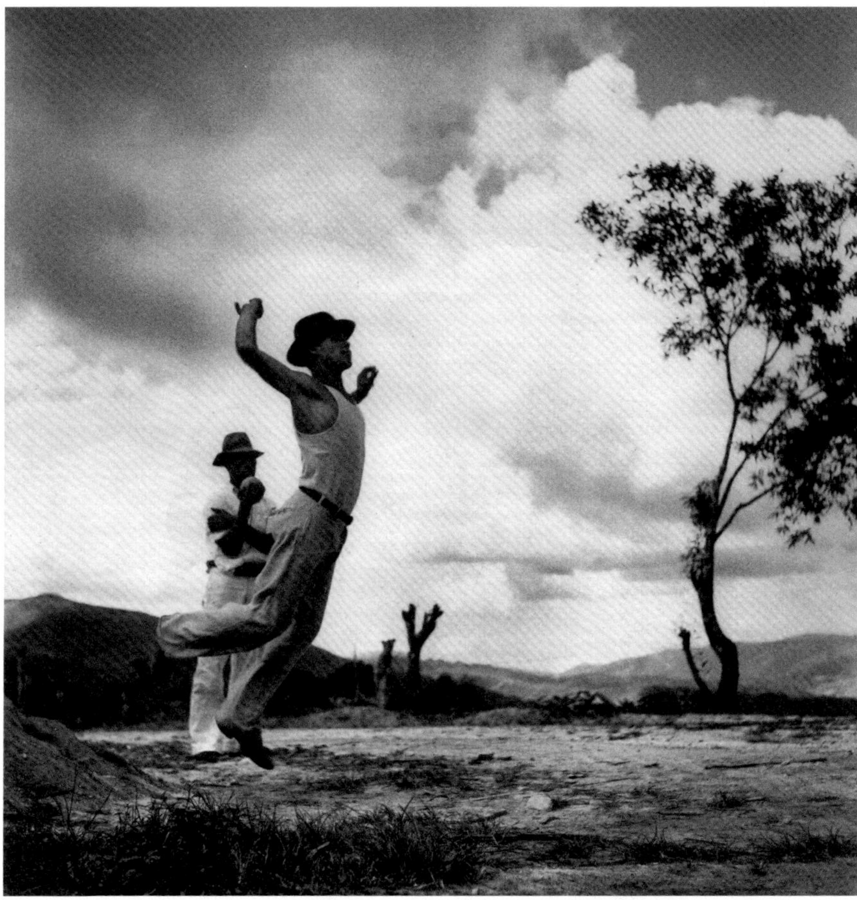

alfredo boulton
Eladio Montiel. c. 1944. Gelatin-silver print. 7 1/2 x 7 1/2" (19 x 19 cm). Alberto Vollmer Foundation, Inc., Caracas

alfredo boulton
Vista de El Ávila desde Los Guayabitos de mañana (El Ávila mountain seen from Los Guayabitos in the morning). c. 1943. Gelatin-silver print. 9 7/8 x 22 7/16" (25 x 57 cm). Alberto Vollmer Foundation, Inc., Caracas

alfredo boulton
Gallinero de Chachopo (Chicken coop in Chachopo). 1939. Gelatin-silver print. 12 1/8 x 11 3/4" (30.8 x 29.9 cm). Alberto Vollmer Foundation, Inc., Caracas

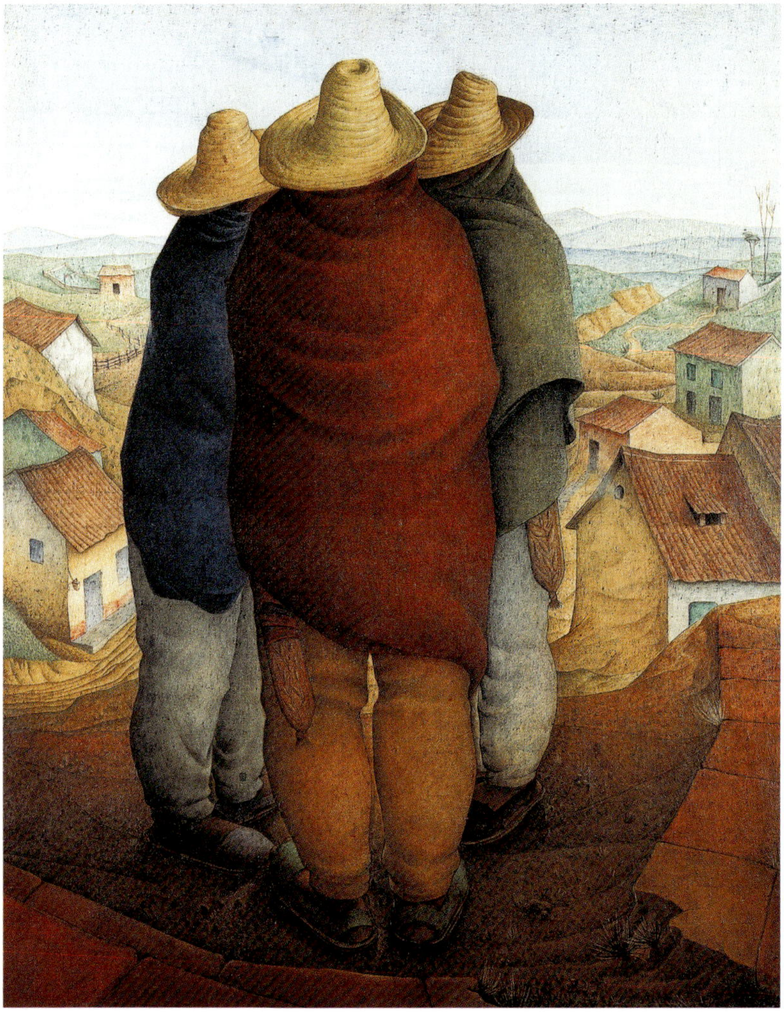

héctor poleo
Los tres comisarios (*The Three Bailiffs*). 1942. Oil on canvas. 35 7/16 x 27 9/16" (90 x 70 cm). Collection Fundación Museos Nacionales. Galería de Arte Nacional, Caracas

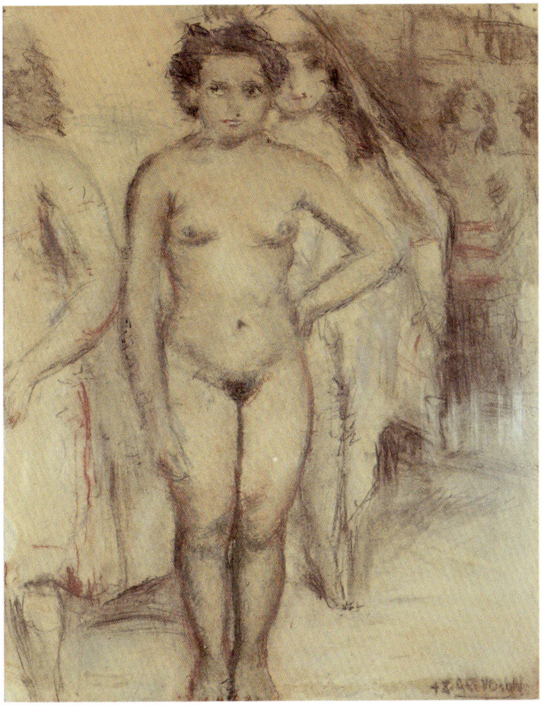

armando reverón
Figuras (*Female Figures*). 1948. Pastel and charcoal on paper, mounted on cardboard. 26 x 20 1/16" (66 x 51 cm). Collection Patricia Phelps de Cisneros, Caracas

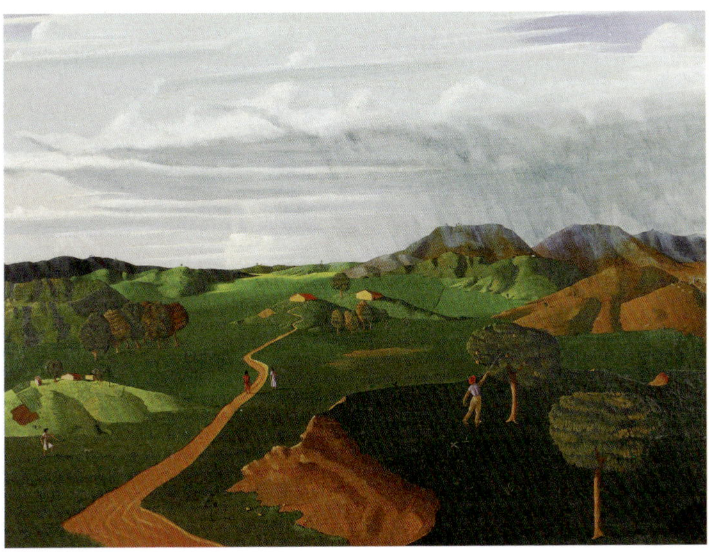

pedro león castro
Armonía (Harmony). 1947. Oil on canvas. 27 7/16 x 35 7/16" (69.7 x 90 cm). Collection Fundación Museos Nacionales. Galería de Arte Nacional, Caracas

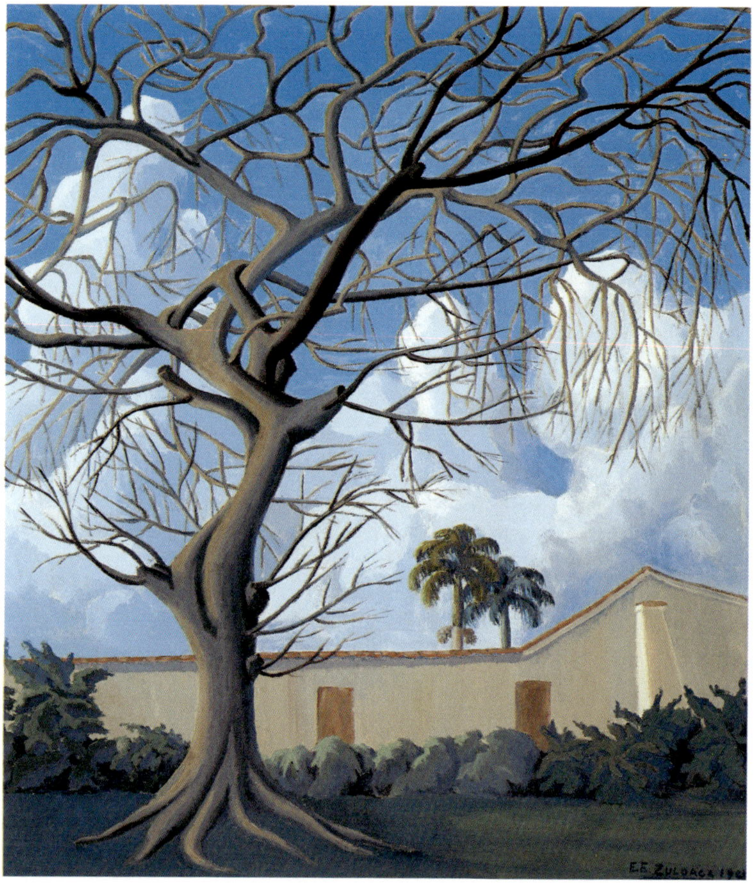

elisa elvira zuloaga
Higuerote. 1945. Oil on canvas. 21 x 17 13⁄16" (53.4 x 45.2 cm). Collection Fundación Museos Nacionales. Galería de Arte Nacional, Caracas

manuel cabré
El Ávila (la silla) desde La Urbina (El Ávila mountain [the "saddle"] seen from La Urbina). 1955. Oil on canvas. 44 5⁄16 x 50 5⁄8" (112.6 x 128.6 cm). Comodato Banco Nacional de Descuento (BND). Museo de Arte Contemporáneo de Caracas, Caracas

pedro ángel gonzález
Desde una colina del sur (From a southern hill). 1957. Oil on canvas. 32 x 49" (81.3 x 124.5 cm). Collection Fundación Museos Nacionales. Galería de Arte Nacional, Caracas

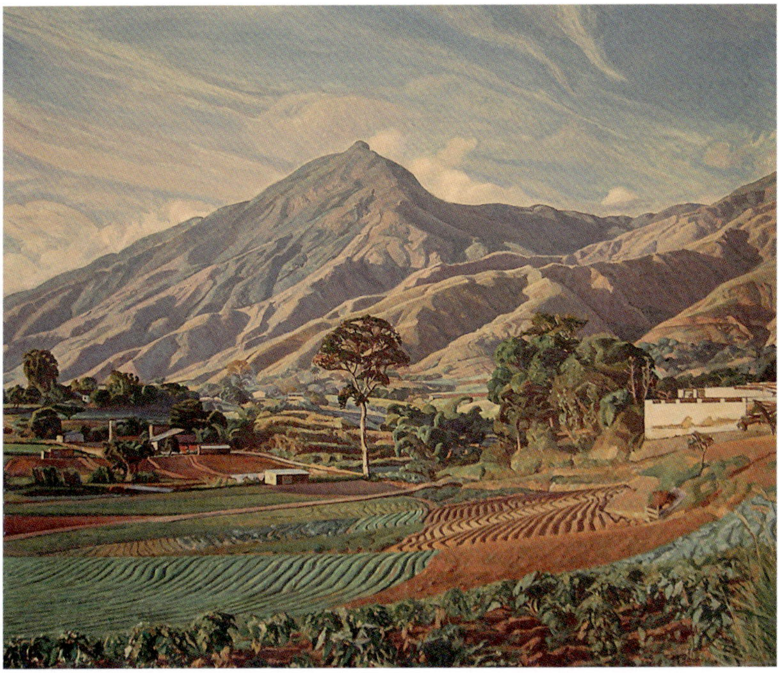

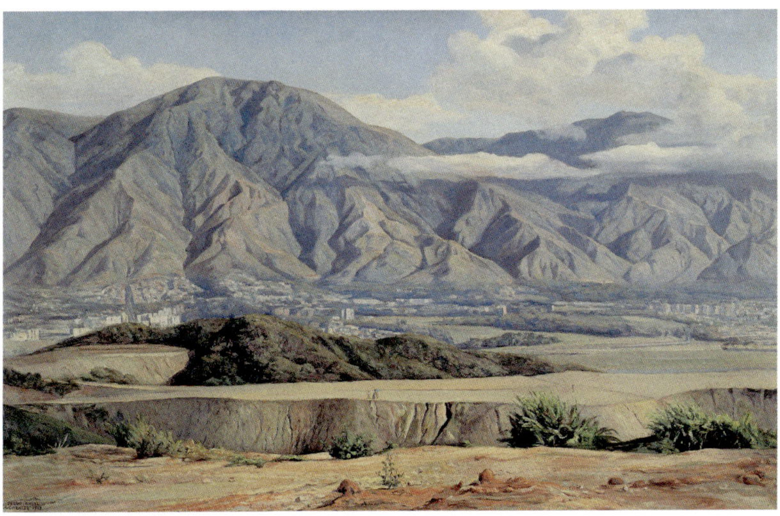

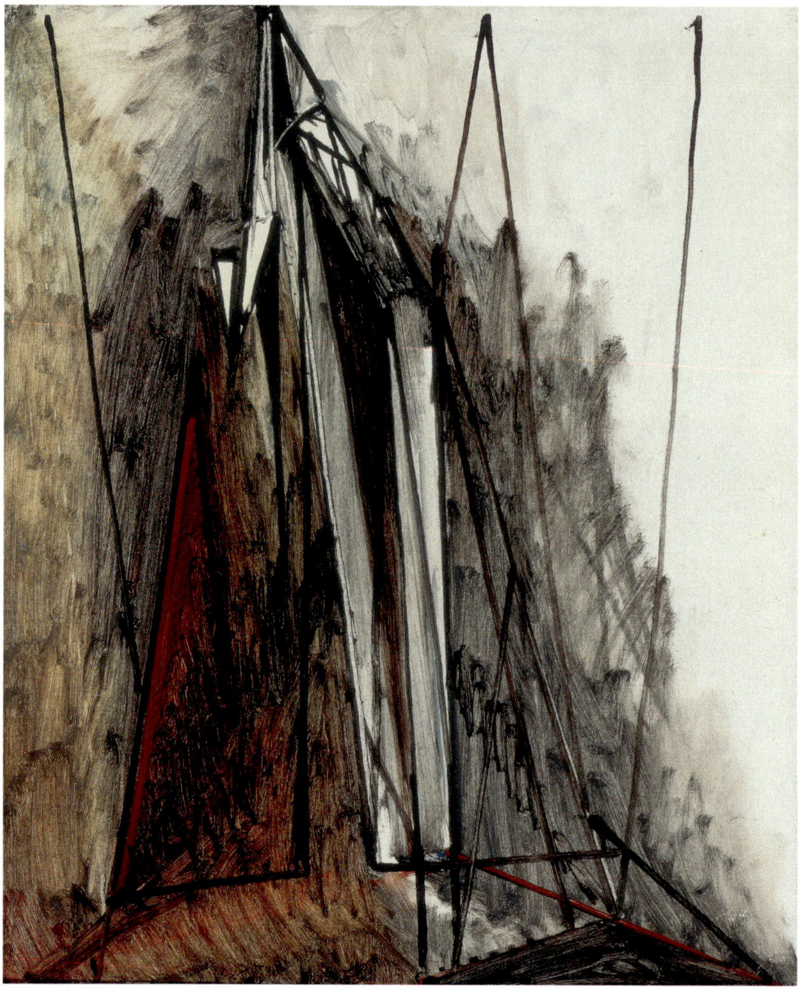

alejandro otero
El pote blanco y la pala marrón (*The White Pot and the Maroon Shovel*). 1947. Oil on canvas. 32 1/8 x 25 5/8" (81.5 x 65 cm). Private collection

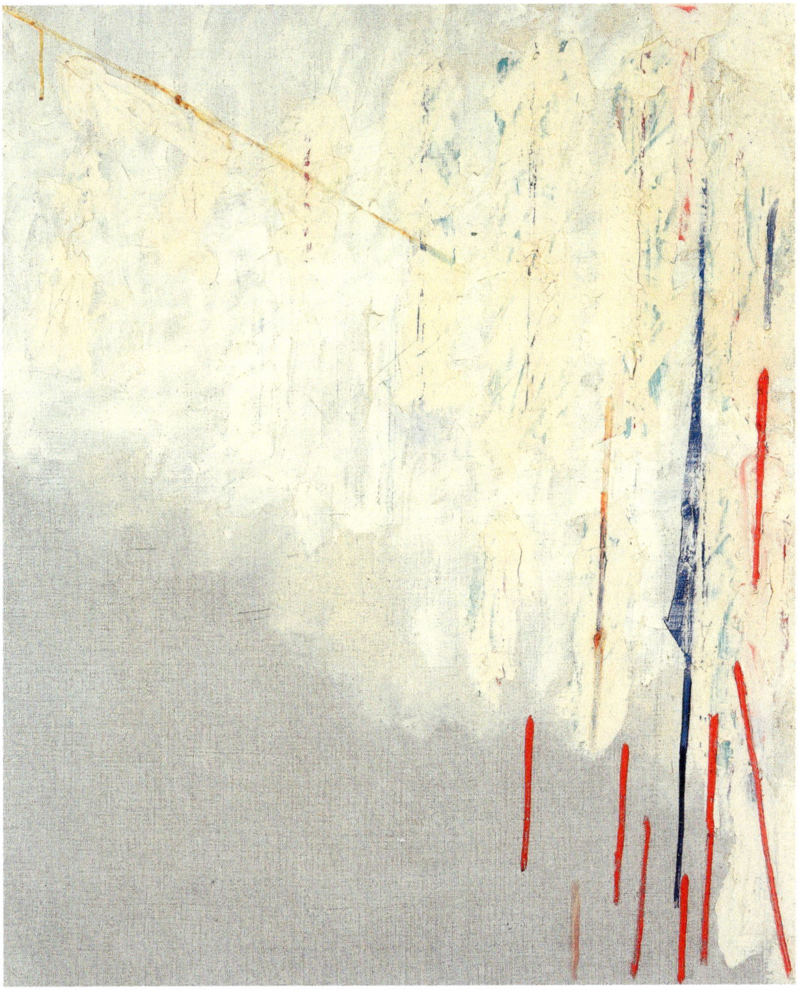

alejandro otero
Líneas coloreadas sobre fondo blanco II (Colored Lines on White Background II). 1951. Oil on canvas. 31 3/4 x 25 5/8" (80.7 x 65 cm). Collection Ignacio and Valentina Oberto, Caracas

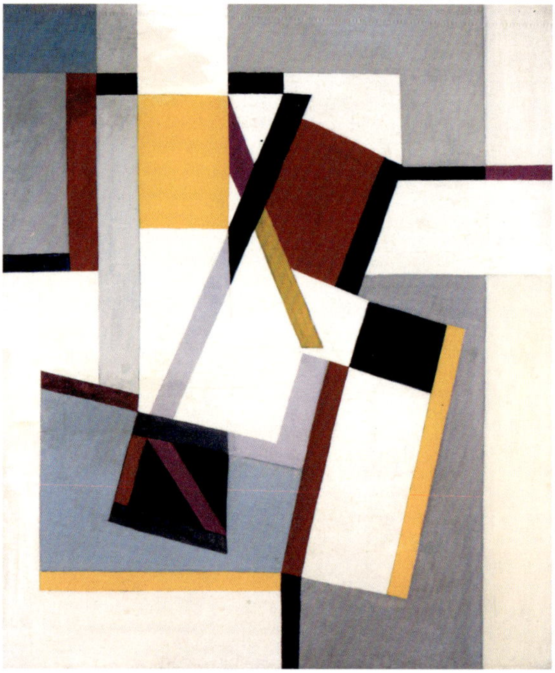

luis guevara moreno
Untitled. 1950. Oil on canvas.
31 1/16 x 25 3/8" (79 x 64.4 cm).
Collection Mercantil, Caracas

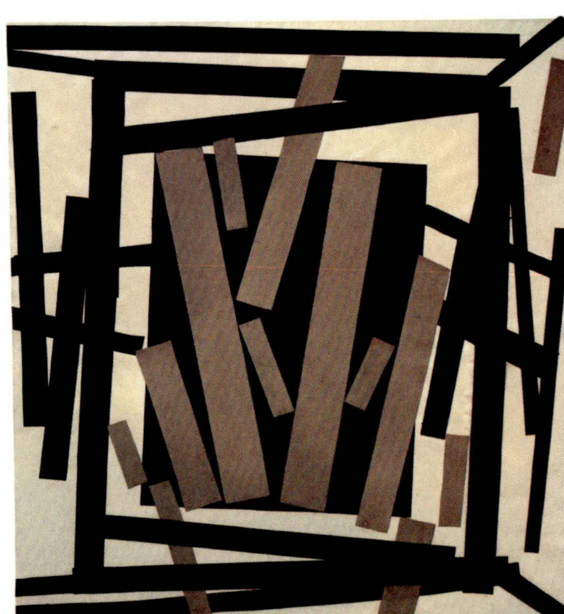

pascual navarro
Estudio (Study). 1950. Collage on paper. 22 3/16 x 20 1/16" (56.4 x 51 cm). Collection Mercantil, Caracas

alejandro otero
Tablón de Pampatar (Pampatar plank). 1954. Enamel on plywood. 10′ 6 3/16″ x 25 5/8″ x 1″ (320.5 x 65 x 2.5 cm). Collection Patricia Phelps de Cisneros, Caracas

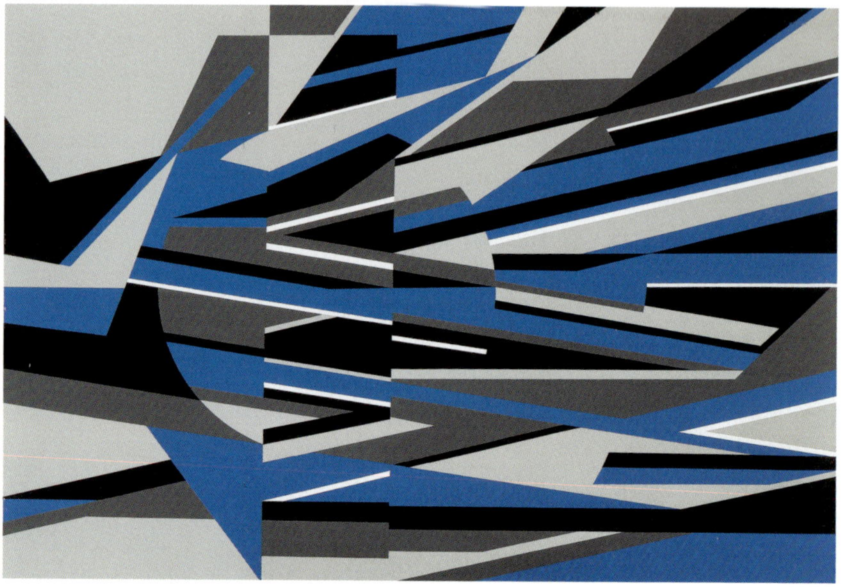

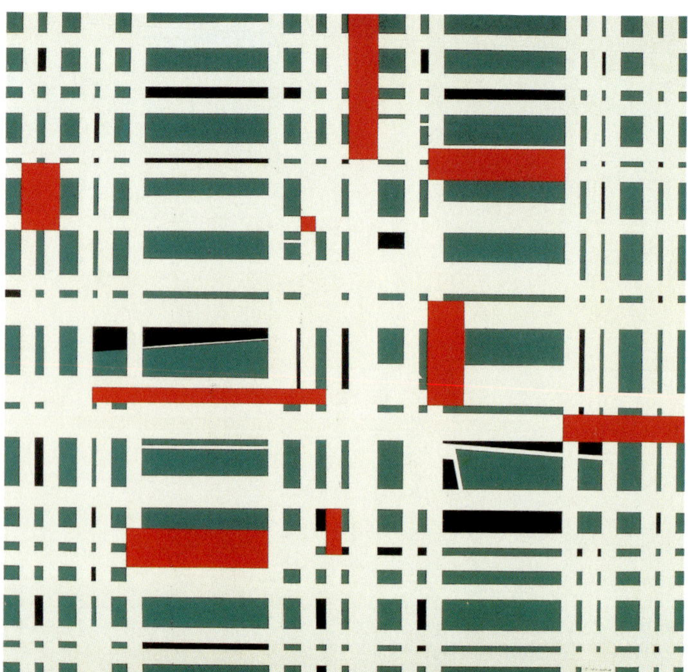

jesús rafael soto
Rotación (*Rotation*). 1952. Oil on plywood. 39 5/8 x 39 5/8 x 3" (100.5 x 100.5 x 7.5 cm). Musée National d'Art Moderne, Centre Georges Pompidou, Paris

aimée battistini
Un soleil pour Milosz (A sun for Milosz). 1964. Acrylic on canvas. 44 7/8 x 63 13/16" (114.5 x 162 cm). Collection Fundación Museos Nacionales. Galería de Arte Nacional, Caracas

omar carreño
Composición geométrica (Geometric composition). 1959. Lacquer on wood. 39 3/8 x 39 3/8" (100 x 100 cm). Collection Fundación Museos Nacionales. Galería de Arte Nacional, Caracas

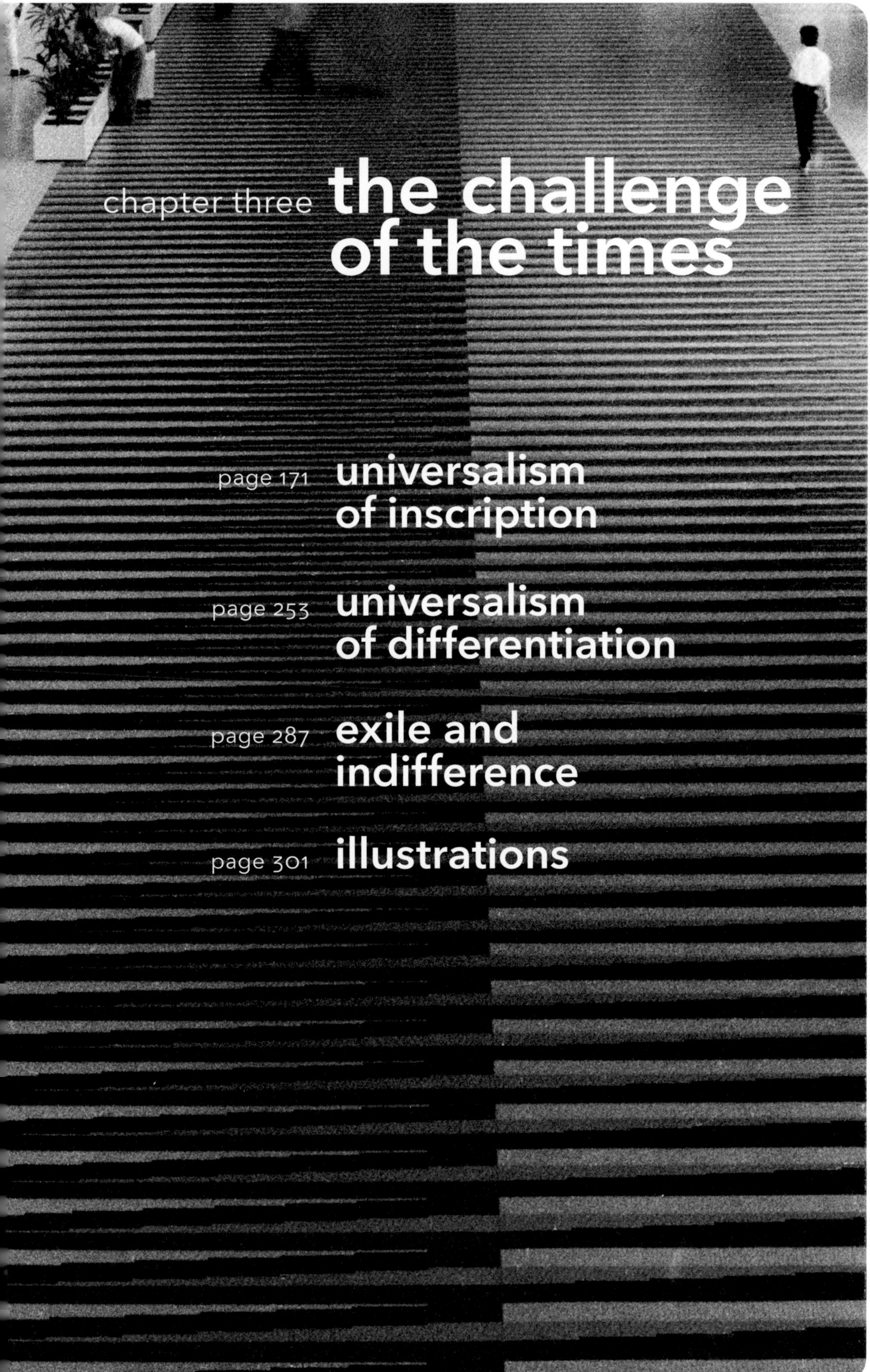

chapter three

the challenge of the times

the challenge of the times, 1949–1974 ariel jiménez

universalism of inscription

The increasingly complex presence of the metropolis was the defining factor of Venezuelan life in the crucial years 1945–50. During this period, the generations that had worked to keep Juan Vicente Gómez in power[1] would be displaced by others who dreamed of constructing a modern country, far removed from a past they fervently wished to forget. The construction of this new Venezuela began under the governments of Eleazar López Contreras (1936–41) and Isaías Medina Angarita (1941–45) following the Gómez dictatorship.

Among the country's artists, the need for progress at this point was categorical and dire, and they saw no possibility for it but a radical break with national traditions. There were several motivating factors in this need for rupture. It was, first, an inevitable reaction to the twenty-seven years of dictatorship that had kept the country in an enforced state of political and cultural infancy—a state that over time had become increasingly intolerable for younger generations. The end of the dictatorship triggered the bursting of a *válvula*, a "safety valve"[2] that had contained the nation's pent-up energies for years.

No small number of Venezuelans felt that the twentieth century began for the country in 1936, with the end of the Gómez regime (as Mariano Picón Salas would iterate in several texts).[3] But the move toward modernity entailed a kind of disregard or erasure of the reality of that coarse and uncultured mass of people—as depicted, for example, in the photographs of Torito (Luis Felipe Toro Mujica)—who stood by and watched with such strange indifference the construction of this new country that was and would be theirs as well. It entailed ignoring the fact that in Venezuela—as everywhere else—time flowed like a river carrying the past along with it, and a sudden swelling of the waters could come at any time, bringing centuries-old residue of distant moments of history into the present with a single wave.[4]

The urgent national drive to break with the past was accompanied by a range of forces of progress and modernity, responses to other forms of "barbarism"—that is, avant-garde currents coming out of Europe—which kindled new ideas and hopes among Venezuelan artists. European modern art, so admired by young Venezuelans, nourished their desire for renewal, provided them with tools and strategies, and even affected the tenor of their writings, leaving its traces in many of the manifestos penned in Latin America, including those in the journal *Válvula* (published in 1928).

An apparent will toward modernism can be seen in letters written to Alfredo Boulton by the young Alejandro Otero, one of the first artists to journey to France in the mid-1940s in search of the new, in search of the future.[5] He wrote in April 1947: "[Matthias] Grünewald and [Pablo] Picasso are predecessors enough to give me confidence, as does Paris, and the faith I have in the painting I create. I think these are the only things I need to be able to do something in painting that, for the first time, will be truly important for my country. Something that will rise to the challenge of the times, something certain of its meaning."[6] For Otero, Picasso represented the very essence of the modern; it was his encounter with the Spanish master's work that incited Otero to begin his own Parisian practice. In those initial moments, the "Americanist" concerns of Otero's colleagues were scarcely important to him. His desire was that his work should be *universal*—that is, not bound by local trends and concerns but engaging on an equal footing with all art—and for this he felt that Grünewald and Picasso were "predecessors enough."

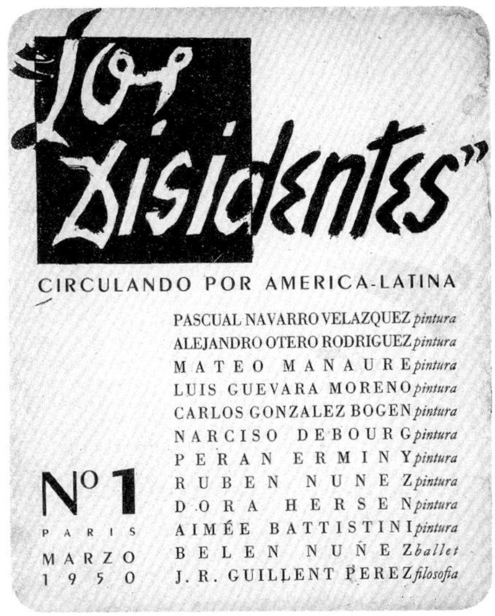

Cover of *Los Disidentes*, no. 1. Paris, March 1950. Collection Ignacio and Valentina Oberto, Caracas

Otero's chief cultural contribution would be innovation: he would point other Venezuelans toward the future. It was in this frame of mind that he began work on his series of Cafeteras (Coffeepots) in 1946, taking as his inspiration the work of Picasso that he had discovered in Paris. With his Cafeteras and other works, Otero initiated a now-classic process of early abstraction: reducing his models to their essential lines and colors, using those lines to build a range of structures, some compact, others more fluid. This was a form of visual "writing," which he describes in his letters as moving little by little toward "pure" painting: that is, sheer lines and colors on the flat surface of the canvas. Otero exhibited this series in Caracas at the beginning of 1949, marking a clear break with national artistic traditions.

The most intense moment in the determined movement to effect this schism came just a few months later, in 1950, when a number of young artists in Paris (Otero among them) founded the group called Los Disidentes—the Dissidents—and published a journal of the same name, in which they articulated their ideas and positions.[7] Despite the youthful naïveté of putting out a magazine in Paris that was plainly strictly Venezuelan in character and scope, the group's guiding principles are effectively set forth in the pages of *Los Disidentes*. They violently disparaged the figures and institutions in Venezuela that supported a system that in their view was utterly outdated. As artists, they sought to transcend national barriers in order to take their place in world history, and they believed that in geometric abstraction they had found a possible way to achieve their goal. They viewed this new genre as a complete rejection of the landscape-oriented traditions that so anachronistically dominated their country, and they were fully convinced of its historical necessity.

Their art education in Caracas had inculcated these young people with a linear vision of modern art history, a history that began with Impressionism and ended with Paul Cézanne and the immediate consequence of his work, Cubism. Abstraction, of which they had heard next to nothing, seemed to them the logical outcome of that trajectory: its most current point. When they encountered in Paris an art scene in which the visual movements that had been halted by the war were being reevaluated, they felt justified in the direction they had chosen, and were ready to commit themselves entirely to abstraction—with the determination of one arriving late to a party, who wishes to erase, through overzealous exuberance, any doubt that he belongs with this group. Since 1944 Denise René's Paris gallery had been championing abstract art, both its masters (many of whom had been forgotten during the war) and its emerging talents.[8] In 1950, artists Edgar Pillet and Jean Dewasne created the Atelier d'Art Abstrait, a workshop for abstract artists where the young Disidentes came to study. Everything seemed to confirm the Venezuelans' decision to follow this route, and to prove that their orientation was indeed integral to universal history itself.

Abstract works were not, of course, the only ones being reevaluated in this period; trends stemming from Surrealism were also very active. *Art informel* stood out as a particularly dynamic iteration of abstract art; but it was *art concret* that caught the attention of the Venezuelans. In concretism, they saw correspondences with their own mission: a commitment to breaking with the past, a decisive move toward a future charged with hope—an order yet to come that would encompass all the realms of Venezuela's burgeoning urban life. And in their view, that future, as touted by geometric and concrete abstraction, could not be located in a more promising context than the Americas, where, they believed, it was possible to achieve what "Old Europe" could not.

The abundant correspondence between Otero and Boulton in the late 1940s and early '50s provides clear testimony of the lively arguments animating this group of artists at the time—and also alludes to the differences that would cause Los Disidentes to disband. Although Otero was at this point the most impassioned defender of universality, which he considered to be in direct opposition to national or "Americanist" character, not all artists agreed with him. The texts of J. R. Guillent Pérez continuously set forth concerns that (as in early modernist works) led to the conception of the foundation upon which a new Venezuela would have to be constructed. Simón Bolívar, El Libertador, reappears in the discourse of Los Disidentes as the one figure around which a consensus might be reached. This Bolívar was not, however, a character constructed by an idolatrous historiography, but a flesh-and-blood man whose central attitude of rebellion, according to Guillent Pérez, demanded emulation: "We need a Bolívar of the arts, a Bolívar of intelligence, a Bolívar of the economy. [. . .] Bolívar's greatness cries out for the birth of his equals."[9] Guillent Pérez makes it clear that these artists felt they were the legitimate heirs to a spirit of rebellion, that in their work and in the radical leap symbolized by geometric abstraction their generation would in fact reach universality: a real and liberating synchrony with Western history.

There are, however, several texts in which we may trace the links that connected these young artists to landscape and nativist traditions of the first half of the twentieth century—the very traditions they so violently condemned. The figure of Bolívar is one of these points of connection; this becomes particularly evident in Boulton's work of the 1950s. Once he had finished his iconographic project on Venezuela, creating such books as *Los llanos de Páez* (Páez's plains; 1950) and *La Margarita* (1952), Boulton declared (in a similar vein to Los Disidentes) that his was a search for the inhabitants of those lands he had captured with his lens.[10] His book *Los retratos de Bolívar* (Portraits of Bolívar) was first published in 1956. There he wrote:

> This book is an epilogue, and concludes the frieze of Venezuelan images culled in my previous work: the imposing gorges of the plateaux, the absolute solitude of the plains and the happy, noisy Caribbean. [. . .] Nonetheless, despite the presence of the men who move through some of these pages, [. . .] beings without a present and without a past whom we place in different sites within these tales, we were missing the absolute and complementary presence of Venezuelan man. It was indispensable to create a physical depiction of him – of his body, his arms, his legs, his face. Perhaps he is small and round like the *indio*, or jet black and slender like the black man, or pale and bearded like the white man. [. . .] It was necessary to seek out and locate the conglomerate being who would correspond superlatively to this state. Only one man could respond to such a difficult and exalted demand: Simón Bolívar, who provides an admirable model in a country replete with contradictions and surprises.[11]

When Boulton says that it is necessary to depict the Venezuelan with "his body, his arms, his legs, his face," he seems to be describing those factors that would complete Francisco Narváez's *Barutaima*, that figure of an *indio* depicted in an idealized manner – without arms, legs, or face – created by the sculptor in 1947 for Boulton's home. On the other hand, the artist's task is also to locate a figure capable of overcoming the racial differences inherent to Venezuelans, not so much through an idealized *mestizaje* – racial mixture – but rather by dint of that person's elevated significance, his "universality." That figure was Bolívar. For Los Disidentes, in a sense, Venezuelan painting reached a level of universality with geometric abstraction that was in every way comparable to that which Boulton found in the figure of Bolívar. Their processes were parallel, and for this very reason they responded to the nativist impulses of the first incarnation of modernity in the same way – that is, by seeking to complete them, to reach by other means their central objective: universality.

If the formation of Los Disidentes marked a charged moment of ideological confrontation between the landscape-oriented and nativist artists of the first half of the twentieth century and the generations of abstract artists that followed, the concept that most clearly characterized Venezuelan modernity was that of "integration of the arts," espoused by the architect Carlos Raúl Villanueva in his design and construction of the Universidad Central de Venezuela in Caracas.[12] Begun during the government of Medina Angarita (1944) and finalized in 1958, this project of integration would be Villanueva's most comprehensive and complex work. It would also constitute a living document in which the differences between the two great phases of Venezuelan modernity would be most clearly manifested: the earlier phase, of landscape-oriented and nativist work, and the later phase dominated by geometric abstraction.

Villanueva's general design for the university, as it was conceived in his 1944 plans, hearkened back to a classical formal structure, specifically in its pronounced central axis around which buildings and gardens are organized symmetrically (see plan, next page). The university hospital is located at the head of the group of buildings to the west of this axis, which on its eastern side

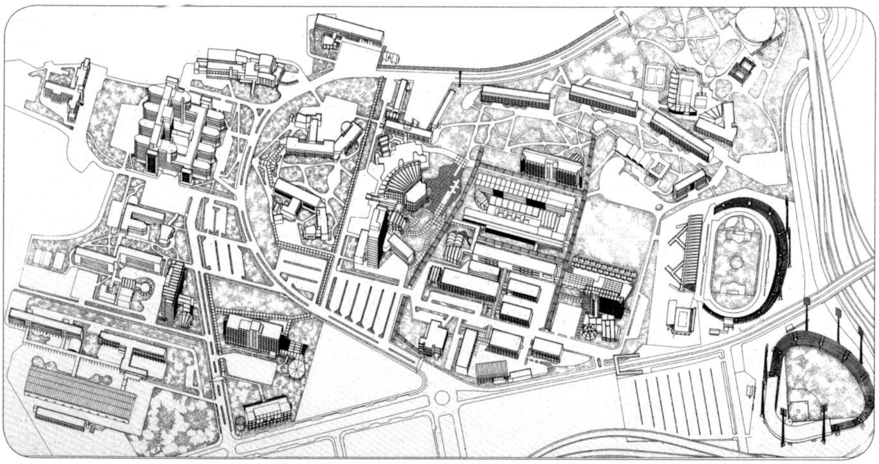

General isometric layout of the Universidad Central de Venezuela. Archivos Fundación Villanueva, Caracas

ends in the Estadio Olímpico (Olympic stadium). The architecture of the hospital and of the entire medical area in general, which constituted the initial phase of the university's realization, were, however, free of the formal references of Villanueva's previous projects—in particular his overhaul of the El Silencio district of Caracas—in which he sought to link design solutions of modern architecture with the traditions of the colonial city.[13] Thus the university buildings have a more decidedly modern aspect than their overall design might suggest. This did not, however, mean that Villanueva had given up the idea of achieving the integration of colonial traditions with the languages of modern architecture; while the connections here are not made with formal references, he established them nonetheless with his choice of structural solutions.

By contrast, Villanueva's ideal of artistic integration underwent a less marked evolution, as seen for example in Narváez's works for El Silencio and those he realized later for this first phase of the Universidad Central. For this first university project, Narváez's subject matter was no longer in the typical nativist mode he had adopted in previous decades—here he depicted such allegorical figures as *La educación* (Education) and *La ciencia* (Science), as well as illustrative murals—but his basic visual language remained largely unchanged. Narváez continued to present the stylized figures that had characterized his nativist painting and sculpture in the 1920s and '30s. The distance between Villanueva's architectural language and Narváez's sculpture was at this point quite apparent.

But the distance between their approaches in this first phase of the university project differed considerably from that in the second phase, which embodied the ideal of total unification that Villanueva attempted to define in the early 1950s. In the second phase, synthesis was made possible because, as the architect put it, "a single concept permeates the world of the plastic arts," and "the same philosophy runs through it."[14] At that point in time, the work of Narváez was not imbued with the same spirit that saturated Villanueva's architecture, which was increasingly oriented toward structural purity.

Regardless of whether Narváez's contribution to this project of integration achieved the level of empathy demanded by Villanueva's architecture, for contemporary observers it clearly illustrates an essential kinship between the nativism of the first incarnation of modernism and the abstract movements in the second phase of the university project. Narváez, like Boulton, was one of the figures who articulated the divide between these two moments; their respective bodies of work not only accompanied the process of modernization from its inception in the 1920s until its culminating moment in the 1970s, they also outlined a range of possible paths that would become apparent in the works Narváez would create for the second and third phases of the university's construction.

We may say that the first phase of modernity ended around 1949, just as Otero was exhibiting his first abstract works, and the coup d'état against Rómulo Gallegos was dimming hopes for democracy. The 1940s were closing, and with them one stage in the process of Venezuela's modernization.

The abrupt shift that occurred at this point was clearly observed in the Universidad Central project—in its overall structure, in its architectural language, and in the nature of the works that would form part of Villanueva's project of integration. In the campus's larger layout, a north-south "avenue" divides the two defining periods of the university's construction, each comprised of its own distinct phases. The medical area, with its central axis, is to the west, and to the east are the elements of the second and third phases—when the central axis shifted, evincing a fundamental change in the general design of the space to one that was more dynamic and open.

On a strictly architectural level, the change was no less remarkable: Villanueva's architectural language grew perceptibly richer, incorporating the use of raw or unadorned reinforced concrete, and introducing a new openness to the spaces and structures. The walls and open planes were covered with Venetian tile, utilizing the element of color in a more organic, more palpably material way than simple paint, and rendering the surfaces truly unique.

The artists—Venezuelan, European, and North American—who were invited to participate in Villanueva's integration-project took on a symbolic role. Together they created, in the heart of the university campus, a space in which to materialize that essential desire for historical synchrony that from its inception guided the modern Venezuelan project. Narváez had worked alone with Villanueva on the first phase of the university, between 1944 and 1949; beginning in 1951 the young Disidentes were to participate in the project, in particular on the Estadio Olímpico,[15] with which Villanueva began the second phase of the university's construction. With these buildings, Villanueva was perhaps attempting to balance the obvious disparity between his own architectural language and Narváez's work. In the early 1950s Los Disidentes were, like their European models, attempting to discover the essence of painting through the practice of abstraction. Their university works are thus "permeated" with a concept similar to those that drove Villanueva's architecture; the result was a greater harmony between the spirit of the works of art and that of the surrounding architecture. Still, Villanueva was obliged to accept the limitations that prevented him from achieving true integration: the works presented by the young abstract artists (Mateo Manaure, Carlos González Bogen, and Armando Barrios) were simply enlarged paintings that were later applied to the open surfaces of his buildings, using a medium (large sheets of fired ceramic) that was not especially well suited to the goals of his project.

Narváez's role in the project began to transform, specifically with a large-scale sculpture titled *El atleta* (The athlete), which for the first time exhibited characteristics remarkably engaged with the spirit of Villanueva's architecture. The sculpture is of a glorified male figure, embodying the confident humanism of a generation and a nation that believe themselves to be in full control of their future. The work is constructed of prefabricated concrete modules, which were assembled on site. Narváez had made the shift from nativist sculpture to an artistic practice that tended toward abstraction—demonstrating that for him there was no contradiction between the nativism of the first half of the twentieth century and the abstraction of the 1950s.

One of the clearest manifestations of this universality was in the central nucleus of the campus. Here Villanueva attained his most eloquent architectural achievements and the most refined examples of integration. He had learned from his previous efforts, in terms of the type of art needed, the ways he might achieve its integration into the architecture, and even the materials the artists should utilize. Ultimately, of course, these efforts were successful also because the most talented Venezuelan and international artists were contributing to them. The architect was not content to provide open spaces where artists would simply insert interventions; rather, he contemplated these spaces and sites for and with specific artists. For the works of Henri Laurens and Fernand Léger, he opened the roof of the Plaza Cubierta (the central covered plaza); the great project that Alexander Calder created for the Aula Magna (great hall) both responds to and resolves specific architectural problems, in this case the acoustic drawbacks of the classroom. Alejandro Otero and Víctor Valera offered artistic interventions for the university's departments of architecture and engineering; they achieved some of the most tempered and elegant examples of integration, not just because of the aptness of their visual solutions, but also because of their skillful use of materials—predominantly Venetian tiles. All these efforts contributed to an urban center that is among the most successful achievements of integration created in Latin America during this period. At the same time, the very space manifests, in the most transparent way possible, an essential will toward historic synchrony.

The legitimacy of this impulse might be contested, of course, with the point that none of the Venezuelans who participated in this project achieved the universal celebrity of artists such as Calder, Léger, and Laurens—and thus the "historic synchrony" they sought was nothing but a hope that never became a fact. This defect in the universalizing strategies of the first incarnation of Venezuelan abstraction had enormous and lasting weight—as it did in all national contexts that in some way depended on other, more dynamic and complex centers—and was a decisive factor in the trajectories of many artists, some of whom would later abandon abstraction to follow other paths and other means of historical validation.[16]

The political climate under Marcos Pérez Jiménez affected all the Venezuelan artists who contributed works to the Universidad Central, but there were two for whom the military dictatorship represented an insurmountable obstacle to their participation in the project. Jesús Rafael Soto and Carlos Cruz-Diez would nonetheless make their own indelible impact on Venezuelan modernism. But politics were not the only reason for their absence from Villanueva's university plan. Cruz-Diez's work in the 1950s vacillated between politically charged imagery (which at that time served as social critique) and a few early, timid attempts at abstraction. It was on the whole out of keeping with the formal dictates of architecture—his paintings of this period were predominantly figurative, descriptive, and presented as conventional tableaux. Cruz-Diez's own political position furthermore prompted him to maintain a great distance from the powers of the day. In Soto's case, too, the political landscape kept him out of the university project; although he constructed a model of the piece he intended to contribute, he withdrew it in the end. But there was another significant obstacle for Soto: he balked at geometric abstraction, which in his understanding was restricted to a rigid formalism that prevented any real evolution toward solutions in painting that would be not only more contemporary, but also more effective as plastic art.

Soto's works—often repetitive structures made with Plexiglas—are spatially open, and require the optical participation of the viewer, of that body "both seeing and seen," of which Maurice Merleau-Ponty speaks in his essays on Cézanne.[17] In this way, Soto's explorations are congruent with the those of such artists as Calder, Paul Bury, Jean Tinguely, Yaacov Agam, Robert Jacobsen, and Victor Vasarely—the group with whose work the gallerist Denise René organized the seminal 1955 exhibition *Le Mouvement* (Movement), a milestone of the emergence of kineticism on the European scene. Soto's participation in this exhibition—indeed, the very fact that a Latin American artist was invited to take part in this event hailing the birth of a new movement, inscribed from its inception into European history—brought an undeniable sense of legitimacy to the Venezuelan scene. For Venezuelans who were striving for such universality, there was no longer any doubt: through Soto and his work the art of their country had at last attained the universality dreamed of since the beginning of the twentieth century by all the protagonists of modernism

Cruz-Diez was one of the artists who saw in these events indisputable proof of the historic validity that had been achieved by abstract art, and particularly kineticism. In 1959 he created the first of his Fisicromías (Physichromes), a series of works in which color was projected off the two-dimensional surface and into space. The eminent modernist thinkers Arturo Úslar Pietri and Boulton would later devote texts to Cruz-Diez and Soto that helped to clarify the many significations of their work, and examined the conclusive historical valorization it provided for the modern Venezuelan scene. In Cruz-Diez and Soto, as in Armando Reverón, Boulton and others recognized genuine world citizens: truly universal Venezuelans.

The inscription of these artists into the European scene was one of the galvanizing factors that would make the kinetic movement into something of an oppressive presence in Venezuela during the 1960s and '70s, damned by certain critics as an "official art," imposed by the country's governing elite. The government, along with nearly all middle- and upper-class Venezuelans who yearned to feel part of the world as a whole, saw in these artists a source of symbolic validation: a formidable number of private and public architectural projects incorporated kinetic works; museums purchased and organized exhibitions on kinetic art, and numerous books were published on the kinetic movement and its protagonists. The inevitable polarization these events brought about in the context of Venezuela – a country so eager for legitimation – exaggerated and undoubtedly diluted any fair perception of the art.

The works of Soto, Cruz-Diez, and others of this era can and should be understood at least in part from a European perspective; certainly the artists themselves perceived their art as a phenomenon essentially disconnected from any local tradition. Still, their works – both in their virtues and in their contradictory effects – also constituted genuine expressions of the desire for modernity, which energized much of Venezuela's population during a significant part of the twentieth century. Without that desire, "local" in its way, their art would not have been created.

universalism of differentiation

In tandem with this eagerness for modern traditions, this yearning for a form of expression that would inscribe Venezuela into the larger Western context, there were other trends driving artists in the country as well. These expressions strove to be deeply rooted in national reality, without being militantly "nationalistic." These artists were also propelled toward an ideal of universalism – but in a distinctive way. While many abstract artists considered themselves leftist intellectuals, these alternate artistic movements tended toward more radical political opposition, particularly in the 1960s.

The most representative manifestations of these currents were found in the expressive paintings of Jacobo Borges, and in the literary review *Sardio*, which gave rise to the group known as El Techo de la Ballena (The roof of the whale). These factions also wished for a universal presence, but their attentiveness to the circumstances of their country and region situated them within what might be termed "universalism under an opposing sign" – or universalism of differentiation. If the abstract artists were compelled to reach the most advanced point in universal history in order to inscribe themselves into it – to continue it and enrich it with their work – the *Sardio* group and El Techo de la Ballena encouraged their members instead to take in everything history might provide in order to imagine themselves as a different reality. Their hope was to achieve universality as a way of marking, in some way, their difference.

Between such polarities there has always existed a more popular type of art, some of it considered "naïve," and some more sophisticated and politically committed. Such works were often spurred by a diametric opposition to Europe – always perceived as the home of the invader, the Other. The visual examples of these trends are of course wide-ranging and at times contradictory; they extend from distinct indigenism (as in the work of Alejandro Colina) – perhaps the most overt rejection of all things European[18] – to an art of political witness and protest, aligned with the ideals of Mexican muralism (as seen, for example, in the paintings of Gabriel Bracho).

There were also the exiles – who were of course as deeply embedded in the national experience as anyone else. Some were "voluntary exiles," and among these certain ones, such as Reverón and Mario Abreu, were "internal exiles." Others, such as Bárbaro Rivas, were involuntary – or perhaps indifferent – exiles.[19] These exiles and exceptions present yet another set of axes in the development of twentieth-century Venezuelan art. It is important, however, not to attempt to schematize too precisely, as the borders that separate the exiles from the "insiders" are often as subtle as the ties that unite them.[20]

It is certain that as the phenomenon of urbanization became more entrenched during the 1950s, the conflicts marking Venezuelan life, too, became more intense. There were contrasts between urban and rural spaces, between organized areas of the city and the vast marginal neighborhoods surrounding them, between cosmopolitanisms and nationalisms. Each of these groups had its own projects and futures, yet at heart all were pursuing a common goal: to create a new, modern, and just nation.

Thus the points of fracture, too, multiplied. One of the most significant was the carefully timed coup d'état on January 23, 1958, against the dictatorship of Pérez Jiménez, who had promoted the boldest modern projects. His fall was accompanied by considerable turmoil, particularly in leftist sectors that were convinced that the historical moment demanded greater political consciousness, and less "aestheticizing." The opening manifesto in the literary journal *Sardio*, published just months after the dictatorship ended, argued this point forcefully:

> No one who is not a militant advocate of freedom can experience the portentous creative adventure of the soul. Faced with the weight of our current history, replete with imminent anxieties, no thinking man can evade such militancy without betraying his own radical condition. The aesthetic categories that prevailed until recently now seem too narrow and sterile.[21]

The imperative of an art focused on – if not always committed to – the material transformation of political and social life began to be imposed as the fundamental basis of these artists' actions. Yet for them, the most efficient way to achieve this goal was located as far from abstract "aestheticism" as it was from that excess of "local color" they criticized in the most narrowly nationalistic movements, or in those that were blindly politicized, populated by faithful followers of Communist party directives. "The man of today faces a vaster and more complex experience," according to *Sardio*'s testimonial, "one that would be useless to simplify with regional or partisan limitations. The man of today is motivated by a profound longing for universality."[22] Such phrases could be deployed by artists from a vast range of trends and movements, so palpable was the yearning for universality that formed the central axis of all modernizing projects of the twentieth century. But sometimes minor differences – as surely as more radical ones – regarding the means of action or the paths to follow may divide entire generations. The Sardio group's understanding of *universality* was not far from the most urgent national needs, and it did not necessarily consist of an opposition to the local: "We should not confuse universality with cosmopolitanism," they wrote.[23]

The 1959 Cuban Revolution and the many attempts to export that revolution militarily to all of Latin America would later radicalize positions that managed to coexist, as long as they were not obliged to take sides for or against violence. In the midst of increasing tensions, Sardio would continue its work and the publication of its journal until 1961, leaving a legacy of one of the most intense and rigorous editorial phenomena in the country.

At this point, a new movement emerged from the ashes of Sardio: El Techo de la Ballena, a group more radically committed to the revolution, ready even to take up arms in order to attain power. Its devotion to the cause was total, leading some of its members to participate in revolutionary actions that were intended to undermine Venezuela's established order. Their strategies were rebellious; like guerrillas, El Techo de la Ballena operated suddenly, aggressively, and without warning. And like the Dadaists and Surrealists, they took great delight in causing an uproar—indeed, most of their actions were more scandalous than truly violent.

On the literary side, the group's contribution consisted of a radically urban literature that was opposed to that Gallegos-esque search for a national essence in the rural interior of the country. This in itself is testimony to the drastic changes that in a mere forty years had transformed a primarily rural population into a society that was essentially urban—despite the inadequate living conditions in Venezuelan cities at the time. Theirs was a literature of denunciation, and in its manifestos the group criticized the cultural environment of the country with the same vehemence as that of Los Disidentes. El Techo de la Ballena fully subscribed to the tradition of rupture that characterized modern avant-gardes, particularly in countries like Venezuela, whose inhabitants lived in constant and painful discord with an unsatisfying reality.

If the ultimate goal of El Techo de la Ballena was to transform society, they did not attempt to achieve this end as the abstract artists did, with humanizing gestures that might enrich a reality that everyone agreed was wretchedly poor. Rather, their medium was confrontation and strong political message (as seen, for example, in Caupolicán Ovalles's 1962 poem "Duerme Usted, Señor Presidente?" [Are you sleeping, Mr. President?]—a direct, even somewhat crass, attack on the governing powers). El Techo's goal was radical political change, in tune with many movements driven by young people in the 1960s in the hopes of reaching total utopian liberation. They supported informalist tendencies in the visual arts, trends that led to a kind of unruly eruption of textures and marks. As Ángel Rama has noted, this "transition from geometric and kinetic art to Informal art, driven by the passage from a combinatorial frame of mind to one focused on the turbulence of life, was accompanied in Venezuela by an aggressiveness unheard of in the rest of Latin America."[24] But although the virulence of El Techo de la Ballena's artistic interventions and actions assured them national notoriety, these same elements would work against them, in the sense that once the struggle ended, with the defeat of the Venezuela's rebel movements in 1968, their aims and strategies lost all pertinence and efficacy. The field was left wide open to the powerful symbolic legitimation kineticism offered to a society hungry for historical recognition.

exile and indifference

Revolutionary or not, Venezuelan avant-garde movements in the 1950s and '60s were responding to the country's fraught cultural circumstances; they wished to create a different reality for Venezuela—they wanted their nation to be more organized, and fully in charge of its own historical destiny. Beyond the ideological and strategic differences among them, these movements concurred in their will to move past colonial limitations. They all dreamed of a country that was no longer a submissive consumer of ideas and products, that would be instead a mature nation, capable of creating its own material and cultural values.

Against this sense of urgency, this exasperated need for modernity, and a political left that seemed to perceive nothing but misery and anguish—the quiet and rather fragile figure of the artist Gego (Gertrude Goldschmidt) posed a significant contrast. Attuned both to the contributions of technology and to the most elemental manifestations of life, Gego was a complex artist; her work's relevance grew as the country's hopes for progress became dimmer and as the urban poverty inundating Venezuelan cities created an increasingly volatile environment.

Gego arrived in Venezuela in 1939, a German Jew fleeing the horrors of Nazism. She was a sophisticated product of a country that was a creative center for new ideas, arriving in a nation that deeply longed to be modern and had its gaze fixed on that center from which she had just escaped. This simple reality is significant, as is the fact that Gego would not bring full focus to her work as an artist until ten years later, after she had been nationalized as a Venezuelan and had settled in Tarma, a small rural locality on the outskirts of Caracas. Here, in this second, self-imposed exile, Gego worked with figurative drawings and watercolors in 1949–50, and in a few years moved on to her first abstractions. In 1956, as the artist herself wrote, she attempted to convert surfaces into volumes, and the following year she sought to "dissolve" volumes into sets of parallel lines. The result is immediately perceptible as a kinetic effect, although she classified it as the accidental result of other explorations.[25]

In 1957, Jesús Rafael Soto had his first show in Venezuela, in which he presented his kinetic structures made of Plexiglas and parallel bars of welded iron (created between 1955 and 1957). The similarities between his works and Gego's were instantly evident, in terms of the artistic solutions at which they had both arrived. This was a peculiar intersection of destinies: Soto, an artist who came from the cultural aridity of the Venezuelan provinces (as described by Otero), who looked toward Europe with its historic modernity and prestige, sharing a moment with this "intelligent and quiet"[26] European woman hidden in the rural town of Tarma. Gego's work was intended to "dissolve" volumes; Soto's to draw within space. She sought something of what he had left behind, while he dreamed about what she had fled. Both artists were products of exile, and they shared the experience of having passed through Caracas—that tangle of hopes—in the 1950s. But their congruencies were momentary, a result of circumstances.

After this circumstantial synchronicity, each artist was to follow a different, even opposing, path in search of what he or she lacked, fleeing her or his phantoms. After a "baroque" period of strong textures and twisted wires (which at times seemed to presage Gego's future works), Soto would, in 1962, embark on a path toward a rigorous control of forms, creating work with a clean finish involving industrial materials. Gego, by contrast, constructed open structures, sensitive to the touch of the hand and to chance, in bundles that seemed suddenly to split off from themselves, becoming ex-centric, fleeing the rigidity of orthogonal, parallel structures, little by little drawing closer to lifelike forms. This work caused Gego to be perceived by the kinetic artists as a kind of ingénue; of course they felt affinities with her work and process, but Gego resisted any manifestation of the systematic, while they sought it out—systematically.

What is most emblematic of the lives and works of all these artists was not located in the conflicting arguments wielded by one faction or another—or not only there—but rather in their similarities, in the peculiar coincidences and contrasts their works exhibited, in that complementariness that made Caracas the lively place it was during this period.

Within that context of contrasting modernities and shared hopes, the life and work of Bárbaro Rivas serves as another very specific example of exile, another strange gap in time. However, his was an "internal exile"—to some extent involuntary—the result of a marginality that left him outside, even indifferent to, the hopes of his contemporaries. His work was thus not consciously inscribed into active efforts toward modernization in the country, but was perceived as the continuation or surviving residue of a popular imaginary that had existed for centuries, and did not require anything further: a simple response to the ubiquitous need for devout images.

In Venezuelan political conflicts in the middle of the twentieth century, the Communist party consistently sought instances of popular culture that might serve as opposition to the modernizing hopes of the country's "elites." When Rómulo Gallegos came to power in 1948, a grand *fiesta* of native traditions was organized in Caracas to celebrate his inauguration; there, popular songs and dances from around the country were presented for the first time in the country's recent history. The "recuperation" of Rivas, beginning in 1949, was part of this renewed interest in local tradition, and was effected largely by Francisco Da Antonio, an art critic and a member of the Communist party who resided in the Petare neighborhood where Rivas lived for some time. Da Antonio's interest in this obscure painter's work—beyond its obvious visual power—lay in the possibility it seemed to speak of for Venezuela and for Latin America's position in Western history. It seemed to promise a way of belonging in the world that would not be exclusively identified with the *new*, thus negating local traditions, but would rather put down roots in the reality of the country, encompassing its entire breadth and depth. For Da Antonio, Rivas was a living example, the survivor, of "an ancient *pueblo* from an agrarian community, recounting for us its history and its reason for being—a people we are inexorably obliterating as if it were an alien past, in our own process of becoming."[27] Plainly, two drives were in conflict: "progress-oriented" forces that sought to sanitize the city and the country, to make them completely new, and forces that wanted to incorporate the dispossessed who had been left behind in the midst of the eradicating power of the bulldozers. And yet there was no impermeable wall separating these two poles completely, as was proven time and again by a multifarious, complex, and subtle network of interconnections among them.

It is an incontrovertible fact that Venezuelan society as a whole, with its many modernization projects, was not able—or did not know how—to locate paths that might allow for the creation of that balanced and fair modern society so many dreamed of then, and dream of still. Thus Venezuelan modernity, or modernities, delineated a truncated history, a history of dreams and exiles, of commitments and dissidences.

Translated by Jen Hofer

notes to the text

1. The young military and political figures who overthrew General Isaías Medina Angarita in 1945 had two essential agendas: the clear continuity of Gómezism, and the refusal of the idea of presidential elections based on universal suffrage, with a direct and secret system of voting.
2. The "válvula," or valve, was the metaphor chosen by the young writers (among them Arturo Úslar Pietri) who put together one of the first avant-garde journals in the country, *Válvula*, published in 1928.
3. Mariano Picón Salas affirmed that the Venezuelan twentieth century began only in 1936, after the death of Juan Vicente Gómez. Picón Salas maintained that before this point, "protected by the harsh mountains on the coast, by the heights of the Andes and the immensity of the savannahs, [Venezuela] had been a country set apart, where one had to make a lot of noise in order to be convinced of belonging to the twentieth century." Mariano Picón Salas, *Regreso de tres mundos* (Mexico City: Fondo de Cultura Económica, CREA, 1985), p. 112 (first published Mexico City: Tezontle, 1959).
4. In just this way, Domingo Faustino Sarmiento's Juan Facundo Quiroga arrives in Europeanized Buenos Aires, as a sudden intrusion from Latin America's "barbarous" provinces. (See Sarmiento, *Facundo: Civilisación y barbarie* [1845]; *Facundo: Civilization and Barbarism* [Berkeley: University of California Press, 2003].) Nearly eighty years later, Juan Vicente Gómez and his cohorts came down from the Andes (as depicted in Rómulo Gallegos's texts) like a horde of savages surging out from the abandoned provinces and from another period in time, to settle in the very center of the city and its history.
5. Alejandro Otero made his inevitable pilgrimage to France on November 13, 1945, shortly after World War II. His trip was made possible by a grant from the Venezuelan government; he obtained it with the help of his cousin Raúl Leoni, the future president of the republic (1964–69), who was one of the civilian leaders involved in the coup d'état against Isaías Medina Angarita.
6. Letter from Otero to Boulton, April 14, 1947. In *He vivido por los ojos: Correspondencia Alejandro Otero/Alfredo Boulton, 1946–1974*, Ariel Jiménez, ed. (Caracas: Fundación Alberto Vollmer and the Fundación Museo Alejandro Otero, 2001), p. 45. This letter appears in the present volume, p. 180.
7. The Disidentes group was formed in Paris in 1950 by young Venezuelan artists and intellectuals, principally Otero, Mateo Manaure, J. R. Guillent Pérez, Perán Erminy, Aimée Battistini, Pascual Navarro, Dora Hersen, Narciso Debourg, Luis Guevara Moreno, and Carlos González Bogen, among others.
8. The Galerie Denise René opened in June 1944, and was notable for its advocacy of abstract art currents. Among other seminal exhibitions at the gallery were the historic 1955 show of kinetic art titled *Le Mouvement* (Movement)—in which Jesús Rafael Soto participated—and Piet Mondrian's first Paris exhibition, in 1957.
9. J. R. Guillent Pérez, "Bolívar, nosotros y hoy" ("Bolívar, Ourselves, and Today"), *Los Disidentes*, no. 1 (Paris), March 1950, p. 15. This text appears in the present volume, pp. 172–74.
10. "In my photographs, I have covered more or less the entire territory of Venezuela, so as to see what this country I did not know was really like. . . . And once I had more or less dominated the Venezuelan landscape, observed by me through photographs, I set out to find the Venezuelan—the man. Who is the most prototypical man who has lived in these lands? So I looked for the most outstanding person among us: Bolívar." Boulton, in Ariel Jiménez, "Conversación con Alfredo Boulton," in *Homenaje a Alfredo Boulton*, exh. cat. (Museo de Arte Contemporáneo de Caracas, September 1987), p. 17.
11. Alfredo Boulton, *Los retratos de Bolívar*, 2nd edition (Caracas: printed by Editorial Arte, 1964), p. 9. (First published in Caracas: printed by Editorial Arte, 1956.)

12. See Villanueva's "El problema de la integración" ("The Problem of Integration") (Caracas: Facultad de Arquitectura, Universidad Central de Venezuela, 1980), pp. 70–71. The text is included in this volume, pp. 197–99. See also Maciá Pintó, "Carlos Raúl Villanueva: The Synthesis with Venezuela" in this volume, pp. 349–66.
13. Although the interior spaces of El Silencio's buildings responded to modern demands for clean, undecorated walls, the exteriors of the buildings incorporate covered passageways and the arcades and columns of many colonial structures, in a clear attempt to draw together new forms and the colonial city. In this way, Villanueva created a structure that was harmoniously inscribed into nativist traditions of painting and sculpture from the first half of the twentieth century.
14. Villanueva, "El problema de la integración" ("The Problem of Integration").
15. See letter from Alfredo Boulton to Alejandro Otero, August 1, 1951, in *He vivido por los ojos*.
16. It is naïve, if not impossible, to ignore the importance of these generationally based collective phenomena of historical legitimation. The presence or absence of society's approval, and particularly of those on the scene most admired for their successes, had real and concrete effects on many people's lives. A number of young abstract artists would go on to abandon geometric abstraction during the 1960s (and with it the pretensions toward universality) in order to anchor their practice to other processes of legitimation, such as those offered by a range of nationalisms, or that provided at the time by Latin American revolutionary movements, particularly after Fidel Castro's triumph in Cuba.
17. See Maurice Merleau-Ponty, "[le] corps . . . à la fois voyant et visible," in *L'Œil et l'esprit* (Paris: Gallimard, 1983; first ed., Gallimard, 1964); in English as "Eye and Mind," trans. Carleton Dallery, in *The Primacy of Perception*, James Edie, ed. (Evanston, Ill.: Northwestern University Press, 1964), pp. 159–90. Revised translation by Michael Smith in *The Merleau-Ponty Aesthetics Reader* (1993), pp. 121–49.
18. In Latin America the *indio* has always represented, thematically at least, an explicit rejection of the European. But creators who use this figure have not always been able to see that this rejection is often expressed through mediums, techniques, and strategies that have deep and obvious European roots. Thus we may observe the *mestizo* reality that characterizes Latin America, in which European elements play a role as important as—and in many cases, more important than—indigenous ones.
19. The complex reality of Venezuelan modernity has led Luis Pérez-Oramas to speak of "voluntary modernity," as in the work of Otero, and of "involuntary modernity," as in that of Reverón.
20. Bárbaro Rivas symbolizes the essential difficulty of contemplating the heterogeneity of the Venezuelan and Latin American contexts. An illiterate and marginal painter, to some degree a naïf, Rivas created work that expresses a true cultural openness toward the West, a type of unlettered cosmopolitanism, as Hugo Achugar aptly suggests in his essay "Latin American Modernities" in this volume (pp. 14–30). This would additionally explain why Rivas was claimed both by the Venezuelan left for his "popular" value and genuine depictions of national life, and by a figure like Boulton in his defense and full expression of universalist tendencies in Venezuela.
21. "Testimonio" ("Testimonial"), *Sardio*, no. 1 (Caracas), May–June 1958: 1. This text appears in the present volume, pp. 254–56.
22. "Testimonio" ("Testimonial").
23. Ibid.
24. See Ángel Rama, "Del terrorismo en las artes" ("Of Terrorism in the Arts"), in *Antología de El Techo de la Ballena* (Caracas: Fundarte, 1987). Published in English in *Inverted Utopias: Avant-Garde Art in Latin America*, Mari Carmen Ramírez and Héctor Olea, eds. (New Haven/London: Yale University Press in association with the Museum of Fine Arts, Houston, 2004). This text is included in the present volume, pp. 258–64.
25. See Gego, "Testimonial 1: Outline of Ideas and Interests Pursued," in *Sabiduras y otros textos de Gego* (bilingual edition), María Elena Huizi and Josefina Manrique, eds. (Houston/Caracas: Museum of Fine Arts; Fundación Gego, 2005), pp. 152–53. The text is included in the present volume, pp. 288–89.
26. Marta Traba, "Gego: Caracas tres mil" ("Gego: Caracas Year Three Thousand"), in *Mirar en Caracas* (Caracas: Monte Ávila, 1974), p. 51. This text is included in the present volume, pp. 289–94.
27. Francisco Da Antonio, "Bárbaro Rivas: Apunte para un retrato" ("Bárbaro Rivas: Note for a Portrait"), in *Textos sobre arte: Venezuela 1682–1982* (Caracas: Monte Ávila, 1980), pp. 304–19. The text is included in this volume, pp. 295–99.

universalism of inscription

bolívar, ourselves, and today **j. r. guillent pérez**

Simón Bolívar was born in Caracas on July 24 in the year 1783 and died in San Pedro Alejandrino on December 17, 1830. This December 17 marks the 119th anniversary of Bolívar's death. One hundred nineteen years have passed and still his fame and glory are sung by all and sundry. Every illustrious poet, writer, and public figure of Great Colombia and Latin America has offered words that attest to these feelings of deep admiration. It has been said over and over again that Bolívar is the only genius the Latin American continent has ever produced. Bolívar has been called a hero, a great politician, a great diplomat, a great orator, a great writer. The enthusiasm for the figure of Bolívar is truly singular; the loftiest of qualities have been ascribed to his person. All this, however, has left the impression that Bolívar's life was a kind of landscape, an exterior landscape far too removed from the rest of us, those of us who are alive today.

Nietzsche once said that to understand a great man, one must be his equal. If we were to consider ourselves in light of this statement, we would have to conclude that Bolívar's life and work have been entirely unknown and foreign to us for 119 years. The majority of the existing analyses and studies regarding Bolívar's personality tend to be filled with grandiose words, vacuous terms, and sentimental phrases that fail to consider the genuine drama and true circumstances of Bolívar's existence. For most of his critics, historians, and admirers, Bolívar has become a ghostly, phantasmagoric figure completely disconnected from mortal affairs, and specifically from those of Great Colombia and Latin America. For these gentlemen, Bolívar is the genius, the hero, the shrapnel, the hurricane. And several other words, to be sure. But words only.

Our historians have overlooked the most important aspect of the true reality of Bolívar: he was a man of the Latin American colony. Bolívar was a Latin American colonial man: here lies the secret and the true reality of Bolívar. The colony is the domain of Latin America; it is the vision of our totality, our "root belief." Bolívar has been stripped of his flesh, removed from the circumstances of his life—and circumstance is the first and foremost element of human life. Too often, people forget that the drama and life of Bolívar run parallel with the drama and life of Latin America. For this reason, before making any attempt to glean anything about the life of Bolívar, we must first ask the question: What is Latin America?

The most fundamental characteristic of Latin America is its colonial identity, an identity that continues to hold sway even today. The colonial identity is our true reality, the vision of our totality. For us, it is our most important historical classification. The colonial character is not something that has been caused—in fact, just the opposite. It is the uncaused cause. We were born as colonial people, and that is what we continue to be. The colonial legacy does not come from outside us; rather, it is something that we possess and that possesses us from within. It is and has been our fate, our destiny. Society is an organized whole, a totalized world; what matters is the whole. Its parts are of secondary importance. We should not say, then, that we are colonial because of the shortcomings of our literature, or the shortcomings of our production processes, or the ignorance and backwardness of our people. Quite the contrary: we are and have been all these things because we are colonial.

The colonial existence is the reality of our overall experience. And all studies or considerations of facts or people must be carried out against the backdrop of that totality. How have the most distinguished figures of our history acted in the face of that totality? And with regard to Bolívar, what did he believe? What particular connections exist between Bolívar and our colonialism? Bolívar was our Libertador—our liberator. The life and work of Bolívar are summed up in that one word. Bolívar was a man of the colony and he was also El Libertador. The gulf between those two positions is insurmountable: they are the two most diametrically opposed notions imaginable. To be colonial means depending on someone or something else, it means being subjected to external powers. Bolívar was the will, the determined spirit that resolved to stop being colonial. Bolívar broke the first link in the chain of colonialism. Bolívar was our political Libertador. After Bolívar, and in a general sense, after (political) independence, the root of Latin American countries changed; a new kind of historical life was born.

Mere political independence can never be enough for a country. Absolute, total freedom is what must be attained. Human life, both individual and collective, is an organized whole, and political freedom is only the official manifestation of freedom. In short, the work of Bolívar and independence must be completed and fulfilled. What good is political freedom if we are still economically and culturally colonial? In other words, Latin America has enjoyed political freedom for 120 years now, but as far as everything else is concerned, we are just as we were before. Only in the official sense have we been free.[1]

Today Bolívar is a topic of tremulous, urgent timeliness for us—that is, the real, genuine Bolívar.[2] What can the Bolívar who is so ardently admired and lavished with praise be worth to us if he is not useful to us in the present? Bolívar is the rebel stance that confronts colonialism and clamors for support. Bolívar should serve as an example for us, not so much through his quotations and proclamations, but rather through his most essential attitude: the rebellious attitude of a man who no longer wishes to be colonial.

All the idolatry of Bolívar has done us a great deal of damage. The manner in which we have treated the figure of Bolívar has effectively blinded us, kept us from understanding him in his true sense, and from understanding ourselves as well. We must never forget that Bolívar was a man of flesh and bone, as [Miguel de] Unamuno would say. Our historians have elevated the figure of Bolívar so far above the rest of the mortal world, so far removed from our real concerns, that today many people would cry sacrilege if we were to turn to Bolívar and ask him to help us in the present moment. The rift we have created between ourselves and the glories of yesteryear is so deep that we have truly disconnected our present from our past. Our past was too great, and our present is too small—and there is nothing more pernicious than the idolizing of the past. The past can only be a genuine past when it functions in the service of a present. The past for the past's sake is anachronism. And the service that Bolívar can offer us today consists, primarily, of his defiance of the colonial realm. We would do well to follow his lead, to ensure that all other orders and aspects of our reality achieve freedom and autonomy. Our economy, our art, and our intelligence continue to exist in the colonial realm. In the resulting order of things, we must adopt a position that is equally defiant, and we must seek out the means and methods for undoing the ties that bind and subjugate us. Thus, we need a Bolívar of the arts, a Bolívar of intelligence, a Bolívar of the economy. But isn't it a sacrilege, isn't it rather offensive of us to ask such things of Bolívar? (With this we return to the concept of idolizing the past, to that spectral distance between us and Bolívar.) No, gentlemen. Bolívar's greatness cries out for the birth of his equals. After all, of what use is his greatness if we cannot understand it or allow it to evolve? Otherwise it can only be a greatness annihilated, mummified, with no basis in true reality. Until today, this is what the life of Bolívar has been for us, in essence.

Why has Latin America enjoyed only political freedom? This is a topic that ought to attract the interest of our historians and sociologists. Why is it that culturally, economically, and in every other real sense we have continued to be as colonial as ever? In all these 120 years, has Latin America ever had any real chance to achieve true, comprehensive freedom? Doesn't it seem, rather, that we have been more or less what we had to be? And for all those people who believed and continue to believe that political independence is everything, our 120 years of Latin American life stand as testament to our real and continuing colonialism. Political freedom is something, but it is not everything. Political freedom was nothing more than a beginning.

As long as we are content to receive and imitate, we will never abandon colonialism. This has been the traditional stance of our forebears. But it is incumbent upon us to reformulate and reconsider, as painstakingly as we can, the traditional issues and heroes of our culture. And before we do this, at least one criterion for evaluation comes to mind: to what degree have the most distinguished figures of our tradition broken our ties to the colonial world? Is, for example, someone like Andrés Bello a liberator of the mind of the continent? And so on. In this matter, we cannot allow ourselves to be satisfied with the middle ground. Independence achieved in parts, or partially, or halfway, is a failed independence. The truth is that in none of the remaining orders of our life and culture is there a single figure worthy of comparison to Bolívar. And as long as this person eludes us, we will remain as colonial as ever.

The colonial Latin American Bolívar was El Libertador. In these pages I have offered an extreme oversimplification of a few bits of the colonial man and Libertador that was Bolívar. But more than that, and most essentially, Bolívar was a Latin American. A Latin American whose figure has never been equaled. Bolívar is neither from Caracas, nor Bogotá, nor Quito – Bolívar is, above all these specifics, a Latin American in the most essential sense. And in truth, what would have been the point of liberating Venezuela and not Colombia? Venezuela without Colombia, Colombia without Ecuador, Ecuador without Mexico, Mexico without Argentina – none would have ever achieved anything truly important. Latin America is a unified reality. And in this sense, too, Bolívar serves as an example – an example not to be contemplated and admired in his greatness, so far removed from the rest of us, but rather to be brought closer to us so that today, just as yesterday, he may serve and aid us through his example.

BOLÍVAR, COLONIAL LATIN AMERICAN LIBERATOR.

– "Bolívar, nosotros y hoy," *Los Disidentes*, no. 1 (Paris), March 1950: 12 – 16.
Translated by Kristina Cordero

on latin america and the west **j. r. guillent pérez**

[. . .] Every respectable philosopher, at least once in his life, ought to cast *doubt* upon everything he knows. Today's young Latin American finds himself in a somewhat Cartesian dilemma: in order to discern the *unequivocal* and *solid* truth of all that is Latin American, he must take all of Latin American culture and life and pass it through the sieve of doubt. The very fact of doubting everything may well be the strongest evidence we have to suggest that we are embarking upon a new kind of history. Doubt is not always a manifestation of weakness or lack of courage; in the Cartesian case, for example, doubt actually represented a pivotal step forward in Western history, by heralding the *unequivocal* terrain of the modern nation. It has been said that a science achieves maturity precisely when it begins to experience a crisis of principles. And in a similar vein, one might say that the crisis of Latin America's *traditional* existence may be the very best evidence we have to suggest that Latin America is entering a period of historical maturity. Of course, a scientific crisis of principles is without a doubt far less dire and less urgent than a crisis regarding existence, especially collective existence.

Our present age is an age of crisis—not so much because it exists in a transitory state of crisis, but rather because *today,* a *permanent* crisis of existence is put forward as the essential condition for authenticity. Contemporary man feels that the traditional beliefs regarding what is "Western" are grossly inadequate. And yet when he tries to suggest new ways of conceiving this term, what he really proposes is a perpetual crisis of all that is traditional. Today, for example, philosophy is expected to exist in a state of permanent crisis: "Philosophy gets underway only by a peculiar insertion of our own existence into the fundamental possibilities of *Dasein* [existence] as a whole" (Martin Heidegger: *What is Metaphysics?* [. . .]). This permanent state of crisis that contemporary man has come to experience is magnificently expressed in the following passage: "In this sense, the 20th century man feels more alone than ever; now he finds himself without a world, without God, and without himself. A most singular historical condition. Intellectually, contemporary man has no other choice but to reside in the ontological place where the reality of the world, of God, and of his own existence could dwell at the same time" (Xavier Zubiri, *Naturaleza-Historia-Dios* [*Nature, History, God*; Madrid: Editora Nacional, 1942], p. 49).

If any meaningful results are to emerge from this crisis of traditional assumptions about Latin America, the crisis itself needs (in the sense of a historical need) to find its source in the same crisis that is presently occurring in the realm of what is generally perceived as "Western."

But wouldn't we be misleading our young people if we were to tell them to *mistrust* all that is *traditionally* Latin American, if we were to tell them to doubt all such things? Isn't it inhumane to propose that men live their lives in a state of crisis? Wouldn't it be better to tell men to *forget* the more critical elements of existence, and instead dedicate themselves to harmless, *humanitarian* endeavors? In the specific case of Latin America, wouldn't it be better to let the traditional conceit, filled with concessions and abnegations, take its course?

With the exception of a few corners of the planet, the Western interpretation of the world is the dominant vision of our time. The Europeans colonized America, Oceania, Africa, and parts of Asia. Ever since the end of the nineteenth and all through the twentieth century, we have witnessed the ever-growing trend of Westernization around the globe. The most notable examples are Japan, Russia, and more recently China. Without question, all of humanity has taken Western civilization as its own, as something entirely *natural*. The label "Western," no longer the exclusive terrain of a specific geographic area, has become the anonymous property of all mankind. Today, Europe is nothing but a portion of the planet—one with a certain amount of privilege—that shares Western civilization with the other communities of the world.

In matters relating to Latin America, Westernization has been overwhelming and absolute. All our institutions, public as well as private, are derived from the Western interpretation of the world. Our political and social beliefs draw from the European interpretation of life. Our justice system has been brought directly from Europe, and our educational institutions have been created in the image and likeness of the European model. The industries that have been developed in our countries are of entirely Western roots. Our family lives, our "societal" lives, our fashions, our leisure, and our sports are all of Western origin. Our ways of communication, our modes of transportation, and our health-care system all find their inspiration in the West. Everything about life in Latin America hinges upon the Western conception of life. There is no manifestation of life in Latin America that does not presuppose, as its most essential element, the Western perception of the world.

At this stage in our modern age, it would be impossible for Latin American life to extricate itself from all that is Western. Proposing a completely original way of life would be a futile task. Far before we knew it ourselves, and without any effort on our part, we were ascribed a place in the Western realm. As such, the only thing that we can reasonably (historically) do about this today is reconquer the Western world in the *intellectual* sense, by reconquering that foundational element of our reality, in order to achieve historical equilibrium.

Whether ingenuously or otherwise, many people believe that Latin America, with all its traditional knowledge and resources, is a truly original culture, essentially distinct from the other cultures of the Western world. Nevertheless, we need look no further than Greek culture, for example, or the life that has been adopted by the modern nations of the West, to begin to express *doubts* as to the *supposed* originality of Latin America. How is it possible for a culture to be original and authentic if it has been created under the aegis of a colonial approach toward existence? The one truly original culture that has ever existed in Latin America was the culture that existed before the [continent's] discovery. Nowadays of course, the Incan or Aztec interpretations of life influence the fate of Latin America in only the most superficial way. Pre-Columbian culture *was* an original culture.

The true originality of Latin America cannot be discerned by studying monuments or testimonies of a bygone era that has only the most negligible influence upon our lives in the present day. Nor is the originality of Latin America characterized by the exuberance of its natural environment or the intermingling of its races. Exuberant natural environments and mixed races can also be found in Africa, Oceania, and Asia. Moreover, natural environments and mixed races are simply not sufficient evidence of a truly original culture in a world that is Western.

Today's Latin American has decided, in every sense, to evade the *responsibility* of his true Destiny. He invents imaginary worlds and purported originalities that neither convince nor fool anyone. Because of this, Latin American life finds itself in the most radically false position: it remains smug in the most superficial kind of originality, while turning its back on its true reality. Instead of seeking genuine contact with all that is Western, and appropriating it *intellectually,* it focuses only on ancillary elements.

Taking possession of the *truth* is the real endeavor that the young people of Latin America must assume to truly understand their existence. This does not refer to a static truth, or even one that already exists. What we need to do is conquer the *truth* so that it may find its place in the minds of Latin Americans and thus become a fundamental part of their lives. Truth is not this or that, or any other thing. Truth is that peculiar manner in which the Greeks *interpreted* the world; it is that peculiar manner that would one day constitute the most essential foundations of the West. And all of us must work toward the conquest of that truth. All of us must work so that the intelligence, the art, and the social life of Latin America are firmly grounded in truth. We must do everything in our power to ensure that the Greek *noûs* [mind] takes root in our lives. When Western intelligence has become the private patrimony of our lives, only then will we possess true intelligence and true art.

Just as the Liberators found it necessary to *break* with the establishment and exorcise all that is traditional, we too must distance ourselves from the traditional Latin American point of view if we wish to embark on the path of truth. And in order for us to do this, we have to *want* to live in plenitude and authenticity–in other words, we have to sincerely want to be the true masters of our destiny.

Truth is only granted to those who have been *freed.* Truth without freedom is illusory. Latin America does not live in truth because the freedom it enjoys is an inferior kind of freedom. Do not be fooled, however, into thinking that our most pressing task is to achieve freedom, which in turn will bring us truth: freedom without truth is impossible. Freedom and truth are always inextricably linked.

There is no way to carry out the task of achieving true freedom in Latin America without questioning the most fundamental assumptions regarding the life of Latin America. Only a crisis of our most basic tenets regarding traditional Latin American existence will truly inspire the need for freedom and truth.

–"Lo Latinoamericano y lo occidental" (part 2), *Los Disidentes*, no. 1 (Paris), May 1950: 13–16.
Translated by Kristina Cordero
This text has been abridged for the present volume.

manifesto **los disidentes**

We did not come to Paris to take classes in diplomacy, nor to acquire "culture" to serve our personal convenience. We came here to confront problems, to struggle with them, and to learn to call things by their real names. For this reason we cannot remain indifferent to the atmosphere of insincerity that constitutes the cultural reality of Venezuela. We intend to contribute to its improvement by ruthlessly attacking its defects, so that the blame may fall upon those truly responsible, or those who support them.

A good deal of the work we have set out for ourselves is none of our business, but given the indifference of the people who should have made it their business, we have not hesitated to make it ours, and we will be as specific and detailed as possible.

We are (and will continue to be) Venezuelan, and we are the first victims of the deplorable state of things. Today we are speaking out against it, and if we do so loudly, it is because it is necessary.

We stand up against all that we believe to be regressive or stagnant, against all that functions under false pretenses. We are the product of and witness to a great deal of nonsense, and we would be in a bad way ourselves if we could not speak our minds, in the way that we believe is necessary.

We want to say "NO," both now and after "Los Disidentes." "NO" is the tradition we want to establish. The Venezuelan "NO" that is so hard for us to utter.

"NO" to the bogus Salones de Arte Oficial.

"NO" to that anachronistic archive of anachronisms that is called the Museo de Bellas Artes.

"NO" to the Escuela de Artes Plásticas and its promotion of bogus Impressionists.

"NO" to the exhibitions of national and foreign merchants who come to the Museo each year by the hundreds.

"NO" to the bogus art critics.

"NO" to the bogus folk-style musicians.

"NO" to the bogus page-filling writers and poets.

"NO" to the newspapers that support so much inanity, and to the public that so obediently walks to the slaughterhouse day after day.

We say "NO" for once and for all; to the Venezuelan *consummatum est* with which we will never be anything but decadent and ruined.

–Introductory text in *Los Disidentes*, no. 5 (Paris), September 1950.
Translated by Kristina Cordero

manifesto of the galería cuatro muros[1]

mateo manaure and carlos gonzález bogen

To be history, not its victim. Herein lies the artist's highest destiny.

No one more than the artist has intuited that time cannot be reversed: "It is not given to us to live back, we can only think back."

This is why in every true artist, as in every creator, there is a destroyer.

To release art from its figurative content keeping it in the plane achieved solely by pure lines and colors has been the task of abstract art.

All true art is more than opticality.

Until now the understanding of the uninitiated has been predominantly *thematic*, therefore what is truly *visual* has escaped their comprehension. Today the pure values of the plastic arts are being restored. Herein lies their educational reach made real: *four walls*.

Cuatro Muros is a continuation of the battle started in the magazine *Los Disidentes*.

To some degree, the origin of this battle is to be found in the vision of an art of such a total renovating power that it is a genuine creation of our time.

We advocate the comprehension and integration of this *new dimension of the plastic arts* within any live manifestation in which balanced visual elements such as shapes and colors play a role.

–"Manifiesto de la Galería Cuatro Muros," Caracas, February 21, 1952.
Translated by Mónica de la Torre

correspondence between alejandro otero and alfredo boulton

letters from alejandro otero to alfredo boulton

Paris, April 14, 1947

Dear Alfredo:

Today the photos go out to you. Numbered in chronological order, from one to eighteen. They also have some other notations: in Roman numerals, the number of the subject, from I to V, and alongside that, the number of the canvas indicating the order in which it should appear in the series. Seen in chronological order, from 1 to 18, you will see the same concerns that come up in writing; in some, you see the evolution of the arrangement of one canvas in the one that follows, and most of all, the *position* from the perspective of nature. All of this, no doubt, exists as nothing more than the seed of an idea and I know it will be very hard to get a feeling for it through a simple photograph that has neither the color nor the quality nor the proportion of the canvas etc. You will see, however, that none of this has anything to do with the art of the eye, even though, in principle, everything has been done in front of a model. It is really more a kind of art-conception that seems to move toward the creation of a reality (here it would make sense to define that reality), and I can say that it is a *voluntary* reality with monstrous tendencies (because here the object, an object, through a will of the spirit, possesses a life, a human signification that makes it strange in the eyes of those who are not accustomed to seeing the human element in anything but man himself, and then, only the gentle side of the human condition).[1]

On these canvases, more visibly in the less abstract ones, there is a *conscious effort* toward deformation that adds character. Not the character of things as they are in reality, but rather the character of the *voluntary object*, of the object-invention and the direct message of the artist.

The strange and new thing about this (I am speaking in the future, given that I have actually created very few of all these so far—you know that I only started working again in October)[2] is the extraordinary reality that one can communicate to an object and to a man with this psychology. In this sense I am pleased with my candlestick and jar in canvases 15 and 18, and of my saucepan in canvas 1. If you want to have some of the photographs published, I would suggest that you pick from 1-4-5-6-9-15-16 and 18. And you baptize them.

[Matthias] Grünewald and [Pablo] Picasso are predecessors enough to give me confidence, as does Paris, and the faith I have in the painting I create. I think these are the only things I need to be able to do something in painting that, for the first time, will be truly important for my country. Something that will rise to the challenge of the times, something certain of its meaning. [. . .]

Your friend, affectionately,
Alejandro

Paris, February 15, 1950

Dear Alfredo:
I haven't sent you the letter I wrote on the 10th because I have been waiting to see how my work comes out—I have worked on many more canvases since then *with no connection to reality.* [. . .] *without any relation to reality. From the perspective of plastic interest, these are as good as the best of my more or less figurative work. That is what I think, and that is what I see, at least up until now. Yesterday I stopped working, to give myself a bit of critical distance, to clear my thoughts and, in the end, to see whether or not I was wrong. (I pray to God the answer is no, because I have put far too much effort, honesty, and enthusiasm into this). If all this is true, I believe that my painting* habrá alcanzado *[will have attained] a greater meaning. I will have reached the freedom of my age, and from here it (my painting) can only continue to evolve.*[3]

The experience today is only the beginning. It is from this point onward that all the problems of painting, and everything else, if they exist, begin to take shape. And what makes me anxious now is nothing other than the desire to continue seeing them from this new world. This is a good day, today, and while I may not feel certain about ideas, I have good, strong faith *and from here I see a future for myself. I see, I see, and I believe it will be mine.*[4]

Ton ami de toujours [Your friend forever],
Alejandro
[. . .]

Paris, April 8, 1950

Dear Alfredo:
I received your letter of the 31st. I have been working nonstop on the photos I promised you, which I thought I would send you this week, but they came out terribly, meaning they don't give even the slightest idea of what the paintings are like. The most interesting thing about them is their color, and in black-and-white all of that gets lost. [. . .]

Regarding what you have said to us about our pamphlet and our position. I cannot help feeling quite touched by the things you say, because I know that you say them from the very core of our friendship, which has always been what it is today, sincere and rooted. My letter to you the other day was, without a doubt, full of passion and not very specific, and it must have taken you by surprise, but if you want to know the reason for it, you don't have to look any further than the accumulation (en masse as I was writing the letter) of all the problems that have led us to adopt the position we defend now. These problems have ballooned to the point that they are about to explode from their own retrograde implications, which places us in a position of repulsion, and fills us with a passion for combat, without question. I would be so happy if you could understand it as only that, and please forgive the belligerence that occasionally comes out when I say things; I know they have a way of changing the terms in which we write to each other.

If we begin with a combative action against figures and groups, it is only because those figures and groups are at the very foundations of the reactionary opposition to our painting, and because it is through that reaction that we may identify our own active position. Personal diatribes are inevitable, as are the personal reactions of all the people involved. The inevitable atmosphere of scandal will descend upon us because of this, to be sure; on the other hand, it will certainly serve to encourage the reconsideration of many of the issues that make up our program.

We did not set out as grant recipients of the national education ministry to attack Venezuelan cultural officials and organizations—grant recipients or not, we are a group of young people who want to take responsibility for the problems that concern us. Those officials and organizations are standing in our path of action and, even more importantly, they are the consequence and cause of everything that needs to be fixed in the grueling march of our incipient culture. We also did not set out as self-styled quixotic figureheads of all the things that need to be done. We want to act like young people, and it is young people to whom we are speaking, in the name of an action that will one day produce results. When you remove that action from the exclusive framework of all that is national, and disconnect it from the local figures involved, it really is nothing more than a simple, logical phenomenon, almost an obligation, that the youth of Venezuela—including us—had ignored until now. This movement is being led, for the moment at least, with the support of twelve young men in Paris, and the men in Mexico and Caracas will join us in the second edition of our pamphlet.

We cannot answer for the life of our activity—and we know that a strong reaction will begin to work against it, but we can answer for the question of the scope of the issues we present. Our action is sincere and true, and our passion is the very root of our principles. Our paintings may be good or they may be bad, but our position will always be authentic, without a doubt. We do not believe in absolute truth, nor do we believe that we are invulnerable to the attacks that may be aimed at us. We are analyzing things with tools that we feel are good, tools that we hope to hand down to those who come after us, with the sole and fervent desire for the result to be a fruitful one. [. . .]

I ask you then to consider all of this as a simple statement of problems and of our decisions, which I hope will not in any way change the friendship we have always had and the moral support that has been, between us, the mainstay of our mutual trust and understanding. [. . .]

Alejandro

Paris, June 15, 1950
5 minutes to 1 A.M.

Dear Alfredo:

I am just back from the meeting this evening. We had a long talk about our problems with painting. A lively, almost violent debate (with all of our usual passion when it comes to these topics), among Pascual [Navarro], Guevara [Moreno], [Rubén] Núñez, and [Perán] Erminy, that lasted all the way to the metro. This was the main reason for the creation of our group, and I think it is useful for all of us. I am still a part of this conversation, and it is this trust, this faith in our work that has made me want to write to you. I am one of them, and yet I feel that I am more than just another member of the group, moved by this desire that drives us to move forward, to understand, to see and to do something.

I have been working all this time, until this afternoon, and I don't know but that may also be part of what makes me feel encouraged. I have been working on the collages for the show, and some color catalogues for [Guillermo] Pardo, and today I painted three canvases. I can't say that I am happy with the work, because it has turned out to be so difficult. I don't mean making the paintings themselves—that part is never more nor less difficult. What I'm talking about is the work in general, because it can only advance so slowly. It makes you feel as though your efforts don't make any difference, as if you were condemned by fate to walk forever at the same, pre-established pace. You know how desperate I can get, but it doesn't do any good. The one thing you need is something that simply won't come until the time is right, despite all your good intentions.[5]

As I was walking, I thought about the possibility of making leaps. My work today is almost the opposite of my previous work, yet I have arrived at this point slowly, step by step; and now that I am really on the path, it gets even harder. Slowly things start to come together inside you, producing a result, consequences of the environment, the reality that you live in, as if you couldn't escape it even if you tried. Everything that is overly evident doesn't work. And you do what you do because it is the only way. As if you were fatefully driven to do it. The painting, my painting, my life itself, what I experience without consciously controlling, but simply experience, has imposed its present reality upon me (currently the reality of my problem), and I have approached this with my usual honesty. On the surface there is no work, there are no dozens of paintings. If I could make them materialize I might be saved, but that is not how things are, nor how I wish them to be. All this has been lived with intensity and that intensity is what counts, I think, and maybe that applies only to me, although sometimes I think that this could also reach the others as well. And so I move along, little by little, honing my position, a point of view, formulating the bases of my testimony, so that it may be worth something. And that is how I play things, day by day, doing what I am doing as purely as possible, which is the best I can do. My various problems are only different mechanisms of the same thing, and today, tonight, I feel them arrange themselves in a whole that *is*. [. . .]

I thought about the dangers, the kind that those people who exist outside themselves call danger. But I don't think there is any danger out there when a person does what he does fully conscious of the danger, in the things that one experiences dangerously. This risk, I think, is where the important things lie, because going through life so absolutely sure of everything is meaningless, because you can only be absolutely sure of everything when you are walking on stable ground, and stable ground does not exist in art. Stability can only be the past or the dead. Only in mediocrity is a person stable. The most important thing of all is what we experience in life, and life is constant risk. If a person does not take risks, it is because he has no courage, and faith is meaningless. Valid faith, living faith, is the faith that a person has in what *might be possible*, through the credit that a person builds for himself. What makes painting so compelling is that constant process of building credit for the adventure that is a possibility, the risk that is a possibility—not by proving it, but by making new risks possible. This apparently insignificant drama of the art adventure is the drama of that risk, of the possibility of *creating* something. That is why the importance of the work itself is secondary, next to the testimony that the work represents of that dynamic movement. And so the work, in addition to the interest it may have as a work of art, is above all something that should be experienced outside itself, between the work and the *act* that creates it, between the work and the credit that was obtained for it by the person who created it, and by the risk taken. The work is nothing more than the testimony of a leap, a leap that *is not* the work itself, but of which the work is the end result. In that sense, the work reveals nothing more than the indispensable. The work *is not a drama in and of itself* (though it may also be that); it is the only concrete thing that remains of an *act* that has been experienced. That act is important because only the act is essential, not the action (the other is combination, manufacture). What one experiences never becomes concrete, it disappears with the act, and that is greater than you or me; that is what can be more than one single person. (This is the most human element between work and creator).

The perspective with which we look at the work, then, must necessarily change, because the work is no longer complete in and of itself as a work (that is, according to the traditional laws regarding these things). It is now a different work, and functions in another way, beholden to another conception of life and art. That is the reason for the elimination. That is the reason for the devalorization of qualities (I am speaking about plastic qualities and the life that one suppresses over time). And this is where all the traditional beliefs regarding the artist's way of life break down. Not because there *exists* one *way* of being an artist, or because a person has to be one way or another. The two realities are simply different. And that is how a person starts to get loaded down with vices when in the company of other people—because that's what other people call them, vices, and then come the labels: abstract painter, expressionist painter, etc., neither abstract nor expressionist painter. Life, with everything that becomes tangible to us because of it, has a way of changing the circumstances of how we live; and we are part of those circumstances that are constantly changing and evolving in different ways.

Our altruistic (or perhaps patriotic) flights of fancy are secondary. When you really think about it, the way everyone else does, you realize that these things have to be done, and these are the moments when you feel overcome with conviction. When you live the life that everyone else lives, the only thing people can say about you (with reservation) is that you are good, and this is where the old morals come in, full force. In this sense as well, we are trying to be the best we can be. The only difference is that our methods, and our results, are completely different. [. . .]

Alejandro
2:30
(to be continued) (6/16/50)

(cont. of my letter of yesterday or this morning)
8 P.M.

Paris, June 16, 1950

My latest canvases are simple: syntheses of three or four tones on white. And in yesterday's canvases, which already I don't like, I returned to a kind of complication with the terms of the picture. To a kind of violence of color and stains. In any case, the problem is a problem of spaces, of great dimensions organized into a given rhythm, colored lines or half-formed shapes arranged dynamically within a given space on the canvas.[6] And more than color harmonies, they are tonal saturations: saturations covering the entire canvas, or saturations with the white itself and very little color, only what is essential to give it depth, and its meaning lies not in translation, nor in one particular shape or feeling. A painting must be enough in and of itself, its own content, its own meaning as a work of art. And its artistic meaning consists, precisely, of taking the "opposition qualities" to a specific *climate*. That climate is the support for the ensemble, without which the work would fall apart. And what I mean by that is that in plastic creation (in my case) there is one instant (which is why I think of it as a question of time) in which the support structure of the work (no matter what it is, whatever the work may be, in terms of its plastic content) stands on its own, and lends the work its true significance—a culminating point, a critical point, that is the value of the work itself, its meaning. Despite the decorative aspect of the work (formal interest), its true meaning lies beyond that aspect, which is ultimately nothing more than a result, a consequence of that other equilibrium, that other harmony, that imponderable support. That "imponderable support," is something that *the viewer can relive*, and it is when the viewer relives it that the work takes on its *true meaning*. Only then does the viewer feel the work. The rest is just primary contemplation, and in that sense the work is of no more interest than any other harmonious form—not necessarily a work of art—that one might find in nature.

What I call "opposition qualities" are the pure plastic terms, the intrinsic qualities of the paint that one works and creates with.

I say "its meaning lies not in the translation of shapes," because I am trying to create paintings without shapes—or, in other words, paintings in which the shapes have no meaning, and which do not wish even to be construed as shapes, despite the fact that in the end the elements of a picture (lines, colors, and spaces) come to resemble shapes. The things that exist in my paintings as shapes are the things that I have not been able to disconnect from nature in the most extreme sense. I refer to them as "shapes that have no meaning at all" because when one decides to work with a particular shape (any geometric form, whether a triangle, circle, square, or any other intermediate invented shape) it always, in the formal sense, has "a meaning." The painter always "wants to say something" with them. Or at least has a "specific" sense about shapes.

And when I said: "its *meaning* lies not in the translation of a feeling," it was because I am convinced that all this is very far removed from all that is feeling. What remains of *expression* in that painting is not the expression of feelings but rather the *expression of a specific conception* about painting. The question of feelings is something else entirely, and I don't believe in "translation" painting, and if translation exists, it would also be the translation of a specific conception of painting.

In my painting, this is nothing new. This is what I have always searched for, but the difference is that today, there are fewer external things in my paintings than before, and I have become clearer and clearer about this problem over time.

Without these antecedents it is very easy to get sidetracked when looking at my canvases. What jumps out at the viewer is a sensation of void, or of senseless complication.

It is very odd: every painter, no matter how realistic, has a "key point" without which any attempt to penetrate his painting is useless. Without that key point one cannot relive the work, and that is its most transcendent meaning. Everything else is nothing more than looking at the painting from the outside, and art is not just appearance, now less than ever before, a time when so many things about "appearance" are either in crisis or overlooked. The bad thing is that people start getting accustomed to these "new aspects" of the work of art, and this prevents them from entering the work. New precepts arise, and people become accustomed to the new (exterior) laws and nothing else.

In the path toward comprehending a work of art, there is nothing more difficult than discovering the "points" or the "key point" and the art critic is almost never of any help with the most contemporary problems. And as a painter, you situate yourself in the present day, in your own life, even before having *understood* the problems of contemporary art (I am talking about those fundamental problems) and maybe you never discover them, and only discover your own problems, with only the most tenuous connection to your contemporaries.

These problems regarding the comprehension of a work of art are very important, I think. Because art is not just one thing alone. There are as many paintings as there are artists, and given that the painting is a personal *testimony*, one cannot read a painting in an *impersonal* way, and it is in the impersonal that one generally experiences and, as such, judges art. For this reason, I believe that one of the noblest attitudes the viewer can adopt is that of accepting art out of respect. Of course, you cannot respect just anyone—even if that "anyone" is a genius—when you cannot identify the qualities that should inform your respect. In that case, what ends up happening is that the viewer respects, or at least recognizes what he has agreed to respect or accept, as long as the artists involved are not friends or those with whom he has immediate contact. That agreement, or contact, is what opens doors for us, and at some point, we end up finally understanding.

"Every mind is a world unto itself," they say, and yet, when a person gazes at a work of art that escapes understanding, the last thing that comes to mind is that there is an entire world behind that work of art, and that one does not understand it because one doesn't know it (and, especially in the case of art, it often may appear simple). The work of art must be at a specific level of comprehension for it to be understood. And it must be agreed beforehand that the question of whether the work is understood is an ancillary one. Every testimony must live, or fulfill its destiny, great or small, for today or for tomorrow (and if it is not today, it is almost never tomorrow), as if nothing could stop it.

A quarter to eleven P.M.

Please let me know when you have received these soliloquies.

Alejandro Otero
(to be continued)
(as with Los Disidentes)
[. . .]

October 5, 1951

Dear Alfredo:
I received your letter in response to the one I wrote from Villard-de-Lans. [. . .]

Of the two compositions I left before going away (one was finished and the other one halfway done), the news is as follows: the second piece is now finished (and very good, I think), and the other one, which was already done when I left, is on hold—meaning that, though it isn't bad, I will take more time to work on it, so that I can incorporate some of the new experiences. You'll see them for yourself, but before getting started again, I am going to get to work on a new one that I have in mind, to see if I can finish all three for the exhibition we want to put together. If not for now, immediately, then for when I have to send them to you.

Now, moving on to the exhibition: Mateo [Manaure] must have spoken to you about a project that Hernán Briceño has been thinking about, that he wants to bring to Venezuela; it is similar to the Venezuelan project, only it also has some other foreigners involved, as well. All this was somewhat up in the air, which is why I decided to do something about it all myself, but I could tell that Briceño was still taken with his project, so we decided to turn the two projects into one, and to activate the thing by collaborating. And so ever since I've been back we have been getting together (with the foreigners), and from our end the project is becoming clearer and clearer. Now, here goes the rest of the list: [Georges] Koskas (Tunisia), [Ellsworth] Kelly (United States), [Albert] Bitran (Turkey), and [Jack] Youngerman (United States), Yonesco, [Horia] Damián, Enard Maussian, [John] Coburn. Later on I will give you the details of the nationalities of these last few. Of these artists, I know Bitran, Koskas, Youngerman, Kelly, who all have some excellent pieces. In general they are large-format paintings, relief objects, and polychrome sculptures, etc. . . .

Many of the sculptures will be sent on as models to be produced in larger dimensions there. Please realize that we are not playing games here. [Carlos González] Bogen and Mateo will do everything with a team that they will put together. One portion of these sculptures (before anything I will send you photos, if you want, so they can get an idea) will be for the exhibition, another group will be for the outside—meaning, so that they can be seen from the street—and then a third group will be placed temporarily in different parts of the city (boulevards, parks, gardens, etc., to add atmosphere). One of these creations will be the emblem or the symbol of the show.

It should not be, as I said to you in my last letter, an abstract art salon or a simple exhibition. It needs to be something much more significant than that, an event of artistic magnitude that will exemplify the notion of *unity* among the *arts* (*in the man and in the city*),[7] the same things we have touched on in our discussions. In other words, we are talking about an intimate collaboration among painting, architecture, sculpture, etc. in the interest of the life of the community.

Painting and sculpture as they relate to architecture and vice versa. Their interrelations and the influence of all this in the practical aspect of objects of daily life in the house, in the street, etc., etc. This is what we should be aiming for, starting with the things we have created and continue to create, and which exude this same spirit.

The promotional literature should be titled "Unity in Art," and it should group together the recent works of the young Venezuelan painters in Paris and some of their fellow artists of other nationalities, also living there (or something along those lines). Forgive me, I know this is all scattered, I am writing to you without a real plan and I want to tell you everything all at once.

For all this, you will see that we won't need to work with young Venezuelan architects (we have two here)—not just to mount the exhibition (which is one of the most important points, since these things should not be exhibited as things *to be applied but rather as things that have already been applied*. Each with its own ambience and its own light, offering the most illumination, revealing its own specific individual value). So, not just to mount the exhibition, but also to organize that part that ought to be represented: architectural projects and examples that reveal the harmony between (modern) architecture and the other plastic arts, maquettes, etc. Of course, most of this will get sorted out from this end, but if we want to make the thing as lively as possible I think it would be a good idea to get as many interesting elements involved as possible over there. Would you help us to establish these contacts and write to us about what they are doing and what they think of it all?

Now, the location: it must be as big as possible (there are pieces that measure five and six meters long by two meters wide, to give you an idea), and that will allow us to put up some walls, made of cardboard or some other material (given that, to a certain degree, *we have to create the architecture* so that it goes with the things that are in the show, and accommodates their needs).

I know that all this is difficult and most of all expensive, but it is the only *way* to do anything interesting or useful. Not something that will come and go, but something that will set a real precedent, a real achievement. Don't you think? Please give me your honest opinion on that.

Of course, I know that everything will have to be fine-tuned, and that is why it is so important for us to establish the dialogue between all of us and those of you who are there, in the field—you are the ones who know what can and cannot be done, and what is or isn't worth getting excited about.

We thought that we might try to secure the material for the constructions by approaching small *domestic businesses* (cardboard, wood, paint, etc.) and getting them to give us the material if we guarantee them good promotion, once the plan is established – by then they will be able to see the scope of the project and the interest it will generate. Some construction outfit might be interested.

All of us thought the idea of the Ciudad Universitaria was a very good one – it sounds like the ideal backdrop, since we also thought of planning the system of visits in a very special way, too, as well as the *system* that will ensure the success of the thing. Leaving aside (for the moment) the issues of doing it at the right time of year, getting a good viewing public, getting this or that critic to cover it, we have other ideas for guaranteeing interest in the show, through other means – for example, *organized visits* led by three or four of us there, for elementary schools, secondary schools, even university students. We can go to the schools and bring them around in packs, walk them through the exhibition, and explain it to them (how many of these visits could we do in a month?). For other sectors of the population we could have a different system and schedule for visits. [. . .]

Thinking of you,
Alejandro

Paris, February 17, 1961

Dear Alfredo:
[. . .]
The show, which opened on February 1, will stay up until the 28th and includes the following painters: [Antonì] Tapiès, [José Luís] Cuevas, [Roberto] Matta, [José] Guerrero, [Wifredo] Lam, [Eduardo] Ramírez [Villamizar], [Edgar] Negret (sculptor), and me. I have received some very enthusiastic letters from David Herbert, among them his last one in which he says: "The show is going very well and lots of people have come to see it despite the terrible weather we've had this month. It's still snowing, and very cold. I think your work is magnificent. The more I look at it the more I admire it. The Coloritmos [Colorhythms] have a power and a movement that are truly extraordinary. Congratulations." [. . .]

About the Boston exhibition, it already happened. Now it's New York's turn but I don't know when it will be. Then it will travel around the country until 1962. Mr. [Thomas] Messer, director of the Institute [of Contemporary Art], who has just been named director of the Guggenheim Museum in New York, has also written me several very kind letters. Regarding the vernissage of the exhibition, he says: "It was an exceptionally successful evening. Rarely have there been so many preview observers and seldom have they shown such interest in the works." Regarding the paintings, he says: "Your paintings are, in my opinion, singularly successful and had [*sic*] a particularly electric and vibrant chord to the exhibition as a whole." He ends with this eloquent postscript: "I greatly regret that we could not reproduce one of your works in color as we had intended. Delay in the arrival of your works was responsible for the omission."[8]

Along with this letter, he sent me a press clipping with a photograph of me alongside two columns, and the following comment. It is frivolous, but it is the only piece mentioned: "And one of the most individual in this showing, though the method is scarcely new, is Venezuela's Alejandro Otero, who brings real pizzazz to his geometrical abstracts. Vibrant color along with handsome blues and browns are woven into paneled strips which seem to emerge and recede before your eyes. Subtle use of small diagonals lend further rhythm and movement to his work. He really brightens the corner where he is."[9]

[José] Gómez Sicre sent me two other clippings, both of which came out in Colombia, talking about the same show. The most important is from Marta Traba from *Estampa* in Bogotá, Feb. 6–12, in which she says: "The splendid Coloritmos of Alejandro Otero, whose severe language, rigorous definitions, incessant rhythmic organization, and faith in intelligence lend his work a permanent sense of vigor and are what make his works the strongest and most original of Latin American plastic art."

Despite all that, none of this has any relation at all to what I am going through now—the Coloritmos are done, they constitute a closed chapter, there is nothing more for them, and since I can't simply begin inventing things, I find myself starting from zero right now. After months of constant introspection I am starting over. And what I am trying to do is make a material that I abandoned ten years ago—oil—speak to me.[10] A series of twenty-eight canvases, done almost without interruption, are the result of this attempt. My impressions? I am happy, not because of what I have achieved but because I think I can continue. The writing and the color are eloquent and furthermore, the canvases work. Something tells me that in the struggle to reach the bottom of my most intimate feelings about painting, even rejecting all forms of support, I have found a path through which I may achieve what I need to achieve, despite the risks and the enormous effort it requires. Why wouldn't I take a stab at it? Anyway, I don't have a choice, really, that is my situation—I just had to face up to it. [. . .]

Love to you, as always,
Alejandro

Paris, July 10, 1961

Dear Alfredo:
I just received your letter of the 6th as well as the *El Nacional* supplement, and anxiously await the catalogue from the show at the museum, which looks superb. [. . .]

Regarding my silence of late about what I am working on, I think it is all because of something by [Henri] Matisse that I was reading around that time, which made quite an impression on me. He says: "If someone wants to seriously dedicate himself to painting, he has to start by cutting out his tongue." I thought this was marvelous, and I felt as if he were speaking right to me. For once, I decided to hold my tongue but now that you are asking me, here goes: I have been working a lot and I am pleased with the change I have been able to make as a painter, I am happy and expect great things. The phase on the rue Delambre is over. During that time I finished a series of canvases, thirty in all but they have been whittled down to eighteen, and in them I believe I have reached a culmination of my 1948–50 paintings.[11] More than that, though, with these pieces I feel I have reached the end of another process that has brought me to a place —a surprising and unsuspected place—from which I have created an entire series of paintings in relief that you will get to look at immediately as I am sending some color photos of them via Miguel [Arroyo].[12] [. . .]

According to the opinion of [Karl] Flinker, a gallery owner, who by the way is going to start showing my work as of next fall, I am among the neo-Dadaists(?). This, because I have slowly moved from painted painting (as in some of the canvases I have sent you) to textures (some of which I also sent you) and even to the use of very obvious matter with all sorts of things mixed in—screws, nails, pins, nuts, rope, etc., etc. You will see this in a blue relief that I sent to Miguel, and also in another piece in white and several other colors that I gave to Mrs. [Hans] Neumann as a gift, and you will see the others in the photos. This experience, it goes without saying, is not something that I invented, nor is it the invention of all those who fervently work this way these days, but what is most definitely mine is the intensity and rawness that I think the pieces contain, as well as the position that is the root of my practice. As far as rawness and intensity, this is the first time I have ever reached such a pitch, and regarding position, you might call it anti-painting. I fight with the material, with the color, with all the things that I use as elements, and what most excites me is that the emerging result possesses the truest kind of expressivity. And they actually come to seem beautiful; I have achieved the best plastic quality without even intending to at all. And I have arrived at this point by taking things step by step, not without violence, but also by letting myself go, simply putting my passion and my love for painting to work at the tensest, most dramatic moments, and searching for a way to the things that words cannot convey, the things that require the expression of the hand, of the painter's life. [. . .]

With a big hug for you to share with our child's godmother, your friend always, fondly,
Alejandro
[. . .]

Paris, December 12, 1962

Dear Alfredo:
I received your letter of the 5th, as well as the clippings that you have been sending on; they are the only record I have of everything that is happening with my show. Needless to say I am thrilled, and I can hardly express the joy you've given me with the acquisition of my blue-gray *Relieve* [Relief], with everything, and to think there is even a place to hang it at Los Guayabitos! That relief was almost a kind of stowaway:[13] nobody realized that one day it might be of some value but for me it is among the most evocative of my recent pieces. All you have to do is find "its" light, which should never be harsh. Only that way will it exude that blue-gray air, that atmosphere of evanescent metal. Just as your letter reached my house, I was over at Carlos [Cruz-Diez]'s place[14] working with some negatives that I had to reproduce and I found the ones of the *Relieve gris-azul* [Gray-blue relief], and I stopped for a minute and gave it the fond

hello that it deserves, and then I went on to the less sentimental task of finishing up the rather pressing work at hand. Now I will copy them for you. That piece went through various phases, and I believe I photographed it at every point along the way. The blue of the slab, which had entered into my world, had been gnawing away at me from the inside, and the piece just didn't meet my expectations and hopes for it. The first time around it had a letter, and believe me, I felt very attached to that little piece that says INRI on El Greco's crucifixion in the Prado, surrounded by warm grays and *bleus meurtris* [bruise-blues]. The *bistre*-colored writing of the letter, with its wrinkles and deathly white, on the blue slab, almost resembled that but I just didn't have the strength for it, or the resources at the time to take it where it needed to go. Then it went through another phase, very simple this time, nothing more than a sheet of metal that moved forward in space. At that moment it already had the air, but it seemed poor. Then after that, it finally took on the quality it has now.

I tell you all this because I want to explain to you how these things happen to me, and of the purely expressive interest they have for me. If they don't "talk," if they don't communicate, they are useless pieces, "be they wires, or brooms," as you say.

I know that in my show there is a lot that can be taken, if you look at it superficially, as an exercise, an experiment, but that has never been my intention. Picasso said: "When I paint a painting, it is almost as if I am throwing myself into the void, I never know if I am going to land on my feet or crack my head open. In that struggle I get ripped apart, I rip apart the painting, and it is not strange that such a disaster turns out to be a guitar."

I believe only in the human testimony of a piece, but to offer testimony you have to cling to something. That something is none other than language. There are artists who, from the start, intuitively know their language, and they stay with it until the end. Others, like [Paul] Klee and like Picasso himself, know that language allows infinite transformations and, through such transformations, the signification of the work is modified as well. And there are even others who feel that a language "already charged" with significations is also viable and that with that language the work takes on a new expressive dimension, which is the case with objects. The object can be compared to the word in the sense that the word always means something, independent of what a poet, for example, can make it mean in the context of a given work.

Without a doubt, painting is passing through a phase that is eminently linked to the poetic experience just as the Cubists and the Dadaists experienced it, the only difference being that the Cubists barely ever removed themselves from the painted work and the Dadaists were not mature enough to take it to its most extreme consequences. Today we can go deeper into that experience and achieve it. I have the feeling that my current work is a contribution in that sense, no matter how it is received for the moment. In any event "*I have no choice*";[15] I feel the need to put myself on that path, I cannot keep myself from doing so. You know me, and you know the honesty with which I approach all these things and that I don't care if I "crack my head open."

At this point in my exhibition, your letter has given me one of the greatest feelings of satisfaction I know, not because it comes from a friend but because you would not have written it if in some way you weren't convinced. You can count on me to keep at it, with more love and more effort as time goes by. [. . .]

I send both you and Yolanda all my love and affection and the warmest regards from all of us,
Alejandro

letters from alfredo boulton to alejandro otero

Caracas, May 8, 1947

Mr. Alejandro Otero
4 rue de Trétaigne
Paris, France

My dear Alejandro:
[. . .] Upon your photographs' arrival, I contacted your mother and I took them to her, and we spent a long time looking at and discussing them. Afterward, I took them to the Escuela where I showed them to Antonio Edmundo [Monsanto],[1] [Juan Vicente] Fabbiani,[2] [Mateo] Manaure, Anderson, etc., etc. The first pronouncement was that you had turned Cubist (obviously, they seem not to know what Cubism is). Others talked about how abstract you seemed and Antonio Edmundo spoke about how you gradually deformed the real object (the two coffeepots) until it became something abstract.

On the whole, they liked your photos, feeling that although the photographs lacked color, there was something that had meaning and that was made with deliberate purpose. Moreover, it is my feeling that if they did not understand it, at least they explained it to themselves. This is already a triumph when it comes to painting. They all commented that the colors were a great complement to the drawing and they discussed the dynamism of certain themes with great praise. As I said before, I was surprised to find such favorable comments. To me, in particular, what you are doing seems extremely interesting and I believe that you are truly on an excellent path. Others who have succeeded never started at the age of twenty-six, as you have.

I must confess to you that I had a vague notion from your correspondence and I feared a small disappointment, but now that I have seen this, I am truly happy with your work. (How pedantic!) [. . .]

Write soon.

[. . .]
Alfredo

Caracas, February 24, 1961

Mr. Alejandro Otero
32 rue Manin
Butte Chaumont
Paris (19), France

My dear Alejandro:
[. . .] The Salon is opening next month. The works sent, as you will see in the article that I am including, have been many, but the comments that have been made, and which do not appear in the newspaper, are that the quality has gone down tremendously. Casualism is in its heyday and our local painters are looking for new subjects and new sensations. I think that painting is entering a new stage, which will turn into a new artistic language, with new expressive elements, looking to distance itself more and more each day from its classical bases. The new generations are constructing, knowingly or not, an art that will have nothing to do with what have been considered the basic concepts of the plastic arts until now.

The new field is widening in such a way, in such a violent way, that not only will men be painters, but the world itself has elements in its own formation concrete enough to make it compete with the artist in the field of casualism. Lichen stains on the bark of trees, damp marks on whitewashed walls, or the drip that damages the ceiling will all become as casual as the waves on the dunes, the clouds in the sky, or the artificial way in which man has managed to reproduce his own feelings and many others still hidden within him, as is the case with so many modern painters. Painting is becoming so diluted in man's life—it is becoming part of his every day; it is invading him, even in his dreams and his subconscious—that it has acquired a new vital meaning that divorces it day by day from what it has been until now.

Where do you find yourself in this tremendous maelstrom?

Hugs to all from,
Alfredo

Caracas, November 15, 1961

Mr. Alejandro Otero
20 boulevard de la Bastille
Paris

My dear Alejandro:
[. . .] I offered you a letter containing my reaction to those works of yours that I saw in Paris. I have given a lot of thought to what I could say to you about them and to the value that my opinion might have. I personally think that the artistic creation of a person of your maturity, with your human qualities, and your artistic trajectory, is above being influenced by others' opinions, even if the person giving them holds you in his highest esteem, friendship, and admiration. I also think

that you personally must not and cannot allow yourself to be influenced by those who like you a lot. Artistic creation is a product of such intimate, particular, and special convictions that under no circumstance should they be subject to modification by anyone but the person who created them, as they are the exclusive product of his affection and sensitivity. Just as you may not change the color of little Mercedes's eye, or the size of Alejandro José's hand, or Gil's hair color – in that same way, you may not alter the feeling you have as you create plastically what you have in your heart. I am sure that Picasso, Matisse, or [Marc] Chagall; or [Jackson] Pollock, or [Piet] Mondrian, or [Vasily] Kandinsky have created their œuvres by looking at themselves in their own mirrors, in their own eyes, seeking to express what they had inside, with their backs to the world, and confident that what they should say was what mattered to them. I am sure that they searched their surroundings with the sole intent of going against them, but never to take them into consideration and to be "followers" of this or that modality. Painting is essentially an individual, personal, one might even say a self-worshipping manifestation, and one does not succeed by following one tendency or another *à contre-cœur* [against one´s will].

In today's world of painting there is an eagerness to be eccentric, to do things that no one else has ever done before; this is a race toward a very dangerous pitfall. One runs toward the unknown without being sure of what one is doing; instead, one simply does it to be "fashionable," so as not to be labeled a reactionary. This is, in certain cases, an insincere and dangerous position. It is braver to confront the enemy resolutely than to follow a pack that rushes madly and without knowing why, toward an overflowing torrent, that is driven by superior forces with their own convictions. And it is precisely because of this that I do not understand how, from such a severe and disciplined subject as were your Coloritmos, you have been able, brutally and abruptly, to use plastic materials that are so absolutely strange to your condition as are those I saw in Paris. A man, an artist, cannot change his language, the way he pronounces words, his way of constructing a sentence, the language that expresses his affections; he cannot change them from one day to the next and make himself understood in a way in which he had never done previously. I cannot speak to you in Marxist dialect or in Zhou En-Lai's Chinese simply because I desire to follow "the fashion of the day." Simply, I must continue doing it in Spanish because that is how I feel it and can make myself understood. And if I have something to say that is burning my heart, and if that something is truly strong, sincere, and worthwhile, it is in Spanish that I will make it understood. [. . .]

A very affectionate hug for *la comadre* and best wishes to you from someone who loves you very much,
Alfredo

Caracas, December 5, 1962

Mr. Alejandro Otero
18 bis, boulevard de la Bastille, 10th floor
Paris, France

My dear Alejandro:
Two fundamental concerns jump out at one in your exhibition: the search for chromatic vibrations and their appreciation, and new appreciation of forms in relation to the object. The ill-prepared viewer might believe that you give this second aspect greater importance than the first one. I believe that objects and forms and their new uses are secondary in your work. What is essential is the importance that color has in your entire œuvre. It is, after all, the continuation of a search on which you are set, from the purple and green skies of your student days to your most recent Coloritmos. The color's rhythm is what has always served to drive your inquiry. If you were to remove the orange from the *Candado naranja* [Orange lock], the green from the *Seda china* [Chinese silk], or the metallic quality from the *Relieve azul-grisáceo* [Gray-blue relief], or even the yellow dot from the Collages,[3] all those recherché structures, as the baroque is recherché, would come crashing down and their structural presentation would not be worth a thing. The blue glove is important not because of the function or form of the object, nor because of the element of surprise with which you present it, but solely because of its rich tonality. The blue of that glove is also beautiful in Mercedes's hand when she used to dry the dinner plates, irrespective of the eccentric way in which you use it.[4]

Painting has, after all, an irremovable intention: the appraisal of forms, of lines and colors, conceived, captured, designed in such a way as to make feelings vibrate. Be they wires, or brooms, or vistas, or compressed automobile bodies, all those combinations of ideas and experiments have but one final objective, to awaken the sensitive fibers of the human heart. He who has attained the greatest depth of feeling is the one who can best enjoy that sensation. In this quest, we find ourselves faced with an attitude that it is important to elucidate. Experimentation, theory, and aesthetic function. I believe that today's painter is starting to travel on paths that, with time, tend to distance themselves from old formulas. He is starting to experiment and to distract himself by what, also with time, could bring him to create a new expressive function, quite removed from the original notions that man has created about painting. Within that order of things, he is determined to expose the beauty of forms and objects, which existed in them most intrinsically, as if they were new bodies with artistic value. Your blue glove had always been beautiful, even before you used it as a pictorial element. A bicycle's wheels are as captivating when they run in the "Tour de France" as when they are used by [Jean] Tinguely. The beauty of forms exists from the moment of their very creation. It makes no difference if it is a tree's bark, a cloud's diaphanousness, or the abstract and conventional use that man wants to give it. An object has its own beauty despite the man and the exotic use he might want to give it. Because of all this, I believe that your exhibition has been of great interest, if only to prove that painting is essentially made through chromaticism's life, even if that chromaticism becomes, as is sometimes the case with Jesús Soto, the strictest monochrome. And even monochrome itself vibrates.

I suppose very few people must have understood what you meant to do. Even if you do not want to say so. You know this all too well, that this is how it is, and that it has very little significance. Artistic expression is still appreciated merely because of a selection. When it becomes the stuff on stamps, that is when it loses its selective function. The great spiritual and material advances would never have been achieved without intellectual minorities.

I like your exhibition, as I have already told you, because of the problem you have identified in your own problem. I might dislike it because of the conventional way in which you sometimes overcome its difficulties. What is important in all of this is to know that you are immersed in a world in which you perceive, through its darkness, the eternal problem of color and of forms.

I have already chosen the wall in Los Guayabitos where I will hang the *Relieve azul-grisáceo* that I acquired yesterday. I am going to speak with Miguel in a few minutes so that I can include your check with this letter, so that you will soon have it in your hands.

Many warm regards and all my affection,
Alfredo
[. . .]

–Excerpts from the epistolary correspondences between Otero and Boulton, in *He vivido por los ojos: Correspondencia Alejandro Otero/Alfredo Boulton, 1946–1974*, Ariel Jiménez, ed. (Caracas: Fundación Alberto Vollmer and Fundación Museo Alejandro Otero, 2001).
Otero's letters translated by Kristina Cordero; Boulton's letters translated by Carlos Riobó
These letters have been abridged for the present volume.

the problem of integration **carlos raúl villanueva**

What are some of the reasons why artistic integration is currently advocated by architects and by painters and sculptors as an important objective, as one of the most urgent purposes to achieve? Why does the painter approach the architect and ask for the opportunity to work with him in the field of architecture?

Why does the architect feel the need to enlist the painter in order to make architectural surfaces vibrate with color? We believe that the reason for this lies, on the one hand, in the architect's desire to develop the meaning of his architecture; he seeks to enrich its painterly values through a wiser, more controlled, and more conscientious use of the tools that have traditionally been the painter's domain: color, line, and form.

The painter and sculptor, on the other hand, have recently left a personal and individualistic tradition behind and entered one that heralds human intervention as a symbol of social commitment, of human and collective sympathy, as a sign of responsibility. The value of communication, which painting and sculpture have abandoned (especially if they are left to individual whim), is reincorporated through an approach to art whose relationship to society is more functional, more direct, and more necessary. Introducing the pictorial or sculptural work into an architectural framework is currently a clear sign of the desire to assume social responsibility.[1] Need we repeat that the contemporary artist can no longer create for himself, within the limits of a personal world that can be understood by only a small circle of people, or within one that floats in the sterile isolation of individual action?

Well, it is precisely in reaction to all this that the artist approaches the architect with an offer to collaborate. He asks that his pictorial vision be allowed to acquire greater meaning and social consequence. This effort to collaborate cannot succeed without first resolving a wide range of problems. It is evident that without team spirit, professional solidarity, and camaraderie, artistic collaborations that ultimately aim at integration will not amount to much. Likewise, painters and sculptors need to have a relatively clear idea of the architect's way of working, of his artistic potential, and of the technical factors that affect his work. The spatial vision that characterizes the architect must be understood and used by the painter. Similarly, the architect must take the painter's or sculptor's particular way of working into account. Whether in surfaces or in volumes, he must respect the creative methods that are specific to each medium. There is a substantial difference between a work of integration and an attempt at decoration. Decoration, these days, is considered a surface embellishment, a superimposition and, as such, useless and perhaps even contrary to the purposes of architecture. Integration, on the other hand, results not only from the recognition of a common purpose but also from a necessary subordination among various forms of expression. It results in the creation of a new architectural-sculptural-pictorial organism that does not betray the least trace of indecision or the slightest fissure between different forms of expression. The necessary function of each artistic perspective must be immediately evident.

Art is the great testimony to each era's cultural meaning; in it we find the markers of historical character. The more the arts demonstrate a unity of concept and participate formally in each other, the more clearly they reveal the social axis around which the man-culture binary turns.

The presence of this axis stimulates the cohesion of artistic expression. In fact, the unity of human content is a fertile and necessary condition for the flowering of total integration. Architecture, painting, sculpture, and technique coalesce around a common purpose, around a common goal. Uniting objectives enables plastic synthesis.

In the context of this synthesis, architecture's concern with questions of functionality makes it responsible for leading the way in defining general concepts and sketching out the initial guidelines for the framework that will shape plastic events.

When a single concept permeates the world of the plastic arts, when a single philosophy runs through it and a single vision enriches its constituent parts, the arts coexist in the same field (often in close contact) but do not necessarily come together in total fusion. No effort at integration is necessary, no total union is needed, either as an objective or as a consequence of collaborative work. Nevertheless, those works that flourish during the same time period, underpinned by the same sentiments, reveal, after careful analysis, an almost constant unity of form. A product of the "spirit of the times," but also of the contact and exchange between cultures, the frequency of this phenomenon has hinged on how easily culture is transmitted and disseminated.

There is no synthesis without discipline. There is no synthesis without enthusiasm. There is no synthesis without faith in human values.

It is worthwhile to remember, along with Michel Ragon, that just as lions should not be in zoos, paintings and sculptures should not be secluded in museums. The natural environment for wild animals is the jungle. The natural environment for works of art is the plaza, garden, public building, factory, and airport—all the places in which man can perceive man as companion, as partner, as helping hand, as source of hope, and not as the wilted flower of isolation and indifference.

—"El problema de la integración" (Caracas: Facultad de Arquitectura, Universidad Central de Venezuela, 1980), pp. 70–71. A longer version of the essay, titled "La integración de las artes," was published in 1966 (Lima: Facultad de Arquitectura, Universidad Nacional de Ingeniería), pp. 9-16.
Translated by Catalina Ocampo

is photography an art? **alfredo boulton**

Is photography an art, you ask? Of course it is. Does anyone debate whether lithography, engraving, or etching are forms of artistic expression or artistic media? What might be debatable is whether the human being, the engraver, the etcher, or the photographer are artists. Now, this subject is already separate from the first question and very distant from the issue raised here. It is rash to doubt that a valuable creation could be made with a new artistic medium. What is important is that the work of art is successful. Would anyone today ask himself, or is it even relevant whether James Joyce's *Ulysses* was typewritten or handwritten, or Bach's old clavichord was used in the orchestration of [Arthur] Honegger's music? That would be an attempt to define the work of art's success merely through the values of old purist formulas. Any unexpected natural talent that might appear in the attempt to improve upon the old formulas is doomed a priori. Photography is a new form—if what was created more than a century ago can be called new—just as canvas, marble, metals, and even ivory were also once new. Enamels, glass, *papiers collés*, cement, and quicksilver—are they not perhaps expressive accessories used by men of sensitivity to create things and forms, the artistic value of which men of little understanding may still ponder? New tools are used indifferently to take creation to its due height by resorting to revolutionary formulas and by obtaining unexpected results. If the captured image contains sufficient visual value, then it should not matter whether it was copied on a canvas, on a rock, or on a simple piece of white paper bathed in penetrating and odorous acids. The work of art is there and that is what counts. It neither matters nor counts that it might have been necessary to turn to mechanical devices to achieve it. Routine and skill can also become mechanical, but the creation of things of indisputable artistic value does not cease because of that. Then why the skeptical and doubtful attitude in this instance?

No doubt the widespread use of photography has deprived the medium of the mystery that surrounds other activities invented and created by small, selective groups. Many people are still mystified by hendecasyllabic meter or the technique for writing a novel. To many people, the mixing of certain colors or the value of certain forms is still a mystery, but anyone who can afford to buy a camera and a roll of film is a photographer. In North America, that means twenty million Kodak customers. There can be no possible mystery among so many people. The charm of the unknown and the labyrinthine chamber of the camera obscura are things that can be learned today from both textbooks and five-cent magazines. The enigma of the creative force, that mystery that very few men perceive and are aware of, does not exist. Most people believe that a simple touch of a lever is all it takes to make things happen. This easy and mechanical action has depreciated the value of photographic expression. Few people believe that as many dramatic and beautiful elements could accumulate on a piece of paper as in a frieze or a fresco. The simplicity of its mechanism has relegated photography to a disrespected position where it has remained with wall plaster or commercial pictures or posters. Yet if we truly appreciate aesthetic reality, if we face the simple facts, is not the very position of the wall plasterer or of the copywriter equal to that of many painters, sculptors, or writers? Most of the time, the latter are but simple, unimaginative makers of things, of paintings, of sculptures, or of novels, and they are nothing more. They are like Kodak's twenty million customers. But, to be that and an artist at the same time is a different matter and something almost exceptional. The mere act of participating, by profession or hobby, in an activity with artistic possibilities does not necessarily mean that one has achieved the necessary degree of quality. The popularization of the term "art" has distorted its interpretation. It is precisely due to that degeneration of its meaning that, today, the word's true value is muddled, perhaps on purpose. As a result, to ask whether photography is art is a matter that may be answered in the same manner as if the question were asked in relation to any other activity that might require human sensitivity for its utmost success. Shouting is not art, but knowing how to sing is; waving your hands and feet is not art either, but knowing how to dance is; neither is pronouncing words art, but speaking well is, as are writing, and drawing, and designing. Art exists in almost every human endeavor, but that does not make every man an artist. This is precisely where the true quality of the human condition comes into play and it is in this succinct and simple formula that we must discover the several shades of sensitivity. This defines the entire range of sensitivity from the sensitive man to the insensitive one. It is from that supreme condition, handled with intelligence, skill, and mastery, that the work of art emerges, be it in literature, painting, poetry, or simply photography.

Seldom has it been possible to describe human life as movingly as do the images we have seen daily in magazines and newspapers for the last half century. No other graphic expression would have yielded up in such a brutally dramatic way the historical aspects that have put life on this planet at death's door. Perhaps photography bears no small responsibility—in the violent clashes among human ideas, in the most perfect understanding of the relations among peoples – in disseminating, to the four corners of the globe, pictures that cleared the way, like tractors in the jungle, for a better understanding among races and beliefs. Perhaps all of this would not have been accomplished if the images had lacked expressive qualities. Let us remember the impact that some of them had at the time. [Mathew] Brady's images of Lincoln; those of Colonel [*sic*: Captain Alfred] Dreyfus on Devil's Island; Rasputin's elegant tea parties; the photograph of the imperial Russian family sunbathing on a Yekaterinburg roof; scenes of the October Revolution in the streets of Moscow; Mussolini's march on Rome, of white *guetas* and frock coats; Leni Riefenstahl's series on the Berlin Olympic Games; Hitler's multitudinous marches in Nuremburg; Roosevelt's contagious smile, and Churchill's bulldog captured by [Yousuf] Karsh's camera as they exited the Ottawa Summit. Who could have described the course of the Nile from Lake Victoria to the Mediterranean better than [George Hoyningen-] Huene? Who could have captured old [J. Pierpont] Morgan's financial ferocity better than [Edward] Steichen when he had Morgan grasp the arm of the chair as if it were a dagger? Who captured the mimes of [Charlie] Chaplin, and [Henri] Cartier-Bresson's life in India, and the underwater atomic bomb of Bikini where the biggest battleships of the world's greatest fleet are mere celluloid boats? All that strength and expressive power cannot be lost, floating about in space without finding its precise place. So much crude reality and so much pure fantasy already have their place secured in the art world; the heaped-up, naked bodies at the Buchenwald crematorium and the images of life in Polynesia definitively consecrate the expressive value of photographic art.

In years past, the magnificent photographer Hoyningen-Heune compiled in several volumes the views he had captured in Greece, Egypt, and Mexico. How many before him visited those same places and wasted yards and yards of film, trying to capture the decayed beauty of the walls of Sakkara or the yellow pyramids of Chichen-Itza? How many of us would have wanted to endow those ruins with the splendid life that the weathered columns of the Parthenon still conserve? However, to achieve this, the artist's sensitivity was necessary to construct, contrast, and arrange the essential values on the pages of a book in order to be able to capture and to make an artistic image out of something that had been lying in ruins for centuries. The stones and the temples have always been there, but no one had ever looked at them the way this artist did. His camera was the instrument for expressing what he saw and what very few people believed they saw. He put within everyone's reach the altar at Delphi, where the Oracle, enclosed between green hills of myrtle, pronounced her prophecy.

Clearly, the subject and the formula are always the great problem. What is different among men is the way of expressing things, or the way they do not know how to express them. There is the subject and there is the lens, but the man who will look at the subject through his lens is not like all the rest; he is the creator of images, he is the Maker. He is not the same as the man who writes page upon page, believing that he has written a novel; he is not the same as the man who has smeared and squandered stretchers and canvases, believing that he has created a work of art. The question, such as it has been formulated, may consequently be answered in several ways, but those different answers are themselves also applicable to other human activities. There is no question that what thousands of strollers do on Sundays when they go out to the country with their cameras in tow is not art, and those seekers of beauty who have spent a lifetime without ever having captured it are just like them. The answer lies in the man himself, and not in the medium that he might use to express his sensibility.

–"Es un arte la fotografía?," *Revista Shell*, no. 3 (Caracas), June 1952: 27–29.
Translated by Carlos Riobó

polemic **miguel otero silva and alejandro otero**

The following are excerpts from the polemical dialogue that took place during March and April 1957 in the pages of the daily newspaper El Nacional. *The debate was sparked by statements issued by the painter Alejandro Otero, criticizing the selection by the judges panel for that year's Premio Nacional de Escultura, and by a public letter that Otero addressed to Miguel Otero Silva.*

concrete concepts about abstract painting **miguel otero silva**

[. . .]

a division without artistic content

Abstract artists seek to divide modern art, and actually art from all time periods, into two great antagonistic currents: abstract and figurative. We maintain that such a division is highly fallacious, and erroneous from an artistic point of view, constituting nothing other than an expression of the inflated opinion that abstract artists have formed of themselves and their school of thought.

In fact, abstractionism properly considered is just one of a number of strains of modern painting that inspired Fauvism by way of [Vasily] Kandinsky, Neo-Impressionism by way of [Robert] Delaunay, and Cubism by way of [Piet] Mondrian. From these same branches, and from the tutelary trunk provided by [Paul] Cézanne, other schools currently in vogue have been born, each as respectable as abstract art. The only difference is that none of these has sought, as abstract art has, from its early inception when it was barely an evolving nucleus, to become fully "half" of universal art. And much less have the members of any other school sought to declare, on their own account and at their own risk, that the opposing "half" consists of all the other schools man has created over a period of centuries, both before and after abstractionism, from the very first stuttering moments of painting up to current trends that have now far surpassed abstract art, considering it overly academic. It is more or less as if the head of a pin were to say: "The universe is divided into two parts: the head of a pin and everything else."

So that our position might be more clearly understood, we will make reference to another sectarianism that is similar to that of abstract artists and should be condemned with equal vehemence. We allude here to those childish leftist extremists who seek to divide painting into categories like "bourgeois and proletarian" or "revolutionary and reactionary," without taking into account the question of visual orientation. They call any painting based on revolutionary political subject matter proletarian, and everything else bourgeois, including abstract artists, whom they consider bourgeois in the first degree. In this way they place truly revolutionary painters, not just in terms of their subject matter but also in terms of how much their creative genius has contributed to the new art (Diego Rivera, [David Alfaro] Siqueiros, [Cándido] Portinari, etc.), in the same category as the fauna of the *pompiers* who paint "starving peasants" or "the striker's children" with conventional lines and photographic faithfulness.

The truth is that the visual arts cannot be classified according to dogmatic principles, with no consideration of the norms that determine and govern their independent development. To divide universal painting into categories like figurative and abstract, or proletarian and bourgeois, or mystical and profane, or materialist and spiritualist would be literary, political, religious, or philosophical. But it is not aesthetic.

Abstract painting (thematically speaking) is what the men who painted the caves at Lascaux made during the Upper Paleolithic period of prehistoric art. Abstract art (thematically speaking) is what Cretans, Arabs, American Indians and nearly all primitive peoples created. But that thematically abstract art is intimately, thematically connected to figurative art of its own era, which used the same visual media yet in no way employed the abstractionism that Mondrian and his contemporaries executed in the twentieth century, under the influences of Cubism, Einstein's theories, and advances in modern architecture.

What is perturbing about abstract artists is not their works, which are at times excellent, but rather the categorical doctrines they seek to impose, far outside the realm of the visual. We do not deny that abstract art is one of the many currents of modern art, of indisputable importance given the truly transcendental discoveries it has brought to the fields of form and color. Furthermore, as an artistic tendency, it must be studied and respected. But when it abandons the territory of visual work in order to preach a dogmatic pseudo-philosophy, when it claims that actual human beings and their difficulties should be removed from the realm of art, when it attempts to become a destructive force against other tendencies in universal aesthetics, when it advocates the idea that painting should cease to exist as art in itself in order to become a utilitarian and functional subordinate craft in the service of architects, then it becomes necessary to combat it without hesitation.

And that is what we are doing.

–"Una división sin contenido plástico" (part 2 of "Conceptos concretos sobre la pintura abstracta"), *El Nacional* (Caracas), March 29, 1957: 12.

* * *

the emergence and development of abstract art

Despite the fact that in recent times followers of abstract art have taken to claiming that this style of painting is the logical visual expression of the "Western world," the truth is that Abstractionism in this century came to us by way of the Russians. Kandinsky, [Kazimir] Malevich, [Mikhail] Larionov, [Vladimir] Tatlin, and [El] Lissitzky are the men who appeared, beginning in 1910, at the forefront of the discovery of abstract painting. It's only fair, however, to note that a year earlier, a half-Spanish, half-anarchist painter named Francis Picabia had shown a tremendous abstract work he called *Caoutchouc* [*Rubber*]. However, though Picabia was acting as an anarchist and as a Spaniard, he was also an Impressionist, a Cubist, an Orphist, a Dadaist, a Surrealist and many other things; therefore, no one now wants to remember that he invented abstract art in 1909.

We shall accept, then, that it was the Russians. The most important was Vasily Kandinsky, the first father of abstract art, a wonderful painter born on the Russian border with China. His abstract watercolor from 1910 and his book *Concerning the Spiritual in Art* are key points of departure for lyric abstractionism. Though historians claim that Kandinsky was inspired by the prints on women's clothing to create abstract painting, it seems to us more apt to say that he was visually inspired by [Vincent] van Gogh's Fauvism, as can be observed in any careful examination of his colors, form, and style. As for the ideological foundation of his visual theories, in large part van Gogh furnished that as well. In fact, the indomitable and tormented Dutch artist always dreamed of painting music itself, of expressing in painting the sentiments of the human spirit. It was just this that Kandinsky later attempted to achieve.

The second father of abstractionism emerged in Holland and was named Piet Mondrian. Calvinist, puritanical,[1] erudite, an aficionado of the sciences, aggressive scorner of literature and poetry, and admirer of mechanics and architecture, he nonetheless possessed an extraordinary creative genius. His pure abstractionism or "Neo-Plasticism" resulted directly from Cubism, particularly that of [Fernand] Léger and of [Pablo] Picasso's Cubist period. But if Cubism was already in itself a source of rigor, constructed to put the brakes on the facile ease and disorder of the early years of the century, Mondrian took that rigor to the extreme of reducing its formal means of expression to the meeting of two straight lines in a right angle and of shifting colors to strictly flat surfaces, in inexorable reflection of his puritanical and scientifically oriented Dutch spirit.

Intelligences as distinct as Kandinsky's, which was lyrical, and Mondrian's, which was mechanical, coincided in the foundational moments of abstract art because a similar intention guided them: to express painting through alternative means. Some artistic genres express themselves in abstract language (music, architecture) while other genres express themselves in figurative language (poetry, painting). When Kandinsky and his disciples attempted to express music through painting (their works are often called "compositions," "improvisations," "fugues," "symphonies," etc.), they fell into abstract painting. Likewise, when Mondrian and his followers sought to express the architectonic world through painting, they too fell, via another route entirely, into painting that was abstract. In the end, abstractionism came to be nothing more than this: painting expressed in musical language (Kandinsky), painting expressed in chromatic language (Delaunay) or painting expressed in architectural language (Mondrian).

Unfortunately, aided by an era of skyscrapers, atomicism, radioactivity, and North American millionaires-cum-critics, Mondrian succeeded in dominating other tendencies in abstract art in the long term. In 1920, Kandinsky himself set aside his music and became an adherent of the geometric conception of abstract art. Currently, only [Hans] Hartung and a handful of other painters keep Kandinsky's lyric flame alive, and it is only [Alfred] Menessier and another group who recall Delaunay's splendid lights. The rest is just frigid, monotonous "Mondrianism."

The same thing has happened in our country. The group of works presented by the abstract artists in the eighteenth Salón Oficial is dominated (with the happy exception of Ángel Hurtado, a student of Hartung's) by Mondrian's mathematical dogma, straight lines and flat colors. Mateo Manaure himself, the last Kandinskian in this region, gave up his vigil and moved over to the topographic camp.

A group of young Venezuelan artists, some of whom are endowed with immense talent, have locked themselves tightly within the confines of this rigid, rigorous view of painting, within these mathematical and conceptual canons that use rulers and compasses as brushes. Turning their backs on their land and their people, decorating buildings and walls, they continue to bury themselves more each day in a uniform and academic formulism. It would be a difficult but noble task to recuperate them for the sake of painting, to yank them out from under the architects' utilitarian rod.

–"Aparición y desarollo del abstracionismo" (part 3 of "Conceptos concretos sobre la pintura abstracta"), *El Nacional* (Caracas), March 30, 1957: 16.

* * *

the social positioning of abstractionism

Though abstract painting has provided us with new formal visual elements, it has simultaneously posed, in the ideological realm, an age-old problem that has been debated for centuries: the disconnect between art with human content and art for art's sake. Abstractionism is, beyond a shadow of a doubt, an exaggeration of the thesis of art for art's sake, taking it to its final consequences: the complete abolition of subject matter, the radical elimination of man and nature as inspirational elements of art, the exaltation of technical media to the point at which these become the very objective of the work.

Yet we should note, before arguing against it, that the thesis of purism in art–that is, of the artist's neutrality or total "escapism" in the face of the problems of men and of communities–has encountered two utterly irreconcilable archetypical adversaries. First, there are those enemies of art for art's sake who represent the most regressive and obscurantist forces of thought and do not accept the evasions of artists, but rather aspire to elicit from them a commitment to the defense of their interests and seek to utilize art as a weapon with which to enslave the community and put the brakes on any possible attempt at reform man might initiate.

Second, and for diametrically opposed reasons, there are humanists and proponents of social renewal who are also enemies of the theory of art for art's sake. They maintain that artists and works of art cannot remain at the margins of humanity's evolution, that like it or not, these are both a reflection and a consequence of that evolution. And they likewise maintain that artists' seeming neutrality, which is based on renouncing content in order to take refuge exclusively in form, is not in the end neutrality, but is rather their resignation to settle for the existing reality.

We should indicate, on the other hand, that the initial impulses of purism in art or the theory of art for art's sake were built on rebellion and nonconformity. Artists who disagreed with the surrounding social milieu, who were unable to openly declare their opposition, attempted to find shelter in their subjective world, to isolate themselves in a pneumatic campaign in order to produce uncontaminated abstract or abstruse works. It is not a chance phenomenon that abstractionism, a trend in the arts that seemed already buried and forgotten, would have been taken up again with such enthusiasm in postwar Europe. Young people without faith and without horizons for the future, dissatisfied with reality but lacking in principles that might contribute to its transformation, turned their backs on men and nature in order to take refuge in the line, in perspective, and in color. That was what occurred beginning with World War I, when a considerable number of painters and poets sought to elude reality via a number of outlandish purist-art "isms"; they were later extracted from the ivory tower these represented by an even more monstrous war than the previous one.

This is the eternal tragedy of abstractionists and evasive spirits. If, as we walk through a forest, we come across someone who is killing a child, and we do not intervene because our convictions of neutrality prevent us from doing so, it is very possible that once we leave the forest we might begin to feel more complicit than neutral.

Another uncomfortable consequence of purism in art, of its disdain for the content of the work of art and its exclusive exaltation of form, is the definitive fact that following this path leads to attempts against the very essence of art. The idealist [Leo] Tolstoy and the materialist [Georgi] Plekhanov agree when they affirm that "art is a means of spiritual contact among men." And if the work of art were to be divested of its human content and restricted only to its formal attributes, art would be reduced to merely "a means of professional contact among people with the same occupation," since only those with the same occupation would be capable of appreciating, in all their depth and value, the artist's technical experiences and formal achievements. It is this we have referred to as the substitution of aesthetic (that is, artistic) evolution for cerebral (that is, technical) appreciation of the work. And this is precisely what is occurring with abstract painting.

–"Ubicación social del abstraccionismo" (part 4 of "Conceptos concretos sobre la pintura abstracta"), *El Nacional* (Caracas), April 1, 1957: 12.

* * *

on the interior world of abstractionists

Abstract artists will not resign themselves to accepting classification as purist artists, nor to the observation that their work lacks human content. On the contrary, they ardently rebel against that statement and emphatically affirm that "all man's gestures are human" ([Alberto] Magnelli), that "artists are part of nature, nature itself" ([Auguste] Herbin). In general terms, they maintain that abstract works are the result of the process artists undergo in their interior worlds, an "expression of what belongs to them" (Kandinsky), an expression that contains, if you will, greater humanity than the objective world called reality. And they insist on this to such an extreme that they even reach the extravagant paradox of using the term "individualists" to refer to artists who provide in their work a reflection of man as a real and common being, those painters who seek their inspiration in the problems of the collective, and they use the term "collectivists" to refer to abstract painters who attempt to express exclusively the interior world of one single individual. [. . .]

Far be it from us to engage in a Byzantine argument with abstractionists in order to prove to them that the interior or subjective world is not precisely the objective world nor is it the real world, or to attempt to demonstrate to them that the individualist is not the collective, nor is the collective the individualist, as they claim. We prefer to be more radical and to deny them outright the smallest premise or the greatest premise of their sophism. In other words, to deny outright that abstract art might be the genuine product of the interior world, of the artist's own personality.

And in order to support this negation on our part, there is nothing more apt than an examination of contemporary Venezuelan abstract painting, which is nearly totally in line with the geometric, scientific Mondrian school. Speaking concretely, who are the abstract painters in this country? Excellent kids born in Upata, Uracoa, Porlamar, Maracaibo, El Tocuyo, Puerto Cabello, or San Cristóbal (you may verify our precision in the catalogue of the eighteenth Salón Oficial), with barely a certificate of any primary instruction, completely lacking any kind of average general culture (not by any fault of their own, naturally), though extremely enthusiastic and possessed of indubitable natural artistic talent.[2] [. . .]

Interior world? Reflection of a modern and complex spirit? "Element of personality"? Rubbish, my dear abstract Venezuelans, rubbish. The works you produce are not, fortunately, the reflection of any interior world, but are rather the application of terribly exterior formulas invented (or pilfered from Cubism) by the wise Dutchman Piet Mondrian, that rigorous Calvinist soul who is programmatically in love with geometry, professor of ice who found poetry ridiculous and sought to subordinate literature to science and painting to architecture. [. . .]

—"Sobre el mundo interior de los abstraccionistas" (part 5 of "Conceptos concretos sobre la pintura abstracta"), *El Nacional* (Caracas), April 2, 1957: 12.

* * *

the return to the functional and the decorative

Another defensive action abstract artists take when they are defined as purist artists and champions of a dehumanized art, is to proclaim that their painting is "functional," useful in the face of man's needs, and thus human. Guided, furthermore, by their zeal for the modernity with which they are obsessed, they rush to add that to make painting into a functional, utilitarian art is to give it "new meaning."

Here they err on two counts. What is functional in art neither implies human content nor is particularly novel. It is obvious that when we refer to the social and human mission of a work of art we are not alluding to the physiological or organic needs of man, but rather to the development of human beings in the context of history. To attribute "human content" to works of art based on the greater or lesser utility they provide man is almost an exaltation of the applied arts (textiles, ceramics, tile-work, etc.) as an elevated expression of humanistic art. The prodigious mystical content of Ghiberti's *Porta del Paradiso* [*Gates of Paradise*] bears no relation whatsoever to the functional fact that people pass through that gate, and it would be equally prodigious if that gate were to lead nowhere.

Otherwise, that "functional" concept of painting is backward and regressive, to call things by their proper names. In the civilizations of antiquity (the Near East, Egypt, Crete, Greece before Pericles, etc.), we find painting subordinated to the decoration of clothing, bricks used for construction, and vessels: completely functional work.

With the development of those civilizations, and later in the Roman era, painting achieved great advances and leapt from objects to begin climbing walls. Yet it was always subjugated to the decorative function attributed to it, which clipped its wings. It was centuries before painting liberated itself. As late as the Middle Ages, the painter was like a mason, in the service of builders and architects, adorning buildings for them with their work.

In the fourteenth century, humanity's vital forces caused medieval structures to collide with the fortified walls of academia. Within the territory of painting, the role of the great liberator fell to Giotto. His profoundly dramatic work, overwhelmingly human and exhibiting great artistic love for nature, initiated the liberation of painting which was then completed splendidly during the Italian Renaissance, while Van Eyck among the Flemish and Dürer among the Germans were engaged in the same glorious mission.

Once liberated, having become a major and undeniably leading art form, painting experienced six centuries of splendor. Through painting, great geniuses of humanity have made themselves known, from Leonardo to Picasso. As for architecture, it has been obliged to resolve its issues on its own.

And now, in the twentieth century, Mondrian appears with his Neo-Plasticism, his scientific abstractionism, his geometric angles and his flat color planes, proclaiming that the only real painting is his painting and that anything "other" is lagging and has been "surpassed." But really, what does he want? He wants painting to cease to be painting for its own sake, in order to become a "complement to architecture." He wants painting to cease to express man's social and spiritual problems in order to become "functional." He is the anti-Giotto. He is architecture's fifth columnist, who got into painting in order to work toward a return to the lost slave galleys.

It seems to us perfectly reasonable that architects and builders would be so pleased with abstract painting, as in general they are. My excellent friend Carlos Raúl Villanueva, for example, exhibits sharp practical intelligence and a great love for his profession as a builder when he proclaims himself an advocate of abstract painting in Venezuela. Carlos Raúl is honestly doing what he does best.

Yet we are not architects, but rather artists who love painting to the core, as a major and rightful art. And from that position we maintain that the painting known as "abstract" should be considered "new art," insofar as it is a visual teaching derived from Cézanne, van Gogh, [Georges-Pierre] Seurat and [Georges] Braque, Léger and Picasso. But it is definitively archaic and regressive when, distancing itself from the pictorial field, it seeks to impose upon us doctrines according to which painting must become once again strictly "functional" (here read utilitarian), as it might have been in primitive civilizations, or a "complement to architecture," as it might have been in the Middle Ages.

–"El regreso a lo funcional y a lo decorativo" (part 6 of "Conceptos concretos sobre la pintura abstracta"), *El Nacional* (Caracas), April 4, 1957: 16.

* * *

[. . .]

orientations of new painting

Venezuelan abstract painters honestly believe they have located the true path of new art, the "only" path of new art. And they defend this conviction with the exalted exclusivity and the uncomfortable pretentiousness that characterize abstract artists from the far corners of the earth.

Is abstractionism truly the genuine expression of new art? This question is currently being debated in all avant-garde artistic centers, particularly in Paris, the city where our abstractionists acquired the convictions they hold dear today. And the truth–our abstract artists must know this from the art magazines–is that abstract painting is receiving severe blows at the hands of new artistic generations, who are openly reacting against a rigid academicism that would close the doors of emotion and tenderness to them, which over the long term is the same as closing the doors of creation to them. In a poll taken a few weeks ago by the French magazine *Preuves*, among forty-eight young painters nearly all declared unconditionally that they are against abstractionism, against its very nature, which they found restrictive, affected, and a castration of the imagination.

This is not the first setback abstract painting has experienced. After the initial popularity of its theories, which were hoisted up as the flag of isolation by a generation devoid of faith and of hope, another era occurred, during which abstractionism was filed away as a post-Cubist experiment that executed conceptual explorations in the pictorial-musical or pictorial-geometric world, but which did not lead anywhere. It did indeed resurface, when Nazism took hold in Germany, when Spain was invaded and sacrificed, when horrendous concentration camps arose in the heart of a Europe in flames. At that point a large group of artists, terrified by human cruelty, escaped into straight lines and flat colors that expressed nothing but at least did not torture or kill or debase mankind.

But after a crisis, humanity always regains confidence in its destiny. Thus the painters of today, returning from abstraction, where they had taken refuge in order not to hear, or see, or speak, once again direct their creative power toward the inexhaustible subject matter of man and nature, primordial and eternal source of painting and poetry.

Venezuelan abstract painters have undergone a very different process. They arrived in Paris during the chaotic postwar period; lit up by their youthful rebellion, spurred by their voracious desire to discover new forms, they affiliated themselves with the abstractionism that was in vogue at the time, without stopping to consider that as an intellectualist and decadent mode it did not fit well with their personality, neither in their cultural makeup nor in the spirit of the country that had given them life. For ten years they have remained shackled within the narrow limits of that doctrine.

They do not want to see that in the face of this new painting other paths are opening that are a thousand times more fertile than the path of abstraction. They forget that in 1910, at the same time that Kandinsky was discovering abstract painting in Europe, the greatest painter the Americas have seen was appearing on the Mexican scene: José Clemente Orozco. Extraordinarily new and creative, yet without shrill displays of novelty, Orozco provided the departure point for a new kind of painting, diametrically opposed to that of Mondrian. He represents the confluence of Giotto and Bosch, Goya and Daumier, Delacroix and Cézanne, yet expressed through an unmistakable personality via an unmistakable creative genius. Beneath Orozco's flags—Mexican and universal, profoundly human and powerfully new—the path was blazed for the restorative work of Rivera, Siqueiros, and [Rufino] Tamayo. Couldn't Venezuelan painters, if they believe themselves endowed with such artistic prowess, attempt to create work that might parallel that of the new Mexican renaissance instead of burying themselves beneath puritanical algebraic dogmas?

There is another path. A path that has a given name and a surname: Pablo Picasso. From Picasso arise innumerable ramifications of contemporary painting—even the abstractionism that is so insatiably nourished by Picasso's Cubist principles. It makes us smile to hear abstract artists repeat that their painting is "the expression of this era," when we all know that it is but the expression of the least artistic facet of this era: cold technicality, the exaltation of machines at the expense of men. If there does exist some visual expression of this era it is named Pablo Picasso, because in his hands all the spiritual, material, and social concerns of mankind in our time come together. In *Guernica*, Picasso leaves abstractionism far behind, not just from the perspective of the poetic emotion and human drama of the work, but also from the perspective of the aesthetic quality and innovation of his expression. *Guernica* is, on its own, a compelling path, wide open to new painting. Couldn't our young painters follow that path, instead of retreating into the cul-de-sac of abstract formulas?

There is another path. There is a path that consists of valuing the visual experiences of abstractionism for what they are: a means, never an end. This path consists of studying it as a means, as an auxiliary apprenticeship, and then, supplied with its valuable technical tools, to undertake the creation of autonomous work. This is the solution adopted by numerous painters from all over the world, among whom we can cite one Venezuelan: Luis Guevara Moreno. Guevara Moreno, who was until not long ago one of our most important abstract painters, bravely made his way out from between the prison bars of abstractionism and is today creating—utilizing his abstractionist experiences as a means, as the material out of which to create secondary regions within his paintings—a labor of unquestionable importance, rooted firmly in the field of new painting. In our judgment, what Guevara Moreno contributed to the eighteenth Salón Oficial is the most outstanding work being exhibited at the museum.

There are many other paths. And innumerable paths yet to be cleared. The prison doors are wide open before our young abstract painters, and beyond those doors is a luminous world where humanity and nature await. If these chronicles serve to help even one among them escape from the aesthetic purgatory in which he has voluntarily placed himself, we will feel marvelously compensated for the bit of work it took for us to write them.

—"Orientaciones de la nueva pintura" (part 8 of "Conceptos concretos sobre la pintura abstracta"), *El Nacional* (Caracas), April 6, 1957: 16.

reply to miguel otero silva **alejandro otero**

1

Miguel Otero Silva sets himself the task of divulging clear information about abstract art in a series of articles he has been publishing in this very newspaper. Yet despite his laudable intentions, he constantly contradicts himself, creating confusion among his readers. The offending contradictions in his texts are the following: in his first published piece, he criticized abstract art for its lack of social concern, preoccupation, and contact with the community. But in his second article, intended to be explanatory and titled "A Division without Artistic Content," he claims the following: "To divide universal painting into categories like figurative and abstract, or proletarian and bourgeois, or mystical and profane, or materialist and spiritualist would be literary, political, religious, or philosophical. But it is not aesthetic." He adds: "What is perturbing about abstract artists is not their works, which are at times excellent, but rather the categorical doctrines they seek to impose, far outside the realm of the visual."

The contradiction lies in the fact that Miguel Otero initially seems to yearn for some contact with humanity and later seems to take on a defense of purist art—that is, of strictly formal art. We responded to his first text by saying that abstract art embodies a new "conception" of the world and the artist—capable of being the passive product of a medium—and in many cases discovers the unforeseen solution, the path to follow, which is present, throbbing, in that very medium. This latter attitude is the one we abstract artists share.

Today's artist can no longer be a chronicler of occurrences, a folklorist, or simply a narrator. He is first and foremost a creator who creates and constructs even from within chaotic circumstances. Thus we do not believe that the only value of our works is their pictorial aspect. Abstract art is subject to the strictest elements of painting, not just in its formal rigor or aesthetic exigencies. The fundamental elements are recuperated—line, value, color—from within a position that regenerates what is most vital in all its force and breadth. Abstract art's subject matter is life, but life as a totality, not reduced to anecdote or allegory, nor even to its symbol. And for that reason it can share its creative process with the processes of architecture, because it is freed from the thesis of "art for art's sake," because it is capable of being active and functional, and because it desires to communicate with what is most anonymous and with the life of men, their daily realities and their customs, seeking to awaken the creative potential latent in every human being. That is our ideological position, of course, with a popular projection, naturally, and incongruent with all that is bourgeois; the bourgeois tends to violently reject anything that presents a new dimension of man—not just in painting but also in the realm of the political, the social, the literary, the musical, etc.—because its prejudices incapacitate it or immobilize it. It is not at all rare for a sensibility educated in the bourgeois environment to complain that abstraction is metaphysical and diffuse. On the other hand, it is not at all common for this to occur with a coarser being who is uncontaminated by ideas about the genre and who conceives the world in a primitive manner.[3] Paintings by Arabs and *indios* from the American continent have nothing to do with what abstract art is, as Miguel Otero discovers. Those primitive drawings nearly always have a symbolic or religious nature. For abstract painting there is no faith other than life itself. Therefore, it lacks symbols. It is an expression of life, and does not symbolize anything. A valorization of the entirety, of the matter in its entirety, draws it undeniably close to the attitude of men who still did not have their "I" readily at hand. This possible relationship between the irrational or religious and the impersonal has many times produced erroneous judgments about artistic expressions that are centuries apart. There are judgments, for example, that misconstrue the vital affinity that exists between the primitive and the abstract, ignoring the distances between their basic organization and consciousness. [. . .]

Here we come to his second contradiction. So as not to exhaust readers, we would like for Miguel Otero to tell us concretely what it is he is defending: form with its content or artistic arabesques? This is not clear in any of his texts. We, abstract artists, are in the first camp. According to Miguel Otero, in his own words, painting cannot be divided into figurative and abstract, or materialist and spiritualist, because what is fundamental is its artistry. Would he prefer to be left with a simple decorative adornment? So why the sudden pining over the problems of man? It would be better for him to make up his mind, because his contradictions multiply. It would seem as if in those pages he were pining for figuration, a painted silhouette and nothing more, since according to his own concepts what is most important, even in the figure, are the visual aspects. Here indeed we cannot agree; figuration depended on a historical process, just as abstraction does. We are not seduced by the ornamental. Art is not a game but a commitment. And if its purpose is full aesthetic realization, that purpose has never been lacking in heartbeat and human searching.

Miguel Otero's third article, titled "The Emergence and Development of Abstract Art" also falls into contradiction. [. . . He writes]: "Intelligences as distinct as Kandinsky's, which was lyrical, and Mondrian's, which was mechanical, coincided in the foundational moments of abstract art because a similar intention guided them: to express painting through alternative means. Some artistic genres express themselves in abstract language (music, architecture) while other genres express themselves in figurative language (poetry, painting)." It is a truism to say that color is the inherent language of painting, as is the word for poetry or sound for music. That word, that color, that sound, are all subject, naturally, to historical changes. No one can write or paint as in the Middle Ages or the Renaissance, not because there were no good writers then, but because we have other exigencies. Thus contemporary painters have resolved to work within color and line, just as painters from other eras subordinated that color and that line to figures, to religious images, to still lifes or bucolic scenes. In one case or another, we are all utilizing visual language, if that is what he is worried about. And what's more, in pictorial terms, a color or a line has more visual artistry than a linear figure or colored nosegay. But only in those cases where figuration appears does painting actually occur, according to Miguel Otero, despite his earlier defense of the purely visual.

This all takes place, however, because the retina has grown accustomed to seeing color embodied in objects. Visual work embodied the love of nature via landscapes, or reflected the conquest of the individual via the portrait and the nude, just as religious passion had been made manifest in ex-votos. There comes a moment, however, when man feels the deepest commitment he has been able to feel: the phenomenon of life with its multiple relationships. The world is understood as a whole, not as divisible. Until then, painting had been, in its content and as a consequence in its subject matter, an adventure of the "I" in the face of the things of the world. Painters situated themselves in front of their well-laid tables and painted them; they did the same with the faces of their friends or relatives, or with their strolls through the countryside. They painted everything, from a personal perspective, at a distance. Miguel Otero claims that "Cubism was already in itself a source of rigor, constructed to put the brakes on the facile ease and disorder of the early years of the century." What facile ease? What disorder? Purely visual representations of these? We imagine he is referring to a situation of a psychic order and not just an expressive aspect of the era. Cubism was in fact a source of rigor; it was almost a hygienic, healthful measure in the face of the reigning individualism. There were reasons it shattered objects and laughed at delicate faces. Color was no longer manifested in objects, but rather in mocking individuality or in breaking with limited zones. Cubism was a source of rigor, but this rigor was not only artistic; it was also critical. Or is it the case, as Miguel Otero seems to suppose, that artistic creations are made outside the world, exactly like an artifice? And now, another question: does one remain indefinitely within a critical and censoring spirit, simply protesting, or does one attempt to reform "the facile ease and disorder" by repositioning man in relation to things? There are those who try, who venture forth toward the prospect of a better life, and there are those who console themselves with a return to the past, with the nostalgia of those days without risk when man found himself confronting things alone, with no other obligation than his own testimony or narrative. Perhaps being only becomes possible once again when we feel capable of renouncing a series of comforting habits. Painters decided to set themselves the task of revision and retraining. It was necessary to begin from the pure medium, from the strictly visual medium: line, value, color. Nonetheless, Miguel Otero says that Kandinsky utilized a musical language and Mondrian used an architectural language, which ends up meaning, more or less, that Mondrian was a well-known midcentury architect and Kandinsky an expert in tremolos. In both cases, what was sought was the possibility of communication, of innovation and expansion. Mondrian linked himself to architecture without discrediting his visuality and Kandinsky revealed that lyricism is a way of uniting and interconnecting things, conceiving them within a unitary phenomenon and not in isolation. Kandinsky provided conception; Mondrian provided practice, which he enacted in its most immediate aspects. Kandinsky's lyrical line was continued by Delaunay, with greater intensity, which led to the expansion of the borders of art as had not occurred up to that time. Delaunay utilized the language of color as no one else had, though Miguel Otero says he did not, that he used another, different language: that of chromatism. What did he wish to say with that statement? To criticize a painter who is chromatic would be like reprimanding a singer who has a voice or a writer who uses words.

"North American millionaires-cum-critics," living in "an era of skyscrapers, atomicism, and radioactivity" who, according to Miguel Otero, aided Mondrian in his undertaking – and note that atomicism and radioactivity could chronologically be Mondrian's grandchildren – might continue acquiring abstract creations for their private collections, aided by someone knowledgeable who could give them counsel strictly based on the works' artistic value. It may be, in the long term, that the vision of a constructive world, linked to architecture and to man's most generous ideals, which function to create unity, might serve these collectors as an impulse and spark. Who knows what a man might be capable of, with dollars and all the rest? For our part, regardless of who acquires our works – as the market is wide open – we remain certain that what we do is not built on simple artistic value. [. . .]

– "Réplica a Miguel Otero Silva" (part 1), *El Nacional* (Caracas), April 9, 1957: 12.

* * *

2

The articles Miguel Otero has been publishing about abstract art remind me of a paragraph by Thornton Wilder from *The Ides of March*: "There is not a single untruth, no – but after ten lines Truth shrieks, she runs distraught and disheveled through her temple's corridors. 'I can endure lies,' she cries. 'I cannot survive this stifling verisimilitude.'" When Otero takes a series of phrases from Kandinsky or others and arranges them to suit his interpretation, I can do nothing more than ape him and say, "Rubbish, Miguel, rubbish." Abstract art is not solely the product of the individual's interior world, and likewise it is not the result of the "process artists undergo in their interior worlds"; rather, it is the result of the process the world undergoes. Nonetheless, the word "result" is not quite right in reference to the phenomenon of abstract art, because it implies a passive and even fatalistic attitude that abstraction is very far from enacting.

We also do not feign to make people believe that our expression "contains, if you will, greater humanity than the objective world called reality." If we were to accept this idea, we would become party to an interpretation that excludes reality. We would have to accept man as a reality independent of exterior reality, and accept that as something separate from and alien to man. We work from a different idea: we believe in an interaction between man and the reality that surrounds him. We believe that man is reality and that his beliefs are also reality; we believe, therefore, that man extends and modifies reality. We cannot imagine man as a static being in the face of the world. His capacity to perceive reality varies, as does his way of perceiving it, interpreting it, and expressing it.

The problems of collectivity are of basic interest, but not when approached in a narrative or passive form. Abstract art is animated by the permanent need to participate in the creation of a world of man and for man. Abstract works are not, therefore, "solely the fruit of an interior process," which Miguel Otero claims someone has sought to "make him swallow." Our concerns are in Upata, Uracoa, Porlamar, Maracaibo, El Tocuyo, Puerto Cabello, and San Cristóbal, but they are also in any place where a new, more generous and broad vision of the world is being revealed to man. We work alongside young people who are anxious and inquisitive, who seek ways to resolve their problems and struggle to develop their possibilities. When we write these explicative texts, we do it above all with those young people in mind, and also with the certainty that we will be understood by those mature artists who, having accumulated research, reflection, and a body of work, can take on the title of masters, given that the mere fact of accumulating years is no guarantee of maturity. Mastery is not a consequence of age, though age gives it power in many cases; mastery seems to us to result from any human activity that is faithful to its responsibility and its destiny. [. . .]

Things must be measured and weighed before they are spoken, and above all, they must be approached with a decisive will for knowledge. It is necessary to seek out and study what the most anonymous man has created.

The distinction Miguel Otero establishes between what he calls "humanistic art" and what he designates as "functional art" seems acceptable to us. At first his definition seems correct as a definition. He attributes to the term *functional* a sense of practical utility and to the term *humanistic* a capacity for human content. However, an obvious demonstration of his error in appreciation—as it is not one of definition—is that he cannot see in all the art of the Middle Ages anything more than something like a work of masonry. His inability to see in the art of the Middle Ages the result of one of the most enormous efforts toward integration in the arts that man has ever realized, the expression of a prodigious movement of conglomeration on the part of human beings in relation to their faith, is the same inability that today makes him see in abstract art merely a series of algebraic formulas and in its integration with architecture a subordinate attitude on the part of painters in relation to architects, and a degradation of painting, which, according to his criteria, reduces it to a minor art. Painters form a union with architecture, which does not imply a limitation for them, but rather an experience of working in common with other artists related to them in a visual sense. Painters collaborate with architects in order to achieve the fusion of two artistic perspectives that, once the work is executed, come to be indissoluble. This is the case with polychromy and with many effects that might be realized in conjunction with architectural elements. But this is not the only feature of integrative works: there are other cases when the work, despite the fact that it might be created with an eye toward the spatial relations architecture provides, conserves all its power as a work in itself, and might even be removed from its particular environment and continue being a work of art. In the Middle Ages, for example, sculptures and stained-glass windows formed an integral part of cathedrals, but each of these, in isolation, is in and of itself an artistic creation. Artists were not disdainful of illustrating a missal, carving a prie-dieu into an altarpiece, making the framing ornamentation for a stained- glass window, engraving a chalice, or creating a graffito with biblical scenes on the very floor of a church, because they had faith in God and because they felt that even in the most imperceptible spaces the common man might alight, a participant in the same belief system. The same may be said of Asian temples, and of Aztec or Mayan temples.

As for Ghiberti's gates, though Miguel Otero might denigrate them, they lead to the Baptistry. Constituting a creative wonder, they are conceived as doors. This is a beautiful example of what art can be when the artist does not consider it a creative diminishment to work with absolutely any element or object, leading it toward expressive power with the goal of valuing it and fusing it with other elements. Yet Miguel Otero seems unaware of all this, because, for him, it seems that art has only been in existence from Giotto to Picasso. It is frivolous to seek to erase entire historical periods, especially when they consisted of such singular capacities, and furthermore, when this confuses and disorients viewers. Renaissance art and its derivatives have no reason to be the definitive norm and end point of artistic creation. Qualitatively speaking, it is not possible to consider any of Giotto's work as superior to the stained-glass window of Notre Dame de Chartres, though the latter might be considered as an integrated work while Giotto's works point to a historical moment when painters began to feel the need to isolate themselves. These works are superlative, fitting, complete, necessary expressions of the moment of their production. But it is necessary to have studied all this with passion and responsible conscience so as to avoid entering into superficialities, random affinities, and contradictions.

Miguel Otero's journalistic experience allows him to play games that are by far more facile than the so-called ontological board game he accusingly attributes to us. Nonetheless, he seems utterly unaware that the Einsteinian concept of space-time is also present in the visual and architectural world of our era. At the same time that Einstein was working to elaborate his theory, Picasso, Braque, and other Cubists, along with many architects, intuitively reached identical or similar conclusions visually. This demonstrates the unity that exists in man's thinking, a unity that causes the most essential manifestations of a single era to correspond with one another.

Guernica, one of the paintings Miguel Otero cites when he references Picasso, is an expression of this idea. A painter with a fourth-grade education could perceive the space-time relation in painting. But if one is not a painter, or has no sensitivity toward painting, it takes more than a doctorate to understand it. Perhaps it is because he approaches these problems in painting with a doctoral mentality that Miguel Otero so readily asks us to change our mode of expression. [. . .]

—"Réplica a Miguel Otero Silva" (part 2), *El Nacional* (Caracas), April 10, 1957.

* * *

3
conclusion

We have come to use the term *abstract art* to refer to an artistic concept that arose in Europe around 1910. This concept excludes any representation of people, symbols of people or objects, and any idea of naturalistic representation. In contrast, the term *figurative* has been used to refer to any work that in some way, even in the most occluded way, takes recourse in an imitative representation of those same beings and things present in nature. This distinction developed with the birth of abstract art, so it would be possible to refer to a phenomenon that was different from everything traditional art had been. It is not worth stopping to argue over whether the terms *abstract* and *figurative* are the most apt for designating these two realities. This question has been debated at length and up to now no more accurate term has been found. A definition always carries the risk of diminishing the scope of the undertaking, and more so when the topic at hand is abstract art—a concept that has existed for barely forty-some years—which has been spoken of, at times, in very confusing ways.

The facts about the birth of this art, its historical affiliations, and the theories that have been able to sustain its early masters are easy to find in any modern-art manual. Yet there is still no text that has sufficient clarity so as to truly penetrate this new phenomenon. The absence of complete documentation is due to the fact that abstract art, from its inception until now, has experienced important changes both formally and conceptually, since from one day to the next it encounters new expressive methods. Those of us who have come to abstract art, not in order to affiliate ourselves with the latest fashionable trend, but rather because we have linked our concerns with an existing reality—one that, though obscure for many, became eminently clear to us under the light of our sensibility—find ourselves obliged not just to give form to that reality through our works but also to make an effort to communicate to others the phases of its particular problematic.

In order to understand the deep signification of painting—from any era or style—it is necessary to possess a guided sensibility, and in order to approach painting at the various stages of its development we must have studied it intention-by-intention, modifying our appreciative criteria alongside that development. It is never the case that a work of art is merely a combination of forms, colors, sounds, or words. For those who work in that way, it is impossible to capture the reality that artists seek to express through the media specific to each genre. Historically, man has made use of the basic elements of painting in order to express realities that have always been changeable. There was an era when it was necessary for painting to be magical, and it was: Altamira, Lascaux, African paintings made on rock. And there were other times when it had to become religious: Egypt, Byzantium, Gothic art. And there was the era when painting had to explain to man what he was corporally: Greece, the Renaissance. And another, when the task was the discovery of the individual: Holbein, Dürer, Rembrandt. Then it became necessary to inventory nature: Hobbema, Ruysdael, Rubens; to point out the frivolities and whims of man: Watteau, Fragonard, Boucher; to critique the problems of human baseness and social problems: Goya, Daumier, Lautrec. There was another era when it was necessary to specify the problems of man's interior world, his rebellions, his nightmares, his internal conflicts—Expressionism, Surrealism, Dadaism—all as a consequence of the need for compensation, for security, for knowledge, with the purpose of dominating in one way or another the forces of nature. Once those eras had come to pass and man had achieved that domination, he needed to experience the creation of a world that would be the complete expression of his most true being. For what man in any century saw as immediate or total reality is for us nothing more than a part of reality. When we contemplate the world or nature fractured into pieces, we also contemplate ourselves divided, as simple spectators incapable of fully penetrating totality. Art is no longer a way of being above the world, and much less of being alongside it, but is rather a means of being within the world, within its indivisibility. When our beliefs were based on religious or individualist principles, it was possible to take recourse in the imitation of the forms of beings and things. A new concept of reality, as distinct from the ones man had previously held, demanded an equally distinct language; man's new situation in relation to the world and his search for a corresponding mode of expression were located at the vortex of the crisis that led artists to a total rupture with tradition. No previously existing form would do, no return to the past was possible. At that moment, there occurred a reconfiguring of what painting fundamentally was, and thus it was that artistic mediums showed themselves to be a primary material, potentially charged with a force to which painters would have the task of giving form and meaning. There was no longer a reality to be imitated, but rather a reality to be created.

Kandinsky's watercolors of 1910 are an expression of that world in formation. With these works, painting had ceased to be what it had been so as to begin once again to be. For the first time, man became master of a total creative power, and he created on equal terms with nature. Painter and sculptor took a wrecking ball to the traditional scaffolding of painting and sculpture and positioned themselves before the future with a new world in their hands. Once that leap had been made, and painters remained free of the support that had traditionally been provided by nature directly, they were left with the enormous problem of inventing new signs, capable of expressing a new and totalizing concept of reality. In the face of all this, who in the world could possibly think that abstract painting is merely a combination of colors and forms? Painting has always been, and abstract painting therefore is, a conception of life and a conception of visuality at the same time. Painting has always been witness to a way of being in the world, and abstract painting, as much as or more than any other mode, discovers and affirms this fact.

Every valid new artistic expression constitutes an explosive invasion into the phenomenon of life and art, an opening of a space within it, a being within it, a penetration into it to achieve the total surrender to and expression of a new reality or situation.

It is very difficult to be certain that in their earliest moment revolutionary artists were intellectually clear as to the fundamental facts of the problem that was driving them to the creation of abstract art, since this problem has become clear only later, with the contributions of philosophers and men of science. They had, however, intuited it and predicted it. We should keep in mind what Kandinsky relates about his experience in the gestational period of abstract art; this experience was nothing more than the revelation of the intrinsic power of painting as an art form in itself and not as an imitation of anything. Kandinsky was looking at an Impressionist painting by Monet, the purpose of which could barely be deciphered. "I had the impression," he said, "that the painting itself was the subject of this work," and then he wondered "if it might not be possible to go further along that same path." As Kandinsky's later work demonstrates – and here I am referring only to his abstract period – going further, for him, signified the creation of a new art, the creation of new signs that, without being imitative, might serve to express the world as he was feeling it. In his writings, Kandinsky called that world his own "interior world." However, given the fact that there were neither symbols nor forms in those paintings that might potentially be interpreted as direct allusions to what that world was – rather, there was a series of signs he had invented that were associated with one another to the extent that they constituted a set of non-dissociated forms and colors organized as a totality with their own value and force – undoubtedly his painting was seeking an idea of reality that was impossible to express by means of direct allusion to objects or beings. Nonetheless, he did not fully penetrate the deep significance of this problem. His later phase clearly demonstrates this. During that earlier phase, called his Paris phase, Kandinsky limited himself to making an inventory of the real images teeming within his imagination, and this is, to synthesize, what he called the "interior world." Even in Kandinsky's abstract phase, form and signs were organized in accordance with the way figurative painting had created space and depth.

Mondrian came from the camp of Cubism and Cézanne's influence, to impose a more rigorous order. He reduced his use of color to the primary tones of yellow, blue, and red, alongside a use of noncolors, like white and black. With his work, painting would encounter its own specific reality: flat color surfaces applied to a canvas that was also a flat surface. Oppositions and tensions in dynamic equilibrium, as he himself put it, but without any simulation of depth. Painting must be painting and not a simulation of what it was not. The importance of the phenomenon of Mondrian was precisely that proposition, that painting should be approached from within a reality that should be all its own and ordered by its own laws – not the reality of nature, ordered by its laws. He approached painting as an art in and of itself, and rejected all confusion. It was through his intervention that painting would achieve independence as an art; it was he who set painting free for us, leaving it dependent on the creative capacity of the painter.

We have faith, fundamentally, in man – but in man as a totality. That idea means that today's true artist, sincere as he must be, must place his sincerity in everything, and do the same in his art as in his friendships, in his public life or private life, and even in his most elemental acts, because the new concept of life further entails a new moral position. What we do, we do with excitement and optimism, because we know what we are constructing and because we know that it is life itself that communicates beauty, dynamism, and truth to our works. Our relationships with what is natural and human are no longer outside ourselves. We do not have to hunt these down, placing our easel in front of a landscape or a human massacre. We live in the world and not upon it or beside it. We are in dialogue with man and we participate in his dramas, not as observers but rather as integral participants in his drama and his being. What, then, is it that we are betraying, and whom? What would art be: a simple untranscendent game? What would an artistic sensibility be: a simple skill for combining forms and colors, sounds or words, with the goal of amusing ourselves?

Art is transcendent because it is a means of delving deep into the unrevealed and it therefore creates disruption each time it takes a new step. Is it possible that none of this can be seen in our works? Nevertheless, we do see it, and simple, uncontaminated people feel it. Might this be what has been called an "already-understood minority clique"? It is possible. The fact that the number of people who understand or feel the contemporary manifestations of art might not be especially copious does not imply that fault lies with the art or with the artists. It is the fault of prejudices, of an absence of culture and a lack of distribution of artistic works, and also of that individualist—and thus regressive—concept held by those who seek a return to man's omnipotent and dominating Renaissance role. Isn't there an eminently reactionary idea embedded in the following sentence: "As late as the Middle Ages, the painter was like a mason, in the service of builders and architects, adorning buildings for them with their work"? Hence an attack against one of the most exemplary and noble collectivist eras in art history, one in which painters and sculptors became anonymous, in which painters-turned-stained-glass-window-makers created alliances with architects, with masons, with artisans, in order to build one of the most unified and magnificent works of man: the Cathedral.

There is an attack against our idea of moving toward architecture and the streets, toward houses and the most insignificant objects so as to draw near to all men, and once again the hierarchical idea of genius and supermen is being proclaimed. Battle is being waged against our idea of making ourselves anonymous in order to construct works with collective intention and collective reach, as are the integrated visual arts works we advocate. There is a desire for us to return to "major art," a desire to recuperate us in the service of the limited, wretched paintings those with money want to enjoy once again, lolling in their armchairs in front of the fire. Where would we go if we took that route, for whom would we have to make our paintings? It goes without saying, not for the majority. Let it be said once and for all that we consider ourselves simply man-as-painter, and as such we are not superior to man-as-doctor, man-as-philosopher, man-as-mason, or man-as-man. We will continue painting in accordance with our beliefs, regardless of what our paintings may become.

But let us go back a moment, in order to say that our work is not limited to constructing a mere performance of what Mondrian dreamed painting was going to be. Our era has expanded and become enriched in every sense, and Mondrian has not been the only artist working to achieve these goals. We believe that anything can be attained through the purely visual, but not because we think that the purely visual in fact contains everything, but rather because it is the fundamental material for painters and sculptors, the material with which everything can be expressed. Is it not through the essential elements of painting that everything that has been said in painting has been said? Proof that with these elements still more can be said. Nevertheless, we must not think, not in the least, that what remains to be said must be said with the same language as before. First of all, the way a thing is said bears immediate relationship to what is said, and additionally, there are things that require an appropriate language in order to be said.

Abstract art is precisely that: a new language in order to express a new reality. In the end, aren't reality and language the same thing, when we are talking about artistic expression? In abstract art this congruence is realized more efficiently than in any previous art form. In figurative painting or sculpture, an image could be interpreted in a wide variety of ways because the symbols were imprecise. In abstract painting or sculpture the form is exactly what it is and nothing else, because an identification has been reached between form and truth. For each problem of expression the artist finds the form or the relation of forms to express it, without having to take recourse in imitation or symbol. That is why abstract art is direct, that is why it is simple, that is why there are no tricks of our trade, that is why its structure is nakedly evident and it is direct in its material and colors. Abstract artists do not attempt to get anywhere with their art, because it is not allusive; rather, what is there is what there is, purely and simply.

Relationships and tensions are the expression of a vital force; color vibrations are active life; the material artists use to paint is a concrete expression; the rhythm artists imprint upon a composition is simultaneously its movement and the very movement of what is not purely pictorial. An abstract composition opens and is unlimited, because the world itself appears to us now as open and unlimited. And with every work new rhythms are created and new forms are approached, seeming to arise almost of their own accord, because we are experiencing a phase of discovery and surprises in every sense. We insist on color; color seems to us always undiscovered, because there is much in the world yet to be revealed. And we are excited about color, and focus our faith there, just as we do with our own children, because for us color is like a newborn whom we want to grow and to live, for its own sake and for the sake of others. We cultivate our painting and we cultivate ourselves, because we respect our painting as we respect ourselves, because painting has the right to be, to grow, and to exist just as this new world we are discovering has the right to be, to grow, and to exist.

If we were to ask ourselves, "What will this world become?" it would be as if we were asking ourselves, "What will our painting become?" We cannot foresee it, because we all know that what might definitively destroy the former is the same thing that might definitively destroy the latter. Thus the relationships established within an abstract painting are transitory, subject to the most fragile equilibrium. The slightest thing could disassemble them and even destroy them. And they are a way of clinging to what is material and concrete, because nothing else sustains us in this world of beings and things. We take refuge in the primitive and the pure because we have a new faith, and given the risk of total world destruction, we cling to painting and to life. But that faith, where is it directed, in the first and last instance, if not toward man himself? We know that each of us as individuals will disappear, and nonetheless we insist on creating our work so that our testimony will stay behind for others to witness.

Did Kandinsky and Mondrian think this way? I don't believe so, although it has been said that "abstract art is simply the mechanical transfer of dogmas manufactured by men with a very different psychology, from a different culture and an interior world diametrically opposed to that of Venezuelan painters." Yet the incontrovertible truth of this entire problem perhaps exists nowhere else but in painting itself. I gravely fear that we might have to take recourse in painting in order to locate its true essence and transcendence. Painting will be what man-as-painter makes of it, as it has always been.

–"Réplica a Miguel Otero Silva" (part 3, conclusion), *El Nacional* (Caracas), April 11, 1957: 16.

–"Polémica" (selection), in *Polémicas sobre el arte abstracto* (Caracas: Museo Alejandro Otero, Colección Delta Solar, 1999).
Translated by Jen Hofer
These texts have been abridged for the present volume

from the *journal de genève* **jesús rafael soto**

Excerpted from the interview granted to the Journal de Genève, *1970.*

When I came to Caracas in 1942, I was introduced to what was known as modern art, especially that of the French school. I was introduced to the work of [Paul] Cézanne and [Vincent] van Gogh. What most caught my attention at that time was a still life by [Georges] Braque, from the era of Synthetic Cubism. I was dazzled by it and immediately began to work in accordance with the concept of pure art–and I am not afraid to use that term. For me, art is a science through which we may arrive at a deeper understanding of the universe. From that moment on I sought out those artists who, throughout history, had adopted this view: Cézanne, the Cubists, etc. Then, all of a sudden, I felt an urgent need to discover contemporary art. With that in mind, I went to France in 1950. In Paris, I found [Piet] Mondrian, [Kazimir] Malevich,[1] and the spirit of the Bauhaus in all its glory, artists whose true dimension and scope were not yet fully understood. Some of these artists were overlooked entirely, while others among them were little appreciated. Nevertheless, I decided to study their works and managed to assimilate them in a relatively short period of time. From then on, my work began to move forward through a kind of evolutionary process. My work is the result of the discoveries and the attitude I adopted then. Around 1950, abstract art had begun to play a role in forging a new kind of writing–it was still very limited, but it was something that we had to use in order to get to the next step, the next frontier. And so, rather than negating space and its dimension, I became determined to make use of it.[2] This situation, then, led me to consider the question of time: how to use it, and how to formulate the fourth dimension as a plastic element. It was, in fact, in this area that our generation made a great leap forward: in the use of this new element as an artistic material. We do not utilize the simultaneous description of the object in the manner of the Cubists. Instead, we use time in a very concrete way, as a plastic, sensitive medium. To this end, I began with the idea of repeating one element, which at the time was the only means by which I might abolish the form as well as the flat surface of the canvas. Through the repetition of one element, ad infinitum, one arrives, imperceptibly, at the universalization of language. I always believed that the task of the artist was to create an object, done to scale, that demonstrated a universal principle. Liberated from representation through the negation of form inherent to repetition, I understood that we were automatically moving closer to a new idea of plasticity, in the most cosmic sense. At that point I still didn't know what that idea might be, but little by little I began to realize that modern man could not view a work of art from a single perspective, as he had done since the Renaissance. Our modern era had given rise to a physical question within the mechanism of visual perception: the viewer was asked to decipher, to look squarely at a work of art in its process of development, as if it were a film, no longer thinking of it as a static work. That was when I became aware of the need to incorporate the element of time into art. The process of figuring out just how to do that (and with what means) was slow, because I didn't want my work to become a decorative "machine." I wanted it to retain a strong purity of meaning—this defines my approach even today as I search for ways to decipher universal meaning through the new possibility offered by time.

In 1951 I created my first objects based on optic repetition. I then began to work with layered spaces made of Plexiglas that took on a life of their own as they were transformed through the movements of the viewer. This marked the discovery of new visual possibilities that eluded the traditional reading of the image. In 1954 I began to create genuine sensations of optical movement; I added progressively more movement to the image, without relying on any medium but the human being. I was determined to find a language driven and fueled by the human being, as I became increasingly aware of the integral role that the spectator would play within the work. I developed from this a kind of symbiosis, a communion of sorts, between the man and the work of art. For me the work of art does not exist independent of the viewer. Consider, for example, what happens with photographs of my pieces: when photographed, their value is no more than that of a traditional image, because their true dimension can only be appreciated in the presence of a viewer, whose movements are conveyed and reflected through them. Through the Penetrables, my most recent effort, that participation actually becomes a "tactile" and, on occasion, auditory experience. Man plays with the world around him. Matter, time, and space comprise an indivisible trinity, and movement is precisely the value that reveals this trinity. Even when a certain level of technology is called for, the truly important thing—at least for me—is this concept of man. All technique must be subordinated to him. I do not see the human being as a creature that merely contemplates the universe—I see the human being as an integral part of the universe in which he lives. For that reason, I no longer believe in the traditional concept of painting. The man who continues to see the universe from the outside lives as a spectator. And we are not mere spectators, we are participants. The mission of the artist in the twentieth century is to sensitively decipher the universe, and then to express this through the work of art. The "penetrable" work is the tangible proof of my vision of the universe. Artists decipher the sensitive state of the cosmos in parallel with men of science, who decipher the measurable states of the universe. A scientist who once came to visit me in my studio remarked how incredible it was that we, as artists, use such simple means to demonstrate the ambiguity that exists in space, whereas [scientists] need to avail themselves of the most extraordinary laboratory equipment to arrive at the same results. It is the concept, then, of aesthetics that separates us from the learned men. I am not afraid to use that term, though it has fallen into disfavor of late. We have to offer an aesthetic explanation of the universe—in other words, a qualitative explanation of the universe. Modern art cannot be representational, not because we reject representation in and of itself, but because representational art came about in an age when man believed himself to be the center of the universe and the witness to universal phenomena. Now, however, we know that we are only an infinitesimal part of that great whole, and as such we can no longer conceive of representational art, nor can we, as a result, continue to be contemplative.

—From an interview with the *Journal de Genève*, 1970, as published in Alfredo Boulton, *Soto* (Caracas: Ernesto Armitano, 1973), pp. 64–66.
Translated by Kristina Cordero

statement **jesús rafael soto**

We declare the existence of relations in every lucid moment of our thinking existence.

We stand amazed at the laws of coincidence without realizing that we are only perceiving relations of which we had never dreamed.

The elements plunge into the work of art like fish into water: all these directions, speeds, accidents, positions are ordered by an all-embracing whole, of which they are tributaries and which conditions their variants. Their force is measured by the number of their revelations.

This state, conscious or not, of the Contemporary artist has given today's Art an astounding wealth of possibilities.

SOTO

—Statement in *Signals* 1, no. 1 (London), November–December 1965: 4.
Translated from the French by Sebastian Brett

dialogue **jesús rafael soto and guy brett**

Paris, rue de Turenne, April 1965

b: Soto, whenever I've heard you speak or read things you've written, I've always heard you maintain that you are a *painter*. Technically speaking, your works are constructions of moving pieces which make use of devices of optical illusion. In what sense are these *paintings*?

s: Well, painting at all times has been in some way or other concerned with illusion, to suggest movement or space of a certain kind within the limitations of the canvas. The kind of illusions I use are completely inseparable from the kind of movement and space I wish to reveal, which in turn I believe to be the kind of movement and space which may characterize our experience of the world. In my painting, I've searched for movement by the device of superimposition; and these superimposed elements act on each other in a way which negates the distance between them. For example, if you take a photograph of a work of mine, so that it appears purely two-dimensional, a sensation of movement in space is created purely optically, though technically the elements are superimposed. It's the same with [Paul] Cézanne; though he was seeking a different sort of structure, he superimposed with what he had—the layers, the screens of paint.[1]

b: In order to create space?

s: Yes; space is the preoccupation of the painter.

b: But no longer in the Renaissance sense of perspective.

s: Absolutely not; perspective implies a single point of view, to give the illusion of depth, as in a landscape. It's surprising how difficult people find it to shake off the idea of space in painting as the illusion of recession. My aim is, by still using two-dimensional means, to give the illusion of mobility, rather than recession. Sculpture recently liberated itself so that its elements might move in space; but in my works it's the *surface* which is moving, that's why it's a manifestation of painting.

b: Can you describe to me the stages by which you arrived at this point?

s: Well, I really started out with the desire to make the work of [Piet] Mondrian move. Mondrian's last three works, the Boogie-Woogie paintings made in New York, affected me deeply; it seemed to me that he had made a sudden leap in the direction of a purely dynamic painting, realized through optical means. It seemed to me that he was about to make the image move optically, and it was this process that filled my mind when I started making works in 1951. I began with repetition—identical forms repeated across the canvas—and always the simplest possible forms, such as rectangles and squares. I have always worked with the smallest number of elements, to get as far away as possible from *description*. French painters have tended always to use "beautiful" forms, forms with a decorative function. I decided to use more anonymous and impersonal forms—the line, the square, and the circle.

b: The fundamental elements of a painting. . . .

s: No, it's better to say they're the least descriptive. I didn't invent the square, but it is an invention, it doesn't exist in Nature. By means of the endless repetition of the square, the square itself disappears and produces pure movement. Before I began to use superimposition in 1952, I was touched by the idea of serialism in music. I worked with small dots of familiar colors, again the least descriptive, so that one's attention is directed on the relationships between them. I organized the intervals precisely. Separating colors, calculating the distance between them, produces a vibration—as in the work of the Impressionists, [Georges] Seurat, the Fauves. The problems of abstract painting, you see, are problems of pure dynamism; the simplified-organic shapes of an artist like [Jean] Arp belong essentially to figuration.

For two years I worked on the idea of superimposition, using sheets of Plexiglas. It was in the last of these, using three planes and the form of the spiral, that the movement was freest, most realized. The whole process had been one of trying gradually to *detach* the elements. After I'd worked with Plexiglas for a little while I got tired of it and there followed a rather baroque period. I became more interested in the *material* of the work.

b: Yes, the informality of these paintings is surprising after the strict, step-by-step progress of the early works. It is as if you suddenly became conscious of what your actual contemporaries were doing. *L'art informel* was at its height in Paris then, wasn't it?

s: Yes, it's true; I wanted to test the relationships between my researches and the researches of painters around me, to be associated with them. It was certainly an experience. At that time I also made very free and complex "sculptures" from wire. Wanting to liberate the elements still further, I began looking for a way to combine illusionary optical movement with *real* movement.

b: And this, of course, brings us to your recent work. I think that here the superimposition ceases completely to look like a device; it becomes sensually inseparable from the visible change that appears to take place in the elements.

s: Yes, what has always interested me has been the *transformation* of elements, the *dematerialization* of solid matter. To some extent this has always interested artists, but I wanted to incorporate the *process of transformation* in the work itself. Thus, as you watch, the pure *line* is transformed by the optical illusion into the pure *vibration*, the *material* into *energy*. Of course it all depends on the elements one uses and the way one uses them, but the transformations can always be different, and really I leave it alone to behave as it likes. But I do use elements which seem to be the purest and most unadorned, because I want this transformation to take place in perfect *equilibrium*.

b: It's interesting that you should use the word "equilibrium," for the quality of the movement in your works has always struck me as being confident, lucid, ordered—like the waves of the sea rising and falling evenly. Do you see it like that?

s: Not exactly. In my case, at bottom, it's a *repetition*. I no longer see waves but the pure repetition behind the waves—blue, gray, green. But what happens when you see the work is that you discover Nature in it. One invents nothing in the plastic arts; all one does is *demonstrate* the existence of things. The artist discovers possibilities. But although it's a question of discovering, of demonstrating, it's also a question of doing it at the right moment. It's no good setting out with the intention of inventing something, some "new reality." One is placed at a certain point in a historical evolution. I am very conscious of this "historical process" in which I am placed, and my ambition is to develop this process from the stage at which I found it. The artist does not look forward, as many people suppose, but looks deeper. The artist "foresees" new visions entirely by discovering new values in what already exists. For example, Arp and [Constantin] Brancusi "discovered" value in forms as simple as pebbles, and after that people began to notice and even treasure pebbles, a thing they would have found inconceivable before. But one must not forget that for Arp and Brancusi to do this it was necessary that art should have evolved to a certain stage. The difference between the artist and the non-artist is that the artist is able to *provoke* the next stage in the evolution. The very strangeness of some of these "provocations" illustrates what I mean. When [Vasily] Kandinsky came home and found his landscape painting upside-down on his easel—in one stroke he thought of abstract art. His discovery was in the form of a sudden revelation—but one must understand all his foregoing preparations for that moment, both spiritual and intellectual, which make it unique, but at the same time logical.

b: I think people still find it difficult to believe that abstract art has its basis in life, that it is as much a personal necessity as any other form. A lot of people seem to think it's a sort of set of rules you can distribute like a book. For this reason, most optical painting seems to me to have a great deal of surface drama, but no real density.

s: Yes. . . . For the bad optical artists it is a system, artificial and stylized, which they just take up one day and exploit. Maybe tomorrow they will be exploiting something else. Stylization is the great enemy of creation—it's a sign that the traveler has turned his back on the unknown and settled down. For me, optical painting is not a system, but a record of day-to-day plastic discoveries, and a means of expressing what I feel—nothing more complicated than that. As you say, it is also a need.

b: I'd like just to come back to what you said earlier about your first desire being to make the works of Mondrian move. It reminds me of a story about a visit [Alexander] Calder made to Mondrian's studio when he first came to Paris—a decisive visit, which gave him what he called "the necessary shock." He found Mondrian's studio like a spatial version of one of his mobiles, with rectangles of primary color carefully placed on the white walls. Calder suggested to Mondrian that all these colored elements might be made to *move*. . . .

s (laughing)**:** I didn't know that; it's very gratifying, because it corresponds to my own work. I wanted to do the same sort of thing. Of course Calder never did anything of that kind because he is a sculptor, interested in objects moving in space, which I am not, as I explained earlier. My works keep their distance—the vibration is not felt as something tangible, as something that involves the body; it's purely optical, without physical substance. The elements I use, I use solely to realize an abstract world of pure relations, which has a different existence from the world of things. My aim is to free the material until it becomes as free as music—although here I mean music not in the sense of melody, but in the sense of pure relations. For me, the first artist who began to see things in this way was Turner. Turner made a conscious move away from figuration. You can say that there was already a feeling for abstract relations among primitive peoples, but for them a naturalistic art was not technically feasible. For Turner it was, but he rejected it. I see him as altogether more remarkable than the Impressionists and post-Impressionists, who were still attached to figuration. In fact, after Turner one can move directly to pure abstraction, to Kandinsky for example.

b: Yes, I think that modern art's gradual discovery of the *spiritual* power of relationships, which have no material existence but are something generated by the interaction of elements, corresponds exactly with modern science's discovery of the *psychical* power of relationships between material elements. Both art and science have been able to reveal these new forces, which simply take no notice of the old barriers that man used to erect between one part of his world and another.

s: Yes. I use anonymous elements to emphasize the purity and sufficiency of the rhythm that may be revealed between them. In representational painting the Surrealists approached the same problem in a different way. You remember that old passage from Lautréamont [Isidore Ducasse] that the Surrealists liked so much—about the sewing machine and umbrella meeting upon the operating-table. Separately these things are nothing, but together something very strange happens. This is the sense in which I understand the "immaterial"—a whole world of new meaning and possibility revealed by the combination of simple, neutral elements. Coming from the material, it has immaterial existence, freedom, purity, and precision.

—"Dialogue: J-R Soto and Guy Brett," *Signals* 1, no. 10 (London), November–December 1965: 13. The text, originally published in English, has been edited for spelling and punctuation in the context of this U.S. publication.

the construction of a language **carlos cruz-diez**

When I graduated from the Escuela de Bellas Artes in Caracas, I believed that the job of the artist was primarily to express himself in the interest of crafting a kind of great chronicle of the unknown and magical world that is Latin America. This, I believed, was also a fundamental affirmation in the face of cultural dependence. This reasoning process resulted in aesthetically conventional paintings and confusion between the atemporality and the political fact of art.[1]

In 1954 I entered the process of reflection that, in theory, all artists come to a certain moment in their lives when they start to have doubts about the validity and transcendence of the paintings they are creating.

During this period I managed to structure a conceptual platform that has allowed me, to this day, to carry out my work based on a nontraditional approach to color.

Through careful study and consistent experimentation it became clear to me that, conceptually speaking, the element of color in painting had not changed over the course of time, as have drawing, chiaroscuro, perspective, and composition.

Ever since the age of antiquity, one sole concept had held its ground: first, the artist drew a shape and then he filled it in, as if color were something to be added to shape.

Only the Impressionists, the Pointillists, the Fauves, and the Expressionists adopted different attitudes toward the chromatic phenomenon, while certain Constructivists and abstract art continued to insist upon the relationship between form and color.[2]

Based on this analysis, I launched a methodical investigation aimed at discovering how artists had treated and written about color throughout the course of history. I also familiarized myself with the realms of physics, chemistry, optics, and the physiology of vision.

I searched for what the philosophers and the humanists had reasoned about the phenomenon of the perception of color.

All this was aided by the knowledge I already possessed about the processes of image multiplication, color photography, photomechanics, and the various different systems of printing on paper.[3]

In short, I can summarize by saying that perception of the chromatic phenomenon is something unstable, in constant evolution, subject to multiple circumstances. This fact has never been dealt with by artists before.

The Impressionists, for example, were unable to move past the contradiction that lay at the core of their experiences.

The Impressionists aspired to be more truthful than the academics by reconstituting the ephemeral qualities of light on a static fabric support. But in the time that elapsed between the moment they observed their models, mixed their colors on their palettes, and finally returned to their canvases, the situation and the color relations had all changed. For this reason their approach to the model was the same as that of the academics: in other words, the artificial, immobile reconstitution of a changing reality.

This discovery, in addition to all my previous experiences with color, helped me conceive of a context that would allow me to manifest and reveal the mutable quality of the chromatic fact.

My solution to the *eternal binary* of form and color was to shatter the form by transforming the colored plane into a succession of vertically positioned color parallels, which I called *chromatic event modules*. This structure allowed me to manifest the evidence that color is in a constant process of creation: it is something that happens over time.

the reflection

I propose . . .

autonomous color

without anecdotes, stripped of symbology, like an evolutionary fact that concerns us.

Through my chromatic trajectory I intend to prove that color is an

ephemeral and autonomous situation.

Color in continuous mutation creating

"autonomous realities"

Realities,

because these events occur in time and space.

Autonomous,

because they do not depend on the anecdotal quality that the viewer is accustomed to seeing in painting.

In this way, between the viewer and the work *another dialectic* is established, as well as

another form of communicating knowledge.

To this end, I venture to cite [Maurice] Merleau-Ponty in "L'Œil et l'esprit" ["Eye and Mind"]. Speaking of Descartes and his opinion of painting, he says the following:

> . . . A closer study of painting would lead to another philosophy. . . . If he [Descartes] had examined that other, deeper opening upon things given us by the secondary qualities [of painting], especially color [. . .] he would have found himself faced with a conceptless universality and conceptless opening upon things. He would have been obliged to find out how the indecisive murmur of colors can present us with things, forests, storms—in short the world; obliged, perhaps, to integrate perspective, as a particular case, with a more ample ontological power. But for him it goes without saying that color is an adornment, mere coloring, and that the real power of painting lies in design.[4]

The viewer may *discover his own* capacity to create and destroy color through his own means of perception, and also to discover his own *emotional resonance.*

As color appears and disappears in the course of our "dialogue" with space and time, we become aware of a phenomenon inherent to human nature. At the same time, however, we also confirm that the information and knowledge acquired and memorized in the course of our life experience is probably not all true – or is at the very least only partially true.

It is possible, moreover, that through color and our growing awareness of "elemental vision,"[5] stripped of pre-established meanings, we may awaken other mechanisms of sensitive capture that are subtler and more complex that the mechanisms that are imposed by cultural conditioning and the mass information disseminated in contemporary societies.

aesthetics and effectiveness

Contrary to conventional belief, I believe that the artist should not work according to "aesthetics," because what is "aesthetic" today was the invention of yesterday.

When I say "aesthetic" I am talking about what the masses call "beauty," which is nothing more than a generational convention. This is the case of the Surrealists, who invented automatic writing because of its efficacy, a technique that became an (academic) aesthetic as time went by.

The very form and structure of a work of art depend on the solution that the artist has found for the problem that concerns him.

The arrangement of forms, the employment of color, and the technique utilized are all determined by the artist who deems them valuable according to their efficacy, not their beauty.

From Romanticism onward, many artists have insisted not on the beauty of their works but on their "truth," their character, or the fact that they are "characteristic" works of art.

This suggests that the artist understands the historical character of the concept of beauty in the sense that a work's importance is determined by the amount of "truth" it may contain or reveal, and not by that conventional quality we call beauty. As such, the efficacy of a formal discourse generates a new aesthetic, a new notion of beauty, which corresponds to the artistic fact created by the painter.

On the other hand, this has been the path of all artists, and if the Pointillists painted the way they did, it was not because a point of color seemed more beautiful than a plane in their eyes, but because this was the method they utilized to reveal the dynamic nature of vision, through the optical mixture of color. The Pointillist aesthetic, like the Impressionist and the Expressionist aesthetic, responds to the efficacy of the plastic discourse.

In the same way, while the great majority of kinetic artists may work at the limits of "normal vision," or what is traditionally accepted as such, they do not do so with the goal of producing an "effect," but rather because this is the method through which they may reveal certain unknown but real aspects of vision. This is how another "form of communicating knowledge" may be established.

When I juxtapose or superimpose two or more *chromatic event modules* by producing critical angles of vision, I do it because it allows me to generate chromatic behaviors that are difficult to perceive under "normal" conditions.

The line, as such, is not an "expressive" or "aesthetic element" but rather the most effective means I have found for multiplying the critical zones of vision between color planes, so that I might generate new and unstable ranges of color. This does not prevent the result from being an expressive, communicative and sensitive fact.[6]

Contrary to the Renaissance artist who ascribed greater importance to form and "colored planes," I try to dissociate color from form, and I have only been able to make this manifest by working at the very edges of normal vision, just as the Surrealists put into play the realm of dreams, the irrational and the absurd, working at the very fringes of the life that is conventionally accepted as "normal."

One of the purposes that guide me in my art is that of broadening the field of human experience, and making it more subtle and more complex.

—"La construcción de un lenguaje," in *Reflexión sobre el color* (Caracas, FabriArt, 1989), pp. 19–32, 59–63.
Translated by Kristina Cordero

the work of armando reverón **alfredo boulton**

Within the panorama of Latin American painting, and from the perspective of its evolution, the figure of Armando Reverón (1889–1954) is indisputably outstanding, although this has been acknowledged only somewhat belatedly. Reverón arose in that space of cultural time still rooted in the Neoclassical, Romantic, and Impressionist schools, whose impact indeed seems to have greater resonance on our continent every day. The present work is intended as a study of Reverón's extraordinary contribution to painting: Reverón as the creator of very advanced chromatic formulas. We shall also see that his message—as time has borne out—was authentic, courageous, and constitutes a major contribution to the field of fine arts by a Latin American artist.

Reverón lived through a difficult transitional stage in Venezuela, when academic trends were beginning to be displaced by the more modern theories of Impressionism, which reached this country only in the first decade of the current century. Some of the formulas, which would later serve him as a springboard onto new paths as yet unknown in painting, became a part of Reverón. Based on the scanty information he had of [Claude] Monet, [Camille] Pissarro, and [Alfred] Sisley, Reverón created an absolutely personal expression within the order of luminist values; great creations span the entire spectrum of the refractions of light. His work, at certain moments, hearkened back, as did that of the Impressionists themselves, to the heights of [J. M. W.] Turner, even though Reverón had never heard of him.

Reverón's White period represents one of the great contributions to the exploration of chromatic phenomena in the development of the plastic arts.[1]

With the hindsight that we now have regarding the evolution of certain theories of the plastic arts, it is possible to appreciate the importance of his contribution: an image in time that allows us to evaluate the artist's figure and to place him, albeit belatedly, in an increasingly important position, for he created a new language and invented a revolutionary concept regarding the question of light. [. . .]

Armando Julio Reverón was born in Caracas on May 10, 1889. [. . .] His father, Julio Reverón Garmendia, came from a distinguished family of Caracas. His mother, Dolores Travieso Montilla, was born in Valencia [Venezuela] to a wealthy, established family. [. . .] Armando was born in the "Quinta San José," in the Parish of Santa Rosalía, [. . .] into a loveless environment. Soon, his mother took him to Valencia and put him in the care of the Rodríguez Zocca family. In that home, which was not his, he grew up with Josefina, the daughter of those kind people; he spent his first years with them and came to consider them as his true family. At the time, an uncle of the artist's mother, Ricardo Montilla, lived in the same town. He was an amateur painter and gave the child his first lessons. [. . .]

In Reverón's case, biographical information is important as, throughout his life, his social conduct was very much bound to his work and greatly influenced its evolution. Thus, we must follow a parallel route in this study covering his life and work.

As a boy, Reverón lived in Valencia. He had mood swings—sometimes he was quite boisterous, and then suddenly he would become melancholy for a prolonged period of time. When he was twelve years old, he contracted typhoid fever, which nearly killed him. After his recovery, he had the mental age of a three-year-old, so infantile were his games and moods. He played with dolls, dressing them up, cuddling them, and putting makeup on their faces. He then became even sadder, gloomier, irascible, and unsociable. His main amusements were drawing and spending long hours with Josefina Rodríguez, his foster sister.

The artist's mother, following the advice of her uncle Ricardo Montilla, decided in 1908 to bring the young artist to Caracas to study at the Academia Nacional de Bellas Artes, then under the direction of Emilio J. Mauri. In the capital, Reverón met César Prieto, Rafael Monasterios, Antonio Edmundo Monsanto, Manuel Cabré, Raúl Santana, Carlos Otero, and Leoncio Martínez, who became his close friends and who helped guide him at difficult moments in his career. [. . .]

It was at this point that a new movement began in Caracas, organized by a group of students at the Academia Nacional de Bellas Artes, which would assume a concrete form in 1912. They intended to leave that training establishment for good and to form a cultural group that would be christened the "Círculo de Bellas Artes." [. . .] They were the first in Venezuela to experiment with the theories of the Impressionists. But when this Círculo de Bellas Artes was formed in 1912, Reverón was already in Spain. In fact, he had gone to Barcelona shortly after his exhibition at the Escuela de Música y Declamación [in Caracas]. [. . .]

Upon his arrival in Barcelona, the artist must have been dazzled by the atmosphere in Europe. Nevertheless, his stay in Catalonia was brief; a short time later, he had to return to Caracas to take care of business concerning the scholarship that the government of the federal district had granted him [. . .]. Reverón, however, returned to Spain—this time to Madrid. [. . .]

The artistic stage on the Iberian Peninsula was dominated by a group of artists who had reacted against academic and affected painting. They represented a new trend that looked back to the dramatic and sad horizons of Goya-esque painting. Some had assimilated the lessons of French painters; others were trying to uncover forms of ancestral fatalism in the Spanish soul, linked perhaps to gypsy folklore. Outstanding among these were Ignacio Zuloaga [and] Darío de Regoyos [. . .]. This group of artists expressed very clearly their search for an exaltation of native, even regionalistic, values that would lead them to the very roots and atavisms of the Spanish soul. They were attempting to reencounter Goya, but they were far from attaining the genius of the Aragonese master. [. . .]

When Reverón returned for good to Venezuela, in 1915, he was twenty-six years old. He was full of admiration for Spanish life – its culture and its painting: Velázquez and his lights, Goya and his mysteries, Zuloaga and his gloomy backgrounds – an admiration that was not, however, reflected in his technique. The influence on his emotions was much greater, although Zuloaga's influence can be detected in certain works by Reverón [. . .]. What really impressed him, more than the technique they used in executing their paintings, was the atmosphere exuding from the work of each of these painters. [. . .]

His short stay in Barcelona, and at the Academia San Fernando in Madrid, indicates that he was not very interested in the search for scientific or academic knowledge of fine arts; they were, however, a helpful means of fashioning his own world. [. . .] In Goya, Reverón discovered the reality of the "tenebrous," which peeked through in the magical elements of the Black paintings, of those witches and giants who, in 1820, inhabited the nights of "La casa del sordo" [The deaf man's house].[2] In Zuloaga, on the other hand, he found the deft theatrical fantasy of a "tenebrism," more zarzuela than great drama, in those figures pretending to be *majas*[3] simply by swaying their slender waists: conventional poses, a style of painting that was rather balladic and folkloric, pursuing a goal that only Goya, with his great sensitivity, managed to attain.

Luis Buitrago-Segura, who has studied Reverón's life, tells us that the artist, upon his return from Spain, settled at his aunt Pepita Reverón de Martínez Zozaya's house, and there covered the walls with frescoes; he became an active member of the Círculo de Bellas Artes, whose activities he had encouraged in earlier years. On the stage of the Teatro Calcaño, Reverón explained Goya's chiaroscuro, and taught his fellow members the still unfamiliar technique of etching. Since he had trained his eye to appreciate the chromatic scale by studying engraving, he spoke with enthusiasm of those experiences. He distributed books, pamphlets, journals, and European catalogues on painting among his friends. He practiced visual memory by choosing particular hues among sixty cards tinted with India ink on one side. He astonished not only his fellow painters, but the literati as well. He talked about [Francisco de] Quevedo, Cervantes, and the entire movement of the Spanish Golden Age, which he had thoroughly assimilated. He recited and acted in plays by Lope de Vega and Calderón, alternating these activities with teaching a course on perspective and scenography. He was an intellectual artist whom, later on, people decided to surround with an aura of primitivism, partly through ignorance of these facts.

In 1915, around July, he must have returned to Venezuela, where he made a sketch of the Paseo El Calvario, which then dominated the whole of Caracas from the west.[4] This work clearly reflects a predilection for somber harmonies, which even then corresponded to his state of mind. This little sketch [. . .] proves beyond any doubt the chromatic atmosphere Reverón brought back with him from Spain. [. . .] Henceforth, the way he conceived volumetric structures—their geometry, balance, and compositional strength—is remarkable. He attacked the subject as it came, with its own structural shape, without the slightest concern for whether it corresponded to the classical norms of preestablished concepts. He copied directly from nature, just as nature had composed the subject. As an artist, he considered it much more important in those days—and this was always the case with him—to capture the idea of spontaneity in the subject rather than its composition. [. . .]

A small painting from 1916, depicting the entry gate to Eduardo Carreño's house, was executed with that same spontaneous determination. The house is shown with the particular effect of twilight in Caracas, where light plays with hues of gray, lilac, purple, and brown, filling the atmosphere. One can clearly see here what would happen later with the intensity of values. It is important to establish this at this juncture, as it will be an important reference point when explaining the Blue period. [. . .]

By this time, the members of the Círculo de Bellas Artes had dispersed. Toward 1916, some of them gathered in a house at Pagüita, which they called "El cajón de los monos" [The monkeys' crate]. Reverón was among them. Nevertheless, he split his time that year among Valencia, La Guaira, and Caracas.

At the end of 1917, Reverón settled in La Guaira, near the Santos Michelena school. [. . .] Reverón made a living giving private lessons to several La Guaira families [. . .]. He was then a rather composed, taciturn man, sometimes hermetic, who had difficulty expressing himself. He was not very sociable, and he was reserved when there more than three people present. During this period he devoted his free time to making charcoal drawings on newsprint; his oil painting was rather scarce [. . .].

During the Carnival of 1918, he met Juanita Ríos, who would become his model, then his female companion, and later his wife. He called the first painting he made of her *La del lorito* [Girl with the little parrot], as she had a little bird standing on her foot.

There is no doubt that the main changes in those youthful years of the artist took place after his return from Spain, when he was already established in Caracas, and when certain immediate and environmental factors made a direct impact on his painting. Such was the case with the influence he received from Samys Mützner, Emilio Boggio, and Nicolás Ferdinandov. It may be assumed that it was then that Reverón truly came into direct contact with certain formulas of Impressionist theories. [. . .] The members of the Círculo de Bellas Artes were familiar with works of the French school through both color and black-and-white photographs. But it was only in 1916 that they were able to appreciate up close the impressionistic paintings done in Venezuela by Samys Mützner, a Romanian born in Bucharest in 1884, who had studied in his country and in France, and who arrived in Venezuela in 1916, fleeing the war. Mützner spent a short time in Caracas before moving to the Isla de Margarita, where he lived until the end of 1918. He returned to Caracas and held an exhibition of his works at the Club Venezuela. [. . .] In 1918, it was possible to admire the works of Emilio Boggio, born in Caracas in 1857, who had lived most of his life in France, where he was a friend of Camille Pissarro and of Henri Martin. Boggio, now an old man, came back to Caracas, where he stayed for less than a year. Before returning to Paris for good, he exhibited some sixty canvases at the Escuela de Música. The new generation's contact with the works of these artists opened the field to a different perception of color. From that moment on, Venezuelan painting was to take new routes.

During these years, Reverón was strongly influenced by Nicolás Ferdinandov, a Russian artist born in Moscow in 1886. Like Mützner, Ferdinandov had arrived in Venezuela in 1916 and went to live on the Isla de Margarita; he left in 1918 to live in a small hut in a little fishing village at Punta de Mulatos, near La Guaira. Ferdinandov was chiefly a watercolorist. His drawings were rooted in the stylistic expression of the "Nevsky Pickwickians," led, during the 1880s, by the Russian painter Alexandre Benois.[5] [. . .] There were also observable traces of the somewhat hackneyed style of Iván Bilibine, in the "Art Nouveau" mode. Ferdinandov's pictorial formulas did not contribute greatly to the evolution of Venezuelan painting at the time, except, of course, for his passing influence on Reverón and the advice he gave him about the value of specific colors and "nocturnal" moods. Reverón, in those years (1919–20), may be considered to have been very receptive to the influences of these three painters. What came later was his own creation. [. . .]

In general, Reverón's production during this period shows a marked search for strong and somber notes. This tendency can be observed in *La quebrada de Morrocotudo* [The Morrocotudo ravine], captured at nightfall; *Juanita*, dated 1919, in which the seminude figure appears reclining and covered by very fine, significant shadows mostly hiding the model's face—these were the first attempts at what would later be better conceived and painted in *La cueva* [*The Cave*], which exemplifies all the poetic and ineffable mystery of the artist's sensibility during his Blue period. [. . .] Those concepts were very much in contrast to the impressionistic essays made at the time by his Caracas colleagues, who were discovering the splendor and vivacity of color through light. [. . .]

This tendency became stronger from 1919 onward, when Ferdinandov, newly returned from the Isla de Margarita, [. . .] became a close and generous friend to Reverón. [. . .]

Ferdinandov—a great bohemian, good designer, and deft decorator, as well as a great lover of the color blue—discovered in Reverón a fertile field in which to sow his theories; as we have seen, Reverón had already, in 1912, 1916, and 1919, shown a clear preference for atmospheres of profundity.

In January 1920, the Russian organized an exhibition of his own works together with those of Reverón and Monasterios. [. . .] It may therefore be thought that Reverón's personality took on new dimensions in 1919 and 1920. Indeed, his friendship with Ferdinandov was of considerable consquence. [. . .]

Reverón's curious psychopathic personality should always be borne in mind when studying his painting. [. . .] His pathological development ran parallel to his artistic evolution. We must, therefore, bear both these elements in mind when describing the different aspects of his work. It is necessary to talk about the new way of life adopted by the artist during his Blue period, and to Reverón's settling in Macuto, after Mützner and Boggio had left Venezuela. The move to Macuto was an important event. Dolores Travieso de Reverón bought a plot of land, twenty-seven square meters, just above the small shack where Reverón had lived since 1920, opposite a bar called Las Quince Letras. It was a plot strewn with boulders, where mesquite trees, coconut palms, orange trees, and breadfruit trees grew. [. . .] It looked like the dry bed of an ancient stream that had dragged those rocks along.[6] The painter built two huts there. A small one, with a roof thatched with palm leaves and walls made of burlap nailed to slender wooden sticks buried in the soil, served as a bedroom. The center of the plot was occupied by a larger, spacious log cabin, which also had a thatched roof. The walls were palisades of cane and wide curtains made of burlap to screen out the light. The floor was of hard earth, kept very clean. The whole building was made of timber cut from local forests. At the end of the big room there was a very narrow mezzanine, where Reverón put his paintings to dry. I remember that there was a great cupboard of very coarse wood below that area, where he stored his paintings. [. . .] He also hung a trapeze in order to do physical exercises, which greatly amused visitors. Pieces of tulle hung from the beams, and light penetrated the cracks of what he called "the arbor." On one side was a wooden platform where his models lay on multicolored cushions filled with dry leaves. Light came in through a round hole, screened with fishnetting, between the roof and the wall. Reverón prepared the settings for his models to pose upon that platform. He cut annatto, palm, and papaya branches, to use as a surrounding chromatic reference. Sometimes it was Juanita who posed in the nude, wearing multicolored feathers on her head, or Otilia, a very young girl who looked Balinese. When he had the model pose in the garden, he placed her on a wooden bench, and took out a dilapidated parasol to shade

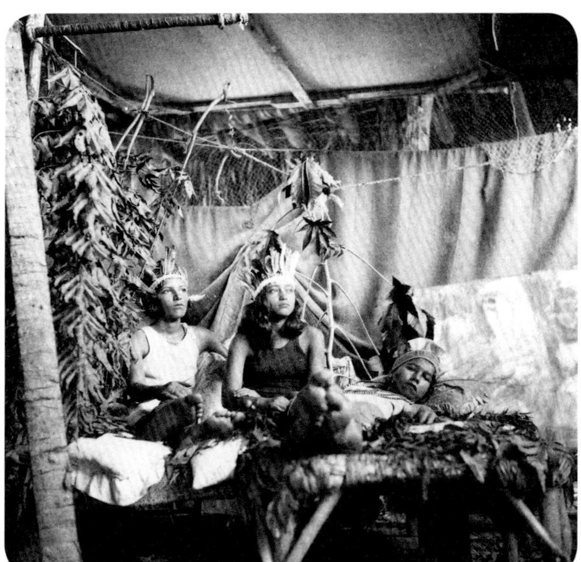

Young women posing as Indians at Armando Reverón's Castillete. Photograph by Alfredo Boulton. c. 1933. Alberto Vollmer Foundation, Inc., Caracas

himself. There was a rough-hewn table where he placed a great white-stained palette and two or three wooden trays containing five or six colors that were fundamental to his composition. He usually painted bare-chested; sometimes he donned shorts, and carried a big burlap bag hung from his waist in which he kept brushes. These were in fact just wooden sticks with cloth attached to one end. He usually worked with his left hand, although sometimes he feverishly painted with both hands at once, in order to go faster.

At such times he was a nervous man, with whom it was difficult to carry on a conversation, for new ideas kept crowding his mind, and he jumped from one subject to the next, without having finished the first. He was like that all his life; making fluid, continuous dialogue with him was next to impossible. His words were accompanied by jerky arm gestures and his face would suddenly light up with his roguish, mocking smile, which made conversation even more difficult to conduct. [. . .]

With time, his way of life evolved. His eccentricities often made him the subject of curiosity. Many people went to visit him as if he were a comic spectacle. This made him slowly begin to raise the walls around his property ever higher, until he was completely isolated from his neighbors. The grace and charm that the place had once had, built as it was within exuberant tropical vegetation, gradually begin to fade away. It became like the fortified castle of a madman.

There can be no doubt that the environment that surrounded him, and in which he developed his way of life, had a great influence on his artistic production. His way of life was reflected in his work. His surroundings led him to consider—very directly—certain problems with light, which he bravely confronted. The solutions he found constitute one of his main contributions to the world's artistic interpretation of light on color. [. . .]

I think that everything in man's work responds to motives and forces of a spiritual character. Reverón was a magnificent example of this. Enrique Planchart, his friend since childhood, recalled that often restlessness made it difficult for [Reverón] to work at ease, and that there came together in the artist "apparent contradictions, for there are also enormous numbers of artificial things, beginning with most of his exterior world." Other contemporaries believed that Reverón had a particularly nervous personality. His psychiatrist, Dr. J. M. Baéz Finol, would later say that he had always been schizophrenic. [. . .] Juanita has related to us several scenes of the artist's illness when he suffered from the epidemic of Spanish flu, at the close of 1918. He would race between Punta de Mulatos and El Pavero as a cure for his illness. Later, upon returning to the hut, exhausted and sweaty, he would dive into a tub of cold water so that he might extinguish the fever. He kept a strict diet at that time and the cures with which he supplied himself were of inconceivable formulas. [. . .]

From this point on, his work began to free itself and the expression of his true temperament blossomed—a process that grew more intense until his style became a reflection of the peculiar plastic mechanism of quick gestures and agitated brushstrokes, with which he built the image, very loosely, by arranging colors on the canvas. It was an extremely free and subtle exercise, during which shapes came to life while his body's movement kept its rhythm. It was a gesticulation that suggested erotic recollections, rather atavistic, like facing the bull, so common with certain Spanish painters. The impetus with which Reverón attacked the canvas could reveal a hidden sexual intention. In those moments the artist isolated himself from every outside contact; he did not touch metals; he plugged his ears with cotton wads or with balls of yarn; and he divided his body into two zones, cruelly tightening a belt around his waist. Then, in a ritual full of gestures and noises, as if falling into a trance before the canvas, with his eyes half-closed, he grunted and simulated the movements of painting until his body's rhythm and gestures had reached enough momentum. With spasmodic motions he would then assault the canvas as if it were the red flag that the bull attacks. Sometimes, in those rushes, he pierced the canvas. There was a conjunction of factors in which that man, isolated from every outside contact, responded intensely to his mind's creation; and seemingly enchanted figures would start emerging from that collision [. . .]. It resembled the integration of human and plastic matter, the result and consequence of the body's total isolation translated into the uncontaminated vision of an extraordinary pictorial language.

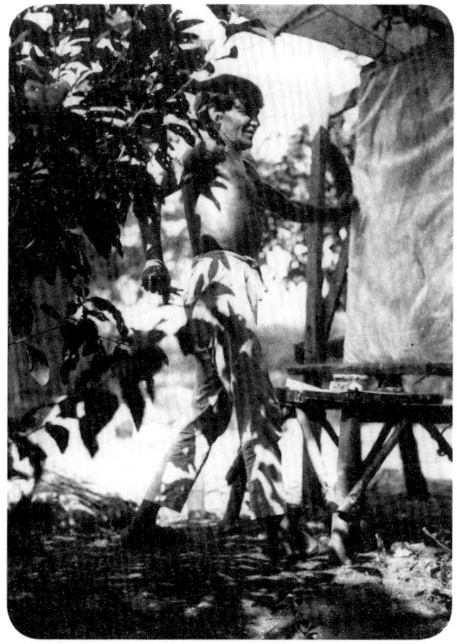

Armando Reverón painting Luisa Phelps. Photograph by Alfredo Boulton. 1934. Alberto Vollmer Foundation, Inc., Caracas

In this sense, it could be said that his pathological state had an influence upon his work, but only through a process of purification, through a filter, which took shape as a result of those physical torments to which the painter subjected himself. [. . .]

Dr. Baéz Finol, who knew him better than anyone else did, as far as his mental illness was concerned, [. . .] explains, "Once the crisis was overcome, and he was in the process of convalescence, his wish to work was the clearest sign of his mental recuperation; but when there were acute crises, when, hallucinating, he began to hear those inner voices, and turned all his creative energy into a religious mysticism, as we observed when he was under treatment at my clinic, every plastic manifestation disappeared. This largely explains why in all his work there is no sign at all of spiritual weakness, no sign that would lead us to discover any characteristics of his mental illness." [. . .]

Baéz Finol thinks that the typhoid fever that Reverón suffered in Valencia when he was twelve, and his mother's death in 1943 were "the most determining episodes of his mental perturbation." He also thinks that the painter's social behavior was dominated by his disease, and hence the eccentricities [. . .]. I think, in this respect, [. . .] that [Reverón's] social behavior did have repercussions upon his artistic production, for in that ritual or pantomime he performed before his canvas, those gestures and thrusts against it, the painting took shape in a series of points, touches, and linear strokes, or planes deriving from his constant movement [. . .]. That *mise en scène* undoubtedly had an effect on the plastic quality of some of his works, at least on those that became damaged by the sea spray, when Reverón planted his easel among the rocks at the beach, and let the foam bathe the canvas, Juanita, and the artist himself, while Juanita, naked, trembling, and shining with water, grasped the rocks. [. . .]

Of the three periods characterizing his painting, the Blue period was the shortest and reached its best expression in the paintings made between 1919 and 1920. That period's most important piece was *La cueva*, painted in Caracas in 1919.[7] It was in this piece that the painter best expressed the artistic concepts he had at the time concerning the poetry and beauty of color, a language wrapped in mysteries and in the blues that kept invading his nights. [. . .] In this painting, Juanita and another model appear reclining, like odalisques. It is a triangular-oblong composition. Its shapes insinuate a soft and sensual cadence of curves, enhanced by the transparency of the fine veils that barely cover the nudity of their bodies. [. . .] The poetic expression of this canvas is achieved through the wise construction of the atmosphere pervading the whole painting, and by very lightly rubbing the materials, there appear hues that seem to disperse and then fuse again as the linear structure of the drawing begins to emerge. [. . .]

The stylistic concept of *La cueva* cannot be included in what might be called pure impressionism. The chromatic problem is posed in different terms. It may be catalogued within a kind of expressionism, but without the professed determination of expression—that aspect so very characteristic of the German school. The plastic feeling of this painting becomes mysterious and poetic, transforming it into a jewel vaguely reminiscent of the gleaming figures of Gustave Moreau. [. . .] There is no imposition of any one value upon another—all of them maintain a great symphonic unity, enhancing the mysteries of the artist's world, his sensual world. Blues of all hues and intensities pervade the light surrounding and building the two figures that are lit by lilac, green, and emerald tones. In a foreground made of finely interwoven reds, purples, and browns, the two odalisques lie as if on a tapestry, expecting to be penetrated by pleasure and light. The trick is done using the granulated consistency of the canvas and thousands of minute brushstrokes that create a sort of surrealistic atmosphere that reaches the limits of magic and mystery. For the first time here, Reverón expresses on canvas what would later become, in his other styles, one of his most valuable characteristics—the transformation of real elements from his environment into highly unreal shapes just by sifting them through the magical sieve of his sensitivity, which is indeed one of the most notable and important qualities of Reverón's painting. [. . .]

The Blue period ends between 1921 and 1924, when the coastal light began to modify the artist's vision. Reverón's palette begins to adjust to the intensity of this light, and the splendor of the coastal landscape. It was a time of transition between absolute blue and total whiteness, and it corresponds to a very important moment in his production. During this time, Reverón lived briefly in the small town of Naiguatá,[8] with Juanita and Ferdinandov. Before six months had passed, he was back at his Macuto studio. That restlessness, that mobility, that lack of stability, which until then had characterized his way of life, were also reflected in his work—in his quest to find a style of his own there is a series of attempts that show that he had not yet reached a stable form of expression. There were new false starts in that search for a style in 1922, 1923, and 1924, when the artist still worked in a staccato manner, and when, as he used to say, "the canvases are resting for a long period." This could be called the process of re-adaptation—of readjustment—to a different environment, to a more intense light, to a new plastic conception. He was passing from the shadowy depths of *La cueva* to the splendor of the sun.

One of the paintings that best expresses this transitional period is *La trinitaria* [The bougainvillea]. [. . .] A technical examination of *La trinitaria* leads to certain conclusions already mentioned, but there are also some aspects just beginning to take shape. The painting was done on a rather rough canvas, covered by a white preparation that serves as background. The general tonal harmony is blue, although the main subject is a red bougainvillea. This is one of [the painting's] chief peculiarities—the substitution of one color for another. The composition is simple, as it generally was in Reverón's œuvre. [. . .]

One of the great characteristics of Reverón—who announces in this work a new development of the true value of the architecture of shapes in relation to colors—is his wise self-discipline, his parsimony of palette. It is worth noting the way he treats the great red mass of *La trinitaria*, with an extreme economy of red, while on the other hand there appear white vibrations gleaming in the air, surrounding the space where everything should have been carmine-red. We may recall Fernando Paz Castillo, who put it this way: "It is the air surrounding things that determines their relationships and gives them shape and color." The violent light of the tropical sun devoured the hues, no matter how strong and solid they were, destroying them, annihilating them, leaving only a luminous vibration, which revealed just a first glimpse of the object—its red; this was scattered in the great mass of light next to the blue, violet, and purple shadows, which acted as contrasting elements.

Two works of the greatest significance belong to the same period of the painting we have just discussed. They are Sra. Carmen Galindo de Maduro's *Paisaje* [*Landscape*] and *Fiesta en Caraballeda* [*Fiesta in Caraballeda*]. The former is one of his major works. It is neither signed nor dated, but because of its style one may surmise that it was made around 1924, when the artist was coming out of his Blue period and entering his White period. It is a very fine worsted canvas, similar to the one used for *La cueva*. The chromatic harmony stands out because of the surprising tonal unity it possesses. The entire composition, which seems as though it were bathed in a subtle blue haze, is brought to life by very soft hues of blue, lavender, and mauve. The technique used on this occasion would be developed more clearly in subsequent years, the formula eventually reaching a purer extreme. [. . .]

The magnificent landscape *Fiesta en Caraballeda* was painted in 1924. It already shows a marked preoccupation with the problem of large white spaces. It may be said that this canvas is very close indeed to the White period, although some blue, lilac, green, and rose tones still survive—tones that were present in the 1920 paintings, but that the artist had been gradually rejecting more and more in favor of the analysis and interpretation of white as the embodiment of light. It is interesting to observe the quick succession of styles that took place within these few years—whereas Reverón had developed in a gradual and orderly way until reaching the first splendors of the sun, announced in *La trinitaria* and present also in the *Fiesta en Caraballeda*, a painting of the utmost importance in the artist's production.

It is necessary at this juncture, however, to look at two very significant elements that had always figured in his painting's technical process, but that from this point on become more noticeable. [. . .] We are referring to the preparation of his canvases, either with casein or red ochre. This is a process that exerted considerable influence on his technique; indeed, it reached the status of chromatic substance with Reverón.

A good portion of his Blue period—*La cueva*, *Procesión de la Virgen en El Valle* [*Procession of the Virgin in El Valle*], *Noche de luna* [Moonlit night]—was created using red ochre tones with which he primed the canvas's background, as though it were a chromatic medium. [. . .]

During the White period, the casein preparation was very lightly colored in different gradations, according to the tonal intensity the artist wished to give his paintings. However, during the stage following that period, after the gouache interlude (1935–36), Reverón left the background of his canvases virtually unprepared, in order to use the natural color of the canvas. This is the reason why many of his works from that time seem altered in their general hue, as oxidation has darkened them. And yet these paintings attained a new intensity that would have thoroughly satisfied the painter.

[. . .] But let us return to 1925, when a new character appeared in all its dimensions. This time, it was light. Formerly it had been "darkness." In just five years, Reverón moved from one extreme of the spectrum to the other, always with violent determination: from the turbulent emotions of the deep *cueva* to the splendor of the sun, which blinds and overwhelms it all. Just as everything was previously overwhelmed by night. [. . .]

The White period started around 1925 or 1926, a moment of gestation, readjustments, and trials, which sometimes caused his production to become nearly paralyzed. In fact, *Luz tras mi enramada* [*Light Behind My Arbor*] is from 1926, the moment when Reverón definitively entered the search for a new synthesis, responding to very concrete propositions about the strength and expressive value of light, ushering in a revolutionary period within the field of objective painting. [. . .] Other important factors were taken into consideration in 1926—the preparation of the canvas itself and its texture, almost as significant as the theory of monochrome itself. The two elements functioned as a single expressive unit. [. . .]

Reverón subjected the structure of shapes, and the linear body delimiting them, to the impact of a powerful luminosity. This destroyed the chromatic play that originally constituted those shapes and dissolved the hues that gave them life. He discarded the linear resources of contours, of volumes obtained through different gradations of shadows. For him, objects had a luminous value of their own; without light, they would almost lack concrete form. Forms were like color masses, color planes, whose details had no importance. The artist was simply exploring the vibration of the light coming from those bodies [. . .].

For Reverón, then, form was color, and color was light, and light became the sun; a white sun, a monochromatic sun, covering bodies and spaces, and mountain ranges, and the sky, sometimes weakening into tenuous blues. Light rushed in violently through spaces and, like fire, it fused them, dissolved them. White reached such intensity that it was practically frightening. The artist submitted all bodies to that fearsome potency. [. . .]

Upon examination of the White period's emergence, several very well-defined aspects may be observed, allowing us to distinguish the various stages of its execution. It is important to analyze the chromatic structure of *Luz tras mi enramada*. This work is presented as a photographic negative, on which forms are silhouetted against light, making the structure of the composition prominent. The problem in this case could only be solved through lights and shadows caused by the clash produced by the contrast over the vertical structures of the subject. It is quite a simple formula, in which only two elements play a role; the artist achieves this with touches of white that penetrate the cracks in the wooden boards, and then by varying their intensity, and with the help of the canvas's texture, he makes the whole atmosphere of the painting reverberate. The composition's subject is used, through its light, as an element forcing the whites to vibrate over any other color element, and to dominate them in the process. [. . .]

Another magnificent example of the chromatic theory of the White period is a small landscape belonging to the successors of Manuel Guillermo Díaz, [. . .] signed and dated "A. Reverón 12 X 1926." [. . .] The background, treated with much diluted casein, makes it possible to appreciate the porosity of the canvas. The composition centers on two coconut trees whose shapes are built with the values of the canvas's background and with very tenuous gray tones. This little canvas admirably expresses the peculiar manner he had of juxtaposing different harmonies of luminous quality in order to create a vibrant and transparent body, as if made of air and light, in which the notes of chromatic balance are formulated by very tenuous blues—pale and evanescent, they are so light—and some brushstrokes of a strong impasto keeping the peculiar green tone that has been noted in previous works. The character of the stroke, with strong and expressive forms, enhances the sparkling, luminous vibration emanating from the movement of the palms' foliage. It is a resource in which the very texture of the materials was used as an expression of reverberating language. [. . .]

This extremely simple proposal would reach its maximum level of purity in the following years, up to 1935. In that process, Reverón achieved an expression based upon the value of light over colors and objects, surpassing what the French Impressionists had done, and what Claude Monet had glimpsed in his London period of 1899. [. . .]

These are the reasons why most of [Reverón's] works painted between 1927 and 1934 are frequently conceived as light, white silhouettes [. . .]. An excellent example of this process is *Paisaje Blanco* [*White Landscape*], in the collection of Doña Belén Clarisa Velutini. It is easy to observe here how the painter uses light touches of the canvas's own cream-color to enhance the whites. He also uses the canvas's texture, and when he cannot achieve the desired intensity, feverishly, as in rapture, he perforates the canvas. New references then appear, which acquire chromatic characters and add new values to the composition. At no point does Reverón's work reach a greater expressive simplicity or a higher exaltation. It is, above all, because of the fine aesthetic quality of the White period that Reverón's name surpasses the conventional boundaries of world painting, and that he is being considered an authentic creator, a pioneer in the search for universal plastic values. [. . .]

The White period ended around 1934–35. I recall that the artist then underwent a brief mental crisis. When he recovered, he painted on very flat surfaces—papers glued to cardboard—so that the brushstroke, very diluted in tempera, could run freely over great spaces that he furiously covered at a very fast pace: blues, ochres, vermilions, and thick white impasto. The painting still kept very clear hues, and in those days he produced some very important works, such as the *Autorretrato* [*Self-Portrait*] [. . .] and *Paisaje de Macuto* [Landscape of Macuto] [. . .].

In October 1934, Sra. Luisa Phelps de Cot took an important group of paintings by Reverón to Paris, where she exhibited them at the Katia Granoff gallery, and where they were enthusiastically commented upon by the local critics.[9] Georges Wildenstein's [*Gazette des*] *Beaux-Arts* said, "This artist's work is very interesting. It is a pity that the gallery's lighting is not the most appropriate: the painter's delicacy, the subtleness of his paintings do not show up as they should. His technique is rudimentary, and yet reaches a certain type of virtuosity. The expression is sincere, enthusiastic, and vigorous. The landscapes have a very lively and luminous charm. The large gouaches representing figures are strong—they reach a true poetic and savage grandeur in spite of the carelessness in the execution." At the end of that year, on December 23, I organized an exhibition at the Ateneo de Caracas of thirty-three paintings covering the last part of the White period. [. . .]

After taking sensuous satisfaction in the very smooth surfaces of paper, Reverón returned to canvas in 1936–37. The Sepia period may be considered to have begun then, even though the task of precisely fixing certain dates is difficult, as has been often noted. For this reason it is not possible, as I would have liked, to set the beginning and the end of the period exactly. [. . .] I should mention here the appearance of a new sensibility in the character of Reverón's work, which starts with a small group of paintings created with great violence and vigor, using the natural sepia color of the canvas in its almost virgin state. This moment could well be considered the beginning of the Sepia period. A tempera on canvas, generously donated by Miguel Otero Silva to the Museo de Bellas Artes, is very representative of this new style. In it, the graphic stroke acquires as much importance as in certain Oriental paintings. In the expressive concept of the artist, the stroke's graphic nature must replace the chromatic values that are absent in his paintings. [. . .]

The sparseness of his palette reached [. . .] the same extremes as it had when he painted using white tones. The main chromatic values were only three: gradations of white, black carbon pencil mixed with glue, and the color of the canvas itself, which served as a linking element. They explode in that violent *Paisaje* belonging to Otero Silva, in which the sky and its reflections on the sea speak a language of high graphic drama. The vertical silhouette of a coconut tree barely maintains the harmony of the composition, made with strong horizontal masses. [. . .]

Toward 1940–41, Reverón again used casein with tempera and glue to prepare the background of his canvases, but he took care to do this according to the needs of the composition of a landscape he intended to paint, in order to use the canvas as an additional color. [. . .]

Reverón was fundamentally a painter of landscapes and shapes. He had a very well-developed appreciation for the atmosphere exuded by his models, for the feverish temperature he discovered in them. It was like a meeting of the senses that would develop between him and particular forms and atmospheres. He, who ended up fading Macuto's landscape into very subtle whites, was the same one who painted the most beautiful sepia and ochre tones in the strong and loving image of a nude *criolla* [. . .]. The exalted beauty of the supine body is a magnificent lesson about the knowledge of academic drawing and about the classical formation that the artist had. [. . .]

The theme of the *La maja criolla* [*The Creole "Maja"*], painted in 1939, has a special, magical sense. The mysterious figure of a dark woman, perhaps out of the nights of Goya, seems to watch over the sleep of a fragile girl. Between them there is the nude figure of a man lying beside the frightened nymph. The artist placed some red flowers over the man's belly. A white hint of the sun is present beyond his left arm, through a luminous gap. The technique used in this work shows a state of nervous agitation due to the constant movement of the body and to the feverish, intermittent, but confident gesturing of the artist. Reverón was at this point on the brink of one of his most acute mental crises, which would manifest itself violently the next year. The expressionism of the language, the anecdotal intention, the aggressive character of the touches, points, stains, rubbings, in its extraordinary rhythm and confidence, gives life to these three enchanted characters, mysterious yet earthly, who seem to be performing some ritual of magic. Light, tempered in soft hues, accentuates the climate of sorcery that surrounds the seated figure, who looks like an old naked priestess, and seems to be presiding over the deflowering of *la maja criolla*. This work has a poetic feeling distinct from everything previously expressed by the artist, and there is a very definite erotic temperature. It is the narration of an event; it is the story of a spell. But the painter does not stop at the simple delight of reproducing the sensual flesh of the feminine body. He penetrates her inner world, in order to narrate its mystery—full of figures, gestures, chromatic climates, mysteries, and incantations, and light illuminating the intimate scene of sensuous pleasure through a curtain. [. . .]

A little later, a violent change took place in Reverón's life. Dolores Travieso de Reverón died in 1943. His mother's death caused a deep and prolonged crisis that would take him to Dr. Baéz Finol's sanatorium in 1945; he remained there for several months. He was practically inactive for almost two years. When he recovered, he looked for a different environment in which to paint, quite opposite to what had been until then the peaceful setting of Macuto. Although he still lived there, he went to La Guaira to paint, amid the bustle of the port. His work reached a new human feeling at this time, when the artist became a chronicler of various activities of harbor life. He captured the silence of noon in the customhouse and the feverish movement in the shadows of the workshop. The noise of the locomotives and their plumes of white smoke served as inspiration for paintings of scenes full of somber masses, in which ochres, blacks, and blues prevail. He painted the wharves, the fishing boats, and also the warships. Amid the smoke and steam, he once placed a red spot, a touch that often appears in his production, wisely corresponding to a settling of the equilibrium of the tones, as in the yellow brushstroke in the white foreground of *La trinitaria*. [. . .]

The Sepia period brought a new conception of how to consider the landscape on the coast. The artist nearly eliminated the blues in the shadows, replacing them with greens, ochres, and siennas of a deeper hue. He seemed determined to transfer the exact tints of the earth itself, of the vegetation, wholly onto the canvas, practically eliminating the play of light in the prism's deceitful reverberations. During this final period he looked straight at the earth, without any artifice, without recourse to chromatic theories. [. . .] This is the least lyrical period of his production, the most direct and earthy; the closest to the traditional romantic language; the least artificial and imaginative. It is the finest hymn to the vital values of the earth. [. . .]

Toward 1945, Reverón returned to his hut in Macuto, after spending several months at Dr. Baéz Finol's sanatorium. Here the painter entered his last stage of production. His visual world was progressively reduced to the small environment of his studio. He filled it up with large rag dolls made by Juanita; Reverón placed these in different positions, forming a variety of scenes; with these depressing figures he painted, nevertheless, two magnificent "genre scenes," the only two in his whole production—*El bautizo* [The christening] and *Fiesta de la Cruz de Mayo* [Feast of the May Cross].

Also from this period is a series of self-portraits, in which we find an expression of deep nostalgia and sadness for a life approaching its end, and which every day became more entangled with inner voices, animals, and the fierce bull that had harassed him since his days in Spain. [. . .] In one of his finest self-portraits, made in 1948, his chromatic subtlety is well expressed. [. . .] Armando's spectral figure appears, his head covered with a piece of canvas—as though he were hallucinating—with pale hues of death already on his face. The dolls, their arms stretched high, are doing the final pirouettes of a ballet, just before they fall down dead. The scene is sublime. It would seem the last real vision the artist had of his own face, when he was still conscious, before he delved into the series of painful self-portraits with beard and top hat. These images, translated via woolly brushstrokes, are a very painful harbinger of imminent death. These, his final works, are sad paintings, in which it is easy to see that the old combativeness had lost its strength. Those impassive faces kept repeating themselves monotonously, as his own ever-shrinking world reflected the little life that was left. They are pessimistic paintings in which violets and reds join the white, but without the rhythm and courage of his previous works. The painter seems to take note of that circumstance, and devotes his time to rapid exercises in figures in notebooks: sketches with colored chalks or carbon pencil, whose execution, as in a ritual, still tied his life to the movements and gestures that, years before, had achieved such rhythm and deftness. But now they were becoming his last. The mental state of the artist, by 1952, was disturbing. His production was notably diminished, and its artistic quality visibly declining.

He made his last works with colored chalk. His final portrait is an extraordinary painting of a female patient in the sanatorium. He used carbon pencil and blood-red powder to color the shapes. He painted it with his fingers, in tactile touches that went on building the robust shape of his last model. For the last time, and in the way he had always done it, with extreme harmony and without harshness, he painted this magnificent portrait in his friend's clinic, to which he had been taken October 24, 1953, thanks to the generosity of Armando Planchart and his old friendship with Manuel Cabré. He stayed at the sanatorium for eight months. When he became lucid again, he painted twelve works. [. . .] On September 18, 1954, Armando Reverón died in Caracas of a cerebral embolism.

The best way to look at Reverón's work, without rhetorical flourish, is to coldly analyze the different concepts it comprises. One of its most characteristic components is the very stroke with which the work is created: its impasto, the brushstroke, its graphic character, its vigor, the linear arabesque, its form and its artistic strength. The stroke's expressiveness always had as much emotional impact as did color. The character of the stroke's structure played an important role in his work. [. . .]

To penetrate even deeper into Reverón's world, it is interesting to observe in the artist a certain type of intellectual detachment from his own work, a detachment that became stronger when he settled in Macuto, and a reflection of which was the fact that, with very few exceptions, the painter did not title his paintings. Reverón almost never concerned himself with naming his works. [. . .]

When narrating the painter's life, I have chosen not to make use of the many anecdotes and facts that are so often mentioned. I think that those elements are of little help in explaining his work. Instead, they depict him in a false light, presenting him as though the madness he suffered and the meaningless sentences he uttered were more interesting than his paintings themselves. That is the reason why there are no quotations in this work of his peculiar way of speaking, or descriptions of his eccentricities. [. . .]

Reverón's painting cannot be considered the work of an intellectual. It never had the content or the literary intention of the Pre-Raphaelite painters, of Maurice Denis or Puvis de Chavannes. It is far removed from [Henri de Toulouse-]Lautrec's picaresque. Except for some works of [Reverón's] Blue period that fell under certain influences, which have been mentioned, his work was essentially an expression of plastic elation. Without any literary message,[10] he reached poetic heights with a language that exclusively used painting's own resources. A short incursion of a "nativist" sensibility was observed—*Las hijas del sol* [*Daughters of the Sun*]—during a few months of his White period, when in Venezuela our ethnic values were being exalted in literature, and when some writers praised the dark complexion of the painter as proof of his indigenous ancestry.[11] An absurd theory, for Reverón descended from old *criollo* families, in which there was no appreciable mixture whatsoever of Indian blood.

His painting had more poetic intention, more elegiac confidence, than that of any other of our painters. He used color to create chromatic worlds instead of re-creating the world's image in conventional colors. His work is outstanding for its expressive character, which contributed some very advanced formulas to the problems of light, and in the international field of painting it may be regarded as one of the most interesting experiments carried out as a consequence of the theories of [Paul] Cézanne, Monet, Pissarro, etc. [. . .]

[Georges-Pierre] Seurat, the Fauves, the Cubists, did nothing but try to solve, each in his own way, the relationship of the dynamic force of light upon objects. Each of them, and Reverón too, took a similar route, but following different paths: the Fauves through pure color; Seurat with his vibrating Pointillism; Cézanne extending the movement of structures so that, in a kind of subvibration, color took on the mutation of light. The Cubists, going deeper than Cézanne, fractured the accidents of shapes into a thousand pieces. Reverón looked at the problem from the point of view of the body's own organic force and discovered an intensity so extraordinary that it managed to dominate all other forces, actually killing the hues and gradations present there. [. . .] His painting was realistic inasmuch as he copied nature. It contained, however, an expressive element that bordered on abstraction's subjectivism. It was an essentially artistic function perceived by one who was familiar with the concerns of the French Impressionists. In him, however, these concerns became an idea that managed to capture the topic's underlying reality, by inventing those spaces where the forms' physical materiality seemed to be about to fade. [. . .]

Concerns about the way of resolving the values of light have always been present and are as ancient as painting itself. [. . .] Indeed, it is not light that has changed its conceptual value. It is the artist who has actually changed the concepts. The elements constituting the body of light have always been the same and have always been present, like black night, and day. [. . .] There have been great moments in the history of painting when the foundations of the values of light have been revised. Leonardo da Vinci and the *sfumato* technique he used on his forms corresponded to the way of appreciating the play of light over contours. Caravaggio broke the darkness and made it play over scenes and bodies. Rembrandt tried to penetrate the material consistency of shadow, as though entering the body of details. Velázquez disregarded those previous concepts and looked at the reflections and gleamings of matter. Delacroix saw light in warm figures moving across his canvases. Turner invented abstract bodies to convert them into luminous skies, in the massive landscapes he painted in the least luminous country in the world. Pissarro, Monet, Cézanne followed that search of the real temperature of elements and discovered chromatic vibrations in the trees, the skies, the air, built as a single body by the refractions of the sun. "Synthetism," a reaction against this concept, was expressed by the Pont-Aven group, headed by [Paul] Gauguin from 1889 onward, and continued, later on, by the "Fauves." The brutal colors of Pont-Aven, like masses of shapeless harmonies, of beating vibrations, would give origin to [Vasily] Kandinsky's *Untitled (First Abstract Watercolor)* in 1910. That same anxiety at finding the true mystery of light was what led Reverón to propose his white theory, just fifteen years after Kandinsky. If in Pont-Aven the organic, molecular, and explosive sense of color was of primary importance, if its force was fundamental as an emotional structure, that same concept, analyzed and studied by subsequent schools of painting, would also lead Reverón—unwittingly, I am sure—to create a language of absolute realism about the most precise manner of perceiving the chromatic refraction moving in space, in the distance between the pupil and the object—the true "spectrum" of light. In that quest, he managed to give color an abstract sense, rearranging the whole problem into a true morphology of plastic matter and creating a revolution against all previously expressed concepts.

—"La obra de Armando Reverón," in *Exposición retrospectiva de Armando Reverón* (Caracas: Museo de Bellas Artes, July 1955); reprinted in *Reverón* (Caracas: Macanao, 1979).
Translated by Carlos Riobó
This text has been abridged for the present volume.

editor's notes to the texts

guillent pérez / bolívar, ourselves, and today, pp. 172–74

1. The need to achieve cultural freedom—the complement to political freedom—for Venezuela has been and continues to be a recurring theme. Los Disidentes believed they had finally begun to achieve this freedom, and they believed it was made possible through a synchrony between their works and the abstract geometric practices they encountered in France.
2. Alfredo Boulton likewise attempted to capture the genuine Bolívar with his iconographic studies in *Los retratos de Bolívar* (Portraits of Bolívar), published in Caracas in 1956.

manaure and gonzález bogen / manifesto of the galería cuatro muros, p. 179

1. The Galería Cuatro Muros was founded in Caracas in 1952 by Carlos González Bogen and Mateo Manaure. It advocated the ideas and works of the geometric abstract artists who were actively involved in the construction of works at Venezuela's Universidad Central at the time.

letters from alejandro otero to alfredo boulton, pp. 180–93

1. Otero is describing pieces that belong to the series that would later be known by the generic name Cafeteras (Coffeepots). In December 1948 Otero had his first solo show with this series. The exhibition, *Alejandro Otero: Still Life, Themes and Variations*, was organized by José Gómez Sicre for the Panamerican Union in Washington, D.C. Later, the show traveled to the Museo de Bellas Artes in Caracas, where it opened in February 1949.
2. Based on this comment, Boulton suggests that Otero likely began work on the Cafeteras in October of 1946.
3. This passage in italics is in French in Otero's original letter: "sans aucun rapport avec la réalité. Du point de vu de l'intérêt plastique elles sont aussi bonnes que les meilleures que j'avais faites dans le plus ou moins figuratif. C'est ce que je pense, et c'est ce que je vois jusqu'ici. Je me suis arrêté de travailler hier pour me donner un peu de recul, pour remettre mes idées en place, et enfin pour pouvoir juger si je me trompe ou non. (Dieu veuille que non, car j'y ai mis trop de bonne volonté, de sincérité et d'emportement). Si tout cela est vrai, je crois que ma peinture *habrá alcanzado* [will have attained—these words in Spanish] une plus grande signification. J'aurai atteint à la liberté de notre époque et de là elle (la peinture) ne pourra que s'épanouir."
4. In French in Otero's original letter: "et de là je vois pour moi de l'avenir. Je vois, je vois, et je crois que j'aurai."
5. In 1950, Otero was going through a period of crisis that lasted until 1951. During this time he left behind the early reference points (Picasso of the 1940s) with which he had begun his series of Cafeteras, and started his series Líneas coloreadas sobre fondo blanco (Colored lines against a white background). This may explain the somewhat overwrought tone of his letters around this time.
6. This is a reference to Otero's series Líneas coloreadas sobre fondo blanco.
7. In French in Otero's original letter: "dans l'homme et dans la cité."
8. The quotation is in English in the original letter.
9. Idem.
10. The reference here is to Otero's Monocromos (Monochromes) series of 1961. In the words of the artist, "the surface of the rectangles was covered by a kind of barely perceptible blot-writing, until the canvas was almost entirely white" (*Alejandro Otero*, exh. cat., Museo de Arte Contemporáneo de Caracas, 1985).
11. Otero is speaking of the Monocromos series here.
12. Otero is referring to his Ensamblajes y encolados (Assemblages and glued pieces).
13. That is, a "stowaway" in the exhibition mentioned in Boulton's December 5 letter to Otero.
14. Cruz-Diez also worked as a graphic designer.
15. In French in Otero's original letter: "je n'ai pas le choix."

letters from alfredo boulton to alejandro otero, pp. 193–97

1. Antonio Edmundo Monsanto was the director of the Escuela de Artes Plasticas y Aplicadas in Caracas.
2. Juan Vicente Fabbiani was a professor of Alejandro Otero.
3. Boulton is referring to Otero's Collages ortogonales (Orthogonal collages), directly influenced by the work of Piet Mondrian—an outcome of the trip Otero took to the Netherlands at the end of his period working on *Líneas coloreadas sobre fondo blanco* (Colored lines against a white background).
4. Mercedes Pardo, Otero's wife.

villanueva / the problem of integration, pp. 197–99

1. Here Villanueva underscores the social consciousness that informed the agents of Venezuelan modernity (the most important ones, at least), a consciousness that was manifested in many urban projects, particularly in projects that dealt with public housing. Villanueva's work successfully sought out links between modern art and the architectural traditions of Venezuela.

otero silva and otero / polemic, pp. 202–22

1. Otero Silva emphasizes Kandinsky's Slavic and Eastern origins, and Mondrian's Calvinist and puritanical tradition, in order to later claim that abstraction pertains to a world that is foreign to occidental, Catholic Latin America, and that abstract artists could not engage in abstraction without turning their backs on their land and their people.
2. The provincial origins of many abstract artists is undoubtedly one of the elements that defined the desire, ardent and naïve, for modernity and progress that was characteristic of their work. It is also a clear sign of the profound way these modernizing hopes took root in Venezuelan national history.
3. Alejandro Otero is alluding here to the privileged education his cousin Miguel Otero Silva received, and to his own "uncontaminated" rural origins.

soto / from the *journal de genève*, pp. 222–24

1. Soto had actually heard of Malevich in 1949, during his time as director of the Escuela de Bellas Artes in Maracaibo. An acquaintance spoke disdainfully of the creator of a white square against a white backdrop. Never having seen the work, and knowing nothing of the artist, Soto said to himself that that was the most efficient way to capture light in a painting, the most simple and eloquent form to express it, and it became a guide that he would never forget.
2. Soto is referring to his analysis of Mondrian, in whose works he saw an attempt to trap the vibration that was emanating from them, specifically in the crossing of its verticals and horizontals.

soto and brett / dialogue, pp. 225–28

1. This sentence makes Soto's reading of Cézanne apparent: Soto favors the transparency of the work (particularly visible in Cézanne's late watercolors) against other artists (the Abstract Expressionists in the United States, for example) who insisted in the materiality of their paintings and the opacity of their pictorial field.

cruz-diez / the construction of a language, pp. 229–32

1. During the 1940s and the early 1950s, Cruz-Diez practiced a kind of "Socialist realism": he sought through his painting to denounce the poverty of marginal areas.
2. Much of Cruz-Diez's reflection was focused on the possibility of moving beyond the experience of Josef Albers with his series Homage to the Square.
3. Cruz-Diez identified the starting point for his first Colores aditivos (Additive colors) and his first Fisicromías (Physichromes) in the work of Edwin Herbert Land during the invention of Polaroid photography. This is the reason for Cruz-Diez's exclusive use of red and green in his first kinetic pieces.
4. The English translation of this passage is from Maurice Merleau-Ponty, "Eye and Mind," Carleton Dallery, trans., in *The Primacy of Perception*, ed. James Edie (Evanston, Ill.: Northwestern University Press, 1964), pp. 159–90.
5. These and similar reflections indicate that kinetics (at its best) cannot be reduced to what Marcel Duchamp described—with some irony—as "retinal" painting.
6. Much of modern art conceives of the artist's work in this way. Paul Valéry in his *Variété V* (1944): "A poet's function . . . is not to experience the poetic state: that is a private affair. His function is to create it in others."

boulton / the work of armando reverón, pp. 232–49

1. Following the model applied to the work of Picasso, Boulton divides Reverón's later work into three great periods: the Blue period (1919–24), the White period (1925–35) and the Sepia period (1936–49), each of which has its respective stages. But Boulton struggles when it comes to setting the exact beginning and ending dates of each period, which he suggests is due in part to "the artist's tendency to sign and date his work at the time of selling each painting, even if he had completed them months or years earlier."
2. That is, the house of Goya, who became deaf in his final years.
3. *Majas* were members of Madrid's art scene in the nineteenth century, who, though generally from the lower classes,

distinguished themselves by their pure, gracious use of the Castillian language and their elaborate manner of dress. Cf. Goya's *La maja desnuda* (*Nude Maja*) and *La maja vestida* (*Clothed Maja*), 1797–98.

4. Reverón's rendition of this scene, *El Calvario* (1915), is included in the catalogue of The Museum of Modern Art's 2007 exhibition *Armando Reverón*. In this essay Boulton discusses several other works that were featured in the exhibition or illustrated in the catalogue: *Juanita* (1919), *La cueva* (*The Cave*; 1920), *Paisaje* (*Landscape*; 1922), *Fiesta en Caraballeda* (*Fiesta in Caraballeda*; 1924, inscribed 1927), *Procesión de la Virgen del Valle* (*Procession of the Virgen in El Valle*; 1920), *Luz tras mi enramada* (*Light Behind My Arbor*; 1926) *Paisaje blanco* (*White Landscape*; 1934), *Autorretrato* (*Self-Portrait*; 1936), *Cocotero* (*Playa*) (*Coconut Tree*; 1944; Boulton refers to this image as "*Paisaje*"), *La maja criolla* (*The Creole "Maja"*; 1939), and *La hija del sol* (*Daughter of the Sun*; 1933; Boulton discusses a related work titled *Las hijas del sol*). See John Elderfield, with Luis Pérez-Oramas and Nora Lawrence, *Armando Reverón*, exh. cat. (New York: The Museum of Modern Art, 2007).
5. Alexandre Benois was the editor of the art review *Mir istkusstva*, which promoted the Aesthetic movement and Art Nouveau in Russia in the early 1880s.
6. The fierce rainfall that battered the country in 1999 completely destroyed Reveron's Castillete (his "Little Castle") in Macuto, because, as Boulton notes here, it was built on a streambed.
7. *La cueva* remained part of Boulton's collection until his death.
8. Naiguatá is on the Venezuelan coast, a few kilometers away from La Guaira, a port that serves the city of Caracas.
9. At this time, Boulton wrote his first article dealing exclusively with Reverón's work, in which he particularly emphasized the favorable reviews the exhibition received from French critics.
10. See Mariano Picón Salas's essay "Armando Reverón," *Revista Nacional de la Cultura*, no. 13 (November 1939): 63–80. This text is included in the present volume, pp. 115–22.
11. See ibid. Boulton is undoubtedly referring to Picón Salas's description of the painter's ethnic origins: "Andalusian Arab and indigenous Venezuelan" (p. 115).

universalism of differentiation

testimonial **sardio**[1]

No one who is not a militant advocate of freedom can experience the portentous creative adventure of the soul. Faced with the weight of our current history,[2] replete with imminent anxieties, no thinking man can evade such militancy without betraying his own radical condition. The aesthetic categories that prevailed until recently now seem too narrow and sterile. To be an artist implies a commitment to style and an exercise of the soul as much as moral strength and a pledge to life. One does not live or cease to live with impunity. One must be fairly burned by history's devouring flames. Man's traces in history must reveal he was in charge of his path. And those who choose to take a stand in the world of culture must also be responsive to the urgent expectations of their time.

To take an idealistic stance toward solving the convulsive problems imposed upon us by politics would be in vain. Politics has ceased to be a taboo or a menacing Minotaur; it has become the vast domain of the intelligence and soul of the people. All aspects of human life are under the positive or negative influence of politics, which determines their destiny, no matter what. Being political is tantamount to being a man. All indolence favors slavery and the humiliation of the soul. Those who neglect this truth forget that certain dark forces, when unleashed in a given moment in history, invariably destroy the dignity of all creations. This is why culture and tyranny are radically incompatible. Dictatorships are more than just the blind imposition of instinct or greed. They are generated by the fundamental denial of the human essence and intelligence.

Given the urgent reconstruction that our country demands after the abysmal decade of the past dictatorship, Sardio declares itself in complete solidarity with such principles. We believe that we have deeply assimilated the invaluable experience of the past years. But if yesterday we were committed activists and militants during that exceptional adventure that was the nation's Resistance, today we aspire only to assume a critical and guiding position—without abandoning our personal civic duties—amid the dizzying dynamics of recovery that currently define our nation. We do not intend to be political leaders, but we do accept the obligations entailed in being writers and artists. We oppose the traditional demagogy of certain intellectuals who still resort to conventionalism and sentimentality to impress the unsuspecting and to obtain influential positions. All social climbing is cultural treason. Intelligence is a more serious and dramatic commitment. Intellectuals are cautionary and controversial beings, capable, on occasion, of going against the grain in order to point out gaps and injustices. Politics, on the other hand, has ceased to be a simple game of proselytism or an accommodating strategy and has acquired the dimensions of a lucid science capable of informing the people's awareness. Today, all rhetoric has been discredited. Even political parties have been forced to abandon their old fetishes and their simple crowd-pleasing emotiveness, and are already presenting themselves as active and defined ideologies. We are facing a reality that requires study and discipline, and not vague, purposeless invectives.

If we do recognize the beginning of a new political style in our country, we nonetheless want to address certain facts. We declare that freedom is not the pure, indiscriminate enjoyment of civil rights, without direction or objectives.

If freedom is the highest universal aspiration of our time, it should be based on the solid, economic self-sufficiency of nations. We are orthodox in our belief that a country can fully exercise its freedom only when it diversifies and maximizes its economy, and when it removes itself from any kind of subservience to foreign nations. We demand, with full awareness, a more daring and patriotic economic policy that safeguards the great resources of our nation's material heritage. This is how we shall attain our sovereignty on the world stage, so often threatened by imperialism from the North.

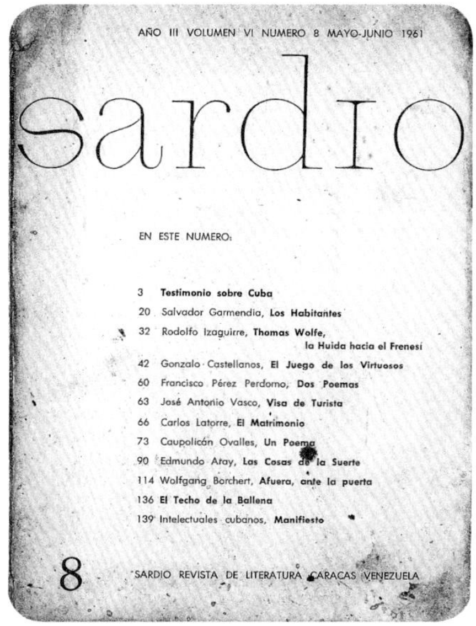
AÑO III VOLUMEN VI NUMERO 8 MAYO-JUNIO 1961

sardio

EN ESTE NUMERO:

3 **Testimonio sobre Cuba**
20 Salvador Garmendia, **Los Habitantes**
32 Rodolfo Izaguirre, **Thomas Wolfe, la Huida hacia el Frenesí**
42 Gonzalo Castellanos, **El Juego de los Virtuosos**
60 Francisco Pérez Perdomo, **Dos Poemas**
63 José Antonio Vasco, **Visa de Turista**
66 Carlos Latorre, **El Matrimonio**
73 Caupolicán Ovalles, **Un Poema**
90 Edmundo Aray, **Las Cosas de la Suerte**
114 Wolfgang Borchert, **Afuera, ante la puerta**
136 **El Techo de la Ballena**
139 Intelectuales cubanos, **Manifiesto**

8 SARDIO REVISTA DE LITERATURA CARACAS VENEZUELA

Cover of the literary review *Sardio* 6, no. 8. May–June 1961. Collection Ignacio and Valentina Oberto, Caracas

Freedom cannot be a deceptive entelechy to which more urgent and concrete imperatives shall be sacrificed. If freedom is to be a dynamic concept that attunes man to his interior potential and his human dignity on earth, it cannot ignore the material and social happiness of the people. To unite all of these ideas into a harmonious system of coordinates is the key objective of democracy. Freedom is only justifiable to the extent that it makes such a conjunction possible.

We declare ourselves affiliated with a left-wing political humanism that provides large, unassisted sectors of the country with rational and democratic education and that incorporates the full enjoyment of the great values of the spirit to our nation. Culture cannot continue to be an elitist or class-based privilege. In order to acknowledge the gravity of our historical destiny we need a luminous and creative nation, sensitive to the realm of ideas and truth.

In keeping with these positions, Sardio must not forget the pledges it has made regarding the nation's culture. We will not be overly emphatic, as emphasis only reveals indecisiveness and intolerance. We should not confuse universality with cosmopolitanism, but it is obvious to us that the excess of local color and all its derivations have damaged a large part of our artistic expressions at their core. Just as we condemn all aestheticism, we also condemn all arrogant and exacerbated nationalism. Although we respect the illuminated soul of our people as it is expressed in folklore and in our best traditions, we believe that certain artists have become irreverent pillagers of this heritage. Likewise, the literature of preconceived schemes and solutions seems insubstantial to us. If we're beginning to resent the anachronism of prophecies, the posture of redeeming aesthetes that some artists have tended to adopt out of convenience is becoming even more anachronistic. We praise the inalienable plenitude of literature and art. They fulfill a social and human function as channels of creation and never as mere masks of biased behavior. The man of today faces a vaster and more complex experience, one that would be useless to simplify with regional or partisan limitations. The man of today is motivated by a profound longing for universality. We should deal with national problems by letting that great aspiration guide us. We must elevate our country's nightmarish issues to a more universal perspective. The anecdotal, the landscape, and the picturesque are nothing but fraudulent visions of reality regarding the needs of our times. We should nurture a solid commitment to style, a vigilant dedication to education, and a more original and modern ideology. Our culture seems deprived of ideas and problems, as if we still lived in an imperturbably blissful Arcadia. We must bring a more dramatic awareness of man and reality to the fore. But it should be a rigorous awareness, overcome by clarity and demands. Naïveté and improvisation must be kept at bay from our purposes. Without flaunting a misunderstood modernity, and without forgetting our great masters, we feel guided by a new vision and a different sensibility. We do not strive to create a school of illuminati; we feel contempt for such pretensions. But we do want to stress the polemical spirit that motivates us. If there is something alarming to us, it is the absence of debate about the problems and motivations for making art, the absence of objective analyses when judging the work of an artist. We live amid prejudices and factions. We lack meditation, transcendence. Our value system is governed by timidity and complacency. But culture is something more than delightful games played by those who indulge in mutual admiration. Culture is the expression of history, which mirrors the joys and tribulations of man. It is the unshakable dominion of truth.

–"Testimonio: Manifiesto Sardio," *Sardio*, no. 1 (Caracas), May–June 1958: 1–3.
Translated by Mónica de la Torre

pre-manifesto **el techo de la ballena**

It is not by happenstance, not through idleness, not as the activity of a group of lazy or supposedly maladjusted intellectuals within the current social apparatus that El Techo de la Ballena [The roof of the whale] has begun to expose the longstanding mediocrity of our cultural milieu; it is, rather as a gesture of frank protest against the country's ongoing cultural farce, and the continued political and economic mistakes of Venezuelan democracy. Proof of this is the exhibition titled *Homenaje a la cursilería* [Homage to flashiness], in which literary texts by some of our most established national writers were used to show the crushing superficiality that limits and characterizes Venezuelan literature.

The members of El Techo de la Ballena, who identify themselves with dynamic artistic tendencies that include and value matter within the extraordinary adventure of art, have organized a show of informalist painting. The exhibition's catalogue alone has had a real impact within artistic circles, given the rebellious nature that drives their chief members.

Following are several texts that outline and foresee the objectives of this group. They include introductions from our exhibition catalogues and a Pre-manifesto.

pre-manifesto

It seems as if every attempt at renewal, or rather at research and experimentation in art, has to take into account, like it or not, the groups that prospered at the beginning of the century, such as Dada and Surrealism. Although it is true that we took such experiences very much into account when founding El Techo de la Ballena, we are not trying to revive acts or resuscitate gestures that time has appropriately allotted to the history of literature and contemporary art. We do not aspire to situate ourselves under any protective symbol. What we want is to breathe vitality into the placid environment of what is called national culture. For this we will take full advantage of any means that come to hand. However, we will not proclaim ourselves priests of the absurd or still less of mockery, both of which are categories that we have all already overcome. Mockery and the absurd will be used as nothing more than means of expression. Art in our times is tragic; it constantly devours itself and continues to do so with every new attempt, much like the serpent devouring its own tail that was once a symbol of alchemy. We want to express ourselves, only to express ourselves. To reach this essential objective, we renounce every cliché that might be attributed to us; other sources provide the quality or insignificance of the forms and aspirations that drive us. We do not want to proclaim ourselves so late as agents of any irrationality or ideas that might be related to the subconscious. We are driven above all by the most absolute lucidity. We do not want the absurd to thrive among us as a state of being, for what we want at the end of the day is to restore magma, the boiling matter, the extinguished luxury of lava. We want to demonstrate that the whale does not need to know zoology in order to survive, for every vertebrate takes risks and the risk that every creative act incites will be the only aspiration of the whale. As we risk asphyxiation, we perceive how museums and academic and cultural institutions rob us of poor ozone in exchange for rarefied and putrid air. The whale wants to restore the atmosphere.

first catalogue   for the restoration of magma

It is necessary to restore magma   the boiling matter   the luxury of lava   to place a piece of fabric at the foot of a volcano   to restore the world   the luxury of lava   to show that matter is more lucid than color   in this way the amorphous cuts away at the superfluous that prevents reality from transcending   it overcomes the immediacy of matter as a means of expression   making it   not an instrument of implementation   but an active medium that explodes   impact   matter transcends itself   matter transcends itself   textures tremble rhythms draw vertigo   violence presides over the act of creation   and leaves evidence of what is   magma must be restored in its decline . . .

informalism returns it to the essence of creative activity   reestablishes categories and relationships that science has already foreseen   informalism also has its own fungus   the beat of arbitrary matter that can be seen even by the most incredulous eyes   the possibility of creation is as evident and real as the earth and rock that shape mountains   because it is necessary to restore magma the boiling matter   adam's prosthesis

second catalogue

To establish a demarcation between the saccharine and the sentimental without being ridiculous is a highly problematic undertaking. We don't know how successful we have been. In any case, we've never tried to establish such a difference. We suppose that in the vernacular both terms have overlapped in subtle ways. However, there are pretentious things—and people—that inevitably become sentimental, an epithet that many in this country fight over and so rightly deserve. We also know that not all sentimentality is saccharine, and that neither saccharinity nor sentimentality can be easily transformed into clichés. All the same, all three categories can be found in the sphere of the ridiculous.

If with this exhibition—which we are already know is flawed because we would have needed to include a large part of our history and of what has been called our CONSECRATED VALUES in order to complete it—we succeed in blurring the differences among these terms, in other words, if we succeed in making saccharinity an extension of the sentimental, which in turn approximates a cliché, then we'll have reached a crucial objective. Although not everything that is sentimental is saccharine, everything that is saccharine is sentimental, and so it is essential to make this public (national) knowledge, to transform saccharinity into a state of consciousness that has been, unconsciously, an indeclinable factor throughout the history of this country (i.e. NATION). In this way and by knowing the rules of the game, maybe the general state of the country will become more malleable and less ridiculous. We therefore declare our exhibition to be strictly vernacular, almost folkloric, even common. As a result, we will transform the repeated and timely slogan VENEZUELA FIRST into a very useful command.

—"Pre-manifiesto," *Sardio*, no. 8 (Caracas), May–June 1961: 136–38.
Translated by Laura Pérez

of terrorism in the arts **ángel rama**

Among the many Venezuelan artistic movements that gave a peculiar, tumultuous tone to the 1960s in Caracas, one stood out for its violence, anarchic spirit, and deliberate public aggressiveness, turning provocation into "an instrument for human research." In a gesture of absolute freedom, it called itself El Techo de la Ballena [The roof of the whale].

Its exuberant stance made this movement more an outburst than a school or a coherent aesthetic system. However, its true importance lay in the fact that it brought together briefly a group of young artists that included some of the poets and fiction writers who would later carry out the literary renewal of contemporary Venezuela. The affiliation of novelists such as Adriano Gonzaléz León[1] and Salvador Garmendia,[2] who were to become important proponents of a new narrative prose; poets such as Juan Calzadilla,[3] Francisco Pérez Perdomo,[4] Efraín Hurtado, Caupolicán Ovalles,[5] Dámaso Ogaz,[6] and Edmundo Aray;[7] and artists such as Jacobo Borges[8] and Carlos Contramaestre[9] is proof of the movement's appeal during the mid-1960s. The painter Contramaestre would most clearly define the movement's initial characteristics and its principal artistic stances.

El Techo de la Ballena was founded in 1961; in March of that year, in a garage in El Conde, a Caracas neighborhood, it opened an exhibition [*Para la restitución del magma*] *For the Restitution of Magma*, and published its first manifesto magazine, a simple folded page with the title [*Rayado sobre el techo*] *Stripes on the Roof*. Simultaneously, a publication in the newspaper *La esfera* offered a brief programmatic text. Various activities followed: statements, leaflets, small plaquettes in prose and poetry that showed a clear and unusual tendency to theorize apodictically. This tendency found in the manifesto its preferred tool, revealing the group's avant-garde conception.

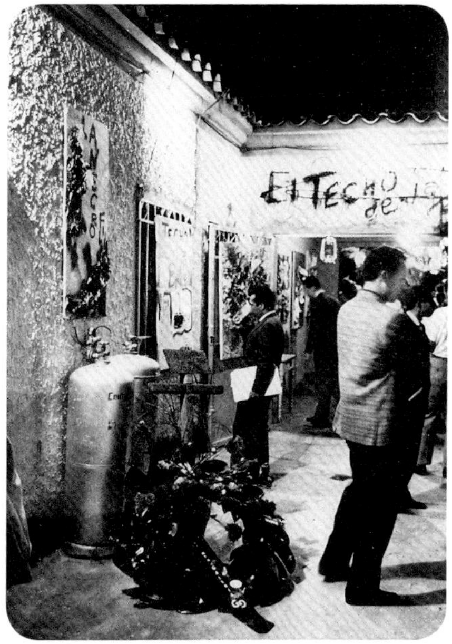

View of Carlos Contramestre's exhibition *Homenaje a la necrofilia* (Homage to necrophilia). Caracas, 1962. Collection Ignacio and Valentina Oberto, Caracas

Still, the movement's main events were art presentations. Two of these attracted particular attention: [*Homenaje a la cursilería*] *Homage to Flashiness* (June 1961), offered as a "gesture of open protest against the country's pervasive and unmovable cultural farce," and Ovalles's [*En uso de la razón*] *Power of Reason* (1963), a "testimony against pseudo-politically engaged frauds and culture builders," which constituted the first attempt to demolish the petit bourgeois concept of culture that prevailed in Venezuela, not only among those responsible for the official activities but even among the opposition.[10] Even more effective than these was Contramaestre's scandalous show [*Homenaje a la necrofilia*] [*Homage*] *to Necrophilia* [. . .], the movement's most powerful exercise in provocation; accordingly, the exhibition produced the desired response from the indignant Caracas bourgeoisie at whom it was aimed.

Merely three years after its creation, and following the publication of its third artistic manifesto, titled *Rayado sobre el techo*, no. 3 [1964], El Techo de la Ballena began to disintegrate as the political-cultural group that had lent its support to the movement started to dissolve. Even so, Contramaestre and Aray, its most committed proponents, were able to keep it more or less alive to the end of the decade, ensuring the dissemination of its guiding principles through art galleries, exhibitions of Informal painting, and literary publications. But by then its surrealistic stance began to appear dated, and in the end there was the predictable slip into a rhetorical mode.

Around 1968, after a period of intensified publishing activities, El Techo de la Ballena brought out *Salve, amigo, salve y adiós* [Hail, friend, hail

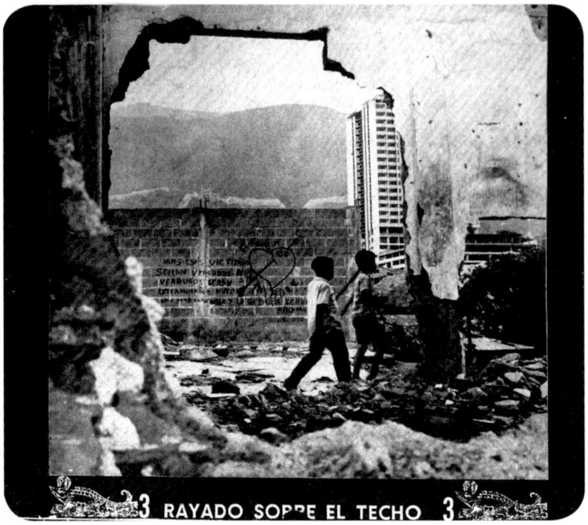

Cover of *Rayado sobre el techo,* no. 3. Caracas, 1964. Ediciones del Techo de la Ballena. Designed by Daniel González. Collection Ignacio and Valentina Oberto, Caracas

and farewell], with contributions by Aray, Contramaestre, Hurtado, Calzadilla, Ogaz, Javier Domingo, Marcia Leyseca, and Tancredo Romero. This volume can be considered the closing act of the group's run. Members began to disperse and to form other groups with different ideological definitions and principles, or they pursued their own individual artistic endeavors. That year marked, on the one hand, the near extinction of guerrilla activities in Venezuela and a great disheartenment among the members of the revolutionary left after the death of Che Guevara in Bolivia (1967). On the other hand were the violent uprisings in the country's universities inspired by the spirit of protest brought about by the "French May," which kindled the so-called renewal movement at the University of Caracas. Discernable in this new student movement were traces of the aesthetic tenets and conceptions about the act of artistic creation professed by El Techo de la Ballena.

Most of the writers in El Techo de la Ballena made themselves known through the pages of the literary review *Sardio*. Its members published eight issues between 1958 and 1961, but the group disintegrated and regrouped following the political events of the times: the founding of the new Venezuelan democracy in 1958 after the ten-year dictatorship of Marcos Pérez Jiménez, which meant an explosion of tumultuous energies and renewed projects; the impact of the Cuban Revolution of 1959 and its embracing of socialist doctrines; and the national problems stemming from the left's insurrectional opposition to the repressive politics of Rómulo Betancourt's government.

The group published texts in its own magazine, *El Techo de la Ballena*, which presented as an organic whole a revolutionary literature that subsequently would be theorized in two separate parts, often in contradictory ways. On the one hand, these texts came to be treated as a literature at the service of the revolution; on the other, as a revolutionary literature to a self-contained, formal aesthetic revolution. Consequently, there ensued debates over the aesthetic line of the Communist party members, who defended the literary models of "socialist realism" or, more generally, of a "literature for the people," often embodied in the trite and even fossilized forms employed by Latin American social fiction.

Oscar Collazos tried to reinstate these principles somewhat haphazardly (prompting a judicious response from Julio Cortázar), but another Venezuelan, Jesús Sanoja Hernández, gave them a more coherent form, structured by the aesthetics of socialist realism and the political philosophy of the Communist party.

In contrast to these positions, the group El Techo de la Ballena proposed a drastic revision of prevailing cultural values and a transmutation of the country's current art and literature. All of this was in support of a militant contemporary project at the service of the revolutionary insurgence. In these kinds of proposals, as well as in the actions of the urban guerrilla groups formed almost entirely by university students, a rebellion of the educated middle class was readily observable. The social and political problems of the petite bourgeoisie led some of its members, a clear minority with no ties to workers, farmers, or even the majority of its own class, to attempt a subversion of the established order. Because of this the movement was shaped exclusively by an avant-garde spirit, a fact that could help explain its prolific theorizing about the creation of revolutionary focuses—a kind of theorizing so pervasive in Latin America in the 1960s and whose insufficiencies were to exact such a high cost.

Various factors help to explain the anarchic spirit of this movement and that of similar movements in different parts of Latin America. On the one hand, there are the members' social backgrounds, their scant doctrinal preparation, and their isolation from the productive sectors of society, specifically from their cultural structure; on the other hand, there are the members' high degree of education, acquired as beneficiaries of national university systems, their freedom to act and think unfettered by dogmatic constraints, and their keen sensibility toward regional changes. Together, these diverse components made for the movement's surprising inventiveness, artistic effectiveness, and revolutionary ineffectiveness, as well as its unabashed violence. Though these combined elements allowed for an apt interpretation of society's circumstances, they fell short of achieving its drastic transformation.

One reproach routinely made against the group calls for careful examination. El Techo de la Ballena often was accused of a too ready adherence to already obsolete twentieth-century *isms*. This was far from unusual, as Caraqueños on the whole, though not Venezuelans in general, have long been notorious for their quick adoption of foreign aesthetic trends and ideologies. José Martí observed this as far back as 1880, and it also can be traced back to the ideology of the War for Independence. In the second half of the twentieth century, after a long period of dictatorships that had limited national culture to provincial and archaic modes, Venezuela experienced a frenetic economic development and opening up to a global culture. Both would inevitably reinforce the tendency toward the ideological fads observed by Martí. Be it the tenets of André Breton, T. S. Eliot, Jean-Paul Sartre, Antonio Gramsci, or Pablo Neruda, an often superficial and indiscriminate flocking toward European values characterized not only by El Techo de la Ballena but also all of the country's intellectual movements of the period. Moreover, the belated incorporation of *isms*

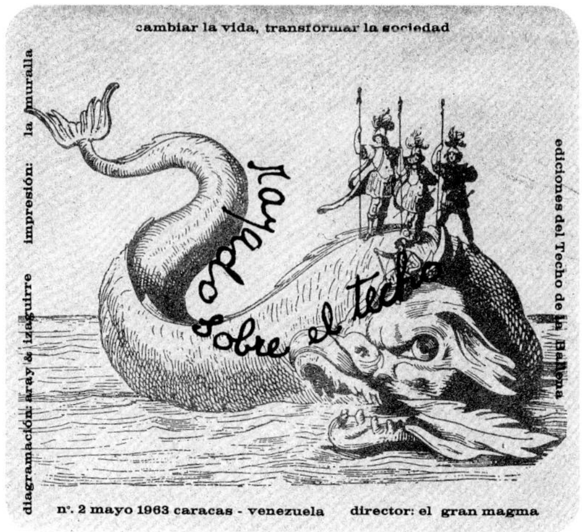

Cover of *Rayado sobre el techo*, no. 2. Caracas, May 1963. Ediciones del Techo de la Ballena. Collection Ignacio and Valentina Oberto, Caracas

from the period after World War I was typical of the workings of the new avant-garde that bourgeoned in the West in the 1950s and whose focal point was the arts and letters of the United States ([Lawrence] Ferlinghetti, [Allen] Ginsberg). The members of El Techo de la Ballena were keenly aware of all this, and in their 1961 "pre-manifesto" they stated: "It seems as if every attempt at renewal, or rather at research and experimentation in art, has to take into account, like it or not, the groups that prospered at the beginning of the century, such as Dada and Surrealism." And in 1963, after a period of gauging the enterprise they had launched, they were able to acknowledge the universal resources that allowed them to defeat the provincialism that ruled the rest of the nation:

> El Techo de la Ballena recognizes at the ballast
> Of its cargo frequent and aggressive sea beasts
> Borrowed from Dada and Surrealism. As well as the existence
> On its beams of signs leading to torrents of abuse
> Of the poets from California. And also, at the poles of its hulk,
> A material heedful of the dialectical premises
> Needed to bring about change.[11]

The editorial board of *Rayado sobre El Techo de la Ballena*, whose first issue was the catalogue for a March 1961 exhibition, evinces its members' decisive predilection for painting. The board included Calzadilla, Contramaestre, Aray, Gonzalo Castellanos, Rodolfo Izaguirre, and Gabriel Morera.[12] Furthermore, the topics broached in these publications all belong to the realm of the visual arts, especially in the two surveys of art and the Official Salon. The publication of this issue signaled a change in Venezuela's art scene: the emergence of an informal group that defined itself against the geometric abstraction and kinetic art so dominant during the 1950s. In a way, Informalism could be considered less a definite aesthetic affiliation than a wholesale revolt against the prevailing order: the medium of painting. The same could be said about the subsequent incursions into figurative art. The transition from geometric and kinetic art to Informal art, driven by the passage from a combinatorial frame of mind to one focused on the turbulence of life, was accompanied in Venezuela by an aggressiveness unheard of in the rest of Latin America. In order to understand the extent to which El Techo de la Ballena subordinated artistic practice to theoretical objectives, it is necessary to examine this difficult fusion in its members' most conspicuous creations.

The behavior of every avant-garde, be it political, religious, or artistic, has usually been ruled by the tension between its scandalous minority status and its universal, absolute claims. On the one hand, its members constitute a very small group of society as a whole; on the other, they uphold their convictions with undaunted force, positing themselves as reservoirs of undeniable universal truths, derived from an all-powerful divinity or from human forces, such as History, previously taken as absolute.

While these deep-rooted convictions invigorate every avant-garde, giving it some doctrinal, proselytizing, and transforming energy, its exponents' lack of any real power makes the realization of these beliefs practically impossible. This force field between opposed poles generates terrorism, understood as the various means needed for imposing one's convictions by force, for defeating the power that resists change, and above all, for hastening victory through effective assaults against the established structure, be it political, religious, or artistic.

In the case of the arts, Dada and Surrealism constituted the models embraced by the rest of the avant-garde movements of the twentieth century. In their turn, these models appeared to be mere imitations of the revolutionary avant-gardes of the nineteenth century. The avant-gardes' characteristic positioning as a minority predetermined their methods and actions and led to the avoidance of known forms of combat legitimized by the established authority from a position of power and for the conservation of power. At the same time, it led to a quest for other forms that, as suggested above, would necessarily be illegitimate and, in order to be effective, also capable of hitting the vulnerable spots of the prevailing structure of domination.

What has been called terrorism is a method of fighting the system that can take the form of an anarchist's bomb lobbed at the carriage of a monarch as well as that of an assault on the private life of an enemy by a writer, a measure legitimized by Manuel González Prada in Peru toward the end of the nineteenth century. In both cases, what characterizes the avant-garde's behavior is the circumvention of the established field of operations, be it the democratic debate or the debate over ideas. Lacking the power to prevail, and appealing to its creative dynamic, the avant-garde is forced to find a different field in which to operate, one in which the adversary is taken by surprise and lacks the necessary defenses and abilities to respond [. . .].

The distinctive conditions of the avant-garde demand a high degree of inner cohesion among its members, which in the end results in bitter disagreements among them, frequent exclusions, and repeated dogmatic theoretical redefinitions. In addition, the smallness of the avant-garde group, and the consequent need to present a united front, require a combative solidarity that extends even to eventual mistakes. These factors also determine the very short span of time during which the avant-garde can operate effectively. In the end, if it fails, the group disintegrates, and if it attains victory, it is institutionalized and loses its peculiarity. These movements are merely flashes, which in the dark social body absorbs to a certain degree, distorting their meaning or taking advantage of if for its own benefit. Even so, ultimately they enrich society.

This process of social confrontation or assault and eventual absorption into the mainstream necessarily marked El Techo de la Ballena. At the same time, wealthy and powerful forces were developing the project of a bourgeois culture with no or scant criticism of the system, mixing provincial and folkloric holdovers with modernizing projects such as those of geometric and kinetic art. In confronting these forces, the group had to intensify its terrorist activities against the enemy. The explosive intensity evident in the members' writings and art pieces derived not only from its minority status but also from the disparity between the warring forces. This imbalance signaled the group's predictable defeat—that is, its failure to lead the social body toward a transforming storm. The movement's inability to impose itself can be observed in the subsequent evolution of some of its iconoclastic figures, who accepted national awards from the same society they had so bitterly opposed.

At the beginning, the situation demanded a terrorist stance, and it has to be admitted that such a stance was theorized and practiced with a commitment and resolve unknown in other similar Latin American movements of the time. The actions of El Techo de la Ballena can be compared only to the Surrealist model of Breton's extreme period, when he advocated going out into the street with a revolver. The fact that this terrorist stance was postulated against a backdrop of armed insurgency, and was considered by the guerrillas to be viable at the moment, increased its force and destructive energy against the official culture of the time.

—First published as "El Techo de la Ballena," 1974. The essay appeared in the present shortened version, titled "Del terrorismo en las artes," in *Antología de El Techo de la Ballena* (Caracas: Fundarte, 1987). This English translation was published in *Inverted Utopias: Avant-Garde Art in Latin America,* ed. Mari Carmen Ramírez and Héctor Olea (New Haven and London: Yale University Press; Museum of Fine Arts, Houston, 2004).
Translated by Julieta Fombona

the great magma (first manifesto) **el techo de la ballena**

under every structure that hopes to capture a dynamic
the seed of rupture already exists
we are less able to organize   this is ob-
vious   that to live   to live is urgent
thus the whale does not need to know about zoo-
logy to live

el techo de la ballena is built on the full and uncon-
trollable luminosity of orgasm   that only insomniacs verify because the whale
is the only valid prism the only prism
with its own barbarism

few realities are as exciting as a name that
breaks all liturgies of language   el techo de la ba-
llena is more than a name

under their binding, all things will have a point of union
with the intangible   such is the meaning discovered in what
the whale has devoured in the skin of the iguana

on the surface of the painting devoured by its own mat-
ter the almanacs do not register everything that can be said
about the whale

it is cosmic hunger demanding its scream   it is a gesture   it is
an attitude   just like popular singers, el techo de la ballena will enjoy
extraordinary popularity

el techo de la ballena is a stone animal that resurrects
the world for the wellbeing of its guests
el techo de la ballena reigns amid frenzied lovers
owner of un-reconquered matter

–"el gran Magma," *Rayado sobre el techo*, no. 1 (Caracas), March 1961.
Translated by Laura Pérez

homage to necrophilia **adriano gonzález león**

Love has always been discussed, even when not from a romantic point of view, as something that transcends daily existence. Whether as a dirty trick or a sacrosanct invention, even the most determined naturalists have wanted to project a passionate lure onto what is known as "the beyond." A need for absolute communion? Fear of this pathetic daily life? Gratuitous gesture? No one knows. Only one thing is certain: during moments of passion, there is not one couple that hasn't wanted to prolong their romantic adventure until death do them part. The evidence can be found from the most high-flown poetry to the most popular love ballads. One might even catch a glimpse of [Francisco de] Quevedo's[1] influence among the rasping voices of radio singers. "I will love you until I die," is uttered as a kind of emotional long-term loan, with which love either becomes more vibrant, or at least continues to be surrounded by flowers, by bouquets that will be traded for wreaths, flowers that, even as they smell like the grave, recall the first date at a café. But there is another proposal made by lovers both inside and outside the world of romantic novels: "Let's grow old together." This is a different type of proposal, a bit of a trap due to the sensations and slowness with which the road to physical disaster is paved. One would have to research whether the Quechua[2] or Egyptian traditions of surrounding corpses with food did not include the mischievous hope for a picnic or fair, where love

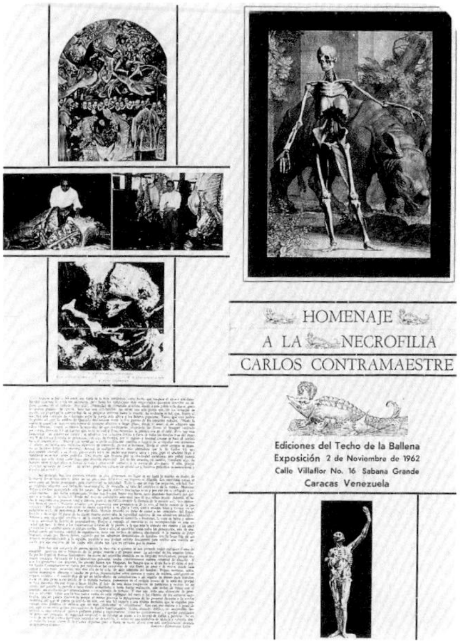

Catalogue of Carlos Contramestre's exhibition *Homenaje a la necrofilia* (Homage to necrophilia). Caracas, 1962. Designed by Daniel González. Ediciones del Techo de la Ballena, Caracas. Collection Ignacio and Valentina Oberto, Caracas

might be caught dancing behind the trees. The most encouraging attitude was that of Charles VI, who clung to his own pain, pressing a saintly and pure death into his chest in the form of an amulet that eventually sank into his rotting flesh. A disturbing death because of its metaphysical obscenity; a poor Christian death that offered the boredom of eternity as payment. The death of lovers, on the other hand, transfers something human onto what some call *nothingness* and others call *to be seated at the right hand of God, the father.* Because they project their passion or semen, tools for revitalizing and bringing us closer to the all-knowing and the dust of infinity.

There is, however, a categorical adventure from another dimension: instead of lasting until death, love functions within death, in a more final gesture, without the passage or delay of time. Necrophiliacs understand love as a postponed event, in order to seize it in its totality. Denial, solitude, or desires inhibited in life acquire an unquestionable yearning for revenge: to redress such wrongs at graveside. Monsieur Ardisson[3] made his desperate confession to the judges: "I could not get living girls and so I was forced to take dead ones." This is how, pale girl by pale girl, bone by bone, he compensated for having felt such humiliation and abandonment in the parks and avenues of the city, where thousands of attractive women were for him only a distant possibility. Also, the act assured him a complete and different type of possession, since necrophiliacs invert the structure of the song in the following way: "We will die until we love." A brave effort that provides life with permanence on the very edge of putrefaction. It even transcends death's fauna and stands firm, against coffins, gravestones, and formalin, in an audacious gesture of persistence. This is why Zoilo Morales moved his dining-room table to a cemetery in the State of Trujillo and stated that his dead wife's juices increased the nutritional value of his squalid repasts. Death's vivifying ability is arbitrary, as it brings the necrophiliac closer to Prometheus—dressing him in hero's clothes and celebrating his activities as a thief of putrefaction. The necrophiliac is often misunderstood by a society so fearful of the ultimate consequences of passion, caring only for death or love if produced by machine guns or civil codes. Despite all this, and just like the persecuted and those accused of enmity against an imbecile system of organization, the necrophiliac has clandestine ways of defending himself. Like George Stransom,[4] as cited by Henry James, who wandered about the dilapidated outskirts of London leaving a trail of his dead in tow, shimmering behind his back, playing with a strange kind of mercy only to hide his unusual devotion to those women whom he only loved once their eyes were closed in death.

There have been attempts to prevent a category of people, maybe the majority of us, from engaging in any form of encounter with or search for our own death and love. The actions of lovers are limited by the Leagues of Good Manners. The number of daily deaths produced in police laboratories[5] constantly assaults our will to choose and thus offends the activity of the necrophiliac in his corrective cleanliness. When faced with police officers who shoot, with large ships that form a blockade, with mushroom clouds that billow toward the sky, the painter Carlos Contramaestre makes compromises in order to recover different ways of loving and dying, in which each copulation, each bone is a reminder of a sovereign act, even beyond life. Intestines, shrouds, unguents, or powdered rubber spill over cardboard boxes and pieces of wood, creating a violent concoction that is far from a beautiful collector's item or the pride of a museum. It becomes instead the burning pursuit of human flesh at the very heart of sordidness, because it must rescue intestines and fecal matter next to the sweet jumble of underpants and *resitex*,[6] in an attempt to overcome so much cowardly refinement, such wonderful achievements that walk arm in arm with murder, whether it be produced by machine guns or instruments of torture. And more: a whole lineup of amorphous foulnesses, in which a new kind of beauty appears among the folds of leather and the entrails of sacrificed lambs. This will not go unnoticed, for at least it provokes repugnance in decent people or a disdainful smile from those who think they know art, with a mental blindness and sadness that prevent them from pronouncing any words of defense other than "dadaism" or "infantilism." And with this, above all and in spite of this, here are some provocative blows by Carlos Contramaestre, the lucid, alienated, sane doctor, the type who prefers experimenting with "all the quintessentials" rather than becoming paralyzed with prize-worthy perfection, commercial security, or calling cards to ladies' salons or painting salons. His intent is to recover certain discredited territories that situate him in an atmosphere of audacity and courage, in which the old codes of art have little worth and even shatter before this naked confrontation with death and love.

—"Homenaje a la necrofilia," accompanying text for Carlos Contramaestre's exhibition *Homenaje a la necrofilia*, November 1962.
Translated by Laura Pérez

why the whale? **adriano gonzález león**

"Why the whale?" someone asked, with that irritating reflexive need sometimes exhibited by those who cannot rightly explain why they were born. There is certainly a way to justify the fact of not having answers: by mucking about pompously, professorially, or with false naïveté, in the middle of the void, with the work of others. In the mental shooting gallery of our culture, amid the rotting gunk of this subjugated and humiliated country, within the rubbish heaps of the great consortiums, such a stance is perhaps to be expected. When faced with the discovery of one's own impotence, the uselessness of the creative impulse, or a lack of daring to blaze a new path, it is not at all surprising that one should take refuge in traditional thinking patterns, babble like a provincial when trying to be universal, or resort to the tricks of the bourgeois even while attempting to be revolutionary. This is how some have adjusted themselves to the general gossiping grounds on which we debate.

And so it is that, within the mindset of a boringly quotidian logic, any risky endeavor seems miscalculated. And so it is that someone may ask: why the whale – a southern or northern creature – and not a caiman, a well-bred species that thrives in our own tropical paradises. This is a matter for the theorist, who wants reality to be reality even when refusing to search for its many different aspects. But, in the same obstructive spirit, this is also a matter pertaining to the housewife, for whom it is much easier to toss a red snapper than a whale into a frying pan.

We shall not provide a straightforward and simple answer. We have always hated the voraciousness of interrogations, and an exam is an exam whether it is held in a classroom, a café, or the headquarters of the police. Like those who show courage and manliness when tortured – there have been so many in recent years! – we shall not tell tales. Like bad students faced with malicious, poorly phrased questions in an exam, we shall cheat. One can reconstruct oneself and have a taste of one's own medicine. Only the wave that we've left in our wake during our three years of difficult and active swimming can provide testimony. If one wishes to know something, the trail is out there, well-marked, with the insinuating mystery of Saint Elmo's fire, the single instance of killing provided by the albatross, or the glimmering traces of any hurricane in the Caribbean waters.

On the surface, on the tracks of these vicissitudes, the fuse of a polemical device is still smoldering, sometimes planted by terrorist methods that have never before been seen in the peaceful and respectful factory of our arts and literature. At a certain point, strategic sabotage was required for so much poisonous safety, so much intrigue, the paralyzing aestheticism that admits only the "finished work of art," and the upholstered safety of the dogmatic. This drove reasonable fishermen mad. The fin-slap that altered the traditional course of the battle shattered old supporting structures of those who had not stripped down fiercely enough, and disoriented those who, wanting change, used methods already worn out by the very system that they had tried to undermine. For the task of changing life and transforming society, the unthinking use of prescriptions could do nothing, precisely because the issue at hand was a dialectic one: for a specific country in a specific moment, the resources for the struggle have to obey a certain need.[i]

The need for action: an action-poetry, an action-painting. To inhabit, to abandon, to declare oneself on strike, to sanction *niples*,[1] to throw things out onto the street. An adventure in which the very risk of the consumption of the artist is in itself valid as an aesthetic and human task. Red-hot activity and passion, because patient work and so-called good judgment have only led people to the academy, deanships, administrative positions, or the benefit of the good paterfamilias. We would not claim, however, that on the road we have traveled thus far we have captured the whole truth. That would mean denying the initial

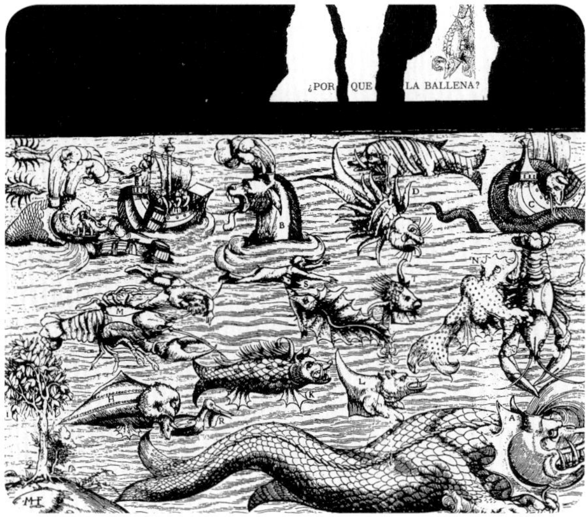

Illustration accompanying Adriano González León's text "Por qué la Ballena?" ("Why the Whale?"), published in *Rayado sobre el techo,* no. 3. Caracas, 1964. Ediciones del Techo de la Ballena. Collection Ignacio and Valentina Oberto, Caracas

objectives of El Techo de la Ballena [The roof of the whale].(ii) Nobody can coldly and crudely manipulate the patrimony of truth. Yet to go in search of it, fearing jellyfish and avoiding the temptation of new discoveries and riches that might be afforded by losing one's way, is to move about protected by a lifejacket and the desire to seize only half of things.

A simple navigation in the waters or of the waste discarded by the Whale reveals, at least to us, the following fact: painting and poetry in our country cannot continue to be a docile amassing of honors obtained with impunity, because there are no peaceful means allowing for the so-called benefit of renown. All titles, documents, surnames, influences, secret gatherings, or prizes, whether they are produced in universities, museums, or patrons' homes, do not derive their validity solely from that and must be subjected to a vigilant line of fire. El Techo de la Ballena draws its vital pride from the disturbing blow it delivers in a pious and conformist environment, when there are no other achievements of which to speak. Thus emerges the vague possibility of accessing a broader world such as that of Latin America. Subjected equally to fraud, theft, and alienation, harassed equally by the naval infantry and oil or banana corporations, all countries have similarly undergone cultural fraud and an idiotizing process. Those responsible are, for a variety of reasons, the *entreguistas*[2] and the servile, as well as those who believe in the inviolable power of dogmas.

Attentive to the ideological changes taking place in the world, at the same time attacking traditionalists and sectarians, El Techo de la Ballena has devoted itself to an activity more mindful of man: even if it takes place in the midst of capitalism or underdevelopment, this activity represents an open rejection and a declaration of the need for change. El Techo de la Ballena recognizes at the ballast of its cargo frequent and aggressive sea beasts borrowed from Dada and Surrealism. As well as the existence on its beams of signs leading to torrents of abuse of the poets from California. And also, at the poles of its hulk, a material heedful of the dialectical premises needed to bring about change. This is precisely the reason for staying on one's feet, pursuing gusts of wind.

But the Ballena is also aware that in all its structure and scaffolding a Venezuelan condition prevails, disheveled and imprecise, perhaps, but full of the courage needed to assert itself. Here, for special reasons, as in the rest of Latin America, no developments in contemporary arts and letters can be foreign to us. The working methods, the expansion of borders, and the vigorous endeavors implemented in different latitudes provide us, as is the case of politics or the sciences, with a wide field of research in which things can be accepted or rejected according to our own demands. To ignore this is to hide one's head in the sand like an ostrich, pure and simple. To access the great universal wave in our own garb, in order to invigorate ourselves, is to grant our condition as artists and writers the only gift that can lead to transcendence: to know ourselves as cultivators of a new land replete with poisonous or unusual foliage and fruits, but no longer as servile imitators of well-kept European groves or poor vegetable farmers into whose souls plagues, folkloric sterilizers, and the plough and ox have hammered underdevelopment.

Why the whale? Precisely because of all this. Because it would have been easy to choose the caiman. Because dandified aesthetes would have chosen the seahorse. And also because the whale is between kindness and horror, subject to the pull of both heaven and earth, with her dignified belly laughing at Jonah and swallowing an oil tanker. Extending itself from one end of the earth to the other, the whale is almost the earth itself, or the tiny bird that pecks at the cavity of the tooth in which fish swim about. Such a vast swimming space, such frenetic slipping and sliding, have allowed us to refuse to answer at first, and then to end up answering, because, despite our hatred of the inquisitor, we had enough answers to nullify his despicable question. The push toward the unknown may strengthen our reason for living and for contaminating our instruments with a corrosive substance that will change life and transform society.

González León's notes:
(i) See the final section of the "Second Manifesto," *Rayado sobre el techo*, no. 2, May 1963.
(ii) See *Rayado sobre el techo*, no. 1, March 1961.

–"Por qué la ballena?," *Rayado sobre el techo*, no. 3 (Caracas), August 1964.
Translated by Mónica de la Torre

terrible evidence **juan calzadilla**

Matter has formed the coffin of abstraction. Informalism has played the role of putrid cadaver in this ceremony. To bury it in haste is something less than a humanitarian act. It is, rather, a beautiful necessity that has made it clear that we are entering the last stage of a generalized death whose funeral–neither modest nor luxurious–will be paid for by abstract art.

For better or worse, informalism has died, and by no means do we intend to invoke the Guaire[i] this time to rescue the bittersweet remains of a much too mordant joke, like the one about the theft of Informalist paintings.[ii] The lock (though now junk) is still on the door, and the walls of the garage are probably now more covered in paint than ever before: a fateful sign of what was to come. The entire neighborhood of El Conde (the rain shelter for the first Ballena) was demolished and turned into an immense toilet, into the great Informalist painting that is visible only from the sky, and which, at one point or another, we all wanted to make. Dowels, worms, lime, and cement are put aside like an unbiased crime, entrails parched by a strange massacre before which informalism never became more than a pocket-sized mirror in the clenched fist of a suicide.

The rules of etiquette have permitted this type of painting to bow its head politely at museum entrances, and to poke its hooked nose in the door without the courage to enter, except for the purpose of installing a time bomb. Disaster is graceful. And so it occurred precisely at the spot where only six months ago a FAN helicopter[(iv)] [*sic*] moved the heavy sculpture of Father Morelos[1] fifty meters eastward, creating the most succulent urban mess of the *adeco* dynasty.[2] And there, in front of the museum, where Abraham with his long knife unhurriedly participates in a different form of sacrifice,[(v)] an event has occurred that would have been unimaginable for General López Contreras in more peaceful times.[(vi)] The beautiful desecration of the museum, a spectacular robbery of French paintings in which the only regrettable thing was, after all, the awful quality of the (French) exhibition, which on the other hand, was a nice excuse and even an alibi for thieves of such refined taste.[(vii)] Madame Dutilh[(viii)] would have had to wait a bit and postpone her return to the City of Lights by a few days, for she undoubtedly would have participated, at least by taking down the five paintings or by pointing to those with the highest insurance policies.

Informalism had no place in a city where peaceful coexistence can only be strictly interpreted as a funerary act, nor was it destined to survive any longer than it takes a beached whale to die during the dry season on the beaches of Miranda State.[(ix)] A city where life insurance policies are basic necessities, where existence becomes an open barrage of machine-guns ready to turn bodies into smoking sieves. This is where right-wing informalism—there is also a left-wing one—begins. This is where visceral painting programs lower their flags for the benefit of the police while the preparations for the international funeral of abstract art take place, to be attended by commissioners with hands on hearts. A toilet is not just a sculptural object;[(x)] it is also an instrument of torture. And this is how democracy keeps its promises[(xi)] and proves itself receptive to the discovery and practice of new artistic forms of murder, while still operating within the legal framework of a constitution[(xii)] whose stink clearly indicates that someone has shat upon it. Artists have also paid for this in jails or hospitals, where they have been committed at the slightest provocation and treated as putrid inmates or common criminals, but in any case as destroyers of the Christian order, according to the police files, though the silence of civil servants and the complacency of judges[(xiii)] are incapable of explaining anything. Sometimes at least they claim that if artists are jailed it is because they are unable to keep their mouths shut and turn art into a harmless machine. But an abstract painting is not a time bomb or a mimeograph.[(xiv)] This is not a silly joke. And it also isn't humorous that democracy cleaned the slate of the art market, transforming painters into vendors of wilted flowers, exhibitions into cultural events, and museums into amusement parks for wealthy fathers who have no place to take their kiddies on Sundays.

The necrophilic element that we prophetically invoked three years ago,(xv) advocating for great art on cracked walls, has contaminated the atmosphere, passing from the body to the disease, rarefying the spirit, leaving behind the turbulent dream of painting, turning it into a pale caricature of a genocidal act, a dirty dish of pastry served in the morgue, a shapeless and betrayed thing, a cadaver in a suit strolling through the rooms of the Pan-American Union.

We have physically turned into that which we had hoped painting, in aesthetic terms, would become. Like a plan destroyed just in time, the government has made from our slogans an entirely funereal use that strikes a deadly blow against conscience. Art is in mourning. All art has died in a city that has become a collective funeral. Our eyes have been horribly yanked out of their sockets beyond what our eyelids would allow if being terrorized by an infantry battalion.(xvi)

We've become cadavers at the first corner without losing the balance that keeps us standing on one foot.

In sum, informalism unmasked itself; it was reduced to a dark prophecy.

It passed the test and left its coat on the barbed wire.

A blasphemy whose fruits are not visible simply because they have already been buried.

Or a slogan snatched from us to further the dictatorship's cause.

Calzadilla's notes:

(i) The Guaire, a river of excrement running through Caracas. Lauded by poets in the nineteenth century, the Guaire was considered sacred four hundred years ago by the Chacao tribe, which imposed severe sanctions on those who relieved themselves in the river's bed.

(ii) El Techo de la Ballena first opened (in March 1961) in a garage located in the neighborhood of El Conde, which has since been demolished to make way for a modern development. A scandal was staged for the opening – and was echoed by the press in its great newspaper headlines – concerning the alleged theft of a number of paintings presumably thrown into the Guaire by the burglars. On the same day, the first issue of *Rayado sobre el techo* published the following report: "LATEST NEWS: We have been forced to withdraw a graphic article about Max Ernst that was to appear in this page in order to report a daring theft that took place in our gallery. The press just made this public with huge headlines: The paintings of the Ballena have been stolen! And with good reason, as this theft sets a precedent in the annals of those who, at least until now, had honestly gone about looting private property. But had they ever stolen any informalist paintings before? What use could they have for paintings that are good for nothing and whose value is unmistakably dubious? Certainly, the success of informalism has helped to refine the taste of the thieves. The most expensive object stolen was the old lock on the door. No money was stolen. El Techo de la Ballena was left intact, without a crack. And, as if filled with indignation, la Ballena vomited up Jonah once more, and its stomach became empty once again. Whatever the outcome or the nature of this theft may be, we should not be alarmed. The works won't go very far (to the Guaire) since informalism will soon have passed!"

(iv) [*sic*: there is no note iii in original] FAN, Fuerzas Armadas Nacionales [National armed forces]. The monument to Morelos was placed in front of the Museo de Bellas Artes after the plaza of the same name was demolished to make way for a complex road system. Protests by art organizations against the use of this statue as an embarrassing monument to sentimentality, comparable only to the Paseo de los Próceres, were in vain. . . .

This should represent, on our part, reparations for the memory of the hero of Mexican Independence.

(v) *El sacrificio de Abraham* [The sacrifice of Abraham], a sculpture by Jacques Lipchitz located in the courtyard of the Museo de Bellas Artes.

(vi) General López Contreras succeeded Juan Vicente Gómez as head of the Venezuelan government from 1935 to 1941. In January 1958 he officially inaugurated the Museo de Bellas Artes; the military band was present. The general weighed only 121 pounds at the time.

(vii) Allusion to the sensational theft of French paintings in January 1963. The Museo de Bellas Artes issued the following communiqué: "At around 3:15 P.M. today, approximately fifteen suspects, including two women, broke into the Museo de Bellas Artes armed with machine guns and pistols. After disarming the members of the Guardia Nacional on duty at the museum at the time, the assailants took over the premises of the museum and prevented by force the movement of administrative and security personnel. When the burglary occurred, the exhibition *Cien años de pintura en Francia* [One hundred years of painting in France] was being visited by students from four public and private high schools of Caracas. The assailants ordered the students and other visitors of the exhibition to remain in the exhibition rooms, and after a maneuver that lasted approximately fifteen minutes, walked away with the following originals from the exhibition: *Bathers* by Paul Cézanne, *Still Life* by Paul Gauguin, *Flowers in a Copper Vase* by van Gogh, *Still Life* by Pablo Picasso, and *Still Life with Pears* by Georges Braque. The assailants fled in two cars that were parked near the museum. During the robbery, one student suffered a gunshot wound."

(viii) Madame Odette Dutilh, the official curator of the exhibition *Cien años de pintura en Francia.*

(ix) Geography. In 1962, a delegation from El Techo de la Ballena visited the beaches of Higuerote (Venezuela) after hearing reports that a whale was a few meters from the shore there. However, the rescue operation could not be accomplished and the whale died. Professor Rodríguez and his students from Guatire managed to rescue the enormous skeleton, which is now on exhibit at their public high school as biological sciences research material. From 1961 to 1963, five beached whales have been found on Venezuelan shores, without counting, of course, the one that can be found indoors.

(x) Reference to Marcel Duchamp's first Dadaist manifestation in the United States. He sent a new toilet model for an official art exhibition to take place in New York in 1915 [*sic*: 1917]. There have been a number of denunciations of the torture of political prisoners at the police headquarters in Caracas, where prisoners have their heads repeatedly dunked in dirty toilets. In 1962, the Venezuelan congress included the issue in a report on physical torture.

(xi) "Democracy keeps its promises" is a slogan used by the Venezuelan government in advertisements for the construction of public works. The government also uses other formulas widely shown on television, such as: "The police succeed in the campaign for the extinction of extremists." Clearly, the reference is to physical extinction.

(xii) [*sic*: notes xii and xiii are apparently out of order] An allusion to certain judges who unconditionally support the government's use of force by issuing police warrants to enter homes, high schools, and universities. Famous among these are Judges Meléndez and Martínez, whose behavior led to a macabre prank: the extremists published invitations to the funerals of both judges in major newspapers.

(xiii) The current Venezuelan constitution was promulgated by legislators under the dictator Pérez Jiménez and supports an eminently presidential regime.

(xiv) In March 1963, the painters Ramón Vázquez Brito and Olga Matute were detained and accused of terrorism. The police placed a mimeograph and subversive propaganda where the painters were detained, and took photographs that they later gave to the official press. This undignified and cowardly way of forcing the detainees to pose with conspiratorial materials in order to accuse them of terrorism is one of the government's most commonly used tactics to jail people without any kind of trial.

(xv) Manifesto "para un arte del futuro" [for an art of the future] and prologue to the Salón Experimental [Experimental salon] of 1960, in which the initial goals of the informalist movement in Venezuela were outlined and to which El Techo de la Ballena was radically committed.

(xvi) "Beyond what our eyelids would allow" is taken from Lautréamont. "An infantry battalion" refers to the Bolívar Battalion, which laid siege to the Universidad Central in Caracas for two days in November 1962. In an article published by the Caracas newspaper *El Nacional,* pseudo-writer and apologist Juan Liscano praised the head of the Bolívar Battalion for his "courage" during the military operation against the defenseless university campus.

–"La terrible prueba," *Rayado sobre el techo*, no. 3 (Caracas), August, 1964.
Translated by Mónica de la Torre

borges: the communicated image **marta traba**

A great painting of 1965 titled *Humilde ciudadano* [*Humble Citizen*] bears witness to a figurative painter being pursued by furies that are highly recognizable – as much for their kinship with [James] Ensor's chromatic liberation as with [Willem] de Kooning's pathological disfiguring – yet are nonetheless powerful, well-crafted, and original, especially given the increasingly aseptic milieu that dominated Caracas from the mid-1950s to the mid-1960s.

The insolent and deformed figures brutally pointing toward the spectators, the bloody birds, and the convulsive faces in the burial-murder materialized in a tombstone that reads "Here lies Jacobo Borges" were all in keeping with the will of the painter who in *Letra roja* manifested his "unremitting determination to not let himself be destroyed," bolstered by a "class decision" he found "nourishing and commendable."

At the time, the aggressive gestures of Borges's paintings certified his personal aggressiveness. "*Letra roja* has asked me to speak about Venezuelan painting," he wrote. "I cannot come up with an abstraction based on my own life, or the lives of my friends, or their deaths, because I suspect that if we are to make any contribution to painting, it needs to come out of all of this, out of our history."

Borges had just returned from Paris, a journey he had taken thanks to *Lámpara y silla* [Lamp and chair], an unremarkable painting that resulted from a strike at the Escuela de Bellas Artes, in which it was demanded that the eternal theme of the little apple be replaced by the no less eternal themes of chairs, coffeepots, and lamps. "These movements are common in Venezuela," Borges commented with his harsh sense of humor, "to substitute one artistic expression that doesn't correspond with the country with a new one that doesn't correspond either."

Gamblers, monstrous, brazen women, bestial and generally ferocious men crouching and exposing themselves started sharpening Borges's œuvre in order to catapult it more effectively against the salon games that had already become the dominant artistic trend in Venezuela. The iconoclastic young members of El Techo de la Ballena adored him and presented him, along with [Carlos] Contramaestre, as the reverse side of the coin in which the Great Magician justly reigned: Jesús Soto.

What artist, what man hovered over the enormous *Humilde ciudadano* canvas? Jacobo Borges in his sealed room, "undergoing an intensive 'shit-therapy' treatment: juice, cigarettes, clocks, soda, bread." Locked up with generals of ubiquitous raised hands, capturing and then releasing images after having vindicated them, engaged in a game of spontaneity, hurling color at the canvas both violently and nonchalantly, seeking dramatic, spectacular, theatrical solutions, complacent and reassured in his way of being – one that for its repetitiveness and rejection of the milieu has always yielded an unmistakable "Borges style."

Thanks to a talent and predatory character that are equally fluid and natural, what Borges did in 1965 was to embody a good neo-figurative painter who bellicosely articulated an alternative to the prevalent neutrality regarding man and his problems and who at the same time appropriated the powerful kinetic movement of Venezuela.

"Man is unmade according to his image," writes [Maurice] Blanchot.[1] Faithful to a similar idea, Borges has unmade man according to man's image. A disagreeable option, almost a bloody one, which kept him in the vulnerable position of a trigger-happy protester by vocation.

I am not adding anything that isn't already present in *Humilde ciudadano*. You can see for yourselves.

Suddenly the debauched carnival of the *Jugadoras de cartas* [Card-playing women], painted by Borges, suffered an eclipse.

From 1966 on, Borges devoted himself in body and spirit—as did a brilliant group of filmmakers, musicians, photographers, architects, and writers—to preparing the audiovisual show that would open on the occasion of the four hundredth anniversary of Caracas.[2] Those years of teamwork dramatically altered his points of view as an easel painter.

The scale of that performance and his decisive participation in a true audiovisual uprising, in which history was revised and reproduced under an unprecedented and dynamic guise, showed him the limitations of painting as an expressive medium. It also taught him the differences between *expressing* (as he had done with the cruelty of *Humilde ciudadano*) and *communicating;* expression was directed at the small and cultivated circle of those chosen and understanding of aesthetic situations, whereas communication was aimed at diverse audiences. Communication and expression seemed to him irreconcilable and he therefore gave up painting. For six years he abstained from making any work, not even a drawing, and he gave up being his country's most brilliant and promising figurative painter.

In 1972, when he decided to return to painting, he cautiously and stubbornly clarified his new ideas: "I am much more of a communicator than a painter. A painter is a medium; a communicator is a person who is aware. A painter is someone absorbed by his instrument. A communicator reflects on it."

By emphasizing his training as a communicator, he intends to have a new relationship with society. He abandons that detonating time-bomb relationship with a society whose vices ought to be denounced through ardent gestures. He abandons the confessional asides and theatrical outbursts. The point now is to know society and the codes driving it so that the image may become a conscious replica that dismantles them, and consequently demystifies them intelligently.

That is to say that the deformed woman who persists at the bar, who is flanked by the contoured fragments of a chair, who is inscribed in a clearly relational space with two sealed windows and a man's silhouette, is only a distant relative of the card players committed to their brutal greed and their unbridled chattering. This new woman has been adjusted to her value as a sign. She is in fact a sign surrounded by other signs, projecting herself as language, as information subjected to the symbolic mediation of art.

With the image of the woman, and the images of the men in the foreground, of hopeless and mysterious gatherings, Borges wishes to be a communicator: that is, someone who in a critical attitude places himself before the very elements that he is in charge of, until he manages to transform them into transmittable signs.

But painting is only a halfway language that could never adjust itself to the conditions and laws of linguistics, and Borges knows it. Painting is nothing but the simulacra of a semiotic system. Is it enough for the artist to satisfy his current communicative passion? "No," he declares, "I use the elements of an individual medium such as painting, within the midst of a culture from which I can't escape, but I think that by provoking a rupture through the new information I transmit with the image I can expose those transitional and precarious aspects of painting, and maybe even—why not—painting's own future extinction."

In other words, Borges thinks that through his paintings he can explode painting in general. (The information that the image provides becomes dense and concrete, yet it cannot communicate itself as a sign due to the constant concrete and symbolic interferences that get in the way.) This does not mean that Borges is prophesying the possible extinction of figurative or abstract painting, but rather that of painting in general due to its inefficiency as a means of communication. Figuration, abstraction, Op art, kinetic art, anti-museums—everything is bound to explode.

What will happen, then, with art? Borges projects himself into the future: "When people become aware that communication is a system, they will be able to see it with critical distance: at that point an art that would remain implicit in much wider levels of communication could be formulated, not because it would be collectively *developed* (an important point here) but because it would be collectively *received*."

This confirms that his passion for communicating springs directly from his growing desire to serve a social function. Borges thinks that if the artist really wants to have a social function, he needs to do it by establishing a relationship in which he feels not superior, but rather an equal part of a whole. This might imply, as has been pointed out many times before, the temporary disappearance of the artist. Yet Borges also knows that if such an emergency doesn't present itself, the artist plays a critical role that the work of art itself can carry out.

Let us turn to his work again. Although his engrossing passion for communication could cool the image, the turmoil of the sight still imposes itself. The image of the woman or the image of the man, frontal and semi-decapitated on the tables, as exposed in their distortions as in their expendable and changeable existences: these corroded and corrupted images, dissolved by the inanity of their actions, continue to be perturbing Borgesian images, mutilated and brazen in their disfigurement, sentenced to isolation in an environment of incomprehensible signs. They continue to be the furious and condemning reverse of a composed and over-refined society.

Let us look at the finger, the cup, the bird, the painting-object where a mutilated woman is held captive, the figure-objects, the closed-off interiors, the baroque offices, the moldings of doors, the backsides of desks, the reiterative anti-landscapes, the geometrical elements that things drag, all entangled and laughable. Gone is the terseness of the plane; the optical effects are aggravated, the normal relationships between things and beings disjointed, close-ups smudged and distorted, silhouettes undone. The security and ever more uncertain power over things has faded. The image is chafed, repainted, blasted, and reworked through artifices replacing the direct and carnal phrasing of the previous works. The image is intent on enriching itself through the accumulation of meanings but, in the end, continues to operate and transmit itself as the personal passion of the painter Borges.

The information that Borges tries to convey to the spectators, so they may become aware of the manipulations to which they are subjected, and so that may react against them, can hardly be grasped. Spectators tend to see signs as clues, and to incorporate them into the mystery of surreal relations. The face of the man blurred against an optical plane, the bird on his shoulder, the clipping of the fruit bowl, and the posterlike imprint of the tire will always be associated with a Surrealist set of symbols.

Surrealism produced an encoded world, and the allure of mystery, of complicity with the mystery, attracts us still. Although the sign's intentions—to articulate an explanation of the world—are diametrically opposed to the intentions of the Surrealists, which articulate an invitation to irrationality, in paintings such as those by Borges the confusion between the two becomes palpable. It is useless for Borges to take on the number one problem of communication: to dismantle language structures so as to make them visible and make their effective transmission possible. His study of structures as systems of dormant relations, bestowed with rhythm and internal self-regulation, cannot be clearly read in the final outcome of his paintings either. Instead, when he plays and uses perceptions and sensations, he begins to tread on more favorable ground. [Pierre] Francastel argues that "the conception of art as structure leads to a dynamic conception of the function of art, to the role of art as transformative, and to the substitution of the passive system of information with the full use of sensations and perceptions."

It is clear that Borges wants to incorporate that full use of perception and sensation into his new work. Many of the elements in these paintings seem completely disassociated from the general context, which is underscored through its explicit markers: unexpected croppings of shapes, geometrical interferences, sudden voids, rotund designs. Others become extemporaneous when they are forced into the canvas in a blatant attempt to augment and unbalance the whole: all geometric forms and optical devices, for instance.

This accumulation of perceptions and sensations undoubtedly provides active information: the image is enriched and motivated in such a way that it elicits the new type of reading that Borges seeks. Unlike his previous spontaneity, which sought to impress the spectators with the dreadfulness of its images, he now aims for his paintings to resist a careful reading, for them to invite the viewer to take them apart piece by piece and reflect on them.

The new work of Borges is his organized passion. His protest is transformed into criticism. His old avowal not to let himself be destroyed is transferred to a larger frame of references that alert spectators to the destruction threatening them.

—"Borges: La imagen comunicada," in *Mirar en Caracas* (Caracas: Monte Ávila Editores, 1974), pp. 23–39.
Translated by Mónica de la Torre

finale: allegro con fuoco **marta traba**

In Caracas, if I were to say that I wish to speak of kineticism (and by "kineticism" I am referring to Op art, geometric abstraction, Concrete art, and of course also kinetic art) without bias, without the slightest animosity, and finish off this series of essays with an *allegro con fuoco* finale—*nobody* would believe me.[1]

This is yet another result of living in societies that have come nowhere near Europe's reflective ability and are led by tribal passions and monolithic ideas that can never be examined with equanimity. It is true that I deem the Venezuelan kinetic art trend to be a sort of official art that has proved convenient for the ruling classes and economic powers since it caters as much to their ideology as to their snobbery. It is true that I have repeated and hammered this incessantly, in an open *campaign*, because I believe that in our countries ideas can no longer be solely *expressed*, instead they have to be *fought for* tooth and nail so some minimal attention can be devoted to them. But if the kinetic movement as a general response to the cultural situation of Venezuelan society seems inadequate to me (to say the least), this does not mean that I have stopped appreciating kinetic art as a valid movement within the art of our times, or that I do not think that some kinetic works have all the formal attributes that allow for an object to become a work of art. My openly admitted admiration for [Josef] Albers and [Victor] Vasarely, and my interest in [Barnett] Newman, [Ellsworth] Kelly, and [Donald] Judd should prove this. However, since I have been irrevocably categorized as the general enemy of kineticism and the personal enemy of [Jesús Rafael] Soto (whom I hardly know and with whom I have never exchanged a single word), I would once again like to clarify my position in this essay, not to right any wrongs, which I consider impossible, but to reinforce my positions.

I maintain that Venezuelan kinetic art is an official art: in the rest of the Americas there are no official art movements (the case of the official Mexican muralism, sponsored by the PRI [Partido Revolucionario Institucional: Institutional Revolutionary Party], doesn't count, since all of Mexico's modern art has been made behind the government's back); yet Venezuela, as I have often said, is a sui generis country.

Venezuelan kinetic art fills both the ruling classes and economic power, if they are not one and the same, with complacency. The Venezuelan ruling class has sought to project a completely progressive image of their country. You will say that this happens everywhere: it could certainly be that all leaders aspire to progress, yet no one determines the future's path more vehemently than Venezuelans. The ruling class invented the myth of the year "2000 and something." This does not happen anywhere else, not even in developed parts of the world. Only in Caracas could the country's most important newspaper celebrate its anniversary dedicating it to the year "2004"; only here could a new newspaper called *2001* be launched. In this space odyssey, it is obvious that the present keeps being erased, with increasing force, and the contempt for the past is constantly growing. It is also evident that a society that embarks on such comic-book futurism disconnects itself from its problems, and that nothing could be more convenient for its rulers than the projection of their people onto the backdrop of the future, where everything enters a context as utopian as it is harmless.

But if futurism is a true political weapon inoculating a society with the virus of progressive utopia, nobody has collaborated better with the Venezuelan ruling classes than economic power. The "dominant culture" of Venezuela was stimulated by the vertiginous fortunes created after the oil and construction boom of the Pérez Jiménez era. Almost all those with money embraced the cause of progress with unprecedented enthusiasm, understandable if one takes into account the newness of their fortunes and their desire to become fully integrated with a highly industrialized society. In Venezuela culture was purchased with the same commendable fervor with which North Americans purchased it at the beginning of their industrial development: the best art collections in the continent are in Venezuela; they have been acquired with a munificence unknown to us before. People bought the progressive and experimental trend: for every refined collector of [Giorgio] Morandis there have been ten collectors of [Alexander] Calders. This is where the boundary of the dominant culture was traced: from then on, money favored those artistic forms that, positioning themselves in the extreme avant-garde, created an image of progress, technology, and scientific advancement that was urgently needed.

Money and the ruling classes in Venezuela are very consistent. They supported kinetic art as well as technical and scientific experimentation and, deeming this point the most convenient in terms of their progressive image, they stopped there. Curiously, while Alejandro Otero was asked to paint water towers in Caracas, Soto was asked to inaugurate the Kinetic Museum of Ciudad Bolívar[2] with great pomp and circumstance, Mateo Manaure was asked to decorate buses, and [Carlos] Cruz-Diez was asked to make his murals of additive color and chromatic induction on the Santo Domingo dam. While kinetic works invade the IVIC [Instituto Venezolano de Investigaciones Científicas: Venezuelan institute for scientific research] in Caracas or the Paseo Ciencias in Maracaibo, the new avant-gardes are not being supported and a distracted indifference, paired with ignorance, surrounds the new artist's break with the past, environmental and Conceptual art, *arte povera*, and art actions. If we stop to think about it, however, it makes sense that the ruling classes, among which sophisticated snobbery predominates, are uninterested in the new avant-gardes. In the current world, avant-gardes are part of a process; they are the necessary result of and the predictable response to the specific situations generated by the process. Here, on the other hand, the kinetic avant-garde does not represent a moment of that process, but instead is the artistic faction chosen to represent as fully as possible the idea of progress. Venezuela did not *go through* kineticism (as Europe or the United States did), it *chose* kineticism; kinetic experimentation was not the final exit toward which other situations were pushing; instead, in Venezuela, it was purchased.

Why? Because an appearance of progress needed to be in tune with an innovative, nontraditional art. It was important to get away from traditional forms with the same energy with which the city was destroyed; new buildings went up, and the past was ferociously and decisively abolished: traditional forms, i.e. painting and sculpture, were considered obsolete and inappropriate given the city's façade of progress. Unfortunately many artists individually adopted this compulsive option that has nothing to do with a genuine process; the case of Manaure and his fine Surrealist sensibility, and the case of [Víctor] Valera and his powerful figurative sculptural vision unfortunately illustrate this: both artists and their works have been annulled by the compulsive kinetic option.

Once the banner of technique and science had been raised, nothing served it better than the experiments of the kinetic artists in Paris. Technique was God, and Soto was his prophet.

In 1967, when the exhibition *Lumière et mouvement* [Light and movement] was presented at the Musée d'art moderne in Paris, Soto, Cruz-Diez and [Narciso] Debourg managed to adhere to the visual experiment even more successfully than the famous "Recherches" group, who a year before, in their show *A Day in Paris* [*sic*: *Une journée dans la rue* (A day in the street)], had opted for the kinetic action and concept over the *object*.[3] The ideas that Soto expressed at the time, underlining the importance of the relations among things, were very much in line with a meticulous and extremely fine search for vibrations and minimal movements that, in my opinion, culminated notably in the works he showed at the Brussels exhibition of 1958 (now in the IVIC), in which he achieved his maximal capacity to enrich those relations. This relational world—therefore basically structural, intelligent, and sensitive—does not seem to be the same as that of the unfortunate mural of the Centro Capriles,[4] in which the relations between the work's components fail; the pressure of the dominant culture seems to have crushed Soto's silent virtues as a maker of vibrating objects. It is not the world of the Penetrables either, whose poor argumentation is not saved by trivial synesthetic reactions. Venezuela validates *any* kinetic result with the same criteria. A culture that stimulates a certain phase of art because it bestows upon it a progressive status is not required to be *understanding* of the artistic act: it simply chooses it and appropriates it. With its promotion in this way, with its application on buses and water towers, buildings and avenues, ornamentation, advertising, and private homes, kinetic art ceased to be an interesting experiment in a given stage of modern life: instead, it went on to illustrate the ambitions of the haute bourgeoisie and of "progressive" leaders. The price it paid for abandoning the artistic process was to become clearly mediocre and decidedly decorative. Whether consciously or unconsciously, it pandered to the megalomania of Caracas and lost interest in all the other services it could provide, even that of tending to the "discreet charm" of the bourgeoisie, which is always more appropriate and conservative. The Museo Soto in Ciudad Bolívar and Cruz-Diez's chamber buried ninety meters underground in Barinas may be understood in this context.[5]

Now I am thinking that all the times I wrote "Venezuela" I should, more accurately, have written "Caracas." Caracas does not differentiate itself from Venezuela with the logical distance that all capitals keep from the countryside. Not even between Buenos Aires and the Argentine interior, or between São Paulo and the Paulista countryside, is there a distance as great as that between Caracas and the rest of the country. This distance is marked by a peculiar fact: Caracas is not the city whose vertiginous (and monstrous) growth has been prompted by monetary and migratory abundance, but rather the city that has been manipulated by the dominant culture to become the model of the year 2000. Caracas has been invented like a city out of [H. G.] Wells, walking all over its own realities, its census-counted population of half a million people who live in ranches and the tremendous contradictions of the present. The invention of Caracas was mutually agreed upon by the ruling classes and economic powers, because nothing else represented the image of progress and technology so completely. Regardless of its being a lie–which is the case with all inventions–and its inability to be confronted with objective reality, regardless of the fact that nobody is more critical of the chaotic and suicidal growth of Caracas than the city's inhabitants themselves, in the end everyone has accepted this fiction. People discuss city planning, they protest over the ravaging of nature, they denounce poverty, but nobody has thought of Caracas as the illustration of the illusory technological level that Venezuela has supposedly reached.

I call it illusory because most of Venezuela is foreign to that fiction; because nobody who has ever traveled within Venezuela can think of technological progress; instead they think of a deserted country, of immense unpopulated lands where the only towns appearing every so often in the west, for instance–even those that are considered the country's second, third, or fourth cities, etc.–are submerged in villagelike underdevelopment, amid the slow deterioration of last century's religious and family values, which have not been altered or substituted for ones more in tune with the present world. Most of Venezuela lives in a world untouched by modern culture, vision, and thought.

Every so often the dominant culture of Caracas looks to the provinces and decides to plant technology, like those who plant trees: no one cares to find out whether the tree can grow in that specific climate or whether it will shortly die emaciated. The act of planting satisfies the dominant culture and convinces it that progress will spread in the land.

Why is a museum of kinetic art planted in Ciudad Bolívar? From the point of view of the museum's mere existence, has anyone paid mind to how the devastating sun comes in through the "brise soleil"?[6] Or to the heat and moisture that make Vasarely's pieces of paper come undone? Or to the leaks? The mildew? The conservation of works that will be destroyed in a few years? And what matters most: has anyone thought about what this museum means with regard to Ciudad Bolívar and its irrevocable dream of an alienated province? About the extent of its public's ignorance? About the museum's lack of connection with contemporary life? About the awe that the museum's works inspire in their viewers? About the lack of any educational effort? Who will see, take advantage of, and benefit from this museum? The opening night posse? The European travelers who will be brought in to see this phenomenon? What can a specific and complex phase of the art of our times mean to an audience who has no relationship with art? Wouldn't this be like forcing someone who has never even heard of philosophy to read an excerpt of Kant's Categories?

I don't consider this surrealism. This is in line with the aristocratic and ignorant attitude of Caracas that goes about planting its false progressive image with complete disregard for what the countryside is, comprehends, and needs. Because the fact that three or four residents of Ciudad Bolívar go into the museum each day and leave it with a face of boundless stupefaction does not mean that they are *below* kinetic art, but rather that the radius of their comprehension and sensibility, as well as their daily experiences, are different—not less important, but certainly diametrically *different*.

The vision of the countryside is still rural and emotive, its artists paint landscapes and portraits, their thoughts are light centuries away from technology. The landscape painters of Lara—a city six hours from Caracas by car, one hour by plane—keep placing their easels before nature, no matter their age or social condition. Barinas is a county with a distinct color, solitude, and temperature that have nothing to do with the colors, sensations, or temperature of Cruz-Diez's chamber. It is also a city where, according to the August 16, 1973, edition of the newspaper *El Universal*, ten children a day die of gastroenteritis due to starvation, nutritional deficiencies, and lack of medical attention.

These insane grafts of the image of progress are completely delirious and not funny in the least. I'll say it again: the surrealism is that Remedios the Beauty[7] should fly unhindered over Aracataca; the construction of an additive color mural is nothing but the persistence to endorse the grand fiction of Caracas's dominant culture. It is justified, then, that in an interview Cruz-Diez claimed that he did not think Venezuela was in a position to provide him with "the means to publicize and integrate his work within the universal world of culture." Evidently Venezuela has little to do with *the universal world of culture*, if such a thing exists, which seems increasingly uncertain. Let us say that it cannot promote or integrate him (nor Soto, nor the young artists developing absolutely incomprehensible nonsense to justify their experiments, nor those in England writing on "art in the street" and occasionally satisfying the brief curiosity of a bored Brit) within foreign and unknown avant-garde situations that Venezuela has never experienced and will never experience.

This is not the case in highly industrialized nations. There artists have been summoned and seduced by industry, to the point that it has persuaded them to turn the studio into a laboratory and meld with the scientific and technical manifestations in a "total art" that more accurately should be called "capitalist realism" since it is marked by the same docility, repetition, and alienation as its counterpart's "social realism." Through institutes, foundations, and promotions of a frankly industrial scale, etc., artists have been convinced to ally themselves with industry: artists are loyal servants, they have lost autonomy and critical distance, regardless of the conservative or cutting-edge means by which they may express their independence. Of course those loyal artists serving the grand industry have also had loyal critics: in this sense, no one has lent more delirious services than Pierre Restany in France. Nowadays every discipline has its family Batman, that is, a half-cartoonish and half-fictive figure pushing all actions beyond rational decisions. Restany is the Batman of contemporary criticism. (How appropriate that the anniversary issue of the Caracas newspaper mentioned above chose Restany as the prophet of the future of the visual arts. His panting efforts to push artists beyond any art comprehensive of social reality and to thrust them into actions sadly lacking in meaning works well on that futurist screen onto which they seek to cast all Venezuelan art.)

In developed countries, regardless of the extravagance of "total art" trends, the coincidence of industrial advances, the projection of that advancement over the entire society, and the situation of artists – who are involved in the process of development as well, and so accept what it demands from them instead of demanding anything from it themselves – are noteworthy.

On the contrary, to make a chamber ninety meters underground in the Venezuelan state of Barinas is as outlandish as building transparent cupolas amid the mysterious jungles of Venus, such as those imagined by Ray Bradbury. When a country's artists choose to channel their works toward science fiction, they succeed most in distancing themselves from reality. I care about the end results less and less: I could not care less if they generate a kinetic, Pop, or Conceptual work. Such unfocused creative behavior can only yield something devoid of signification, and therefore expendable and meaningless to the community.

Does this mean that the new artists who persist in kinetic art because they have let themselves be persuaded, honestly or dishonestly, by the dominant art trend, or those who go about Europe aping the anti-art actions of Europeans or North Americans, should drop the magnetic balls, Plexiglas, sand, wire, metals, synthetic and discarded materials, and start painting *araguaney* trees like the landscape painters of the state of Lara?[8] *Of course not*. But art needs to serve a social function (social, not political) by immersing itself in the real facts of a society. And in Venezuela there are two societies: one pastoral, provincial, and nineteenth-century-like. Another, fabricated in a Caracas stronghold for the year 2004. This two-headed nation is the social framework for today's artists: they should figure out how to situate themselves in it, how to reconnect themselves with one of its two faces or with both at the same time, or how to rectify the error and horror of its front and back, or how to really respond to a true society, or how to relate to a present that, despite its weighing on the dominant culture, is there every day. I mean that in Venezuela the only artist with the possibility of redemption is the one who sees this split society clearly and is able to solve the problem outside the tyranny of kinetic art and the inconceivable fossilization of the *araguaney*.

Because if the work of an artist is destined to reorganize the visible and reveal the invisible, what is it that the officialized kinetics reorganize and reveal? What slice of reality are they operating on? Their works are nothing but decorative objects: very few have avoided this desire to please, to flatter the monarch. In some young people, however, one can perceive a reaction against this stratified situation. The dolls of Lilia Valbuena, the "people-boxes" of [José] Campos Biscardi, [José Antonio] Quintero's landscapes, William Stone's tents, the characters of Ana María Mazzei, and the people of Lourdes Blanco and Sonia Márquez, the Conceptual objects of Margot Römer, some boxes by [Manuel] Mérida, some drawings by Oswaldo Parra, [Diego] Barboza, [Ángel] Peña, [Julio] Pacheco Rivas, Villasmil Herrera. . . . All these are good explorations into other territories that, by responding to an avant-garde that has not been codified by the dominant culture, represent an act of independence and a clarification of the problem, at least at a personal level.

So that one *looks at Caracas* with sufficient attention, this official kinetic art movement needs to be as visible as the reactions of these younger artists and the vertical disconnection of the provinces. Yet also, like any other happily Latin American country, Venezuela has a margin of imponderables.

That is the reason why, for instance, the lost town of Cajaseca, with its single street and battered plaza, can give rise to someone like Henry Bermúdez, a brilliant draftsman and elementary-school teacher who invents, in the manner of the most refined representative of secular culture, oriental birds and wreaths formed out of hundreds of feminine bodies. That is why Cabimas, a hallucinating city with a landscape of iron artifacts endlessly perforating the ocean and the sky, and already marked by the depletion of oil, can give rise to a painter like [Emerio Darío] Lunar, a creator of imaginary, plundered, and strict architectures, where lifeless creatures intensely await from a void more dreamlike than [René] Magritte's.

Like any other country in the Americas, Venezuela has a potential reserve of fictions: they do not yield as much revenue as oil but, in the end, they are all the more important.

–"Finale: Allegro con fuoco: Cinéticos y experimentadores," in *Mirar en Caracas* (Caracas: Monte Ávila Editores, 1974), pp. 123–33.
Translated by Mónica de la Torre

editor's notes to the texts

sardio / testimonial, pp. 254 - 56

1. *Sardio* (or *sardónice*, from the latin *sardius lapis*) means "sardonyx," a gemstone characterized by layered veins of sard and onyx.
2. January 23, 1958, marked the fall of Marcos Pérez Jiménez's dictatorship in Venezuela, at which time leftist intellectuals saw the possibility of a new revolutionary government. Art, in their view, could not remain disconnected from these political conditions. In this respect, their position came to resemble that expressed by André Breton, Leon Trotsky, and Diego Rivera in their 1938 "Manifesto: Towards a Free Revolutionary Art."

rama / of terrorism in the arts, pp. 258 - 64

1. Adriano González León, who died in 2008, was a Venezuelan writer, and editor of the journal *Sardio*. He was a central member of El Techo de la Ballena. His books include *Asfalto infierno* (Asphalt Hell; 1963) and *País portátil* (Portable country; 1968).
2. Salvador Garmendia was the author of such books as *Los pequeños seres* (Small beings; 1958), *Los habitantes* (The inhabitants; 1961), and *Los escondites* (Hiding places; 1961).
3. Juan Calzadilla is a poet, painter, and art critic. He is the author of *Dictado por la jauría* (Ruled by a pack of dogs; 1962), among other books.
4. Francisco Pérez Perdomo was a poet and critic. He was a founder of the journal *Sardio* and a member of El Techo de la Ballena. Perdomo was the author of *Fantasmas y enfermedades* (Ghosts and maladies; 1961); *Los venenos fieles* (Faithful poisons; 1963), and *Depravación de los astros* (Depravity of the stars; 1966).
5. The poet Caupolicán Ovalles was one of the most active members of El Techo de la Ballena. His poems include "Duerme usted, Señor Presidente?" (Are you sleeping, Mr. President?; 1962) and *En uso de la razón* (*Power of Reason*; 1963).
6. Víctor Manuel Sánchez (Dámaso) Ogaz was both a visual artist and a writer. His early work was abstract, later becoming figurative in the Surrealist vein.
7. Edmundo Aray is a poet and filmmaker; he participated both in the journal *Sardio* and in the group El Techo de la Ballena.
8. On Jacobo Borges, see Elías Pino Iturrieta, "An Appraisal of Contemporary Venezuela," in this volume, pp. 31 - 45, n. 10.
9. Carlos Contramaestre was a physician, writer, and visual artist. He was a founding member of El Techo de la Ballena. His 1962 exhibition *Homenaje a la necrofília* (Homage to necrophilia) was the most controversial of the group's shows. See Adriano González León's "Homage to Necrophilia" in this volume, pp. 265 - 67.
10. Caupolicán Ovalles, *En uso de la razón* (Caracas: La Muralla, 1963).
11. Adriano González León, "Por qué la ballena?" ("Why the whale?"), *Rayado sobre el techo,* no. 3 (Caracas), 1964. This text, in a slightly different form, is included in the present volume, pp. 267 - 70.
12. Gabriel Morera is a visual artist who created the series Cabezas filosóficas (Philosophical heads; exhibited in 1962) among other works.

gonzález léon / homage to necrophilia, pp. 265 - 67

1. Francisco de Quevedo was one of the most important writers of the Spanish Golden Age.
2. Quechua: South American Indians living in the Andes from Ecuador to Bolivia; also the language of the Inca empire, later the lingua franca throughout the Andes.
3. Victor Ardisson was a mortician in a small town in nineteenth-century France. According to some estimates, he had sex with over a hundred corpses.
4. George Stransom is the protagonist of Henry James's short story "The Altar of the Dead," published in 1895.
5. This is an allusion to the fierce repression of leftist militants by the military and police during the government of Rómulo Betancourt (1959 - 64).
6. *Resitex*: a type of polyester.

gonzález léon / why the whale?, pp. 267 - 70

1. *Niple*: a type of pipe-bomb that makes a lot of noise and dispenses confetti-like pamphlets when exploding, but that causes no bodily harm. *Trans.*
2. *Entreguistas*: those who advocate that foreign companies be granted permission to exploit the country's natural resources. In the 1960s, in Venezuela, this referred specifically to the extraction of oil prior to the nationalization of the oil industry. *Trans.*

calzadilla / terrible evidence, pp. 270 - 73

1. José María Teclo Morelos y Pavón was a priest and insurgent who led the independence movement in Mexico. He was executed in 1815.
2. *Adeco* refers to Acción Democrática, the Social Democratic party of Venezuela.

traba / borges: the communicated image, pp. 274–77

1. Maurice Blanchot, *The Space of Literature*, ed. and trans. Ann Smock (Lincoln: University of Nebraska Press, 1982), p. 260.
2. This is a reference to the multimedia performance *Imagen de Caracas* (Image of Caracas), directed by Jacobo Borges and presented in downtown Caracas in 1967 as part of the festivities celebrating the city's quatercentenary. The audience was shown a particular vision of national history projected by eight film projectors and forty slide projectors onto large, moving cubes.

traba / finale: allegro con fuoco, pp. 278–84

1. This essay was the closing text, or "finale," in Traba's 1974 collection of critical writings *Mirar en Caracas*.
2. The museum Traba refers to is the Museo de Arte Moderno Jesús Soto, which was created by the artist in 1974 in Ciudad Bolívar, his birthplace, during the first term of Rafael Caldera's government (1969–74). The museum's collection includes representative works by Soto and other artists of the period, especially the French *nouveaux réalistes*.
3. The Groupe de Recherche d'Art Visuel (GRAV) was formed in Paris by a group of artists including François Morellet, Julio Le Parc, Francisco Sobrino, Horacio García, Joël Stein, and Jean-Pierre Yvaral, and lasted from 1960 to 1968.
4. This mural is installed in the tower of the Empresas Capriles in Caracas. Soto made a large-format mural for the building's main façade; unfortunately, due to the work's considerable scale, the artist's "dematerializing" strategies were ineffectual.
5. Carlos Cruz-Diez created this monumental work, *Ambiente cromático para la Central hidroeléctrica de Santo Domingo, Venezeula* (*Chromatic Ambiance for the Hydroelectric Plant at Santo Domingo, Venezuela*) in 1973 in Santo Domingo, in Venezuela's state of Barinas.
6. Architect Carlos Raúl Villanueva, the designer of the Museo de Arte Moderno Jesús Soto, had contemplated a structure without air-conditioning that would be ventilated naturally. It was Soto himself who directed the efforts to rectify this mistake.
7. Remedios the Beauty is a character in Gabriel García Márquez's 1967 *One Hundred Years of Solitude*.
8. The *araguaney* tree (*Tabebui Chrysanta*) was declared Venezuela's national tree in 1948. It produces a peculiar yellow flower that has been painted by countless Venezuelan landscape artists.

exile and indifference

testimonial 1: outline of ideas and interests pursued

gego (gertrude goldschmidt)

The years refer to the beginning of the idea or proposal

1956 Give flat surfaces volume. Starting off with flat surfaces.
Trials on paper.

1957 Dissolve these surfaces into lines
separated by specific distances
(with the thickness of the lines
being the same as the distance between them)
in order to achieve transparency
and integrate the space on each side of the surface.

The visual effect has been classified as "kinetic."
This was not the intention, but it turned out like that.
The "paralactical charm" was born and I loved it.

There were technical problems to be resolved,
with the help of metalworkers.
The materials were iron and aluminum or copper.
Paper maquettes and technical drawings
served to communicate with the craftsman.

The charm of parallel or quasi-parallel lines
was then extended to many drawings and etchings.

64 Trials to get around the technical problems
by using material I could handle myself
without the help of craftsmen.
The material used was iron wire, soldered just once.
I modulated the strips and planes.
Experiments with joining wires together
by purely mechanical means, in spirals, with plastic tubes, etc.

67 Purely structural solutions.
Total elimination of form and volume.

69 Escape from the scheme of intercrossing parallel or
quasi-parallel lines.
Beginning of drawings with clearly interwoven lines
forming flat or modulated nets.
Highlighting of crossover points.
To give these meshes real reality in space
with articulated intersections to control modulation,
the field between the lines had to be triangular.

RETICULE AREA[1]
After using enameled iron (from flower shops) and aluminum wire,
I found that stainless-steel wire of 1 mm thickness
was the best means to work with
(it being understood that for big projects in streets, buildings,
and squares, the material had to be chosen according to the
circumstances).
71 Thicker streams of wire mostly in polished aluminum
joined together in the same manual way as in the *reticulárea*.
Parallel lines again,
but this time the accumulation of lines
does not produce flat surfaces or enclose volumes
but rather creates mass.
71 Square *reticulárea*
with different manual solutions for the intersections
and with copper twists
which highlight perfectly the wire crossings
so that the fields between the wire are clearly defined.
72 Stimulated by serious studies of geometry,
I experiment with double-curve surfaces
and with self-supporting tubular surfaces
and suspended spheres.
76 The drawings on paper are replaced by paperless frameless
drawings.

—"Testimonial 1: Planteamiento de problemas e intereses perseguidos," explanatory text written at the time of Gego's 1977 retrospective exhibition at the Museo de Arte Contemporáneo de Caracas, and later used in Hanni Ossott's essay in the exhibition's catalogue. This English translation was published in *Sabiduras and Other Texts by Gego*, ed. Maria Elena Huizi and Josefina Manrique (Houston and Caracas: Museum of Fine Arts Houston; Fundación Gego, 2005), pp. 152–53.
Translated by Mark Gregson

gego: caracas year three thousand **marta traba**

There is a rare genius in Venezuela who has been surprisingly underestimated: Gego [Gertrude Goldschmidt] is her name. An admiring essay like the one written by Lourdes Blanco introducing *Reticulárea*,[1] exhibited at the Museo de Bellas Artes in 1969, or conventional and rather bewildered reviews like those in issue 15 of *Papeles* in 1972, are not enough to make up for the noticeable omissions regarding her work in the setting of the red desert of Caracas. It is certain that those omissions exist: the inventor of environments who preceded all of the unanimously celebrated works of [Jesús Rafael] Soto and [Carlos] Cruz-Diez is never mentioned in the third volume of Alfredo Boulton's *Historia de la pintura en Venezuela* [History of painting in Venezuela], a volume that, despite featuring "painting" in its title, dedicates page after page to the towers and penetrable sculptures of [Alejandro] Otero and Soto and ends with [Soto's] *Penetrable de Pampatar* (Pampatar Penetrable), which is infinitely less evocative, rich, and original than Gego's *Reticulárea*. And just as people seem to forget that her 1961 piece for the Banco Industrial pioneered the embedding of a formal project into an architectural space, her subsequent works in public buildings do not seem to have been sufficiently understood or appreciated, since they have not given rise to serious monographs or essays, nor even articles that might lead one to give them the careful attention they deserve.

It is true that Gego lacks the courtesan attributes and the type of promotional skills that attract prizes, distinctions, and favors. This intelligent and quiet being, who expresses herself with difficulty and awkwardness, and who prefers the direct vigilance of her works "with a cigarette in mouth," as her husband Gerd Leufert[1] says affectionately, to any procession with the Caracas coterie, works like an enlightened European despite having resided in Venezuela since 1939.

Gego has operated in this country, accepting the challenge and the opportunity offered to her by the construction boom and the fabulous growth of Caracas. She needed opportunities, buildings, and a budget—all of which she had here, certainly, to a degree she would not have encountered elsewhere—in order to develop her big public works. But though she was offered launching pads, from the Banco Industrial in 1961 to the Parque Central in 1972[2]—which means she was able to do enormous works in only ten years—the extraordinary production she has been delivering has been followed by a critical void. It is in this regard that this country—this city—variously characterized as a "tabula rasa" by Darcy Ribeiro and with the caustic label "saloon" by the acidic intelligence of Isaac Chocrón, is fully lacking in cultural discernment.

The "desert" and the "West" are vague epithets, true; but only by admitting that there might be some validity to them is it possible to understand the silence regarding Gego, given that the powerful society of Caracas, as I have noted in previous articles, readily claims the paternity of the avant-garde projects of its favorite artists.

Could it be that Gego is not *sufficiently* avant-garde? Her work, however, is completely innovative, in the explorative and adventurous sense of the word. Could it be that her investigative spirit is too serious, that she faces her work as if it were a relentless, elaborate, and difficult construction, and therefore also radically distant from frivolity and improvisation? Could it be that Gego is truer than her milieu, more profound than her milieu, more complex and cultured than her milieu? Could it be that she goes beyond "visual games" and therefore surpasses the framework of reception that comfortably settles in amid such games?

I believe there is some truth to all these hypotheses. For a European *artist*, to become Venezuelan is almost an ontological impossibility: Gego cannot *be* Venezuelan, she will never truly have endogamous or tribal relationships with the national spirit. The dominant trend of Venezuelan art directs all its attention to the chromo-interfering towers, to the effector batteries of Ciudad Bolívar, and to other, equally pyrotechnic statements: nothing is more pleasing to it than Venezuelan artists without a distinctive identification, who knowingly and with poise conceal their place of origin under protective technological cloaks. But it is an entirely different thing to deeply appreciate a work conceived naturally by a European spirit, in which technique and science do not hide anything, but rather constitute the points of departure for the liberation of the creative imagination.

Gego graduated from the University of Stuttgart, in Germany, as an engineer-architect. It would have been impossible for her to develop her work without that technical and professional foundation. She thinks as an architect, solves problems as an engineer, and projects as an artist. In this *thinking as an architect*, the notion of space prevails over all the others and Gego is necessarily subjected to her relation with the space containing her. By *acting as an engineer*, she is able to solve technical and scientific problems that allow her to come ever closer to her goal of positioning forms in space with a progressive autonomy regarding the supporting element. By *projecting as an artist*, she manages to dismantle the scientific order to appropriate emptiness, dynamize space in a hallucinatory manner, and achieve ephemeral sensations, unreality, poetry, and unexpected discoveries. Only by relying on these three different lines of thought, which are more dialectical than convergent, can one explain the permanent tension and complexity of her works. They are not born of a simple technical display, as one might presume given Gego's precision in linking, finishing, connecting, and tightening; they are not a combination of spaces derived from her accurate architectural understanding of the empty or the full and from the field of vision that characterizes great architects. The flexibility of her artistic temperament, her imponderables, and her surfeits interfere with her audacious solutions and skillful articulations. *Reticulárea*, an extraordinary work presented at the Museo de Bellas Artes de Caracas and at the Center for Inter-American Relations in New York, aptly represents Gego by combining, with a powerful sense of balance, the work's perfection, spatial clarity, and the mysterious and wild net transformed into something living. I mention this work again because I believe that in it, more than in any other work, the three determining factors of Gego's œuvre are present with the same degree of intensity, without any one of them overpowering the others.

In the Banco Industrial (Martín Vargas, architect) the passion for elevating articulated parts and an astounding degree of care made it possible for anodized aluminum tubes to support themselves at a height of nearly forty feet. This feat seems superior, for instance, to the imaginative flight and the creation of spaces that in this particular case appear to contract and protract themselves simultaneously in a single vertical structure. The splendor of this structure results from the extreme control over the following elements: the combination of round and square tubes of different shades of gray, the impeccable insertion of some into others, and the progressive genesis of the tower, etc.

In the arrows of Chacaíto (which unfortunately I saw only in photographs, as the piece had been taken down), Gego seemed to achieve a level of shared intensity. Unmatched in her way of placing extremely fragile tensors in order to make aerial constructions of the highest subtlety, her ability to insinuate and her poetic humor were fully present in that work (*Flechas* [Arrows], 1968, aluminum and nylon: aerial structure designed for an interior patio at the Chacaíto shopping center.)

In the Tower of the Cediaz shopping mall (1967–68, steel, concrete, nylon, and neon light), which she conceived in collaboration with Gerd Leufert, all her efforts point to the construction of a signpost, slight but at the same time fully visible, following the *constant* that she has achieved so stupendously in all her works of imposing the delicate, of unsettling via the imperceptible. The point here is not to *elevate* a tower, which is seemingly simple, but to elevate it sweetly, in an enveloping and almost inadvertent way so that its height of over seventy-seven feet might be redeemed by the process and might constitute itself in much more than a mere statement concerning height, in a *rhythm* capable of rising, and also of descending, on its own. The idea of a round tower with an ascending and descending rhythm is fulfilled completely, but unfortunately now the tower has been contaminated by its deadly proximity to all types of billboards: there is no space to see it, it is at the edge of a street whose crosswalk is surrounded by deadly perils. The fierce bustle of Caracas has managed to erase it and make it invisible during the day, and the red signal at night is not fully able to recapture its value.

The most fruitful period of this formidable artist's career spans from 1968 to 1972.

Between 1968 and 1969, also with the collaboration of Leufert, she placed the corner murals made of tubes in the terrific building of the INCE [Instituto Nacional de Cooperación Educativa: National institute for educational cooperation] created in 1959 by Tomás and Eduardo Sanabria. More than 656 square feet of anodized aluminum combined with enameled steel and set on mosaic serve only to explain the technical importance of a relief whose complexity and movement transcend these facts. While at the entrance, due to the minimal angle at which the tubes are placed, an illusory sense of movement of the wall is achieved—a *trompe l'œil* that she later reinforced in her sculpture for the IVIC [Instituto Venezolano de Investigaciones Científicas: Venezuelan institute for scientific research]—in the exterior wall and the corner of the building a wide linear rhythm is displayed, solidly inserting itself into the architecture's structures, softening them without contradicting them, in one of the best relationships conceivable when it comes to this material. That is, the relief does not function as the architecture's guest—which is so often bothersome—the architectural design does not swallow up the relief, and neither do they "tolerate each other" in the precarious wedding of the "decoration of buildings."

Against these three types of relationships, which are the norm and can be verified in numerous public buildings in Caracas, Gego and Leufert proposed a fourth, that of acting *within* the architectural design as an autonomous structure that simultaneously reveals the design's force and originality. This explains the complex proposition of curving, ample rhythms within the rectangular structures of the INCE and the beautiful way in which the curve of the relief penetrates the corner of the building and continues along the adjacent wall. What prevails in this work, I believe, is Gego's architectural vocation, as well as her understanding and her respect of architecture.

At the IVIC (*Cinco Pantallas* [Five screens], 1968–70) the decorative element is also transcended owing both to the generosity of the piece's rhythmic pattern and to the breath and richness of the screens formed by tubes. Optical illusions are inscribed upon spatial problems: the empty spaces between the screens and their correspondences and visual partitions play a role. The alternation between them generates a constant counterpoint between the concave and the convex whose result is an energetic hollowing of the air in order to embed within it a strong three-dimensional illusion and a powerful open volume, one that is continually generated in the circulating air that the screens cause to move.

We may situate the Reticuláreas and the Chorros (Streams), presented at the Betty Parsons Gallery in New York in 1971, as well as the structure for the Parque Central, alongside these great achievements.

For the Reticuláreas Gego takes over a room with a structure comparable to a very fine mesh of enameled iron, whose power of conviction, and even of enchantment, is directly related to the *invasive*, *compulsive* quality of the project that traps the spectator in that unendingly fractured world of fine lines that are in turn manifold divergences from the eternal right angle amid which man lives. In order to increase the sense of being inside a lattice, inside an interwoven fabric, and to contribute to that dimension in which the anthropocentric perspective is diluted, Gego hung a white canvas tent from the ceiling of the gallery in New York to hide the room's angles from view and avoid having any reference (lintels, baseboards, ceiling, etc.) that would contradict this new dimension.

Gego executed this delirious and lyrical expansion of lines within a circular white space with a faultless, masterful hand: the indefatigable perfection of joints, always studied as if they were the true protagonists of the work, the finesse and great delicateness of the materials used, and the constant intention to valorize them are as present in the Reticuláreas as in the Chorros.

Destined to appear amid barbaric tropical vegetation, amid mastic trees of opulent dark leaves, and to fall from above, precipitating themselves amid the verdure, the Chorros, made of aluminum rods measuring nine feet and broken up by joints as fragile as the rods themselves, come together in surrealistic, restless, mobile waterfalls in which glimmers and transparencies are as fleeting as water itself. But this fugitive quality is a still, crystallized one, as if a real image had been cropped and fixed through the artistic process.

These solid, unexpected alliances between the poetic and the mathematical are born of the same certainty with which Gego manipulates *scientific fact*, accepts its processes and the resistance tests of its materials, and uses physics and engineering calculations, never forgetting that she makes her decisions in a *different territory,* brimming with imponderables. Such is the *aesthetic* fact: free and complex language.

In a work like the nylon-rope structure for the Parque Central (Siso-Shaw Associates, architects) Gego's clear, parallel command of art and science becomes manifest. The result could have many analogies with the spatial representations of mathematical equations. But the quest for rhythms, the search for inner relations between them and with the architectural space as well, point clearly to an aesthetic fact.

Unlike the work at the INCE, here the work launches itself to open space instead of adhering to the architecture; instead it becomes a sort of accompanying text profoundly inscribed in *structural values*. As is the case in all of Gego's œuvre, encroaching culture never weighs on her: on the contrary, her works live within it as if in their natural environment. The autonomy of the noteworthy structure of the Parque Central, its interrelational value, the importance and adjustment of its parts in relation to the whole, the qualification of the work as an open process always bound to establish new relations with its surroundings: all this takes place as if the beauty of the structures were being illustrated and as if a new, unpretentious and subtle light were wanted to be cast on them.

Far from being incidental, that fluidity and naturalness of the artistic fact is a cardinal virtue in Gego's œuvre. Indeed, as is the case of perfect works, it seems to rise and develop effortlessly, with an organic vitality and truth.

My own well-known and admitted boredom with regard to so many kinetic works makes many people think that I cultivate a systematic and generalized hatred of the genre. That is not true. My judgments are discerning. First: my lack of interest is concentrated on artists who, in Latin America, are making kinetic art following the dictates of North America and Europe, which to me seems senseless, illogical, and lacking an adequate connection with an environment dominated by misery, chaos, and irrationality—even in those urban centers that attempt to inscribe themselves mimetically in the developed world. Second: not all kinetic works can be put in the same bag just for promoting certain more or less skilled optical illusions. Indeed, because kinetic art is a general system of representation to a greater degree than it is a representation resting on an individual vision, one has to do extraordinary things to achieve aesthetic value within its realm. The third point is almost a consequence of the second: among the hundreds of practitioners or relatives of kinetic art, a select few make *works of art* and the rest make *toys*. Works of art and toys can be important and fun with regard to their own ambitions when I see them like a fish in the water of American and European scenarios, but who knows what violent moral longing (perhaps it is my hopelessly bad habit of observing my surroundings intensely) makes me scorn toys if their makers are Latin American. I think that given the state of affairs on our continent, *artists have no right to make toys*, and I doubt that anyone can prove me wrong here. On the other hand, I have profound respect for those who in our difficult and unfortunate milieu have managed to make *works of art* within the deprived and austere zone of contemporary art: [Edgar] Negret from Colombia, [Eduardo] MacEntyre in Buenos Aires, and Alejandro Otero, whose Coloritmos [Colorhythms] I will always think of as assets in the realm of the continent's modern art. It is in this zone where Gego's œuvre stands out with ever more clarity and firmness.

When Caracas, in the year three thousand, has a hundred levels of highways and dozens of toys spread out in all of its neighborhoods, Gego's work will have to be shown in a way that is completely unlike that in which the toys are exhibited: those will look outdated, but Gego's œuvre will continue to be preserved by mathematics and poetry, and by the combinatory genius that presides over both.

—"Gego: Caracas tres mil," in *Mirar en Caracas* (Caracas: Monte Ávila Editores, 1974), pp. 51–59.
Translated by Mónica de la Torre

bárbaro rivas: note for a portrait **francisco da antonio**

My childhood, like that of all children, was graced by the presence of those popular characters whose generally mysterious lives thrillingly enliven the fantasies of our early years.[1] Bárbaro Rivas, one such figure, was to my imagination a man who with each step underwent a Last Judgment in miniature, complete with trumpets and punishments, in the feverish passage of his bristling sensibility. However, around 1949, when I first met this undeniably talented painter, Rivas had ceased to be a significant object of that childhood curiosity, which the years tend to overcome. No small labor and a great deal of time were needed in order to approach the most intimate recesses of his creativity, particularly considering that his natural withdrawal was exacerbated by justifiable suspicions awakened in him by my own status as a painter, which was not unknown to him. When I managed to draw near, demolishing the last barriers erected by this artist—until then universally disregarded, and furthermore stigmatized as a madman by many—the first duty I assumed was to salvage his work, which up to that point had been scattered randomly and was in the process of disappearing, and to undertake, at the same time, the difficult task of restoring him to his pictorial labors, which he had abandoned since 1950. The first few months of 1953 passed; a simple inventory of that time illustrates Rivas's state of mind in terms of his misgivings about the exterior world, which were also illustrated by the number of times that, for several reasons and despite my interest, I experienced a certain need to act simultaneously unconcerned and attentive in the presence of one whom I could not succeed in convincing that his work was worthwhile as painting, as art, as emotional testimony to his life and his people.

Let us just say it outright: Bárbaro Rivas is now understood as the most important contemporary figure in Venezuelan naïf painting. And if the mere fact of an extensive trajectory doesn't constitute sufficient argument for such a claim, it is then imperative to note that long before the appearance of names like Feliciano Carvallo,[2] Federico Sandoval,[3] and Víctor Millán,[4] among others, Rivas's work—unknown until recently, but no less positive and honest than that of those artists—had been developing, nourished by elemental resources and discoveries, almost from the start of the 1920s when he made his first attempts.

It will become clear that this is not a matter of the "appearance" of a new "extemporaneous" painter. His works, though few in number, began around 1926. Of the ones that have been recovered, two oil paintings, for example, date from that time: *El rebaño* [The flock] and *Paisaje de Baruta* [Baruta landscape]. From then until 1953, only ten works in good condition have been located. All the rest, even much of what was painted on walls both indoors and out, have disappeared under harsh conditions of deprivation. This, then, is how Rivas comes to be the "primitive" painter with the most extensive body of pictorial work in our country, and at the same time probably constitutes the greatest guarantee of his integrity and spontaneity. He was born in 1893 of humble origins; the occupations of railroad worker, mason, carpenter, and housepainter were the most readily available to him over the course of his life.

Lacking the most elemental theoretical concepts, his painting is replete with all the force, candor, and ingenuity of a child and a visionary.

Possessed of a profound yearning to create, as if deep within he carried a solemn and unknown truth, he constructs his paintings from an emotional belief in a message not yet transmitted. Or at times it is the voice of an ancient people from an agrarian community, recounting for us its history and its reason for being – a people we are inexorably obliterating as if it were an alien past, in our own process of becoming.

Now then, up to what point is it possible to undertake a visual analysis, an exhaustive review of the technique, processes, and contributions inherent to the language of an artist who must implicitly be located at the margin of all learning or intellectual discipline? Despite the danger of falling into the anecdotal and literary, in relation to a spontaneously formed artist there will always be a sequence of relative values, sometimes absolute values, which are viable fields of study and in the face of which any judgment will be made independent of those selective criteria commonly applicable to cultured artists.

Mastery of craft achieved through effort and constant work with the material; the more or less uniform use of certain visual resources; and a familiarity with the range of solutions to problems presented by both color and design, for example – all these constitute relative values. These are, of course, difficult to establish as immutable principles, since anything made by a "primitive" might successfully move us, and even fill us with that deep emotion experienced in the presence of works of immense quality, despite, in most instances, obvious contradictions, deficiencies, and improprieties in the formal order of the work. This is not the case with cultured art from every era and school, in which scant or poor discipline in the craft will lead to nothing more than mediocrity, though virtuosity may not necessarily be one of the foundations of art either.

Absolute values will be more reasonably conditioned by a series of distinct factors that are psychological and even – or rather particularly – social. When a work attempts to reflect or successfully expresses one or more of those factors – abstract in form and profoundly real in terms of content – in isolation or in conjunction with one another, we immediately recognize a reference to those values. Personality, and likewise the concepts exposed through a particular type of response to a specific orientation – because with any naïf the message or anecdote incorporated in his own sphere of expression will predominate – are the most meaningful, the most fundamental. It goes without saying that a determined personality, a product of the range of factors that inform the absolute value of that personality, can never be sketched out except through value-processes, which one might say are relative and to a certain extent common with regard to their formal development. In the last instance as in the first, these will signify to us, through stylistic imprint, that this or that thing corresponds to this or that author. Thus we arrive at a concept of visual personality, which is valid at least in the most general sense.

the artist and his creative sensibility

But let us situate ourselves in relation to Bárbaro Rivas and his work. This work is clearly valuable, all the more precious since so few examples exist from a thirty-year period of constant creation and tremendous deprivation, because of which – apart from any didacticism or moralizing – we may discern a profound anguish, like an accusing sprite with a tormented soul, which from time to time will cloud with shadows what was created for the illumination of human understanding and faith. Painting of this sort cannot correctly be called "naïf" in the same way as work we have known by that name until now. Neither the dazzling restlessness nor the melancholy climate in which grays, black, and an entire range of cold colors rule over white, incorporated always into cadmium and earth tones, escapes the romantic and obviously dramatic emotion inherent in things.

Unlike naïf artists with whom we are already familiar, for the time being Rivas eludes any charming descriptive logic and that folkloric style, replete with anecdotes and local color, which those artists so often exploit. His painting, like that of primitive medieval artists, does not exist in harmony with any pure image received from the outside world. It defines an extra-artistic intention that is both instructive and exemplary. Thus what we see in the painting is not what is observed, but rather the juxtaposition of the image projected by experience and the image projected by the emotional being of this experience. In this way *Placita de Petare en 1901* [Small plaza in Petare in 1901] and *Entrada de Petare* [Petare entryway] appear after fifty years exactly as they might have been seen in Rivas's childhood and youth; the images are created with an intense eagerness to transmit not the objective impression of the landscape-subject but rather a spiritual testimony to a less-burdened collectivity and a way of being that is perhaps more pure—we do not know. *Placita de Petare en 1901*, painted in 1953, reflects this intention like no other work. What is depicted is the secondary plaza in his hometown, surrounded by large houses and by a sky interrupted by telegraph wires. We climb the weighty stone stairs toward it. It is the same small plaza with its leafy *copei* trees blossoming with children, the fountain with its copper swans covered in rust, and the wooden benches beneath the filtered green shade of the tunnel of trees, which might see, faraway beneath a night of other years, the parochial incidence of Halley's Comet, an aerial wonder the painter still recalls.

From its unyielding religiosity to its recalling of primitive Christian art of North Africa and the Latin Occident, Rivas's work coincides at more than one point with these other currents in one of its principal features: "continuation" painting, in which the action is developed on a surface with "cinematographic" mobility. And of course it also shares to a lesser degree some features of Byzantine art, though without the brilliance and splendor, due more to a dearth of materials and elements available for use than to a lack of creative talent and imagination. Thus, if in some way Rivas coincides—in a manner of speaking—with the mysticism of Federico Sandoval, that modest policeman painter who seems of no interest today, it is because of his concern for divulgence, which leads him to develop biblical themes; from these he seeks to extract greater benefit from his faith, which he shares with others like him. Through the most meaningful aspects of the life of the Savior, he signals the most perfect lesson of love and tenderness, or sounds the alarm about evil when he conceives of that apocalyptic image *La salida de este mundo* [The departure from this world], created in 1953. This piece pertains completely to the most formal problematic of Rivas's work. It has to do with an unusual conception that expresses a series of "unconscious" images—seen during daydreams—periodically "revealed" by the clarity and elucidation of the interrogations proposed by the investigative and vigilant spirit of the "Christian." (It is truly interesting to note some of the terms Rivas employs in order to define facts and mysteries. In biblical references, he tends to refer to the Christian as a *pagano* [pagan][5] with the same precision he uses in calling the heretic a "Jew," because a Christian is one who suffers and pays, with his pain and with his life, for proclaiming his faith before the "Jew," whom only God's miracles can "*atorrizar*"[6]—intimidate, incite to panic—with His Ubiquity and His Power.) The figure of the Son of Man rescued from the netherworld, from death, presides over the structure of this small painting. Above Him is the dove-symbol, white against the blue of the background, and the earth is at His feet. Toward the top is a sky framed in semicircumferences, where the souls of the wholesome ascend, while below, toward a flaming finale, the remains of the condemned are released. A grave philosophical spirit surrounds the thematic terrain that includes certain elements with decorative-symbolic functions: a bat that represents night and evil; a serpent, as sin; and a lake, a strange unimaginable place, complement of the sublimation of life, spirit, earth, fire, air, and waters in well-balanced metaphysical sentiment or presentiment, of an extra-human vision. Of definitive punishment or compensation, where God turns out to be an object, a negation of what has been created.

We continue, then, to discover a purpose, a single goal with each new step the artist makes; a seemingly infinite thirst for teaching, for demonstrating paths toward love, toward what is Above, toward God. And this attitude, absent in Venezuelan painting since the disappearance of the anonymous colonial artists of the eighteenth and nineteenth century, an attitude that in principle might be objected to in a cultured artist (as Don Eduardo Crema criticizes [Andrés] Bello's constant juxtaposing of pedagogical and moralizing intention with his artistic work)—this attitude constitutes in Bárbaro Rivas's work, by contrast, one of the most meaningful qualities.

the painter and his experiences

Around 1939, Rivas painted *La Palomera* [The dovecote]. The subject could not be simpler: a small house with its garden and gate. Across from the front door, near the steps that lead to the path, a figure examines the small garden. And this single figure, cut out of cardboard and fixed a posteriori onto the base, comes to be an extremely unpretentious experiment in a gluing technique that for Rivas, clearly unlike the Cubists, is a transcription of his great figurative objectivity and his consequential and equally obligatory search for three-dimensionality on the surface of the painting (and in this we do in fact see something of Cubism), which will repeatedly lead him toward modeling. This is because, unaware of the theoretical principles of the laws governing perspective, he will find in the most general of those spheres favorable ground for solving the problems implicit in the volume of a truly faithful and logistical form in the face of his firm rational conceptualization of things. Two clay reliefs of remarkable proportions, one of *San Francisco y el ángel* [Saint Francis and the angel] (1948) and one depicting a stove with a hearth (1953), constitute the most magnificent examples of his exploration of the territory of visual ornamentation.

Approximately seven years after *La Palomera*, in *Domingo de Ramos* [Palm Sunday], which dates from 1946, the use of "collage" responds more to an apparently decorative intention than to any analytical concern. The work depicts Jesus' entrance into Jerusalem. In the midst of a disorderly crowd that follows him, waving palm fronds all around, the Savior rides in on a mule. The extra-pictorial materials in this work—sequins—are used as a clever resource with a decorative function. The figure of Jesus and the gate to the city are not the only elements to be treated in this way; thanks to its Divine Rider, so is the mule itself, which plays an important role in illustrating [the artist's] use of gluing techniques.

With the quantitative absence of pieces executed before 1953, with the disappearances and losses resulting from so many years of neglect, we might encounter the greatest obstacle impeding our access to a more extensive and well-documented view of the painter's trajectory. It is thus even more lamentable that it is impossible to answer, among other things, the question of whether any continuity existed in the use of extra-pictorial elements; if others were used and on which occasions, or if *La Palomera* and *Domingo de Ramos* were isolated examples or momentary solutions with no larger significance whatsoever. Nevertheless, keeping in mind the experiments noted here, we would like to underline this, one of the relative values of greatest transcendence in the artist's painting practice.

To conclude, it is indispensable to note that another of the most steadfast values in Bárbaro Rivas's work is his remarkable interpretive capacity. We see him "copying" his chosen models and at the same time separating himself from them, in both instances working from a similar intention and using his ideas to improve upon it. We might use *La Oración* [The prayer], for example, as the illustration of an entire chapter. The work involves a reproduction from Millet, and suddenly there is no further connection between the "original" and the "copy" other than a common vision of what is expressed. Observing, on the other hand, an accentuated faithfulness to the original, [Rivas] paints a gouache copy of Bartolomé Esteban Murillo's painting *Los niños de la concha* [The boys with the conch shell]. However, his faithfulness ends at the point where Murillo organizes his own elements to form a setting. From that ambiance of clouds and vaporous angels with which the Spanish painter surrounds his small characters and the sheep that observes them, Rivas constructs a scene that is probably more real, with a plethora of colors: a small stream bordered by greens and recognizable plants, framed by giant rocks in the far background. It is a world closer to his concept of landscape and nature, as we have seen through his sensibility and his rich life experience.

—"Bárbaro Rivas: Apunte para un retrato" (Caracas: Cromotip, 1956). The essay was later published in an expanded version in *Textos sobre arte: Venezuela, 1692–1982* (Caracas: Monte Ávila Editores, 1980), pp. 304–19.

Translated by Jen Hofer

editor's notes to the texts

gego / outline of ideas and interests pursued, pp. 288 - 89

1. The term *Reticulárea* (translated here as "Reticule area") was coined by the Venezuelan art critic Roberto Guevara for the works that Gego produced beginning in 1969, when the artist turned from the use of parallel lines and began to work with lines interweaving in space.

traba / gego: caracas year three thousand, pp. 289 - 94

1. German-born Gerd Leufert was a visual artist, designer, and photographer. His varied, mainly abstract œuvre includes the noteworthy series Listonados. He was Gego's second husband.
2. Gego's *Escultura* (Sculpture; 1962), for the Banco Industrial de Venezuela, consists of a series of grilles of parallel lines that interweave vertically. Her *Cuerdas* (Cords; 1972), a sculpture made of suspended nylon and stainless-steel strips, constructed like a spider's web between two buildings, was created for the Parque Central complex in Caracas.

da antonio / bárbaro rivas: note for a portrait, pp. 295 - 99

1. Francisco Da Antonio grew up in the town of Petare, where Bárbaro Rivas was a local figure. Originally located a few kilometers east of Caracas, Petare has now been absorbed into the city and is one of Caracas's most popular and populous neighborhoods.
2. Feliciano Carvallo was a self-taught painter who worked for Armando Reverón as a mason and learned basic painting techniques from him. He was one of Venezuela's most outstanding autodidact artists.
3. Federico Sandoval is a self-taught or "naïf" Venezuelan painter. He showed his work for the first time at the Taller Libre de Arte (Free arts workshop) in 1950.
4. Self-taught painter Víctor Millán showed his work for the first time at the Taller Libre de Arte in 1951.
5. In Spanish the term *pagano*, or "pagan," also refers colloquially to "one who pays the way of others" – hence the pun to which Da Antonio refers here. *Trans.*
6. Da Antonio's term "*atorrizar*" would seem to be a direct transcription of Rivas's pronunciation of *aterrorizar*, to terrorize. *Trans.*

illustrations

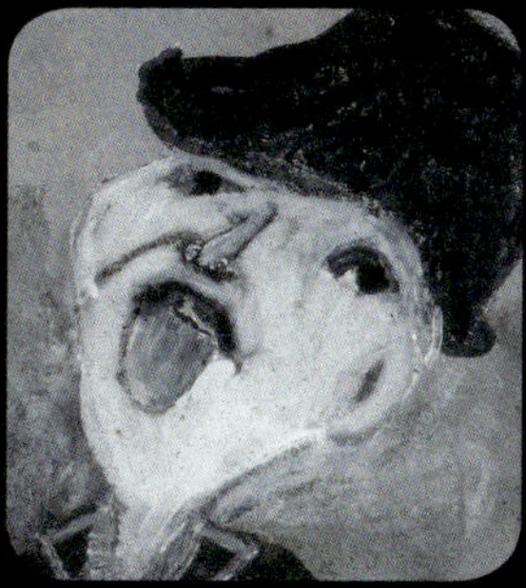
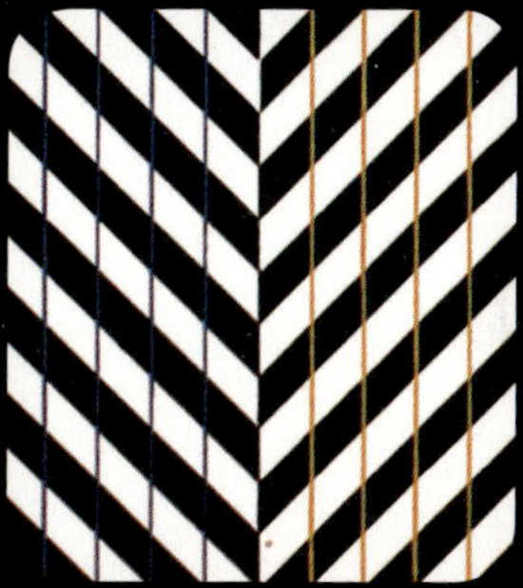
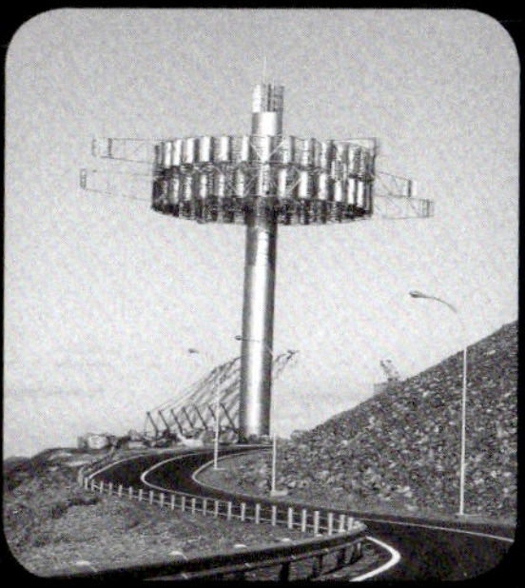
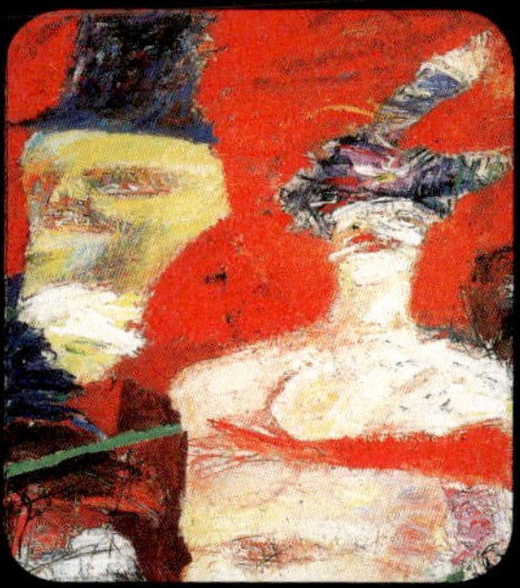
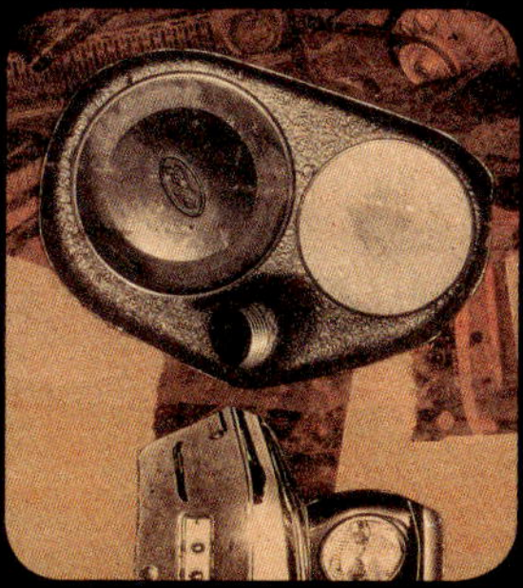
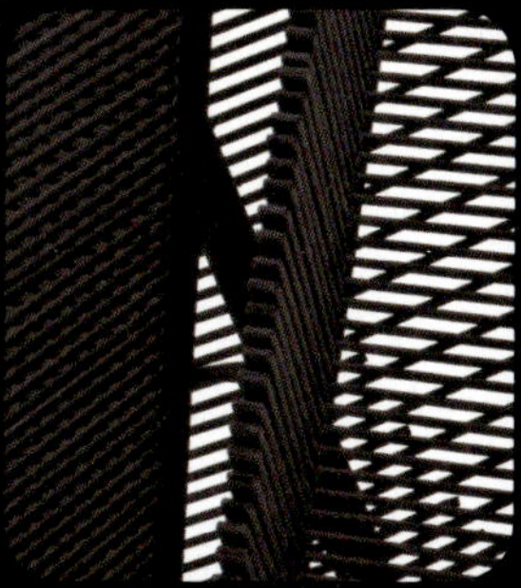

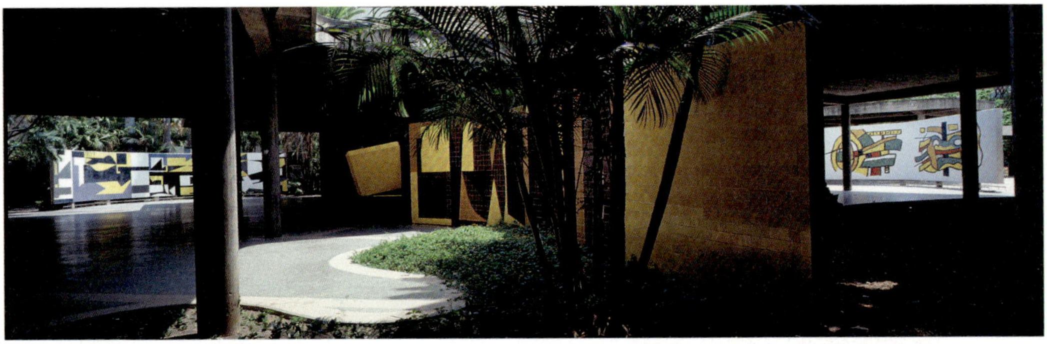

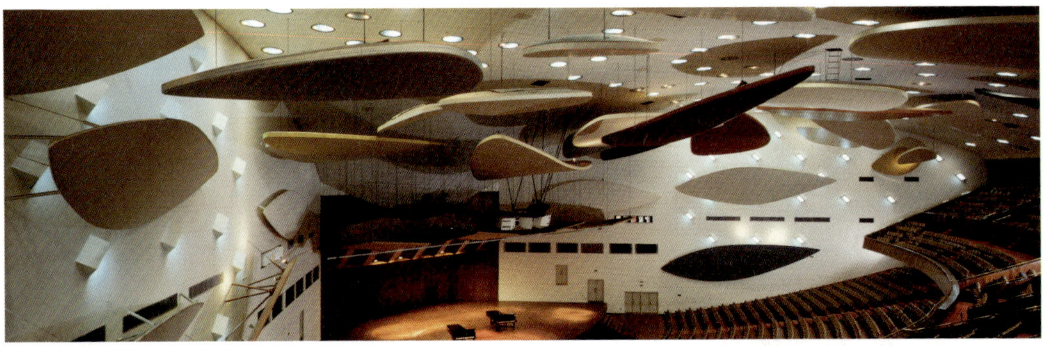

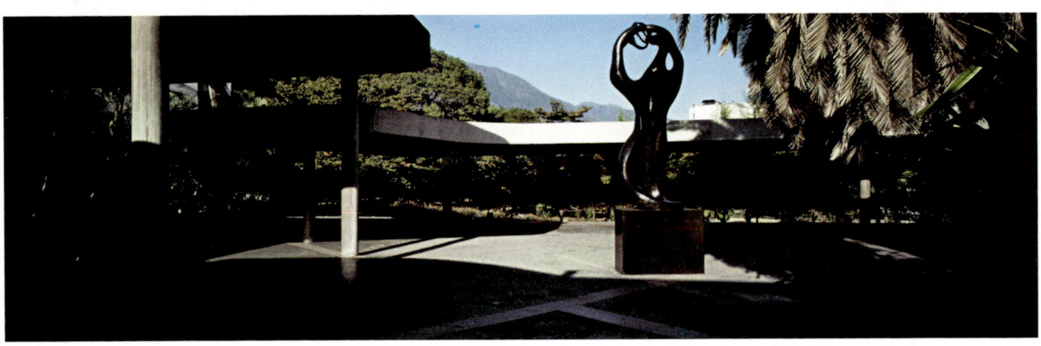

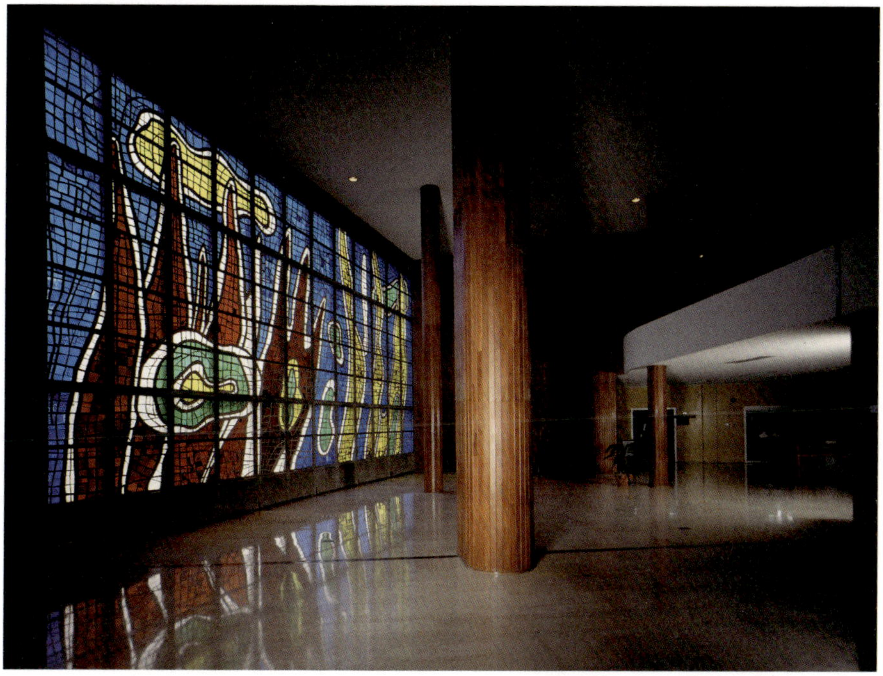

Stained glass (1954) by Fernand Léger in the library of the Universidad Central de Venezuela. Photograph by Paolo Gasparini. 1985–89. Archivos Fundación Villanueva, Caracas

Central area of the Plaza Cubierta (covered plaza), Universidad Central de Venezuela. Photograph by Paolo Gasparini. 1985–89. Archivos Fundación Villanueva, Caracas

View of the Universidad Central de Venezuela's Aula Magna (great hall) showing Alexander Calder's *Acoustic Clouds* (1952–53). Photograph by Paolo Gasparini. 1985–89. Archivos Fundación Villanueva, Caracas

View of Henri Laurens's *Amphion* (1953) in the Plaza Cubierta (covered plaza) of the Universidad Central de Venezuela. Photograph by Paolo Gasparini. 1985–89. Archivos Fundación Villanueva, Caracas

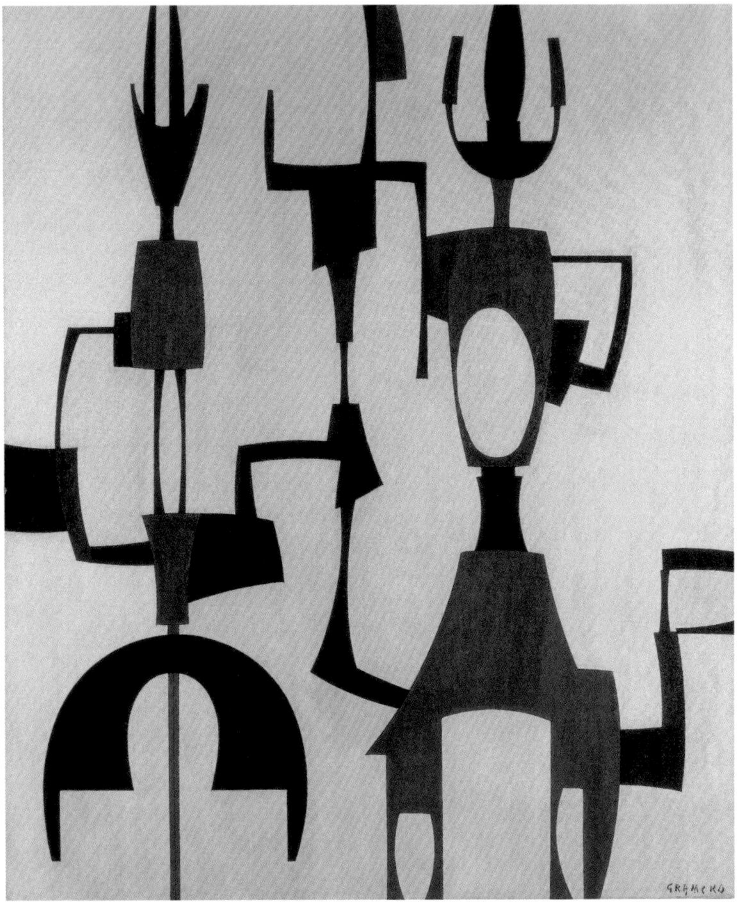

elsa gramcko
Untitled. 1957. Oil on canvas.
29 9/16" x 23 5/8" (75 x 60 cm).
Private collection

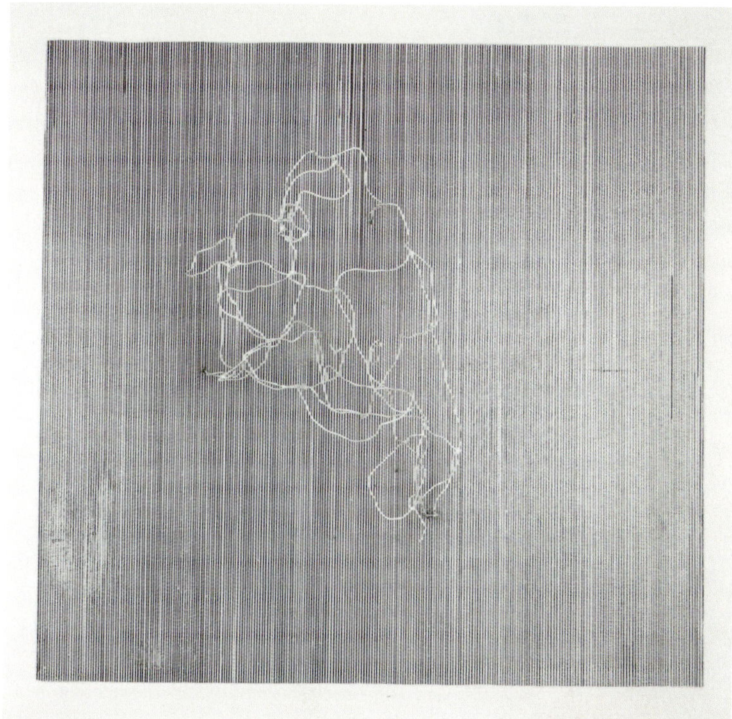

jesús rafael soto
Primera vibración (First vibration). 1957. Paint on metal and Masonite. 23 5⁄8 x 23 5⁄8 x 5 15⁄16" (60 x 60 x 15 cm). Private collection

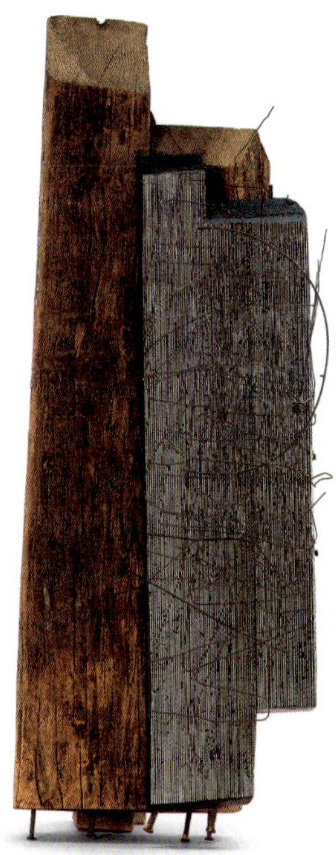

jesús rafael soto
Untitled. 1959–60. Wood, painted wood, metal, and nails. 35 3⁄8 x 11 3⁄4 x 13 3⁄8" (89.9 x 29.8 x 34 cm). The Museum of Modern Art, New York. Committee on Painting and Sculpture Funds

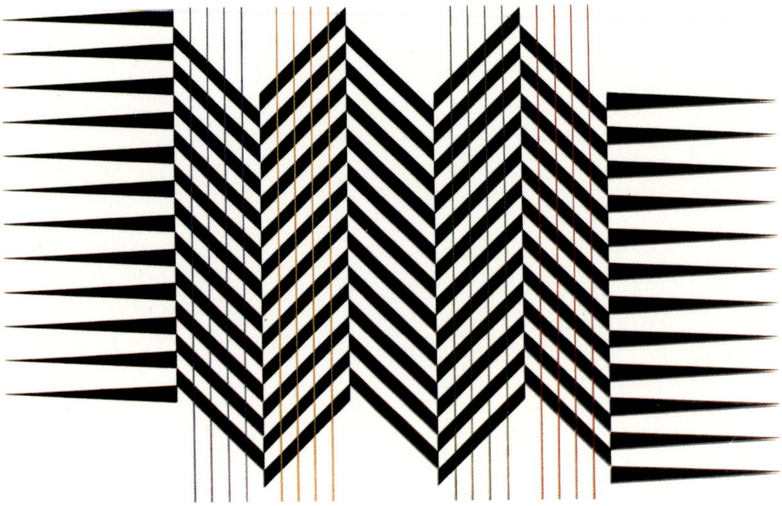

carlos cruz-diez
Doble animación de un plano (Double animation of a plane). 1959. Paint, wood, and casein. 40 3/16 x 23 5/8" (102 x 60 cm). Private collection

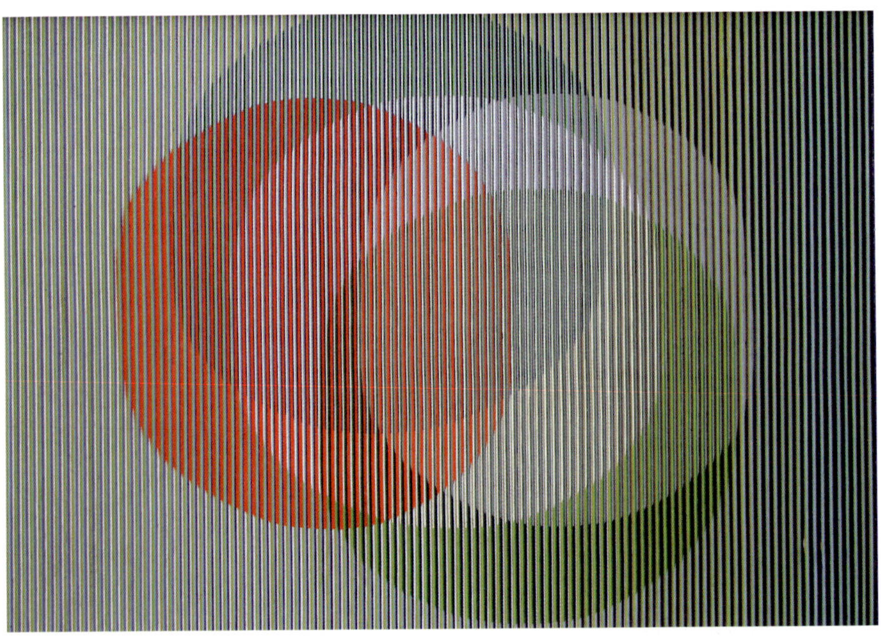

carlos cruz-diez
Physichromie no. 285 (*Physichrome no. 285*). 1966. Casein on cardboard and wood. 31 7/8" x 24" (81 x 61 cm). Private collection

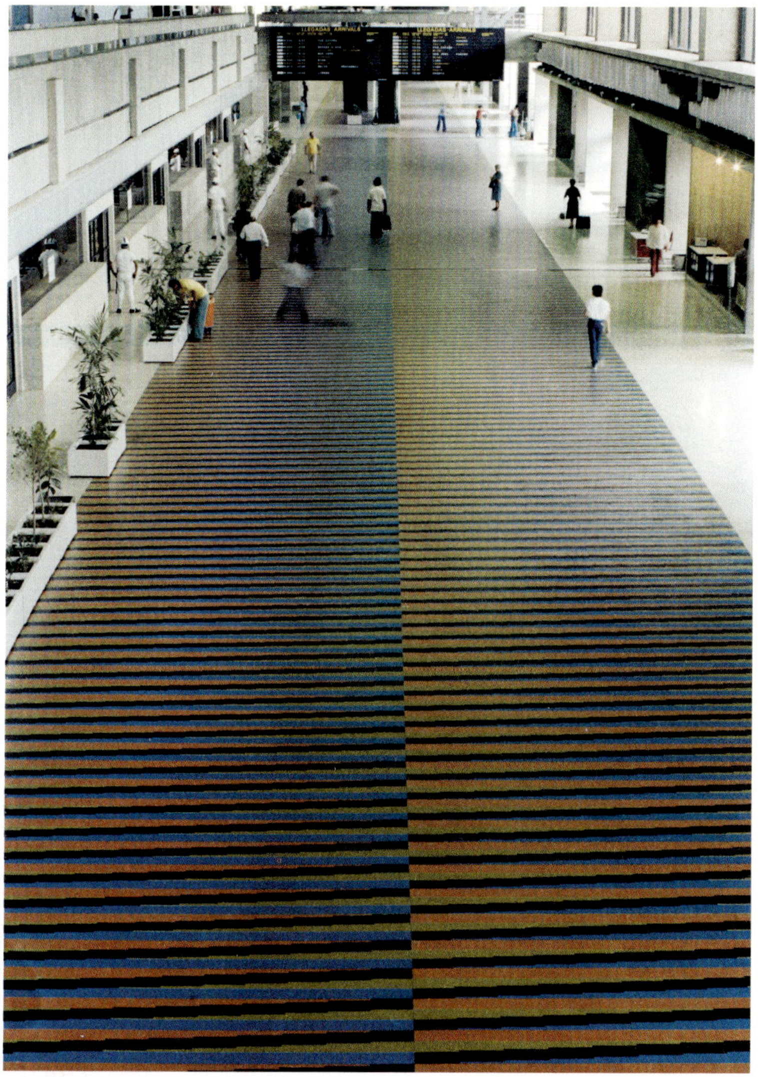

carlos cruz-diez
Ambientación cromática (Chromatic environment). 1974. Additive color walls and floors in the central hall of the Aeropuerto Internacional de Maiquetía Simón Bolívar, Venezuela (Montemayor and Sully, architects). Glazed Sialex tiles. 887′ 8 ½″ x 29′ 6 5⁄16″ (270 x 9 m). Collection Instituto Autónomo Aeropuerto Internacional de Maiquetía Simón Bolívar

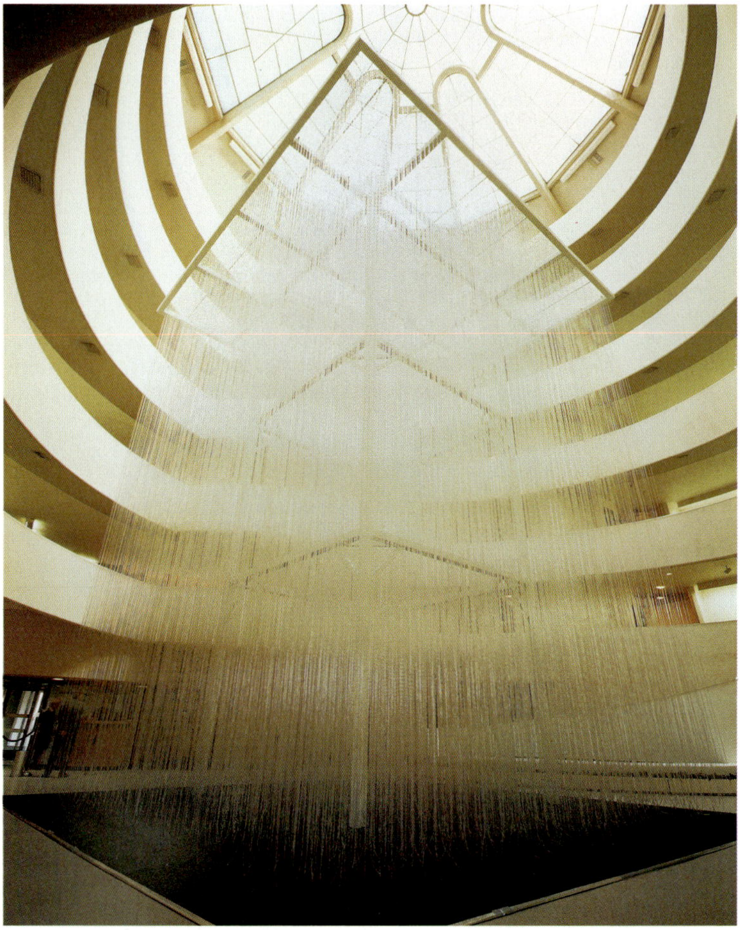

Installation view of Jesús Rafael Soto's *Penetrable*. 1974. Ephemeral work created for *Soto: A Retrospective Exhibition* at the Solomon R. Guggenheim Museum, New York

Alejandro Otero's *Torre solar* (*Solar Tower*; 1986). Photograph by Alfredo Boulton. 1987. Alberto Vollmer Foundation, Inc., Caracas

Installation view of Carlos Cruz-Diez's *Cromosaturación de Gelsenkirchen* (Chromosaturation of Gelsenkirchen). 1998. Ephemeral work constructed for the exhibition *Carlos Crus-Diez: Und gebe dem Raum die Farbe* (And give color to space) at the Städtisches Museum Gelsenkirchen, Germany. Private collection

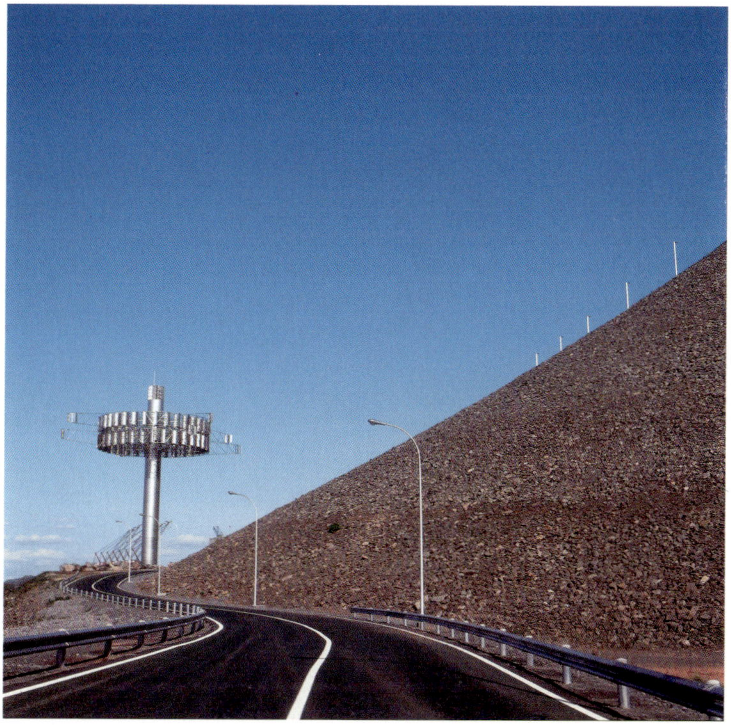

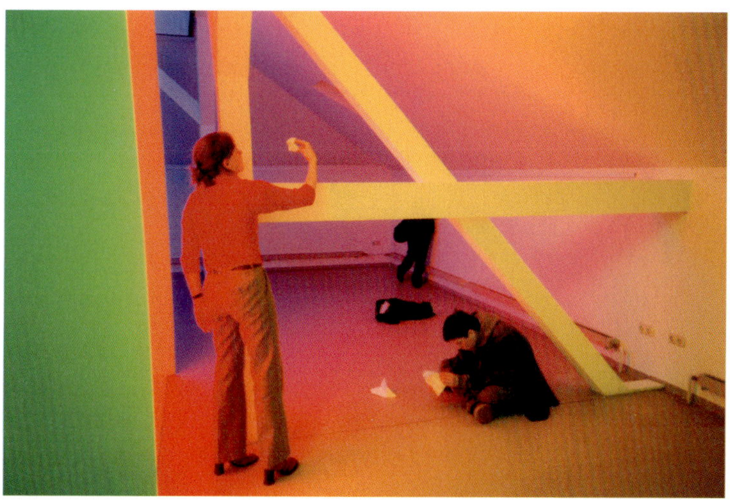

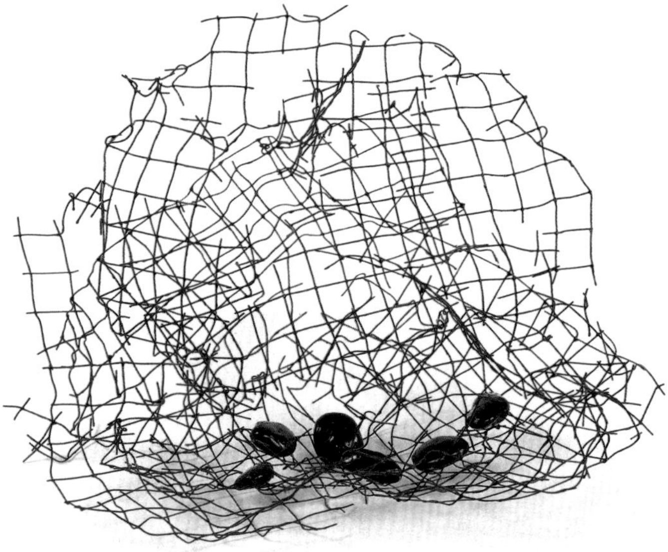

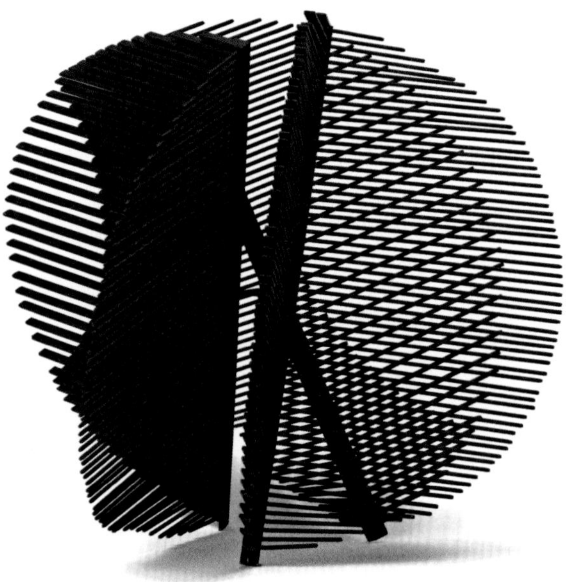

top: **gego (gertrude goldschmidt)**
Bicho 87/11 (*Critter 87/11*). 1987. Wire mesh and stones. 10 3/4 x 18 3/8 x 14 1/4" (27.2 x 46.6 x 36.2 cm). Collection Patricia Phelps de Cisneros, Caracas

bottom:
gego (gertrude goldschmidt)
Esfera (*Sphere*). 1959. Welded brass and steel, painted. 22" (55.7 cm) diameter. The Museum of Modern Art, New York. Inter-American Fund

opposite, top:
gego (gertrude goldschmidt)
Cuerdas (Estructuras aéreas ambientales) (*Cords [Environmental aerial structures]*). 1972. Nylon rope and iron tensioners. 59' x 57' 5" x 72' 2" (18 x 17.5 x 22 m). Collection Centro Simón Bolívar, Parque Central, Caracas

opposite, bottom:
gego (gertrude goldschmidt)
Reticulárea (ambientación) (*Reticulárea [Environmental work]*). 1968. Stainless steel and lead rods. 11' 5 13/16" x 17' 8 5/8" x 16' 4 7/8" (3.5 x 5.4 x 5 m). Collection Fundación Museos Nacionales. Galería de Arte Nacional, Caracas

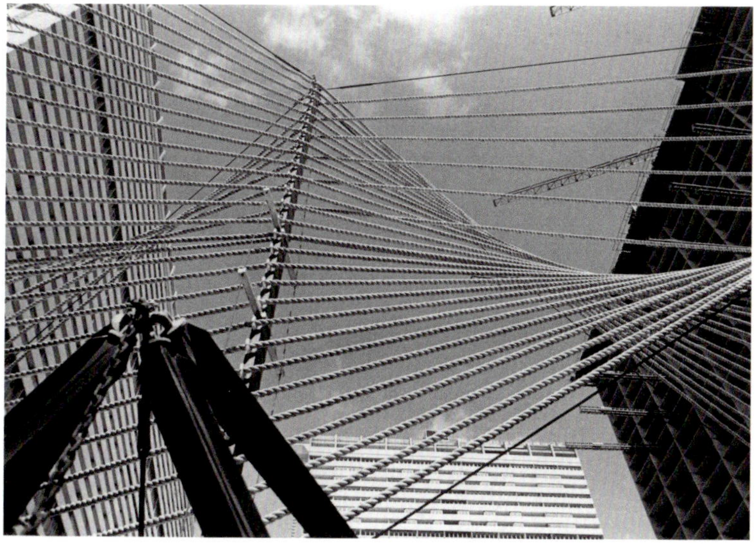

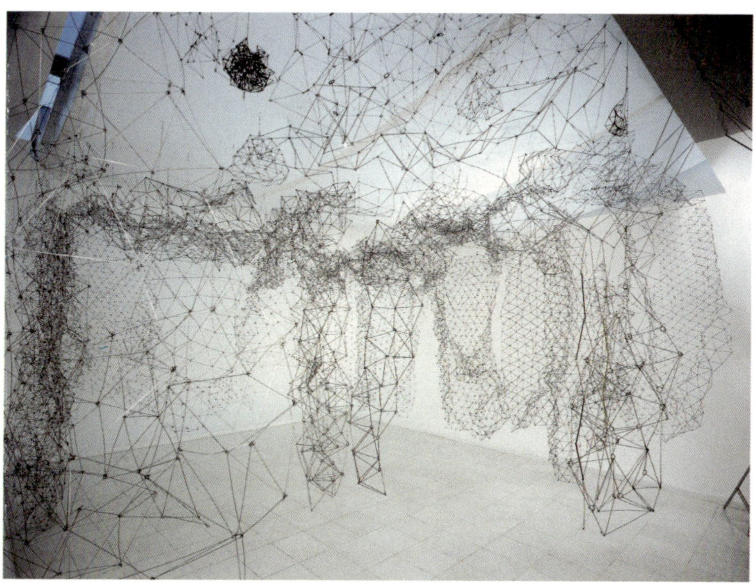

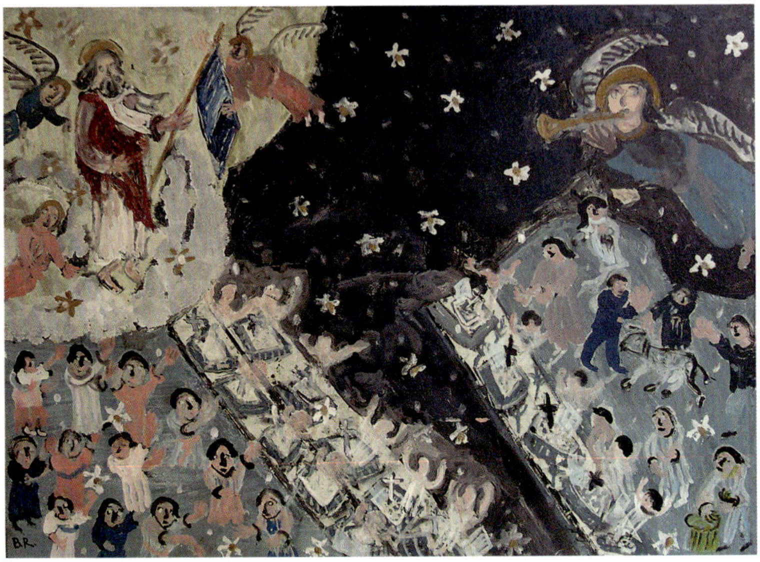

bárbaro rivas
El Juicio Final II (*The Last Judgment II*). c. 1957. Lacquer on Masonite. 24 x 32 5⁄16" (61 x 82 cm). Collection Banco Central de Venezuela

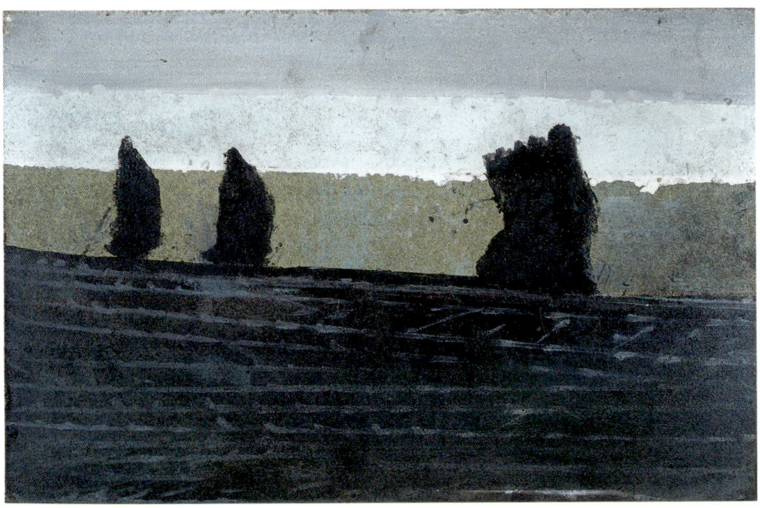

bárbaro rivas
Las rocas (*The Rocks*). c. 1965. Enamel on Masonite. 15 15⁄16 x 24" (40.5 x 61 cm). Private collection

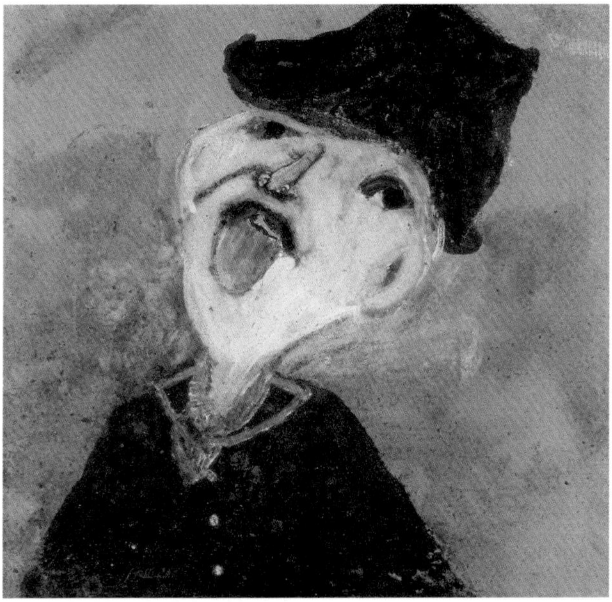

bárbaro rivas
Autorretrato (*Self-Portrait*). c. 1966. Enamel on Masonite. 15 7/8 x 15 7/8" (40.3 x 40.3 cm). Private collection

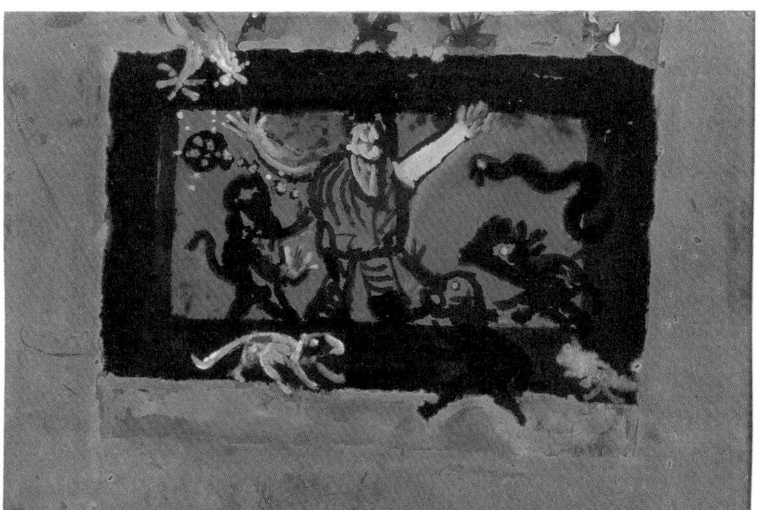

bárbaro rivas
El hombre luchando contra las enfermedades (*The Man Fighting Illnesses*). c. 1966. Enamel on Masonite. 14 9/16 x 20 13/16" (37 x 52.9 cm). Private collection

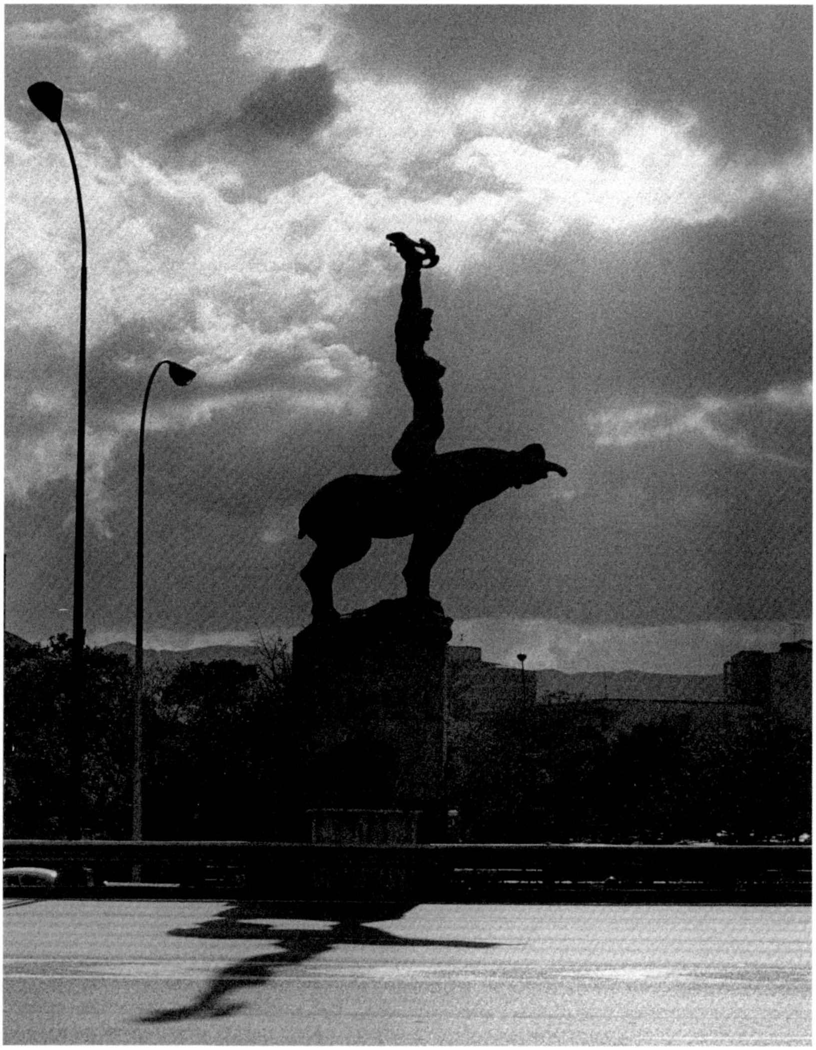

alejandro colina
María Lionza. 1951. Faux stone.
19' 4 1/4" x 3' 11 1/4" x 12' 3 1/4" (5.9 x 1.2 x 3.74 m). Autopista Francisco Fajardo, Caracas

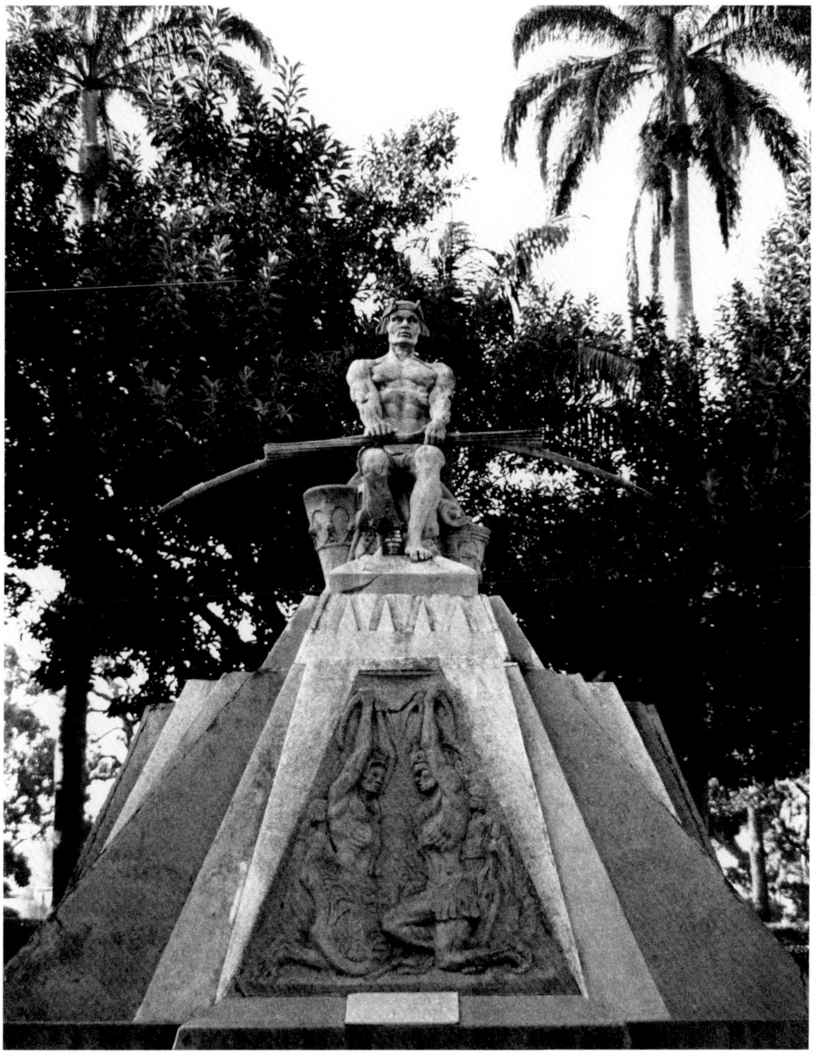

alejandro colina
El cacique Tiuna (Tiuna the cacique).
1951. Faux stone. 7′ 6 1/2″ x 6′ 6 9/16″ x
6′ 6 9/16″ (2.3 x 2 x 2 m). Plaza Tiuna,
Avenida Roosevelt, Caracas

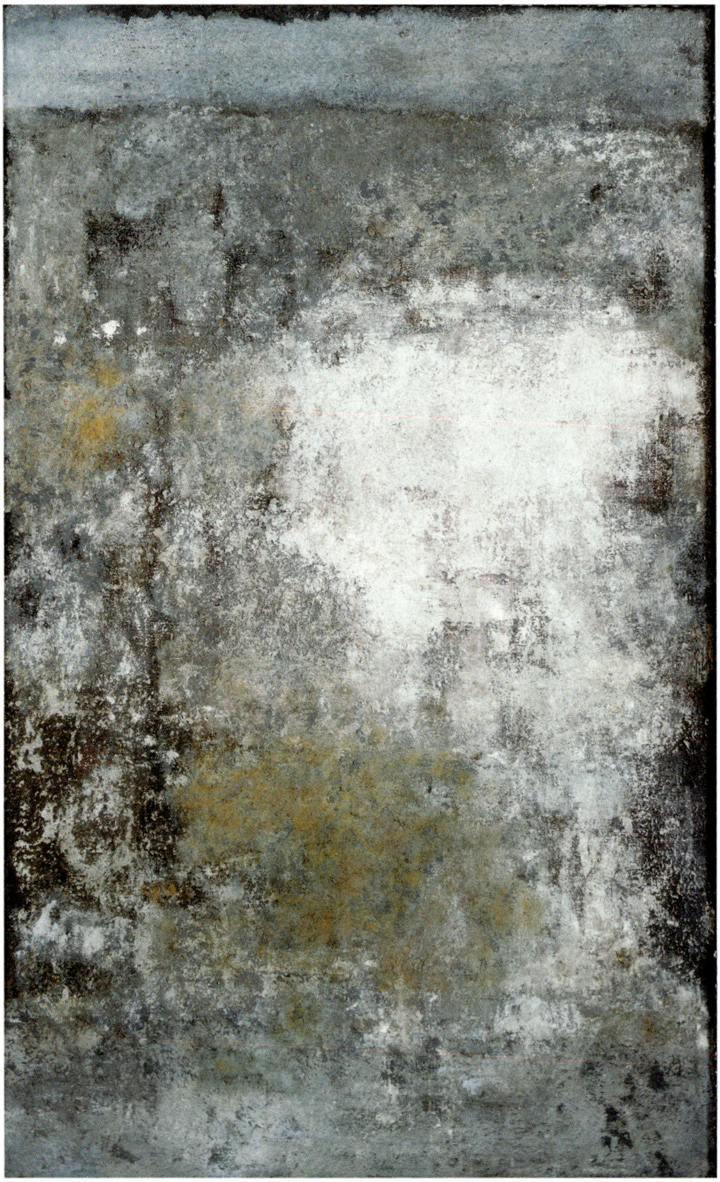

luisa richter
Composición (Composition). 1958.
Mixed media on canvas. 62 5/8" x 37 7/16"
(159 x 95 cm). Collection Mercantil,
Caracas

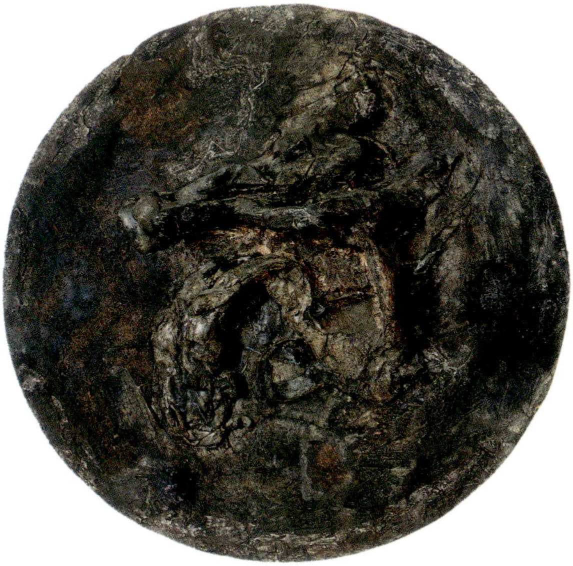

fernando irazábal
Occiso (Murdered). c. 1960. Mixed media on wood composite. 16 15⁄16 x 16 15⁄16" (43 x 43 cm). Collection Mercantil, Caracas

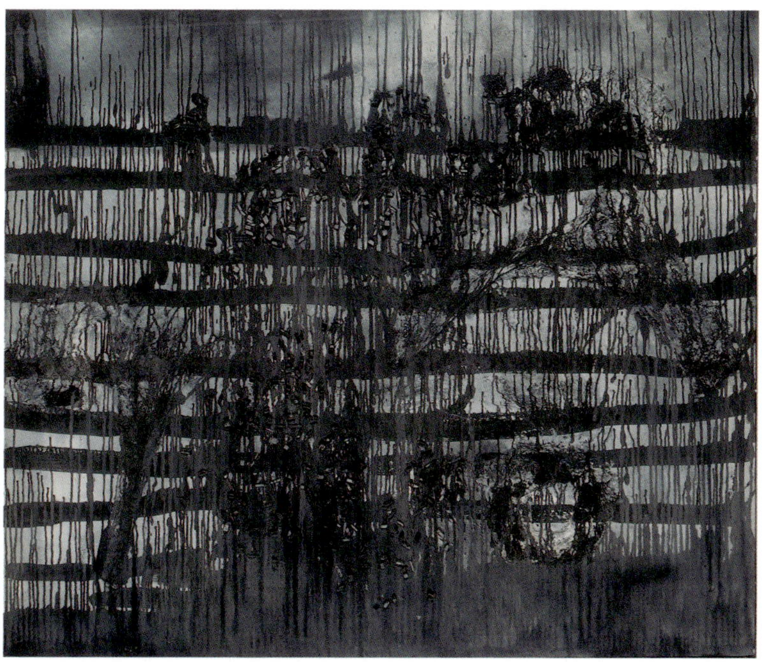

maruja rolando
Vuelo sideral (Sidereal flight). 1961. Oil and mixed media on canvas. 54 5⁄16 x 63 3⁄4" (138 x 162 cm). Collection Ignacio and Valentina Oberto, Caracas

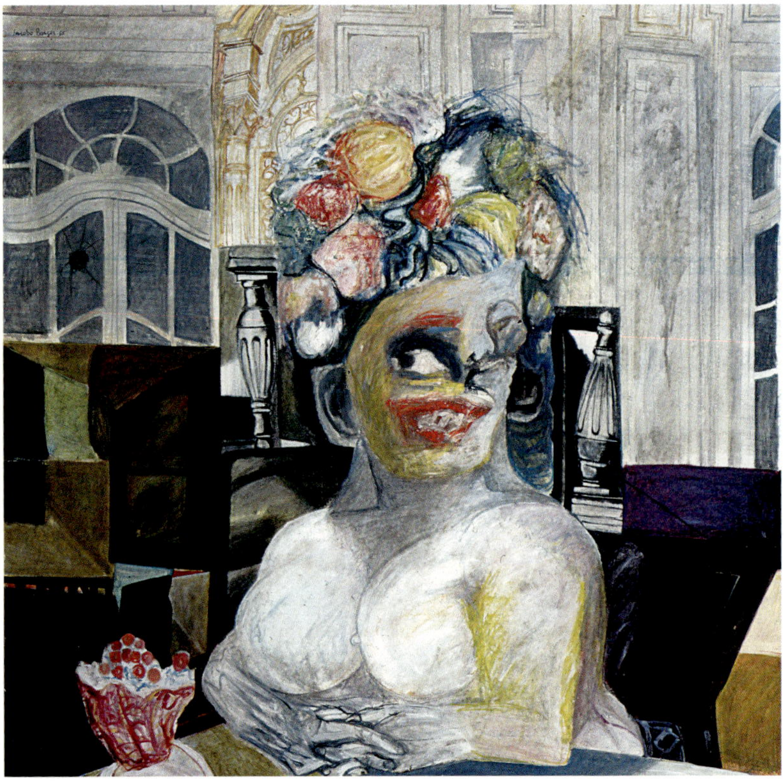

jacobo borges
Algo se ha roto (*Something Has Broken*). 1965. Oil on canvas. 58 ⅞ x 58 ⅞" (149.4 x 149.4 cm). Solomon R. Guggenheim Museum, New York

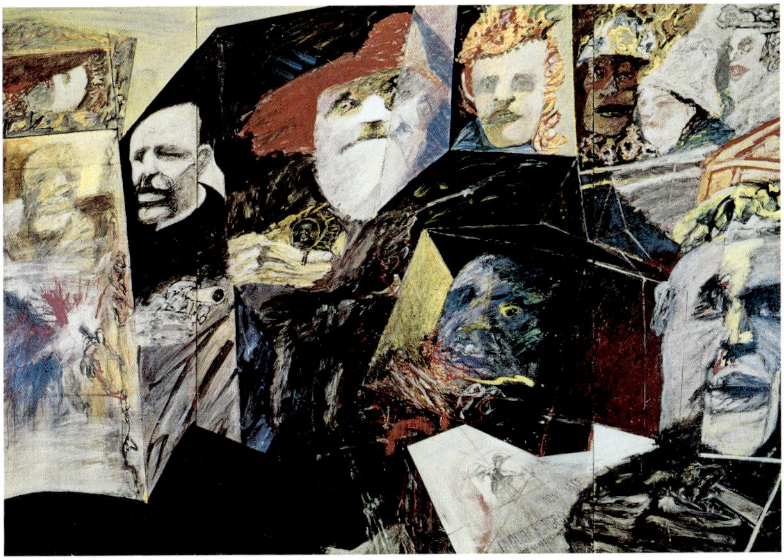

jacobo borges
Humilde ciudadano (*Humble Citizen*). 1964. Oil on wood. 6′ 6 ¾″ x 9′ 2″ (2 x 2.794 m). Collection Fundación Museos Nacionales. Galería de Arte Nacional, Caracas

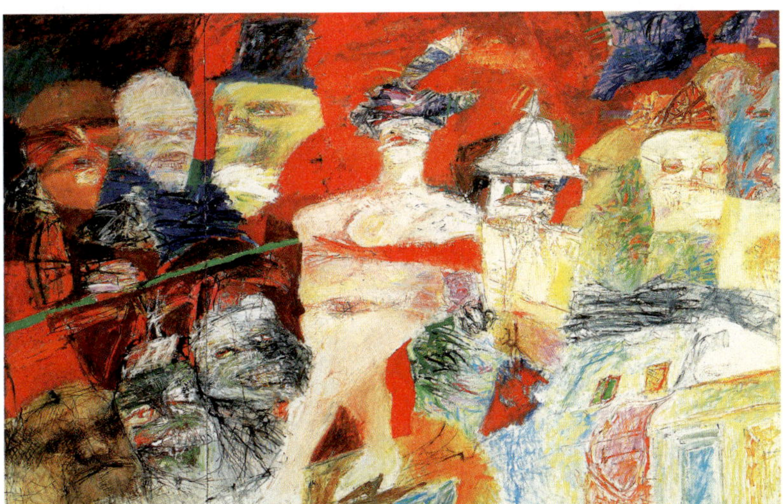

jacobo borges
Ha comenzado el espectáculo (*The Show Has Begun*). 1964. Oil on canvas. 71″ x 8′ 10 7/16″ (180.3 x 270.4 cm). Collection Fundación Museos Nacionales. Galería de Arte Nacional, Caracas

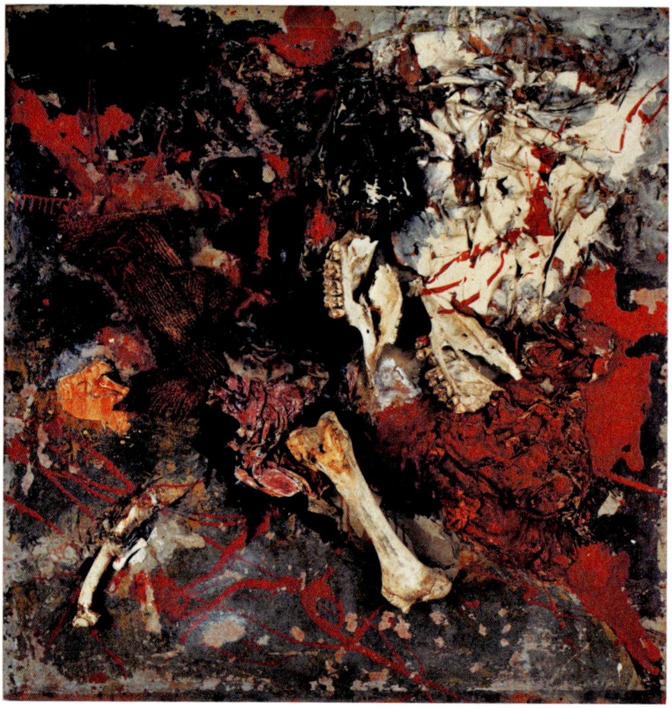

carlos contramaestre
Estudio para verdugo y perro
(Study for executioner and dog).
1962. Mixed media on canvas.
47 1/4 x 44 1/8 x 5 7/8" (120 x 112 x
15 cm). Collection Ignacio and
Valentina Oberto, Caracas

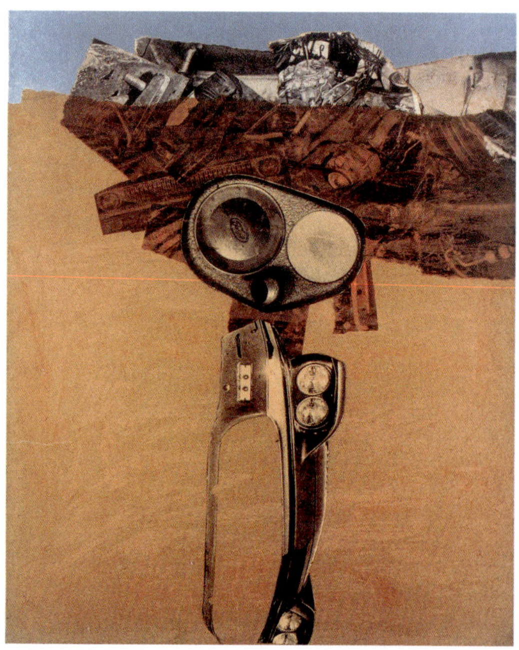

daniel gonzález
Untitled. 1963. Collage on paper.
4 9/16 x 11 7/16" (37 x 29 cm).
Collection Ignacio and Valentina
Oberto, Caracas

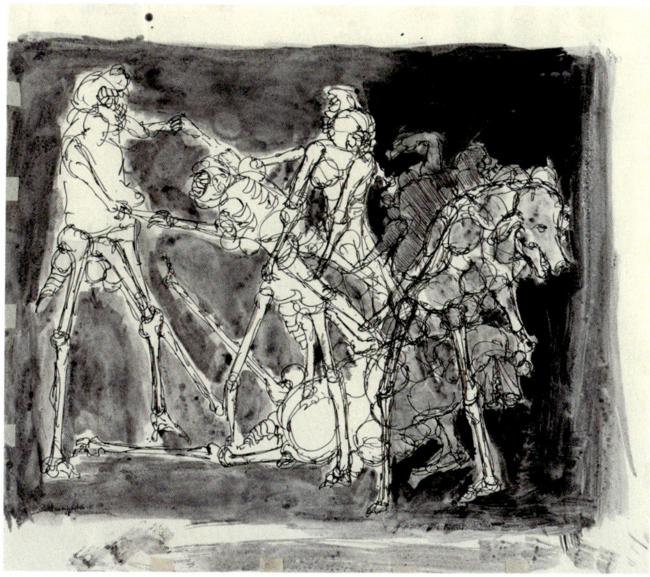

carlos contramaestre
Untitled (*Caballeros luchando*) (Knights battling). 1963. Chinese ink on card stock. 24 3/8 x 26 7/8" (62 x 68.2 cm). Collection Fundación Museos Nacionales. Galería de Arte Nacional, Caracas

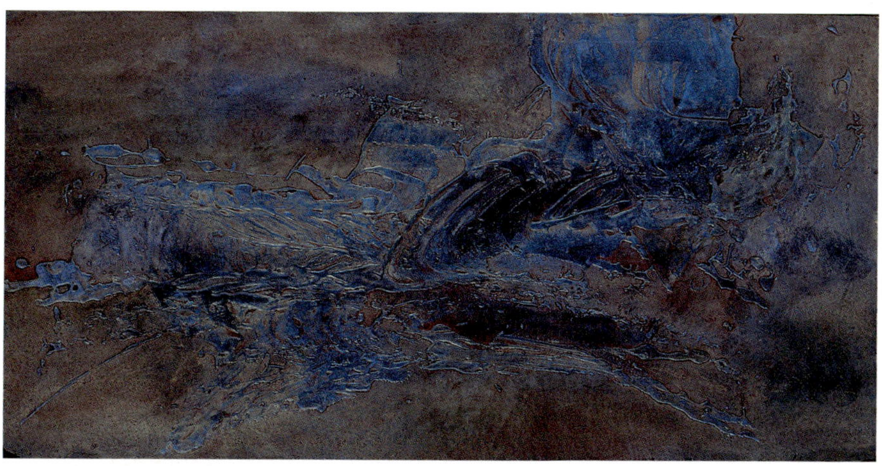

ángel luque
Untitled. 1965. Mixed media on Masonite. 21 1/4 x 40 15/16" (54 x 104 cm). Collection Ignacio and Valentina Oberto, Caracas

chapter four **critical nexus**

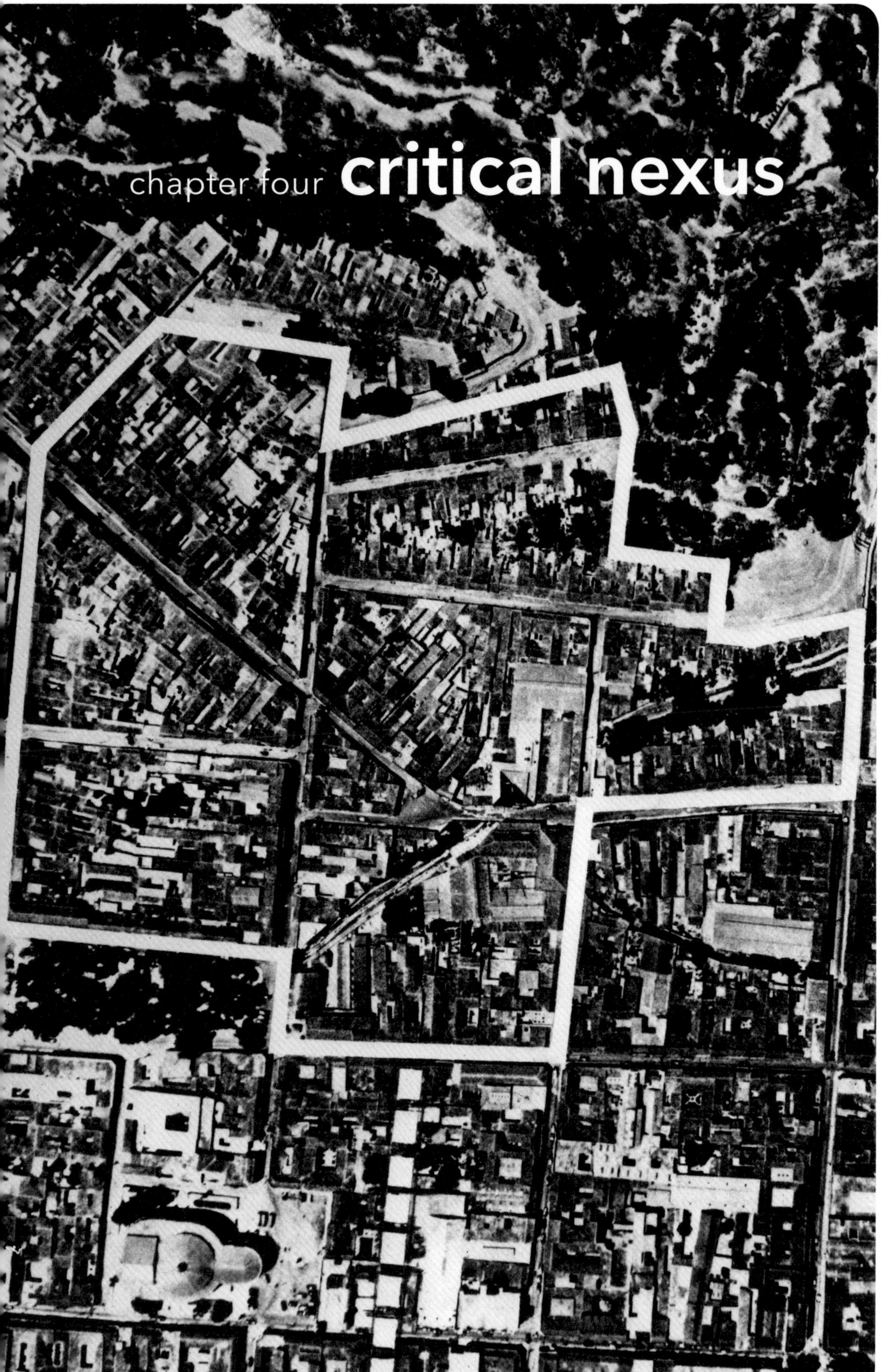

inventing modernity in the land of adam: alfredo boulton, armando reverón, and bárbaro rivas

luis pérez-oramas

Thirty years elapsed—three decades from the first line to the last—between Alfredo Boulton's first truly significant text on Venezuelan painting and what was perhaps his final great text on the art of the Caribbean nation that witnessed his birth, to which he dedicated his entire life, and with it his work as an intellectual, collector, and art connoisseur. The first essay focused on the work of Armando Reverón;[1] the last discussed the "outsider" artist Bárbaro Rivas.

During those thirty years from 1954 to 1984 many things developed in Venezuela, including, not insignificantly, the only political system in the country's history to be civic and democratic, and to allow for the effective alternation of parties. The emergence of that system galvanized a fragile but portentous hope in Venezuelan society, a hope for this political goal that had been harbored in vain since the country's first days of independence—a hope that exists to this day.

During those three decades both modernity and its history took shape in Venezuela: modernity understood as a system of social, infrastructural, and aesthetic aspirations, and its story—a controversial chapter in the existence of the nation. Venezuelan society became conscious of the main protagonists of this modernity: it identified its pioneers and founders; it recognized, discussed, and celebrated their achievements, and thus the nation became a subject of that very modernity, which was undertaken as a continual and never-ending project.

It is striking that Boulton should have written his first great critical text on Reverón. For reasons that must be unraveled in light of the author's work and life, Boulton chose a self-marginalized subject—a man who was absolutely unlike himself. Boulton willingly chose this subject, so distanced from the central action of the art world, to mark the beginning of his task as a historiographer and with it, retrospectively, the foundation of modern art in Venezuela. Boulton wrote this text presumably between September 1954, the month of Reverón's death, and July 1955, when it was published as the central piece in the catalogue of the first retrospective show of the artist's work, at Caracas's Museo de Bellas Artes.[2]

Thirty years later, in June 1984, what was then called the Museo de Arte Contemporáneo de Caracas Sofía Imber presented the most important retrospective exhibition devoted to the self-taught artist Bárbaro Rivas, perhaps Venezuela's most significant popular artist and one of the indisputable protagonists of pictorial modernity in Venezuela. In the catalogue of that exhibition, organized by Boulton and Francisco Da Antonio (two figures as well-respected as they were unlike each other), Boulton published his last great critical text on Venezuelan art.[3]

The origin and destiny of this art historiographer's work, the legacy of this tropical and patrician Vasari, are thus bound up in two artists who resemble each other in that neither came from the disciplinary—and disciplined—world of art; they shared a common alienation, resplendent and painful, and both removed themselves from the world through their decision to stay out of the politics that govern art and the *civis*. Furthermore, both were separated from the world of the art academy: Reverón had to forget his artistic training so as to reinvent his art in conditions that were extremely challenging, conditions that were chosen and determined by him, alone in his solitude, while Rivas never had to "free himself from any ties that bound him to any artistic movement whatsoever, to any *ism*," to borrow Boulton's words.[4]

I recall a conversation with Da Antonio, in which he spoke of Reverón's portrait of Boulton: a wash drawing on paper depicting the historian as a young and elegant man, made with those nervous and ostensibly formless strokes that were typical of Reverón's work in the period 1933–34, when he produced numerous tempera drawings; this was shortly before his great Arcadian scenes of the late 1930s, but with the experience of his 1920s white landscapes still close at hand. These are exultant, intense, festive works, perhaps the most intuitive and immediate ones of Reverón's entire œuvre. As Da Antonio pointed out, Boulton's portrait is striking because of the distance between the artist and his sitter, because of the explicitly guarded pose of the subject. It is as if that image muted or mediated the proximity of the friendship between Reverón and Boulton, acknowledging an insurmountable difference between them, as if Reverón wanted in this work to identify the opulent presence of that visitor, his English gentleman's manners, as if that sophisticated friend embodied, through the likeness by which the painter represented him, the distance between Reverón's own Castillete—his isolated "little castle"—and the world of the salons, where art and banquets take place, with its rational gardens, its ancient and modern palaces, the city, urbanism, urbanity, power.

Boulton visited Reverón numerous times, but it seems doubtful that they ever became intimate friends. Boulton probably avoided visiting him during those periods when Reverón's mental health and eccentricity became troubling accomplices of the artist's own masks.[5] He certainly did not write about Reverón's work systematically or begin the project of constructing Reverón's historiography until after the artist's death, the occasion that no doubt prompted Boulton to write his 1955 essay.[6]

That Reverón had unintentionally inaugurated a new form of modernity in Venezuelan painting was, for Boulton, a retrospective certainty. It is interesting to see this in contrast to our critic's convictions about the significance of Francisco Narváez's sculpture or of Alejandro Otero's or Jesús Soto's work while they were still alive. Reverón must have been, for all of them, including Boulton, both profoundly admirable and nearly incomprehensible: a man of their generation who might have shared their world, but who decided to escape to another place, an alien place, a country of his own.

Reverón's was an unknown and therefore an obscured country whose light—sometimes supremely bright, even blinding—requires an eccentric disposition, a kind of alienation, to perceive it. This was a country that Caracas had only recently been made aware of in 1948, when the young poet Juan Liscano was put in charge of organizing the Fiesta de las Tradiciones (festival of Venezuelan folk traditions) to celebrate the advent of the first popularly elected government in Venezuela. Here, for the first time, the country's capital saw the *tamunangue* folk dance performed before a massive audience, and for the first time heard the deafening noise of the black drums that had long been relegated to workers' celebrations in the back roads of the great haciendas or in remote coastal towns – drums that would from here on set the rhythm of the nation.

The year 1948 also brought Venezuela's first exhibition of abstract art, at the Taller Libre de Arte (Free arts workshop) in Caracas. Even to this day in Venezuela a basic fact seems insufficiently examined: that political modernity, social democracy, and artistic modernity all burst onto the nation's consciousness in tandem with deeply telluric traditions; folklore became commonly acknowledged and its popularization was one of the effects and most palpable characteristics of the country's modernization. Just as Venezuela discovered the timeless works of its artisans and popular musicians, hidden or disregarded until then, the country also discovered the art of the future, and what the writer Mariano Picón Salas dubbed the modern *mensaje de celeridad* – the message of celerity, of forward motion.[7]

Boulton's interest in Venezuelan folk culture is another topic yet to be studied in depth. The historian seems not to have taken much interest in the work of artisans, in spite of his later research into pre-Hispanic ceramics and his unceasing focus on the native landscape, the racial types of the country's inhabitants, and the physical beauties of Venezuela's people. Boulton was from an old and well-established Venezuelan family, proudly rooted in a nation whose people he loved, but his work as an intellectual always emphasized the formative accomplishments of the elites – heroes of independence (and among these the most patrician: Francisco de Miranda and Simón Bolívar), explorers (and among these the most sophisticated and intelligent: Alexander von Humboldt and Camille Pissarro), and avant-garde artists, such as Francisco Narváez, Jesús Rafael Soto, Carlos Cruz-Diez, and Alejandro Otero.

And yet Boulton's work as an art historian and historiographer opens and closes with Reverón and Rivas, two exceptions, two eremitic Venezuelans, two artists excluded from the great civic banquet, two men of the earth. As if to point out that humanity and its glories – among them creative intuition – cannot endure standards of urbanity or "civilizing" norms, Boulton chose these two great artists to open and close his personal history of modern art in Venezuela, perhaps because in the end they represent the Venezuelan character above and beyond all civilizing constraints, creation beyond "culture," and ultimately the invention of modernity in the land of Adam.

Boulton's take on Rivas was very different from his approach to Reverón. "The life and work of Bárbaro Rivas," he writes, "are clear proof that talent does not depend exclusively on an individual's cultural training."[8] This phrase, so light and simple, written by Boulton at the end of his life, is an entire continent, revealing the beautiful process of learning about Venezuela that constituted his life's work. It might be said, at this difficult moment in the nation's history, that *citizenship* too depends not on formal culture, or on institutional education, but simply on the creative and free choice of individuals. And Rivas, a hermit and a genius, the "great storyteller" of Venezuelan painting (to use Boulton's words once again), is the undeniable and complex proof of that choice, embodied in unprecedented works capable of entering into dialogue with the modern art of his time – from the art of the young Jacobo Borges in 1960s Caracas to that of the CoBrA group in Europe (although contemporaries of Rivas, CoBrA in all likelihood knew nothing of the genius of Petare).

Boulton did not ignore the facts—on the contrary, he celebrated them—that Rivas "made the world sublime," as he put it, that the artist demonstrated technical mastery in his "control of harmonies," or that his work was surprisingly close to the "Spanish picaresque," endowed at once with an unprecedented narrative efficacy and an admirable "inventive candor."

Boulton's essay on Rivas was a conclusive gesture, in keeping with his general approach to Venezuelan art: his life's work closed with a reflection on a figure who had much in common with Reverón, the critical consideration of whom had marked the starting point of Boulton's career. But the piece on Rivas is also an exception within Boulton's work, for two reasons. First, it is the critic's only approach to Venezuelan popular arts, and more than just an analysis of the artist: it is a theoretical reflection on the universality of art, on the mystery of "pictorial intuition" personified in a self-created genius who lacked any formal education, who could not write, who thus lacked "culture." The second element that makes the Rivas essay exceptional within Boulton's œuvre is that it concludes with the author giving up the floor. In his very last lines, he opens a door—at once literary and symbolic—to the voice of others with the following statement:

> [Rivas's] forms of expression are so diverse that his work sometimes seems as if made by a hundred different hands, each one a unique way of entering the landscape or the character, but always with the same particular audacity. Yet it was only one hand. It was the hand of Bárbaro Rivas as if it were the hand of a hundred painters set out to renovate Venezuelan art. Who was the man called Bárbaro Rivas? Who was that great artist? Francisco Da Antonio, who discovered and took him under his wing, will tell you.[9]

Boulton seems to have recognized that Rivas distilled within himself the humanity of an entire nation—those "hundred painters" in unison; Boulton saw the work of absent multitudes in the intuition of a single exceptional artist. It is as if, on the eve of his own silence as a historian, he also knew that his critical œuvre was destined to be complemented, discussed, refuted, and transcended in the work of others to come. The words of his colleague Da Antonio follow Boulton's in the subsequent pages of that introductory text on Rivas, the last text of indisputable significance that Boulton would write about a Venezuelan artist.

Boulton's argument to justify his own unprecedented foray into the realm of popular arts was, in fact, that Rivas was *not* a conventional popular artist, that as an intuitive genius he deserved a place in the Parnassus of art next to Le Douanier Rousseau, or indeed Armando Reverón. But it is still significant that Boulton took such an interest in an artist who was so firmly installed in the constellation of the popular arts—even if it involved a theoretical denegation of Boulton's long-established art-historical proclivities. It brought the critic onto a new path, a path that here he does not exhaust but instead leaves open (as he did in other texts that leave behind new "disciplinary" clues) so that those with greater authority—in this case, Da Antonio—might one day continue upon it. Boulton's work was a kind of cartographic sketch for the territory of art historiography, or for the foundation of visual anthropology in Venezuela: he does not exhaust anything in its entirety, yet he leaves no field untouched – pre-Hispanic civilizations, colonial society, the establishment of republics, the invention of the landscape and of local nature, civic art, the modern arts, the physiognomy of the heroes of independence, popular arts. He thus shaped, capriciously but definitively, the destiny of art historiography and of the national adjective "Venezuelan."

The question remains: *why* did Boulton begin and conclude his work as an art historian and critic by considering these two marginal, alienated, and eremitic figures? I would like to interpret this phenomenon as a coincidence – surely accidental – that takes on meaning in light of a retrospective consideration of Boulton's own œuvre, ultimately becoming a definitive gesture (yet open to endless discussion).

The ideological bond in Boulton's work that links the foundational text on Reverón to the concluding text on Rivas is yet another significant symptom of what may be termed Venezuela's national "Adamism." These two figures, in truth, led tragic lives overwhelmed by the weight of the surrounding society. But under Boulton's gaze they become proof of the primordial potential of Venezuelan civilization. Boulton is, in this respect, no different from the majority of Venezuelan humanists who lived during his time: Mariano Picón Salas and Mario Briceño Iragorry, Arturo Úslar Pietri and Guillermo Meneses, Rómulo Gallegos and Isaac Pardo all seem to have awakened to the truth of Venezuela through the disgust produced by its nineteenth-century wars and misery; all devoted themselves to finding, beyond the tragedy, the nation's Arcadian core.

This is the crux of meaning in the photographic images that Boulton took of the Caracas Valley and of the waving Andean heights, of Páez's plains and of the Isla de Margarita. This constitutes his fascination with the men of the earth: to discover a Venezuelan Adam, to affirm the existence of an origin and the inevitable complexity of human liberty (the truth that humanity is always responsible for its own misery), so as to found on this land – presumably virgin and full of grace, and thus of course fictitious – the possibility of modernity.

Upon sailing the waters of the Paria peninsula, Columbus witnessed "great indications of this being the terrestrial paradise." In a letter sent in 1498 to King Ferdinand and Queen Isabella of Spain from the island of Hispaniola, in which he describes his arrival in Venezuela, Columbus claims with certainty that he has seen the Garden of Eden in that land, which he calls the "Tierra de Gracia" or "Land of Grace."[10] A long and significant ellipsis in Venezuelan thought runs from this reference all the way to that famous chapter in Rómulo Gallegos's 1935 novel *Canaima*, in which the author describes an extraordinary scene of purification. The book's main character is a worldly man who apparently gets lost and, after encountering the soul of the jungle in the density of a rainstorm, becomes once again an Adamic figure – that is, both flawed and pure. As it turns out, and as that heraldic novelist of Venezuela discerned, in the modern world every Adam is condemned to ostracism and incomprehension: to being, in other words, an antihero.

As were, in fact, Reverón and Rivas: two antiheroes in whom Boulton saw the beginning and end of modern art in Venezuela and with whom he began and ended his own work. The idea of a modern-day Adam is neither new nor particularly original. There has always been an apparent collision (which is in fact a secret ideological complicity) between modernity and primitivism, from Paul Cézanne's desire to see the world as if it were an unintelligible, unnamable blotch to the compulsion that gripped both the architect Walter Gropius and the artist Kurt Schwitters to build "Adamic" shelters.[11] Reverón's house, as the birthplace of modern Venezuelan art, is in this sense just another Adamic house in Paradise.

But we all know that Paradise is a fiction. And thus the vision of Venezuela as an Adamic place or setting was, and remains, a fiction. Like any work of fiction, it feeds and illuminates reality, but never coincides with it. Like any work of fiction, what it provides is a place without place: a place outside of place. The Adamism of our modern humanists consisted of a desire to construct a possible country based on a narrative of definite redemption, in which modernity was seen as an epic enterprise of purification. In order to take hold in historical events, this enterprise needed to be sure of the existence of a virgin humanity, untainted by the horrors of its past: an innocent (or perhaps merely victimized) humanity, a humanity untethered to civic responsibilities.

Such are the pure men and women described and spoken of by Boulton, Úslar Pietri, and Gallegos. Such is the idea of a country, gratified by its own unexpected natural gifts, that is called to transform them into creative energies, forever unburdened of its debts to history, as if the threat of a brutal return to the labyrinth of the country's anthropological contradictions did not weigh upon its destiny at all. Such are the symbolic manifestations of this Adamism: perhaps a painting whose whiteness made Boulton deem it immaculate – in spite of the shadowy figure of its creator, Reverón – but which is actually a gnarled and dirty latticework made entirely of discarded scraps. Such are Rivas's pictorial accounts, which Boulton realized were bound to the artist's personal tragedy, but which he also read as children's parables, even if they were – and still are – the humble recourses of a man who suffered in order to escape the pain of the world, transforming it into painting: the unexpected, bitter, warping alibis of anguish. Boulton's power of discernment (and denial) was such that he discovered, accidentally, in the work of these two extraordinary outsiders the image of a pure *tierra de gracia* – unwieldy, complex, and protean though it may be.

Translated by Catalina Ocampo

notes to the text

1. Alfredo Boulton, "La obra de Armando Reverón" ("The Work of Armando Reverón") in *Exposición retrospectiva de Armando Reverón* (Caracas: Museo de Bellas Artes, 1955); reprinted in *Reverón* (Caracas: Macanao, 1979). An abridged version of this essay is included in the present volume, pp. 232–49.
2. On the 1955 *Exposición retrospectiva de Armando Reverón*, and Alfredo Boulton's text, see Maria Elena Huizi, "Una exposición sin precedentes," in *Armando Reverón: La exposición de 1955*, eds. Maitena de Elguézabal, Rafael Romero, Juan Ignacio Parra (Caracas: Asociación Proyecto Armando Reverón, 2007).
3. Alfredo Boulton, *Bárbaro Rivas: La intuición pictórica* (Caracas: Museo de Arte Contemporáneo de Caracas Sofía Imber, 1984).
4. Ibid., p. 7. Quote translated by Catalina Ocampo.
5. See *He vivido por los ojos: Correspondencia Alejandro Otero/Alfredo Boulton, 1946–1974*, Ariel Jiménez, ed. (Caracas: Fundación Alberto Vollmer and Fundación Museo Alejandro Otero, 2001), p. 63.
6. The first great critical text on Reverón, and certainly one of the most thorough, was written by Mariano Picón Salas in 1939. See Picón Salas, "Armando Reverón," *Revista Nacional de la Cultura*, no. 13 (November 1939): 63–80; reprinted in *Armando Reverón: 10 Ensayos* (Caracas: Consejo Municipal del Distrito Federal, 1975), pp. 43–50. The text is included in the present volume, pp. 115–22.
7. See Mariano Picón Salas, *Suma de Venezuela: Antología de páginas venezolanas* (Caracas: Editorial Doña Bárbara, 1966), p. 22.
8. Boulton, *Bárbaro Rivas*, p. 18. Quote translated by Catalina Ocampo.
9. Ibid., p. 28. Quote translated by Catalina Ocampo.
10. Christopher Columbus, "The History of a Voyage which Don Christopher Columbus Made the Third Time that He Came to the Indies, When He Discovered Terra Firma, and which He Sent to Their Majesties from the Island of Hispaniola," in *Four Voyages to the New World: Letter and Selected Documents*, trans. and ed. by R. H. Major (Gloucester, Mass.: Corinth Books, 1961), p. 137.
11. The reference is to Gropius's Sommerfeld house in Berlin, and to Schwitters's Merzbau, which he intended to build on untouched natural settings. See Joseph Rykwert, *On Adam's House in Paradise: The Idea of the Primitive Hut in Architectural History* (New York: Museum of Modern Art, 1981).

the desire for emancipation: origins and destiny

sandra pinardi

> *Has it not happened to some of you, walking distracted through the Cuban jungle, the Brazilian forest, the Andean cave, or the Venezuelan prairie, that you quiver suddenly with the idea that you will imminently happen upon an already-adult man, recently born, naked, covered only in his own pelt, not born of parents but rather sprung up from the earth, standing immobile, with his feet still buried in the sludge, devouring the strangeness of the world with an astonished gaze, his mouth half-open with his first stammered sound?*
>
> *This has happened to me, at any rate, on a number of occasions. And that is because in these lands of ours, with their impressive silence and tragic solitude, it is easy to feel that the sixth day of Genesis has not yet ended, that the creator's breath still blows through them.*
>
> – Rómulo Gallegos, "Las tierras de Dios" ("God's Lands"), 1931[1]

The Americas were "discovered" – they appeared at the dawn of modernity as a reward for and an affirmation of the West's civilizing project and its impulse to construct. This "discovery" has marked the course of Latin American history and the political and cultural challenges that its nations have faced throughout that history; it is a foundational gesture that constantly reappears in Latin America's ways of considering itself and meeting its own needs.

In order to delve into Venezuelan modernity and the role that the visual arts have played in it, it is necessary to point out two factors associated with this particular "origin." First, Latin America's appearance on the Western cultural map constituted a "discovery" implies a tension and a conflict from which the region has never been able to break loose: a thing can be *discovered* only if it already existed but has remained hidden. There is a paradox to this "discovery": on one hand, it confirms that Latin America's appearance in the West was not "originary" but arose though a process of naming – an enunciation, an imposition – and on the other, this "discovery" obliterates, annuls, and excludes Latin America's anteriority. It appeared; it emerged – it was not born; it is a being that erupted from a concealed preexistence. This emergence, which is its founding contradiction, brings together the majority of Latin America's projects and trajectories with a dire need to contruct and consolidate themselves in an "originary" manner – devoting themselves to the exploration of their own identities, permanently vexed by the need for self-recognition. Indeed, because of its location in this tense space between its emergence through enunciation and its effaced anteriority, identity in Latin America is not something to be grasped, but a difficult, lingering, and inapprehensible question. And as something to be explored, not grasped, identity has been a recurring problem in the history of these nations, a problem that has defined their efforts and their process of development, forcing them to emerge in a protracted process of inauguration: simultaneously an "origin" and an erasure. Facts come to be based on a *having-been* that remains hidden and thus fails to establish itself as their substratum.

Second, what the Western imagination discovers is deemed a "new world": a pure "continent"[2] (from the Latin *continere*, to contain), a terrain ready for edification that, as the word itself implies, *is* not, but *will be*. In this "continent" of Latin America—an exuberant and untilled "virgin" territory—notions of foundation and beginning are determined by physical circumstances: these are terrains and not experiences, places and not meanings, spaces and not legacies. With the Latin American continent, the pure space of possibility (or the space of pure possibility)—perpetually *to come*, a topos without tracks or imprints, a potential way of life—enters the cultural geography of the West. This poses another paradox. Latin America is always "modern" precisely because it is something that is *yet to be*—a factually impossible, pure, and ideal potential, a vague territory in which the realization of "modernity" is suspended in plans for its potential destiny. Latin America is modern, then, from a position of *exception*: nascent modernity—which discovers it and names it—affirms that it must distance or detach itself from the very materiality and territory that constitute it. At work in this modernity is a force of law-without-law that is invoked as it is revoked, and that emerges as its own space of crisis and critique. This is why, in Latin American nations, the modern project is always an aspiration and never an achievement, a norm and not a praxis, putting these nations' ways of life at risk by implanting, grafting, imposing here an ideological and symbolic system linked to external powers and subjectivities.

This "non-originary origin," this obscured and absent *having-been*, this "excepted" modernity, compels Latin American nations to understand and think of themselves as projects, constitutions geared to the future, subjunctive structures in which desire prevails, in which being is idealized and presented as a state-to-come. Modernity and identity are deeply interrelated phenomena here, not only because Latin America's process of forming identity is also its process of instituting modernity, but because (in keeping with modernity) Latin America constantly reinaugurates itself, is always in the process of being founded.

Latin American modernity, undermined by a desire for identity and legitimation, has become manifest in strategies of cultural differentiation. This modernity is marked by projects of self-valorization and critical appropriation of that world in which the continent was "discovered," in which it emerged as a permanent *will-be* without ever having been. This search for "origins" and significant substrata has been expressed in the mythical but ill-defined idea of emancipation—that is, of a practical freedom conquered rather than given, reclaimed rather than possessed, an autonomy presented as a demand, goal, destiny, and work. As the philosopher J. R. Guillent Pérez urges: "Absolute, total freedom is what must be attained. . . . Bolívar should serve as an example for us . . . through his most essential attitude: the rebellious attitude of a man who no longer wants to be colonial."[3]

This idea of emancipation is conceived as the practical "condition of possibility" for genuine freedom and action. As a practical idea, emancipation is also ideological, given its intermediary position among the ideals to which it gives rise and the material conditions it seeks to modify or transform, and the fact that it involves context-specific actions: the constitution of a being in its very place of becoming. Emancipation is a Western aspiration, not just a Latin American one. It resembles the texture of language (and is expressed in speech): it is marked equally by universalism and by specificity, by idealist aspirations and by material resistance. Yet unlike language, emancipation is mostly a will, a desire. In this sense, *freedom* – the guiding principle of enlightened modernity – makes its appearance in Latin America, but only in its practical guise: as emancipation, a fact that signals the existence of significant cultural differences, insofar as freedom can be acheived. *Freedom* is a fact, whereas *emancipation* can only be stated and desired.

In Latin America – this new territory of a perpetual *will-be*, this indeterminate space of problematic identities – nation-building and cultural development have always been discontinuous processes. Shaped by a foundational impulse, continuously reinstituting a beginning, these processes disregard and efface Latin America's anteriority in the process of a recurring "discovery," obliterating and invalidating its breakthroughs and achievements. The founding event in our national imagination, the event that always takes us back to the "origin," requires the conquest of an appropriate place for the country's freedom to function. This conquest is the "condition of possibility" it needs to realize our subjunctive being, the utterance that, always to come, shapes our identity. This "state-to-come," this "not yet," this "postponed today" implies that Latin America's political and cultural discourses are inextricable from discourses about identity and freedom.

During the twentieth century, emancipation emerged as a modernizing impulse embodied in a series of political, social, cultural, and economic projects. However, this modernizing and forward-looking impulse was linked to the same questions and cultural uncertainties about identity, the authenticity of our development and representations, and the adaptation of norms and institutions to our particular circumstances.

a devouring and adaptive territory

Venezuela is a limit, a port, an entryway, and a thoroughfare. Its status as a port and a border has marked the country: it has given rise to an outward-looking nation that welcomes and forgets, a nation forged of a condition of transition. Its status as a port is compounded by a territory and a natural landscape that absorb and resist all abstract or rational constructions and have, symbolically, imposed their particular form of generation and growth upon the nation.

This territory never becomes a mere site for construction, a mere substratum on which to build; on the contrary, it shapes and marks structures, adapting them to its patterns, to its needs, throwing established structures out of order and restructuring all projects and ideals. Venezuela's territory is one of the nation's fundamental elements, not only in that the space contains the nation and all its processes, but because it is always more than just a contained place, a site.

Leoncio Martínez described the Venezuelan territory in 1912: "Our land, abundantly endowed with the luxuries of a tropical sun, sets before our eyes its uncultivated models, landscapes of flourishing verdure, surprising decorations for retinas unaccustomed, in the hazy Nordic mists, to such extravagances of light."[4] Venezuela's territorial conditions impose themselves categorically, shaping all institutions and all norms. They not only represent symbolic referents or moments of recognition; they also assert their processes and modes of being. This "excessive territory" marks our actions and gives rise to a history that, like life itself, is produced in an ongoing process of generation and degeneration, substitutions and new beginnings, leaving no room for permanence or continuity, and never leading to cultural, intellectual, and institutional culminations.

Transit and substitution, a certain "nomadic" condition – in both the cultural and the political realms – outweigh any desire to settle, any attempts to construct and *establish*. The Venezuelan nation remains open to the possibility of abandoning itself and becoming an Other; its existential impulse is to collect whatever comes from outside its realm, to appropriate those forms and ideas that it finds, and to make them its own.

The port status of Venezuelan culture is emphasized by the country's "excessive territory," which leaves an imprint on its projects and aspirations, becoming something of an expansive storehouse for belonging. Identity and legitimation tend toward those realms in which recognition happens *from* and *in* the body, materiality, and place, rendering all ideal conditions provisional and easily replaceable. This is why Venezuelan culture is characterized by immediacy, by images and signifiers, by presences and places rather by what takes place in it. It is a culture of forgetting and change, of substitutions, replacements, and relocations.

This devouring and adaptive territory elicits from its inhabitants the notion that groups and individuals function and recognize themselves in their practices and actions, in their modes of perception and interaction – this is the basis for all discussions about "identity." This "identity" – marked by the desire *to be* – in still *not* being, embeds itself in the feeling of symbolic and telluric belonging in the unfinished process of nation-building. Identity and nationality collapse into one another and become one by means of various cultural mechanisms, both artistic and political, that relate positively to the territory's forms. These cultural mechanisms are, moreover, the only means of articulating and relating experiences as well as the desire for being; they are the only means of establishing a formal system of signification that can work the territory's unending attempts at reinauguration into a cohesive story.

Venezuela is a port, an open and welcoming space, and its identity is linked to that essential openness that continually makes it lean away from itself, that allows it to incorporate new processes and discourses. The nation's transitory nature and ability to forget are by no means deficiencies – they are, rather, precisely what gives rise to that being that is never anything more than its own potential and possibility.

the modernizing impulse

Guided by the principle and the horizon of emancipation, Venezuelan *modernity* in the twentieth century may be understood as a drive toward *modernization*. Implicit here is the idea that any type of freedom is determined by a nation's ability to achieve a level of cultural and sociopolitical development that allows it to establish living conditions that are more equitable and less out of keeping with the times. *Modernity* thus becomes *modernization* under the imperative of a technical rationale that holds a vague promise of that much-longed-for emancipation, through submission to international standards. This is a "technical vision," economically based and focused on the future: the need for emancipation that devotes itself to adjusting appearances and infrastructures—assuming, based on the national myth of an overwhelming territory, that forms (presences) carry and impose their contents (meanings). The agenda of Caracas's urban planner Maurice E. H. Rotival clearly shows the impetus behind this modernizing impulse. He wrote in 1939: "The people have a profoundly developed urban sensibility, and recognize that the first vertebra of the complex system to reconfigure the city is the place where tomorrow's history will be written, where the song of the 'urbs' will be heard."[5] Like Venezuela's so-called Rotival Plan, this modernizing impulse is executed and implemented in projects that are, for the most part, utopian and authoritarian.

Modernization in the sociopolitical sphere (where it continuously fails) is faced with the difficulty of consolidating and maintaining a democratic republic, and with the persistent breakdown of institutional structures for which development—meaning progress and continuity—seems impossible. In the cultural realm, on the other hand, particularly in the visual arts and in the field of urban development, one encounters building and tangible achievement, solid ground and shelter: the modernizing impulse is fully realized and embodied in images and in the infrastructures that make habitation possible.

Most likely due to Venezuela's transitory condition, this modernizing impulse—particularly after the 1950s—crystallized in the nation's self-proclaimed appropriation of the latest European and North American discourses, in a clear attempt to establish a "contemporary" context. But in the ports, merchandise moves on and is forgotten. Accordingly, modernization was carried out in the framework of pure presences and always provisionally; it took place in images and infrastructures, as scenery and representation.

emancipation, landscape, and race

Alfredo Boulton clearly revealed Venezuela's originary drives through his efforts to "figure" the nation—that is, to provide a singular, conceptual image of it—and to render an account of its foundation. He did this after photographing Venezuela's territory extensively, giving form to its characteristics and to the elements that shaped it. Boulton "figures" Venezuela by concretizing it in two ways: first he registers, organizes, evaluates, and delimits the iconography of the heroes of independence, and later he elaborates a history of Venezuelan art in and through painting, concluding that the realm of images is where emancipation—understood as a universalizing process—becomes effective and possible. He gives faces to the heroes of independence (emblems of emancipation), granting them reality as humans and physical bodies, as living beings. In his examination of the history of paintings (emblems of images), he finds a way of redefining the country's dimensions, a space in which the nation becomes presence, authentic experience, in which its desire for identity and belonging seem to find solid footing. The "new continent," the territory of the *will-be*, once again calls out with urgency via this gesture that gives faces and bodies to discourse. It discerns independence not through its ideas but through its actors, and definitively establishes the "image" as the field, and the "medium" as charged with the task of inscribing Latin Americans into meaning, of exploring and exploding content.

In the twentieth century—with its driven modernizing impulse—the problem of emancipation was played out in two stages. The first, focused upon territory, was geared toward recognizing and making space for differences, for the variety of circumstances and particularities that characterize Latin Americans; the second, more formal and ideological stage critiqued and dialectically explored, negated, and affirmed the manifestations of culture in which recognition was achieved.

The first stage and its agenda were outlined by Martínez in his 1912 speech to the newly inaugurated Círculo de Bellas Artes. In his words, with their distinctly romantic tone, Martínez gives both a definition of art ("seeing and transmuting, feeling more deeply than people generally feel, appreciating the soul's moments in our gestures and the soul of the landscape in the environment") and an ideal course of action (to "make art that is our own genuine art, Venezuelan art, availing ourselves of the simple, beloved elements around us, without taking recourse in exotic practices that do not fit our subjects and our aims").[6] *Art* is understood as expression—not the expression of a subjectivity that creates and belongs to the world, but of an observant and permeable being who, closely linked to the landscape and to his "race," can recognize both the characteristic "soul" of the world and, in it, the forces and peculiarities that define him. The ideal course of action—the future of art and its expression—is, as Martínez puts it, the "fatherland": the affective and filial nation, both sensed and recognized, the nation as lived experience.

The modernizing impulse seeks this emancipation through an organic adherence to those universal discourses that define the West's imperatives. The modernizing impulse begins with and continues via a search that will allow it to establish its own particularities and determine its own traits, to contain and comprehend itself. In this sense, it tries to dismantle its condition of "exception," offering representations and scenery that correspond to the problematic identity it questions and debates.

During this first stage, work and reflection are focused on two areas. The first is the territory, subsumed in and embodied through the landscape, or understood as a "human construct," as the refuge of man and society. The second consists of the territory's inhabitants, as figured within the framework of "the race" and understood through the lens of *mestizaje*, or racial mixing. Both of these factors are constructed as "origins," and are made into the depositories and sources of essential statements that can substantiate and contain the nation, which may function as both substratum and framework. Their essential nature is played out in the realm of identity, in those differences that would legitimate the discovered "margin" of the modern Western world as a mode of signification in its own right, and not just as an "excepted" continent.

The national subject conceives itself, self-reflectively, by appropriating the banner of *mestizaje*, conditioned by the imperative of "race" with its rigid, rational (indeed, arithmetical) structure of mixes and percentages, additions and subtractions. On the other hand, the landscape domesticates the territory. The territory becomes recognizable in the landscape and is rid of its excess;

the subject itself becomes classifiable as a *mestizo*. In both cases, the attempt to recognize territory and people somehow betrays their subjunctive "soul," their continuing effort to *be*, their state of perpetually being their own project, the longing that, since the "discovery" of the Americas, has marked Latin Americans' appearance in and encounter with the world.

The landscape abandons its ties to the territory and asserts itself wherever it is idealized, while man is placed within the framework of a vague and ever-changing race that establishes the notion of origin as a beginning rather than as a determining factor. These mechanisms are paradoxical since, in both, recognition is informed by and formulated through the notion of *having-been* that negates what *is*. The difference that makes seeing and understanding oneself possible is produced in the displacement from existential, inhabited spaces to ideally conceived spaces, recaptured as forms of desire. Both ways of understanding oneself thus reinscribe the initial gesture of the "discovery"—and now appropriate that discovery as their own.

How does the need for emancipation work at this initial stage of recognition? What are the conditions of possibility that are shaped or affirmed at this point? Venezuela gains access to a simulacrum of emancipation in the space of its symbolic and representational practices, both by establishing an idealized landscape and by affirming a mixed, or "impure" race. It emancipates itself from the only thing that might radically define and differentiate it: its own subjunctive condition, its being always a possibility-of-being. By eradicating its excessive, generous, and imposing territory, and by creating the figure of a "race" for itself, Venezuela negates and (once again) conceals its own putative openness. This is a purely ideological emancipation—that is, both its problems (race, territory) and their solution follow a logic that, derived solely from ideas, fails to acknowledge the experiential conditions that shaped its emancipation.

alternating currents

This initial emancipation through recognition is predicated on the landscape and the images that recover Venezuelans' condition as *criollos* and *mestizos*. The notion of such an emancipation has been countered since the 1950s by a modernizing impulse that proceeds even while neglecting specific differences—making a space for itself in the contemporary Western world, appropriating this space and asserting itself in it. In the realm of the visual arts, the two first stages—widely acknowledged as the true beginning of Venezuelan modernism—were embodied in two opposing tendencies, or two movements, represented by the group known as Los Disidentes on one hand and by the Sardio and El Techo de la Ballena groups on the other. The path taken by Los Disidentes appealed to formalism and universality, taking a fully "enlightened," aggressive, and avant-garde stance. Sardio and El Techo de la Ballena, by contrast, situated themselves in the shadows of that formal luminosity, in its unfinished spaces, in its needs and demands: in those places that remained unclaimed.

Los Disidentes abandoned the problems of territoriality and identity in the pursuit of a place in the history of Western art, with no provisos; this tendency toward "universality" allowed them to settle debts and doubts with respect to their own cultural development. They retraced the steps of the European avant-gardes in the name of experimentation and ideal liberty, claiming abstraction as their own space in which to work and grow. Like any experiment in the realm of reason, Los Disidentes' abstraction had the advantage of being crafted in the spaces of pure formalism. As Alejandro Otero points out, this formalism recaptures and transforms the elements that shape the country. Abstract art, he notes, can be "active and functional, because it desires to communicate with . . . the life of men, their daily realities and their customs, seeking to awaken the creative potential latent in every human being."[7]

Los Disidentes, together with the entire current of abstract art in Venezuela—and in particular kinetic art—joined the ranks of architecture with monumental works that synthesized the two realms in which the modernizing impulse operated: images and the infrastructures that allow for habitation.

Sardio and El Techo de la Ballena, on the other hand, appealed to the universality of content and meaning (or meanings), and opposed the intellectual notion of a "universality of forms." The works and aims of both movements embodied larger (sometimes vindictive) agendas whose structure was politically based. They tried to construct their world on the basis of radical difference, and to transform Venezuela's "exception" into an irreconcilable Otherness, increasing and magnifying debts and doubts and making them the starting points of a "revolutionary" struggle. They challenged Venezuela's institutions and achievements, its present and its future—declaring, "Our culture seems deprived of ideas and problems, as if we still lived in an imperturbably blissful Arcadia. We must bring a more dramatic awareness of man and reality to the fore."[8] Along the same lines, Adriano Gonzáles León, a member of El Techo de la Ballena, states in 1964 that the group "has devoted itself to an activity more mindful of man: even if it takes place in the midst of capitalism or underdevelopment, this activity represents an open rejection and a declaration of the need for change."[9]

Both factions conceived of emancipation as negation and universalization. In the case of Los Disidentes, their work in the space of forms, in the realm of purity and ideas, and their radically autonomous conception of the work of art and of the aesthetic task emancipated them from the apparent exclusion inflicted by the West. However, their position neglected fundamental aspects of their particular context and its demands, which they failed to consider. Because of its relation to architecture and its monumental nature, abstract art became the ornament of established power structures and gave them its symbolic support. Marta Traba, in her 1974 essay "Finale: Allegro con Fuoco," refers to Venezuelan kinetic art as "an official art," so associated with bourgeois values and ambitions that it lost all purpose. "The price it paid for abandoning the artistic process," she writes, "was to become clearly mediocre and decidedly decorative."[10]

In the case of Sardio and El Techo de la Ballena, which were consolidating an identity understood as an Other, emancipation was achieved through a revolutionary attempt to re-create Venezuela's cultural and theoretical constellation, denying its foundations and its legacy in the interest of an ideological universality that tried to dismantle its own context by transcending itself.

The controversy between Miguel Otero Silva and Alejandro Otero provides a sense of the tone of these contrasting and complementary courses of action. Both result from a foundational heterogeneity that does not understand itself fully, and that pretends to become universal, to "purify" itself aesthetically, to become a totality in and of itself, thus negating the "Otherness" and the "not-yet" that also define it.

The paths traveled by the visual image in twentieth-century Venezuela omit and conceal – and thus reaffirm – the subjunctive and territorial nature of its status as a port. This is why Venezuela's modernity has been marked by a discontinuous succession of emancipations and reinaugurations in both the visual arts and the rest of the cultural and political realms. Every stage in the nation's cultural development has, in its own way, attempted to provide the necessary "conditions of possibility" for the nation to exercise its freedom and to act authentically. Perhaps it has been regularly forgotten that the power of the port and the border lies precisely – as the historian Luís Castro Leiva once said – in the subjunctive quality that marks Venezuela's cultural and political discourse, which allows Venezuelans to reflect on their fundamental condition as "orphans," and to think of the absence of an "origin" not as a lack or deficiency, but as a space of options and possibilities.

Venezuela did not understand or consider the weave and texture of its modernism, nor of modernism's manner of being and existing. The country and its people are still in the process of becoming something neither given nor possessed – something, therefore, that it is up to Venezuelans to fulfill.

Translated by Catalina Ocampo

notes to the text

1. Rómulo Gallegos, "Las tierras de Dios" ("God's Lands"), lecture delivered at the Nicholas Roerich Museum in New York City on September 1, 1931. In *Rómulo Gallegos: Una posición ante la vida* (Caracas: Centauro77, 1977), pp. 112 - 44. This text is included in the present volume, pp. 103 - 7.
2. See Eduardo Subirats, *El continente vacío* (Madrid: Grupo Anaya Editores, 1994), pp. 203 - 79.
3. J. R. Guillent Pérez, "Bolívar, nosotros y hoy" ("Bolívar, Ourselves, and Today"), *Los Disidentes* 1 (Paris), March 1950. The article is included in the present volume, pp. 172 - 77.
4. Leoncio Martínez, "Ideas y propósitos: Palabras en la instalación del Círculo de Bellas Artes" ("Ideas and Aims: Some Words on the Establishment of the Círculo de Bellas Artes"), *El Universal* (Caracas), September 4, 1912. The speech is included in the present volume, pp. 94 - 96.
5. Maurice E. H. Rotival, "Caracas marcha hacia adelante," in *Carlos Raúl Villanueva: Caracas en tres tiempos* (Caracas: Comisión de Asuntos Culturales del Cuatricentenario de Caracas, 1966), pp. 171 - 82.
6. Martínez, "Ideas y propósitos" ("Ideas and Aims").
7. Alejandro Otero, response to Miguel Otero Silva, in *El Nacional*, April 9, 1957. This text is included in the present volume, p. 212.
8. "Testimonio" ("Testimonial"), *Sardio* 1 (Caracas), May - June 1958. This text is included in the present volume, pp. 254-56.
9. Adriano González León, "Por qué la Ballena?" ("Why the Whale?"), *Rayado sobre el techo,* no. 3 (Caracas), 1964. The essay is included in the present volume, pp. 267 - 70.
10. Marta Traba, "Finale: Allegro con Fuoco," in *Mirar en Caracas* (Caracas: Monte Ávila, 1974). The text is included in the present volume, pp. 278 - 84.

making a space for modernism: criticism as landscape, and the example of alfredo boulton

rafael castillo zapata

The representation of territory is by no means limited to its most predictable artistic or aesthetic manifestations—that is, as *landscape*. It is a cultural operation that comprises many modes and mechanisms: geographic, cartographic, literary, photographic, historical, and critical. Such mechanisms played an important role in the process of recognition and affirmation of a range of Latin American national identities, beginning in the early nineteenth century. The combined products of these practices of territorial representation constitute a complex legacy of "figurations" that made up the corpora—both spatial and human—of Latin American republics. Not only did these products define the conditions of organization, exploitation, and enjoyment of real spaces and their occupants, they also foreshadowed future possibilities for those spaces and occupants, through interpolations of what was to come: in the cultural imaginary, the modern future.

There is a distinctly performative power in this double effect of topical description and utopian projection of territory. It is as if, when the empty spaces in a place still alien to civilizing transformations are illustrated, the premonitory specter of that coming transformation is evoked. This concept is expressed metaphorically and utilized politically in the work of two Cuban poets and thinkers: José Lezama Lima[1] and Cintio Vitier.[2] In *La exprésion americana* (*The American Expression*; 1957), Lezama Lima develops an explicative model of Latin American culture, using as his starting point the notion of landscape as an *operación civilizadora*, or "civilizing action." Vitier, by contrast, proposes an opposition between the *land* as a devouring force and the *landscape* as a collective adventure of spiritual domination over that hungry menace. Indeed, for Vitier, land without landscape is purely telluric and savage, while landscape is nothing less than a spiritual construction that subjugates and organizes the land, which otherwise lacks both *cosmos* (order) and *telos* (purpose).

The history of visual representations of territory in Latin America, and particularly in Venezuela, suggests that the need to create landscape is tantamount to a need to dominate that which distances us from an ideal of progress—an ideal that Latin Americans have pursued since the colonial era. But in that same history landscape may also function as a sort of semiotic operation—encompassing literature, cartography, photography, and painting within a single set of signifying operations—that produces the entity *place*, and permits the comprehension, control, and use of a territorial or human space that is both rich and complex.

Of the many semiotic operations leading to this "production of place," art history and art criticism are of particular salience. They function metacartographically, as narrations of landscape-oriented operations (in both painting and photography) and as landscape-oriented operations in and of themselves, consciously imposing an order on a variety of types of work. Octavio Paz proposes a notion of criticism as an invented intellectual space in which works of art are systematically related.[3] In the telluric territory of art, historiography and criticism have constructed their own kind of landscape for this space: a reasoned order of connections.

The historian, art critic, and photographer Alfredo Boulton laid the groundwork for much of today's understanding of Venezuelan art, and provides a pertinent point of departure for such considerations. Boulton's work, and his example as a figure in the history of Venezuelan modernist thinking, prompt a consideration of historiography and criticism as fundamental components of the semiotic operation of the production of place.

Over the course of Latin America's cultural history, the region cultivated a distinct idea of landscape that derived from two important factors. First there were the specific historical conditions of the Spanish colonies: their prolonged dependent development and the accelerated process of independence, which took place via a series of martial actions that for most countries on the continent transpired during the course of the nineteenth century. Second, the landscape itself served as the agent of recognition and affirmation of a cultural identity that many Latin American nations sought to hone once they were liberated. Both of these processes evolved throughout the nineteenth and twentieth centuries and were reflected in all the actions and products that were characteristic of the region even while it was still in a formative state, its societies in conflict, permeated with extremely diverse social, racial, economic, political, linguistic, and aesthetic currents.

An examination of the geographic and cartographic legacy of colonial times reveals that the republic's early inhabitants were largely ignorant of their territorial surroundings—an important symptom of the Spanish colonies' circumstances. In order to learn about this territory, the republicans organized projects of exploration and description. Thus the understanding of landscape was, from the very beginning of Latin America's republican cultural history, more anthropological and political than aesthetic. The reason for this tendency becomes apparent if we accept the idea of landscape as an operation related to the production of place, as a mechanism for quantitative and qualitative ordering involving a variety of processes: recognition, documentation, description, and representation of territory. The first people to be engaged with the landscape in the region were the military engineers who explored and studied national territories with a view to political and military dominance. These were the topographers and surveyors who measured the dimensions of a space that was often inhospitable and inaccessible; their goal was to conceptualize it in order to make it "workable," to convert it into a space where the operations of a "civilizing action" might take place. Latin America's first "landscapists," then, were geographers and cartographers who reworked colonial maps, submitting them to empirical corroboration by journeying to the territories in question in order to represent them and denominate them anew.

So the two fundamental actions of the semiotic operation we call *landscape*—contemplation and journey—were initially determined by political motives of republican states undergoing a process of formation and consolidation. And the Latin American understanding of landscape generally continued in this vein; the aesthetic experience of territory—which might offer a more "disinterested" contemplation—would be relegated to the background in the face of the urgent demand for territorial precision of a pragmatic nature. This is not to say that the most interesting documents of territorial image did not also constitute aesthetically valuable depictions; in fact, in some of these (such as the *Geografía* [Geography] published by the Italian-Venezuelan Agustín Codazzi[4] in 1841) technical language and sublime discourses are wonderfully combined in pictorial descriptions of the lands being traversed. In such cases landscape proves to be a semiotic operation that fulfills both political and poetic exigencies.

The concept of landscape as an operation of territorial control was not only set forth in geographic and cartographic texts; it was also seen in travel books and other literature, some of which were inherited from colonial times and "corrected" by republican revisionists. This was the case, for example, with Juan Manuel Cajigal's[5] 1833 re-readings of some sections of Alexander von Humboldt's *Viaje a las regiones equinocciales del nuevo continente* (Voyage to the equinoctial regions of the new continent; 1814);[6] and on a broader level with history texts, early novelistic sketches, poetry, and drama.

Also expedient in the mechanism of landscape and the production of place were the *cuadros de costumbres* ("portraits of local customs"), a popular narrative form inherited from Spain, which tended to take on political overtones in the young American republics. As their name suggests (*cuadro* meaning painting or tableau), the *cuadros de costumbres* were strongly linked with pictorial and theatrical practices; they were, in a sense, attempts to verbalize processes from the realm of visual representation, and also borrowed conventions of segmentation and exposition normally associated with theatrical representation. At the same time, in the tradition of *costumbrismo*, they often wove a moralizing discourse around a particular society's habits and ways of developing. The *cuadro de costumbres* thus belongs in several realms: that of fictional discourse (close to narrative and theater), that of ethical discourse (close to social critique and morality), and that of mimetic discourse (in line with visual representations).

These *cuadros de costumbres*, common throughout the nineteenth century in Latin America, offered ironic depictions of fledgling republican societies, underlining (sometimes with comic strokes) the negative elements impeding those societies' economic, social, and cultural development. In this sense, these narratives provided another form of landscape, in that they imposed an organization onto social territory, orienting it toward the achievement of a series of modernizing benefits. The *cuadros de costumbres* thus also constituted productions of place: they set the stage for the possibility of a modernizing experience that did not yet have a position in these "backward," peripheral societies, except as a contrast to what existed. The *cuadros de costumbres* invoked the modern by demonstrating, with exaggerated features, a situation in dire need of modification—a situation for which modernism offered an alternative. This was a genre, then, that truly belonged to Latin American culture; its appearance and proliferation at this juncture was, it might be said, a response to a generalized need to discipline those telluric forces that were resistant to processes of modernization.

As such discursive operations were being produced in geographic, cartographic, and literary texts, the Latin American territory was also being developed in the cultural imaginary through pictorial practices, in which the idea of landscape was further defined and shaped. In the case of Venezuela in particular, it is symptomatic of the nation's specific cultural context that the visual arts developed, beginning in the second half of the nineteenth century, with such an emphasis on representations of battle scenes; the depiction of nature (or any non-military theme) was subordinated to the commemoration of the epic conflicts and heroic deeds that brought about independence. The focus of Venezuela's painting had been predominantly religious during the colonial era; in the republican period it now turned toward the representation of the foundational legacy of the nation. Venezuela's landscape—those vast natural settings and vistas—provided the backdrop against which the figures of heroic warriors were inscribed, the space for a representation of the military foundations of the republic.

The landscape, as depicted in the nation's early pictorial expressions, thus constituted a mechanism of representation that served to organize and fix an image of Latin America's past—an image that the republican elite urgently needed in order to legitimate an institutional order. It is important to take this into account in order to understand the contradictions in the process of modernization in Latin America (and in Venezuela specifically). Telluric attitudes that abide to this day were shaped by the ferocity of battles and by the fecundity of the fields where those battles took place. It became clear that the civilizing and disciplining powers of landscape operations were in the service of the nation's authoritarian organizing forces. This might be interpreted as a symptom of the persistent imaginary of the heroic caudillo along a horizon of perspectives and expectations of our modern political landscape.

Through all of these discursive modalities—from maps and geographical descriptions to landscapes of the battlefield, written histories, and *cuadros de costumbres*—there was an ideological constant: the political and ethical nature of territorial representation. It was not until the appearance of the Círculo de Bellas Artes in Caracas in 1912 that a new kind of landscape painting, free of didactic connotations, began to be seen. At the same time, the works of the so-called Escuela de Caracas—a group that included many plein air painters who produced a varied and abundant range of landscapes (principally of the Caracas Valley)—continued to function as mechanisms of the production of place. Through these paintings, the possible existence of an "experiential modernity" was projected in a performative mode. It is possible to recognize—in their sublime representations of the palpable sensuality of the mountainous Caracas setting, for example—the empty space opened by a strongly telluric territoriality as a site for the modernity soon to come, projected as a utopian impulse and compulsion. The cataloguing of territory, the sublimation of nature to aesthetics were declarations of the implicit will toward a future technical domination of nature—as if the exuberance of the natural setting might forcibly invoke the implementation of modernizing processes that would exploit the land's topographical richness.

This powerful drive toward the future is manifest in the gamut of discursive forms mentioned here. These are the cultural "texts" that organized the natural and human territories of Venezuela, functioning as landscape mechanisms that set the stage for the possibility of modernity, making promises about the future – a future that did not yet have a place in the materiality of practical experiences of territory. In the geographic and cartographic realms, this performative power is more literal, because of the virtual nature of their diagrammatical design. Cartography, as some specialists recognize, is both a description and a construction of territory: this production of place entails a projection of spatial virtualities. In the case of Latin American cartographies of the nineteenth century these projections were strongly inflected with notions of modernization: maps and geographic descriptions abound with notions of a virtual modernity that may be inferred in industrial and urban *voids*; the telluric persistence of the territory offered itself up as the ideal medium through which to exercise a will toward modernizing appropriation and domestication. These maps register not just the existing territory, but also the possible spaces that *might* exist in that territory, most often imagined as modern spaces. The *cuadros de costumbres* likewise clearly implemented this performative power, by hyperbolically illustrating the defects of the existing social territory in order to expose the need for modern, positive antidotes to those defects.

All these discursive forms, all these semiotic operations involved in the production of place functioned as foundational national discourses, ordering the national territory and presenting it anew under the conditions of a modern landscape that, although it did not yet exist, was urgently desired.

Photography also played an important role in the processes of recognition, comprehension, and subjugation of Venezuela's national territory in the nineteenth century. Numbers of traveling photographers traversed the nation, working to construct a "map" of images that might function with the same performative force that other discursive practices were exerting. Their photographs were testimonies of journeys through a sparsely populated, miserably poor national territory, with rural and sometimes atavistic customs; the images served as fodder for the pages of magazines and illustrated journals, often accompanied by a positivist discourse invoking the need to achieve modernity – a process that seemed to be endlessly postponed. There was also, of course, abundant documentation of timid advances in modernization as embodied in material projects: the construction of a hydroelectric dam, or the laying of track for a railway. But the bulk of these photographs provide a rude vision of the deficiencies of Venezuela's precarious modernization, and had an expressly provocative intent: to mobilize the enterprising conscience of the country's citizens.

Venezuelan photography in the nineteenth century thus served a largely documentary function; its power to "create" landscape lay partly in its ability to order and make practicable the spaces where modernity should take place. In the twentieth century, as photography grew to be more independent of its documentary function, the medium continued to play an important role in the "creation" of the Venezuelan landscape by contributing to the figurative ordering of the nation's human and geographic spaces.

Landscape is plainly a critical element in the production of place. Historiography and art criticism, too, serve as mechanisms in this process, in terms of ordering cultural territory – in particular the territory of artistic practice. In the history of

Venezuela, historiography and art criticism have functioned as "territorial cartographies" that outline the space for virtual experimentation with modernity, and that today provide a reading of the legacy of the nation's visual art practices. Historians and art critics charted a critical landscape of Venezuela's desire for modernity and of the country's effective (if not always efficient) processes of modernization.

It is perhaps no coincidence that our first attempt at an art-historical text was the work of a military man. Ramón de la Plaza, author of *Ensayos sobre el arte en Venezuela* (Essays on art in Venezuela; 1883), was a musician, painter, and historian who reached the rank of general in the Guerra Federal (1859–64), Venezuela's final and most devastating civil war. Working alongside General Antonio Guzmán Blanco, who came to power in 1870, de la Plaza was made the director of the Instituto Nacional de Bellas Artes, which opened in 1877. The publication date of de la Plaza's book is symptomatic of political events relating to the symbolic organization of nationality—a central focus of Guzmán Blanco's autocratic government. The year 1883 marked the hundredth anniversary of the birth of Simón Bolívar, and a series of commemorative endeavors were undertaken in celebration of the date—including the publication of de la Plaza's *Ensayos*, a collection of writings about the history of music and painting in Venezuela. A diplomat and congressman as well as soldier and artist, de la Plaza is a clear example of the particularities of Venezuela's cultural landscape during the nineteenth century: a multitude of civic, military, political, and artistic projects all embodied in one man. His several roles demonstrate the demand that the country's narrowly limited erudite elite placed on its members to engage simultaneously in a variety of activities in the service of the society they led.

The early twentieth century brought little change on this front. The lengthy period of Juan Vicente Gómez's dictatorship, from 1908 to 1935, did not contribute much to the development of the disciplines of historiography and criticism. There were, however, some important cultural phenomena linked to the evolution of painting that took place in this era. The creation of the Círculo de Bellas Artes in 1912 was a central event for the future of Venezuelan painting. Invoking the rebellious spirit of the Impressionists, this group opened the possibility for an artistic practice freed from the shackles of academicism, which since the nineteenth century had been upholding (and mandating) the tradition of historical or mythological subject matter. The Círculo also promoted the development of plein air painting, giving rise to a new group of landscape-oriented painters. In 1928, Marcos Castillo's teachings at the Escuela Nacional de Artes Plásticas helped to form a new generation of painters who were better prepared and better informed about new trends and techniques taking place in the global art world.

During this period—with a particular surge in 1912—painting in Venezuela increased in complexity and refinement, and the country's modern art began to take off. Art history and criticism did not follow the same trajectory. José Nucete Sardi's 1940 *Notas sobre la pintura y la escultura en Venezuela* (Notes on painting and sculpture in Venezuela), the various essays published over the course of the 1940s and '50s by the eminent historian Mariano Picón Salas, and Enrique Planchart's 1956 book *La pintura en Venezuela* (Painting in

Venezuela) all illustrate that historiography and art criticism were still at an incipient stage. Nonetheless, these contributions to the discourse have value as "landscape" in that they contributed much to setting the stage, creating the space for organized comprehension of the history of visual practices in Venezuela.

Octavio Paz has said that criticism is nothing more than the creation of an intellectual space in which works can develop mutual relationships and resonate within the combinations they form.[7] The attempts to map the territory of Venezuelan visual arts during the first half of the twentieth century were limited in this capacity, largely because they lacked the sustenance of serious research, and did not manage to successfully integrate the process of artistic production with the more general processes of our historical evolution. There were, furthermore, few or no efforts toward integration with similar experiences in other places on the continent.

Alfredo Boulton's historiographic project constitutes a more systematic and consistent attempt to approach an "organic" critical landscape of Venezuela's visual arts. Boulton was probably the most influential historian of modern art in Venezuela, beginning with the publication, between 1964 and 1972, of his three-volume *Historia de la pintura en Venezuela* (History of painting in Venezuela). Without any academic specialization, Boulton was an interesting heir to de la Plaza and other erudite figures of nineteenth-century Venezuela who performed a number of social functions with only the scant training provided by very general knowledge of various related disciplines.

Boulton began to take photographs at a young age, upon his return to Venezuela in 1928 after his studies in Europe. In addition to a few surrealist experiments and a series of portraits of Venezuelan personalities made in the 1940s, his most important photographic contribution consisted of his images of the national territory: villages and cities in the provinces, the human geography of the country in all its regional and physiognomic diversity. As such, he meticulously followed in the footsteps of the great nineteenth-century traveling photographers, close as they were to the *costumbristas* in their attempts to catalogue the customs and particularities of national life in order to contribute to its betterment and modern extension. Having crossed the country a number of times, Boulton converted Venezuela's geographic and human space into landscape—that is, into an entity that could be culturally assimilated into the patrimonial imagery of nationality.

Boulton worked as a landscape artist in two senses: he depicted rural and urban settings with a documentary and historical intention, and he catalogued them from an emotional, sentient perspective, as a critical witness to the conflicts of Venezuela's still-unrealized modernization and as an idealistic contemplator of the exuberance of its natural settings, its cities and towns, of their inhabitants and their heroic dramas. In all these spheres of the national space, Boulton, as a photographer, functioned simultaneously as a geographer, a cartographer, a sociologist, and a historian. As he himself declared, it was through his observation of the national territory that he arrived at an understanding of the history of the people of Venezuela. He was an enthusiastic traveler—traversing the ruins of forgotten settlements, abandoned Spanish forts, desolate battlefields—and during his journeys he learned to reconstitute history through its empty spaces, even while projecting images of modernization onto those voids.

Boulton's geographic experience and "landscapist" sensibility led him directly to a study of history. He was an itinerant photographer whose eye and spirit—both sensitized to the spaces he was traversing—provoked an interest in his country's past. And so he became an excavator of archives: his systematic perusal (and plundering) of them provided him with the building blocks for the first volume of his *Historia de la pintura en Venezuela*, on the origins of Venezuelan painting and its development during the colonial period.

The richness of the landscape-oriented contributions in this book would diminish in the later volumes of his study, as Boulton began to approach the era and space from which he spoke—as if vicinity and velocity, as dynamics in more recent art, were bewildering to him and did not allow him to find the stability he needed to be able to provide an order for them. His stimulating documentary and critical acumen declined in such a way that the foundations of his investigations began to lose the richness of their unstudied, unexplored quality. Nevertheless, the second volume of the series, dedicated to the nationalist period in Venezuelan visual arts, is an exemplary and important text. The third volume, on the contemporary period, illustrates a radical shift in Boulton's documentary and discursive strategy. A longtime and consistent defender of the direct links and parallels between the development of a society and the development of its arts—particularly in relation to the visual arts practices that came into being in Venezuela during the second half of the twentieth century—Boulton was now at a loss to establish correlations that might explain these connections. He took recourse in a sort of monographic method, offering a panorama of individual painters rather than a comprehensive view of the full landscape of Venezuelan painting in the twentieth century.

Boulton was the first to recognize his own limitations. In this sense, his critique is also a critique of art criticism itself. When he became aware of the exigencies imposed on critical activity by the complexity of modern art, in terms of theoretical knowledge of aesthetics and critical methodology, and acknowledged his own insufficiencies in relation to them, he duly made space for the next critic—more engaged or more specialized—to appear on the scene. Boulton made a landscape out of his own landscape-oriented function, illustrating, performatively, a critical possibility that he himself could not enact in the moment, but that he considered indispensable and urgently necessary. Here—as with the *cuadros de costumbres,* or with aspects of Codazzi's *Geografía*—an unattained modernity is presaged in the very space of its absence, and when that space is delimited modernity is also incited in the act, as a spectral operation of calling into existence what should or must exist.

The historiography and art criticism for which we are indebted to Boulton constitute a fundamental legacy of Venezuela's cultural tradition. His contributions and the example he provided with his commitment to an organic operation of territorial comprehension as manifest through Venezuelan painting have allowed new historiographic and critical claims to be staked. The last three decades of the twentieth century brought the accelerated development of new theoretical skills and an increase in information and internationally based contacts, all of which allowed for the exercise of more efficient criticism and historiography. More recently, Venezuela has witnessed the appearance of high-level academic institutions, and up-to-date and competitive agendas for museums and museum studies; these productive elements have contributed to the growth and consolidation of the nation's cultural landscape.

Still, Venezuela suffers an ongoing lack of any systematized professional art criticism, in large part due to the paucity of spaces that welcome confrontation and open exchange of information. In this sense, the country still has a need for political maneuvers (academic and governmental) geared toward the production of a more consistent and complex landscape reflecting the diverse range of contemporary artistic practices.

The example provided by Boulton continues to be central to this future task. New explorers of our cultural territory believe their work is urgently necessary in order to further his cartographic practice. Currently, many of these intrepid souls have taken up the challenge posed in that prophetic invocation and have embarked upon analytic operations that produce place – offering multiple types of landscapes within the space of Venezuelan art.

Translated by Jen Hofer

notes to the text

1. José Lezama Lima was the author of the novel *Paradiso* (Paradise; 1966), and of the collection of essays *La cantidad hechizada* (The enchanted quantity; 1970). He was also the editor of the journal *Orígenes*.
2. Cintio Vitier was a poet and essayist associated with the magazine *Orígenes*. His collections of poetry include *Víspera* (Vespers; 1953).
3. Octavio Paz, "Sobre la crítica" ("On Criticism"), in *Corriente alterna* (San Angel, Mexico: Siglo XXI, 1979), pp. 39–44; English translation in *Alternating Current* (New York: Arcade, 1990), pp. 35–45.
4. Agustín Codazzi was an Italian geographer, explorer, and soldier who came to Latin America and took part in the campaigns for independence, during which he met José Antonio Páez. In 1830, when Venezuela separated from Great Colombia under Páez's leadership, Codazzi was entrusted with the task of creating a complete map of the new nation, including concrete physical data and statistics.
5. Juan Manuel Cajigal was a man of science and the director of Venezuela's Academia Militar de Matemáticas, founded in 1831.
6. Humboldt's text was first published in France, under the title *Relation du voyage aux régions équinoxiales du nouveau continent*, in 1814.
7. Indeed, according to Octavio Paz, "Criticism is responsible for the creation of what we call a literature, which is not so much the sum of individual works as the system of relations between them: a field of affinities and oppositions." Paz, "On Criticism," p. 35.

carlos raúl villanueva: the synthesis with venezuela

maciá pintó

villanueva: the synthesis

Carlos Raúl Villanueva left us an enduring legacy, a deeply meaningful, transcendent œuvre that set the groundwork and played a key role in building and shaping Venezuela. In light of the great example he set as a citizen, his work may be seen as representative of the country's identity, imbuing a universal quality into something inherently local.

As a man, he set an example with a life's project consistent with his ideals, through his track record of professional rigor, and his lifelong commitment to both architecture and Venezuela. His work ethic, his sense of the public function of architecture, as well as the responsibility he evinced in the fields of urban planning, architecture, and the visual arts earned him a place among a generation of illustrious Venezuelans. His ideas, his writing, his work as an educator, his projects, and his buildings are all part of a coherent body of work in which Venezuela can recognize itself as a country.

Villanueva employed a practice intimately linked to the process of construction but always carried out according to the clearest ideas and motives; his indisputable achievements reveal the strength of his belief system and the wisdom of his vocation. His life and work are two inseparable aspects of his perpetual attempts at synthesis.

In his architecture, space is understood primarily as an interior that is, at the same time, exterior. The materiality of Villanueva's works arises from an "inner" space that infuses them with life – a faithful expression of his "adjectival" understanding of architecture and the representation of an essential substance modeled from within, rooted in man and his *being-in-the-world*. In his architecture, space is transformed along with its inhabitants, growing more complex in the ever-changing experience of everyday life.

This particular conception of space in Villanueva's work is characterized by life, shaped by measure, and animated by light and movement. In this sense, space is life expressed through thought and its realization. As measurement, it is also number and an expression of procedure and moderation. It is made both by and for the light of a particular climate and place, and unfolds as it moves in the continuum of experience.

By and large, synthesis in Villanueva's output has been understood as the integration of architecture and the visual arts, but we should also see it as an intrinsic part of both his working process and his work. In his projects, synthesis is an act of understanding as well as a working tool that becomes the foundation of the creative act. Understood as an activity of reason, synthesis is an expression of both sensitivity and thought. As a method, it occurs through action and the anticipation of a totality. It is part of his work's internal structure and expresses itself as a result; through language, synthesis achieves autonomy and asserts its existence as an independent value.

Space and synthesis are fundamental elements of Villanueva's work: space as the raw material of his œuvre and the greatest virtue of his architecture, and synthesis as the most faithful expression of his life, his most finely honed tool.

Villanueva's unwavering commitment to visual art was an essential element of both his personality and his work. In addition to his accomplishments as an architect of museums and exhibition spaces, he was an artist who created assemblages and collages, as well as an avid follower of the artistic movements of his age. He frequently promoted and organized exhibitions, constantly encouraged young people, and was a notable collector of works made by friends at the forefront of the artistic avant-garde. He also developed the notion of the "synthesis of the arts," both by participating in conferences and seminars and by implementing his ideas in powerful works of his own.

Villanueva's work extends beyond the boundaries of architecture. His "museographic" spaces broke free from museums to become public places, as happened with the Ciudad Universitaria – the "university city" – the main campus of Venezuela's Universidad Central. His own homes became intimate museums, inhabited with his artist friends, who were represented through their works. Likewise, his sketches, in which built spaces were redrawn to indicate the placement of artworks, provided a permanent and ever-changing mise-en-scène for art in architecture.

Over the course of this long and fruitful life process, certain events and connections underscore the essential elements of Villanueva's personal relationships with art, artists, and their work. In examining his life and career, the distances and differences as well as the synergies and synchronies between America and Europe become apparent. The trajectory of his ideas may be traced decade by decade, highlighting periods, dates, and moments that are particularly relevant to an interpretation of synthesis, following a vision that hopes to be both inclusive and "synthetic."

the precepts of synthesis

Villanueva came into the world at the dawn of the twentieth century in the Venezuelan consulate in London, and for nearly thirty years he lived and grew up in Europe. Venezuela, however, was always present in his home: his father and paternal grandfather were directly involved in the country's politics as public servants and members of the diplomatic corps, and both were historians and scholars of life in the Americas. The earliest phase of Villanueva's education during the 1910s and '20s took place in France and included some travels around Europe, particularly to Malaga, Spain. But it was Paris that left an indelible mark on his spirit and his sensibilities: for the rest of his life he maintained a connection to Paris, the city that set the stage and the standards for the artistic avant-garde until the 1950s.

Villanueva's French upbringing gave him an intellectual framework based on reason and passion, Cartesian logic and artistic sensitivity. Rationalism and the Beaux Arts provided solid foundations – deeply rooted in history and composition – that would allow him to make full use of his faculties in his later work and address problems with good judgment. His vision of space as life, and synthesis as a fundamental activity, led to the creative synthesis reflected in his own work. The idea of synthesis took shape at the beginning of his professional career and continued to manifest itself until the end of his life: this idea was central to his œuvre's didactic purpose.

For Villanueva, space was above all an expression of life, used and experienced by humans: the space of architectural practice was an expression of the activities it houses and the uses it is given, space inhabited by and immersed in a culture. For him, as an architect, space was the site of a never-ending practice, his very reason for being. Idea, work, and life were for Villanueva components of a single reality, a single space understood as the expression of being transformed into knowledge. This space made of ideas was not necessarily an abstract space, but an *idea* of space built in his mind as well as in his daily practice. It emerged in the journey from thought to architectural materialization, and was the expression of that wisdom born of experience and tempered by an idea that qualifies it and gives it meaning. His thought was structured by the rigors of logic, understood as the expression of a "particular common sense" with regard to his position in time-space, as well as by his relationship with others and the reality in which he lived.

Synthesis, understood as knowledge, unifies purely conceived multiplicity. Synthesis is expressed through concepts but also through intuition and imagination; both thoughts and a certain kind of sensibility converge in it. Villanueva always kept this attitude toward reason and understanding, and maintained a respect for and acceptance of differences, divergent points of view, and different solutions to design problems. He was always willing to change aspects of the projects he was developing, keeping an open mind to new ways of seeing and feeling, exploring and experimenting, never content with a single solution. For Villanueva, unifying the objectives of different arts facilitated synthesis; unifying knowledge through synthesis turned projects into instruments of creation, into "intelligent" projects that juxtaposed their "unreality" with what they sought to transform.

At the start of the twentieth century, ideas were often expressed through manifestos in which the artistic avant-garde and the modern movement in architecture subscribed to the precepts of artistic synthesis. Villanueva first came into contact with the world of art through the Académie des Beaux-Arts in Paris, which functioned according to established aesthetic canons, but also forged links with the parallel development of the avant-garde, as well as with the new, modern architecture that was beginning to make its presence felt through conferences and a first few significant constructions. Although historically synthesis or integration among the arts has existed in various eras and cultures, the "spirit of coexistence" that emerged during the first half of the twentieth century was unprecedented. It is remarkable to look back on the commonality of interests between artists and architects who were connected to Villanueva, either personally or through their work, and whose philosophies and ideas came together to reformulate the links among the arts. Naum Gabo and Antoine Pevsner, Le Corbusier and Theo van Doesburg, Marcel Duchamp and László Moholy-Nagy, Jean Arp and Sophie Taeuber-Arp were just a few of the iconic figures in this change of direction that prompted artists to branch out in a multitude of directions, movements, and "isms." Space and time, color, light and movement, expression and language, figuration and abstraction, the possibilities of technical reproduction and many other concepts offered countless opportunities for shared reflection on a certain kind of synthesis, whose most immediate reference seems to have been "constructive and geometric abstraction."

In this context, proponents of Constructivism and Neo-Plasticism began to develop new ways of integrating art into architecture. Architecture provides both a constructive and a material support: it allows for a dialogue of sorts between fixed and constant elements, between variable and intermediate elements. Scale is one key element in the elaboration of a space shared by art and architecture; it includes the observer or user and ultimately becomes a work of art from within by revealing the "nonvisible" relationships elaborated by synthesis.

In their early days, abstract art and architecture converged with a single objective: to pave the way for the achievement of modern synthesis. In this, the "architecture" of painting and the "visual art" of architecture found a common denominator. Of all the artists working in this vein, Le Corbusier was possibly the most relevant for Villanueva in encouraging the synthesis of the major arts. These notions mixed and mingled in his writing and his works, as well as in his personal life. The guiding idea in the lives of both men was above all that of "constructing oneself," of "constructing the man along with the work"; while neither conceived of this as an end in and of itself, they both sought and desired it with effort and persistence.

The tenets of synthesis formulated during this time often bore little relation to the works that were carried out, but they did foreshadow what would one day be a productive convergence of purposes. Villanueva kept abreast of these countless events and their protagonists who, through their ideas and their creative work, championed the synthesis of visual art and architecture. Many of these artists and their followers would be selected by Villanueva to contribute to his "synthesis of the arts" project. Their experience and contributions to it were essential.

interiorizing synthesis

The 1930s marked the start of an entirely new period for Villanueva. He arrived in Venezuela in 1928 and, following a brief trip to the United States, executed his first works in Maracay in 1930. The worldview he had developed during his formative years would reach a level of maturity, leading him to a personal philosophy that would culminate in his projects of the 1950s. He underwent a process of adaptation during the period 1930–50. During this time he familiarized himself with the stimulating milieu in which he found himself, an environment whose traditional architecture offered a wealth of underappreciated ideas and solutions. The country, however, was still characterized by a multitude of technical and cultural limitations and a resistance to change, which forced Villanueva to adjust the evolution of his work to the opportunities that presented themselves, and to plan the execution of his first efforts in accordance with the pace of the country's modernization process.

This was also a time of personal adjustment for Villanueva on two fronts. On one hand he was trying to superimpose and achieve coherence between the teachings of the Académie des Beaux-Arts (teachings that Villanueva never renounced) and the modern principles of his new education. On the other hand, he had to adapt an idealized modernity to a particular context and to the practical demands of its realization, while coming to terms with an identity and a series of values, both for himself as an individual and for Venezuela as a country. The changes that had begun to take place in the visual arts in both Europe and Venezuela, concurrent but at different rhythms and according to different time frames, constituted another element that affected Villanueva's work during this period.

In the first decades of the twentieth century, the early phase of Villanueva's education, the possibility of a new synthesis in the arts and architecture had begun to take shape in the European cultural milieu. During the period that followed, as Villanueva's vocation and beliefs began to crystallize, two worlds coexisted in him – Europe and the Americas – as did two modes of thought that were also inevitably contradictory – tradition and modernity.

During the 1930s and '40s, there were three notable milestones in Villanueva's life: his encounter and relationship with painter and sculptor Francisco Narváez; the beginning of his extended project with the Museo de Bellas Artes in Caracas; and his participation in the 1937 Exposition Internationale in Paris (titled *Arts et Techniques dans la Vie Moderne* – Arts and techniques in modern life). Also worthy of mention are the many homes that Villanueva built with his father-in-law, Juan Bernardo Arismendi, as well as his achievements with the Venezuelan ministry of public works and the Banco Obrero, in particular the redevelopment of the El Silencio district of Caracas.

Narváez contributed to the majority of Villanueva's projects, from the Carabobo Plaza in 1934 to the Ciudad Universitaria in the 1950s. At the time, Narváez, who had also spent his formative years in Paris, was working along parallel lines that would take him from figuration to abstraction and from "nativism" to geometry.

The Museo de Bellas Artes in Caracas is perhaps the most complete example of this process of connecting life and work, art and architecture, which began at the start of Villanueva's architectural career and reached its apex almost at the end of his life, maintaining a permanent presence throughout his life in his practice of architectural execution.

As an architect, Villanueva practiced synthesis even in his earliest works by incorporating elements such as reliefs and sculptures into his architectural pieces, but he also achieved a broader, more in-depth synthesis that corresponds to both his life and his work: the consolidation of his developing body of ideas. This synthesis was characterized by a special kind of "synergy" – a convergence of emerging impulses – as opposed to the more dimly viewed "syncretism," which merely combines bits and pieces from different places. With his education at the Académie des Beaux-Arts, Villanueva had formed early relationships with architects Le Corbusier and José Luis Sert, as well as the artistic avant-garde in Paris – the focal point and center of all these manifestations. Combining this familiarity with his own intelligent appreciation of traditional colonial Venezuelan architecture, the synthesis-in-progress gradually evolved as Villanueva internalized values that would ultimately be critical in the execution of his most significant works.

Cultural and architectural synergy, theoretical and constructive practice converged in a synthesized totality that encompassed measure and method. In Villanueva's works, the scale and measure of space is pleasing: space is endowed with an added value that suits it to its purpose. As such, space is defined by a general value according to proportional relationships, a "this-much-by-this-much"; it is a totality that incorporates both the quantitative and the qualitative, quantity and form, dimension and value.

Space—the material of architectural ideas—is abstract, defined by numbers and represented by geometry, but with Villanueva it is also the vital space of inner experience, reduced through economy to its essential elements. It is the space of reduction and synthesis. As a result of balanced measurement, it attests to an ethics of the necessary that eliminates the superfluous, the accessory. It is a space of measure and moderation; it is the art of measurement but also the art of good taste, a contained, latent space, a manifestation of temperance and restraint.

On the other hand, synthesis is a cognitive method and can also be understood as the bringing-together of scattered perceptions, establishing necessary relationships between opposing ideas. Particularly remarkable about Villanueva are the inclusive and conclusive qualities of the variables in his design, his capacity to make the different intentions of a project converge and cooperate, preserving an overall value, a single idea or entity that prevails over the parts or details, a conceptual simplicity and clarity that drive his work.

Synthesis, for Villanueva, was both a tool and a methodology. It gave him the flexibility to change directions in his design process at any moment, by anticipating results, finding answers without having to reconstruct previous stages, and testing solutions based on experience and the understanding of the intricate path that leads from an idea to its execution—through a succession of "progressive" syntheses. Creative synthesis consists in identifying opposites. The "method" most certainly involves practical skill, because Villanueva was, above all, a "maker."

Villanueva's encounter with and recognition of Venezuela through this convergent synthesis, his reformulation of popular and colonial Venezuelan architecture and the postulates of international modern architecture, led him to contextualize his work through a rigorous process in which he first explored the country and then formalized a new national project.

The 1937 Exposition Internationale, the most encompassing and controversial fair held in Paris as well as the largest in scope and number of participants, was a decisive event for Villanueva. Two of his fundamental themes were emphasized in it: the synthesis of the arts and the integration of technology. Villanueva participated by designing the Venezuelan Pavilion with architect Luis Malaussena, but it was the pavilion of the Spanish Republic, by José Luis Sert and Luis Lacasa, that caught Villanueva's eye. Both the Venezuelan and the Spanish Pavilions, in their contradictory relationships to regional traditions and modernity, revealed a dialectic that led him to broaden his vision. Seeing his work in contrast to that of others from outside his country inspired Villanueva to adopt a language of his own. His architecture was a product of the confluence of tradition and modern rationalism; it was free of eclecticisms and historicisms, but always advocated for certain materials, climates, and lifestyles, and reaffirmed his inexorable commitment to functional and constructive architecture.

Villanueva remained in Paris for seven months, until 1938, studying at the Institut d'Urbanisme and attending the fifth Congrès Internationale d'Architecture Moderne (CIAM). He spent time with his friends Léon-Joseph Madeline, Jacques Lambert, Paul Lester Wiener, and Maurice E. H. Rotival, who would later become involved in urban planning projects in Venezuela and other Latin American countries. Villanueva himself, upon his return to Venezuela, joined the Dirección de Urbanismo that would formulate the master city plan for Caracas.

When he visited Paris again, after World War II's long and tragic interruption, Villanueva resumed contact and relationships with the artists and architects of the "École de Paris," which operated as something of an influential common-interest group, including André Bloc, the Espace group, the magazine *Art d'aujourd'hui*, and the artists and works represented by such art galleries as Denise René, which from 1944 played an essential role in the defense of abstraction. Villanueva returned to France in 1948 (the year Alejandro Otero exhibited his series of Cafeteras [Coffeepots] in Paris), to prepare the projects and works that, starting in 1950, marked the beginning of a new era in the architecture of the Ciudad Universitaria in Caracas.

Villanueva's book *La Caracas de ayer y de hoy* (Caracas of yesterday and today), published in Paris in 1950, symbolizes and encapsulates this period of study and learning and Villanueva's process of interiorizing the synthesis between Venezuela and himself.[1] Paulina Villanueva, his daughter and an architect in her own right, believes that through this book Villanueva personally acknowledged the lasting quality of the principles that characterized his architecture, which attest to the common sense that allowed him to adapt to specific environmental conditions.

The incorporation of many traditional elements of Venezuelan architecture into Villanueva's work had by this time become apparent. Villanueva reinterpreted and juxtaposed them against more modern elements in a thought-provoking dialogue. Despite the formidable influence of his European education, Villanueva had most definitely found his roots in Venezuela.

the constructive achievement of synthesis

The 1950s began for Villanueva with a major project that culminated in the construction of Caracas's unique Ciudad Universitaria. Work had started back in 1944, with the first studies and the sketch of a tentative general plan. After making headway on the medical complex and a number of other important buildings, Villanueva introduced substantial changes in 1949 and went on to design the stadiums that were built in 1950 and inaugurated in 1951, heralding the beginning of a new, modern phase with the development of the university's Conjunto Central (central complex).

All of this was made possible by the very particular set of circumstances affecting the country at the time. For political, economic, professional, and most of all personal reasons, Villanueva set the guidelines for the work through the clarity and coherence of his concepts, his directed focus, and the support and efficiency of a well-prepared team. He was able to negotiate the obstacles before him thanks to his equanimity and powers of persuasion, the favorable

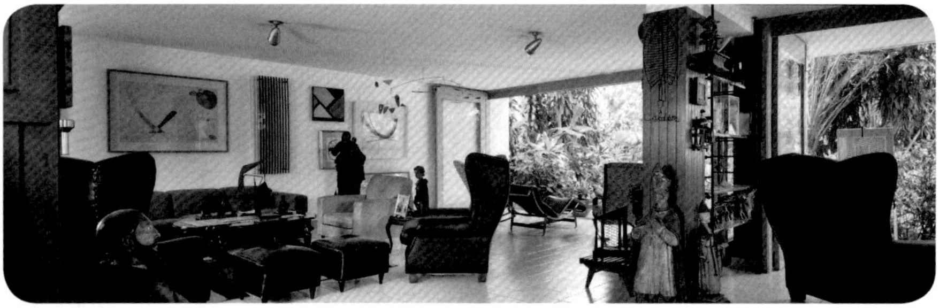

Interior of the Casa Caoma, primary residence of Carlos Raúl Villanueva. Photograph by Paolo Gasparini. 1985–89. Archivos Fundación Villanueva, Caracas

impression and appreciation he inspired in those around him, and his ability to elicit confidence and respect—never forgetting that his work could only be executed in a specific context and that the overall project depended upon its realization. In the end, Villanueva's effective direction of the construction process confirmed the wisdom of on-site solutions to problems arising along the way; this approach allowed the project to become an architectural reality.

A number of significant events occurred during the prolific 1950s: the consolidation of Villanueva's home, Casa Caoma, as a "living museum" with the participation of his artist friends and their works; the institution of an "open museum" in the university's covered quad, the Plaza Cubierta, featuring works by a distinguished group of Venezuelan and foreign artists; and ultimately that unprecedented work, that consummate example of synthesis: the university's Aula Magna, or great hall, which was opened in 1954.

This period also marks the beginning of Villanueva's productive and meaningful friendships and professional relationships with two prominent artists, Alexander Calder and Jesús Rafael Soto, both of whom were connected to the 1955 exhibition *Le Mouvement* (Movement), held in Paris at the Galerie Denise René. Villanueva and Calder met in 1951, and immediately became close friends. Calder saw the university's Aula Magna during his only visit to Venezuela, to attend the 1955 exhibition of his work at the Museo de Bellas Artes, organized by Villanueva, Miguel Arroyo, and Alejandro Otero. It was at this point that Villanueva's support of abstract art in Venezuela took on special significance.

The Caoma "living museum" has been dubbed by Paulina Villanueva a *casa crisol*: a "crucible house," containing the origins and foundations of this encounter between tradition and modernity, spaces and works, inhabitants and artists. Designed in 1952, together with the Aula Magna, as part of a coherent constructive philosophy of "synthesis of the arts," Caoma embodied the encounter of modern conceptions of space and language with Venezuela's cultural and physical climate.[2]

Villanueva's personal and professional lives are both essential to the interior world of Caoma, in which synthesis occurs everywhere. Here, the ostensible context for works of art is revealed to be a "work" in itself, which integrates both the space and the time in which things occur, in which thinking and acting take place. The house served as a model for the implementation of ideas: it was a kind of protected environment in which an inner world took shape

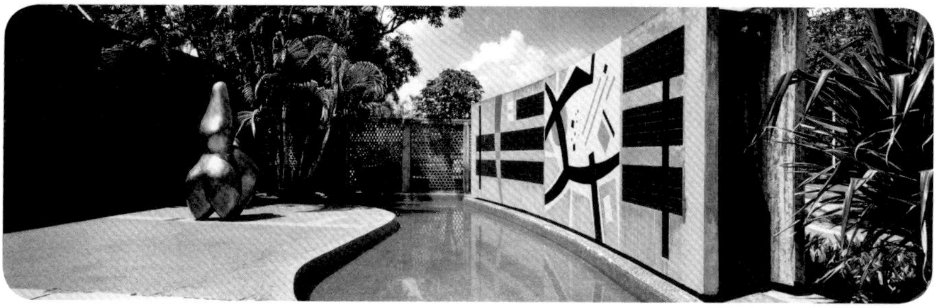

Plaza Cubierta (covered plaza) of the Universidad Central de Venezuela, showing Jean Arp's *Berger de nuages* (Cloud shepherd; 1953), and Mateo Manaure's *Composición* (Composition; 1954). Photograph by Paolo Gasparini. 1985–89. Archivos Fundación Villanueva, Caracas

before its public appearance. Objects, furniture, paintings, sculptures, murals, and spaces filled with light and vegetation, freedom and tranquility, provided an "intimate" counterweight to "public" space.

Villanueva's "synthesis of the arts" project and its "movements" ran parallel to this orchestrated universe within the controlled space of the house and in the mind of the individual/architect; he designed and executed his "synthesis-project" from 1950, working most intensely from 1952 and 1953 and finishing it in 1954. The era came to a close in 1957, when Villanueva erected the buildings for the Universidad Central's department of architecture and urban planning, the school of engineering and oil in Maracaibo, and his other dwelling place, Sotavento.

The Plaza Cubierta, as a synthesis of the arts, was, like Caoma, an experimental laboratory that incorporated both extant works of art and others created expressly for a particular space within the project. The scale and materials of the pieces were carefully gauged—some were left as freestanding structures and others incorporated into a wall or the roof of the building—through a process that made this open museum into a place of counterpoint between artist and architecture, artwork and architecture, user and spectator.[3]

The Plaza Cubierta embodied a museography that was at once immutable and changeable, that established both the relations and the context for the presentation and enjoyment of works of art, but within a variable system that exposed them to the changing seasons in open spaces, as well as to the multifarious uses of architecture. This phenomenon, which is present in every corner of the Ciudad Universitaria, made this project one of the most important monuments to modernity.

The Plaza Cubierta was likewise the product of a complex combination of elements, which the spectator perceives as natural, as a continual and stimulating sensorial space that links and encompasses different places and buildings. The Venezuelan writer Guillermo Meneses, a friend of Villanueva, expressed this most eloquently: "Without making a fuss, as if it were the most natural thing in the world, the loveliest art in the world came to fill the plazas and walls of the Ciudad Universitaria in Caracas."[4]

The Plaza Cubierta is primarily a roof that frames a structure, a shadow that constructs a place, but it is also a floor that gives continuity to its use, a door for the free passage of the body. It is a window multiplied, a frame for the gaze. It is, in short, simply a space in which architectural "materiality" disappears

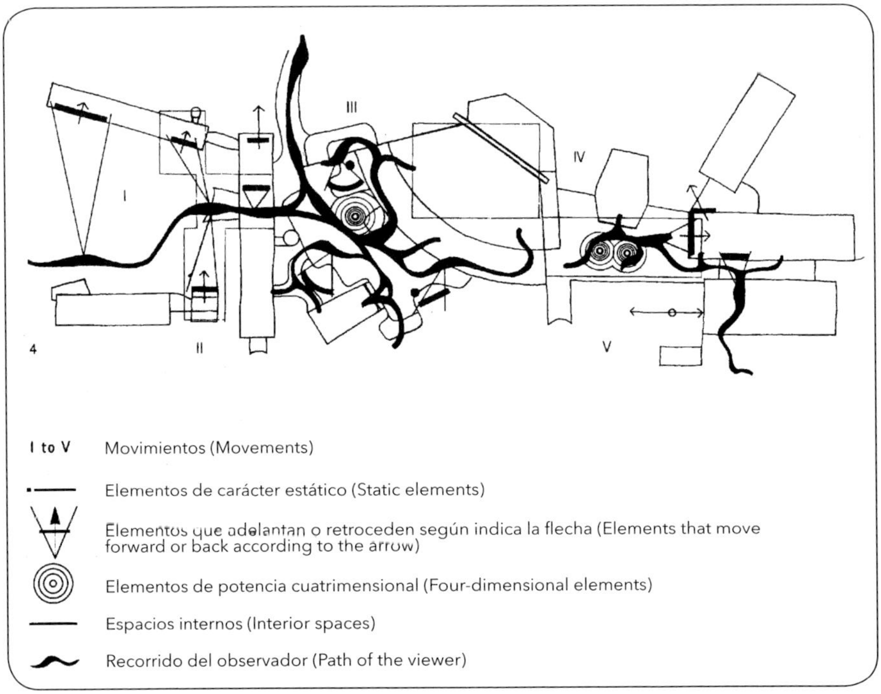

Flow diagram for Carlos Raúl Villanueva's "integration of the arts" project at the Universidad Central de Venezuela's Plaza Cubierta (covered plaza). Archivos Fundación Villanueva, Caracas

and yet continually manifests its temporal presence, constantly repeated and preserved in memory.

The plaza is part of a system that leads to another plaza and to exterior spaces, but also connects various buildings to one another: the university president's office, the Aula Magna, the concert hall, and the library. It is a space of permanence and circulation that branches out into covered passageways and parking lots. Designed with continuous and recurrent movement in mind, incorporating different routes and series of perspectives, connecting focal points to draw attention and orient circulation, the plaza's architecture is largely based on visual perception, but enjoying it leads to haptic experience and sensory synaesthesia. Light and shadow, contour and color, space and time are transformed into the movement of the living body, into the cycle of hours and years. These elements contribute to the persistence of the plaza's continuing mise-en-scène, to its daily making and unmaking.

The plaza's entire "work" lies in the apprehension of an external visual experience, an encounter with a "real" body accompanied by an "unreal" interior experience. Yet, because the work of art always incorporates part of its environment, it presupposes a journey from the work's own "unreal" space to the "real" space where it is located. The spaces of art and architecture are superimposed and interact: sculptures and murals create environments of their own but are at the same time inscribed within the context that determines them. The task of the synthesis is to shape this "cohabitation."

The university's Conjunto Central features works by Jean Arp, Armando Barrios, André Bloc, Carlos González Bogen, Alexander Calder, Pedro León Castro, Henri Laurens, Fernand Léger, Balthazar Lobo, Mateo Manaure, Francisco Narváez, Pascual Navarro, Alirio Oramas, Antoine Pevsner, Héctor Poleo, Victor Vasarely, and Oswaldo Vigas—an illustrious group of Venezuelan and international artists who commune as equals through their pieces, with Villanueva's architecture as their common denominator.

In the short span of less than two years, works of art and architecture were executed in teams and from a distance, through the exchange of letters, plans, and projects, sketches and ideas, maquettes and models. The Plaza Cubierta and the Aula Magna were inaugurated on March 2, 1954, during the opening ceremony for the tenth Inter-American Conference.

Arp's *Berger de nuages* (Cloud shepherd; 1953), Laurens's *Amphion* (1953), Pevsner's *Projection dynamique dans l'espace au 30° degré* (Dynamic projection into space in the 30th degree; 1953), and Lobo's *Maternidad* (*Maternity*; 1953) were pre-existing sculptures that had to be adjusted in size and scale for the space. Léger, with his 1954 *Bimural* and stained-glass mural, as well as Vasarely, with his *Sophia*; *+ - (Positif-Negatif)* (+ - [Positive-negative]; 1954); and *Hommage à Malevitch* (Homage to Malevich; 1954),[5] were different cases for several reasons: these artists created site-specific works with particular purposes, engendered in a stimulating, labor-intensive collaboration between architect and artist—particularly Vasarely, who developed three different works and participated actively in a process that included theoretical reflection. Vasarely, a promoter of kinetic and Op art, believed that art was a social phenomenon and that the work of art existed in order to be re-created, multiplied, transmitted, and disseminated by new cultural mechanisms.[6] His *Positif-Negatif* is a truly kinetic work, a special piece conceived as a "mural-sculpture" and an "artistic-architectural" space, through which time, air, light, and the gaze might pass and create movement.

The art of "feeling and making" had given way to the art of "conceiving and making," and all the pieces in the Plaza Cubierta—especially Vasarely's—participate in this expansive notion that here became accessible to a greater number of spectators and compelled them to participate by means of subtle resonances that reverberate through space and time.

At the heart of the Plaza Cubierta, yet functioning as an intrinsic part of it, is the Aula Magna, an interior space within a larger interior-exterior space: the crown jewel of this project. This is where synthesis is finally achieved, an experience difficult to explain or believe without having "felt it." Built with only the most essential elements, the Aula is monumental. A unique piece—stark and exact, stripped of all rhetoric yet at the same time exuberant and exquisite—it reflects a subtle equilibrium between the creative genius of two artists, Calder and Villanueva, whose efforts are difficult to dissociate and who came to express themselves in this work as a single mind with exceptional force and clarity.

The Aula Magna, with its protected interior, is a fundamental, irreplaceable element in Villanueva's great project of synthesis—and its most celebrated example. Like the soloist who stands out in a musical ensemble, it is, despite or perhaps because of this, the project's most universal element, a work of exceptional quality that can transcend time and is meaningful in any context.

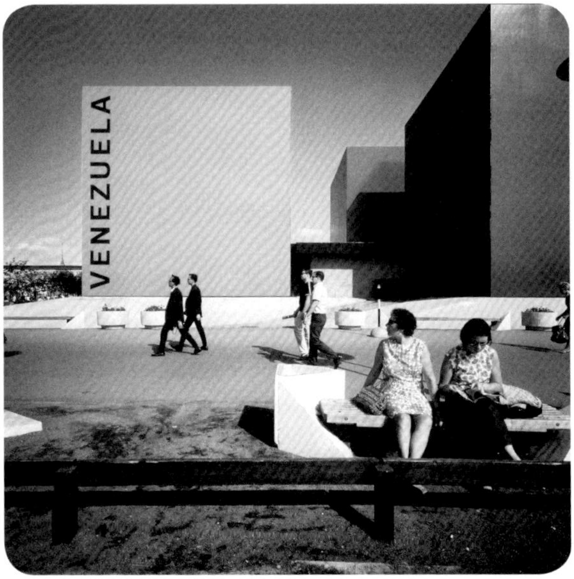

View of the Venezuelan Pavilion at the 1967 Montreal World's Fair. Photograph by Paolo Gasparini. Archivos Fundación Villanueva, Caracas

The significance of the Conjunto Central as a whole is reinforced by every one of its individual parts, a multitude of works within the unity of another work. Its coherence makes it a spiritually and physically unified site created by Villanueva's singular poetic vision.

The "synthesis of the arts" was a mission that had long been attempted in Europe, but was finally achieved by Villanueva in Venezuela, in an interior-exterior space filled with light and color. In Villanueva's case, synthesis was no longer conceptual but was embodied in a work through the reification of art and architecture, nature and artifice, geometric abstraction and constructive concretion.

The Ciudad Universitaria was also the embodiment of a model city, in which the best utopian visions of modern urban planning were made into reality. For the Venezuelan writer Salvador Garmendia, in the Ciudad Universitaria "Caracas found its own heritage for the first time, a voice of its own in the way it organized space and reclaimed form. As such, it was an emblem of identity and perhaps its only lasting manifestation of creativity."[7] This conviction was upheld in 2000—the centennial of Villanueva's birth—when the Ciudad Universitaria of Caracas was declared a World Heritage Site by UNESCO.

the semantic simplicity of synthesis

Following the feverish activity of the 1950s, Villanueva reached his most mature period in the 1960s. Saturated by the activity that had taken place over the previous decade, he turned to introspection, research, and teaching, as well as the dissemination of his work and thought. His architecture and his example of dedicating his life to creative work were widely recognized and admired.

This period of engagement with art and architecture culminated with the construction of the Venezuela Pavilion at the 1967 Montreal World's Fair[8]—a sign of rejuvenation and a unique minimalist piece, implemented in collaboration with Jesús Rafael Soto. Villanueva also undertook in this period the design and execution of the Museo de Arte Moderno Jesús Soto in Ciudad Bolívar. These efforts sealed Villanueva's prolific and widely celebrated œuvre as modest expressions of what he believed to be most essential to architecture. The latter project also reveals the significance of his relationship with Soto.

The 1960s was a period of reflection that allowed Villanueva to take a step back and assess his accomplishments, a time to think about the significance of that living music in the "movements" of the synthesis of the arts.

This decade also witnessed a more general change in the plastic arts in Venezuela, as artists returned to figurative work and *informel* painting, producing pieces that incorporated a rich variety of mediums, and whose content addressed rupture or political and social protest. For a brief period, Soto too began to incorporate rough materials and surfaces, wires and irregular fragments of wood and metal into his work, arranging these elements with no concern for geometric rigor, though he later returned to the precise lines that characterize his artistic project.

Villanueva, for his part, created his Collages and Ensamblajes (Assemblages), using discarded materials and pieces worn out by time. He combined and structured these elements in a crude, unrefined way, but with tremendous poetic resonance. He also spent this period working on notes for his classes, directing his workshop, the Taller Villanueva, teaching design at the department of architecture and urban planning at the Universidad Central, and participating in the October 1962 Royaumont Colloquium and various other conferences and congresses where he kept the discussion about the synthesis of the arts alive.

The 1963 Le Havre exhibition *Venezuela du paysage a l'expression plastique, 10 artistes contemporains* (Venezuela from landscape to plastic expression: 10 contemporary artists), organized and presented by the Fundación Fina Gómez with the assistance of Alejandro Otero, provided an ideal opportunity to demonstrate the "synchrony" among the theses of various projects and the scope of their results in worlds as different as Europe and the Americas.[9]

It was also the moment for acknowledging both local specificities and their attempts at universality, as Otero's long meditation in a January 1963 letter to Villanueva demonstrates. Here Otero initially states that it is necessary "to give the fullest possible account of the Venezuela that has sustained us—its exuberant landscape, its people, its way of life—starting with the man who expressed himself by lightly scratching a stone on the blue of a wall, all the way to our day, lingering as long as we need to on that creative undertaking that is the Ciudad Universitaria." On the second page, Otero adds a revelatory bit of introspection regarding "our" modes of working and understanding reality:

> As I made the maquette that gave shape to the exhibition, I realized that there exists a unique Venezuela, eminently determined by our landscape, of which I was previously unaware. Naturally, this is not the only factor that affects us, but it is the one that seems to unify all others, particularly in the realm of the visual arts. Our sensitivity to color and space, the way we develop our sense of scale, the internal dynamics of our work, the almost unbridled freedom that manifests itself in our work and seems to defy

> all unity, the expansiveness with which we embrace everything, even our particular way of making progress by leaps—all these things seem rooted in the natural landscape that surrounds us, in which we have settled, full of love and wonder for it.

On the third page of the letter, Otero concludes:

> Without attempting to prove this thesis once and for all with the exhibition we are currently organizing, I thought it quite useful and necessary to provide a complete overview of our reality as seen through the visual image when preparing the first show of Venezuelan painting in Europe. The reasons are obvious: because of the lack of information about us—within the cultural realm in which we are inscribed, which is the West—we are viewed as people from exotic countries from whom people expect some sort of astonishing originality. They are tremendously disappointed to find that our expressive language is the same as the one that prevails in Europe. It is no wonder that we are taken for "snobs" or, at the very least, imitators. Much of the criticism of the Latin American exhibition that we organized [last] summer at the Musée d'Art Moderne in Paris accused us of this, and we shouldn't make the same mistake twice. When this misunderstanding is cleared up, no one will deny that we indeed have an accent all our own. We can aspire, at least, to this much and this exhibition tends to emphasize it.[10]

This need to look at, assess, and recreate ourselves, to claim an identity shared with Europeans and Americans but with specific local references that have universal value, is admirably represented by figures like Villanueva and his architecture, and by a distinguished group of visual artists, writers, and poets.

A number of international exhibitions and publications served to spread the word of Villanueva's work in Europe and the United States from the mid-1950s and throughout the 1960s. To a large degree, his relationship with Sibyl Moholy-Nagy and the 1964 publication of her book on his work[11] were instrumental in Villanueva's recognition, and both occupied a substantial part of his time during this decade. Along with Soto and Calder, Sibyl Moholy-Nagy was one of the people closest to Villanueva, and he maintained a prolific correspondence with her.

Among his letters, Villanueva saved a six-page text that he called (in English) a "tentative outline," in which he discusses the initial organization of the book, and which is significant for the clues it provides to his thinking. The first part enumerates three criteria for evaluating buildings—"form, space, and context"—as well as three identifying characteristics of colonial architecture that one should keep in mind when approaching his work—"non-organic or formalistic, simplified-basic, economic functional tradition." A special note is made of the idea that "function means usable space rather than aesthetic beauty." Also evident are the influences in his use of materials: "Concret Brut," and then (written out by hand in tiny letters), "I love concrete! Perret, Corbu, Freysenet, Maillart, and Nervi." It also mentions three thematic ideas: urbanism, structures, and aesthetics—as well as three variables: landscape-climate, economy, polychromy. Finally, it notes three characteristics of the work: "Climatic adaptations for houses in the tropics. Open Plan and Exteriors-Interiors Plans. Balcony and Perfored Wall" (written in English, *sic*). Sibyl Moholy-Nagy expressed her admiration for "the variations within the unity" of the Ciudad Universitaria. According to her, if the word *organic* had any meaning in the vocabulary of Villanueva, it was in Frank Lloyd Wright's sense of the term: "growing in logical stages, as everything in nature."[12]

This synthesis of multiplicity within unity is extremely important in Villanueva's work, particularly in the Ciudad Universitaria. It consists of the unending transformation of a language that constantly accepts new challenges through a process of inquiry and learning—a process of "growth" conceived as the formation and formulation of a philosophy—in conjunction with the harmonious development of the sum and the parts of a massive collection of works juxtaposed in space and time. For Sibyl Moholy-Nagy, moreover, Villanueva's architecture is so filled with "kinetic" elements that it is almost kaleidoscopic.

During the 1970s, the Venezuela Pavilion in Montreal and the Museo Soto reconfigured the relationship between art and "kinetic" architecture. From the moment that Alfredo Boulton introduced them, Villanueva and Soto maintained an active epistolary friendship. Villanueva held Soto's work in high esteem, and empathized with his evolution both as a person and as an artist. For Soto, on the other hand, Villanueva was a point of reference, a useful context within which to inscribe his own project and work, and a source of encouragement and support.

In their first letters, written in 1955, Villanueva and the artist were making arrangements for the inclusion of Soto's works in the exhibition *Le Mouvement* at the Denise René Gallery. The tone of the writings changed once the men met personally: in Villanueva's letter to Soto of June 22, 1956, he writes: "I have had the great honor of meeting you, of gazing at your noble *condottiere*'s profile, worthy of the Florentine quattrocento, of hearing your agreeable voice in an ambience 'du gros Robert,' at three in the morning in Suresnes."[13] In subsequent letters from 1956, Villanueva proposed an exhibition of Soto's work in Caracas in 1957, with the support of Boulton and Inocente Palacios.

Between 1965 and 1966, their correspondence continued. Soto participated in the Córdoba Biennial, this time as a special guest (he had received a prize at the previous fair). Villanueva, a member of the biennial's jury, pointed out the paintings that interested him and began to discuss the possibility of Soto's participation in the Montreal exposition. The year 1967 was an especially active one of letter-writing between the two men, with their collaboration on the pavilion in Montreal. The topic of Ciudad Bolívar began to appear in their letters of late 1967 and early 1968, after the first preparatory visits for what was to become the Museo Soto.

The creation of the pavilion in Montreal and the Minimalist art movement were two key events in the ever-changing relations between art and architecture that had special significance for Villanueva and Soto. Now Villanueva would create "art" with his architecture and Soto finally witnessed the complete synthesis of his work with Villanueva's.

Architectural sculpture, intransitive art, a sign of the times, or perhaps an architecture of synthesis transformed into art, the Venezuela Pavilion in Montreal contained elements and qualities of both artistic expression and minimalist architecture: geometric purity, structural clarity, constructive precision, changes in scale, repetition of elements, and abstract expression. The pavilion—

idea-architecture or object-building—achieved a tremendous significance with a great economy of means. The ubiquitous trinity of volume, space, and color were reflected and duplicated in the multiple faces of three cubes, which revealed the space within through their polished surfaces, simultaneously communicating both interior and exterior, strengthening the relationship between the work of art and its context on different levels by including Soto's work in a stark white interior where the relationships that interested Soto evoked the universality of space.

According to Soto, "Space is not an all-pervasive condition; space itself intervenes as sculpture."[14] Space becomes one; Soto's and Villanueva's spaces become indivisible.

These two projects also reveal Villanueva's use of "architectural dematerialization": in the pavilion's archetypal "cube," paradoxically, because of its abstract, objectlike quality and lack of architectural references. It is also seen in the Museo Soto's empty "boxes," through which Villanueva achieved supreme simplicity, a basic space, the expression of an interior space that steps out and becomes exterior.

In Villanueva's and Soto's work, we find logic and intuition, permanence and change, the destruction and construction of a new organism characterized by relationships and movement. Composing with identical elements multiplied within the work, and destroying the singularity of form through repetition or through its prototypical character—all these are attributes of the pavilion's minimalist language that are also present in Soto's earliest efforts.

With works of both art and architecture, the user discovers through his or her own movement that balance always entails a state of perpetual change. Calder and Villanueva's Aula Magna—like Soto and Villanueva's Montreal cube—reverberates with this contained movement. In this ineffable experience, the spectator and the space become indivisible. In the dense space of these two pieces, the spectator-user becomes aware of this "penetrability" and feels part of a dynamic equilibrium that stimulates the senses until he or she reaches a plenitude of experience and feels the pleasures of the intangible.

The Museo Soto and the kinetic art of the 1970s are part of the synthesis of movement and represent a final opportunity to appreciate the collaboration between Soto and Villanueva. The museum is characterized by clarity and simplicity of form, architectural logic and precision, constructive and geometric abstraction, movement and synthesis. It is physically composed with a constructive language that used serial elements, repetitions, and combinations that could make it seem a "plain" work of art without particular appeal. Yet it shows the courageous poverty of dematerialization, which strips the building of all superficial or accessory elements in a deliberate, measured use of economy, appropriate to the circumstances of the moment. Made to follow a simple, logical order, it reveals the moral dimensions of simplicity.

Comprised of a number of large, empty "boxes" arranged irregularly in space, and made with a minimum of resources and materials, this piece comes close to Villanueva's express wish of making "the invisible visible," making the space itself the protagonist or of making the material, the construction itself, "invisible." He achieves this not through a real or suggested "transparency," but through a dematerialization of form and function, through the visual "disappearance" of matter; although architectural dematerialization is not literally possible, it occurs in this piece due to an exterior-interior inversion, by transposing and manifesting the essence of the interior space. The unification of sizes, materials, and colors, constructive simplification, the continuous interpretation of spaces and elements, and equal or equivalent bodies all come together to make the Museo Soto a coherent whole that aims at synthesis. Its expression of essential elements goes beyond minimalism's precise reductions, and thus differentiates it from the objectlike quality of the Venezuela Pavilion in Montreal.

A work created with no excess whatsoever, the museum reveals itself through the emptiness of its interior, in which space is the raw material of architecture, becoming visible through the very "invisibility" of its starkness. Minimalism and simplicity, or rather "essential" space and "poetic" synthesis, are the results of Villanueva's process of spatial and temporal distillation, of the convergence between art and life and the construction of a personal architectural language whose allusions to a specific context provide its identity and character.

Syntactic and semantic values, minimalism and simplicity, the power of poetic evocation and ethical consistency: all these elements are present in Villanueva's work at the close of the 1970s, and comprise the final chapter of a life dedicated to synthesis and reflected in his complete and total identification with Venezuela.

Translated by Kristina Cordero and Catalina Ocampo
This essay is part of the forthcoming publication by Maciá Pintó: *Villanueva la Síntesis* (Villanueva: The Synthesis), in two volumes: *Espacio y Síntesis en Carlos Raúl Villanueva* and *Síntesis de las Artes y Abstracción Constructiva* (Caracas: Fundación Villanueva, 2008).

notes to the text

1. Carlos Raúl Villanueva, *La Caracas de ayer y de hoy, su arquitectura colonial y la reurbanización de "El Silencio,"* with texts by Carlos Manuel Möller and Maurice E. H. Rotival, and photographs by Alfredo Boulton and others (Paris: Draeger Frères, 1950). A longer version of the text was included in Villanueva's *Caracas en tres tiempos: Iconografía retrospectiva de una ciudad* (Caracas, Ediciones Comisión Asuntos Culturales del Cuatricentenario de Caracas, 1966) published for the four hundredth anniversary of the founding of Caracas; this book includes an additional essay by Mariano Picón Salas. In his introduction to the latter volume, Villanueva calls the book "a testimony that acknowledges the endurance of the principles and norms that prevailed in colonial architecture" (p. 9), while Picón Salas celebrates Villanueva's "aesthetic concerns and his commitment to Venezuela," adding, with reference to El Silencio, that "Villanueva built a great complex at once international and very Venezuelan" (p. 15).
2. See Paulina Villanueva and Paolo Gasparini, *Villanueva en tres casas* (Caracas: Fundación Villanueva, Facultad de Arquitectura y Urbanismo, Universidad Central de Venezuela, 2000). The book addresses the three houses that Villanueva designed and built for his family to live in, providing three paradigms with which to interpret his work: Los Manolos in 1934, Caoma in 1952, and Sotavento in 1957. The first provides an idea of the "model" in the most literal sense, the second displays knowledge of historical "types" and their modern reinterpretation, and the third is an example of "synthesis" as the expression of a highly personal language and a particular kind of poetry. The notion of Caoma as a *casa crisol*, in which the encounter between tradition and modernity is forged, derives from this book. See "Epifanía II, Caoma: El arte como vida" (pp. 9–125) and "Caoma" (pp. 127–78).
3. An essay on Villanueva, descriptions of his works, and a complete biography-chronology, can be found in Paulina Villanueva and Maciá Pintó, *Carlos Raúl Villanueva* (Madrid: Tanais, 2000;

also published in English by Princeton Architectural Press, in Italian by Logos Art; and in German by Birkhäuser, all 2000).

4. Guillermo Meneses, "Los artistas extranjeros de la Ciudad Universitaria de Caracas," *Farol,* March–April 1957: n.p.
5. The original name of the small piece by Jean Arp is *Formes de lutin* (Elvish forms), 1949; this is the title that appears in the contract that corresponds to the execution of this piece. Arp, in a poem he sent to Villanueva, named the expanded piece *Berger de nuages* (Cloud shepherd), 1953 (Archivos Fundación Villanueva, A-II-1-1-3). *L'Amphion* by Laurens dates from 1937 and the university piece *Amphion* to 1953. In an early letter to Villanueva, Pevsner refers to his piece as *Projection dynamique dans l'espace au trentième degré, 1950–51* (Dynamic projection into space in the thirtieth degree). He names the 1953 university piece *Projection dynamique au 30° degré*.
6. See letters exchanged between Vasarely and Villanueva in 1953. Reference numbers: A-II-14-1-1, A-II-14-1-2, A-II-14-3-1, Archivos Fundación Villanueva.
7. Salvador Garmendia, "La Agresión al Espacio," in *Carlos Raúl Villanueva*, exh. cat. (Caracas: Museo de Bellas Artes, 1976).
8. Villanueva designed the pavilion in collaboration with the Venezuelan engineer Ricardo De Sola and the Canadian architect Arthur Erickson. Jesús Rafael Soto created the large work *Volumen suspendido* (*Suspended Volume*) for the occasion.
9. Along with Otero, Graziano Gasparini, Ana Teresa Serna, and María Teresa Isava were with the exhibition's organizing committee; Gaston Diehl provided the introductory texts. The ten participating artists were: Armando Barrios, Carlos Cruz-Diez, Gerd Leufert, Francisco Narváez, Pascual Navarro, Alejandro Otero, Mercedes Pardo, Héctor Poleo, Jesús Rafael Soto, and Oswaldo Vigas. The exhibition ran from May 18 to June 15, 1963. See *Venezuela, du paysage à l'expression plastique: 10 artistes contemporains*, exh. cat. (Le Havre: Musée Maison de la Culture du Havre, 1963).
10. Letter from Otero to Villanueva, January 14, 1963. Registry number A-II-9-1-1, Archivos Fundación Villanueva. The Paris exhibition to which Otero refers was *L'Art latino-américain à Paris* (Latin-American art in Paris), Musée d'Art Moderne de la Ville de Paris, 1962.
11. Sibyl Moholy-Nagy, *Carlos Raúl Villanueva y la arquitectura de Venezuela (Carlos Raúl Villanueva and the Architecture of Venezuela)*, English-Spanish edition (Caracas: Editorial Lectura; New York: Praeger, 1964). Republished in a facsimile edition by the Instituto de Patrimonio, 2000.
12. Cited in ibid, p. 93. *Organization of the Book* The Work of Carlos Raúl Villanueva, *Tentative Outline,* seven-page document, s/f. Archivos Fundación Villanueva A-II-17-1-132. In the promotional materials for the U.S. edition of Moholy-Nagy's book the following comment appears: "The fascinating story of the architect who transformed a nation." Archivos Fundación Villanueva reference numbers A-II-17-1-133.
13. The term "gros Robert" is not elucidated; it may be a reference to the café/restaurant of the chef known as "gros Robert," famous for his fine *coq au vin*. Alternately, the "ambience 'du gros Robert'" may refer to the home of the sculptor Robert Jacobsen – likewise known as "gros Robert" – a mutual friend of Soto and Villanueva.
14. Jesús Rafael Soto, interview in the journal *CAV* (Caracas), 1967. In reference to his piece in the pavilion designed by Villanueva for the Montreal World's Fair, Soto had this to say: "My work is nothing more than a partial detector of the infinite vibrations that Villanueva's cube delineates in the universe." Letter from Soto to Ricardo De Sola, published in the journal *Dada* 1, "De Arquitectura, Diseño y Autores; Separata" (Caracas), April 2000.

references

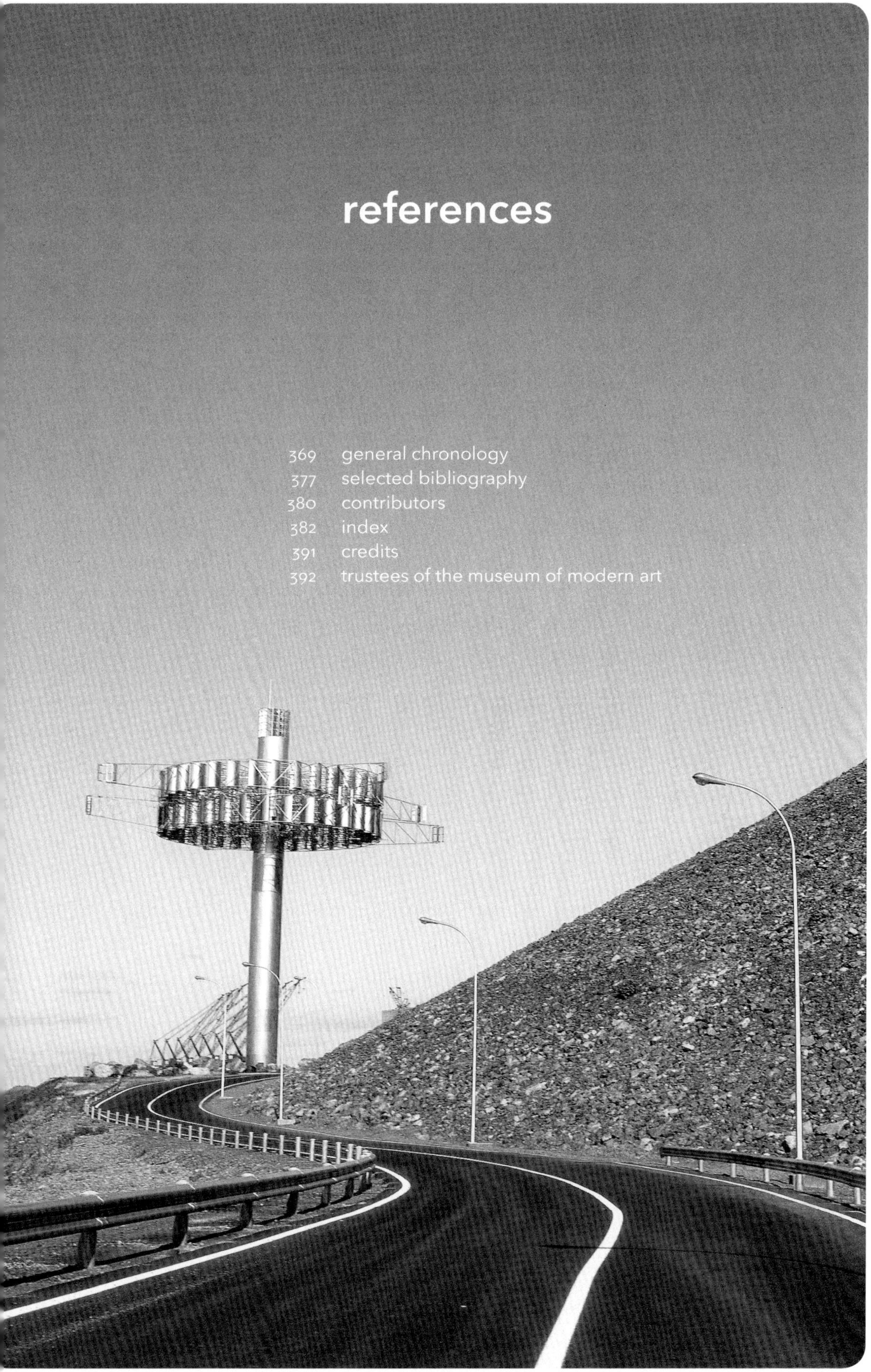

general chronology

of principal political and cultural events in venezuela, 1910–1972

1910
– Venezuela's population is approximately 2,804,511 (source: Julio Páez Celis).
– Venezuela's congress legalizes the dictatorship of General Juan Vicente Gómez, who takes over the leadership of the country from General Cipriano Castro.

1911
– Roadway construction begins in Venezuela, including the route connecting Caracas and La Guaira, the country's main port city.
– Armando Reverón travels to Spain to study at Barcelona's Escuela de Artes y Oficios.

1912
– The Universidad Central de Venezuela is closed by Gómez's government; the school will not reopen until 1922.
– Oil development begins.
– The Círculo de Bellas Artes is established; it is spearheaded by a group of students opposed to the prevailing academic methodologies at the Academia de Bellas Artes under the direction of the painter Antonio Herrera Toro.
– Leoncio Martínez publishes his text "Ideas y propósitos: Palabras en la instalación del Círculo de Bellas Artes" ("Ideas and Aims: Some Words on the Establishment of the Círculo de Bellas Artes") on September 4 in the newspaper *El Universal*.

1913
– The Círculo de Bellas Artes organizes the first annual painting Salon in Caracas.
– Tito Salas begins his series of paintings on the life of Simón Bolívar for the Casa Natal de El Libertador, Bolívar's birthplace, in Caracas.

1914
– The transnational company Caribbean Petroleum's first large-scale oil exploitation of the Zumaque 1 oilfield initiates an oil boom in Zulia, the most important oil-producing state in Venezuela.
– The Círculo de Bellas Artes' second Salon takes place.

1915
– Venezuela's congress carries out a constitutional reform, extending the presidential term to seven years. Juan Vicente Gómez is proclaimed president for the term 1915–1922.
– The journal *El cojo ilustrado*, since 1892 the country's most important source of cultural news, ceases publication.
– The Círculo de Bellas Artes' third Salon takes place.
– Armando Reverón returns to Venezuela.

1916
– Romanian painter Samys Mützner and Russian painter Nicolás Ferdinandov arrive in Venezuela, fleeing World War I.

1917
– Following complaints from neighbors about nude models in the studio, the Círculo de Bellas Artes' workspace is shut down by Gomez's police force, effectively bringing the organization to an end.

1918
– The appearance of the journal *Cultura venezolana* and the emergence of the "Generation of 1918" spark the first iterations of avant-garde Venezuelan poetry.
– Samys Mützner exhibits his work at the Club Venezuela.
– Armando Reverón's Blue period begins.

1919
– Laureano Vallenilla Lanz publishes *Cesarismo democrático* (*Democratic Caesarism*), a text with a positivist slant that justifies Gómez's presence, casting him as a "necessary policeman."
– Artist Emilio Boggio exhibits his work at the Academia de Bellas Artes in Caracas.

1920
– Venezuela has a population of 2,362,895; nearly 83 percent of the country's inhabitants live in rural areas (source: Instituto Nacional de Estadística).
– Rómulo Gallegos publishes *El último Solar* (The last of the Solars) and founds the journal *Actualidades* (which will be in circulation until 1922).

–Manuel Cabré exhibits his work at the Academia de Bellas Artes in Caracas.
–Armando Reverón settles in Macuto, near La Guaira, and paints *La cueva* (*The Cave*); according to Boulton this is the most representative work of Reverón's Blue period.

1921
–The Casa Natal de El Libertador opens. Tito Salas's early paintings are featured inside.
–The *Monumento del campo de Carabobo* (Monument to the field of Carabobo), designed by architect Alejandro Chataing and engineer Ricardo Razetti, is erected on the field where the decisive battle in the country's fight for independence took place.

1922
–The Barroso 2 oil-well blowout establishes Venezuela as a major producer of oil.
–José Rafael Pocaterra publishes the collection *Cuentos grotescos* (Grotesque tales) and is exiled from Venezuela.
–Boulton travels to Europe to attend boarding school in Lausanne; he will stay in Switzerland until 1925, and will subsequently move to England, where he will live until 1927.
–The Semana de Arte Moderna (Modern art week) takes place in São Paulo.

1923
–Juan Vicente Gómez's brother Juan Crisóstomo (Juancho) is assassinated, leading to a period of intense repression.
–The weekly humor magazine *Fantoches* begins publication under the direction of the writer and artist Leoncio Martínez.

1924
–Teresa de la Parra publishes her novel *Ifigenia* (*Iphigenia*).

1925
–Radio transmissions begin in Venezuela with the establishment of the radio station AYRE in September.
–Venezuela's first large-scale national roadway, the Trans-Andean Highway, connecting Caracas to the Andes Mountains, opens. Roads from Caracas to San Fernando de Apure and from Caracas to Ciudad Bolívar are also completed.
–José Antonio Ramos Sucre publishes *La torre del Timón* (Timón's tower). Rómulo Gallegos publishes *La trepadora* (The climber).
–In his book *La raza cósmica* (*The Cosmic Race*), Mexican writer José Vasconcelos speaks of *mestizaje* as the product of a new stage in the life of humanity, in which he foresees the future of humankind.
–Armando Reverón's White period begins.
–The Mexican muralist movement is underway.

1926
–Venezuela has a population of 2,890,720 (source: Instituto Nacional de Estadística).

1927
–José Rafael Pocaterra publishes *Memorias de un venezolano en la decadencia* (Memoirs of a Venezuelan in the age of decadence) in Colombia.

1928
Students at Caracas's Universidad Central de Venezuela engage in a series of protests against the regime, leading to the formation of the "Generation of 1928."
–The Universidad Central is again shut down; students are jailed and sentenced to hard labor.
–The first and only issue of the journal *Válvula* is published.
–Francisco Narváez exhibits his work at the Club Venezuela before traveling to Paris.
–In Brazil, Oswald de Andrade drafts the "Manifesto Antropófago" ("Anthropophagite Manifesto").

1929
–The U.S. Stock Exchange crashes, and the Great Depression begins. Venezuela's economy, which relies mostly on cocoa and coffee production, abruptly falls by nearly 40 percent.
–Carlos Raúl Villanueva returns to Venezuela and joins the country's ministry of public works.
–Rómulo Gallegos publishes *Doña Bárbara*.

1930
–Juan Vicente Gómez pays off the entirety of Venezuela's foreign debt, which had burdened the country since the days of independence.
–In Paris, the Cercle et Carré group (founded by Michel Seuphor and Uruguayan Joaquín Torres-García) brings geometric abstract artists together, and Theo van Doesburg founds the journal *Art Concret*. (Both the group and the journal will have a significant impact on Venezuelan art beginning in the 1950s.)

–Manuel Cabré returns to Venezuela from France.

1931
–The Venezuelan Communist party is created clandestinely.
–Arturo Úslar Pietri publishes *Las lanzas coloradas* (*The Red Lances*).
–Tito Salas begins work on the Panteón Nacional, the monument to Venezuela's heroes where Simón Bolívar is buried; Salas will complete this project in 1942.

1932
–From their exile in Colombia, Rómulo Betancourt and Raúl Leoni create the leftist revolutionary organization Agrupación de Izquierda (ARDI) and develop the Plan de Barranquilla, an agenda of actions to be taken against the Gómez regime.
–Boulton organizes an exhibition of Francisco Narváez's work at the Ateneo de Caracas.

1933
–Boulton begins his career as an art critic with articles in the journal *Elite* and in the newspaper *El Universal,* published under the pen names Bernardo Pons and Bruno Plá.

1934
–Luisa Phelps exhibits a series of Armando Reverón's works at the Katia Granoff Gallery in Paris.
–Boulton organizes an exhibition of Armando Reverón's work at the Ateneo de Caracas.
–Joaquín Torres-García returns from Europe to settle permanently in Montevideo.

1935
–Juan Vicente Gómez dies, December 17.
–General Eleazar López Contreras, Venezeula's minister of war and the navy, assumes power temporarily.
–Rómulo Gallegos publishes his novel *Canaima*.
–Diego Rivera finishes one of his most ambitious projects: the frescoes for the monumental stairway in Mexico City's Palacio Nacional.
–Joaquín Torres-García delivers the lecture "La escuela del sur" (The school of the South) in Montevideo, propounding the possibility and necessity of new art in Latin America.

1936
–Venezuela has a population of 3,364,347 (source: Instutito Nacional de Estadística); 61.7 percent of inhabitants live in cities and 38.3 percent in rural areas (source: Universidad de los Andes).
–Large protests break out against the officials who were involved in Juan Vicente Gómez's regime. Their property and residences are attacked and the protests degenerate into violent looting.
–Eleazar López Contreras is named president by the Venezuelan congress for the next presidential term.
–The Programa de febrero (February program) is enacted, establishing guidelines for resolving Venezuela's national priorities. This program calls for a new constitution, a nationwide sanitary campaign, and a program of public works and services. As part of this plan, minister of education Rómulo Gallegos calls on painters Antonio Edmundo Monsanto and Manuel Cabré to undertake a general reform of the Academia de Bellas Artes, in collaboration with a group of art history professors with the Chilean Misión Pedagógica.
–The literary group Viernes is formed.
–Boulton photographs La Rotunda prison shortly before its demolition.
–Armando Reverón's Sepia period begins.

1937
–Luis Malaussena and Carlos Raúl Villanueva design the Venezuelan pavilion for the Exposition Internationale in Paris.

1938
–Augusto Mijares publishes the collection of essays *Interpretación pesimista de la sociología hispanoamericana* (Pessimistic interpretation of Latin-American sociology).
–Eleazar López Contreras inaugurates the Museo de Bellas Artes in Caracas; the building is designed by Carlos Raúl Villanueva.
–Boulton exhibits his own work for the first time, at the Ateneo de Caracas. This is the first photographic exhibition in Venezuela.
–Héctor Poleo travels to Mexico, where he meets Diego Rivera and studies the Mexican muralist movement.

1939
–Arturo Úslar Pietri is named Venezuela's minister of education.
–Urban planner Maurice E. H. Rotival unveils his "monumental plan" for Caracas, later known as the Rotival Plan.

– Gego (Gertrude Goldschmidt) leaves Germany for Venezuela.

1940
– Arturo Úslar Pietri drafts Venezuela's education law.
– Miguel Otero Silva publishes *Fiebre* (Fever), a novel about the struggle against dictator Juan Vicente Gómez.
– Boulton publishes *Imágenes del Occidente Venezolano* (Images from the Venezuelan West) and exhibits photographs from this series at the Ateneo de Caracas.

1941
– Venezuela has a population of 3,850,771 (source: Instituto Nacional de Estadística); 60.6 percent of inhabitants live in cities and 39.4 percent in rural areas.
– General Isaías Medina Angarita is named president by the Venezuelan congress. He will serve until 1945.
– The Acción Democrática (AD) political party is formed. AD will be highly influential in Venezuelan political life for the remainder of the twentieth century.
– Héctor Poleo sets out on a journey through Colombia and Ecuador, examining social conditions in both countries. He also travels through Venezuela's Andean region.

1942
– Héctor Poleo's painting *Los tres comisarios* (*The Three Bailiffs*), created after his travels through the Venezuelan Andes, wins the Premio John Boulton in the fourth annual Salon of Venezuelan painting.
– In Uruguay, Joaquín Torres-García writes *Introducción al universalismo constructivo: Contribución a la unificación del arte y la cultura de América* (Introduction to constructive universalism: Contribution to the unification of America's art and culture).

1943
– The newspaper *El Nacional*, founded by Miguel Otero Silva, begins publication.
– Boulton takes his most emblematic pictures of El Ávila mountain.

1944
– Mariano Picón Salas publishes *De la conquista a la independencia* (*A Cultural History of Spanish America, from Conquest to Independence*), a key text on Latin America's cultural development.
– Boulton exhibits his photographs of the Isla de Margarita at the Museo de Bellas Artes in Caracas.
– Carlos Raúl Villanueva presents the first small-scale model of the Ciudad Universitaria, the main campus of the Universidad Central de Venezuela in Caracas.
– The first and only issue of the journal *Arturo* is published in Buenos Aires. Argentine artists Carmelo Arden Quin and Gyula Kosice are both contributors to the journal: Arden Quin with the "Manifiesto invención" (known in English as the "*Arturo* Manifesto") and Kosice with "Arte abstracto" (Abstract art).

1945
– A military-civilian coup backed by Acción Democrática overthrows Isaías Medina Angarita. In what later comes to be known as the Revolución de Octubre (October revolution), Rómulo Betancourt assumes leadership of the revolutionary junta.
– Women's suffrage is approved in municipal elections, and direct voting is approved in congressional elections. The Communist party is legalized in Venezuela.
– Construction of Caracas's El Silencio urban-redevelopment project comes to an end. Carlos Raúl Villanueva's design for the project includes two fountains with sculptures by Francisco Narváez (*Las toninas* [The river dolphins]).
– Poet Vicente Gerbasi publishes *Mi padre el inmigrante* (My father the immigrant).
– Alejandro Otero travels to Paris, where he will remain until 1952.
– The Asociación Arte Concreto-Invención is created; Tomás Maldonado is the association's central figure.

1946
– The Comité de Organización Política Electoral (COPEI), the Social Christian party of Venezuela, is formed. The party will play a leading role in Venezuela's political life for the remainder of the century.
– The literary organization Contrapunto is formed, with a view to critical examination of the state of culture in Venezuela.
– The Madí movement is launched in Buenos Aires, with Carmelo Arden Quin and Gyula Kosice at its center. Kosice drafts the "Manifiesto Madí" (Madí manifesto).
– The Asociación Arte Concreto-Invención drafts the "Manifiesto invencionista" (Inventionist manifesto) in Buenos Aires.
– Italian-Argentine artist Lucio Fontana publishes the "Manifiesto blanco" (White manifesto).

1947
– Rómulo Gallegos is elected president in Venezuela's first general elections conducted through direct, secret suffrage.
– Engineer Cipriano Domínguez begins work on the Centro Simón Bolívar with the construction of the El Silencio towers, one of Caracas's modern icons.

1948
– In November, nine months after his election, Gallegos is overthrown in a military coup. A military junta is set up, with Carlos Delgado Chalbaud as president.
– Construction begins on the Avenida Bolívar, which becomes one of Caracas's main urban axes.
– As a form of subtle protest against the coup that overthrew Isaías Medina Angarita, Boulton organizes a photographic exhibition that includes portraits of key opponents to the coup.
– The *Exposición panamericana de pintura moderna* (Pan-American exhibition of modern painting) opens at Caracas's Museo de Bellas Artes in February, to coincide with Gallegos's inauguration as president. It is followed by the exhibition *Tres siglos de pintura venezolana* (Three centuries of Venezuelan painting). Juan Liscano organizes the Fiesta de las Tradiciones, which features folkloric traditions from around the country.
– The Taller Libre de Arte (Free arts workshop) opens its doors in Caracas. During its first year, the Taller hosts an exhibition featuring Argentine abstract artists from the group Arte Concreto-Invención.

1949
– Mariano Picón Salas publishes *Comprensión de Venezuela* (Understanding Venezuela).
– Alejo Carpentier publishes the novel *El reino de este mundo* (*The Kingdom of this World*).
– Alejandro Otero returns from Paris and exhibits his Cafeteras (Coffeepots) at the Caracas Museo de Bellas Artes.
– Work on the second stage of the Universidad Central begins with the design and construction of the Estadio Olímpico (Olympic stadium).

1950
– Venezuela has a population of 5,523,999 (source: Instituto Nacional de Estadística); 52.6 percent of inhabitants live in cities and 47.4 percent in rural areas (source: Universidad de los Andes).
– Carlos Delgado Chalbaud, president of the military junta, is kidnapped and murdered.
– Boulton publishes *Los llanos de Páez* (Páez's plains) and exhibits a series of photographs of the Piaroas *indios* at Caracas's Museo de Ciencias.
– Juan Liscano publishes *Folklore y cultura* (Folklore and culture).
– Los Disidentes publish a programmatic text (later known as the "Manifiesto No" [No manifesto]) in the pages of the September issue of their journal.
– Jesús Rafael Soto leaves for Paris after exhibiting his work at Caracas's Taller Libre de Arte.
– The journal *Taller* is published by the Taller Libre de Arte.
– The Paseo los Próceres and the Círculo Militar, both designed by the architect Luis Malaussena, are constructed in Caracas.

1951
– The Guasina concentration camp for political prisoners is created.
– Juan Sánchez Peláez publishes his book *Elena y los elementos* (Elena and the elements).
– Roman Chalbaud writes his first play, *Caín adolescente* (*Adolescence of Cain*).
– Work begins on the basic elements of the "integration of the arts" project, led by Carlos Raúl Villanueva, at the Universidad Central de Venezuela.
– The first São Paulo Bienal takes place in Brazil. Swiss artist Max Bill receives the festival's first prize in sculpture.

1952
– Venezuela's higher military ranks refuse to recognize Jóvito Villalba's victory in the elections and place Marcos Pérez Jiménez in power.
– Vicente Gerbasi publishes the poetry collection *Los espacios cálidos* (The warm spaces).
– José Agustín Catalá clandestinely publishes *El libro negro* (The black book), an indictment of Venezuela's military dictatorship.
– Boulton publishes *La Margarita*.
– The second phase of building advances at the Universidad Central: the Estadio Olímpico, the main lecture hall, and the Plaza Cubierta (covered plaza).
– Alejandro Otero and Mario Briceño Iragorry have a heated dialogue about abstract art in the pages of *El Universal*.

–Mateo Manaure and Carlos González Bogen draft the "Manifiesto de la Galería Cuatro Muros" ("Manifesto of the Galería Cuatro Muros").
–The group Ruptura drafts the "Manifiesto Ruptura" (Rupture manifesto) in São Paolo, marking the official beginning of the *art concret* movement in Brazil.

1953
–A highway opens between Caracas and La Guaira; it is hailed as one of Latin America's most modern works. The Pan-American Highway opens: a network of roads linking the mainland nations of the Americas.
–Mario Briceño Iragorry publishes *El fariseísmo bolivariano y la Antiamérica* (Bolivarian hypocrisy and the anti-America).
–Alejo Carpentier publishes *Los pasos perdidos* (*The Lost Steps*).
–Armando Reverón receives Venezuela's Premio Nacional de Pintura for his *Desnudo acostado* (*Reclining Nude*).

1954
–Eighty-five public-housing projects, designed to house nearly 145,000 people, are built in Caracas between 1954 and 1957.
–The Centro Simón Bolívar opens in Caracas, December 6, as part of the program known as "Venezuela bajo el nuevo ideal nacional" (A new national ideal for Venezuela).
–Ángel Rosenblat publishes *La población indígena y el mestizaje en América* (Native population and *mestizaje* in America).
–Juan David García Bacca publishes *Antología del pensamiento filosófico venezolano* (Anthology of Venezuelan philosophical thought).
–Gio Ponti designs and builds Caracas's Villa Planchart, a project that synthesizes his work in architecture and interior design.
–Carlos Cruz-Diez makes his first abstract pieces, including *Proyecto para un mural* (Project for a mural).
–Armando Reverón dies in Caracas.

1955
–Carlos Raúl Villanueva, in collaboration with a group of other architects, designs the 2 de Enero (2 January) public housing project (later redubbed 23 de Enero).
–Miguel Otero Silva publishes *Casas muertas* (Dead houses).
–Caracas's Museo de Bellas Artes hosts a retrospective exhibition of the art of Armando Reverón, featuring more than four hundred of his works.
–Alejandro Otero begins work on the series Coloritmos (Colorhythms).

1956
–Boulton publishes *Los retratos de Bolívar* (Portraits of Bolívar), an iconographic study of Simón Bolivar.
–Ángel Rosenblat publishes *Buenas y malas palabras en el castellano de Venezuela* (Good and bad words in Venezuelan Spanish).
–Bárbaro Rivas's first retrospective exhibition opens at the Museo de Bellas Artes in Caracas.
–The Museum of Modern Art in New York acquires Alejandro Otero's *Coloritmo no. 1* (*Colorhythm 1*).

1957
–The Hotel Humboldt opens its doors; designed by the architect Tomás José Sanabria, the hotel is located on El Ávila mountain.
–Boulton's *Exposición iconográfica del verdadero rostro de Bolívar* (Iconographic exhibition of Bolivar's true face) opens at Plaza Diego Ibarra in Caracas. The show draws some thirty thousand visitors in the first ten days.
–Alejandro Otero exhibits his first Coloritmos at the Galería de Arte Contemporáneo.
–Miguel Otero Silva and Alejandro Otero engage in a polemical dialogue about abstract and figurative art in the pages of *El Nacional*.
–Bárbaro Rivas represents Venezuela at the São Paulo Bienal.
–Jesús Rafael Soto creates the first works of his Vibración (Vibration) series.

1958
–On January 23, a military-civilian movement overthrows Marcos Pérez Jiménez and a military junta is established, led by Wolfgang Larrazábal, commander of the Venezuelan navy.
–After the coup d'état, the Instituto de la Ciudad Universitaria, the university's administration, is closed. Villanueva's project of the integration of the arts and architecture comes to an end.
–AD, COPEI, and the Unión Republicana Democrática (URD) sign the Punto Fijo pact in the hope of strengthening the nascent democracy with the support of all political forces in the country.

– The literary group Sardio publishes a journal of the same name.
– Alejandro Otero receives Venezuela's Premio Nacional de Pintura.
– Jesús Rafael Soto creates two murals and a vibrating tower for the Brussels World's Fair.

1959
– Rómulo Betancourt assumes the presidency of Venezuela, selected through direct elections.
– Boulton publishes *Miranda, Bolívar y Sucre: Tres estudios iconográficos* (Miranda, Bolívar, and Sucre: Three iconographic studies).
– Salvador Garmendia publishes the novel *Los pequeños seres* (The small beings).
– Juan Sánchez Peláez publishes the poetry collection *Animal de costumbre* (Creature of habit).
– Poet and critic Ferreira Gullar drafts the "Manifiesto neoconcreto" (Neoconcrete manifesto). The movement of the same name is founded.
– Carlos Cruz-Diez creates his *Fisicromía no. 1* (*Physichrome no. 1*) in Caracas.

1960
– President Rómulo Betancourt survives an assassination attempt plotted by Rafael Leonidas Trujillo of the Dominican Republic.
– The Organization of the Petroleum Exporting Countries (OPEC) is created through the initiative of Venezuelan economist Juan Pablo Pérez Alfonso.
– Rafael Cadenas publishes the collection of prose poems *Cuadernos del destierro* (Notebooks from exile).
– Painter and playwright César Rengifo publishes the play *Lo que dejó la tempestad* (What the storm left).
– Jesús Rafael Soto receives Venezuela's Premio Nacional de Pintura.
– Carlos Cruz-Diez moves to Paris.

1961
– Venezuela has a population of 7,523,999 (source: Instituto Nacional de Estadística); 37.9 percent of inhabitants live in cities and 62.1 percent in rural areas (source: Universidad de Los Andes).
– Venezuela's congress approves a new constitution, which will remain in force until 1999.
– Political unrest results in kidnappings and bombings. Venezuela's extreme left-wing forms a guerrilla movement.
– The radical art group El Techo de la Ballena forms in Caracas, and produces a manifesto titled "el gran Magma" ("The Great Magma").

1962
– Rómulo Betancourt's government is challenged by four civilian-military uprisings, the most important of which is known as the Porteñazo.
– Caupolicán Ovalles publishes his poem *Duerme usted, Señor Presidente*? (Are you sleeping, Mr. President?)
– Writer Guillermo Meneses and his wife, journalist Sofía Imber, start the journal CAL (*Crítica, Arte, Literatura*).
– Carlos Contramaestre shows his work in the exhibition *Homenaje a la necrofilia* (*Homage to Necrophilia*), which is accompanied by a text by Adriano González León.
– Marisol Escobar creates her emblematic work *La familia* (*The Family*).

1963
– Adriano González León publishes *Asfalto infierno* (Asphalt Hell) with photographs by Daniel González.
– El Techo de la Ballena inaugurates the publishing organization Ediciones Tubulares with the publication of Caupolicán Ovalles's poem *En uso de la razón* (*Power of Reason*).

1964
– Raúl Leoni assumes the Venezuelan presidency: this is the first time that a Venezuelan president transfers power to the president-elect in a democratic manner.
– Leaders of the country's far left faction are detained due to a surge in subversive activities.
– Construction begins on the Guri hydroelectric dam, on the Caroní River.
– Boulton publishes the first of three volumes on the history of Venezuelan painting, *Historia de la pintura en Venezuela: Época colonial* (History of painting in Venezuela: Colonial period).
– The journal *Zona Franca* is founded in Caracas under the direction of Juan Liscano.
– The Salón Espacios Vivientes takes place in the state of Zulia, establishing Informalism as a new current in Venezuelan art.

1965
– The Venezuelan government responds to guerrilla insurgency by training special

troops and setting up anti-guerrilla squadrons.
– Argentine art critic Marta Traba publishes the essay "El arte latinoamericano: Un falso apocalipsis" (Latin-American art: A false Apocalypse), attacking geometric abstraction and characterizing Latin American art as mimetic and depersonalized.
– Carlos Cruz-Diez makes the first small-scale models for his Cromosaturaciones (Chromosaturations).

1966
– A state of national emergency is declared due to political instability.
– Isaac Chocrón stages his play *Asia y el lejano oriente* (Asia and the Far East).
– Boulton publishes monographs on the artists Camille Pissarro, Alejandro Otero, and Armando Reverón.
– David Alfaro Siqueiros completes the mural *Del porfirismo a la revolución* (*From the Dictatorship of Porfirio Díaz to the Revolution*) at the Museo Nacional de Historia in Mexico City.

1967
– On February 6, there is a massive escape of political prisoners from the Cartel San Carlos in Caracas, including several members of the Communist party and guerrilla factions, among them Antonio García Ponce, Pompeyo Márquez, and Teodoro Petkoff.
– The Angostura bridge, linking the plains and the Amazonian states in southern Venezuela, is built over the Orinoco River.
– A strong earthquake hits Caracas.
– Carlos Raúl Villanueva designs the Venezuelan pavilion for the Montreal World's Fair, which includes Jesús Rafael Soto's *Volumen suspendido* (Suspended volume).
– Numerous cultural events are organized for Caracas's centennial celebrations, including Jacobo Borges and Mario Robles's *Imagen de Caracas* (Image of Caracas).
– Bárbaro Rivas dies in Caracas.
– Jesús Rafael Soto creates his first Penetrable.

1968
– Rafael Caldera, the candidate for the Social Christian party, wins Venezuela's presidential elections.
– Adriano González León publishes *País portátil* (Portable country).
– Boulton publishes the second volume of his *Historia de la pintura en Venezuela*, subtitled *Época nacional* (National period).

1969
– Rafael Caldera assumes the presidency of Venezuela; he will remain in office until 1973.
– Boulton publishes a monographic study of the artist Rafael Monasterios.
– Major solo shows of Jesús Rafael Soto are organized at the Musée d'art moderne in Paris and at the Stedelijkmuseum in Amsterdam.
– Gego installs her Reticulárea at the Museo de Bellas Artes in Caracas.

1970
– Boulton is named Chairman of the Board of the International Council of The Museum of Modern Art in New York.
– Influenced by Brazilian Hélio Oiticica's retrospective at London's Whitechapel Gallery (1969), conceptual artist Diego Barboza stages *30 muchachas con redes* (*Thirty Girls with Nets*), his first action work, on the streets of London.

1971
– Venezuela has a population of 10,721,522 (source: Instituto Nacional de Estadística); 27.2 percent of inhabitants live in cities and 72.8 percent in rural areas (source: Universidad de los Andes).

1972
– Boulton publishes the third volume of his *Historia de la pintura en Venezuela*, subtitled *Época contemporánea* (Contemporary period), as well as *20 retratos del General José Antonio Páez* (20 portraits of General José Antonio Páez). He is awarded Venezuela's Premio Nacional de Literatura.

– Compiled by Carlos Palacios

selected bibliography

by and about alfredo boulton

Boulton, Alfredo. *A Reverón, pintor venezolano*. Caracas: Creole Petroleum Corp., 1956.

——. *Alejandro Otero*. Caracas: Oficina Central de Información, 1966.

——. *Camille Pissarro en Venezuela*. Caracas: Impr. Editorial Arte, 1966. English: *Pissarro in Venezuela*. New York: J. B. Watkins, 1968.

——. *Cruz-Diez*. Caracas: E. Armitano, 1975.

——. *Historia de la pintura en Venezuela: Época colonial*. Caracas: Editorial Arte, 1964.

——. *Historia de la pintura en Venezuela: Época nacional*. Caracas: Editorial Arte, 1968.

——. *Historia de la pintura en Venezuela: Época contemporánea*. Caracas: E. Armitano, 1972.

——. *La Margarita*. Caracas: Alfredo Boulton, 1952. Printed in Barcelona: I. G. Seix y Barral Hnos.

——. "La obra de Armando Reverón." In *Exposición retrospectiva de Armando Reverón* (Caracas: Museo de Bellas Artes, 1955); reprinted in *Reverón* (Caracas: Macanao Ediciones, 1979).

——. *El rostro de Bolívar*. Caracas: Macanao Ediciones, 1982.

——. *Soto*. Serie Pintores venezolanos. Caracas: E. Armitano, 1973.

——, ed. *Los llanos de Páez*. Paris: Draeger Frères, 1950.

Boulton, Alfredo, and Arturo Úslar Pietri. *Imágenes del occidente venezolano*. New York: Tribune Print, 1940.

Esteva-Grillet, Roldán. "Alfredo Boulton y la historiografia del arte." *El Universal* (January 31, 1988): 1–2.

Homenaje a Alfredo Boulton: Una visión integral del arte venezolano. Caracas: Museo de Arte Contemporáneo de Caracas, 1987.

Otero, Alejandro, and Alfredo Boulton. *He vivido por los ojos: Correspondencia Alejandro Otero/Alfredo Boulton, 1946–1974*. Edited and with introduction by Ariel Jiménez. Caracas: Alberto Vollmer Foundation, Inc. and Fundación Museo Alejandro Otero, 2001.

venezuelan politics and culture

Baptista, Asdrúbal. *Bases cuantitativas de la economía venezolana, 1830–2002*. Caracas: Fundación Empresas Polar, 2006.

Betancourt, Rómulo. *Venezuela, política y petróleo*. Caracas: Editorial Senderos, 1969. English: *Venezuela, Oil and Politics*. Boston: Houghton Mifflin, 1979.

Calderón, Fernando G. "América Latina: Identidad y tiempos mixtos." In *Imágenes desconocidas: La modernidad en la encrucijada postmoderna*. Aníbal Quijano and Fernando G. Calderón, eds. Buenos Aires: Consejo Latinoamericano de Ciencias Sociales, 1988.

Carrera Damas, Germán. *Una nación llamada Venezuela: Proceso sociohistórico de Venezuela (1810–1974)*. Caracas: Monte Ávila Editores, 1991. (First ed. 1984.)

Cornejo Polar, Antonio. *Escribir en el aire: Ensayo sobre la heterogeneidad sociocultural en las literaturas andinas*. Lima: Editorial Horizonte, 1994.

Gallegos, Rómulo. *Reinaldo Solar*. Bogotá: Ediciones Lerner, 1985.

Gallegos, Rómulo, with Efraín Subero. *Doña Bárbara*. Caracas: Biblioteca Ayacucho, 1977. (First published 1929.) English: *Doña Bárbara*. New York: Peter Smith Publisher, 1948.

García Canclini, Néstor. *Culturas híbridas: Estrategias para entrar y salir de la modernidad*. Buenos Aires: Editorial Sudamericana, 1992. English: *Hybrid Cultures: Strategies for Entering and Leaving Modernity*. Minneapolis: University of Minnesota Press, 1989.

Garmendia, Salvador. *Los pequeños seres*. Caracas: Monte Ávila Editores, 1972.

González León, Adriano. *País portátil*. Caracas: Rayuela, 2003.

Gruzinski, Serge. *La pensée métisse*. Paris: Fayard, 1999. Spanish: *El pensamiento mestizo*. Biblioteca del Presente, vol. 12. Barcelona: Paidós, 2000.

——. *The Mestizo Mind: The Intellectual Dynamics of Colonization and Globalization*. New York: Routledge, 2002.

Martí, José, Juan Marinello, and Cintio Vitier; Hugo Achugar, ed. *Nuestra América*. Caracas: Biblioteca Ayacucho, 1977. English: Martí, José, and Philip Sheldon Foner. *Our America: Writings on Latin America and the Struggle for Cuban Independence*. New York: Monthly Review Press, 1977.

Negrón, Marco. *Ciudad y modernidad, 1936–2000: El rol del sistema de ciudades en la modernización de Venezuela*. Caracas: Instituto de Urbanismo, 2001.

Otero Silva, Miguel. *Casas muertas*. Barcelona: Seix Barral, 1975. (First ed. 1955.)

——. *Fiebre*. Barcelona: Seix Barral, 1975. (First ed. 1931.)

Picón Salas, Mariano. *Cinco discursos sobre pasado y presente de la nación venezolana*. Caracas: Editorial La Torre, 1940.

——. *Comprensión de Venezuela*. Caracas: Monte Ávila Editores, 1976.

Picón Salas, Mariano, and Rafael Ángel Rivas Dugarte. *Formación y proceso de la literatura venezolana*. Caracas: Monte Ávila Editores, 1984.

Pino Iturrieta, Elías. *Positivismo y gomecismo*. Caracas: Facultad de Humanidades y Educación, Instituto de Estudios Hispanoamericanos, Universidad Central de Venezuela, 1978.

Pocaterra, José Rafael. *Memorias de un venezolano de la decadencia*. Caracas: Monte Ávila Editores, 1979. (First ed. 1927.)

——. *Gómez, the Shame of America: Fragments from the Memoirs of a Citizen of the Republic of Venezuela in the Days of Her Decadence*. Paris: A. Delpeuch, 1929.

Rama, Ángel. *La ciudad letrada*. Hanover, N.H.: Ediciones del Norte, 1984. English: *The Lettered City*. Durham, N.C.: Duke University Press, 1996.

——. *La novela en América Latina: Panoramas, 1920–1980*. Montevideo: Fundación Ángel Rama, Universidad Veracruzana, 1986.

Rodríguez Campos, Manuel, and Sara Colmenares. *Diccionario de historia de Venezuela*. Caracas: Fundación Polar, 1997.

Rojas-Mix, Miguel. *América imaginaria*. Palabra imaginaria, 1. Barcelona: Editorial Lumen, 1992.

Rosenblat, Ángel. *Población indígena y el mestizaje en América*. Buenos Aires: Editorial Nova, 1954.

Semprum, Jesús. *Visiones de Caracas y otros temas*. Caracas: Ediciones de la Corporación Venezolana de Fomento, 1969.

Úslar Pietri, Arturo. *De una a otra Venezuela*. Caracas: Ediciones Mesa Redonda, 1949.

——. "El mestizaje y el nuevo mundo." In *La antigua puerta de América: En busca del nuevo mundo*. Mexico City: Fondo de Cultura Económica, 1969, pp. 131–33.

——. *¿Existe América Latina?* Caracas: Instituto de Altos Estudios de America Latina, Universidad Simón Bolívar, 1984.

——. *Las lanzas coloradas*. Madrid: Zeus Editorial, 1931. English: *The Red Lances*. New York: Alfred A. Knopf, 1963.

——. "Sembrar el petróleo." *Ahora* (July 14, 1936): 1.

Vallenilla Lanz, Laureano. *Cesarismo democrático: Estudios sobre las bases sociológicas de la Constitución efectiva de Venezuela*. Caracas: Empresa El Cojo, 1919.

venezuelan artists and art history

Alejandro Otero. Caracas: Museo de Arte Contemporáneo de Caracas, 1985.

Bayón, Damián Carlos. *Aventura plástica de Hispanoamérica: Pintura, cinetismo, artes de la acción (1940–1972)*. Mexico City: Fondo de Cultura Económica, 1974. English: Bayón, Damián Carlos, and Galen Douglas Greaser. *Adventures in Contemporary Spanish-American Painting, Kinetic and Action Arts, 1940–1972*. Paris: Damián Bayón, 1973.

Bonnefoy, Françoise, et al. *Jesús Rafael Soto*. Paris: Galerie Nationale du Jeu de Paume, 1997.

Cárdenas, María Luz, and Lía Caraballo. *Una visión del arte contemporáneo venezolano: Colección Ignacio y Valentina Oberto, Fundación Noa Noa*. Caracas: Fundación Noa Noa, 1995.

Carpentier, Alejo. "Arte abstracto." *El Nacional* (August 15, 1952): 14.

Cruz-Diez. Caracas: Museo de Arte Contemporáneo de Caracas, 1981.

Cruz-Diez, Carlos. *Reflexión sobre el color*. Caracas: Fabriart, 1989.

Da Antonio, Francisco. *Textos sobre arte: Venezuela, 1682–1982*. Caracas: Monte Ávila Editores, 1982.

Diccionario biográfico de las artes visuales en Venezuela. Caracas: Fundación Galería de Arte Nacional, 2005.

Esteva-Grillet, Roldán, and María Antonia González Arnal. *Fuentes documentales y críticas de las artes plásticas venezolanas, siglos XIX y XX*. Caracas: Universidad Central de Venezuela, Consejo de Desarrollo Científico y Humanístico, 2001.

Gego (Gertrude Goldschmidt), Iris Peruga, and Josefina Núñez. *Gego: Obra completa, 1955–1990*. Caracas: Fundación Cisneros, 2003.

Jiménez, Ariel, and Jesús Rafael Soto. *Conversaciones con Jesús Soto/ Conversations with Jesús Soto*. Caracas: Fundación Cisneros, 2005.

López Méndez, Luis Alfredo. *El Círculo de Bellas Artes*. Caracas: Editora El Nacional, 1976.

Moholy-Nagy, Sibyl. *Carlos Raúl Villanueva y la arquitectura de Venezuela*. Caracas: Editorial Lectura, 1964. English: *Carlos Raúl Villanueva and the Architecture of Venezuela*. New York: Praeger, 1964.

Noriega, Simón. "La critica de la pintura en el siglo XX." In *La crítica de arte en Venezuela*. Mérida: Universidad de los Andes, Facultad de Humanidades y Educación, Escuela de Letras, Departamento de Arte, 1979.

Nucete-Sardi, José. *Notas sobre la pintura y escultura en Venezuela*. Caracas: Ediciones González y González, 1957.

Otero, Alejandro. *Papeles biográficos: Memorias de infancia*. Upata: Fondo Editorial Predios, 1994.

Pérez Oramas, Luis. *Mirar furtivo*. Colección arte y crítica, no. 2. Caracas: Consejo Nacional de la Cultura, 1997.

Quintana Castillo, Manuel. "Comentario sobre el arte 'Otro.'" *El Nacional* (August 7, 1958): C1.

Schwartz, Jorge. *Las vanguardias latinoamericanas: Textos programáticos y críticos*. Crítica y estudios literarios. Madrid: Cátedra, 1991.

Traba, Marta. *Dos décadas vulnerables en las artes plásticas latinoamericanas, 1950–1970*. Mexico City: Siglo Veintiuno Editores, 1973.

———. *Mirar en Caracas: Crítica de arte*. Caracas: Monte Ávila Editores, 1974.

Villanueva, Carlos Raúl. *Escritos*. Caracas: Universidad Central de Venezuela, Facultad de Arquitectura y Urbanismo, División de Extensión Cultural, 1965.

———. *Caracas en tres tiempos*. Caracas: Ediciones Comisión de Asuntos Culturales del Cuatricentenario de Caracas, 1966.

Villanueva, Paulina, and Maciá Pintó. *Carlos Raúl Villanueva*. Serie Maestros latinoamericanos de la arquitectura. Madrid: Ediciones Tanais, 2000.

Villanueva, Paulina, and Paolo Gasparini. *Villanueva en tres casas*. Caracas: Facultad de Arquitectura y Urbanismo de la Universidad Central de Venezuela, 2000.

contributors

Hugo Achugar has published essays on culture, literature, and art in Latin America, as well as poetry and novels. His most recent book is *Planetas sin boca: Escritos efímeros sobre arte, cultura y literatura* (Montevideo: Trilce, 2004). He has taught at universities in his native Uruguay as well as in Venezuela, Argentina, Brazil, Spain, and the United States. Achugar is currently a full professor at the University of Miami, as well as director of the Observatory of Cultural Policy at the Universidad de la República in Uruguay.

Rafael Castillo Zapata is chair of the department of literary theory at the Universidad Central de Venezuela. He has been a visiting professor at Brown University (1993) and at Rutgers University (2006), as well as a researcher at the Centro de Estudios Latinoamericanos Rómulo Gallegos. A poet, essayist, and literary critic, Castillo Zapata is the author of *Fenomenología del bolero* (Caracas: Monte Ávila Editores, 1991); *El semiólogo salvaje* (Caracas: Fundarte, 1996); and *El legislador intempestivo* (Caracas: CELARG, 2006). His critical essays have been published in magazines such as *Communications, Revista de crítica latinoamericana, Revista iberoamericana, Hispamérica,* and *Cuadernos hispanoamericanos.*

Roldán Esteva-Grillet studied Hispanic-American literature at the Universidad de los Andes (Mérida), and medieval and modern art at the Università di Bologna; his doctoral studies in art history were completed at the Universidad Nacional Autónoma de México. He has curated exhibitions of Venezuelan art for museums in Caracas and Valencia, and has published widely in his field. He is a full professor of Latin American art at the Universidad Central de Venezuela.

Ariel Jiménez is a historian and curator of modern and contemporary art. He studied art history and architecture at the Sorbonne (Paris), and has curated numerous exhibitions at both public and private institutions in Venezuela and elsewhere in Latin America. Presently he is the curator of the Colección Patricia Phelps de Cisneros (Caracas), and of the Museo de Arte Moderno Jesús Soto (Ciudad Bolívar). Among his publications are: *La primacía del color* (Caracas: Monte Ávila Editores, 1992); *He vivido por los ojos: Correspondencia Alejandro Otero/Alfredo Boulton, 1946–1974* (Caracas: Fundación Alberto Vollmer, Inc., and Fundación Museo Alejandro Otero, 2001); *Conversaciones con Jesús Soto* (Caracas: Cuadernos de la Colección Cisneros, 2001); and *Soto* (Caracas: Fundación Jesús Soto and Banco de Venezuela, 2007).

Marco Negrón studied architecture and urbanism at the Universidad Central de Venezuela, where he is currently a professor lecturing in urban theory with the doctoral program of the department of architecture and urbanism. He has been a visiting professor at universities in Latin America and Europe. He was vice-president of the Inter-American Planning Society from 1978 to 1980, and dean of the architecture and urbanism department of UCV from 1990 to 1996. Negrón led the development of UCV's Zona Rental from 1997 to 2003. He is the editor of the magazine *Urbana* and a member of the editorial board of the Instituto de Urbanismo at UCV's department of architecture and urbanism. Negrón is the author of several books, including *La cosa humana por excelencia* (Caracas: Fundación para la Cultura Urbana, 2004) and *Ciudad y modernidad* (Caracas: Ediciones Instituto del Urbanismo, 2001).

Sandra Pinardi earned her doctorate in philosophy from the Universidad Simón Bolívar (Caracas) in 2000. She is currently a full-time professor in the doctoral program in philosophy at the Universidad Simón Bolívar, and also teaches contemporary philosophy at the Universidad Católica Andrés Bello (Caracas). Pinardi is the founding director of the Instituto Universitario de Artes Plásticas Armando Reverón. She has written numerous articles about the visual arts, aesthetics, and philosophy for magazines and journals, and has participated in many international conferences and events on philosophy and aesthetics.

Elías Pino Iturrieta received his doctorate in history from the Colegio de México. He is the director of Venezuela's Academia Nacional de la Historia, and teaches at both the Universidad Central de Venezuela and the Universidad Católica Andrés Bello (both Caracas). Pino Iturrieta has published many books, including *Positivismo y gomecismo* (Caracas: Ediciones de la Facultad de Humanidades y Educación, Instituto de Estudios Hispanoamericanos, UCV, 1978), *Las ideas de los primeros venezolanos* (Caracas: Editorial Trópikos, 1987), *El pensamiento conservador* (Caracas: Monte Ávila Editores, 1992), *La mirada del otro: Viajeros extranjeros en el siglo XIX venezolano* (Caracas: Fundación Bigott, 1993), *La mentalidad venezolana de la emancipación* (Caracas: El Dorado, 1996), *Venezuela, país archipiélago* (Caracas: Fundación Bigott, 2001), *El divino Bolívar* (Madrid: Catarata, 2003), and *Nada sino un hombre: Los orígenes del personalismo en Venezuela* (Caracas: Editorial Alfa, 2007).

Maciá Pintó Saloni began his career as a draftsman and architect in 1972. He has taught at the Universidad de los Andes (Mérida); and at the Universidad Simón Bolívar, the Universidad Central de Venezuela, and the Universidad José María Vargas (all Caracas). At the Universidad José María Vargas, he was the founding dean of the department of architecture and plastic arts, as well as the coordinator of the Circle of Architecture Deans at the National Council of Universities. In the professional realm he is an architect, publication designer, and curator of art and architecture exhibitions. He has also participated in many colloquia and seminars on art, education, graphic design, and industrial design both in Venezuela and abroad, and has published articles, research papers, and other writings on the topic of architecture. He is on the advisory panel of various institutions, including the Fundación Villanueva.

Luis Pérez-Oramas is a writer, poet, and art historian. He received his doctorate in art history at the École des Hautes Études en Sciences Sociales, Paris, in 1994. He taught art history at the Université de Haute Bretagne-Rennes (1987–91), and at the École Régionale Supérieure des Beaux Arts de Nantes (1992–94). He returned to his native Venezuela to teach art history and modern Latin American art at the Instituto de Estudios Superiores de Artes Plásticas Armando Reverón in Caracas (1995–2002), and in the same period worked as a curator at the Colección Patricia Phelps de Cisneros, Caracas. From 2003 to 2006 he was Adjunct Curator in the Department of Drawings at The Museum of Modern Art, New York, where he is currently the Estrellita Brodsky Curator of Latin American Art.

index

Page references in *italic* refer to illustrations.

credits

photographs and illustrations

pp. 144, 148, 149, 151, 155, 305, 306, 307, 309 © 2008 ARS, New York/ADAGP, Paris; p. 153 © 2008 ARS, New York/ADAGP, Paris/CANC/MNAM/Dist. Réunion des Musées Nationaux/Art Resource, NY; p. 305 © 2008 ARS, New York/ADAGP, Paris, photograph The Museum of Modern Art, New York; p. 308 © 2008 ARS, New York/ADAGP, Paris, photograph The Solomon R. Guggenheim Museum, New York; p. 137 © 2008 ARS, New York/AGADU, Montevideo; p. 312 © 2008 photograph by Luis Becerra; p. 152 © 2008 Ludmila Bedouin; pp. 141, 145 © 2008 Bolivarian Republic of Venezuela; pp. 136, 140 © 2008 Bolivarian Republic of Venezuela, photographs by Miguel Ángel Clemente; pp. 318, 319 © 2008 Jacobo Borges; pp. 136, 147 © 2008 Estate of Manuel Cabré; p. 152 © 2008 Omar Carreño; p. 145 © 2008 Pedro León Carrillo; pp. 314, 315 © 2008 Fundación Alejandro Colina, photograph by Alexis Pérez Luna; front cover © 2008 Paolo Gasparini; p. 311 © 2008 Archivo Audiovisual Fundación Gego; pp. 310, 311 © 2008 Fundación Gego; p. 320 © 2008 Daniel González, photograph by Carlos Germán Rojas; p. 150 © 2008 Luis Guevara Moreno, photograph by Luis Becerra; p. 81 © 2008 Estate of Carlos Herrera, photograph by Carlos Germán Rojas; p. 317 © 2008 Fernando Irazábal, photograph by Carlos Germán Rojas; p. 321 © 2008 Ángel Luque, photograph by Carlos Germán Rojas; p. 147 © 2008 Horacio Moros González; p. 139 © 2008 Fundación Francisco Narváez; p. 304 © 2008 courtesy Asociación Civil Proyecto Armando Reverón; pp. 312, 313 © 2008 courtesy Asociación Civil Proyecto Armando Reverón, photograph by Renato Donzelli; p. 316 © 2008 Luisa Richter; pp. 150, 157, 255, 259, 260, 262, 266, 269, 320, 321 © 2008 photographs by Carlos Germán Rojas; p. 317 © 2008 Estate of Maruja Rolando, photograph by Carlos Germán Rojas; pp. 46, 47, 49, 50, 56 © 2008 Gina Rossi; inside flaps, pp. 132, 302, 303, 356, 357, 358, 360 © 2008 Archivos Fundación Villanueva; frontispiece, back cover, pp. 13, 22, 23, 75, 86, 116, 132, 138, 142, 143, 144, 160, 237, 239, 323 © 2008 Archivo Boulton, Alberto Vollmer Foundation, Inc.; p. 146 © 2008 Mauro Antonio Tóvar Zuloaga.

text copyrights

p. 14 © 2008 Hugo Achugar; p. 225 © 1965 Guy Brett; p. 270, © 1964 Juan Calzadilla; p. 340 © 2008 Rafael Castillo Zapata; p. 229 © 1989 Carlos Cruz-Diez; p. 295 © 1980 Francisco Da Antonio; p. 60 © 2008 Roldán Esteva-Grillet; p. 103 © 1977 Estate of Rómulo Gallegos; p. 288 translation: © 2005 Museum of Fine Arts, Houston, and Fundación Gego. Spanish language text: © 1977 Fundación Gego; pp. 265, 267 © 1962 Estate of Adriano González León; pp. 11, 76, 156 © 2008 Ariel Jiménez; p. 179 © 1952 Mateo Manaure and Estate of Carlos González Bogen; p. 46 © 2008 Marco Negrón; p. 178 © 1950 Estate of Alejandro Otero; p. 202 © 1999 Estate of Alejandro Otero and Estate of Miguel Otero Silva; p. 324 © 2008 Luis Pérez-Oramas; p. 115 © 1975 Estate of Mariano Picón Salas; p. 331 © 2008 Sandra Pinardi; p. 31 © 2008 Elías Pino Iturrieta; p. 349 © 2008 Maciá Pintó Saloni; p. 258 translation: © 2004 Yale University Press, in association with the Museum of Fine Arts, Houston. Spanish language text: © 1987 Estate of Ángel Rama; p. 254 © 1958, p. 256 © 1961 Grupo Sardio; p. 222 © 1973 and p. 224 © 1965 Jesús Soto; p. 264 © 1961 Ediciones del Techo de la Ballena; pp. 274, 278, 289 © 1974 Estate of Marta Traba; p. 98 © 1928, p. 101 © 1928, p. 102 © 1931, and p. 122 © 1974 Fundación Casa Arturo Úslar Pietri; pp. 127, 197 © 1966 Fundación Villanueva; p. 107 © 1933, p. 111 © 1937, p. 199 © 1952, and p. 232 © 1979 Alberto Vollmer Foundation, Inc.; p. 180 © 2001 Alberto Vollmer Foundation, Inc. and Estate of Alejandro Otero.

trustees of the museum of modern art